Lecture Notes in Computer Science 7286

Commenced Publication in 1973
Founding and Former Series Editors:
Gerhard Goos, Juris Hartmanis, and Jan van Leeuwen

Editorial Board

Ken Peffers   Marcus Rothenberger
Bill Kuechler (Eds.)

Design Science Research in Information Systems

Advances in Theory and Practice

7th International Conference, DESRIST 2012
Las Vegas, NV, USA, May 14-15, 2012
Proceedings

Springer

Volume Editors

Ken Peffers
Marcus Rothenberger
University of Nevada Las Vegas, Lee Business School
4505 S. Maryland Pkwy, Las Vegas, NV 89514, USA
E-mail: k@peffers.com, marcus.rothenberger@unlv.edu

Bill Kuechler
University of Nevada Reno, Information Systems /026
1664 N. Virginia Street, Reno, NV 89557-0208, USA
E-mail: kuechler@unr.edu

ISSN 0302-9743   e-ISSN 1611-3349
ISBN 978-3-642-29862-2   ISBN 978-3-642-29863-9 (eBook)
DOI 10.1007/978-3-642-29863-9
Springer Heidelberg Dordrecht London New York

Library of Congress Control Number: 2012936047

CR Subject Classification (1998): H.4, H.5, I.2, H.3, D.2, C.2

LNCS Sublibrary: SL 3 – Information Systems and Application, incl. Internet/Web
and HCI

Typesetting: Camera-ready by author, data conversion by Scientific Publishing Services, Chennai, India

Printed on acid-free paper

Springer is part of Springer Science+Business Media (www.springer.com)

Preface

The growing interest in design science research in information systems continues unabated in 2012. Scholars and design practitioners from many areas such as information systems, computer science, medical informatics, and software engineering are drawn to this area for its ability to extend the boundaries of human and organizational capabilities. The outputs of DESRIST, new and innovative constructs, models, methods, processes, and systems provide the basis for novel solutions to design problems in many fields.

The seventh DESRIST conference, DESRIST 2012, held in Las Vegas built on the tradition and foundation of six prior highly successful international conferences held in Claremont, Pasadena, Atlanta, Philadelphia, St. Gallen, and Milwaukee.

The title of this volume, *Design Science Research in Information Systems: Advances in Theory and Practice,* reflects the breadth of the field, the continuing interest in DESRIST theory formulation and development, and the degree to which this highly practical form of research is influencing design practice in business and government. The subheadings of the table of contents for the proceedings reflect the extent of design science research and its applications: Theory and Theory Building (13% of submissions), DSRIS Methodologies and Techniques (6.5%), Social and Environmental Aspects of DSRIS (19%), DSRIS in Practice (45%), and Evaluation of DSRIS projects (16%). This year a substantial majority of the papers described the application of design science research to real-world design problems in both industry and government. This was an interesting shift that complemented the proceedings of the previous DESRIST conferences in which theory and theoretical papers dominated.

Forty-four papers were submitted to the conference for review. Each paper was reviewed by at least two referees. The reviews were double blind, meaning that each of the two groups – authors and referees – remained anonymous to one another. Twenty-four papers were accepted as full length research papers and seven papers as short papers.

We thank the authors who submitted papers to DESRIST 2012, and trust the readers will find the papers as interesting and informative as we did. We would like to thank the members of the Program Committee as well as the additional referees, who took the time to provide detailed and constructive reviews to the authors. We would also like to thank the other members of the Organizing

Committee, as well as the volunteers, whose dedication and effort helped bring about another successful conference. We believe the papers in the DESRIST 2012 proceedings provide several interesting and valuable insights into the theory and practice of design science, and they open up new and exciting possibilities for research in the discipline.

May 2012

Ken Peffers
Marcus Rothenberger
Bill Kuechler

Organization

DESRIST 2012 was organized by the Lee School of Business, University of Nevada, Las Vegas

General Chairs

Hemant Jain   University of Wisconsin – Milwaukee, USA
Atish Sinha   University of Wisconsin – Milwaukee, USA

Program Chairs

Ken Peffers   University of Nevada Las Vegas, USA
Marcus Rothenberger   University of Nevada Las Vegas, USA

Proceedings Chair

Bill Kuechler   University of Nevada, Reno, USA

Doctoral

Samir Chatterjee   Claremont Graduate University, USA

Consortium Chair

Henk Sol   University of Groningen, The Netherlands

Communications Chair

Michael Lee   University of Nevada Las Vegas, USA

Program Committee

Ahmed Abbasi   University of Wisconsin-Milwaukee, USA
Stephan Aier   University of St.Gallen, Switzerland
Richard Baskerville   Georgia State University, USA
Udo Bub   Deutsche Telekom Laboratories, Germany
Tobias Bucher   Phoenix Group, Germany
Sven Carlsson   Lund University, Sweden
Roger Chiang   University of Cincinnati, USA
Chen-Huei Chou   College of Charleston, USA
Ulrich Frank   University of Duisburg-Essen, Germany

Mike Goul	Arizona State University, USA
Shirley Gregor	Australian National University, Australia
Alan Hevner	University of South Florida, USA
Lakshmi Iyer	University of North Carolina at Greensboro, USA
Joakim Lilliesköld	KTH Royal Institute of Technology, Sweden
Björn Niehaves	University of Münster, Germany
Volker Nissen	Ilmenau University of Technology, Germany
Andreas Oberweis	University of Karlsruhe, Germany
Jinsoo Park	Seoul National University, South Korea
Jeffrey Parsons	Memorial University of Newfoundland, Canada
Stacie Petter	University of Nebraska at Omaha, USA
Jan Pries-Heje	Roskilde Universiy, Denmark
Erik Proper	Radboud University Nijmegen, The Netherlands
Sandeep Purao	Penn State University, USA
Sudha Ram	University of Arizona, USA
Matti Rossi	University of Helsinki, Finland
Michael Schermann	Technical University of Munich, Germany
Arun Sen	Texas A & M University, USA
Henk Sol	University of Groningen, The Netherlands
Mark Srite	University of Wisconsin - Milwaukee, USA
Kevin Sullivan	University of Virginia
Tuure Tuunanen	University of Oulu, Finland
Vijay Vaishnavi	Georgia State University, USA
John Venable	Curtin University, Australia
Ramesh Venkataraman	Indiana University, USA
Jan Verelst	University of Antwerp, Belgium
Jan vom Brocke	University of Liechtenstein, Liechtenstein
Joseph Walls	University of Michigan, USA
George Widmeyer	New Jersey Institute of Technology, USA
Roel Wieringa	University of Twente, The Netherlands
George Wyner	Boston University, USA
Huimin Zhao	University of Wisconsin-Milwaukee, USA
Jack Zheng	Southern Polytechnic State University, USA

Conference Sponsors

University of Nevada, Las Vegas, Lee School of Business
University of Wisconsin, Milwaukee, Sheldon B. Lubar School of Business
University of St. Gallen

Table of Contents

DSRIS in Practice

DSRIS Methodologies and Techniques

Social and Environmental Aspects of DSRIS

Theory and Theory Building in DSRIS

Evaluation of DSRIS projects

Towards a Comprehensive Online Peer Assessment System
Design Outline

Dmytro Babik, Lakshmi S. Iyer, and Eric W. Ford

The University of North Carolina at Greensboro
{d_babik,lsiyer,ewford}@uncg.edu

Abstract. The business of business education is rapidly evolving because of changing economic and social conditions. At many institutions, class sizes are growing, more curricula is being offered online and traditionally successful pedagogical standards are being threatened unless they are adapted to the emerging economic realities of the 21st century. In response to the economic threats and consumers' preferences, numerous IT artifacts are being created to facilitate online teaching in the hope that both quality and cost concerns will be ameliorated (albeit not always using the precepts of design science). The purpose of this 'work-in-progress' paper is to apply design science principles to outline an algorithm for a computer-aided peer assessment system, named Double-loop Mutual Assessment (DLMA). The project's goal is to emulate the case method online, improve students' learning experience and increase grading efficacy. The DLMA yields two IT artifacts: a method and an instantiation. The DLMA method artifact involves two loops of assessment: 1) a summative and formative mutual peer assessment algorithm for essays; and 2) a summative peer assessment of the feedback's quality. An instantiation of DLMA system – a prototype and a beta-version has been implemented and described. Future directions of researching behavioral and operational aspects of the system are outlined. Potential applications of the artifact's capabilities beyond the business necessity are discussed.

Keywords: design science, design artifact, design process, online, prototype, peer assessment, double-loop mutual assessment.

1   Introduction

The business model for business education is changing at many universities. In particular, the costs of delivering courses in-person and in real-time have risen significantly in recent years (*Declining by Degrees*, 2005). The shift in cost structures has led to changes in the way classes are delivered and in the way consumers want their learning systems to be organized. Rising cost pressures have led universities to increase class sizes beyond the thresholds where resource-intensive, in-person, in-structor-dependent pedagogical tools, such as case studies or creative writing, can be implemented effectively (Gibbs & Jenkins, 1992). Besides, tuition inflation has

K. Peffers, M. Rothenberger, and B. Kuechler (Eds.): DESRIST 2012, LNCS 7286, pp. 1–8, 2012.

changed consumers' preferences for how they receive their educational experience. Many students work full or part-time to afford college, do not live on or near campus, and prefer asynchronous modes of delivery to meet competing time demands.

One solution that universities have turned to as a means of addressing both their own financial constraints and the consumers' preference is the large-section (i.e., 50-plus students), online, asynchronous courses. A drawback of such curricular designs is that they make instructor-moderated assignments difficult to execute using existing online information systems (IS) and technologies. For example, the time cost to the instructor of moderating discussion boards is high and the ability to discern an individual student's unique contribution and assign an accurate grade is difficult – if not impossible. Further, commercial learning applications (e.g., Blackboard, Moodle & Pearson) do not have the flexibility to emulate the student-centered, self-regulating, multi-cycle feedback mechanism that allows for complex problem exploration through essay writing activities.

The purpose of this 'work-in-progress' paper is to apply Design Science principles to the development of a peer assessment system that would accommodate complex educational instruments, such as case method or creative writing, while at the same time requiring minimal or no moderation by the instructor. The research question of this study is how to design a self-regulated IS that simulates a dialogue (discussion) experience around creative writing assignments in large-scale, online, asynchronous learning environments and delivers benefits of summative and formative assessments. Further, the IS should be a 'safe' learning environment where potential biases are minimized and the grades are not compromised due to flawed evaluations by any one peer (i.e., a faulty sub-system). The proposed Double-loop Mutual Assessment (DLMA) system creates two types of IS artifacts (of the four types defined by Hevner, March, Park, and Ram (2004)). The first artifact is the double-loop peer assessment method. The second artifact is a purposeful instantiation of an online system for conducting case-study analyses in a virtual course environment.

The DLMA IS artifacts address the wicked problem (Hevner et al., 2004; Rittel & Webber, 1973) faced by educators where there is a critical dependence upon students' social abilities and creativity to generate both summative and formative feedback for peers. The complexity and ambiguity of evaluating creative essays requires flexible systems. The IS artifacts presented in this paper address the constraints introduced by large-class sizes and asynchronous online environments that make instructor-centric facilitation strategies, such as the case method, far more difficult to execute. If design is concerned with how things ought to be and devising artifacts to attain those goals, then building a peer assessment IS that more closely approximates the case method for online environments is a worthwhile endeavor (Simon, 1996).

2   The Role of Peer Assessment and Computer-Aided Peer Assessment in Education

Over the last three decades, researchers and instructors have been debating, researching and experimenting with peer assessment of student performance (Topping, 2005).

Peer assessment is a method that requires students to review other students' work, evaluate its quality and provide feedback. In contrast to self-assessment techniques, generally limited to basic cognitive levels (Anderson et al., 2001; Bloom, Krathwohl, & Masia, 1956), peer assessment enables learning at higher cognitive levels (Bouzidi & Jaillet, 2009). Moreover, well-structured peer assessment permits students to develop competencies by following examples and responding to feedback of their peers and, thus, engage students in social learning (Bandura, 1962; Bandura & Walters, 1963). Feedback is an important aspect of learning that focuses on the details of content and performance. Moreover, it is an important feature of everyday social interactions outside the classroom (and on the internet) and a core management competency to be mastered. Peer assessment adds value as a learning tool by exposing students to the practice of evaluating others' performance and receiving feedback on one's own performance (Brutus & Donia, 2010). Peer assessment is a skill that can, and should, be honed through purposeful practice in controlled settings rather than through trial and error on the job (Sluijsmans & Prins, 2006).

Most of the existing designs of peer assessment systems focused predominantly on summative assessment rather than formative assessment (Trahasch, 2004). Summative assessment is intended to measure a student's attainment at a particular time, often for purposes of external accountability (typically in the form of a score, grade, mark etc.). Formative assessment, in contrast, is a set of formal and informal evaluation procedures employed by an instructor during the learning process with the express purpose of improving student competencies through behavior modification (Crooks, 2001). Formative assessment typically involves qualitative feedback rather than quantitative scores (Huhta, 2008).

In the past, computer-aided assessment (CAA) has been primarily concerned with multiple-choice tests because they relieve instructors of time-consuming grading. The complexity of manual, multiple-peer, double-blind, repeated assessments with paper as the medium, makes such assignments difficult to administer in large classes. Most computer-aided peer assessment systems provide a means to create feedback, and in some instances grade recommendations, but few create a dynamic learning experience. Thus, such systems do not produce the formative assessments that, in turn, lead to the skill-level gains that higher education is designed to produce. What is needed is a reliable and valid algorithm capable of handling summative and formative peer assessments efficiently in a manner that also creates an effective scoring sub-system.

3   Developing DLMA IS Artifacts: Design Principles and System Requirements

In developing the DLMA system, we applied the general methodology of Design Science framework for IS research (Hevner et al., 2004) to show how our research is both relevant and rigorous and contribute to the IS knowledge base by solving a rising problem in higher education (see Figure 1). For the design process, we follow the five-steps proposed by Vaishnavi and Kuechler (2007). At Step 1: Awareness of the problem – we have defined the business need by building the case of limited feasibility of case study method in business education in large online classes. At Step 2: Suggestion – we looked at the role of peer assessment in education, discovered what deficiencies existing peer assessment systems have, and proposed a computer-aided peer assessment solution that is presumably immune to those deficiencies. In Step 2 we also defined a tentative conceptual set of elements that the solution to the problem should have. Step 3: Development – yielded two artifacts, namely, the me-thod of DLMA (including the description of the workflow of DLMA data-generating process of summative assessment), and the instantiation of a physical DLMA IS. Step 4: Evaluation – will include a set of experiments to collect and analyze performance measures of the DLMA system. Step 5 involves making the results of research public-ly available. Steps 1 through 3 are completed in this work-in-progress paper. The plans for completing steps 4 and 5 are then discussed.

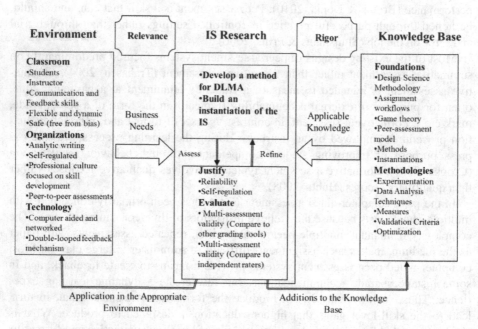

Fig. 1. Relevance / Rigor of DLMA Research (adapted from Hevner et al., 2004)

Computer-aided peer assessment systems available today typically have at least one of the following deficiencies (Aoun, 2008; Doiron, 2003; Topping, 1998):

1. They do not induce sufficient stimuli for students to provide honest and actionable feedback without direct instructor's intervention;
2. They are too complex or cumbersome to be applied frequently in a large class without using unaffordable human resources;
3. They are limited to only either summative or formative assessment;
4. They result in poor quality of feedback (questionable usefulness) or grading (ques-tionable fairness and objectivity).

Bostock (2000) suggested that peer assessment weaknesses can be addressed by using anonymity, multiple assessors, and instructor moderation. Therefore, a generic comprehensive online peer assessment system has to offer several distinct benefits for instructors and students. For instructors, the system needs to:

1. Be scalable, that is, adaptable for classes of various sizes;
2. Accommodate an intensive stream of creative assignments even in large classes;
3. Enable accurate grading without cumbersome and/or resource-intensive scoring process;
4. Allow early identification of underperforming students and offer ways of improving their learning performance.

For students, the system needs to:

1. Intensify learning by engaging in more frequent creative assignments;
2. Facilitate pluralistic, timely and actionable formative feedback to enforce continuous improvement during the course;
3. Guarantee quality and objective summative feedback (scoring) even in large classes;
4. Enhance students' understanding of how they perform in the educational marketplace.

Consequently, a peer assessment system that claims to satisfy the demands outlined in the business need has to have the following elements: 1) process automation, 2) peer anonymity, 3) random allocation of peer groups, 3) reciprocal assessment of essays on common topics, and 5) multiple-peer feedback.

In order to address the business need outlined above, the design principles of distributed cognition system, namely ownership, multiplicity, easy travel, indeterminacy, emergence, and mixed forms (Boland Jr, Tenkasi, & Te'eni, 1994), were used to design DLMA. The DLMA system facilitates the workflow consisting of the following events:

Event 1: Students anonymously submit essays;
Event 2: Students rank-order (or rate) essays submitted in Step 1 by several of their peers and provide anonymous feedback to each of the peers in reciprocal manner (that is, in a small group of students, everyone evaluates everyone else's essay);
Event 3: Students rank-order (or rate) feedback submitted in Step 2 in the same manner.

In addition, based on the class design, students can be placed into groups randomly or non-randomly; a single assignment or multiple assignments may be required; students may be matched with a new or the same group for each assignment. Thus, the DLMA system has to have the following functional properties:

1. Be able to facilitate anonymous (double blind) exchange of essays and feedback in student groups; essays can be pooled either randomly or non-randomly;
2. Be able to utilize either ranking (relative comparison) or rating (absolute comparison), or both ways of comparison to generation of scores of summative assessment;

3. Enable the monitoring of peer assessment process by instructor (including real-time monitoring and comprehensive reporting);
4. Enable flexible setup of assignment parameters (such as essay length, scoring structure, scoring scales);
5. Be adaptable for non-academic settings (for example, non-college online courses).

4   Prototype and Beta-Version of Computer-Aided DLMA

To physically realize the concept of DLMA in a working IS, we built a prototype in the summer of 2011. The prototype used MS Excel as a processing platform and Google Docs and Google Forms as the student-user interface. The prototype was successfully used in four courses during summer and fall semesters of 2011 in the Bryan School of Business and Economics at the University of North Carolina at Greensboro, with undergraduate and graduate classes ranging from 18 to 60 students. The prototype model showed that DLMA is operational, demonstrates high levels of student-student and student-instructor inter-rater reliability (empirical studies evidencing this will be submitted for publication as a separate paper) and is generally accepted by students. While the prototype was essentially capable of replacing the instructor grading function with an IS artifact, it demanded a substantial level of human involvement to maintain data integrity. In spring 2012, the prototype was replaced by a fully-functional web-based beta version of DLMA that entirely automates the process (http://baeloop.uncg.edu/).

5   Expected Outcomes and Evaluation of System Performance

Based on the review of the literature on peer assessment, we hypothesized that a group of students is capable of assessing each other's "essays", such as case analyses, short papers, compositions, visual presentations and similar projects, with the overall outcome superior to, or at least not worse than that of an assessment by a single instructor. The results of such assessment entail:

a) Pluralistic (based on opinions of several people), timely, and actionable feedback on student essays (formative assessment);
b) The distribution of quality of student essays that results in a certain distribution of scores or grades (summative assessment).

We argue that a sequence of creating an essay, providing feedback, receiving feedback, evaluating others' feedback, and having own feedback evaluated constitutes an organic and powerful experience that results in better learning outcomes. Moreover, the impacts on formative learning outcomes are increased significantly if the sequence is repeated several times during a course. Further, this sequence creates a self-regulated in-class economy that ensures a "right" set of stimuli to provide honest and constructive feedback. Finally, if implemented appropriately, this process may remove the burden of grading a large number of essays from an instructor, thus permitting a more diligent focus on disseminating knowledge.

Based on the above rationale, we put forth the following propositions regarding the outcomes of the DLMA peer assessment system:

Proposition 1 (Summative assessment proposition): The distribution of a student performance metric generated by the DLMA system, when the students' performance is not directly observed, is the same as the distribution of the students' performance metric generated by an instructor directly observing student performance.

Proposition 2 (Formative assessment proposition): Given the same set of assignments being evaluated, the learning effectiveness of students in a class with the DLMA assessment system is greater than without the system.

These propositions will be tested in a series of experiments using the beta-version of the DLMA system. We expect to submit the results of the evaluation for a journal publication.

6 Conclusion and Further Research

This paper proposed an outline of the design of a new computer-aided peer assessment IS. The following premises stipulate the needs for such system. First, peer assessment approaches' validity has been supported continuously by the research literature and its popularity is increasing in higher education as a result. Second, unresolved issues exist around computerized peer assessment calling for further research and development. Third, solutions to these issues require more sophisticated workflows and complex algorithms, making manual processing impractical and often infeasible. Such solutions, however, could be effectively implemented using computer-aided design.

Further research on DLMA system will entail several new studies. First, an algebraic representation of data-generating process of summative assessment, as well as empirical evidence of validity and reliability of this process, are planned to be submitted for publication as a separate complete paper. We will collect empirical evidence supporting the validity of DLMA-based summative assessment vis-à-vis other metrics of student performance (e.g., GPA, and multiple-choice tests). In addition, instructor-versus-student reliability and student inter-rater reliability will be demonstrated. Second, an empirical study of students' attitudes and learning effects produced by the system is expected to support the argument that the system delivers superior learning experience to students compared to traditional forms of assessment. Finally, the implementation of such system will open a wide range of behavioral questions that we plan to set off and explore. Although there is yet to be much discovered about computer-aided peer assessment systems, they have the potential to deliver competitive advantages to both business schools and their students through improved competency attainment.

Acknowledgements. We thank Alexey Babik and Irene Babik for developing and testing the beta-version of DLMA. We also thank three anonymous reviewers and the Editor for their constructive comments.

References

1. Anderson, L.W., Krathwohl, D.R., Airasian, P.W., Cruikshank, K.A., Mayer, R.E., Pintrich, P.R., Raths, J., et al.: A Taxonomy for Learning, Teaching, and Assessing: A Revision of Bloom's Taxonomy of Educational Objectives. Longman (2001)
2. Aoun, C.: Peer-Assessment and Learning Outcomes: Product Deficiency or Process Defectiveness? In: Proceedings of The 34th International Association for Educational Assessment (IAEA) Conference. Cambridge University (2008)
3. Bandura, A.: Social Learning Through Imitation. University of Nebraska Press (1962)
4. Bandura, A., Walters, R.H.: Social Learning and Personality Development. Holt, Rinehart and Winston, New York (1963)
5. Bloom, B.S., Krathwohl, D.R., Masia, B.B.: Taxonomy of Educational Objectives; The classification of educational goals, by a committee of college and university examiners. In: Bloom, B.S., et al. (eds.), 1st edn. (1956)
6. Boland Jr., R.J., Tenkasi, R.V., Te'eni, D.: Designing Information Technology to Support Distributed Cognition. Organization Science, 456–475 (1994)
7. Bostock, S.: Student Peer Assessment. Centre for Learning Technology. Keele University (2000)
8. Bouzidi, L., Jaillet, A.: Can Online Peer Assessment Be Trusted? Educational Technology Society 12(4), 257–268 (2009)
9. Brutus, S., Donia, M.B.L.: Improving the Effectiveness of Students in Groups with a Centralized Peer Evaluation System. The Academy of Management Learning and Education (AMLE) 9(4), 652–662 (2010)
10. Crooks, T.: The Validity of Formative Assessments. University of Leeds (2001)
11. Declining by Degrees: Higher Education at Risk. PBS (2005)
12. Doiron, G.: The Value of Online Student Peer Review, Evaluation and Feedback in Higher Education. CDTL Brief 6(9), 1–2 (2003)
13. Gibbs, G., Jenkins, A.: Teaching Large Classes in Higher Education: How to Maintain Quality with Reduced Resources. Psychology Press (1992)
14. Hevner, A.R., March, S.T., Park, J., Ram, S.: Design Science in Information Systems Research. MIS Quarterly 28(1), 75–105 (2004)
15. Huhta, A.: Diagnostic and Formative Assessment. In: Spolsky, B., Hult, F.M. (eds.) The Handbook of Educational Linguistics. Blackwell handbooks in linguistics, pp. 469–482. Blackwell Publishing, Malden (2008)
16. Rittel, H.W.J., Webber, M.M.: Dilemmas in a General Theory of Planning. Policy Sciences 4(2), 155–169 (1973)
17. Simon, H.A.: The Sciences of the Artificial, 3rd edn. The MIT Press (1996)
18. Sluijsmans, D., Prins, F.: A Conceptual Framework for Integrating Peer Assessment in Teacher Education. Studies in Educational Evaluation 32, 6–22 (2006)
19. Topping, K.: Peer Assessment Between Students in Colleges and Universities. Review of Educational Research 68(3), 249–276 (1998), doi:10.3102/00346543068003249
20. Topping, K.J.: Trends in Peer Learning. Educational Psychology 25(6), 631–645 (2005), doi:10.1080/01443410500345172
21. Trahasch, S.: From Peer Assessment Towards Collaborative Learning. In: Presented at the 34th Annual ASEE/IEEE Frontiers in Education Conference, FIE 2004, Savannah, GA, pp. F3F–16 (2004)
22. Vaishnavi, V., Kuechler, W.: Design Science Research Methods and Patterns: Innovating Information and Communication Technology. Auerbach Pub. (2007)

Designing Digital Innovation Contests

Anders Hjalmarsson[1,2] and Daniel Rudmark[1,2]

[1] Viktoria Institute, Sustainable Mobility, Gothenburg, Sweden
anders.hjalmarsson@viktoria.se
[2] University of Borås, School of Business and IT, Borås, Sweden
daniel.rudmark@hb.se

Abstract. In recent years, the phenomena of open data have lent a promise to expand the innovation network of an organization. By allowing this type of access to organizational resources, developers beyond the organizational realm may hence generate new innovative artifacts surpassing existing capabilities. However, as an organization utilizes these innovation capabilities they simultaneously loose significant control over the innovations' alignment with existing organizational goals. One way to nurture and harness this type of innovation is to arrange a contest where third party developers are invited to attend. Using a Design Science Research approach, such a contest - a type of artifact we coin Digital Innovation Contest - was designed and field-tested in 2011. The contest, WestCoast TravelHack 2011, summoned 76 developers distributed on 20 teams and was based on an idea to both generate novel digital service prototypes and having these applications promote the organizational goal of less energy-consuming ways of everyday travel. We conclude that by following our empirically grounded and theoretically informed guidelines, this type of contest can indeed increase the likelihood of both producing innovative artifacts and aligning these innovations with organizational goals.

Keywords: Digital Innovation Contest, Open Data, Design Science Research, Digital Innovation.

1   Introduction

Innovation of novel digital services can be performed in closed or open settings. In the latter, organizations may invite third party developers to pursue innovation driven either by non-profit grounds [1] or business models [2]. In recent years, open and distributed digital innovation has been propelled through the provision of open data (e.g. traffic, transport and environmental). The rationale for distributing data in a more open fashion is to attract outside innovators to design new services going beyond what existing services provide [3]. However, as organizations adopt such a distributed way of pursuing innovation it also means that they simultaneously looses significant control of the direction of the innovation work performed. A challenge and insofar unresolved quest is hence how to perform distributed innovation in open

K. Peffers, M. Rothenberger, and B. Kuechler (Eds.): DESRIST 2012, LNCS 7286, pp. 9–27, 2012.

settings promoting that the digital services both becomes novel and adhere to organizational goals.

One concept to stimulate open innovation of ideas and novel products are *idea competitions* [4]. Events of this kind are based on the nature of a contest to drive and encourage open innovation processes. Transferred into the realm of distributed digital innovation, we argue that the concept of idea competitions can be materialized into a sub-concept coined Digital Innovation Contest (DIC). A DIC is defined as an event in which third-party developers compete to design and implement the most firm and satisfying digital service prototype, for a specific purpose, based on open data.

The emerging body of knowledge about idea competitions has generated several tentative guidelines [c.f. 4-6] for how to design idea competitions, which we argue could inspire to support the design of DIC. However a review of this body of knowledge indicates that existing guidelines are still missing important aspects of DIC's. Although idea generation is an important activity in a DIC, software design, implementation and testing are also examples on crucial activates which have to be performed in a successful DIC. This gap points towards the need for a grounded and theoretically anchored contest design process complementing those principles currently available. The research question addressed in this paper is consequently *How can digital innovation contests be designed to generate results that both are novel and adhere to organizational goals?*

Design science research (DSR) is proposed as research approach to use when viable artifacts should be developed in the form of a construct, a model, methods or an instantiation [7]. In the next chapter we describe how we have utilized DSR as research method to develop guidelines for DIC Design. In the following four chapters we describe how we have utilized the applied research method to 1) identify challenges and opportunities when designing DICs, 2) based on observations and existing literature formulated requirements and hypothesize on implementation principles for the artifact, 3) materialized these hypotheses on the design of DIC to enable testing in the field, and 4) evaluated the designed artifact. In the last chapter reflections are made regarding our contribution and the paper is concluded with suggestions for future work.

2   Research Approach and Process

This paper presents developed, field-tested and evaluated guidelines for DIC Design. This contribution constitutes the artifact generated by a five-step DSR process, depicted in table 1. The three DSR Cycles presented by [8] have been used to derive and organize the steps in the research process. To further govern the work performed the seven DSR Guidelines provided in [7, 9] was used to guide the planning of the research and used as an approach for the research work performed in the different activities.

Table 1. Research Approach and Process

Research Process	Research approach			Chapter in paper
	DSR Cycle	DSR Guideline(s)		
Identify challenges and opportunities in contemporary DIC Design	Relevance cycle	Guideline 2: Problem relevance; Guideline 6: Design as a search process	Guideline 1: Design as an artifact	3
Derive implementation principles	Rigor cycle 1	Guideline 5: Research rigor; Guideline 6: Design as a search process		4
Design and field-test DIC Design Guidelines	Design cycle	Guideline 6: Design as a search process		5
Derive principles for and perform evaluation		Guideline 3: Design evaluation		6
Report contributions and communicate research	Rigor cycle 2	Guideline 4: Research contribution; Guideline 7: Communication of research		1, 2, 3, 4, 5, 6, 7

3   Challenges and Opportunities in DIC Design

This study is a part of a larger innovation and research program in Western Sweden entitled Innovation for Sustainable Everyday Travel (ISET) [10, 11]. This program is driven by a vision to create a service ecosystem for sustainable innovation, that 1) supports the provision of open data for distributed innovation of digital services that enhance sustainable mobility, 2) facilitates that the provision of data is turned into new services for sustainable everyday travel through distributed development, and 3) that the services developed in turn become viable and improves everyday travel in western Sweden (www.viktoria.se/projects/iset). ISET is organized as a cluster of industrial and science partners. It currently runs three projects from 2009 to 2013 with a total turnover of €3 million euro. ISET is structured in three phases: infrastructure innovation, service innovation and systems innovation. The first phase was completed in the second quarter of 2011 and aimed to facilitate the release of traffic, transport and environmental data to the public. The work within this phase resulted in a digital infrastructure - a developer zone - that promotes distributed development of digital services that supports sustainable everyday travel (www.trafiklab.se).

In spring of 2010 the second phase in ISET - service innovation - was launched in parallel to the ongoing first phase. The aim with this second phase was to promote and establish a viable use of the developer zone and stimulate the development of novel services that promoted sustainable travel. Early on, the cluster formed the idea that a contest might be the vehicle to use to elevate distributed innovation of services based on the open data provided by the developer zone. In June of 2010 however, the contest idea was merely a blur opportunity. As a first step a team was put together to 1) understand and assess the value and the challenges of a contest given, and 2) if feasible, turn the ideas into realty. Members from the team visited two different 24 hour competitions held in Sweden in 2010 and 2011 to seek out and collect experiences regarding the development contest as phenomena.

The first competition visited was *CODEmocracy* (www.codemocracy.se), which summoned some 50 developers in September of 2010 in Stockholm, Sweden for a 24-hours contest. For the members of the ISET contest team this event – through the quality of the participants and the resulting artifacts – validated on one hand the contest as a potential vehicle to promote innovation of digital services based on open data, but on the other hand also illuminated a number of challenges which needed to be addressed.

They also got a first sense of the community participating in the event. During the contest they informally inquired into why participants chose to spend an entire weekend programming for virtually no reimbursement (a significant portions had even paid to travel across the country to attend). Various reasons was given as response: some expressed a need to do something fun and non-work related (compared to their daily work as company developers – one programmer termed this as "to come up and breathe from the 'enterprise development swamp'"), others enjoyed the laid back and friendly atmosphere and some saw this as a way establish themselves in the (Smartphone application) development community.

One identified challenge was connected to the observation that most solutions (with some notable exception) were very technology-oriented. While they utilized new and emerging technological capabilities, the user interface was often crude and a clear value for users was mostly missing. We connect this to three observations: 1) *primarily programmers participated in the event.* ISET is driven by the idea that novel and viable digital services can contribute to a more sustainable society, however in order to produce services that achieve such impact an assumption is that services cannot just be based on innovative technology. They must also offer substantial value for various users (travelers) in the everyday travel situation. Further, they need to be designed with the capacity to promote sustainable travel and themselves be sustainable over time to be able to have an impact. This in turn required that participating teams not only had to include capabilities such as programming, but also user interface design, ideas on business design and sustainable development. 2) *CODEmocracy was primarily organized around open data as contest resource.* The challenge for the ISET DIC was to provide both interesting open data as the crucial "juice" for the design work during the competition, but in addition, we saw a need to provide additional resources that adhered to the overall goals for the competition (which for CODEmocracy meant increasing transparency and public influence); e.g. user needs, tools for assessing user value, attractive descriptions of future vision and ways of supporting the teams during the contest. 3) *The criteria for the competition were vague.* Even though the event were organized as a contest, very little information on what grounds the winner would be picked were given prior to the contest, which gave participants little guidance on how to design a winning contribution.

In March 2011 members from the ISET DIC team visited *Appening* 2011 in Sundsvall, Sweden (www.appening.se). This DIC was an open data contest with the purpose to stimulate distributed innovation of digital services based on data provided by different governmental agencies on a national and regional level. The event was similar to CODEmocracy as it was organized as a 24-hour contest. The rules were simple. Teams should include no more than 5 individuals. All contributions should use public data. The contribution should not be published in any other form prior to the event and the contribution had to be made available to the public after the event. Similar to CODEmocracy the criteria used to decide the winner was however vague. It begun with a three-hour preparation wherein the contest was presented together with the data sources available for the teams. At 16:00 the competition was commenced and ended 24 hours later. A presentation and evaluation segment wherein the teams presented the contributions to a jury who evaluated the contributions and selected the winners followed the competition segment. A number of prizes ranging from cash prizes to technological rewards (Smartphone's) constituted the award in the contest.

In order to prepare the final evaluation the jury visited the teams before the deadline and received information about the progress so far and the expected outcome. In addition the data providers also provided teams continuously support on demand in accessing data in the real operating systems or by the provision of a temporary data environment for the competition. When asked the participants especially said that they appreciated this on demand support.

The experiences collected by the ISET DIC contest team at Appening 2011 once more confirmed the opportunity to use DIC as vehicle to promote service innovation based on open data. The team was however also reinforced about challenges identified during CODEmocracy. User value was generally not prioritized in the contributions, and in addition, despite of introductions to organizational goals given during the presentation segment prior to the competition, the outcomes preliminary were focused on being technological firm rather adhere organizational goals.

4   Principles of Implementation

We therefore as organizers of a DIC, with the purpose to enhance sustainable mobility, concluded that we had to in different ways motivate the participants to develop firm applications based on open data as resources that also adhered organizational goals, so that the innovation performed created contributions beyond current borders of existing services for sustainable travel. In order to theoretically inform the design of appropriate guidelines that ensured this double aim of a DIC, we next initiated as a second step a rigor cycle with the purpose to derive suitable implementation principles for designing guidelines for DIC Design.

Turning to organizational goals, one lens through which researchers has viewed the process of aligning development activities and organizational goals is *control* [12, 13]. Kirsch [12] defined control as "any attempt to motivate individuals to behave in a manner consistent with organizational objectives" (p. 374). Inherent in current control theory lays an often implicit assumption of agency, materialized as a controller - controlee relationship, where a controller (e.g. manager or group) exercises formal or informal control over a controlee (e.g. developer). The basis for this uneven distribution of power is contractual, where the controlee is financially compensated for its work as an employee, contractor or sourcing partner. However, as new forms of development organizing emerge - such as the digital innovation contest - the foundation for the relationship is fundamentally altered [14]. As noted in the attended contests, rather than full or partial financial reimbursement for time spent developing software, many individuals are motivated intrinsically by personal growth, subcultural recognition, or pure personal enjoyment [3]. Nevertheless, any sponsoring of organizational development efforts needs to be driven by the promise of meeting some organizational goal. Given this backdrop it is important to find ways of aligning the motivation of the participants with organizational goals. As a first requirement to be met by a digital innovation contest we hence propose:

Requirement 1: In a digital innovation contest, organizers need to find innovative ways of motivating voluntary contestants to meet business objectives.

As mentioned above, we suggest that the reason for attending a DIC is primarily rooted in intrinsic motivations, which offers a challenge for organizations as organizational goals per definition are external. However, through the introduction of a contest, some means for formal control are introduced as the DIC thereby contain a set of evaluation criteria against which all submissions are judged and compared. Thus, by arranging a contest and carefully crafting the evaluation criteria according to organizational goals, organizers are able to exercise a form of *output control* on the contestants [12, 13]. However, given that the participation by developers is not primarily rooted in organizational objectives [1], imposing too restrictive criteria may repress intrinsic motivations and cause the organizing entity to come off as parasitic [15] as well as hamper innovation. To this end we also suggest that significant measures of *facilitative actions* are incorporated into the design.

Turning to facilitation, this notion literally means activities put in place to make social processes easy [16], by the implementation of supporting tools and through the behavior of appointed facilitators, acting using different facets and styles [17]. As noted above, a DIC need to 1) stimulate that teams participating in the DIC adhere to organizational goals during the competition and to 2) stimulate that the innovation work performed during the competition results in novel service prototypes. However, given the limited space of prescribing contestants' behavior, we suggest to add facilitative actions to the overall design. Hord [18] provides a six-component framework to describe facilitative actions that underpins change and innovation, which includes creating an atmosphere and culture for change, developing and communicating a vision for change, planning and providing resources that enable innovation. In a DIC we thus propose:

Design hypothesis 1: In a digital innovation contest, organizers should complement control through organizationally driven contest criteria with facilitative actions, both prior to and during the contest.

Another issue for organizations engaging in DIC concerns the transfer of domain knowledge e.g. about prospective users. Any contemporary application development method will include components dealing with the transfer of user needs into software development, typically formalized into some sort of user requirements. Whatever the notation of these requirement are materialized into, such artifacts serve at least dual purposes. On the one hand, they convey user needs which the developers are assumed to meet by developing appropriate system functionality. However, since developers are financially reimbursed as e.g. employees or contractors, requirements also form the basis of a contract about the work developers commit to [13] by e.g. estimating the time necessary to develop the specified functionality. As described above, we see that the room for dictating the solution space as limited. Thus we conclude, if an organization wants its knowledge of prospective users to be reflected in the designs of contest participants, they need to represent such needs in a non-contractual fashion.

Requirement 2: In a digital innovation contest user needs can help meet organizational goals but must be communicated in a non-prescriptive way.

In recent years *personas* has emerged as a new type of user needs representation [19]. A persona includes a textual description of typical, yet fictional users – *archetype users* [20]. Personas have been explored in the HCI community and draws on explicit descriptions of both contextually important factors (such as age and interests) as well as the goals of the archetype user. Based on potential constraining factors and personal goals, designers are able to explore different scenarios where a new artifact may support a particular activity [20]. This way, it has been argued, the concept of the user becomes less abstract and fluid throughout the entire design process [21]. Even more importantly, several authors argue that one of the main strengths of the persona is its ability render engagement and interest for the user [22, 21]. By describing users this way the shared mental image of a hypothetical future user is more likely to become used throughout the whole design process. Furthermore, personas have been argued to carry the potential to be ingrained with a multitude of both qualitative and quantitative data [20]. This enables the designers of personas to inscribe organizationally important characteristics to both current and future users.

Design hypothesis 2: In a digital innovation contest, user needs can be communicated by introducing personas as a complementary resource.

A concept closely connected to user needs is *user value*. Albeit understanding user needs is important to deliver useful innovative artifacts, correct understanding does not guarantee artifact user value [23]. In fact, it lies at the very heart of these types of transformational processes – such as a DIC - to find ways of promoting maximum user value [4]. Furthermore, given the technology-orientation of the participants in these types of contests, both our observations and parallels from the open source movement suggest to expect a high level of technical expertise and interest among intrinsically motivated programming participants [24]. Previous work has shown that this orientation of participants may yield solutions suitable for experts rather than typical end-users [4] which may jeopardize substantial adoption of contest-developed services. We thus see a need to avoid development of elegantly engineered prototypes missing a user base and to this end suggest.

Requirement 3: In a digital innovation contest, resulting submissions need to articulate user value.

A common way of articulating the value for the user is through a *business model* [25, 26]. In fact, the perhaps most important component of a business model is the user value proposition [25, 26]. The value proposition either defines ways of executing a certain task in a more efficient or less expensive way, or suggests how to open up new avenues of potential user action. Furthermore, a business model typically includes the target user niche, ideas on how the product or service should be distributed and how revenues are created [25, 26]. In sum, by introducing a technique for business modeling into the artifact development process, it ideally helps balancing the focus between technological possibilities and user uptake in the target context. To balance an anticipated technological focus of services we thus suggest.

Design hypothesis 3: In a digital innovation contest, introduction of a toolbox for business modeling by the organizers helps balancing issues of technological innovation and user value and adoption.

The generation of new and innovative IT-based artifacts is the main driver for pursuing an innovation contest. We use the definition by Yoo et al. [27] of digital innovation as "as the carrying out of new combinations of digital and physical components to produce novel products". It has been argued that perhaps the main driver of this digital innovation is *digital convergence* [28]. As different pieces of information, insofar unconnected, becomes available in a digital format, they also become subject for potential combinations and thus new, innovative artifacts [27]. Furthermore, through the usage of existing software and/or hardware bundles - platforms [29, 30] - software developers may rapidly connect and reiterate digital information pieces to explore new innovations [27]. Moreover, the perhaps most striking takeaway from earlier contest observation was how programmer found innovative ways of combining and presenting existing information. For organizations considering hosting a DIC it thus becomes important to offer their information in an innovation-friendly format:

Requirement 4: In a digital innovation contest, information addressing the contest space must be available in a way supporting rapid re-configurations and deployment on common platforms.

In recent years an increasing number of organizations are turning to open organizational data to outside innovators and thereby may draw on large numbers of developers building new and innovative artifacts for organizational users. Typically this is achieved by adhering to a specific architectural style for web based distributed programming (c.f. SOA, REST, Semantic Web) which allows outsiders to easily incorporate organizational data in their applications. Considering this potential, it is not surprising that boundary resources such as API's will be of utmost strategic importance for organizations seeking outside innovators to support their business [27]. Our final design hypothesis hence reads.

Design hypothesis 4: In a digital innovation contest, web-based API's can be used to enable rapid re-configurations and usage on common platforms.

Next we turn to how these design hypotheses were materialized and tested in the field.

5   Design and Field-Test of DIC Design Guidelines

As third step, design and field-test preparations was performed between April and October of 2011. With the implementation principles as base, these were transformed into a tentative DIC Design, as presented in table 2.

Table 2. Implementation Details of Field Tested DIC

Requirement	Design hypothesis	DIC Design Guidelines (incl. mean grading)

In a digital innovation contest, organizers need to motivate contestants to meet business objectives.	In a digital innovation contest, organizers need to strike a delicate balance between contest criteria and facilitative actions.	1) Motivate participants to address organizational objectives by both output control through careful design of evaluation criteria (see below) and help contestants meet these criteria through different facilitative actions (see below)
		2) Output control
		   a. Incorporate a specific overall, heavy weighing criterion that the service does support organizational objectives [200 points] (57 %).
		3) Facilitative action:
		   a. Prior to the contest, present major challenges connected to sustainable everyday travel in various and engaging ways
		   b. During the contest, support the teams in interpreting the challenges at hand and provide a workshop in how to self-evaluate the feasibility of solution ideas

Table 2. (*continued*)

| In a digital innovation contest, personas can be used to communicate user needs | In a digital innovation contest, personas can be used to communicate user needs. | 1) Output control
    a. Services should support presented personas today [150 points] (63,5%)
    b. Services should support presented personas in a near future [100 points] (57%)
2) Facilitative action
    a. Prior to the contest, present personas in an engaging way
    b. Prior to the contest, present expected societal near future developments and trends
    c. During the contest, support the teams in interpreting and clarifying presented personas and trends |
| In a digital innovation contest, resulting innovations need to provide user value. | In a digital innovation contest, introducing a toolbox for business modeling helps balancing issues of technological innovation and user value. | 1) Output control
    a. Present a business model (following the ideas of Osterwalder [26]) [50 points] (100 %)
    b. Present a concise selling description (i.e. value proposition) [100 points] (61,35 %)
    c. Suitability for target user niche [100 points] (63,85%)
    d. Testable without paying (i.e. distribution) and ideas on how the service will survive over time (e.g. revenues) [100 points]. (60,1 %)
    e. Realization complexity (i.e. key activities) [100 points] (57,85%)
2) Facilitative action
    a. Prior to the contest, present a business model toolbox
    b. During the contest, perform a workshop on business modeling to support the teams in designing business models |

Table 2. (*continued*)

In a digital innovation contest, information addressing the contest space must be available in a way supporting rapid reconfigurations and deployment on common platforms.	In a digital innovation contest, web-based API's can be used to enable rapid reconfigurations and usage on common platforms	1) Output control
		   a. Use of 1 API thought to support organizational goals [100 points] (42,55 %)
		2) Facilitative action
		   a. Prior to the contest, present all available data in an engaging way
		   b. During the contest, support contest with API issues

The DIC was coined WestCoast TravelHack 2011 (www.travelhack.se) and in June 2011 ISET announced that on October 8-9 2011 TravelHack 2011 would reward the team who developed the most innovative, best implemented, and impactful digital service prototype, that facilitate people to shift from overly energy consuming travels to other more sustainable ways of travelling. The participating teams would compete for awards exceeding the total amount of SEK 100.000 (approx. €10.000) together with wide exposure of their contributions. The prototype built should be operational and could be any kind of software application.

Fig. 1. Snapshots from WestCoast TravelHack 2011

A jury, specialized in this domain (see ch. 6 for further details on jury composition) was recruited and after presenting them with the criteria's, minor revisions were made. As advocated by Hevner & Chatterjee [9] the output from designing the artifact must be returned into the environment for study and evaluation.

Following the tentative guidelines, the contest team further designed a set of coherent facilitative actions. These actions were performed both prior to the competition as well as during the contest. Two months prior to the contest major challenges and visions connected to sustainable mobility were published on www.travelhack.se The motive behind this action was to prepare participants that the DIC had a specific purpose adhering to certain organizational goals. The aim was to build up capabilities within the teams to meet one or several of the challenges described.

The event commenced on October 8 at 8.00 am. After arrival and registration the team received their working areas. During the first contest day prior to the contest start the team was once more introduced in the challenges underlining the importance to develop a contribution in line with the challenges at hand (c.f. figure 1). This dialogue-based seminar on sustainability challenges for everyday travel was also accompanied with seminars about 1) all the data sources available at the competition (over 20 APIs), 2) Eight traveler personas representing different life situations and current trends in the society, and 3) a toolbox for business model design[1]. In addition fourteen real life user needs, generated through a traveler competition, was posted on the walls in the contest facilities in order to stimulate innovation. Most of the associated resources (personas, visions etc., however not the data or the real life user needs) had incrementally been released on www.travelhack.se the months prior to the competition in order to build up the capabilities within the different teams. In this sense, the seminars merely completed the preparation phase prior to the contest.

The contest started at 1.00 pm on October 8. During the contest phase facilitative actions were also performed in various ways to support the participants in their innovation work. A workshop was given to support the teams to interpret the sustainability challenges at hand and to support them to self-evaluate feasibility in solution ideas before implementation. This workshop was followed up with two "health checks", one after 12 hours and one after 18 hours, in which the organizers visited the teams in their working spaces and gave them the opportunity of self-evaluate their progress. Another workshop was in addition given early in the competition to support the participants to develop a business model for the digital service prototype utilizing the toolbox provided. Support was also given to the teams in interpreting and clarifying presented personas and trends. And in addition the data providers supported with API issues during the 24-hours that the competition ran. In all nine data providers participated providing more than the 20 APIs with released data.

The contest phase was ended on October 9 at 1.00 pm. As a final sequence of this phase, the jury visited all the teams and received a demonstration of the prototype. Ultimately on WestCoast TravelHack 2011, 76 individuals competed organized in 20

---

[1]   The seminars was streamed live via Bambuser. In total these broadcasts were viewed live by 756 viewers (http://bambuser.com/channel/travelhack). Slides used during the DIC were published on Slideshare (www.slideshare.net/travelhack)

Fig. 2. Snapshots of the digital service prototypes innovated at WestCoast TravelHack 2011

teams. A total of 1824 hours of innovation work was performed during the DICs 24 hours resulting in 20 digital service prototypes (c.f. figure 2 and table 3). The submitted contributions (represented by screen shots of the service prototype, a description of its functionality and a business model of the intended service) were published by the teams as projects on the developer zone prior to the jury evaluation. (www.trafiklab.se/travelhack2011bidrag). After the deadline the jury elaborated during two hours evaluating the different contributions. At 3.00 pm the teams was summoned in the grand hall and the different winners were announced. After this final ceremony the event was ended.

Table 3. Submitted digital service prototypes on WestCoast TravelHack 2011

Title	Digital Service Prototype Description
Barker	Barker is a digital service aimed toward event organizers. The organizer can create a "find us" page, which easily can be incorporated on the event web page. This page has all necessary information about how to get to the event utilizing car, public transportation and ride sharing. All modalities have attributes such as travel time and CO2 emissions. This guides the event participants in choosing sustainable means of transportation to and from the event

Table 3. (*continued*)

BeThere	BeThere will be a seamless integrated, non-intrusive automatic reminder that makes sure that the user is at the right place at the right time. It utilizes the users calendar while encouraging you to use public transportation.
BusStopInfo	BusStopInfo provides the means to present information about different public transportation stops to the user. The intention is that information about stops on different routes can act as incentives for increased usage of public transportation services. It also provides functionality to send feedback to the operators informing about the current status at a specific stop.
Buynearby.se	Buy Nearby is a service that incorporates information about homes for sale with information about travel and means of public transportation. The service provides criteria to search home for sales in relation to travelers occupations. Suitable homes for sale are displayed on a map together with information how to utilize public transportation including travel time and when to departure in order to reach an occupation utilizing public transportation.
Carpal	Carpal is a rideshare service integrated with existing services e.g. Facebook and Spotify. Provides functionality to select ride shares based on pictures, age, number of friends and music taste. It utilizes the Facebook wall to spread information about trips and trip requests.
Commute GBG	Commute GBG promote eco-driving by providing information about the CO_2 emissions produced by the user as a car commuter. The service is constructed in an idea that congestion fees in urban areas will become variable in relation to the amount of pollution a commuter generate.
Commutify	Commutify encourage in a fun way to climate smart traveling by providing functionality which facilitate that travelers can challenge themselves to travel more climate smart by challenging friends or celebrities to travel climate smart. Enhanced travel behavior will be rewarded by different incentives such as offers, improved personal health and a better environment.
Compass	Compass is designed as a dashboard with widgets. The user decides which widgets should be included in the specific Compass. The widgets have are developed to inform the user about public transportation, how to utilize means in the public transportation systems, plan trips, evaluate trips etc. The service will be provided in two configurations: one towards the public and one towards companies and other type of organizations.
Daily CO2 Emissions	The service will be integrated with Google Calendar. The aim is to include time for travelling, ticket purchase, SMS-alerts and CO_2 information for the trip when a meeting is arranged using Google Calendar.
Dev.ia.tion	This prototype is a hub (an API) through which travelers as well as traffic coordinators, drivers or systems can share and receive traffic deviations. The API in turn promoted distributed development of other services improving sustainable smart mobility
EnoughTime	This service will eventually support the traveler to make public transportation or car traveler more reliable by incorporating live-information about disturbances in the traffic system in travel planning. The aim is to improve advance planning and coordination before and during trips (e.g. commuting).
Find me a ride	Find me a ride allows users to search for, create and join rides from wherever in the city (or between cities eventually) to wherever. A ride is a set of point-to-point journeys (each belonging to one user) that makes a reasonable route; it is a trade-off between stops, passengers, times and fuel consumption.

Table 3. (*continued*)

Go Green Game	GGG is a game that assigns points to the users based on the way they travel in a city. Users need to press start a journey button and after they reached to their destination, press on finish journey. GGG automatically identifies transportation types and calculate desire points. GGG has designed as the way that gives highest points for zero-emission journeys and lowest for cars.
Moving In	The prototype was constructed based on the vision that the service should support people when they are moving making an informative decision based on traffic and public transportation information. Suitable objects (houses, apartments etc.) available are chosen and visualized based on the possibility to utilize.
My Public Transportation	Travelers are via the services provided support to give feedback, ask questions or provide information about deviations to the public transportation operator during the travel.
SmallButBig	SmallButBig transforms the traveler to the main character in a game. By entering the game a tournament begins against other travelers to conquer public transportation stops and compete quests of different sorts. All with the purpose to attract travelers to utilize public transportation.
SocialTrip	The service is based on the idea of making public transportations social. The prototype is built on a social network of travelers who plans their trips based on collective actions of other actors on the network. In so doing, travelers will be encouraged to use public transportations more than they used to and/or encourage travelers to shift from private to public transportations.
TimeTraveller	The service will provide functionality that supports the user to add favorite trips and view these trips for different themes: time, environment and price. Relevant data for the user is presented when the traveler choose a specific theme. The service will also provides alerts to inform the user when he or she should leave the home/office in order to not miss a specific departure from a public transportation stop.
TravelBot	TravelBot is integrated with Facebook. By creating a user utilizing the login credentials on Facebook all FB friends is integrated in TravelBot. By adding the travelers favorite routes TravelBot informs the user about weather on the route and also disturbances in the traffic systems. TravelBot will also provide alternative routes to avoid disturbances, and in addition provide functionality to simulate alternative directions as well as what impact a change of modality will create.
TravelCheck	TravelCheck provides functionality that makes it easy for the traveler to log the travels that he/she makes. Every trip generates a receipt about the CO_2 effects, time traveled, distance etc. The aim with the service is to keep track of the effects created by the individual travel behavior.

6   Evaluation

To assess whether our hypotheses in ch. 4 hold true we matched the result of our design against the two overarching characteristics of successful DIC's, innovative submissions which are aligned with organizational objectives. To investigate whether the resulting submissions were innovative, we compared submitted applications towards existing ones in the domain.

Of the 20 submissions, 15 were applications for Smartphone's. We thus searched the three major Smartphone platforms (Apple, Google Android and Windows Mobile) for applications on everyday travel. We used keywords such as "traffic", "transit", "parking", "bicycle" etc. to find such existing applications. We excluded those search results which evidently fell out of the scope of the competition (such as applications for promoting driving schools). In total we found 44 applications addressing everyday travel in Western Sweden on the three platforms. We then studied the descriptions of the existing applications and compared them with those submitted in the DIC. In our assessment we found that one submitted application to some degree existed on two Smartphone platforms (an automated public transit-based tourist guide), however the remaining 14 we considered novel and non-existing. Of the remaining five, three were web-based applications. Since it is not possible to inventory web sites in the same manner as Smartphone applications, we manually searched for web-based applications similar to those submitted. Of these three we found one which existed as a prototype but not as a fully operating application. For the remaining two submissions, one based on Facebook and one publically available API for open reporting of traffic disturbance we found no equivalents. Thus, as we found only two submissions to be already existing (although only partly) we conclude that the goal of innovative artifacts is met.

The other major foundation of a successful DIC is that the services produced meet organizational objectives. Since we wanted a researcher-independent assessment of the contributions' alignment with organizational goals we recruited an external jury judging the viability of the submissions. The jury consisted of the CEO of the region's public transit company, a business development manager for public transit on a national level, a business angel and social media expert, an official from the Government Offices of Sweden (national coordinator of public open data initiatives) and a technology reporter from the largest newspaper in Gothenburg. The primary goal was to generate services which promote more energy efficient everyday travel. This overall goal is divided into several important aspects manifested as contest criteria. A closer examination of the expert-based assessment reveals that the mean of all submission was about 60 % and that the top three submissions received between 80 % and 90 % of the maximum points available[2]. Given that the criteria are correct and the independent expert-based evaluations of the submissions are done in a rigorous way, evidence points towards that a significant portion of the submissions carry the possibility to meet organizational goals.

7   Final Reflections and Future Work

The DSR presented in this paper points towards the conclusion that it is indeed possible to perform DIC Design and create a contest that better meet the intended objectives; and thus to generate innovative artifacts adhering to organizational goals. By

---

[2]   As a backdrop, one of the main governmental funding agencies expects ISET to produce at least three services in this vein.

carefully designing the contest in accordance to the observed environment, guided by the extended literature review, we managed to finally extract a number of firm and novel digital service prototypes. We can based on this argue that this paper presents derived and evaluated DIC Design Guidelines.

However, our study has some shortcomings. First, we have only made a single field study. One interesting expansion is to compare our findings with a control group in which the competitors have received the same challenge but not received the guidelines put forward here and then compare the outcomes innovated. Our study also only focuses on the 24-hour on-site form of a DIC and not virtual or lengthier formats for DIC's. We believe that a comparison between formats is valuable in order to investigate the effects that length and location might have on the quality as well as the market readiness of the outcome produced from DIC's.

Further, this study was made in the vein of personal transportation, an area which seems to be attractive to work with from the developer community. Hence we do not know how well these findings may be transferred to other domains. Further, from a temporal perspective, we only study the actual competition. However, in order for a competition to be truly successful, the resulting submissions must be deployed and utilized by users in the environment which the time frame of this paper did not allow us to do. To this end, we invite other scholars to study and test whether these guidelines actually help promoting the applications in the phase following the competition; all in all to expand and improve the body of knowledge regarding DIC's.

Acknowledgement. The authors want to thank all the members of the contest organizing team behind WestCoast TravelHack 2011, as well as the participating organizations in the ISET Innovation and Research cluster for their effort in making the event a success. WestCoast TravelHack 2011 and ISET 2009-2013 is in addition made possible by grants provided by Sjuhärads Kommunalförbund, Västra Götalandsregionen / InMotion and Vinnova, the Swedish Governmental Agency for Innovation Systems.

References

1. Kuk, G., Davies, T.: The Roles of Agency and Artifacts in Assembling Open Data Complementarities. In: ICIS 2011 Proceedings (2011)
2. Ceccagnoli, M., Forman, C., Huang, P., Wu, D.J.: Cocreation of Value in a Platform Ecosystem. MIS Quarterly 36(1) (2012)
3. Boudreau, K.J., Lakhani, K.R.: How to manage outside innovation. Sloan Management Review 50(4), 69–75 (2009)
4. Piller, F.T., Walcher, D.: Toolkits for idea competitions: a novel method to integrate users in new product development. R&D Management 36, 3 (2006)
5. Bullinger, A.C., Moeselin, K.: M.: Online Innovation Contests – Where are We? In: AMCIS 2010 Proceedings (2010)

6. Bullinger, A.C., Neyer, A.-K., Rass, M., Moeslein, K.M.: Community-Based Innovation Contests: Where Competition Meets Cooperation. Creativity and Innovation Management 19(3) (2010)
7. Hevner, A., March, J., Park, J., Ram, S.: Design science in information systems research. MIS Quartely 28(1), 75–105 (2004)
8. Hevner, A.: A three-cycle view of design science research Scandinavian. Journal of Information Systems 19(2), 87–92 (2007)
9. Hevner, A., Chatterjee, S.: Design Research in Information Systems: Theory and Practice. Springer, New York (2010)
10. Hjalmarsson, A., Lind, M.: Challenges in Establishing Sustainable Innovation. In: ECIS 2011 Proceedings (2011)
11. Hjalmarsson, A., Lind, M., Rudmark, D., Carlson, R.: Challenges when Digital Services for Sustainable Everyday Travel is Innovated. Sprouts: Working Papers on Information Systems 11(11) (2011), http://sprouts/aisnet.org/11-11
12. Kirsch, L.J.: Deploying Common Systems Globally: The Dynamics of Control. Information Systems Research 15(4), 374–395 (2004)
13. Kirsch, L.J.: The Management of Complex Tasks in Organizations: Controlling the Systems Development Process. Organization Science 7(1), 1–21 (1996)
14. Tiwana, A., Konsynski, B., Bush, A.A.: Research Commentary–Platform Evolution: Coevolution of Platform Architecture, Governance, and Environmental Dynamics. Information Systems Research 21(4), 675–687 (2010)
15. Dahlander, L., Magnusson, M.G.: Relationships between open source software companies and communities: Observations from Nordic firms. Research Policy 34(4), 481–493 (2005)
16. Webne-Behrman, H.: The Practice of Facilitation: Managing Group Process and Solving Problems, LaVergne, TN (1998)
17. Rosemann, M., Hjalmarsson, A., Lind, M., Recker, J.: Four Facets of a Process Modeling Facilitator. In: ICIS 2012 Proceedings (2012)
18. Hord, S.M.: Facilitative leadership: The imperative for change Austin. Southwest Educational Development Laboratory, TX (1992)
19. Cooper, A.: The inmates are running the asylum: why high-tech products drive us crazy and how to restore the sanity. Sams, Indianapolis (1999)
20. Pruitt, J., Grudin, J.: Personas: practice and theory. In: Proceedings of the 2003 Conference on Designing for User Experiences. ACM (2003)
21. Blomquist, Å., Arvola, M.: Personas in action: ethnography in an interaction design team. In: Proceedings of NordiCHI, vol. 2, pp. 197–200 (2002)
22. Grudin, J., Pruitt, J.: Personas, participatory design and product development: An infrastructure for engagement. In: Proceedings of PDC 2002, vol. 2002, p. 7 (2002)
23. Cockton, G.: From quality in use to value in the world. In: Proceedings of CHI 2004 on Human Factors in Computing Systems, pp. 1287–1290. ACM (2004)
24. Nichols, D., Twidale, M.: The usability of open source software. First Monday 8(1) (2003)
25. Chesbrough, H., Rosenbloom, R.: The role of the business model in capturing value from innovation: evidence from Xerox Corporation's technology spin-off companies. Industrial and Corporate Change 11(3), 529–555 (2002)
26. Osterwalder, A.: The business model ontology: A proposition in a design science approach. Academic Dissertation, Universite de Lausanne, Ecole des Hautes Etudes Commerciales (2004)

27. Yoo, Y., Henfridsson, O., Lyytinen, K.: Research Commentary - The New Organizing Logic of Digital Innovation: An Agenda for Information Systems Research. Information Systems Research 21(4), 724–735 (2010)
28. Yoffie, D.: Competing in the age of digital convergence. Harvard Business School Press, Boston (1997)
29. Gawer, A., Cusumano, M.A.: Platform leadership: How Intel, Microsoft, and Cisco drive industry innovation. Harvard Business School Press, Boston (2002)
30. Evans, D.S., Hagiu, A., Schmalensee, R.: Invisible Engines: How Software Platforms Drive Innovation and Transform Industries. The MIT Press, Cambridge (2006)

Evaluating APIs: A Call for Design Science Research[*]

Bala Iyer[1] and George Wyner[2]

[1] Babson College
Wellesley, MA USA
biyer@babson.edu
[2] Boston University School of Management
Boston, MA USA
gwyner@bu.edu

Abstract. In a business world characterized by ecosystem-based competition, APIs are key determinants of success. However, there is very little guidance on how organizations should go about making decisions about APIs. API design must account for the needs of both present and future application developers who use the API, and API outcomes depend on the success of the applications which incorporate that API. As a result, the design of APIs poses unique challenges that would benefit from design science inquiry. At the same time, these multiple sources of input in API design pose special challenges for carrying out design science research. This paper focuses on developing a foundation for future design science research in the API domain by addressing the first two steps of the design science research methodology recommended by Peffers et al: We view these as preliminary steps towards the development of a methodology for the design of APIs.

Keywords: API, kernel theory, modularity, stakeholders, strategy.

1   Introduction

A business ecosystem consists of firms embedded in formalized, significant, and enduring inter-firm relationships [1]. These business ecosystems permit a focal firm to access resources and capabilities external to the firm. The information flows in the ecosystem have the potential, when combined with the focal firm's resources, to positively impact firm performance [2].

The dynamics within the software industry call for simultaneous firm cooperation and competition. Thus, every software firm faces the challenge of ensuring product interoperability with other firms' products. Interoperability is critical because no single firm provides all the software required by users. The value to end customers is based on coordinated product launches of complementary products that work together seamlessly [3].

Consider the case of Facebook and Zynga. Zynga developed games like Farmville and Cityville and launched them on the Facebook platform. Thus Facebook becomes

---

[*]   The authors contributed equally to this paper and are listed in alphabetical order.

K. Peffers, M. Rothenberger, and B. Kuechler (Eds.): DESRIST 2012, LNCS 7286, pp. 28–35, 2012.
© Springer-Verlag Berlin Heidelberg 2012

a platform provider and Zynga a complementor [4]. In order to support this arrangement, Facebook opened up its platform in 2007 and provided Application Program Interface (API) driven access to its internal functionality and data.

An API is an interface provided by a software system to expose specific services to external applications. Today there are billions of API calls being made per month on Google, Twitter, Facebook and Netflix. In what becomes a battle for control and strategic advantage, a platform provider provides APIs to make it easy for complementors to develop applications. While it is providing support, the platform provider is simultaneously trying to make sure that it is not substituted by the complementor and the complementor is trying to make sure that it stays interoperable with this platform and is portable to other platforms. In this arena, decisions related to API design and adoption have significant business implications. For example, when, in May 2010, Facebook and Zynga came to a standoff over revenue sharing, Facebook turned off Zynga's access to some of its APIs and thereby denied Zynga users the ability to use Facebook features like status updates. Facebook forced Zynga to settle on a 5-year revenue sharing agreement.

As our stakeholder analysis below will emphasize, the value an API provides to its stakeholders is mediated by the applications which developers build on top of the API. This indirect element of an API's design impact has profound implications both for the importance of engaging in design science research on APIs and the difficulty of carrying out that research.

Because the functions provided by an API are incorporated in complex ways into other design artifacts (the applications built using the API), certain design decisions made by an API's architect are highly visible to the application developers who make use of the API in their creations. In particular, the interfaces defined by the API must be understood precisely by developers. Thus the design of an API will receive very close scrutiny by potential adopters and it becomes all the more important for API designers to understand the principles which govern API design.

A second issue driving the importance of developing a strong theory of API design is the high cost of changing an API. As Jacobsen et al [5] observe, API developers must consider carefully how changes to their interfaces will impact existing applications. A change to an interface has the potential to break existing applications thus requiring use of a versioning system or requiring developers to rework their applications. Clearly design decisions carry special weight in an API context, with important ramifications for the existing code base as well as for opportunities for downstream innovation.

For these reasons API designers and companies seeking to invest in API development would stand to benefit from the kind of careful investigation of design decisions and their consequences that design science can provide.

The same indirect element of API design that makes it such a promising area of inquiry for design science also creates interesting challenges for that research. While APIs are certainly not unique among design artifacts in requiring designers to focus on the requirements of multiple stakeholders, the problem is perhaps more severe in the API context because the functionality provided by an API to the end user is mediated through the applications developed using the API. The API designer must provide functionality that will be provided in applications of which she may be unaware and over which she has no control. Evaluating an API design is exceptionally challenging for similar reasons: the value and success of an API depends both on its direct appeal to the developers who use it in their applications and the success of the applications those developers create. Evaluation will be more difficult because of the need to measure impact on both these levels. As Jaroslav Tulach has observed, an additional challenge is that APIs are being designed for both present and future developers and changes in APIs must take into account the issue of backwards compatibility with past developers as well [6].

This paper seeks not only to call attention to the potential benefits of this research, but to begin the work of developing a foundation for future design science research in the API domain by addressing the first two steps of the design science research methodology (henceforth referred to as DSRM) recommended by Peffers et al [7]:

1. We explicate the API design problem by carrying out a stakeholder analysis. We argue that such an analysis is important to scoping the problem by bringing in additional dimensions that go beyond the core technical concerns.
2. We begin the process of identifying objectives for API design. Rather than focusing on a specific API design problem in this paper we want to lay the groundwork for such specific research by identifying general characteristics that might be used to distinguish a good API design. Our approach to this question will be to consider the relevance of various candidate kernel theories. As Walls et al have observed, such kernel theories serve as a basis for deriving "meta-requirements" for a given design domain [8]. Identifying the strongest candidate kernel theories is a first step towards this goal.

2   Stakeholder Analysis

We describe requirements for defining, designing, developing, and deploying APIs from four perspectives: owner, architect, builder and end-user. Figure 1 shows what each stakeholder expects as inputs and what they expect to achieve from using APIs.

Owner. This stakeholder looks at APIs from the perspective of building a competitive advantage and the various business models it can enable. A business model describes the rationale of how an organization creates, delivers, and captures value [9]. Thus the owner will expect business models to be at an appropriate level of granularity for their purposes and will expect the models to allow each asset to be reused and monitored. Owners will study the feasibility of various combinations of business assets. Ultimately, they would want to answer the question "How can APIs liberate the trapped value in my enterprise and allow me to experiment with various business models?" The answer to this question results in identifying the various business assets that need APIs, the budget allocated, and metrics for performance.

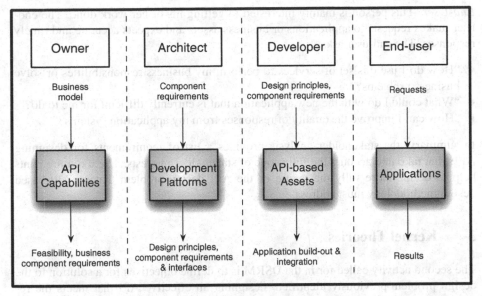

Fig. 1. A Stakeholder Analysis of an API

Architect. An architect will help define the platform on which various business models can be enabled, including the APIs to be provided. This person defines the design principles, components, interfaces and tests to the platform. The architect asks:

- "What principles and commitments will guide the design of the required business assets?"
- "Which of those business requirements could we provide using APIs?"
- "What are the advantages/disadvantages of delivering the requirement using an API?"
- "Which business assets should be built and what functionality should they encapsulate?"

For a company to have a strong position within an ecosystem, the architecture decisions should be made in a transparent manner and be subject to close scrutiny by a community of users.

Developer. A developer implements and integrates components using the architecture design principles and the API capabilities as defined by the architect. A developer asks:

- "What supplier provided solutions will I deploy to implement and integrate?"
- "What granularity of components should I select?"
- "How long would it take, and what would it cost to develop each application?"
- "What new skills would we need to acquire to develop these API-based business assets?"
- "What products/tools/technology should we purchase?"

End-User. This person is mainly interested in getting his or her work done. The end-user makes requests to applications or business assets and expects accurate and timely responses. The end-user asks:

- "How do I use this set of services to perform my business responsibilities or solve business problems?"
- "What could I do with the new application that is currently difficult for me to do?"
- "How can I improve the quality of responses from my application systems?"

In summary, the stakeholder analysis provides a list of requirements for designing APIs that take into account the full scope of stakeholder interests. These requirements help to define more fully the nature of the API design problem that an API-based design methodology must address.

3   Kernel Theories

The second activity called for in the DSRM is to define objectives for a solution to the design problem previously identified: designing an effective API that meets the requirements of all the relevant stakeholders. A set of objectives for designing an API is of necessity going to be very dependent on the specific context: the purpose of the particular API being designed and the specific goals of the stakeholders involved. Thus, as noted in the introduction, our agenda at this point is to elucidate some general principles to guide the discovery of such objectives given a specific API design problem. To arrive at such principles we will consider a number of kernel theories that may offer insight into what counts as good API design.

3.1   Modularity

One place to look for guidance in the design of APIs is the theory of modularity [10], given that APIs are modules separated from the applications which consume their services. Messerschmitt [11] lists five key attributes which characterize good modular design:

- *Functionality*. Each module offers a set of functions which are conceptually connected so that the overall scope of the module seems to represent a natural grouping.
- *Hierarchy*. Modules can be further decomposed into sub-modules and this internal structure is not typically visible externally.
- *Separation of concerns*. Each module is only loosely coupled with other modules.
- *Interoperability*. Modules can easily interact with each other.
- *Reusability*. Modules can be reused in multiple systems.

While these attributes can be used to guide the design of any software including an API, there are particular aspects of how these principles apply to API design that should be made explicit:

Functionality. The more intuitive the functionality offered by each element in an API, the more easily developers can learn which function to use for a given purpose, thus making the API easier to learn and code easier to maintain.

Hierarchy. The degree to which the internals of an API exhibit hierarchical design would appear to be less directly relevant to its adoption by developers since, as defined by Messerschmitt, this concerns internal issues which are not exposed to the API's consumers. However, as with any complex system, there is the potential benefit of hierarchical design as a way to manage the internal complexity, and thus the stability and maintainability, of the API's implementation.

Separation of concerns. In the context of API design there are two kinds of coupling to be considered: coupling between elements of the API and coupling between the API and the applications which use it. For the first of these: to what extent does successful use of one function call rely on use of other calls? While some interaction among calls is inevitable, the more complex those interactions the more difficult use of the API is likely to be. In the case of coupling between the application and the API, issues might include to what extent the developer needs to understand the internal state of any data structures maintained by the API.

Interoperability. While by its very nature an API is designed to be interoperable, one might assess the complexity of the mechanisms employed to interact with the API. For example one has the issue of whether to use lighter weight technologies such as REST and JSON or more powerful XML-based techniques for accessing APIs over the web.

Reusability. While an API inherently offers the potential for reuse in that its functions are available to be called by multiple applications, in practice reuse will depend on the extent that the functionality embodied in an API is usable across a wide range of potential applications.

3.2   Design Patterns

Given that many modern APIs are object-oriented in nature, an important possible resource for good API design would be the classic book on Design Patterns by Gamma and colleagues [12]. In this book the authors set forth a series of best practices for object-oriented design. The best practices are expressed as design patterns following the approach proposed by Alexander and colleagues [13], in which a design best practice is given a memorable name and situated in the context in which its use is most appropriate.

The patterns proposed by Gamma et al are sometimes known as the "Gang of Four Patterns" or "GoF Patterns" because of the number of the book's authors. The GoF patterns taken one at a time each represent a kind of mini-design theory in that they document best practice as it already exists in the field based on the judgments of experts in the field. However, there remains much latitude as to which pattern to use in what circumstance and how specifically the pattern is to be realized for a given software project.

GoF patterns can play several distinct roles as a kernel theory to support API design: first, the patterns constitute a theoretical vocabulary for describing object-oriented designs. Thus any given API can be described in part in terms of the patterns it uses. Second, while in some cases the choice of a pattern may not be obvious, there are cases where the presence or absence of a particular design pattern can have clear normative implications.

For example, the *Singleton* pattern would apply to an API when some data structure needs to be globally visible and unique. The Singleton pattern suggests that an API provide a dedicated function for locating such a global object rather than, for example, requiring applications to use some agreed upon "hard coded" object name.

Beyond the GoF patterns there are other contributions to the patterns literature that seem promising for our purposes: Fowler has proposed a set of patterns of enterprise application architecture which address a number of issues which relate to API design, for example alternatives for defining the interface between the business logic layer of an application and the database layer [14]. One of the patterns Fowler has identified in this regard, *Active Record*, has been explicitly adopted in a number of APIs including the Ruby on Rails web framework.

The point here is not that API developers should be using software patterns in their work. Clearly this is already the case. However, as Tulach has observed, the patterns which are appropriate for developing an object-oriented application are not necessarily the patterns that are best for developing an API [6]. There is additional work to be done to clarify what patterns apply to API design and in what circumstances, and to discover new patterns specific to API design. Tulach has made a very important contribution in this area, based on years of experience developing APIs and guiding others in doing so. The result is a body of knowledge that can serve as an important resource as we move forward in using design science research methods to develop an API design methodology. To do so, we must take into account technical knowledge such as that embodied in Tulach's work together with the broader scope of requirements we have identified in our stakeholder analysis.

4   Conclusions

In this paper we have argued that the domain of APIs represents an important area for future design science research. As a first step we have articulated the scope of the API design problem by conducting a stakeholder analysis, and have identified some potential kernel theories that can provide the elements of a theory of API design.

In future work we expect to further develop the stakeholder analysis by modeling the interdependencies and interactions among the stakeholders. Moving forward, the next steps in our work are clearly defined by the DSRM. Having described the API design problem we need to articulate the objectives for API design. In this paper we have explored the potential applicability of two existing kernel theories: modularity and software design patterns. To further develop our understanding we plan to undertake a series of interviews with API developers and strategists to clarify the design objectives, challenges, and strategies which emerge in the practice of API design. As the DSRM suggests, this clarification of objectives should then lead to the construction and evaluation of a design artifact. In our case the design artifact will take the form of an API design methodology. Such a methodology will be informed by existing best practice and kernel theories and will provide API designers and other stakeholders with guidance for developing API designs that take into account the broader strategic context we have begun to surface with our stakeholder analysis. Our hope is that pursuing this line of inquiry will lead to a significant contribution to the design-science knowledgebase [15].

Acknowledgments. The authors would like to thank the anonymous reviewers for their valuable suggestions on how to improve the paper.

References

1. Gulati, R., Gargiulo, M.: Where do interorganizational networks come from? American Journal of Sociology 104, 1439–1493 (1999)
2. Venkatraman, N., Lee, C.H., Iyer, B.: Interconnect to Win: The Joint Effects of Business Strategy and Network Positions on the Performance of Software Firms. In: Baum, J.A.C., Rowley, T.J. (eds.) Network Strategy: Advances in Strategic Management, pp. 391–424. JAI/Elsevier, Oxford (2008)
3. Shapiro, C., Varian, H.R.: Information Rules: A Strategic Guide to the Network Economy. Harvard Business School Press, Boston (1999)
4. Gawer, A., Cusumano, M.: Platform Leadership. Harvard Business School Press, Boston (2002)
5. Jacobson, D., Brail, G., Woods, D.: APIs: A Strategy Guide. O'Reilly Media, Sebastopol (2011)
6. Tulach, J.: Practical API Design: Confessions of a Java Framework Architect. Apress, New York (2008); Distributed to the book trade worldwide by Springer-Verlag New York, Berkeley, CA
7. Peffers, K., Tuunanen, T., Rothenberger, M., Chatterjee, S.: A design science research methodology for information systems research. Journal of Management Information Systems 24, 45–77 (2007)
8. Walls, J., Widmeyer, G., Sawy, O.E.: Building an information system design theory for vigilant EIS. Information Systems Research 3, 36–59 (1992)
9. Osterwalder, A., Pigneur, Y.: Business Model Generation. John Wiley & Sons, Hoboken (2010)
10. Baldwin, C.Y., Clark, K.B.: Design Rules: The Power of Modularity. The MIT Press, Cambridge (2000)
11. Messerschmitt, D.: Understanding Networked Applications: A First Course. Morgan Kaufmann Publishers, San Francisco (2000)
12. Gamma, E., Helm, R., Johnson, R., Vlissides, J., Grady, G.: Design Patterns: Elements of Reusable Object-Oriented Software. Addison-Wesley, Reading (1995)
13. Christopher, A., Ishikawa, S., Silverstein, M., Jacobson, M., Fiksdahl-King, I., Shlomo, S.: A Pattern Language. Oxford University Press, New York (1977)
14. Fowler, M., Rice, D.: Patterns of Enterprise Application Architecture. Addison-Wesley, Upper Saddle River (2003)
15. Hevner, A.R., March, S.T., Park, J., Sudha, S.: Design science in information systems research. MIS Quarterly 28, 75–105 (2004)

Designing for Recombination: Process Design through Template Combination

Arvind Karunakaran[1] and Sandeep Purao[2]

[1] Sloan School of Management, Massachusetts Institute of Technology,
Cambridge, MA, United States
arvindk@mit.edu
[2] College of Information Sciences and Technology, The Pennsylvania State University,
University Park, PA, United States
spurao@ist.psu.edu

Abstract. Process design remains an important yet difficult concern for postindustrial organizations. We posit that processes 'become' processes in these organizations only via their anchoring in concrete artifacts. Consequently, we identify and refine two design principles: processes as anchored in concrete material artifacts (not abstract process representations); and process design through recombination of existing processes (instead of designing anew). Our research starts by building a research artifact, ReKon, that instantiates these two principles. The paper describes this artifact with the meta-model, an implementation and the fine-granular process units, as template chunks created from ~1,200 real-world templates, to populate the tool. We revise and refine the design principles via successive cycles of implementation of the research artifact, formative evaluation with student teams, and insights obtained from an ongoing field study. We conclude by pointing to directions for future research.

Keywords: Business Process, Templates, Artifacts, Granularity, Recombination.

1   Introduction

Process design and management is a crucial aspect of postindustrial organizing. The past two decades have seen significant scholarly activity and practitioner interest in this area [1-4]. Many techniques and methodologies, such as Quality circles, Total quality management, Business process management, Six Sigma, and Method Engineering have been proposed for the design, reconfiguration and management of business processes. Scholars have proposed Process Handbooks [5], Process Grammars [6] as well as tools to generate innovative business process ideas [7].

Although these efforts have produced a rich body of scholarship on process design and management, fundamental problems remain. Existing approaches are neither able to keep existing processes in sync with changes in the business environment nor able to generate new processes in response to shifts in customer demands. Many extant studies show that existing approaches aimed at designing and managing processes often lead to suboptimal outcomes [8-12] and at times, entrap the organization [12-14]. These unresolved issues provide the broader motivation for our current study: *how do we generate and implement processes to respond to ongoing changes in the business environment?*

K. Peffers, M. Rothenberger, and B. Kuechler (Eds.): DESRIST 2012, LNCS 7286, pp. 36–51, 2012.
© Springer-Verlag Berlin Heidelberg 2012

The solution we propose is based on the following argument. We posit that existing conceptualizations of 'process' are too abstract and coarse-grain. They fail to notice that processes are materially anchored in concrete artifacts, such as project templates, forms, checklists, slide decks, boilerplates and more. Due to this oversight, approaches for process design cannot easily translate new processes to work practices, and end up being ineffective at infusing process changes onto the day-to-day fabric of work. We advocate the position that processes *become* processes only when they materially anchored in concrete artifacts. Existing approaches to process design do not address this important dimension, and instead, remain trapped at higher levels of abstraction and granularity. The research challenge, thus, is how to facilitate process design through a recombination of materially anchored processes.

Our approach to addressing the research challenge starts with two foundational design principles: (i) processes are anchored in concrete material artifacts of some form, and hence, process design should be orchestrated through these artifacts; (ii) new processes are generated through the extension and recombination of existing processes. Together, they suggest that process design should be supported via artifacts such as templates that are modularized for subsequent recombinations. In doing so, our core argument remains: artifacts such as templates represent material anchors of processes, which can facilitate process (re-)design.

We follow the canonical design research approach [15] that aims at knowing via building [16], aided by empirical field work. We build multiple iterations of ReKon, a tool that allows recombination of fine-granular template chunks to generate new processes. The paper elaborates theoretical foundations of the tool, derives design principles from the specific implementation, and outlines formative evaluation results that have lead to evolution of the design principles. We conclude with future research steps.

2   Background

We begin with a motivating example, followed by a review of relevant prior work.

Consider a scenario faced by EntArch, Inc., a large IT services firm, specializing in the migration, integration and maintenance of banking and telecom systems. With over 400 clients, including many major US banks and telecom carriers, and 1000+ completed projects, their primary methodology is incremental commitment and test-driven development. Over the years, EntArch has derived these from past projects: a large repository of process knowledge, a best practice toolkit including rules, routines, checklists and procedural guidelines, and a methodology for capturing and representing workflows from their clients along with past examples of ER Schemas, DFDs and Petrinets. They are now dealing with a new client, TeleCorp, and deciding how to approach a new systems integration effort. The project requires constructing a catalog of maintenance timelines and service-level agreements from a scheduling application, and outlining procedures to replicate it with other legacy applications. EntArch, Inc. has done similar projects in the past, and would like to reuse these processes where possible. However, they realize that these processes will need adjustments to address new project needs and are unsure about how to do this. EntArch, however, has several practice artifacts, in the form of word documents, spreadsheets, slide decks, forms, checklists and more, each codifying best practices used in past projects. Each runs into several pages, contains instructions and worksheets for tasks such as requirements gathering, business process modeling, database designing, and testing. The project team is more comfortable with the possibility that their project can benefit from these artifacts and would like to leverage the artifacts appropriate for this project. They realize that no single artifact can fully address their concerns and several artifacts contain more than what they might need. The sheer number of artifacts, and conflicting and overlapping choices, is making it difficult for them to move forward, and leverage these process knowledge assets.

In situations like these, the traditional response involves use of techniques such as Business Process Management (BPM) or Method Engineering (ME), i.e., a return to prescriptive and coarse-grain methods to design and reconfigure processes. Such a response ignores practice-related knowledge such as rules, routines and best practices from past projects codified in artifacts. Artifacts, as we have suggested above, act as material anchors of processes. They provide a more concrete alternative to the high abstraction of BPM [3] and ME [17] that end up hindering translation to practice [18, 19]. We elaborate this in the review of prior work next.

2.1 Process Design

Early interest in the design of processes can be traced to the industrial era [20], where the design of processes and work activities could be mapped against the physicality of the manufactured product and its hierarchical decomposition [21]. The shift to a post-industrial era brought on challenges of invisible and tough to measure work, making it difficult to design business processes by partitioning work activities ex ante [22, 23, 24]. BPM was, therefore, seen as a useful approach for partitioning and formalizing intangible work into processes, and formalizing these for mapping against organizational functions [25, 26]. Digitization, coupled with knowledge management initiatives, formalized this further with mechanisms for creating, reconfiguring and maintaining processes [27-29]. These processual assets [30, 31] provided a source of competitive advantage [32-34].

Despite these theoretical arguments and empirical evidences, efforts to design and maintain business processes have remained tenuous at best (see [10, 35, 36] for related arguments). Scholars have repeatedly documented why these efforts become counterproductive [9, 37], and have showed how and how firms fall into capability traps [11, 12] due to self-confirming attribution errors that arise during the dynamics of process design.

2.2 Method Engineering

A more recent analog to process design research is found in research aimed at addressing limitations posed by generic systems development processes [17, 38, 39]. An example is Method Engineering [17]. It suggests adapting methods such as ER, PetriNets and FDM or deriving tool-kit approaches that respond to the needs of a particular project. This may take the form of selection from a set of methodologies to selection of a path within a methodology to compiling a method outline or even modular method construction [40].

Although the potential benefits of method engineering seem obvious, its feasibility has remained a concern [41, 42]. Mathiassen et al. [43], for example, argue that the primary customers of method engineering are not those who are 'working with methods' but those who are 'learning the methods'. Thus, expert practitioners and actual work context assume only a secondary role for structuring and presenting new methods. Method engineering also involves substantial effort to examine current methods before mapping these to project characteristics or fragmenting methods to derive them as needed [41]. And even after expending these efforts, method fragments turn out to be either too abstract to use in practice or too tightly coupled to the larger technique, leading to redundancy and loss of integrity. Researchers suggest that the coarse granularity of fragments present key obstacles to making method engineering relevant to practice [41, 43]. Together, these problems can be traced to an abstraction mismatch between 'method' and 'day-to-day practice,' similar to those outlined for process design.

2.3   Concrete Artifacts and Process Design

The two streams of research summarized above have lead to a healthy skepticism about Business Process Management, Method engineering and other such approaches [1, 44]. Attempts to re-examine this problem have, however, remained at a coarse-granular level, e.g., inter-divisional [45], capabilities [46, 47] or systems [14]. We argue, based on the example outlined and the review above, that there is a need to return to fine-grain and concrete artifacts for process design. In doing so, we extend the arguments from others who have implicitly made the point about the importance of artifacts in dynamic postindustrial environments [48-54].

3   Research Approach and Methods

To address our research question, we employ design science research [15] aided by empirical work, through five overlapping stages (See Figure 1).

In stage 1, we interviewed individuals in four organizations to understand their process management concerns. The software services domain was selected (following purposive sampling) because of its process-intensive nature [55], and the organizations were selected based on the criteria that a) they were in operation for at least 25 years, and b) they had a stabilized set of business and project management processes. During this stage, the organizations also contributed ~1200 real-world templates.

In stage 2, we analyzed the templates starting with qualitative artifact analysis [56, 57]. We examined the attributes such as format, length, and content of each template to make claims [57] about ways in which they may enable or constrain software development work. Based on this, we derived a meta-model and designed heuristics for categorizing, chunking and placing the template chunks into specific phases and tasks where they could be used.

In stage 3, we designed and built the first version of a research artifact, ReKon, aimed at facilitating navigation through and recombination of template chunks. For example, the tool would allow accessing template chunks given a phase/task, and allow users to combine the templates as needed. Stages 2 and 3 unfolded in an iterative manner.

Concurrent and Ongoing Stage: Reflect and Continually Refine Design Principles

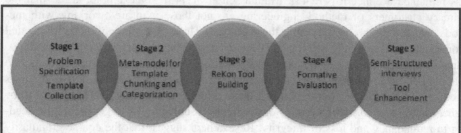

Fig. 1. Research Approach

In stage 4, we conducted formative evaluation [58] with users involved in working on real-world, process-intensive projects to implement integration solutions as part of a course. The evaluation consisted of two steps. First step, conducted prior to the introduction of the research artifact, ReKon, assessed the size and number of template chunks compared to having coarse-grain templates. The second step, conducted after the students explored ReKon for a few weeks, assessed properties such as appropriateness and relevance for project needs.

In stage 5, we conducted semi-structured interviews in 2 of those 4 software services organizations to obtain more in-depth insights about how project templates are created, institutionalized and put to use. This included 11 from one organization engaged in legacy application support, characterized as high process intensity, with more than 3000 employees worldwide; and 7 from the other organization engaged in information management, characterized as very high process intensity, with more than 220,000 employees worldwide. Based on the obtained insights, we have we returned to iterating the research artifact, ReKon.

The five stages (that took place from January 2009 to December 2011) were accompanied by a concurrent and ongoing stage (similar to Sein et al., [59]) to reflect on the efforts and outcomes. This ongoing reflection has allowed derivation and continual refinement of design principles. We elaborate next on the tangible outcomes as well as design principles.

4   Recombining Templates for Designing Processes

We describe the research outcomes – design principles as well as tangible instantiations –derived through the research process. In doing so, we add more detail to the research approach, for example, describing the techniques used for developing the research artifact, and outlining the choices made for the evaluation cycles.

The first stage, initial conversations with individuals from four software services organizations provided us a glimpse of the problem. We understood that process design did not stop at the conceptual level. Constructing a process by specifying dependencies among activities was merely considered a starting point. We realized that processes are realized only through their anchoring in concrete artifacts such as forms, screens and reports. The specific form of artifacts that was implicated most in the design of processes was templates. Consider some examples (Figure 2). Here, the first template (on the left) captures best practices for a requirements gathering task, and includes pointers that project participants can use to structure the task, including potential sub-tasks. The second (on the right) is a code review template that includes a checklist for the overall structure and sequence for conducting a code review.

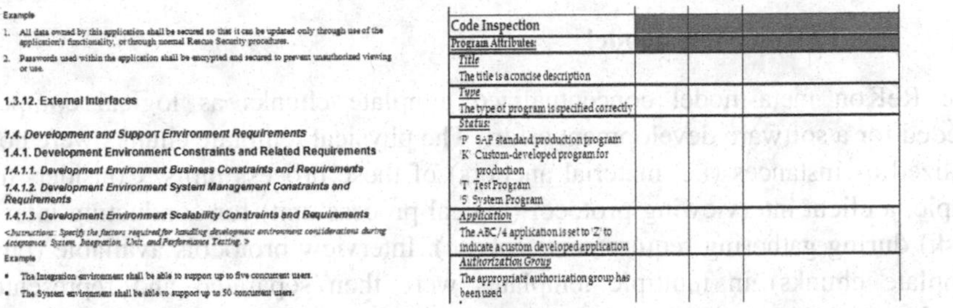

Fig. 2. Templates for (a) Gathering Requirements, (b) Code Review

Such templates are abundant and include, for example, functional specification documents, high-level and low-level design templates, effort estimation spreadsheets, boilerplate contract documents and others. They do not represent an abstracted workflow or method fragment. Instead, each provides an instance of *concrete* and *realizable* process knowledge, experientially derived, symbolically articulated and materially anchored [34]. There are, however, problems associated with the reuse of these templates. They are too many and too varied, so the search costs to locate an appropriate template tend to be high. Each can run into several pages - only a portion is likely to be relevant to a new process, yet, no single template can fully support a task - the needed knowledge is spread across multiple templates. Based on these, we derived initial design concerns for the class of problems. Figure 3 specifies these concerns.

> How to facilitate (re)-design of processes by utilizing concrete artifacts that carry experientially derived process knowledge? How to overcome problems such as coarse-granularity and minimize search costs when working with these artifacts?

Fig. 3. Specifying Design Concerns for the Class of Problems

These provided the motivation to the design research process. In response, our initial design of the research artifact, ReKon, followed two foundational design principles that we derived from prior work (see Table 1).

Table 1. Initial Design Principles drawn from Prior Work

Principle	Description
Anchoring in *Material Artifacts*	Processes are, in real world, anchored in concrete material artifacts of some form, and hence, process design should be orchestrated through artifacts
Process design is *Re-design*	New processes are generated through the tinkering and recombination of existing processes

These initial design principles were supported by extant theories and prior empirical studies (reviewed earlier), and reflected what we learned from initial conversations with the four software services firms. The next steps on ReKon involved designing the meta-model and deriving the template chunks.

4.1   The ReKon Meta-model

The ReKon meta-model conceptualized template chunks as logical components needed for a software development effort. The physical template chunks were conceptualized as instances (i.e. material anchors) of these process units. Consider, for example, a client interviewing protocol (logical process unit) for conducting interviews (task) during gathering requirements (phase). Interview protocols available (physical template chunks) in multiple templates were then separated and represented as chunks. Project members could access these (retrieval) and combine to create new templates (target template). Figure 4 describes the ReKon meta-model.

Process Units and Software Development Efforts

$p \in P$ Phases in a Software Development Effort
$t, u \in T$ Tasks in a Software Development Effort
$l, m \in L$ Logical Process Units
need (l,t,p) Process Unit l is needed for Task t, Phase p $\{0,1\}$

Template Chunks

$s \in S$ Project Templates contributed by four Consulting Organizations
$j, k \in K$ Physical Template Chunks constructed from Project Templates
part (k,s) Physical Template Chunk k is part of Project Template s $\{0,1\}$

ReKon Repository

instance (k,l) Physical Template Chunk k is an instance of Logical
                Knowledge Unit l $\{0,1\}$

Target Template

$d \in D$ New templates constructed by recombining Physical Template
            Chunks

Operations on ReKon

$\{k \mid (\text{retrieve (instance } (k,l) \mid \text{need } (l,s,t))\}$
                Retrieval of a set of Physical Template Chunks $\{k\}$ that represent
                instances of Logical Knowledge Units (l) needed for task t, phase p

$k \in \{k\}$ Selection of the appropriate Template Chunk instance k

---

Fig. 4. The ReKon Meta-model

4.2   Chunking and Categorization

Based on this meta-model, we designed and implemented the ReKon artifact. We populated this version of ReKon, with template chunks derived from the ~1,200 templates acquired from those four software services organizations. To generate the template chunks, we started with qualitative artifact analysis [56, 57]. First, we examined the format, length, and other attributes (such as the number of sections, sub-sections, labels etc.) of each template, and recorded these. We then made "claims" [57] about the ways in which these templates could be used, and how they could enable or constrain process design for software development work.

Using these, we chunked and categorized each template. Each chunk was placed in a matrix of Phases and Tasks constructed by consulting Project Management Institute's PMBOK and Lam and Shankarraman's [60] "enterprise integration" methodology. Some examples of Phases include: Planning, Market Research, Requirements Gathering, Implementation, and Testing. Some examples of Tasks include: IP Waiver, Status Reports, and Client Interaction. The intersection Phases and Tasks provided "cells". Each cell was populated with template chunks.

To ensure fidelity for this chunking and categorization process, multiple coders worked through multiple rounds. First, a random sample of 122 documents (~10% of the set) was chosen. Coders established common guidelines for chunking and categorizing these templates. They identified headings and sub-headings of individual templates, and parsed these to decide if a template chunk could fit into a particular cell. For example, a client interview protocol represents a template chunk that fits in the cell at the intersection of conducting interviews (task) and gathering requirements (phase). Interview protocols available in multiple templates – say, for different variety of clients (e.g., Small businesses, Large enterprises), or for different types of projects (e.g., Web Development, Legacy System Maintenance) - were separated and placed in this cell. Multiple rounds of chunking and classifications allowed comparisons and discussions (to resolve differences) across coders. Table 2 shows the results and inter-coder agreement during the two rounds, suggesting high levels of agreement [61].

Table 2. Inter-Coder Reliability for Chunking and Coding Templates

Round	Templates Coded	Number of Coders	Inter-Coder Agreement
1	122	2	78%
2	122	3	86%

The complete set (~1220 templates) were then divided and assigned to coders who chunked each into logical fine-granular units for placement in a cell in the matrix. The templates assigned to each cell were then examined to select the best templates following simple heuristics, such as number of sections, thoroughness of descriptions, and availability of examples. Figure 5 shows a screenshot of the ReKon artifact built to contain these template chunks. It outlines the Phases along the leftmost column, and the Tasks along the top row. Choosing a Task in the top row shows the template chunks available to structure the task for each Phase. This screen (in Figure 5) captures the Task RFP development and the template chunks available for this task for the Phases: Planning and Market Research.

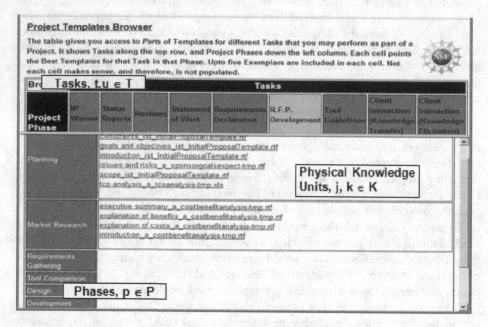

Fig. 5. A Snapshot of the ReKon Prototype

Reflecting on this first implementation effort for the ReKon artifact suggested several revisions to the design principles. Table 3 outlines these revised principles.

Table 3. Revised Design Principles after Implementation of Research Artifact

Principle	Description
Process Anchoring in *Templates*	Processes are anchored in generic templates; appropriately chunked, these template chunks represent parts of existing processes
Template Chunks as *Knowledge units*	Template chunks represent concrete knowledge units that represent organizational expertise about existing processes
Navigation of Template Chunks via Phases/Tasks	Phases and tasks from existing processes provide a navigation mechanism for template chunks
Design via Template Chunk *Recombination*	New processes can be generated by recombination of template chunks, each representing a part of an existing processes

4.3   Formative Evaluation

The ReKon research artifact was subjected to formative evaluation [58] in two steps. Users were recruited from a second course in a series (titled Advanced Enterprise Integration) engaged in working on real-world projects to implement integration solutions (systems of systems). The first step, conducted prior to the introduction of the ReKon platform assessed the use and relevance of (sections within) coarse-grain templates traditionally used. The students were also asked to comment on comparative usefulness of a coarse-grain template versus a hypothetical scenario where different sections from the template would be available separately. The second step, conducted after allowing the students a few weeks to explore the ReKon platform assessed concepts such as granularity, size, appropriateness of classification and relevance of knowledge units, as well as usefulness for project needs. Table 4 shows selected comments from step 1 of the formative assessment.

Table 4. Coarse-Grain Templates versus Hypothetical Availability of Sections

Select Prompts	Representative Comments
Although I may not have used all sections, it is useful to have the complete template	(Positive) … useful to have the template because most of the information we have to come up with ourselves so to have a guide line to fill in is very helpful to the success of this project
	(Negative) …it is difficult to determine if a section is relevant or not. Figuring out what needs to be included is work in itself
It is better to have each section available separately, so we can create the document we need by combining the sections relevant to our project.	(Positive) Most groups will not use all sections and it may be easier to make your own document.
	(Negative) … I'd rather error on the side of caution when it comes to including all possible sub-sections. Having the sections available separately poses the risk of missing something

The responses suggest strong ambivalence among the users. To understand these further, the students were asked to rate the relevance of individual sections of a template. Although some sections of the template were found useful across the board, others were not considered relevant. The answers had a large range: 97% found a particular section (scope definition) to be relevant, while only 33% found another section (related projects) to be relevant. Together, these results clear supported the argument in favor of fine-grain template chunks.

Although this first step indicated a preference for template sections (instead of templates), the exact nature of these sections was open to question. In the second step, the ReKon platform was populated with template chunks created from the ~1200 templates contributed by the four organizations. The second step was, therefore, aimed at assessing properties such as granularity, size, appropriateness of classification, and relevance of template chunks for project needs. On a scale of 1-5, the users indicated that they rated the size of template chunks to be 2.65 (1=too small and 5 = too long). Their rating for whether the template chunks satisfied project needs was 2.71 (1= all and 5=very little). The rated the relevance of template chunks as 2.82 (1=all relevant, 5=none relevant).

The results are encouraging because it is difficult to operationalize rules of thumb such as how large a template chunk should be. A more direct assessment was provided by whether the template chunks units satisfied the project needs, and was considered relevant. These were assessed for a knowledge unit that the participants randomly chose.

Comments from the respondents provided further suggestions for improvement. One suggested the need for additional meta-data: *"further explanation may be needed in the templates. ... to have a better understanding."* Another suggested: *"... quick view feature that open it up in a tiny thumbnail to view"* to locate and retrieve appropriate chunks quickly. One commented that some: *"some of the "chunks" ... should possibly be re-worked to make them easier to understand"*. Together, the responses provided formative feedback, and also added support to and refined the underlying design principles (see Table 5).

Table 5. Refined Design Principles after Formative Evaluation Cycles

Principle	Description
Process Anchoring in *Template Chunks*	Processes are anchored in generic templates; appropriately chunked, these template chunks represent parts of existing processes
Template Chunks as *Knowledge units*	Template chunks represent concrete knowledge units that represent organizational expertise about existing processes
Quick Navigation of Template Chunks	In addition to phases and tasks, a quick preview and navigation mechanism for template chunks
Making sense of Template Chunks	Providing drill-up access to source templates to understand context from which template chunks are drawn
Process Design by Recombining Template Chunks	New processes can be generated by recombination of template chunks, each representing a part of an existing processes

4.4   Iteration and Ongoing Refinement

Based on the insights obtained from the formative evaluation, we decided to design the next iteration of the research artifact. We also returned to the field to understand how templates were actually created, deployed and used within organizations. We conducted semi-structured interviews in 2 of the 4 software services organizations. Analysis of data gathered from the interviews revealed additional themes. First, we found that templates are created for the purposes of standardization of operations that would allow the organization scalability across project and clients. Second, we found that it is through these templates that project-management related processes get modified over time and across a series of projects. These two themes further strengthened our design principles. Moreover, we also found that these templates were more than just *encodings* of process knowledge. Rather, they represented a far more complex *entanglement* of material scaffolds with human knowledgeability. As a software engineer reflected, *"I'm building templates for projects that will predefine the phases that will go on. The deliverables are going to have to come out of those phases in terms of documents not product. .... All the document framework that has to be filled in, so when a new project comes along, they will use that template"* (Italics ours for emphasis). In other words, these templates were not just used to *facilitate* software services work, but instead, were *intrinsic* to it.

Other themes we found included the length of templates, how engineers look for relevant templates, how they make sense of the categorization of the templates, and more. Importantly, we found that most of the newly recombined templates often stays within the laptop/workstation of the individual engineers, and rarely gets back into the central document repository where it could be referred to and reused by other employees. Current document repositories and process and knowledge management systems lack the needed workflows and design features to facilitate the feedback process. Consequently, we plan to iterate the tool and incorporate three major features: (a) social tagging of templates; (b) tracking user-metrics; and (c) approval workflows. This work is still ongoing, and we plan to generate a new version of the research artifact to infer more refined design principles.

5   Conclusion and Future Work

In this paper, we have described ReKon, a research artifact for effective process design through recombination of templates. We have outlined the research process that started with first directing research attention to real-world artifacts, which are used to support in day-to-day software development activities. We also argued that the coarse grain nature of existing process design methods and its abstract definition hinders its translation to work practice. In addition to the abstract conceptualization of processes and process design methods, the very phenomenon of process is in itself abstract and ungrounded in day-to-day work activities. To overcome this, we proposed that processes are, in real world, anchored in concrete material artifacts of some form, and hence, process design should be orchestrated through these artifacts. In addition, we also posited that new processes are generated through the recombination of existing processes; and hence, artifacts should be modularized in a manner to allow for their subsequent recombinations. To realize these principles and subject them to evaluation and refinement, we focused on a particular type of artifact, templates, to build a research artifact.

The research artifact, ReKon, consists of fine-grain template chunks, which could be recombined to generate a process that is tailored to the needs of the project. Formative evaluation was carried out in two phases. The first phase established the ambivalence that project participants express in having access to complete templates versus granular knowledge units that they can combine as needed – a result that fits the need to balance the conflict described above. The second phase assesses the quality, relevance, size and number of knowledge units contained in ReKon. The combined results indicate that the fundamental ideas underlying recombinable template chunks are likely to be valuable for meeting the emergent needs of postindustrial organizations, such as the software services firms. Throughout the process, we have reflected on our own research activities to identify, revise and refine design principles that underlie the research artifact. These represent our response to the class of problems identified, and the core contribution of this research. Ongoing work is aimed at improving the ReKon artifact, a field study to further understand how the complex relationship between templates and process design, and a summative evaluation in the field.

Acknowledgements. The work reported has been funded by the National Science Foundation under award numbers 722112 and 722141. Any opinions, findings and conclusions or recommendations expressed in this material are those of the author(s) and do not necessarily reflect the views of the National Science Foundation (NSF). We also acknowledge contributions of project templates by and discussions with consulting organizations.

References

1. Davenport, T.H., Prusak, L.: Working knowledge: how organizations manage what they know. Harvard Business Press (1998)
2. Davenport, T.H., Short, J.E.: Information technology and business process redesign. Operations Management: Critical Perspectives on Business and Management 1, 1–27 (2003)
3. Hammer, M., Champy, J.: Reengineering the Corporation. Harper Collins Publishers, New York (1993)
4. Markus, M.L., Majchrzak, A., Gasser, L.: A design theory for systems that support emergent knowledge processes. MIS Quarterly, 179–212 (2002)
5. Malone, T.W., Crowston, K., Herman, G.A.: Organizing business knowledge: the MIT process handbook. The MIT Press (2003)
6. Lee, J., Wyner, G.M., Pentland, B.T.: Process grammar as a tool for business process design. MIS Quarterly 32(4), 757–778 (2008)
7. Bernstein, A., Klein, M., Malone, T.W.: The process recombinator: a tool for generating new business process ideas. Association for Information Systems (1999)
8. Alavi, M., Leidner, D.: Review: Knowledge Management and Knowledge Management Systems: Conceptual Foundations and Research Issues. Knowledge Management (2005)
9. Grover, V., Davenport, T.: General Perspectives on Knowledge Management: Fostering a Research Agenda. Journal of Management Information Systems 18(1), 5–21 (2001)
10. Schultze, U., Stabell, C.: Knowing what you don't know? Discourses and contradictions in knowledge management research. Journal of Management Studies 41(4), 549–573 (2004)
11. Sterman, J.D., Repenning, N.P., Kofman, F.: Unanticipated side effects of successful quality programs: Exploring a paradox of organizational improvement. Management Science, 503–521 (1997)
12. Repenning, N.P., Sterman, J.D.: Capability traps and self-confirming attribution errors in the dynamics of process improvement. Administrative Science Quarterly, 265–295 (2002)
13. Fahey, L., Prusak, L.: The Eleven Deadliest Sins of Knowledge Management. California Management Review 40, 265–276 (1998)

14. Garud, R., Kumaraswamy, A.: Vicious and Virtuous Circles in the Management of Knowledge: The Case of Infosys Technologies. MIS Quarterly 29(1), 9–33 (2005)
15. Hevner, A., et al.: Design Science in Information Systems Research. MIS Quarterly 28(1), 75–106 (2004)
16. Kuechler, B., Vaishnavi, V.: On theory development in design science research: anatomy of a research project. European Journal of Information Systems 17(5), 489–504 (2008)
17. Welke, R.J., Kumar, K.: Method engineering: a proposal for situation-specific methodology construction. Systems Analysis and Design: A Research Agenda, 257–268 (1992)
18. Tolvanen, J.P., Rossi, M., Liu, H.: Method engineering: current research directions and implications for future research. In: Proceedings of the IFIP TC8, WG8, 1(8.2), pp. 296–317 (1996)
19. Karlsson, F., Wistrand, K.: Combining method engineering with activity theory: theoretical grounding of the method component concept. European Journal of Information Systems 15(1), 82–90 (2006)
20. Okhuysen, G.A., Bechky, B.A.: Coordination in Organizations: An Integrative Perspective. The Academy of Management Annals 3(1), 463–502 (2009)
21. Simon, H.A.: The architecture of complexity. Proceedings of the American Philosophical Society 106(6), 467–482 (1962)
22. Boehm, B.W., Papaccio, P.N.: Understanding and controlling software costs. IEEE Transactions on Software Engineering 14(10), 1462–1477 (1988)
23. DeMarco, T.: Why does software cost so much?: and other puzzles of the information age. Dorset House Publishing Co., Inc. (1995)
24. Heath, C., Staudenmayer, N.: Coordination neglect: How lay theories of organizing complicate coordination in organizations. Research in Organizational Behavior 22, 153–192 (2000)
25. Grint, K.: Reengineering history: social resonances and business process reengineering. Organization 1(1), 179 (1994)
26. Hammer, M.: Reengineering work: don't automate, obliterate. Harvard Business Review 68(4), 104–112 (1990)
27. Leonard-Barton, D.: Wellsprings of Knowledge. Harvard University Press, Boston (1995)
28. Swan, J., Newell, S., Robertson, M.: The illusion of 'best practice' in information systems for operations management. European Journal of Information Systems 8(4), 284–293 (1999)
29. Wagner, E.L., Scott, S.V., Galliers, R.D.: The creation of "best practice" software: Myth, reality and ethics. Information and Organization 16(3), 251–275 (2006)
30. Kogut, B., Zander, U.: Knowledge of the Firm, Combinative Capabilities, and the Replication of Technology. Organization Science 3(3), 383 (1992)
31. Garud, R., Nayyar, P.R.: Transformative capacity: Continual structuring by intertemporal technology transfer. Strategic Management Journal 15(5), 365–385 (1994)
32. Berman, S.L., Down, J., Hill, C.W.L.: Tacit knowledge as a source of competitive advantage in the National Basketball Association. Academy of Management Journal, 13–31 (2002)
33. Grant, R.M.: Toward a knowledge-based theory of the firm. Strategic Management Journal 17, 109 (1996)
34. Nonaka, I.: The knowledge creating company. Harvard Business Review 69, 96–104 (1991)
35. Mathiassen, L., Pourkomeylian, P.: Managing knowledge in a software organization. Journal of Knowledge Management 7(2), 63–80 (2003)

36. Mathiassen, L., Pries-Heje, J., Ngwenyama, O.: Improving software organizations: from principles to practice. Addison Wesley Longman Publishing Co., Inc. (2001)
37. Benner, M.J., Tushman, M.: Process management and technological innovation: A longitudinal study of the photography and paint industries. Administrative Science Quarterly, 676–706 (2002)
38. Brinkkemper, S.: Method engineering: engineering of information systems development methods and tools. Information and Software Technology 38(4), 275–280 (1996)
39. Henderson-Sellers, B.: Method engineering: Theory and practice. Information Systems Technology and its Applications, 13–23 (2006)
40. Brinkkemper, S., Saeki, M., Harmsen, F.: Meta-modelling based assembly techniques for situational method engineering. Information Systems 24(3), 209–228 (1999)
41. Ter Hofstede, A.H.M., Verhoef, T.: On the feasibility of situational method engineering. Information Systems 22(6-7), 401–422 (1997)
42. Mathiassen, L., Purao, S.: Educating reflective systems developers. Information Systems Journal 12(2), 81–102 (2002)
43. Mathiassen, L., et al.: Method engineering: Who is the customer? (1996)
44. Alvesson, M., Kärreman, D.: Odd couple: making sense of the curious concept of knowledge management. Journal of Management Studies 38(7), 995–1018 (2001)
45. Gupta, A.K., Govindarajan, V.: Knowledge flows and the structure of control within multinational corporations. Academy of Management Journal 16(4), 768–792 (1991)
46. Gold, A.H., Malhotra, A., Segars, A.H.: Knowledge management: An organizational capabilities perspective. Journal of Management Information Systems 18(1), 185–214 (2001)
47. Dosi, G., Nelson, R.R., Winter, S.G.: The Nature and Dynamics of Organizational Capabilities, pp. 1–22. Oxford University Press, Oxford (2000)
48. Beunza, D., Stark, D.: Tools of the trade: the socio-technology of arbitrage in a Wall Street trading room. Industrial and Corporate Change 13(2), 369 (2004)
49. Callon, M.: Society in the making: the study of technology as a tool for sociological analysis. The Social Construction of Technological Systems: New Directions in the Sociology and History of Technology, 83–103 (1987)
50. Carlile, P.R.: A pragmatic view of knowledge and boundaries: Boundary objects in new product development. Organization Science, 442–455 (2002)
51. Nicolini, D., Mengis, J., Swan, J.: Understanding the Role of Objects in Cross-Disciplinary Collaboration. Organization Science (2011) p. orsc. 1110.0664 v1
52. Latour, B.: Visualization and Cognition: Thinking with Eyes and Hands. In: Kuklick, H., Long, E. (eds.) Knowledge and Society: Studies in the Sociology of Culture Past and Present, pp. 1–40. JAI Press (1986)
53. Latour, B.: Where are the Missing Masses? The Sociology of a Few Mundane Artifacts. In: Bijker, W., Law, J. (eds.) Shaping Technology/Building Society, Cambridge, pp. 225–264 (1992)
54. Star, S., Griesemer, J.: Institutional ecology,'translations' and boundary objects: Amateurs and professionals in Berkeley's Museum of Vertebrate Zoology, 1907-39. Social Studies of Science, 387–420 (1989)
55. Ramasubbu, N., Mithas, S., Kemerer, C.F.: Work dispersion, process-based learning, and offshore software development performance. Mamagement Information Systems Quaterly 32(2), 437–458 (2008)
56. Bechky, B.A.: Analyzing artifacts: material methods for understanding identity, status, and knowledge in organizational life. Sage Handbook of New Approaches in Management and Organization, 98 (2008)

57. Carroll, J., Rosson, M.: Getting around the task-artifact cycle: how to make claims and design by scenario. ACM Transactions on Information Systems (TOIS) 10(2), 181–212 (1992)
58. Weston, C., McAlpine, L., Bordonaro, T.: A model for understanding formative evaluation in instructional design. Educational Technology Research and Development 43(3), 29–48 (1995)
59. Sein, M.K., et al.: Action design research. MIS Quarterly 35(1), 37–56 (2011)
60. Lam, W., Shankararaman, V.: An enterprise integration methodology. IT Professional 6(2), 40–48 (2004)
61. Cohen, J.: A coefficient of agreement for nominal scales. Educational and Psychological Measurement 20(1), 37–46 (1960)

Design Principles for Inter-Organizational Systems Development – Case Hansel

Heikki Lempinen, Matti Rossi, and Virpi Kristiina Tuunainen

Aalto University School of Economics,
Information Systems Science, Helsinki, Finland
{heikki.lempinen,matti.rossi,virpi.tuunainen}@aalto.fi

Abstract. In this paper, we report new findings of an on-going action design research (ADR) study in a public organization, Hansel Ltd, the central procurement unit of the Finnish government. A procurement organization acts as a middleman in public sector procurement. In order to coordinate large-scale procurement supported by a third party, inter-organizational systems (IOS) are needed. However, it is challenging to develop these, as the stakeholders are scattered and not necessarily interested in supporting the development of systems. Our goal is to identify and formulate design principles for efficient and effective inter-organizational systems development in the procurement context. With the particular focus on power relations between the involved organizations as well as their separate interests in the IOS being built, we develop design principles for such systems. In addition to being useful for our case company, we illustrate how these design principles can be applied to a class of similar problems.

Keywords: information sharing, public procurement, power relations, interest in IOS, action design research.

1 Introduction

Globalization, rapid technological change, and government reforms are creating increasing pressures for organizations to improve information sharing and integration capabilities across organizations [1]. To cope with these changes and as an attempt to reduce costs and increase purchasing efficiency, many organizations are looking for ways to exploit purchasing synergies [2] [3]. One way to do this is to employ centralized purchasing and corporate-wide framework agreements. The purpose of these centralized contracts is to enable the negotiation of lower prices, as well as to save costs through reduced duplicated effort in the purchasing process, including supplier search, negotiations and contract management [4]. Efficiencies are also sought from inter-organizational systems (IOS) that enable organizations to share information and to electronically conduct business across organizational boundaries [5]. Generally, IOSs as "planned and managed cooperative ventures between

K. Peffers, M. Rothenberger, and B. Kuechler (Eds.): DESRIST 2012, LNCS 7286, pp. 52–65, 2012.

otherwise independent agents" [6], (p. 280) are aimed at reducing both transaction costs and organization costs of one or more of the companies involved in the relationship [5].

In Finland, Hansel Ltd (hereinafter Hansel), acts as the central procurement unit that negotiates and maintains central framework agreements that are used by other governmental units, such as ministries, ministerial offices, state agencies and publicly owned enterprises, for purchasing of goods and services. Hansel aims at creating savings for the Finnish government through centralized purchasing.

So far, Hansel has collected information on the contract usage through a web portal in which suppliers are required to report their framework agreement purchases once a month. Based on this information, the suppliers pay their service fees to Hansel. This data collection procedure is burdensome for the suppliers who have consequently been very dissatisfied with it. Furthermore, the existing system has not particularly encouraged compliance in supplier reporting, rather the opposite. As a consequence, Hansel has not been able to collect all the due service fees, and it receives incomplete information about the use of the framework agreements.

To address the issues with the reporting system Hansel started a development project to design an efficient and effective supplier reporting process and a related Inter-organizational system (IOS) between Hansel, the government units that are its customers, and the suppliers.

In the previous phase of the project, a new concept was introduced for automated inter-organizational reporting (for more details, see [7]). In this paper we present findings of a pilot project during which the suggested system and related processes were tested through a real-life application at Hansel.

We will next introduce our case company, research approach and theoretical grounding. In the following sections, we describe the results of our study. The paper then closes with conclusions and directions for future research.

2   Case Organization

Hansel is a non-profit organization that is financed by service fees collected from the suppliers participating in the framework agreements. The purchase volume channeled through Hansel frame agreements has increased notably over the past five years; the total annual purchase volume has more than doubled since 2006, reaching €553 million in 2010. The service fees are at most 1.5% of the value of these purchases, and are at the moment based on purchase information provided by the suppliers. The inefficiency and ineffectiveness of the current data collection procedure motivated Hansel to start a development project in which the reporting system and the process were being reconsidered and redesigned. In the first phase of the project, a new concept was introduced for automated inter-organizational reporting. The suggested technological solution was based on electronic invoice (e-invoice) duplication that would obliterate the need for separate reporting, as shown in Fig. 1.

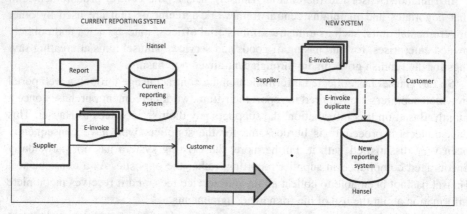

Fig. 1. Old and new reporting system and process concept

In the current system, suppliers generate separately largely the same purchase information to their customer invoices and to a separate report sent to Hansel. In the new reporting concept, purchase data could be copied directly from the e-invoices, making the separate reporting procedure unnecessary.

With a power and interest perspective of multiple parties on the IOS being developed [5], and Action Design Research [8] as our research method, we identify and formulate design principles relevant for inter-organizational procurement systems development based on the pilot phase of Hansel's new system project.

3   Research Approach and Theoretical Grounding

In this section we first briefly describe the Action Design Research approach employed in this paper and then the theory base used for the IOS development.

3.1   Action Design Research

Action Design Research (ADR) is a new research method that combines action research and design research for the purpose of generating prescriptive design knowledge through building and evaluating ensemble IT artifacts in an organizational setting [8].

In action research, theory is regarded as tentative, applied and then improved by successive cycles of application and reflection until the practitioner-defined problem is adequately addressed [9]. In ADR, the initial research opportunity is more strongly based on existing theories and technologies [8], in our case on web based systems and theories of interest and power in IOS [5]. Our aim is to develop a system and a process that align the interests of all parties during an IOS development project, while identifying design rules for such systems. The existing e-invoicing technology serves as a basis for designing the IT solution.

The ADR method is essentially set up to deal with two seemingly disparate challenges of; 1) addressing a problem situation encountered in a specific organizational setting by intervening and evaluating, and 2) constructing and evaluating an IT artifact that addresses a class of problems typified by the encountered situation [8]. The goals of this research project are well aligned with these challenges: the project is both about building a new reporting system for Hansel through an action research project, as well as about applying the design research approach in building the IT artifact. The ADR method is useful both in supporting the research process along the way, and in helping to make a theoretical contribution by creating results that are generalizable also outside the case context. Overall, the case project complies with the principles of the ADR method of practice-inspired research and building a theory-ingrained artifact.

The trigger for the first stage of ADR is a problem perceived in practice or anticipated by researchers. This stage includes determining the initial scope, deciding the roles and scope for practitioner participation, and formulating the initial research questions [8]. Critical issues in this stage are securing the long-term commitment of the organization and formulating the identified problem as an instance of a class of problems. The second stage of ADR uses the problem framing and theoretical premises adopted in stage one to carry out a change in the target organization. This BIE (building, intervention and evaluation) phase interweaves the building of the IT artifact, intervention in the organization, and continuous evaluation of the project, resulting IT artifact, and the research effort. For this project we employ organization dominant BIE where the primary source of innovation is organizational intervention. During the iterations in this form of BIE, the ADR team challenges organizational participants' existing ideas and assumptions about the artifact's specific use context in order to create and improve the design. This stage draws on three principles: reciprocal shaping, mutually influential roles, and authentic and concurrent evaluation. [8] Reflection and learning continues throughout the ADR process. This stage emphasizes that the ensemble artifact reflects not only the preliminary design but is shaped by organizational use, perspectives and participants. Finally, in spite of the situated nature of ADR, learning from the project is further developed into general solution concepts for a class of similar problems. This stage aims therefore to formalize learning through design principles derived from the design research outcomes. See Fig. 2 for general ADR phases.

In the following we describe each phase of the ADR project in the Hansel case and elaborate on how the principles were identified and formulated.

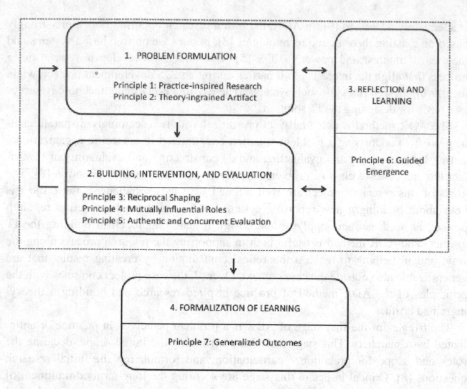

Fig. 2. Action Design Research Process [8]

3.2   Problem Formulation

Suppliers' criticism towards the current reporting system initiated the development project. The fundamental problems related to the inefficient reporting process that causes excessive workload for the suppliers. Furthermore, the current system is not satisfactory for Hansel either, due to the inherently weak control over reporting compliance. In the first phase of the project a conceptual solution for mitigating the problems in the current reporting system was suggested [7]. The overriding aim of the project for Hansel was to develop an effective and efficient system for supplier reporting so that Hansel can:

1) offer better service for the suppliers (efficiency);
2) enhance the control of supplier reporting and decrease the number of unreported purchases (effectiveness); and
3) ensure appropriate quality level of reporting information.

However, not all questions could be answered through the initial conceptual design. The remaining open questions and challenges were related to the IOS technology and the issues of involving all necessary parties in the use of the system. Table 1 below summarizes these identified problems.

Table 1. Problems with the existing reporting system

Problem (previous phase)	Reporting system in use
Laborious reporting for the suppliers	Dissatisfied suppliers Low overall reporting efficiency
Weak control on reporting compliance	Incomplete purchasing information Poor visibility to performance, difficulties in managing internal resources Service fees are not collected to the full
Problem (this phase)	**Projected reporting system**
How to make the IOS work?	Technology issues: data standards and technology integration between parties? Power and interest issues: how to engage all parties in the project from the beginning?

The first set of problems was the focus of the planning stage of the development project and was addressed in the selected process concept and the planned, new reporting system. Now, in the pilot stage, the main focus is on ensuring the performance of the new IOS by addressing technological as well as organizational and social concerns.

3.3 Theory Ingrained Artifact: Division of Power and Different Interests in IOS

With IOS, an information system essentially aimed at supporting links outside the organization, it is crucial for management of the organization developing the system to focus on the external users. While the new system can be driven by cost and control issues, as in Hansel's case, the interests and power of external users, such as suppliers in our case study, must not be ignored.

This calls for effective knowledge sharing to be carried out throughout the development stages, particularly, in the efforts of planning for and implementing information integration technologies [1]. The scope for the design of an effective IOS has been found to be dependent on a combination of technical, economic and social factors, which are intertwined (see e.g. [5]). These include a wide range of issues related to abilities, awareness and knowledge of the involved parties that can have a substantial effect on the different organizations' willingness as well as capability to adopt and use an IOS. More focal to our study, however, are the factors related to technology, interest and power relations.

Technical factors are related to issues such as standards and compatibility of both software and hardware. Even though these are not trivial matters and need to be duly addressed when designing and developing an IOS (or any IS, for that matter), but especially the increasing availability of the Internet, among other developments, has decreased the problematic nature of these.

Organizational interest in the IOS depends on the potential IOS users' perception on the economic and/or strategic advantages the new system could bring about. The expected benefits from the use of the information system can include both direct (e.g. operational savings) and indirect benefits (e.g. impacts on business processes). If the interest of a party in an IOS is low, the organization does not expect to gain much by the use of the system or, it expects that the disadvantages (e.g. increased operational costs or incompatible internal and external technologies) offset the potential benefits. A high degree of interest, in turn, relates to the perception that the IOS could significantly contribute to the overall goals of the company [5]. Accordingly, in the case of Hansel's planned IOS, the perceived interests of the involved organizations are pronounced in terms of how much each of them believes to be able to benefit from using the IOS and whether the benefits will outweigh the costs.

Power relations between the involved organizations impact on the likelihood of being able to involve and engage all the required or desired parties. This kind of organizational power manifests itself in our case context in situation in which Hansel is not able to make the suppliers to use the system, or when the suppliers have the power to ignore the system.

Demands on an organization to adopt a given technology or an information system can result from both formal and informal pressures exerted on the organization by other organizations upon which they are dependent [10] [11] [12]. A powerful party with a strong interest in an IOS can coerce the less powerful parties to use the IOS, even independent of their perceived interest in the IOS [12]. The concept of power can be viewed from processual, institutional and organizational perspectives [13]. Since our focus is on the relations between organizations, we will concentrate on processual (i.e., the social interaction between interest groups) and institutional (i.e. the bases from which power is mandated to organizations) perspectives on power.

Boonstra and De Vries [5] categorize IOS by dividing participants in terms of power and interest. Whereas a balanced IOS can be developed and used when all the relevant parties have a clear interest in an IOS, in unbalanced situation, an IOS is characterized by contradictory interests or at least by contradictory perceptions of the costs and the benefits involved in the system. Earlier research suggest that in order to achieve a balanced IOS, the participants involved need to cooperate (e.g. [6]) and the participants' interests must be aligned and brought together into a common structure and vision [14]. We seek to ensure that these issues are taken into consideration already in the development phase.

4   BIE at Hansel

4.1   Preparation and Organization of the Pilot Project

After the concept design phase, the executive board at Hansel gave permission to continue the project to the next phase and build a pilot system. The rationale was that of using a prototype for further testing of whether, and under which conditions, the new reporting system and process is actually applicable. The pilot project started in May 2011 and is still on-going.

At first, Hansel made the necessary preparations, went through a thorough tendering process during the summer and received offers from three software vendors for building the pilot system in early October. Hansel decided that instead of building a heavy pre-version of the future system, a proof-of-concept (POC) would be most suitable at this point. The goal of the pilot project was essentially to learn and document the lessons learned in order to utilize it in the future development of the full-scale system.

As for the project organization, Hansel first set up an internal pilot project team, including representatives from the IT, finance, and legal departments, and one of the ADR researchers. This project team has held bi-weekly meetings to keep track of the project status. The technology provider and its sub-contractor coordinated the building and actual coding of the system through a POC steering committee. One of the ADR researchers was also part of the POC project team. Other parties whose involvement was needed included suppliers who would test the system and provide invoice data, customers who would simply agree that their invoices could be used for testing, and the potential information intermediaries; the financial shared services center (FSSC) and the e-invoice operator of the Government. All stakeholder groups and their roles and responsibilities in the project are listed in Table 2 underneath.

Table 2. Stakeholder issues

Stakeholder	Role/responsibility
ADR researchers	IOS development, documenting learning gained from the project
Hansel management/IT/finance	Project ownership, user testing
Hansel project team	Project management in Hansel, engaging other stakeholders to the project
POC project team	Building the IT system, monitoring progress
POC management team	Management of the IT system building
Pilot customers	Agreement to use invoice data for testing
Pilot suppliers	Agreement to use invoice data for testing, pilot system testing
E-invoice operator	E-invoice data conversion and transfer to Hansel

The scope for the design of an effective IOS has been found to depend on a combination of technical, economic and social factors, which are intertwined [5]. We will address these in the following sub-sections through issues related to IOS technology, interest and power.

4.2 Technology-Related Issues

Building the user interface (which is also the most visible part of the system) proved not to be very complicated and co-operation with the software provider and the sub-contractor worked very well. The POC project team held regular demo meetings to monitor the incremental development of the system and discuss possible changes and new features. All members of the POC team had browser-based access to the pilot system at all times during the development period. The complete user interface was constructed with little trouble within three months and was completed in January 2012.

The technology issues that arose were related to data standards and building the IOS linkages. In order to actually test how the pilot system works, Hansel needed access to real invoices sent by the suppliers to their customers. In the concept development phase one of the critical tasks was to determine the most technologically viable point of the process from which the XML invoice data should be drawn from. It was decided that a centralized solution should be used in which the data would be drawn from either the financial shared services center (FSSC) of the Government, or the recipients e-invoice operator. At first, the centralized option was left out from the scope of the pilot project because of the presumably high set-up costs.

Instead, the idea was to make the sourcing of data easier by collecting invoices directly from those suppliers who agreed to take part in the pilot project. It was soon discovered that this was not possible: Hansel could not get enough data for testing because all of the suppliers did not use Finvoice 1.3, the e-invoice standard that the pilot system was capable of handling. Although Finvoice 1.3 is a widely used standard, it is not the only one used by Finnish organizations. Hence, Hansel was forced to reconsider adopting the centralized solution already in the pilot project. In the centralized solution the invoice operators convert the invoices and subsequently supply them in a consistent format to Hansel's customers through the FSSC.

Both centralized alternatives, the FSSC and the e-invoice operator, were investigated in detail and finally Hansel decided to work with the operator in the pilot phase. Importantly, the pilot system thereby directly replicates the process of the future system and hence genuinely serves as a proof-of-concept (see Fig. 3).

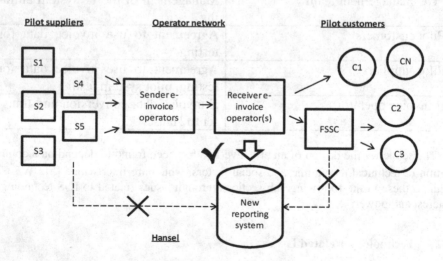

Fig. 3. The modified reporting system

4.3   Interest-Related Issues

Although there were still some technological questions that had to be solved in the pilot system, the real challenge was to gain the IOS parties' commitment. Since this was only a pilot project, there were no direct benefits for the different user groups except for Hansel. Since the incentives were clearly not great enough to promote voluntary active participation, Hansel had to put substantial effort in achieving other stakeholders' commitment.

To have a set of testable data, Hansel needed a permission both from a supplier and from its customers to use their invoices as testing material. The pilot customers were not required to take an active role in the project, only to agree that Hansel could use their invoice data for testing purposes. The new reporting system will not create any benefits the customers, neither directly nor indirectly; their interest towards the IOS was low, as could be expected. In addition, they still needed to go through a contractual procedure to agree on the use of the invoices, which might have hindered the engagement further for some customers, especially when there were no benefits for them.

The pilot suppliers were expected to test how the system works with their own invoices. This was only for testing purposes, and they were still required to use the old reporting system for the monthly reporting as before. Although the system would very much benefit the suppliers in the long run in the future, the suppliers who were asked to join the pilot project hung back on the decision. Hansel negotiated with potential suppliers during the entire pilot system building phase, and in the end, managed to find five suppliers who would participate in the pilot. To put this number into context, is should be mentioned that Hansel currently has more than 300 suppliers.

Despite the five suppliers agreed to take part in the pilot, Hansel could not get the invoice data from them due to technical problems, and the system testing was at risk to fail altogether. Hansel then decided to turn to an e-invoice operator to gain access to the needed data. The operator's commitment was not easy to achieve, either. Although they had been involved in the concept design phase, they did not respond very actively to Hansel's requests to join the pilot project before they were offered financial compensation for their co-operation. The operator agreed to provide consultation and to transmit invoice data to be used in testing, but could not make all the necessary arrangements right away. Due to these challenges, the actual user-testing phase had to be postponed.

4.4   Power- Related Issues

A powerful party with a strong interest in an IOS can urge the less powerful parties to use the IOS, even independent of their perceived interest in the IOS [12]. Power to control IOS can stem from: independence of partner organization, formal authority and legal requirements, control over technology, and/or from inter-organizational alliances, networks and control of informal organization. Related power relation issues between the most critical IOS stakeholders - Hansel, the suppliers and the e-invoice operator - are discussed next (see Table 3 for a summary).

Generally speaking, Hansel has strong power over the suppliers because the public sector is a large and reliable customer, and the suppliers are, to a varying extent, dependent on the public contracts. The same goes for the e-invoice operator. This dependence is expected to give Hansel leverage in persuading the partner organizations to participate in the IOS.

In some cases, Hansel can exercise its formal authority over the suppliers by adding certain demands to the framework contracts. Hansel has not made such contractual demands during the pilot project, and hence it has not been able to control the suppliers through it. However, an attempt to gain formal authority over the e-invoice operator was made prior to the pilot project, as the Finnish Government renegotiated their contract with the e-invoice operator. Through the new contract, the operator was obliged to "co-operate with Hansel in the development of a new supplier reporting system". This did not, however, ensure the commitment of the e-invoice operator.

The new reporting system brings considerable advantage to the suppliers who at the moment struggle with the existing one. These suppliers cannot ignore the possibility of using the new IOS. However, some suppliers have developed their own IT-based solutions to better cope with the existing reporting system, and hence are more likely to disregard the new reporting system. Since the new IOS depends on the information intermediaries in data collection, the e-invoice operator is in great control over the technology. Without the commitment of the e-invoice operator, the IOS concept is not feasible to begin with.

The new reporting concept is an interesting initiative also from the perspective of the information intermediaries as it promotes further usage scenarios of also other types of data and information that they mediate. Hence, the operator is not expected to ignore the development of such an IOS. Hansel has also managed to build alliances with some suppliers who are supportive of development of public procurement. These suppliers are not likely to ignore a possibility to benefit from participating in the IOS either.

Table 3. Power and control relations in the case

Sources of power to control IOS	Operationalization within IOS Hansel vs. suppliers	Operationalization within IOS Hansel vs. operator
Independent of partner organization	Strong	Strong
Formal authority, legal requirements	Weak	Some
Control over technology	Strong, but not over all suppliers	None, operator has full power
Inter-organizational alliances, networks and control of informal organization	Some, specific suppliers	Strong

4.5   Summary of the BIE Phase

During the first cycles in the ADR project, a new concept for inter-organizational reporting was developed. This was done through multiple iterations within the extended ADR team comprising of the ADR researchers, and practitioners from Hansel and other interest groups. In this study, the focus was on the Pilot IT system cycle in which the involvement of all stakeholder groups was required (see Fig. 4).

The pilot project can be further divided into two sub-cycles: system building and system testing. In the first sub-cycle, it became evident that in the case of the IOS, building the user interface was not an issue, but the challenges related to data standards and integrations between the IOS parties. Furthermore, the IOS integrations needed to be tested for a true proof-of-concept. To cope with these challenges, close co-operation with the IOS parties was needed. However, despite the enthusiasm towards the project, all parties were not prepared to put effort to developing the IOS.

Stakeholders' engagement proved to be a critical issue also in the second sub-cycle. It was impossible to test a system without the users and data for this purpose. In Hansel's case, the suppliers held back on deciding whether to join the pilot project or not. A technology-related set back experienced with the data standards as the original plan to get the test invoices directly from the suppliers failed, forced Hansel to co-operate with the information intermediaries. Although one e-invoice operator finally volunteered to supply the data, the process was not totally frictionless and required further compensation for co-operation. In summary, it was noticed that not all the parties had great enough interest towards the IOS and were able to ignore it, particularly in the cases where Hansel was powerful enough to coerce them to join or they were not compensated for joining.

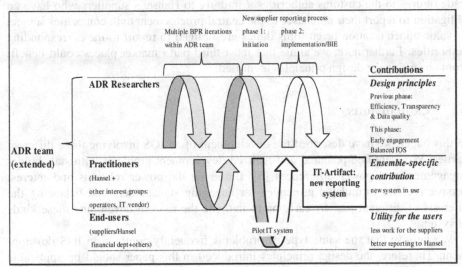

Fig. 4. BIE at Hansel

5   Reflection and Learning

This stage of the ADR process moves from building a solution for a particular instance to applying that learning to a broader class of problems. During the process we identified two general design principles for IOS development: early engagement and balanced IOS. These two principles are elaborated on in Table 4 below.

Table 4. The formulated design principles

Design Principle	Description
Early engagement	To avoid problems and delays in IOS adoption, all stakeholders should be engaged in the development project already at an early stage
Balanced IOS	Stakeholders' interest towards the IOS and power in relation to the other parties define their willingness to take part in the IOS

The first design principle draws on the power relations of the key stakeholders [5] and the importance of exerting pressure, providing incentives or otherwise engaging all necessary parties early on in the development initiative. The second principle is almost a truism based on earlier IOS research on the need to cooperate and find a common vision [6] [14], but in practice the alignment of interests and benefits can be extremely difficult.

The findings of the Hansel case can be generalized to similar problems related to inter-organizational systems for mandatory third party reporting. Examples include companies reporting their VAT sales to the tax authorities or international trade figures to the customs authorities. Similarly to Hansel's suppliers who have an obligation to report their purchases to the central procurement unit, companies subject to value-added taxation or customs duties are obliged to report to the corresponding authorities. Furthermore, we argue that most third party market places could benefit from observing the design principles identified.

6   Conclusions

In this paper, we have described the development of an IOS involving three different parties. We identified potential and realized development problems with stakeholder engagement and power differences [5]. Based on the power relations and interest perspective, we formulated principles for engaging stakeholders and balancing the interests of different partiers early on to mitigate the risks of developing these kinds of systems.

We believe that the same type of problems frequently common in IOS development. Therefore, the design principles introduced in this paper should be applicable for many if not most IOS development initiatives. The interplay of technology, standards and power relations among the participants is in most cases complex and not easily foreseeable. Thus, the principles of engagement and balancing of interests, while general and seemingly straightforward, can help to overcome recurring problems in this kind of systems development.

In the future we shall continue to work together with Hansel in developing the IOS. Once the pilot project is completed, the feasibility of the new reporting system and process will be re-evaluated. Based on the results a decision will be made whether to continue to a full-scale implementation of the IOS. If so, the principles of early engagement and balanced IOS will be applied in the implementation phase of the final, full-scale system.

References

1. Pardo, T.A., et al.: Knowledge sharing in cross-boundary information system development in the public sector. Information Technology and Management 7(4), 293–313 (2006)
2. Faes, W., Matthyssens, P., Vandenbempt, K.: The Pursuit of Global Purchasing Synergy. Industrial Marketing Management 29(6), 539–553 (2000)
3. Smart, A., Dudas, A.: Developing a decision-making framework for implementing purchasing synergy: a case study. International Journal of Physical Distribution & Logistics Management 37(1), 64–89 (2007)
4. Karjalainen, K., Kemppainen, K., van Raaij, E.: Non-Compliant Work Behaviour in Purchasing: An Exploration of Reasons Behind Maverick Buying. Journal of Business Ethics 84(2), 245–261 (2009)
5. Boonstra, A., De Vries, J.: Analyzing inter-organizational systems from a power and interest perspective. International Journal of Information Management 25(6), 485–501 (2005)
6. Kumar, K., van Dissel, H.G.: Sustainable collaboration: Managing conflict and cooperation in interorganizational systems. MIS Quarterly 20(3), 279–300 (1996)
7. Lempinen, H., Tuunainen, V.K.: Redesigning the supplier reporting process and system in public procurement – Case Hansel. International Journal of Organisational Design and Engineering 1(4), 331–346 (2011)
8. Sein, M.K., et al.: Action Design Research. MIS Quarterly 35(1), 37–56 (2011)
9. Lee, A., Baskerville, R.L.: Generalizing Generalizability in Information Systems Research. Information Systems Research 14(3), 221–243 (2003)
10. DiMaggio, P.J., Powell, W.W.: The Iron Cage Revisited: Institutional Isomorphism and Collective Rationality in Organizational Fields. American Sociological Review 48(2), 147–160 (1983)
11. Teo, H.H., Wei, K.K., Benbasat, I.: Predicting intention to adopt interorganizational linkages, an institutional perspective. MIS Quarterly 27(1), 19–49 (2003)
12. Standifer, R.L., Wall, J.A.J.: Managing conflict in B2B e-commerce. Business Horizons 46(2), 65–70 (2003)
13. Fincham, R.: Perspectives on Power: Processual, Institutional and 'Internal' Forms of Organizational Power. Journal of Management Studies 29(6), 741–760 (1992)
14. Koch, H., Schultze, U.: Stuck in the Conflicted Middle: A Practice Perspective on B2B E marketplaces. MIS Quarterly 35(1), 1–24 (2011)

Using Design Science Research to Develop a Modeling Technique for Service Design

Lysanne Lessard and Eric Yu

Faculty of Information, University of Toronto
140 St. George Street, Toronto, ON, M5S 3G6, Canada
{lysanne.lessard,eric.yu}@utoronto.ca

Abstract. Knowledge-intensive business services (KIBS) such as consulting and research and development services are important factors of performance and innovation in industrialized economies. However, current modeling techniques aimed at supporting service design do not account for their core characteristics such as the relational nature of exchanges among providers, clients, and other actors. Using data from a case of academic research and development service as a type of KIBS, we present a modeling technique that can support the design of successful service engagements in this domain. This work is guided by the understanding of service as a process of collaborative value creation, or value cocreation. Beyond the contribution of the modeling technique to KIBS design, our work shows the strength of using a Design Science Research methodology in creating design artifacts that are strongly aligned with the problem domain for which they are developed.

Keywords: Design Science Research, KIBS engagements, service design, value cocreation, modeling technique.

1 Introduction

Knowledge-intensive business services (KIBS) such as information services, computing, and research and development services are important factors of performance and innovation in industrialized economies [1]. While current literature on KIBS helps us understand their core characteristics and patterns of innovation, it has rarely addressed how best to support their design. The understanding of service as a process of collaborative value creation, or value cocreation [2], could provide a framework guiding KIBS design. It allows us to understand parties engaged in KIBS relationships as service systems - collections of specialized resources (people, technology, information, etc.) organized in a manner that enables collaborative value creation, or value cocreation [3]. However, a full understanding of the value cocreation process has yet to be developed [3]; moreover, this understanding needs to be transformed into design tools in order to provide practical design support to KIBS professionals. Using a Design Science Research methodology, our work aims to identify generative mechanisms of value cocreation in KIBS and express them through a modeling technique that can support the analysis and design of service engagements in the domain of KIBS.

K. Peffers, M. Rothenberger, and B. Kuechler (Eds.): DESRIST 2012, LNCS 7286, pp. 66–77, 2012.

We propose to derive the modeling technique from Agent-Oriented modeling, in particular *i** (short for distributed intentionality) [4]. *i** offers a socio-technical perspective on organization and information system design, viewing people, organizations and technologies as actors that depend on each other to reach their goals. Such an approach can be contrasted with current service-specific modeling techniques such as Service Blueprinting [5] and a number of other process-based techniques. While these techniques support the design of service activities, they are unable to link activities to expected benefits and high-level interests of actors engaged in service relationships.

Beyond the contribution of the modeling technique to KIBS design, our work shows the strength of using a Design Science Research (DSR) Methodology in creating relevant design artifacts for a given domain. We use an extended DSR framework, which explicitly adds 'understanding of the domain' to the original 'build' and 'evaluate' research activities [6, 7]. This allows us to anchor our modeling technique in empirical data. Specifically, we are conducting a multiple-case study of service engagements in academic research and development services as a type of KIBS. The key mechanisms of value cocreation identified through the case study first lead to the development of a design framework comprised of identified generative mechanisms and resulting design-oriented questions. Our modeling technique is then adapted from *i** and other techniques in order to both express generative mechanisms and help answer design-oriented questions of the design framework.

2   Research Problem and Objectives

As with many design problems, developing a modeling technique to support the design of Knowledge-Intensive Business Services (KIBS) involves addressing two nested problems: a knowledge problem and a practical one [8]. Core characteristics of KIBS are their knowledge intensity, the involvement of clients in production, and the relational nature of exchanges among providers, clients, and other actors [1, 9]; these characteristics need to be taken into account when designing for KIBS. Service is increasingly being understood as a process of collaborative value creation, or value cocreation [2]. Taken as a framework, value cocreation addresses these core characteristics through its focus on knowledge and skills and their embodiment in technology, on the collaborative process between provider and client, and by situating the creation of value in a wider value configuration space. However, a full understanding of the process of value cocreation has yet to be developed [3]. A better understanding of how value is cocreated in KIBS is thus needed before this framework can be used as a basis for their design.

The practical problem relates to transforming this understanding into tools that can support the design of successful KIBS engagements. Because of their communicative and analytical affordances, models are key service design tools. Many modeling techniques have been proposed in this regard, including Service Blueprinting [5] and a number of other process-based techniques. These service-specific modeling techniques focus on provider-client interactions and sequential activities; they are not able to express key concepts of value cocreation such as collaboration, subjective value determination and network relationships. Modeling techniques from other fields thus have to be explored. However, the choice of a relevant modeling technique to support KIBS design first relies on a better understanding of value cocreation in this domain.

Guided by key concepts of value cocreation identified in literature, our first research objective is to identify the key generative mechanisms that lead to the cocreation of value for parties engaged in a KIBS relationship. This objective stems from a Critical Realist perspective that helps us to understand service engagements as structures that possess inherent mechanisms leading to observed outcomes [10]. By directing attention to questions of why, when and how particular mechanisms are activated, Critical Realism enables an understanding of what fosters or hinders value cocreation in KIBS. Our second research objective is to provide practical support to KIBS professionals through the development of design tools able to support KIBS design. We propose to arrive at this objective by developing a modeling technique able to both express key mechanisms of value cocreation and support the analysis of KIBS engagements.

3   Methodology

A methodology in line with the precepts of design science research (DSR) is used for this research project. DSR is posed as a type of research alongside behavioral, social, and other scientific approaches aiming to understand a phenomenon. By contrast, DSR aims at intervening in a phenomenon; while this may necessitate to first understand it, the practical goal of intervention always predominates in DSR [8]. DSR thus aims at developing practical solutions that can be used by professionals in their field [6, 11]. More concretely, solutions – or design artifacts - can take the form of constructs, models, methods or instantiations [6, 12].

The initial DSR framework mainly consists of the development and evaluation of design artifacts from foundational knowledge and methodologies taken from an existing knowledge base, but driven by a real-life problem or need identified in the environment [6]. This framework is thus particularly useful when mature theories are available to guide the development of design artifacts. When this is not the case, for example in new research areas, design solutions can be developed from field research, in particular case studies [7]. Doing so expands the initial 'build and evaluate' DSR framework by explicitly devoting a phase of the research to 'understanding' the domains for which artifacts are being built. However, understanding for design cannot be limited to descriptions or explanations of a phenomena; it should point to design opportunities, thus to intervention that can lead to more desirable outcomes in a given domain. Such design-oriented understanding also referred to as design theories, can be derived from the understanding of how generative mechanisms produce observed outcomes in specific contexts [13].

As we discussed in the previous section, this research aims at developing a modeling technique able to support the design of KIBS engagements in a way that fosters value cocreation. However, while key concepts of value cocreation have been proposed in literature, a theory of value cocreation has yet to be developed [3]. We thus use an expanded 'understand, build and evaluate' DSR approach. We further separate 'building' into the development of a design theory and of a design artifact from that theory. The main activities of this research are thus to 1) Understand: identify generative mechanisms of value cocreation in real-life instances of KIBS engagements; 2) Build a design framework: identify design-oriented questions that need to be answered to foster value cocreation 3) Build a design artifact: develop a modeling technique supporting the design of KIBS engagements; 4) Evaluate: strengthen the validity of the design framework and artifact through a multiple-case study design and evaluation of the modeling technique by KIBS professionals. This paper focuses on the first three phases of our research.

Our research design includes a multiple-case study of academic research and development service engagements as a type of KIBS. We specifically follow the case study strategy of explanation building, where initial theoretical propositions both guide a study and are refined through evidence from a number of cases in a iterative manner [14]. We apply this strategy to the first three research activities; thus, the understanding of generative mechanisms, the accompanying design framework and the resulting modeling technique will be further developed and refined through a number of cases. Such a strategy strengthens generalization by helping to identify the conditions under which the same results can be attained [14].

We present the results from a first case, a service engagement between a team of university professors and students, and departments in a Canadian municipality. These parties collaborated in the creation of a virtual event aiming to inform city residents about available services in an innovative manner. Data consist of two series of interviews with four key stakeholders, observations during key meetings, and a review of the project's documentation. The data were first analyzed inductively to identify emerging categories. Categories were then interpreted as generative mechanisms through key concepts of value cocreation identified in literature [2], [3]; the inductive coding of data also enabled us to identify mechanisms that had not been accounted for in current literature.

Generative mechanisms identified through the case study served to identify questions that can guide the design of relationships among actors looking to engage in a service relationship. The modeling technique was then developed so as to express the conceptual model in terms of mechanisms and their relationships, and provide analytical means to answer its design questions.

4   Design Framework for Value Cocreation

The results of our first case study led to the identification of seven direct mechanisms and four supporting mechanisms of value cocreation. Direct generative mechanisms are those that cause the evolution of the process of value cocreation; supporting mechanisms intervene in direct mechanisms throughout the service engagement. Due to space limitation, we will focus on the direct and supporting mechanisms that shape the conditional phase of the service engagement. This phase covers actors' initial situation, their identification of opportunities from a potential collaboration, and the resulting commitment to the service engagement. Below, we introduce each generative mechanism in turn:

- *Development of high-level interests.* High-level interests are the general interests, vision or objectives pursued by an actor. Actors' high-level interests guide who they interact with and why, shaping their perception of potential benefits to be gained from engaging with other actors. The concept of high-level interests points to the presence of a larger value-configuration space in which actors create value from their perspective [3]. In our case study, high-level interests of the City included exploring electronic means of connecting with their residents, while those of the University Team included getting research funding.

- *Perception of benefits.* Actors perceive potential benefits to be directly gained from a service engagement, in particular from what others can offer (their *value proposition*). This process can also lead to the perception of potential risks by actors. Importantly, actors not only perceive benefits for themselves, but also actively infer benefits to be gained by others. This generative mechanism emphasizes that value resides in the actions and interactions made possible by the acquisition of an offering, not in the offering itself nor in the activities necessary to produce the offering [15]. In our case, perceived benefits included accessing needed expertise and resources for the City, and testing new technologies for the University Team.

- *Creation of a value proposition.* A value proposition is what one party offers to another; this consists of resources such as time, people, and knowledge, but can also be the actor's context or reputation. Actors have conversations and engage in negotiations in order to adapt their value proposition in relation to others' *perceived benefits*. This mechanism implies that the provider cannot embed a good with value before delivery, but can only propose to apply its knowledge and skills to produce something desired by the customer [16]. In our case, the City provides a test-bed for research to the University Team, which in exchange offers to develop assets for the virtual event.

- *Organizing resources.* The resources needed to fulfill actors' *value propositions* are not readily available to them. They must be planned, allocated, arranged, created – in other words, organized. Actors commit to organizing resources because of the benefits that they hope to gain; they thus seek to balance the amount of resources needed to benefit others with *perceived benefits* from the relationship. This mechanism is in line with a Service-Dominant Logic of economies and societies, which states that economic entities possess specialized knowledge that they apply for the benefit of others, in exchange for others' application of their own specialized knowledge [2]. For example in our case, the University Team brings expertise in virtual worlds to the service engagement, while the City brings its domain knowledge and IT support.

- *Reconciling different values.* Reconciling different values among actors involved in a service engagement concerns among other things the negotiation of one's and others' offering, and the alignment of perspectives, visions, and expectations among organizational and individual actors. Reconciling actors' values is key to aligning *value propositions* with *perceived benefits*. The need to reconcile actors' different values is inherent to the collaborative dimension of value creation in service engagements [15].

These generative mechanisms of value cocreation are in line with current literature, but emphasize the strategic intentions of actors driving value cocreation. A modeling technique able to support the design of KIBS relationships needs to express and support the analysis of this intentionality.

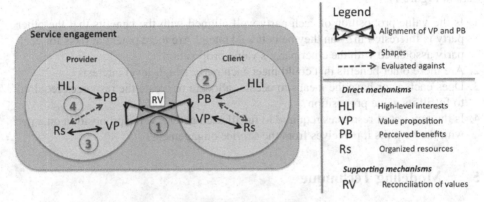

Fig. 1. Generative mechanisms of value cocreation – conditional phase

Figure 1 illustrates the way in which key generative mechanisms of the conditional phase of a KIBS engagement conceptually relate to each other. We draw on the concept of service systems to express the interactions between generative mechanisms. A service system can be understood as a collection of specialized resources (people, technology, information, etc.) organized in a manner that enables an entity to cocreate value with other entities offering complementary specialized resources [3], [17]. While the actual unit being referred to by the term "service system" differs according to authors, we take it to encompass at minimum a provider, its client, and the target of their engagement [18], [19]. We apply the concept of service systems to actors that commit to service engagements in the context of our case study.

Figure 1 attributes generative mechanisms to a provider and its client (in our case, the academic R&D group and the municipal department) in a service engagement, thus forming a service system. The crossed arrows between the provider's and client's perceived benefits (PB) and value propositions (VP) emphasize that value propositions are not fully pre-defined but rather adapted to the other party's perceived benefits through a process of reconciliation of values (RV). They also show the interdependency of actors within service systems. Solid arrows between mechanisms show a directional or bidirectional influence between mechanisms. Specifically, they show that actors' wider high-level interests (HLI) shape the perception of specific benefits (PB) to be gained from the engagement, and that value propositions (VP) lead actors to organize resources (Rs) but that they are also constrained by resources that can be organized. The dotted, bidirectional arrow between organized resources (Rs) and perceived benefits (PB) represent the cost-benefit type of analysis that actors undertake before committing to the service engagement.

Relating generative mechanisms helps to identify important questions to support the design of future service engagements. Firstly, these questions concern the understanding of direct mechanisms, thus knowing what each actor's high-level interests, perceived benefits, value propositions and available resources are. Secondly, questions concern the relationships among direct and supporting mechanisms (see numbers in Figure 1):

1. Is the value proposition of each party well aligned with the benefits that the other party is interested in? Can they be better adapted? Are there potential risks for each party associated with the other party's value proposition?
2. Are there other benefits that could meet each party's high-level interests?
3. Does each actor have the means to access, allocate or create the resources required to fulfill its value proposition?
4. Is the amount of resources required to fulfill each actor's value proposition on a par with the benefits it perceives from the service engagement?

5   Modeling Technique

We propose to express key mechanisms of value cocreation through i*, an Agent-Oriented modeling language. In i*, agents are viewed as social entities that depend on each other to reach their goals [4]. Agents are characterized as intentional in the sense that goals and perceived means to reach these goals are the driver behind their interdependency, and social because they depend on a network of other agents to reach their goals [20]. This understanding is in line with the strategic dimension of the generative mechanisms of value cocreation presented in the previous section. By attributing goals to specific actors, i* also enables the expression of different and potentially conflicting goals among them.

Figure 2 illustrates the use of i* in a simplified model of our case study. The modeling technique uses i* constructs, but changes their semantics in order to express identified mechanisms. We further propose a new construct, 'commitments', to emphasize crossed dependencies between service providers and clients in KIBS.

- **High-level interests** are expressed through the *softgoal* construct, thus as qualitative goals that can only be satisficed (more or less satisfied). This contrasts with hard goals (not used here), which are either fully satisfied or denied. Like softgoals, high-level interests are not precisely defined and do not have clearly predefined criteria for success. The softgoal construct also means that the actor to whom the goal is attributed does not care "how" the goal is achieved. *Contribution links* are thus used to represent relationships between perceived benefits and high-level interests. The use of a "some +" contribution link implies that other alternatives could be proposed to satisfice actors' high-level interests. For example, the City could have decided to collaborate with another organization, or to collaborate with the City's IT department in order to extend its existing website. Alternative perceived benefits can be expressed in *i** using an "or" contribution link between them and high-level interests (not shown for legibility purposes).

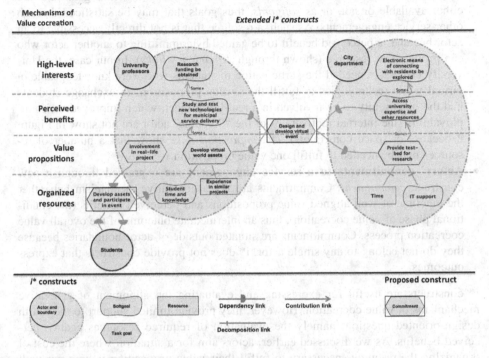

Fig. 2. Adaptation of i* to express generative mechanisms of value cocreation

- **Perceived benefits** are also expressed as *softgoals*. While perceived benefits are defined more precisely than high-level interests, they typically cannot be satisfied in a binary manner. *Contribution links* are again used to connect value propositions to perceived benefit. This expresses the possibility for actors to offer different value propositions in order to gain perceived benefits. However, the presence of dependency links from actors' perceived benefits to each other's' value propositions (through the proposed commitment construct explained below) shows that actors depend on each other to realize these benefits. For example, the University professors had the expertise to develop other technologies able to help the City connect with its residents, but offered to develop virtual world assets because the City specifically wanted to explore this kind of technology.

- **Value propositions** are expressed through the *task goal* construct, thus goals that imply specific activities to be carried out by the actor offering the value proposition. A value proposition is carried out in response to the other actor's perceived benefits, as shown through the use of *dependency links*. However, the "some +" *contribution link* reminds us that actors develop value propositions first and foremost because they are a means to achieve something that is beneficial from their own perspective. Thus, offering a test-bed for research is a means for the City to access University expertise and resources, but only because the University professors are interested in such opportunities.

- **Organized resources** are either expressed as *resource* goals, thus goals that are either available or not, or as *softgoals*, thus goals that may be satisficed through other service engagements. As such, a resource that is not directly accessible to an actor becomes a perceived benefit to be gained by committing to another actor who can provide that resource (shown through *dependency links*). In our case, the University Professors needed the participation of students who were knowledgeable in virtual world technologies to fulfill their value proposition. In exchange students had the opportunity to be involved in a real-life project, which improved their employability (the internal motivations of the "Students" actor are not show in Figure 2 because of space constraints). *Decomposition links* show that a number of resources may be needed to fulfill one value proposition.

- **Actors' commitments to a service engagement** are expressed through a new construct, *commitment*. Commitments are not a generative mechanism but rather the outcome of well aligned value propositions and perceived benefits (the conditional phase of value cocreation), thus an intermediate outcome of the overall value cocreation process. Commitments are situated outside of actor boundaries because they do not belong to any single actor. i* does not provide constructs that express outcomes.

i constructs are useful for expressing and evaluating the alignment of generative mechanisms of value cocreation. However, they provide limited support to the fourth design-oriented question, namely the evaluation of required resources against perceived benefits. As we discussed earlier, actors aim for a situation where the cost of organizing the resources necessary to fulfill their value proposition is on a par with the benefits they hope to reap from the engagement. While i* does provide a procedure to analyze goal satisfaction in models, it would be difficult to apply this procedure to do this cost-benefit type of analysis.

Value network analysis was developed to analyze tangible and intangible exchanges among actors within an organization or part of a larger network [13]. This technique provides analysis tables that are particularly useful to evaluate if the overall ratio of risks or costs and benefits will lead each actor to commit to the service engagement. We have thus adapted impact analysis and value creation analysis tables in order to proceed with this evaluation. Figure 3 shows a partial analysis table where one of the parties, the City department, evaluates its willingness to commit to a service engagement with the University Team.

The section of the table shown in Figure 3 analyzes the risks/costs and benefits of an incoming value proposition. In line with the data, benefits can be identified from the collaborative process itself (e.g., relationship building), and from the deliverable (e.g., reaching out to a bigger portion of residents). An actor can also perceive risks (e.g., accountability to another actor) and costs (e.g., resources) associated with another actor's value proposition. Combined with adapted i* models, these analysis tables can support the design of service engagements that will be perceived as beneficial by all actors involved. Indeed, data from the case study show that participants – both from the provider and client side – already think in terms of identified mechanisms when setting up and managing their relationships. For example, they both actively identify benefits that they may gain from collaborating with others, and try to infer benefits that others may perceive as beneficial so as to develop desirable value propositions. However, they do not do so comprehensively or systematically.

Table 1. Analysis table of an actor's willingness to commit to a service engagement (partial)

Commitment: *Develop virtual event*								
Actor: *City department*								
1		Analysis of the impact of others' VP						
Value proposition (VP)	From	Perceived benefits from collaboration	Perceived benefits from deliverable	Perceived risks of collaboration	Perceived risks of deliverable	Overall risk as beneficiary	Overall benefit as beneficiary
Develop virtual world assets	University team	Develop relationships for future projects	Promote City services to more residents	Failed event if University team does not deliver as promised – mitigated by pilot status of event	Negative perception or disinterest from residents	Medium	High

For example, students wanted a greater involvement in the social media dimension of the event, which would have involved the production of non-moderated content about the city. Thus, this tentative value proposition - developing social media content for the virtual event - was perceived as a risk rather than as a benefit by the City. Using our modeling technique may have helped to identify what students' desire meant in terms of value propositions, and find alternative ways to meet students' perceived benefits (getting real-life experience in social media marketing) in ways that were positive for the city. This technique would thus provide actors engaged in KIBS relationships, in particular providers, with a means to think systematically about the key dimensions of new service engagements and improve chances of successful outcomes for all parties.

The modeling technique presented in this paper accounts for why actors engage in service relationships and how they evaluate the value of a service engagement. It also focuses on the relational level of service engagements by illustrating the networks that are created through actors' need or desire to access others' resources, including knowledge. This contrasts with current service-specific modeling techniques such as Service Blueprinting [5], which focus on sequential activities within service transactions between a provider and client. These techniques thus support the design of service activities, but are unable to link those to actors' motivations for engaging in them.

6   Conclusion

We have shown that a Design Science Research methodology can lead to the development of design artifacts that are grounded in empirical data. Specifically, we have identified key mechanisms of collaborative value creation in knowledge-intensive business services (KIBS) through the study of a real-live case of KIBS engagement. We have then proposed a design framework for KIBS engagements, composed of questions that emerge from the understanding of what fosters collaborative value cocreation this domain. We finally proposed a modeling technique able to express both key mechanisms of collaborative value creation and help answer design-oriented questions from the design framework. Specifically, the modeling technique is derived from i*, an agent-oriented modeling language [4], and value network analysis [21], a technique which provides analytical tables able to help determine actors' willingness to commit to a service engagement. This modeling technique can complement process-based design approaches focusing on the activities involved in the service process, but that are unable to link these activities to the expected benefits pursued by collaborating actors.

This paper outlines the first steps in better supporting the design of service engagements, in particular those found in the domain of knowledge-intensive business services. The results presented in this paper are limited to one case and will be strengthened and refined through a second case within the same sub-domain of academic research and development services. The second case will concern a service engagement between a research group in a different type of academic institution and a for-profit client. The difference in context will ensure that identified mechanisms of value cocreation are not limited to a particular situation or organizational culture. Results from the second case study will also help to refine our design framework and modeling technique. The modeling technique will then be validated through its application to a third case.

References

1. Muller, E., Doloreux, D.: What we should know about knowledge-intensive business services. Technology in Society 31, 64–72 (2009)
2. Lusch, R.F., Vargo, S.L., Wessels, G.: Toward a conceptual foundation for service science: Contributions from service-dominant logic. IBM Systems Journal 47, 5–14 (2008)
3. Vargo, S.L., Maglio, P.P., Akaka, M.A.: On value and value co-creation: A service systems and service logic perspective. European Management Journal 26, 145–152 (2008)
4. Yu, E.: Agent-Oriented Modelling: Software versus the World. In: Wooldridge, M.J., Weiß, G., Ciancarini, P. (eds.) AOSE 2001. LNCS, vol. 2222, pp. 206–225. Springer, Heidelberg (2002)
5. Bitner, M.J., Ostrom, A.L., Morgan, F.N.: Service Blueprinting: A practical technique for service innovation. California Management Review 50, 66–94 (2008)
6. Hevner, A.R., March, S.T., Park, J., Ram, S.: Design science in information systems research. Management Information Systems Quarterly 28, 75–105 (2004)

7. Van Aken, J.E., Romme, G.: Reinventing the future: Adding design science to the reper-toire of organization and management studies. Organization Management Journal 6, 5–12 (2009)
8. Wieringa, R.: Design science as nested problem solving. In: Proceedings of the 4th Inter-national Conference on Design Science Research in Information Systems and Technology. ACM, Philadelphia (2009)
9. Briggs, E., Grisaffe, D.: Service performance-loyalty intentions link in a business-to-business context: The role of relational exchange outcomes and customer characteristics. Journal of Service Research 13, 37–51 (2010)
10. Dobson, P.J.: The Philosophy of Critical Realism: An Opportunity for Information Sys-tems Research. Information Systems Frontiers 3, 199–210 (2001)
11. Van Aken, J.E.: Management research as a design science: Articulating the research prod-ucts of mode 2 knowledge production in management. British Journal of Management 16, 19–36 (2005)
12. March, S.T., Smith, G.F.: Design and natural science research on information technology. Decision Support Systems 15, 251–266 (1995)
13. Van Aken, J.E.: Management Research Based on the Paradigm of the Design Sciences: The Quest for Field-Tested and Grounded Technological Rules. Journal of Management Studies 41, 219–246 (2004)
14. Yin, R.K.: Case study research: design and methods, 2nd edn. Sage, Thousand Oaks (1994)
15. Ramirez, R.: Value co-production: Intellectual origins and implications for practice and re-search. Strategic Management Journal 20, 49–65 (1999)
16. Vargo, S.L., Lusch, R.F.: Service dominant logic: Continuing the evolution. Journal of the Academy of Marketing Science 36, 1–10 (2008)
17. Spohrer, J., Maglio, P.P., Bailey, J., Gruhl, D.: Steps Toward a Science of Service Sys-tems. Computer 40, 71–77 (2007)
18. Gadrey, J.: The misuse of productivity concepts in services: lessons from a comparison be-tween France and the United States. In: Gadrey, J., Gallouj, F. (eds.) Productivity, Innova-tion and Knowledge in Services. New Economic and Socio-Economic Approaches. Ed-ward Elgar, Cheltenham (2002)
19. Ferrario, R., Guarino, N.: Commitment-based Modeling of Service Systems. In: Interna-tional Conference on Exploring Services Sciences. Springer, Geneva (2012)
20. Yu, E.S.: Social Modeling and i*. In: Borgida, A.T., Chaudhri, V.K., Giorgini, P., Yu, E.S. (eds.) Conceptual Modeling: Foundations and Applications. LNCS, vol. 5600, pp. 99–121. Springer, Heidelberg (2009)
21. Allee, V.: Value network analysis and value conversion of tangible and intangible assets. Journal of Intellectual Capital 9, 5–24 (2008)

Towards a Decision Tool for Choosing a Business Process Maturity Model

Amy Van Looy[1,2], Manu De Backer[1,2,3,4], and Geert Poels[2]

[1] University College Ghent, Faculty of Business Administration and Public Administration,
Department of Management and ICT, Ghent, Belgium
{amy.vanlooy,manu.debacker}@hogent.be
[2] Ghent University, Faculty of Economics and Business Administration, Department of
Management Information Science and Operations Management, Ghent, Belgium
{Amy.VanLooy,Manu.DeBacker,Geert.Poels}@UGent.be
[3] University of Antwerp, Faculty of Applied Economics,
Department of Management Information Systems, Antwerp, Belgium
Manu.DeBacker@ua.ac.be
[4] K.U.Leuven, Faculty of Business and Economics, Department of Management Informatics,
Leuven, Belgium
Manu.DeBacker@econ.kuleuven.be

Abstract. The importance of maturity models and business process management (BPM) is already recognized, resulting in many business process maturity models (BPMMs) to progress in BPM. Nonetheless, practitioners have no overview of existing BPMMs and their differences, which makes an informed choice difficult. Choosing the right model is, however, important, as our previous research indicated a great diversity of BPMMs. Therefore, we will design a decision tool that organizations can use to select a BPMM that best fits their needs. The current article introduces possible decision criteria for the tool. Furthermore, the methodology and the conceptual model are discussed. It is argued that the final decision tool can be extended with additional criteria and BPMMs, and translated towards other (maturity) models.

Keywords: business process maturity, design research, decision tool, decision table, consensus-seeking decision-making, Delphi method, multi-criteria decision-making, Analytical Hierarchy Process.

1   Introduction

As from the 1970s, maturity models are recognized as important tools for organizations to progress. Meanwhile, a great amount of maturity models have been designed for different domains, also for managing business processes, e.g. CMMI [1]. In order to improve their design, maturity models are an upcoming research topic within the design-science paradigm [2,3].

Figure 1 introduces the conceptualization of a business process maturity model (BPMM) for this study. A BPMM assesses (AS-IS) and improves (TO-BE) business process maturity. The latter is a collection of capabilities, i.e. abilities or competences, which are needed for a business process to perform excellently. Maturity levels

K. Peffers, M. Rothenberger, and B. Kuechler (Eds.): DESRIST 2012, LNCS 7286, pp. 78–87, 2012.

indicate the overall growth through all capabilities, whereas capability levels indicate the growth per capability. The business process may consist of several sub processes, and defines how an organization operates. For cross-departmental processes, the organization is one legal entity. However, for cross-organizational processes, the organization is a business network of multiple legal entities [1].

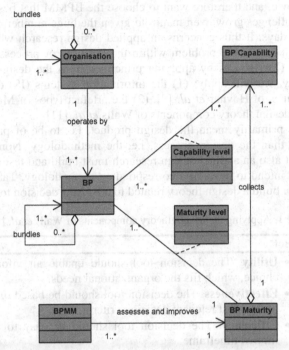

Fig. 1. The conceptual model of a BPMM (limited version)

Nevertheless, the current BPMM proliferation [1] raises questions about the substantial differences between BPMMs. To our knowledge, the BPMM literature is mainly restricted to the design of particular BPMMs, e.g. [4]. Some comparative overviews have been made, albeit without a comprehensive study on a large number of BPMMs [5]. Consequently, organizations have an incomplete state of knowledge on how to select a BPMM that best fits their organizational needs. Besides confusion, information asymmetry makes a rational BPMM choice difficult [6,7]. Moreover, it contradicts rational decision-making theories, such as the multi-attribute utility theory which assumes that decision-makers use relevant criteria to choose a model out of a set of alternatives in order to maximize utility, i.e. value [8].

As examining how an organization must choose a BPMM is paramount, our research question is:

RQ. Which criteria help organizations choose a business process maturity model?

The next section motivates how this research question belongs to the design-science paradigm. Section 3 elaborates on the methodology. Preliminary results are discussed in section 4, followed by limitations and future research. Finally, we summarize the findings.

2   Linking Our Research to the Design-Science Paradigm

Our research is situated in the design-science paradigm by building and testing a BPMM decision tool to solve the incomplete state of knowledge on BPMM selection. This tool will be of practical use for managers wishing to progress towards business (process) excellence, and therefore want to choose the BPMM that best fits their specific context. Challenges grow even manifold given the huge number of BPMMs that are around these days. It thus concerns an applied design research which is (1) relevant for solving a real-world problem within the business or process-oriented community, but also (2) rigorous by applying principles from the design-science paradigm. Particularly, we will apply: (1) the information systems (IS) design research cycle and guidelines of Hevner *et al.* [9], (2) the artefact types of March and Smith [10], and (3) the design theory components of Walls *et al.* [11].

With tool, we primarily mean the design product, i.e. to be of practical use for managers, rather than the design process, i.e. the methodology. Nonetheless, some authors agree that also an applied design research must build and test theories [9,11]. As such, we also intend to develop a corresponding methodology. Table 1 illustrates how our study can build a design theory related to a BPMM decision tool.

Table 1. Applying the design theory components of Walls *et al.* [11]

1. Design product	
1.1 Meta-requirements	• **Utility**. The decision tool should enable an informed BPMM choice, which fits the organizational needs. • **Effectiveness**. The decision tool should be based on a limited set of the most relevant decision criteria. • **Efficiency**. The decision tool should be easy to use, within a limited timeframe. • **Quality**. The output must be clearly and briefly summarized.
1.2 Meta-design	• Conceptual model of the BPMM decision tool (constructs) • Overview of decision criteria and their weightings (model) • Questionnaire (model) • Decision table (method) • Decision tool (instantiation)
1.3 Kernel theories	• Theory of bounded rationality [7] • Theory of information symmetry [6] • Theory of managerial work [12]
1.4 Testable design product hypotheses	• **Utility**. Organizations are more satisfied with the chosen BPMM if the decision tool is used. • **Effectiveness**. For each use, the decision tool results in at least one BPMM. If more BPMMs are obtained, additional information is given to support final decision-making. • **Efficiency**. Organizations using the decision tool are satisfied with the time spent. • **Quality**. Organizations using the decision tool are satisfied with the presentation of the output.

Table 1. (*continued*)

2. Design process	
2.1 Design method	• Content analysis of existing BPMM design documents • Consensus-seeking decision-making (i.e. Delphi method) • Multi-criteria decision-making (i.e. AHP method) • Decision table design
2.2 Kernel theories	• Multi-attribute utility theory [8] • Theory of collaboration [13]
2.3 Testable design process hypotheses	• Delphi experts are satisfied with the decision criteria and their weightings. • Organizations using the decision tool are satisfied with the decision criteria, their question formulation, and their weightings. • The design evaluation guidelines of Hevner *et al.* [9] are met.

March and Smith [10] distinguish four IS artefact types that are commonly accepted in IS research [9]: (1) construct, (2) model, (3) method, and (4) instantiation. Translated to our research, the constructs of the decision tool are visualized in Figure 2.

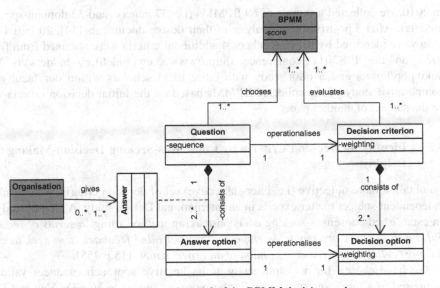

Fig. 2. The conceptual model of the BPMM decision tool

The final decision tool will be based on a set of relevant decision criteria with corresponding options, a priori identified by subject matter experts through consensus-seeking decision-making. The experts will also weigh the criteria and options through multi-criteria decision-making. These relative weightings will allow evaluating existing BPMMs with a final score, and will determine the sequence in which decision criteria are presented in the tool. Regarding this presentation, the decision criteria and options will be translated into questions and answer options. Hence, organizations interested in BPMM selection, will answer a questionnaire, i.e. a mandatory set of questions, and the tool will present BPMMs that best fit their needs.

Two models will be designed: (1) an overview of the final decision criteria and options, including their relative importance as weightings, and (2) a questionnaire. A decision table will be designed as a method, based on the overview, to process the questionnaire. It will explain how answers suggest a BPMM choice. Finally, the instantiation will be the physical implementation into a working tool that organisations can practically use to choose a BPMM.

After designing a proof-of-concept, the number of BPMMs to be evaluated and selected can increase without repeating the identification and weighing of criteria. Similarly, the methodology remains applicable when updating the tool with new criteria. Furthermore, by replacing the upper construct by another model type, the conceptual model becomes transferable to other domains. Also the methodology can be easily generalized (section 3).

3   Methodology

3.1   Initial List of Decision Criteria

In 2010, we collected a sample of 69 BPMMs (i.e. 37 generic and 32 domain-specific models). After a positivist text analysis of their design documents [14], 20 initial criteria were identified by the researchers. 4 additional criteria were obtained from feedback on the EIS2011 conference (http://www.st.ewi.tudelft.nl/~hidders/eis2011/doku.php/home) and a pilot study with other BPM scholars within our faculty. A comparative study of the collected BPMMs based on the initial decision criteria will be the subject of another paper.

3.2   Identifying Decision Criteria by Consensus-Seeking Decision-Making (i.e. Delphi)

To obtain a more objective (i.e. inter-subjective) set of decision criteria, we consulted independent subject matter experts in an international Delphi study. A Delphi study is an established consensus-seeking decision-making method using '*a series of sequential questionnaires or rounds, interspersed by controlled feedback, that seek to gain the most reliable consensus of opinion of an expert panel*' [15,p.458].

We have chosen for a Delphi study as its iterative approach enhances validity, compared to a single questionnaire. Furthermore, according to Van De Ven and Delbecq [16], it generally results in a higher quantity and quality of ideas than other group decision-making methods. The experts are also anonymous, which minimizes group pressures [13]. Moreover, a Delphi study is widely used for exploring ideas and structuring group communication on framework development and rating. Delphi examples are also present in IS research in general [17], and business processes in particular [4].

In November 2011, the Delphi study started with 22 BPM experts, i.e. 11 academics and 11 practitioners, each from five different continents. The academics had credible BPM(M) publications in academic journals, and the practitioners designed a BPMM, applied BPM(M), or were interested in BPMM selection. The selection procedure conforms to [17], introducing different backgrounds to minimize bias [13]. Nevertheless, the initial criteria allowed orienting all experts to the study by providing common ground. Table 2 summarizes the Delphi rounds.

Table 2. The use of the Delphi method

Round	Input of the codification panel	Output of the expert panel

1	**Phase 1: brainstorming**
	
	• Propose initial list of criteria
	• Request missing criteria
		• Per initial criterion:
		  — rate its importance
		  — give open comments
		
		• For all criteria:
		  — rate overall importance
		  — give open comments
		
		• Propose missing criteria

2-3	**Phase 2: narrowing down**
	
	• Consolidate criteria
		• Per criterion:
		  — rate its importance
		  — give open comments
		
		• For all criteria:
		  — rate overall importance
		  — give open comments

4	**Phase 3: weighing**
	
	• Determine final criteria
	• Request weightings
		• For all criteria:
		  — rate overall importance
		  — give open comments
		• Weigh criteria and options

Consensus conditions were a priori defined for a 7-point Likert scale, based on measures of location (i.e. frequencies) and spread (i.e. interquartile range) [18]: (1) 50% of the experts must agree on the two most extreme scores (i.e. either 1-2 or 6-7), (2) 75% must agree on the three most extreme scores (i.e. either 1-2-3 or 5-6-7), (3) the interquartile range must be 1.50 or less, and (4) no opposite extreme score given by any expert (i.e. either 7 for the first case or 1 for the second).

At the time of this writing, the Delphi study was in its second round. Per round, the responses are anonymously analyzed by the researchers and an independent coder. This codification panel will stop iterating when the consensus conditions are met, or when results become repetitive. Hence, a Delphi study typically takes three to four rounds [4,18]

3.3   Weighing Decision Criteria by Multi-criteria Decision-Making (i.e. AHP)

In the final Delphi round, the experts will weigh the decision criteria that reach consensus, including the options. We recall that the resulting weightings will be used to determine the sequence of criteria within the decision tool, but also to evaluate existing BPMMs. The latter ultimately allows a critical view on the many BPMMs. Moreover, BPMMs with the lowest evaluation scores could be omitted beforehand to guarantee the quality of the decision tool's output. Given this purpose, weighing implies eliciting which criteria and options are more important, but also how much more, i.e. their relative importance.

Three commonly used ranking methods within Delphi studies are [19]: (1) simple ranking (e.g. item A > item B), (2) scale rating, as used in the previous Delphi rounds (e.g. item A = 6/7 and item B = 3/7), and (3) pairwise comparisons (e.g. item A is three times more important than item B). Only the third method calculates relative importance, albeit time-consumingly. Hence, the final round will use multi-criteria decision making without consensus-seeking, particularly by the Analytical Hierarchy Process [20]. AHP is a distinghuised method that calculates weightings based on pairwise comparisons and normalised principal Eigen vectors. Besides a thorough calculation procedure, AHP guarantees the quality of weightings by measuring a consistency ratio per expert judgement. Hence, only consistent judgements are taken into account ($CR\leq0.1$) [20]. Furthermore, AHP has been widely used for three decades, also within Delphi studies. Therefore, it has overcome the initial validation concerns of new methods, compared to other multi-criteria decision-making methods [8].

3.4   Decision Table and Questionnaire

If possible, the final decision table will be designed with the PROLOGA decision table tool [21]. PROLOGA also supports the conversion into an automated questionnaire.

4   Preliminary Results

In the first round, 24 criteria were introduced: (1) number of assessed organizations, (2) lead assessor, (3) certification, (4) benchmarking, (5) number of assessors, (6) functional role of respondents, (7) business versus IT respondents, (8) data collection technique, (9) number of assessment items, (10) assessment duration, (11) rating scale, (12) capabilities, (13) number of business processes, (14) type of business processes, (15) architecture type (i.e. staged with maturity levels or continuous with capability levels), (16) number of lifecycle levels (i.e. maturity levels or capability levels), (17) level calculation, (18) level representation, (19) labeling of levels, (20) external view of levels, (21) architecture details (i.e. with descriptive or prescriptive improvements), (22) creation methodology, (23) validation methodology, and (24) the direct costs to access and use the BPMM.

Two missing criteria were proposed by the experts: (1) the purpose for which the BPMM is intended to be used, i.e. it combines the initial criteria of 'benchmarking' and 'certification', and (2) whether the assessment items are publicly available.

All these criteria to be considered in the Delphi study are BPMM characteristics, and thus, inherently fit into the BPMM conceptual model of section 1. Conform to [1], Figure 3 visualizes that a BPMM is used by assessors, and consists of an assessment method (i.e. to rate the current level and identify a gap with the desired level), and an improvement method (i.e. a road map to evolve from the current to the desired level).

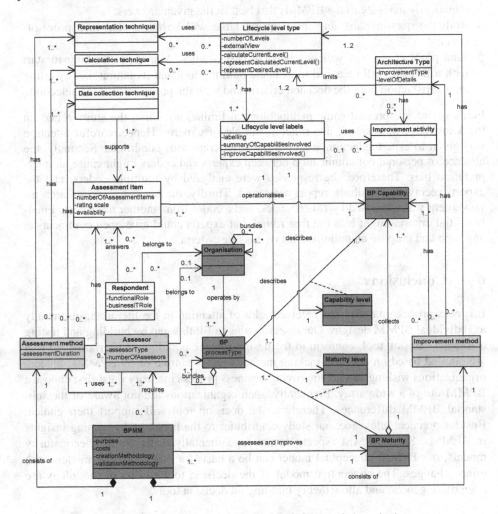

Fig. 3. The conceptual model of a BPMM (extended version)

5 Research Limitations and Future Research

This article concerns a work-in-progress, which is its most important limitation. When the Delphi study is finalised, the decision criteria with consensus and their options will be used to build a proof-of-concept of the decision tool.

1. The evaluation scores of collected BPMMs will be calculated, according to the obtained weightings. BPMMs with the lowest scores might be omitted.
2. The criteria and options will be translated into a questionnaire, and pilot tested.
3. The questionnaire will be coupled to a decision table, which comprises a mapping to the BPMM sample. By answering the questionnaire, the decision table will systematically navigate to the BPMMs that best fit the given answers.
4. Both the questionnaire and the decision table will be automated in a proof-of-concept.
5. This proof-of-concept will be tested in case studies. Managers, wishing to start with a BPMM, will be asked to evaluate both the tool and its output, i.e. by rating their satisfaction with the decision criteria and with the proposed BPMM selection.

Furthermore, we present some methodological limitations. First, the study relied on the knowledge of a small, non-random sample of experts. Hence, careful attention was given to expert selection and defining strict consensus conditions. Secondly, the absence of personal communication between experts and coders might cause an interpretation bias. Therefore, the responses were analyzed by multiple coders, and the experts received a feedback report per round. Thirdly, the bias of prior research involvement was addressed by Likert scales, and a coder from another university. Finally, initial criteria might bias the first round, but experts could give open comments at any time and propose an unlimited list of missing criteria.

6   Conclusions

Business process maturity has received a lot of attention in the literature, but mainly as individual BPMM designs. Our research tries to fill this gap by building and testing a BPMM decision tool, conform to the design-science paradigm. Criteria for the tool are elicited based on decision-making methods and a sample of 69 BPMMs. Indeed, organizations wishing to start improving business process maturity must first choose a BPMM out of a wide array. Frequently, such organizations are not aware of the substantial BPMM differences. Therefore, the decision tool will support their choice. Besides practical relevance, our study contributes to the literature by gaining insights in BPMMs. Since BPMM aspects do not fundamentally differ from other maturity models, our BPMM conceptual model can be a basis for other maturity models with minor changes. The conceptual model of the decision tool and its methodology are even more generic and allow theory building on decision tools.

Acknowledgements. We truly thank the independent coder and the expert panel for their continuing participation throughout the different Delphi rounds.

References

1. Van Looy, A., De Backer, M., Poels, G.: Defining Business Process Maturity. A Journey towards Excellence. TQM & Business Excellence 22(11), 1119–1137 (2011)
2. Mettler, T., Rohner, P.: Situational Maturity Models as Instrumental Artifacts for Organizational Design. In: 4th DESRIST Conference, pp. 1–9. ACM, Malvern (2009)

3. van Steenbergen, M., Bos, R., Brinkkemper, S., van de Weerd, I., Bekkers, W.: The Design of Focus Area Maturity Models. In: Winter, R., Zhao, J.L., Aier, S. (eds.) DESRIST 2010. LNCS, vol. 6105, pp. 317–332. Springer, Heidelberg (2010)
4. de Bruin, T., Rosemann, M.: Using the Delphi Technique to Identify BPM Capability Areas. In: 18th ACIS Conference, Toowoomba, pp. 642–653 (2007)
5. Maier, A.M., Moultrie, J., Clarkson, P.J.: A Review of Maturity Grid based Approaches to Assessing Organizational Capabilities. In: Academy of Management Meeting (2008)
6. Afzal, W., Roland, D., Al-Squri, M.N.: Information Asymmetry and Product Valuation: an Exploratory Study. Journal of Information Science 35(2), 192–203 (2009)
7. Simon, H.A.: Rational Decision Making in Business Organizations. The American Economic Review 69(4), 493–513 (1979)
8. Wallenius, J., et al.: Multiple Criteria Decision Making, Multiattribute Utility Theory. Management Science 54(7), 1336–1349 (2008)
9. Hevner, A.R., et al.: Design Science in Information Systems Research. MIS Quarterly 28(1), 75–105 (2004)
10. March, S.T., Smith, G.F.: Design and Natural Science Research on Information Technology. Decision Support Systems 15(4), 251–266 (1995)
11. Walls, J.G., Widmeyer, G.R., El Sawy, O.A.: Assessing Information System Design Theory in Perspective: How Useful was our 1992 Initial Rendition? JITTA: Journal of Information Technology Theory and Application 6(2), 43–58 (2004)
12. Mintzberg, H.: Managerial Work: Analysis from Observation. Management Science 18(2), B97–B110 (1971)
13. Harvey, C.M., Koubek, R.J.: Cognitive, Social, and Environmental Attributes of Distributed Engineering Collaboration: a Review and Proposed Model of Collaboration. Human Factors & Ergonomics in Manufacturing 10(4), 369–393 (2000)
14. Lacity, M.C., Janson, M.A.: Understanding Qualitative Data: a Framework of Text Analysis Methods. Journal of Management Information Systems 11(2), 137–155 (1994)
15. Dalkey, N., Helmer, O.: An Experimental Application of the Delphi Method to the Use of Experts. Management Science 9(3), 458–467 (1963)
16. Van De Ven, A.H., Delbecq, A.L.: The Effectiveness of Nominal, Delphi, and Interacting Group Decision Making Processes. The Academy of Management Journal 17(4), 605–621 (1974)
17. Okoli, C., Pawlowski, S.D.: The Delphi Method as a Research Tool: an Example, Design Constructions and Applications. Information & Management 42, 15–29 (2004)
18. Hasson, F., Keeney, S., McKenna, H.: Research Guidelines for the Delphi Survey Technique. Journal of Advanced Nursing 32(4), 1008–1015 (2000)
19. Scheibe, M., Skutsch, M., Schofer, J.: Experiments in Delphi Methodology. In: Linstone, H.A., Turoff, M. (eds.) The Delphi Method, pp. 257–281. Addison-Wesley, London (1975)
20. Saaty, T.L.: Relative Measurement and Its Generalization in Decision Making. The Analytical Hierarchy/Network Process. RACSAM 102(2), 251–318 (2008)
21. Vanthienen, J., Wets, G.: Integration of the Decision Table Formalism with a Relational Database Environment. Information Systems 20(7), 595–616 (1995)

Implementing Design Principles
for Collaborative ERP Systems*

Wendy Lucas and Tamara Babaian

Bentley University, Waltham, MA 02452, USA
{wlucas,tbabaian}@bentley.edu

Abstract. Enterprise Resource Planning (ERP) Systems are notoriously difficult for users to operate. We present a framework that consists of a data model and algorithms that serve as a foundation for implementing design principles presented in an earlier paper for improving ERP usability. The framework addresses the need for providing user, task and process context of each system-user interaction. It is intended to form an integral part of the system's data model, which can be queried in real time to produce the information required for a variety of user interface enhancements. We have implemented the framework within an ERP prototype and used it in a laboratory emulation of ERP usage. Using the log data from this laboratory emulation, we present examples demonstrating how the framework meets its design goal of providing contextual and historical information.

Keywords: Usability, human-computer collaboration, enterprise systems, ERP, human-computer interaction.

1 Introduction and Motivation

Enterprise Resource Planning (ERP) systems integrate data and information flow from throughout the organization. Companies rely on them for standardizing their processes around best practices. Rather than the system conforming to the way a particular company does business, the company must conform to the system-prescribed approach in order to reap the maximum benefit. Representing industry-wide rather than company-specific practices places a heavy burden on the user, who must undergo extensive training to learn how to perform particular tasks with the system. Users typically memorize how to do those tasks, as the underlying processes are hidden behind very complex interfaces and little guidance or support is provided by the system. The poor usability of ERP systems has been noted in industry reports [16,22,15,17] and our own field studies [26,10], yet

---

* This material is based in part upon work supported by the National Science Foundation under Grant No. 0819333. Any opinions, findings, and conclusions or recommendations expressed in this material are those of the authors and do not necessarily reflect the views of the National Science Foundation.

K. Peffers, M. Rothenberger, and B. Kuechler (Eds.): DESRIST 2012, LNCS 7286, pp. 88–107, 2012.
© Springer-Verlag Berlin Heidelberg 2012

usability problems still abound. Considerable advances in research on human-computer interaction [19] have also not resulted in significant improvements in ERP system design.

The work presented here is part of a comprehensive research effort aimed at achieving a breakthrough in the usability of enterprise systems by applying the human-computer collaboration paradigm [25] to system design and evaluation. This paradigm is grounded in theory of collaboration and requires that the system act as a partner that supports its users in the increasingly complex environments of modern applications [13]. To be a collaborative partner, the system must do its part by sharing information and adjusting its behaviors based on its knowledge and awareness of the user, the context of the interaction, and its own functionality. (Note that this is different from Computer-Supported Cooperative Work (CSCW), which is concerned with computing technology that supports human collaboration).

In previous work [7], we derived four design principles based on system-user collaboration for addressing the usability issues identified in our field studies. In this paper, we present a representational framework and algorithms that serve as a foundation for implementing these principles. In validating our approach, we focus here on two of these principles, which are referred to as Design Principle 2 (DP2) and Design Principle 4 (DP4). DP2 concerns providing context- and user-appropriate navigational and progress guidance to the user. DP4 focuses on improving access to data and actions that are most likely to be relevant and useful. The other two principles, which involve mechanisms for customization and error handling, are also supported by our framework and are topics of ongoing research that is beyond the scope of this paper.

Our framework specifies a model that represents the system's task structure, interface components, and usage log of all user-system interactions. It has been specifically designed to enable the system to make effective use of usage histories during system-user interactions. This model, which we refer to as the Task-Interface-Log, or TIL, model, provides the requisite information for supporting the design principles by explicitly associating low-level user inputs with higher-order processes. Our approach is further distinguished by its use of logged data in support of system-user interactions in real time, as opposed to the off-line processing of logged data for process mining and discovery purposes [2,23], which is the more common focus of research involving usage logs in the enterprise system domain.

We have implemented the TIL model in SQL and embedded it in an ERP prototype. To evaluate the capabilities of both the TIL model and the algorithms for supporting the design principles, we conducted an emulation of the use of ERP systems in a laboratory setting. The usage data collected from this emulation was used to validate our approach.

The next section of this paper presents related work. This is followed by descriptions of the design principles. We then present our representational framework and examples that illustrate the framework's utility using empirical data. We conclude with a discussion and directions for future work.

2   Related Work

Usage data has been used extensively for extending the functionality of automated tutoring, recommender, and adaptive hypermedia applications (e.g. [21,9]). Jameson [20] provides a review of interfaces that adapt their behaviors in order to better meet the needs of the user. In these applications, the possible set of actions that a user can perform is typically well-defined, and the emphasis is on modeling the user in order to provide suitable recommendations, guidance, and support.

The ability to reason from usage logs for supporting users in real time within the context of complex enterprise systems is far less commonplace. Günther et al. [14] describe how event logs are recorded at very low levels of abstraction, making them difficult to relate to activities within a process. As noted by Ivory and Hearst [18], keystroke data is easy to record but difficult to interpret. Our framework overcomes this hurdle by associating interface components with both contextual information and usage histories, making it possible to analyze and utilize data ranging from the keystroke level to the task level, from a single user to multiple users.

While ERP users are constrained by the business logic of the system, there are no strictly enforced process models. Rozinat and Aalst [23] have shown that activities followed in completing a process, as mined from ERP system logs and other administrative systems, often deviate from the prescribed process. A variety of algorithms and techniques exist for constructing process models from low-level events in a usage log [2]. Investigating system usage by applying such techniques for deriving workflow models that can then be analyzed off-line is the focus of much of the work in this area (see, for example, [4,5,11,6]).

Our own interest lies in developing design models that enable a system to provide dynamic guidance and support to users based on process sequences corresponding to actual organizational practices, which is the subject of far less research. Aalst et al. [3] describe an application that focuses on processes that have not yet completed for checking on conformance, estimating completion times, and making recommendations on steps for minimizing overall flow times. Schnonenberg et al. [24] propose a recommendation service that guides users by giving recommendation on possible next steps based on past process executions. It has been implemented in ProM [4], an open-source process mining framework for implementing process mining tools. A partial case from the user who is seeking guidance, consisting of a sequence of performed steps, is sent to to the recommendation service. The case is then compared to the log, and a recommendation is generated.

The above works are all based on discovering processes from usage log activity traces that are contained within the time period between the predefined starting and ending activities. This approach is complicated by the noise that comes from the non-process related tasks that are commonly interleaved with the process-related ones within the identified time period. Aalst [1] notes that there are several shortcomings to existing algorithms due to processes being highly concurrent and the existence of complex dependencies between activities.

In our framework, we avoid many of the challenges inherent in mining-based approaches because our model contains the specification of tasks included in the process. Our approach is distinguished by the ability to automatically and accurately identify process instances based on log records, by virtue of the direct representation of tasks, processes and the flow of domain objects in the TIL model.

3 Design Principles

Given the integrated nature of ERP systems and the complexity of their design, approaches that specify isolated patches for addressing particular issues will not succeed in improving overall system usability. Rather, a systematic approach for evaluating and addressing usability issues is required. Our field studies of ERP system users revealed common categories of usability issues that can be explained as examples of non-collaborative behavior between the system and its users. We applied collaboration theory [8,13] as the unifying perspective for viewing human-computer interactions in deriving our design principles [7], which are presented in figure 1. What we refer to throughout this paper as *processes* are referred to as *transactions* in these principles.

DP1   The user interface should provide a mechanism for customizing the vocabulary of terms used by the system in its communication to the user, the composition of business transactions, and the content of the system's informational output to match the practices of the organization. There should be a mechanism for incorporating the customizations from an earlier version of the system to a later one.

DP2   **The system should provide navigational and progress guidance to a user performing a transaction, indicating the broader context of each interaction in terms of the related business process components and specifying the completed and remaining parts. A sufficiently competent user should be able to turn off this guidance if it becomes a distraction.**

DP3   When the system detects a problem, it should identify the possible causes and ways of resolving it. If the fix is obvious, the system should inform the user and perform it. If it isn't obvious, the possible causes and resolution scenarios should be presented to the user and be readily executable. If the system is unable to identify resolution strategies, it should present the user with the relevant data and transactions.

DP4   **In presenting selection choices, the system should utilize what it knows about the user, the organization, the task, and the context, and provide faster access to the more likely choices than the less likely ones. Where the choice of data or action is obvious, the system should have an option of not waiting for the user to enact it. The user should have an option to replace/cancel the system's provided choice of data/action.**

Fig. 1. Design principles for greater ERP usability

DP1 grew out of reported instances of users needing to undergo a lengthy process, characterized by some as "brutal" and "intimidating," of learning the language of the system and adapting to its practices. DP2 arose from the difficulties users face in understanding the process flow and navigating the system, with little support on how to proceed or what progress has been made. DP1 and DP2 are meant to address the failure of the system to be a good collaborative partner by *communicating* its knowledge concerning the steps that need to be taken, the means for performing them, and the progress made toward achieving the goal.

Numerous reports by users of their inability to determine the cause of an error, decipher error messages, or figure out how to address the problem led to the statement of DP3. In such cases, the system is failing to *help* a partner in need. Lastly, DP4 grew out of observed and reported cases of the system presenting all possible choices, even those that will not work in the current situation, in search interfaces, lists, etc., and failing to take the user's previous entries and actions into account. In these cases, the system has not provided appropriate *support* to assist the user in daily operations.

The framework presented in this paper provides the information needed for supporting all four principles. We have limited our validating examples in the next section to two of these, DP2 and DP4, due to space limitations. Examples related to DP1 and DP3 will be presented in future work.

4   Representational Framework

In this section, we present the representational framework that we developed to support implementation of the design principles. The design goals behind this framework originated from the requirements on the system's awareness of historical and contextual data, as necessitated by the design principles:

1. to represent the system's task and interface structure in a way that enables reasoning about their relationship to each other and to the ERP domain data in the context of a business process,
2. to capture and store the history of each system-user interaction in a way that enables a quick identification of the task and user context of all past and on-going interactions, as well as recording the lower-level keyboard and mouse input details, and
3. to make the knowledge included in the first two items accessible to the system at run-time for supporting a variety of implementations of the design principles.

The framework includes the Task-Interface-Log (TIL) data model, algorithms for deriving process-related data, and input-aware components. The following sections describe the model and algorithms. While the components have also been implemented, they are not reviewed here.

4.1   Overview of the TIL Modules: Task, Interface, Logging

At the core of our representational framework is the TIL data model for representing Tasks and their inclusion in business processes, the Interface components that implement them, and usage Logs that store the details of system-user interactions.

The *Task* module of the TIL model captures the description of tasks that the system implements and their inclusion in business processes. The set of interface pages associated with each task is described in the *Interface* module. This module also describes the composition of each interface page from user input controls, such as input fields, buttons, and menus. The descriptions within the Task and Interface modules are *static*, in that they do not change with use of the system, with one exception that allows the system to be configured with business process specifications as desired collections of tasks. The data within these two modules is used to render interface pages, when the user invokes a task interface, and for tracking the task and process context of each interaction.

The *Logging* module records user interactions with the system on two interconnected levels: the task level and the interface level. Logging on the task level involves keeping track of *task instances*, i.e., the user's engagement with the system on a particular task. A task instance can extend over multiple user-sessions, and the Logging module chronicles the execution of a task instance from the beginning to the end.

The interface layer log stores the detailed key-press level information regarding the user's interactions with input controls within the task. To support usage data capture, we have implemented and used a library of user input components that record the interaction data. Taken together, the information contained within these two layers of the Logging module enables a quick and complete reconstruction of a sequence of events as they occurred over time.

The records of organizational data, such as customers, vendors, and invoices, are stored in the ERP system database, which we refer to as the *Domain* module. We call Domain module entities *domain objects* and their corresponding tables *object types*.

Definition 1. *A domain object is a record from a table in the Domain module. The domain object type, or simply object type, is the name of the table in the Domain module storing the domain object.*

All three modules of the TIL model are also related to the Domain module - these relationships specify the flow of organizational data through the tasks. In particular, each task description (Task module) includes a specification of the type of organizational data object that the task produces, called the task's *output object type*. For example, the *Add Material* task produces a record in the *Material* table; thus, it's output type is *Material*. The references to the actual objects (e.g. a concrete *Material* record) produced as a result of a specific task instance are contained within the Logging module's record of task instances.

Along with the output object type for a task, the TIL model also includes information on each task's *input object types*. Each user input component description in the Interface module specifies the type of object that should be entered in the field. Since each input component is associated with a task, the TIL model enables the derivation of the set of input objects used in a task.

4.2   TIL Relations

This section introduces the details of the TIL model that are essential to the algorithms and derivations that follow. Boldface is used to denote the names of the relations, and italics is used for the attributes. The relations are defined over standard SQL types, such as varchar, int and datetime. Please refer to figure 2 for descriptions of the attributes of each relation that we review below.

The Domain Module represents the ERP organizational data and is not part of TIL, but TIL model relations reference the Domain module tables that store a variety of domain objects. The **User** relation of the Domain module has a special significance, because it is linked to all usage log related records. For the sake of simplicity, we model the **User** relation as consisting of the single identifier attribute *UID*. Other attributes describing the user's relationship with a particular organizational unit, role, or set of permissions within the system could be added for greater richness of informational queries from the log data, but such treatment of **User** is not included in this paper.

The Task Module consists of three relations: **Task**, **Process** and **ProcessTasks**. The *DTableOut* attribute of the **Task** table refers to the task's output type which, as we defined in section 4.1, is the name of a table from the Domain module that stores the output objects associated with that task. The **Process** and **ProcessTasks** tables list the business processes and specify which tasks are included in each process, respectively.

The Interface Module represents user interface components and their organization and relationship with the Task and Domain modules. Each **Task** is associated with a set of distinct **TaskPages** which, in turn, consist of **Groups** of **InputControls**.

The **InputControl** table describes interactive GUI elements such as buttons, text fields, lists, and menu items. Input control records for text fields specify in the *DTable* column the type of object that must be entered into the text field. For example, a field designated for a customer number will have the *DTable* attribute value equal to **Customer**, which is the table storing customer information in the Domain module. The *DTable* column of input controls used for entering non-domain object data, such as an order quantity or a delivery date, has no value.

The Logging Module records the usage history and describes the relationships between click-level and keyboard-level data, users, and tasks.

Module	Relation and Abbreviation		Description	Attributes and their descriptions	
Domain	User	U	*User description*	UID	*User Identifier (PK)*
	others omitted				
Task	Task	T	*Task description*	TID	*Task Identifier (PK)*
				Tname	*Task name*
				DTableOut	*Task output type(Domain table name)*
	Process	PR	*Process Description*	PRID	*Process Identifier (PK)*
				PRName	*Process name*
	ProcessTasks	PRT	*Tasks included in process*	PRID	*Process identifier*
				TID	*Task identifier*
				Opt	*Task optional or required status*
Interface	Task Page	TP	*Interface pages associated with each task*	PID	*identifier*
				TID	*Task identifier*
	Group	G		GID	*Group Identifier*
			Group of input controls on a page	PID	*Task Page Identifier*
	Input Control	IC	*User input component*	ICID	Input Control Identifier (PK)
				GID	*Group Identifier*
				DTable	*Input Object Type (Domain table name)*
Logging	User Session	US	*User session - continuous period between the time user logs in and out of the system.*	SID	*Session Identifier (PK)*
				UID	*User Identifier*
				t_s	*Time session started*
				t_e	*Time session ended*
	Task Instance	TI	*Task instance - an instantiation of a task, possibly spanning multiple user sessions between start and completion.*	TIID	*Task Instance Identifier (PK)*
				TID	*Task Identifier*
				t_s	*Start time of task instance*
				t_e	*End (completion) time*
				OutPKVal	*Output object produced by the task instance*
	Session Task Instance	STI	*Task instance breakdown by user session*	STIID	*Session Task Inst. Identifier (PK)*
				TIID	*Task Instance Identifier*
				SID	*Session Identifier*
				t_s	*Start time of session task instance*
				t_e	*End time of session task instance*
	Entry Field	EF	*Input control instantiations*	EFID	*Entry Field Idenetifier (PK)*
				ICID	*Input Control Identifier*
				SID	*Session Identifier*
				TIID	*Task Instance Identifier*
	User Entry	UE	*Timed user input per entry field*	UEID	*User entry record (PK)*
				EFID	*Entry Field Idenetifier*
				t_s	*Start time of user input (focus-in)*
				t_e	*End time of user input (focus-out)*
				V_s	*Value in field at the start time*
				V_e	*Value in field at the end time*
				E	*user input*

Fig. 2. A summary of the essential components of the TIL model and the Domain module

The **UserSession** relation represents periods of time during which the user is continuously logged in to the system. It is used to relate each interaction to a particular user.

The **TaskInstance** relation records instantiations of tasks. A new task instance record is created each time the user opens a new task. The task instance end time corresponds to the moment when the user either cancels the task instance or completes it, in which case the output is saved in the Domain database.

The identifier of the output object is stored in the *outPKVal* column of the Task Instance record.

As the task instances can span multiple user sessions, the **SessionTaskInstance** relation is used to record the task instance execution times within different sessions.

Taken together, the **UserSession**, **TaskInstance** and **SessionTaskInstance** relations specify the user and task context of system-user interactions. The detailed log of system-user interactions within the task instances is stored within the **EntryField** and **UserEntry** relations, described next.

The **EntryField** table represents the instantiations of input controls corresponding to a specific task instance and user session. The *ICID* attribute refers to the instantiated input control. *SID* and *TIID* are references to the session and task instances, respectively, in which the entry field was created.

The **UserEntry** relation records the user input directed to the specified entry field. The start and end times of the period when the entry field is in continuous focus are defined by t_s and t_e. Attributes V_s and V_e record the value in the text field at the start and the end of that time period, while E denotes a string recording the user's input as a sequence of keystrokes or mouse events.

4.3   Task and Process Graphs and Algorithms

To provide context-aware guidance and navigational support for design principle DP2 requires that the system be aware of the relationships between the tasks and the input-output flow of objects between them. The TIL model specifies the input and output types of tasks in a process and, during runtime, records the actual domain objects that are instantiated. This information enables the automatic determination of the relationships between task and task instances in a chain comprising a business process. Figure 3 illustrates the types of task and process-related information that we focus on in this section.

Task Graph. Figure 3(a) presents a fragment of a system *task graph* that can be composed from descriptions contained within the Task and Interface modules. The nodes correspond to tasks, and an arrow from one node to another designates that the output of the source task may be used as an input to the target task. For example, arrows from task a, Add Material, lead to tasks b, c, e, and f. This is because these four tasks have Material as part of their input, which can be established by querying the TIL model records on the input fields for these tasks.

The task graph is composed from the TIL model data using procedures *DInput* and *DOutput*, which stand for Domain Input and Domain Output and are depicted in figure 4. We use relational algebra operations [12] of natural join ($*$), projection (π), selection (σ) and renaming (ρ). We use the abbreviated names of the TIL relations, as presented in the third column of figure 2. Uppercase letters used here and throughout the paper denote relations, while the names of scalar values and individual tuples begin with a lowercase letter.

Procedure *DInput(paramTID)* returns a set of domain input types of task *paramTID*, i.e. the types of domain objects that can be entered as an input to

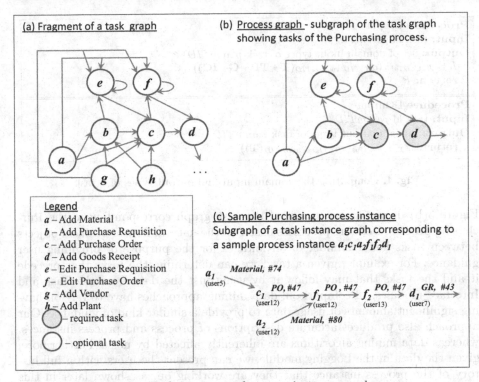

Fig. 3. Task, process and process instance graphs

task *paramTID*. (We refer to the tuples from our data model by their identifier value, as described in the fifth column of figure 2.) *DInput* computes the result by collecting the set of table names associated with all of the task's input controls. Procedure *DOutput(paramTID)* returns the value of the *DTableOut* attribute, which specifies the output table for the task with identifier *paramTID*.

Definition 2. *A task graph is a directed graph in which the set of nodes corresponds to the tasks, and a link from task a to task b is drawn if and only if* $DOutput(a) \in DInput(b)$.

Process Graph. In our framework, the processes are specified as a set of tasks, which must be related via their inputs and output. We define business processes as being comprised of one or more required tasks and zero or more optional tasks. Optional tasks are those that are not required by the system to complete a process. Process compositions from tasks can be configured by organizations to match their own practices.

Definition 3. *A process is a set of tasks, which form a weakly connected subgraph in the task graph. Some steps in a process are designated as required, while the rest are optional.*

Procedure DInput
Input: task id *paramTID*
Output: set of domain input types of task *paramTID*
1 $R = \pi_{\mathbf{IC}.DTable}(\sigma_{\mathbf{T}.TID=paramTID}(\mathbf{T} * \mathbf{TP} * \mathbf{G} * \mathbf{IC}))$
2 return: R

Procedure DOutput
Input: task id *paramTID*
Output: domain output types of task *paramTID*
1 return: $\pi_{\mathbf{T}.DTableOut}(\sigma_{\mathbf{T}.TID=paramTID}(\mathbf{T}))$

Fig. 4. Computing the domain input and output types of a task

Figure 3(b) demonstrates a part of the task graph corresponding to the Purchasing process. Defining processes based on the natural flow of business objects between tasks has a number of advantages for the purpose of providing user guidance. For example, given a task, we can determine the tasks that precede it and the tasks that may follow it by using just the data from the Task and Interface modules. In comparison, data mining approaches have to rely on having significant amounts of usage data to provide a similar kind of guidance. Our approach also produces accurate descriptions of process and process instances, whereas data mining algorithms are inherently affected by noise. Furthermore, given the data in the Logging module, we can present the users with a full history of the process instance that they are working on, as shown later in this section. An illustration of one such process instance derived from empirical data that corresponds to the process in figure 3(b) is depicted in figure 3(c).

Definition 4. *We say that task a precedes task b and that task b follows task a in a given process p if a, b ∈ p and there is a path from a to b in the task graph.*

In the multi-user environment of ERP systems, the precedence relationship between tasks does not necessarily correspond to the temporal order of the task instances involved in a process. Instead, a precedes task b reflects that a is involved in producing input to b, and, in turn, b is involved in handling the output from a.

An algorithm that computes the set of tasks preceding a given task in a specified process is depicted in figure 5. Procedure *PrecedingTasks* is a breadth-first traversal of the process subgraph of the task graph starting from the given task in the reverse direction of the arrows. The procedure starts from the given task *paramTID* (step 2), identifying all of its input types (step 6) and adding the tasks within the process that produce objects of those types to the set Θ_1 (steps 7,8). The same process is performed for each task in Θ_1 and so on until no new tasks (i.e. tasks that are not already found in the union of all visited tasks $\cup_{i=0}^{n-1}\Theta_i$) are discovered. The set of tasks following a given task is computed by a similar traversal in the direction of the arrows.

Procedure PrecedingTasks
Input: task id $paramTID$, process id $paramPRID$
Output: set of tasks preceding task $paramTID$ in process $paramPRID$
1   $n = 0$
2   $\Theta_0 = \{paramTID\}$
3 **do**
4      $n = n + 1$
5   **for each** $taskTID \in \Theta_{n-1}$
6        $InputTypeSet = DInput(taskTID)$
7   **for each** $objType \in InputTypeSet$
8          $\Theta_n = \Theta_n \cup ProducerTasks(objType, paramPRID) - \cup_{i=0}^{n-1}\Theta_i$
9 **while** $(\Theta_n \neq \emptyset)$
10 **return:** $\cup_{i=1}^{n}\Theta_i$

Procedure ProducerTasks
Input: domain object type $paramObjType$, process id $paramPRID$
Output: task ids for task from process $paramPRID$ outputting objects of type $paramObjType$
1 **return:** $\pi_{\mathbf{T}.TID}\left(\sigma_{\mathbf{T}.DOutputType=paramObjType \wedge \mathbf{PRT}.PRID=paramPRID}(\mathbf{T} * \mathbf{PRT})\right)$

Fig. 5. Computing the set of tasks preceding a given task in a specified process

Task Instance Graph and Process Instance Identification. The TIL model also provides for an easy and noiseless reconstruction of process instances, i.e. sets of task instances corresponding to a specified process, regardless of the order in which they have been executed and the number of users involved.

We introduce below two auxiliary procedures, $TIIn$ and $TIOut$, which stand for Task Instance Input and Output, respectively. Shown in figure 6, these procedures return the actual inputs and output objects of a given task instance. Both are used in a process instance identification procedure, whose definition follows in figure 7. The identification procedure is based on a domain object produced as an output and can be best understood as a breadth first traversal of the *task instance graph*.

Procedure $TIIn(paramTIID)$ returns a list of $(objectType, objectID)$ pairs for those objects entered into the entry fields associated with $paramTIID$. To determine which object id was entered, a query selects the chronologically last value of an entry field recorded in the **UserEntry** relation. To perform this selection, steps 1-2 of the procedure compute the complete set of user entries into the entry fields associated with task instance $paramTIID$. Based on the timing of the user entries, steps 3-4 produce the set of final values for each entry field, i.e. the values that were actually submitted. From those final values and the description of their domain type stored in the **InputControl** relation, step 5 composes a set of $(objectType, objectID)$ pairs, where $objectID$ is the value entered in the field, and $objectType$ specifies its domain type.

$TIOut(paramTIID)$ returns the output object type and id of the task instance $paramTIID$ from the **Task** and **TaskInstance** relations.

Procedure TIIn
Input: task instance id $paramTIID$
Output: set of pairs $(objectType, objectID)$ used as input to $paramTIID$
1 $J = \sigma_{\mathbf{TI}.TIID=paramTIID}(\mathbf{TI}) * \mathbf{EF} * \mathbf{IC} * \mathbf{UE}$
2 $K = \sigma_{\mathbf{IC}.DTable!=null \wedge \mathbf{UE}.V_e!=null}(J)$
3 $L = \rho_{Last(EFID,t_e)}(_{EFID}\mathcal{F}_{MAX_{t_e}}(\mathbf{UE}))$
4 $M = \sigma_{\mathbf{UE}.t_e=Last.t_e}(K * L)$
5 $R = \rho_{TIIn(objectType,objectID)}(\pi_{\mathbf{IC}.DTable,\mathbf{UE}.V_e}(M))$
6 **return:** R

Procedure TIOut
Input: task instance id $paramTIID$
Output: pair $(objectType, objectID)$ describing the type and value of domain output of $paramTIID$
1 **return:** $\pi_{\mathbf{T}.DTable,\mathbf{TI}.OutPKVal}(\sigma_{\mathbf{TI}.TIID=paramTIID}(\mathbf{TI} * \mathbf{T}))$

Fig. 6. Procedures computing the input and output of a specified task instance

Definition 5. *A* task instance graph *is a labeled directed graph in which the set of nodes corresponds to the task instances, and a link from task instance a to task instance b with label $o = TIOut(a)$ is drawn whenever $TIOut(a) \in TIIn(b)$ and $a.t_e < b.t_s$, where t_s and t_e refer to the task instance start and end time.*

The process instance information can be explored in a number of useful ways, including:

1. identifying all complete or incomplete instances of a given process, or for a given user,
2. given an object, such as a goods receipt, identifying all the task instances within the process involved in creating that object, and
3. identifying all instances of a process that use a given object, such as a purchase requisition, as their input.

As an illustration, figure 7 presents a procedure called *ObjectHistory* that determines, for a given process and a given domain object, the part of that process that led to the current state of that object. The algorithm is a breadth-first traversal of the task instance graph induced by the Logging module. The traversal is performed in the reverse direction of the arrows, starting from the chronologically latest task instance that has the given domain object as its output. The traversal is complete when all task instances that are a part of the given process are identified. The output of the procedure is a set of task instances that correspond to the steps of the input process up to the point of the latest modification of the input object.

Procedure *Producer*, shown in figure 7, is called by *ObjectHistory* and returns the task instances corresponding to a given process $paramPRID$ that have a specified object as their output. Only task instances that ended before a specified time are returned.

Procedure ObjectHistory

Input: process $PRID$, domain table name $objType$, domain object identifier $objID$

Output: a set of task instances from **TI** that correspond to the process $PRID$ and precede the latest task instance outputting the object $objID$

1 $TIs = Producer(objType, objID, CurrentTime())$

2 $latestTime = \mathcal{F}_{MAX_{t_e}}(TIs)$

3 $\Theta_0 = \pi_{TIID}(\sigma_{\mathbf{TI}.TIID \in TIs \wedge \mathbf{TI}.t_e = latestTime}(\mathbf{TI}))$

4 $n = 0$

5 **while** $(\Theta_n \neq \emptyset)$

6     $n = n + 1$

7     $\Theta_n = \emptyset$

8   **for each** $ti \in \Theta_{n-1}$

9        $\Upsilon_n = TIIn(ti)$

10   **for each** $tiinput \in \Upsilon_n$

11          $\Theta_n = \Theta_n \cup Producer(tiinput.objectType, tiinput.objectID, ti.t_e) - \cup_{i=1}^{n-1} \Theta_i$

12 **end while**

13 **return:** $\cup_{i=1}^{n} \Theta_i$

Procedure Producer

Input: process $parPRID$, domain table name $objType$, domain object identifier $objID$, time value t

Output: a set of task instances from **TI** ending before or at t of tasks from process $PRID$ that outputted object $objID$ of type $objType$

1 $K = \pi_{TIID}(\sigma_{\mathbf{PRT}.PRID=parPRID \wedge (objType, objID) \in TIOut(\mathbf{TI}.TIID) \wedge \mathbf{TI}.t_e <= t}(\mathbf{TI} * \mathbf{T} * \mathbf{PRT}))$

2 **return:** K

Fig. 7. Determining the object's history within a specified process

$ObjectHistory(paramPRID, objType, objID)$ starts by calling $Producer$ to obtain all task instances that had the parameter object as their output. From that set, steps 1-3 determine the task instance that ended most recently (we assume a domain object cannot be edited simultaneously by different task instances). That task instance, stored in Θ_0, is the starting point of the traversal. The traversal can be characterized as a series of computations of sets Θ_n, for $n >= 1$, comprised of task instances adjacent to those in Θ_{n-1} in the task instance graph, which continues until no new task instances can be discovered. Only task instances corresponding to the tasks in the specified process $paramPRID$ are considered. The procedure returns a set of all task instances discovered via the traversal. This set contains all instances of the tasks from the given process linked via the input-output chain that have the given object as their output.

The data model and algorithms presented in this section are used in the illustrative examples presented in the next section.

5 Empirical Validation

To evaluate how the TIL framework meets its design goals and evaluate its usefulness for supporting collaborative system-user interactions, we have built a prototype ERP system that utilizes the TIL model. We have conducted an emulation of ERP usage in an organization using our prototype in a laboratory setting. The emulation involved 15 users performing typical ERP tasks over a period of 27 days, with overall logged usage time of a little under 12.5 hours. There were 39 user sessions that resulted in 6,691 separate user entries. The users accessed a total of 15 different task pages, which created approximately 450 different task instances.

We have tested all algorithms presented in the previous section on the usage data collected during the emulation. Here, we present examples that demonstrate the usefulness of our framework for supporting design principles DP2 and DP4 using the emulation data.

5.1   Example 1: Implementing Design Principle 2

Design principle 2 mandates that the user performing a business process be assisted by having the system display navigational guidance through completed and remaining tasks. This guidance should take into account the task and process context. It is easy to see that the TIL representation and algorithms presented in the previous section directly support derivations of context and process guidance information.

Figure 8 shows a design of an interactive display visualizing the tasks that precede and follow the user's current task. This display was constructed from the emulation data using the data and algorithms presented in the previous section. It includes the Purchasing process task information and references to the task instances related to the *Add Purchase Order* task instance.

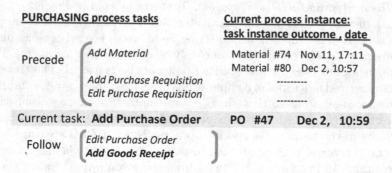

Fig. 8. An interactive display showing a Precede/Follow list, providing quick access to related tasks, objects and task chronology

The left side of the display in figure 8 specifies the tasks, separated into those that can precede the current task and those that can follow it. As defined in section 4.3, preceding tasks are those that are involved in producing the input to the current task and are obtained by executing the *PrecedingTasks* procedure (fig. 5), which derives the information from the **Task** and **Interface** modules of

TIL. The Precede/Follow list highlights in boldface the tasks that are required for the process. It also serves as a useful reminder of the tasks related by the input-output flow and as a navigation tool: given that each task is associated with its interface page specification, a task name can also link to the appropriate task page.

The number of instantiations of each preceding task and the timing of each is included in the instance-specific information on the right side of the interactive display. The figure shows that the currently active task instance of *Add Purchase Order* was preceded by two *Add Material* instances. The other two preceding tasks are optional, and are not present in this process instance. This data is produced using the algorithm presented in figure 7, which returns a list of task instances within the process that are involved in producing the object created by the current task. The data includes the objects created by each preceding task instance and the date that the task instance was completed. Clicking on the object description (e.g. *Material #74*) will display the object. The user can also sort the list of preceding instances by the completion date to see the actual chronology of the process instance.

5.2   Example 2: Implementing Design Principle 4

A core proposition of DP4 is that the system should make use of what it knows about the user, the organization, the tasks, and the context to provide faster access to more likely choices. Software systems often do make use of prior user interactions for assisting with data entry. For example, in filling out a form on the Web, the browser will typically display one or more values that the user had previously entered to a field. With the knowledge represented by the TIL model, the system can provide access to values previously entered by the current user as well as by other users performing a particular task. The latter can be especially helpful to users with limited usage histories of their own. The granularity of usage data in our model also makes it possible to determine the users experience at a detailed level, so that appropriate assistance can be offered not only to users who are novices with the system overall, but also to those with limited experience in a particular task or even with a particular component within a task.

To demonstrate the type of information available to the system for use in tailoring the support it offers on a task-by-task basis, table 1 contains data from our laboratory study showing the users who submitted the Purchase Requisition (PR) Enter Header and Defaults page during a two-day period, the number of times they submitted, and the date of their most recent submission.

For those users with recent and frequent experience in submitting purchase requisitions, default values based on prior entries are likely to be the most useful. For someone with little or no experience, however, knowledge of the values entered by other users performing the same task can be very helpful. Values previously entered to a field can be sorted by frequency of entry, the most recent

Table 1. Count of submissions and time stamp of most recent submission of PR Header and Defaults page during a two-day period

User ID	Frequency	PR Line Items - Most Recent Submission
user10	2	24-NOV 13:15
user9	2	24-NOV 12:16
user8	2	23-NOV 14:55
user7	3	23-NOV 14:27
user6	2	23-NOV 10:50

date of entry, or any other useful property. Table 2(a) shows the values entered by all users into the Plant field in the PR header and defaults page during a two-week time period. The most frequently entered value during that time period was 15, which was also the value entered most recently. This type of information can be used in guiding a user with limited experience in filling out any form within the system.

Table 2. (a) User-entered values during two-week period into Plant field in PR Header and Defaults page; (b) Access counts for all input controls in the PR Header and Defaults page

Value	Frequency	Most Recent Entry Date
15	3	2-DEC 14:34
11	2	2-DEC 13:34
10	2	2-DEC 9:23
12	2	24-NOV 13:15
14	2	2-DEC 10:56
13	1	2-DEC 12:45
7	1	2-DEC 10:45

(a)

Input Control (IC)	IC Name	Data Type	Access Counts
1	Plant	int	67
2	Delivery Date	DATE	60
3	Storage Location	int	88
5	Vendor	int	65
601	Add Plant	menuitem	0
602	Edit Plant	menuitem	0
701	Add Vendor	menuitem	0
702	Edit Vendor	menuitem	0

(b)

DP4 also specifies that, if a choice of data or action is obvious, the system should have the option of enacting it, with the user able to replace or cancel that action. If a user almost always enters the same plant value in filling out a PR, for example, then it would make sense for the system to enter that value for the user. Similarly, if the user typically enters multiple PRs, as evidenced from the log, then the system should let the user cycle through the PR process multiple times, while also providing easy access to other frequently performed tasks.

The data captured to the usage log also provides insights into the practices of the organization that can be used for assisting the user. As an example, consider the fields that the organization requires users to fill in versus those required by the ERP system. While the latter may (or may not) be marked as required in the system, there is typically no discernible way for users to see what fields must be entered in order to adhere to organizational practices; this is because customization is costly and difficult to maintain when systems are upgraded. The system, however, does have knowledge of which fields are most often completed, or left blank; which options are most typically selected, or ignored, etc. Highlighting fields that are typically filled in can help improve the users' efficiency in filling out forms, particular those with which they have less experience.

As an example, table 2(b) shows the number of times each of the input controls in the PR header and defaults page were accessed. While storage location is not a required field, it was the most frequently accessed field. Table 2(b) also shows that none of the menu items were accessed from this page, as there were other ways of navigating that were chosen instead. Because ERP systems are designed to meet the needs of a vast array of users in varying industries, there will typically be fields or options on every page that are not needed by particular groups of users. The system can be designed to not include those components when rendering the interface. In particular, the removal of fields that are never filled in because they are not relevant to a particular organization's practices can lessen interface complexity and improve user efficiency. For other components, such as the menu items in Table 2(b) and other navigational aids, it could be that the user is just not aware of them but they could actually be beneficial (as evidenced by another group of users making frequent use of them, for example). The system could be designed to direct the user's attention to hitherto unexplored options based on its knowledge of overall system usage.

6   Conclusions and Future Work

We have presented a framework, consisting of the TIL data model and algorithms, that was designed as a foundation for implementing design principles for achieving greater ERP system usability. The framework was implemented within an ERP prototype and tested using data obtained in a laboratory emulation of ERP usage in an organization. The evaluation confirmed that the TIL model meets its design goals of supporting context-aware system interactions by enabling real-time querying of contextual and historical information in support of the design principles from section 3.

The task and process specifications contained within the TIL model structure alone (without the usage log data) make it possible to identify all of the tasks that lead to the creation of a specific type of object and all of the subsequent tasks in which that output can be used. The TIL model can also be exploited for providing support to users by informing them, for example, of the flow of outputs through the system leading to the task currently being worked on. Analysis of the usage data within the TIL model provides the larger picture of the many possible ways that users can complete processes with the system, which can be applied to navigational support, guiding the user in input choices and actions, and providing access to data and actions that are most likely to be useful.

A limitation of the presented framework is that tasks are described as having only one output: while many ERP tasks can be characterized in this way, there are some tasks that produce more than one object type. The model and algorithms can be extended to handle multiple output objects in a straightforward way.

Compared to the related work in workflow mining, which addresses some of the same aspects of system behavior, our approach is both model- and log-data-driven rather than being based solely on usage log data. This results in several advantages, including accurate and complete process instance identification regardless of the number of process instances in the log, and the ability to provide user guidance that is based on the model of tasks, processes and object flow.

In this paper, we provided examples illustrating the utility of the framework for implementing two of the four principles, DP2 and DP4. The framework also provides a foundation for several aspects of the other two principles. Indeed, the declarative description of tasks and related user interface components enables the easy customization of the system's vocabulary. The process descriptions in the TIL model provide a mechanism for process customization, as required by DP1. DP3 involves reasoning about errors, which is not addressed by the model presented here, but the TIL model already contains components that are a necessary part of error-related support of the user. In the future, we will extend the framework to fully support all four design principles. We will also develop proof-of-concept implementations of the kinds of interface features described in section 5 and evaluate them in user studies.

References

1. van der Aalst, W.M.P.: Process discovery: Capturing the invisible. IEEE Comp. Int. Mag. 5(1), 28–41 (2010)
2. van der Aalst, W.M.P.: Process Mining: Discovery, Conformance and Enhancement of Business Processes, 1st edn. Springer Publishing Company, Incorporated (2011)
3. van der Aalst, W.M.P., Pesic, M., Song, M.: Beyond Process Mining: From the Past to Present and Future. In: Pernici, B. (ed.) CAiSE 2010. LNCS, vol. 6051, pp. 38–52. Springer, Heidelberg (2010)
4. van der Aalst, W.M.P., Reijers, H.A., Weijters, A.J.M.M., van Dongen, B.F., de Medeiros, A.K.A., Song, M., Verbeek, H.M.W.E.: Business process mining: An industrial application. Inf. Syst. 32(5), 713–732 (2007)
5. van der Aalst, W.M.P., Weijters, T., Maruster, L.: Workflow mining: Discovering process models from event logs. IEEE Trans. Knowl. Data Eng. 16(9), 1128–1142 (2004)
6. Agrawal, R., Gunopulos, D., Leymann, F.: Mining Process Models from Workflow Logs. In: Schek, H.-J., Saltor, F., Ramos, I., Alonso, G. (eds.) EDBT 1998. LNCS, vol. 1377, pp. 469–483. Springer, Heidelberg (1998), http://dl.acm.org/citation.cfm?id=645338.650397
7. Babaian, T., Lucas, W., Xu, J., Topi, H.: Usability through System-User Collaboration. In: Winter, R., Zhao, J.L., Aier, S. (eds.) DESRIST 2010. LNCS, vol. 6105, pp. 394–409. Springer, Heidelberg (2010)
8. Bratman, M.E.: Shared cooperative activity. Philosophical Review 101(2), 327–341 (1992)

9. Brusilovsky, P., Cooper, D.W.: Domain, task, and user models for an adaptive hypermedia performance support system. In: IUI 2002: Proceedings of the 7th International Conference on Intelligent User Interfaces, pp. 23–30. ACM Press, New York (2002)

10. Cooprider, J., Topi, H., Xu, J., Dias, M., Babaian, T., Lucas, W.: A collaboration model for ERP user-system interaction. In: Proceedings of the 43rd Hawaii International Conference on System Sciences, HICSS 2010 (2010)

11. Dustdar, S., Hoffmann, T., van der Aalst, W.M.P.: Mining of ad-hoc business processes with teamlog. Data Knowl. Eng. 55(2), 129–158 (2005)

12. Elmasri, R., Navathe, S.B.: Fundamentals of Database Systems, 4th edn. Addison-Wesley Longman Publishing Co., Inc, Boston (2003)

13. Grosz, B.G., Kraus, S.: Collaborative plans for complex group action. Artificial Intelligence 86(2), 269–357 (1996)

14. Günther, C.W., Rozinat, A., van der Aalst, W.M.P.: Activity Mining by Global Trace Segmentation. In: Rinderle-Ma, S., Sadiq, S., Leymann, F. (eds.) BPM 2009. LNBIP, vol. 43, pp. 128–139. Springer, Heidelberg (2010)

15. Hamerman, P.: ERP applications 2007: Innovation rekindles. Forrester Research (2007)

16. Hestermann, C.: Key issues for enterprise resource planning. Gartner (2009)

17. Iansiti, M.: ERP end-user business productivity: A field study of SAP & Microsoft: Keystone strategy (2007),
http://download.microsoft.com/download/4/2/7/427edce8-351e-4e60-83d6-28bbf2f80d0b/KeystoneERPAssessmentWhitepaper.pdf
(downloaded December 21, 2009)

18. Ivory, M.Y., Hearst, M.A.: The state of the art in automating usability evaluation of user interfaces. ACM Computing Surveys 33(4), 470–516 (2001)

19. Jacko, J.A., Sears, A.(eds.): The human-computer interaction handbook: fundamentals, evolving technologies and emerging applications, 2nd edn. L. Erlbaum Associates Inc. (2008)

20. Jameson, A.: Adaptive interfaces and agents. In: Sears, A., Jacko, J.A. (eds.) The Human-Computer Interaction Handbook: Fundamentals, Evolving Technologies and Emerging Applications, 2nd edn., pp. 433–458. CRC Press, Boca Raton (2008)

21. Linton, F., Joy, D., Schaefer, H.P., Charron, A.: Owl: A recommender system for organization-wide learning. Educational Technology & Society 3(1) (2000)

22. Otter, T.: Case study: Ness combines consumer application ease of use with erp robustness. Gartner (2008)

23. Rozinat, A., van der Aalst, W.M.P.: Conformance checking of processes based on monitoring real behavior. Inf. Syst. 33(1), 64–95 (2008)

24. Schonenberg, H., Weber, B., van Dongen, B., van der Aalst, W.: Supporting Flexible Processes through Recommendations Based on History. In: Dumas, M., Reichert, M., Shan, M.-C. (eds.) BPM 2008. LNCS, vol. 5240, pp. 51–66. Springer, Heidelberg (2008)

25. Terveen, L.G.: Overview of human-computer collaboration. Knowledge-Based Systems 8(2-3), 67–81 (1995)

26. Topi, H., Lucas, W., Babaian, T.: Identifying usability issues with an ERP implementation. In: Proceedings of the International Conference on Enterprise Information Systems (ICEIS 2005), pp. 128–133 (2005)

Applying Design Science Research for Enterprise Architecture Business Value Assessments

Martin Meyer[1], Markus Helfert[1], Brian Donnellan[2], and Jim Kenneally[3]

[1] Dublin City University,
Dublin, Ireland
{mmeyer,markus.helfert}@computing.dcu.ie
[2] National University of Ireland,
Maynooth, Ireland
brian.donnellan@nuim.ie
[3] Intel Labs Europe,
Leixlip, Ireland
jim.kenneally@intel.com

Abstract. In the effort to measure the business value and impact of Enterprise Architecture (EA), we need to adapt an appropriate form of information systems research in order to cope with the encountered challenges. For this purpose, we employed Design Science Research (DSR), a problem-driven approach to provide a solution represented as artifacts to provide the required utility to our stakeholders. The main contribution of this research is the detailed focus on how artifacts are actually conceived in an organizational context and the realization that a complex environment demands for more than just one artifact. Therefore, we are in need of a flexible research methodology. The DSR in this case is conducted within a well-known information systems research framework and follows widely accepted principles and guidelines. We explain the business need that arose from the current business practices in the course of a case study and describe the flexible research methodology we pursue and how we intend to solve the problems we identified as current DSR approaches lack the necessary flexibility we were looking for in practice. This flexibility greatly improves the management of our project in the organizational environment in terms of planning and implementation. Furthermore, we outline the evolutionary state of the artifacts during our adapted research process.

Keywords: Design Science, Enterprise Architecture, Business Value Assessment.

1 Introduction

Conducting research in the field of information systems involves many challenges, especially when considered in the context of business and industry demands. We constantly encounter problems which need to be solved or emerging business needs that have to be satisfied. For this purpose, we must follow a rigorous procedure to deliver

K. Peffers, M. Rothenberger, and B. Kuechler (Eds.): DESRIST 2012, LNCS 7286, pp. 108–121, 2012.
© Springer-Verlag Berlin Heidelberg 2012

the adequate solution. As a means of achieving this, we have Design Science Research (DSR) at our disposal which creates novel solutions that serve human purposes as contrasted by natural science that tries to understand reality. Hence, Design Science is the research of the artificial and produces different kinds of results such as constructs, models, methods and instantiations which are referred to as artifacts [1], [2]. In our case, we want to apply this kind of research to the field of Enterprise Architecture (EA) and more specifically to the way we measure and assess the business value and impact of EA as perceived by different stakeholders. In collaboration with an industry partner, we identified the business need to facilitate a more sophisticated way of assessing EA in an organizational context. This calls for an appropriate methodology of research and hence, the satisfaction of this business need shall be given by designing various artifacts. Consequently, this work is focused on artifacts in terms of development as well as the context in which they are intended to be applied and we therefore our research methodology is centered on the artifacts and we discuss the state of these throughout the research process.

2   Design Science Application

Despite many existing options to conduct IS research, we chose DSR since it demands a rigorous identification of problems or business needs respectively. This course of action is of utmost importance since the design of the artifacts is dependent on the outcome of this analysis. Another reason for choosing DSR is that actual research processes enriched with guidelines and principles exist in literature on which we can base our adapted research method.

For designing our artifacts, we explore the academic knowledge base, an activity which results in a rigorous literature review. Due to the fact that our artifacts are created within an organizational context, we further capitalize on the knowledge base available within the company in addition to other forms of publications and best practices prevalent in industry.

We will now describe our adapted IS research framework in the next section followed by the principles and guidelines that accompany this kind of research methodology.

2.1   Research Framework

For our work, we employed the IS research framework proposed by [1]. As illustrated in Fig. 1, our environment consists of stakeholders, the strategy, processes and the current EA function within the company. Arising from this environment we can identify relevant problems or business needs. The IS Research itself is dominated by the employed research methodology for both artifacts and theories, i.e. design science and behavioral science are complementary approaches. We apply readily available knowledge from the knowledge base, such as the company's IT frameworks and the employed maturity framework IT-CMF [3]. Furthermore, methodologies found in other disciplines such as Business Intelligence and Operations Research are examined and adapted as required. The results of this research will enrich the practitioner environment as well as the knowledge base in terms of insight and added value.

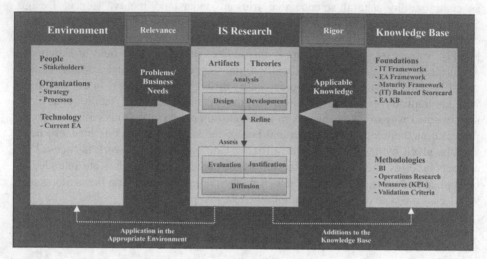

Fig. 1. Adapted DSR Framework (cf. [1])

2.2   Research Principles and Guidelines

Research, as in many other disciplines, needs principles and guidelines. They ensure that the result of the contribution achieves a certain level of quality. As suggested in [4], we adopt the following principles when designing our artifacts.

— *Abstraction:* Each of our artifacts must solve a class of problems.
— *Originality:* Each of our artifacts must contribute to the knowledge base.
— *Validation:* Each of our artifacts must be justified.
— *Benefit:* Each of our artifacts must yield some kind of business value for the stakeholders.

In addition, we follow the seven guidelines proposed in [1]. These are summarized in Table 1 in context of our work.

2.3   Research Methodology

We employ the basic research methodology outlined in [4]. Although other methodologies can be found in the literature, such as [5] and [6], we focus on four basic phases for our design science application although we consider these methodologies as sub-steps of our process. The main phases or activities respectively are Analysis, Design, Evaluation, and Diffusion. Each main phase consists of several sub-steps in which a particular deliverable is produced (cf. Fig. 2). This research process will be explained more detailed in the course of our case study in section ref. But before we go in to detail on the research process, we will describe the application domain and the organizational context in section 3.1.

Table 1. Design Science Research guidelines for our application

Guideline	Our Application
Design as an Artifact	We design a main construct which comprises further artifacts: a method, a model and another construct (cf. 3.2).
Problem Relevance	The problem relevance is shortly covered in the introduction and will be further detailed in section 3.2. Generally spoken, problems that are solved with a projected increase in business value are always relevant.
Design Evaluation	Since the artifacts will be implemented, the evaluation will take place in an organizational context.
Research Contribution	Our research contribution is centered on the designed artifacts and the corresponding environment and knowledge base. It clarifies the artifact creation at various stages of the research methodology.
Research Rigor	For both the design and evaluation we utilize adequate methods to embrace the required research rigor.
Design as a Search Process	Since every step of our design process takes place in collaboration with an industry partner, we satisfy the environmental needs and adhere to the environmental rules and regulations. Because of this collaboration, we have an extended knowledge base at our disposal, i.e. the means to conduct such a search process are diversified and meant to reach a designated end.
Communication of Research	Our work combines business and technological knowledge and therefore is presentable for both the management-oriented and the technology-oriented audiences.

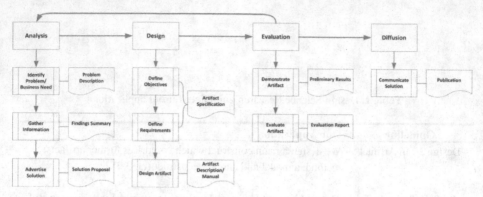

Fig. 2. Used Research Methodology as a Process including deliverables

3   Case Study

For our case study, we employ our approach in an organizational context in order to evaluate and validate its practical utility. First, we shed light on the actual context which is the assessment of EA business value (EABV).

3.1   Context: Enterprise Architecture and Business Value

The discipline of Enterprise Architecture is meanwhile a core practice for large companies within the IT Domain. Furthermore, the number of contributions from academia underlines the importance of EA as a relevant research topic. Another hint on how important the EA community views this topic is the myriad of available EA frameworks as the title of [7] suggests. Large companies, in particular, leverage the benefits of such frameworks in order to improve the effectiveness of their IT function and corresponding organizations. In many large companies, IT organizations are meant to undergo a transformation from cost centers to value centers which is where EA frameworks deliver means to accomplish this. While the value proposition of employing such frameworks may seem obvious, it is still not clear enough how to exactly measure and assess it in terms of business value and maturity [8].

Value Proposition
The value propositions of EA are manifold. It is a means of generating business value, reducing complexity, improving business-IT alignment (BITA), reducing costs and so on. Generally spoken, it increases overall organizational performance and delivers business value to all stakeholders. The most important outcomes of successful EA adoption are classified by [9] as follows:

- Reduced IT costs (operation and maintenance)
- Increased IT responsiveness
- Improved Risk Management

- Increased management satisfaction
- Enhanced strategic business outcomes

The problem now is that we do not automatically know how to measure the promised value. We will discuss EABV assessment in the next section.

EABV Assessment

Assessment of EABV is not a trivial task as there will always be a gap between real and perceived value with differences for every stakeholder group [10]. Little guidance on how to capture EABV and the difficulties of finding the adequate metrics for EA adds up to an ongoing struggle for EA practitioners and EA researchers alike [8]. This is why we find several contributions to address the difficulties of EA measurement in literature. In [11] an IT management assessment framework is presented while in [12], a quantitative analysis at firm-level provides insight on outcomes and success factors of EA by means of employing a conceptual framework. The value from a model-driven analysis is subject of [13]. A classical approach from performance measurement, the Balanced Scorecard, is applied to EA in [14]. The question which EA practices and techniques influence EA benefits is answered in [15].

When it comes to EA assessments, we differ between maturity assessments and EA performance measurement where the former evaluates the overall EA capability periodically while the latter is focused on the operational and organizational performance which is measured continuously. Regarding our case study, our company conducts EA maturity assessments with the IT Capability Maturity Framework (IT-CMF) [3] which itself is also a practical DSR application [16]. With our focus on continuous EA performance measurement, we want to align with the maturity assessment and provide a solution where both assessments complement each other in order to elaborate the EABV.

3.2   Applied Research Process

Analysis

During the first phase of our research process, we rigorously analyze the current state of the EA function and the relevant problems that come with it. As we outlined in section 2.2, we design our artifacts to be applicable to a class of problems adhering to the abstraction principle. A crucial part of the analysis is the identification of relevant problems existing in the environment by conducting surveys and expert interviews with our stakeholders in an exploratory manner. The summary of our problem analysis is outlined in Table 2, Table 3, and Table 4.

The first problem class is of the perception/definition type, i.e. what is EABV and how is it viewed by stakeholders. Then we have the visibility/transparency problems which arise from the fact that the EABV is not or just hardly to find and once found how to measure it. Finally, we deal with improvement/optimization problems. In our case this means how can we improve or optimize respectively the EA adoption, i.e. the acceptance and execution of the EA function, the EA collaboration between stakeholders, EA Governance, EA decision making in terms of overall IT strategy, EA practices, EA maturity and Business-IT Alignment (BITA).

If we now consider the environment, we can give a problem statement and/or the business need and provide the intended solution or IT artifact for it. Based on this analysis we can deliver a first solution proposal in form of four artifacts: EABV Framework (EABVFW), an EA Measurement Process (EAMP), an EA Balanced Scorecard (EABSC) and an EABV Model (EABVM). We will explain these in the following section where we commence with the design of these artifacts.

To summarize, the analysis phase is divided into three steps (cf. Fig. 2). The first is the problem/business need identification where we generate a problem description document. Based on that description, we gather information within the environment and knowledge base and produce a findings summary which describes how to best address such kind of problem and what has been learned so far. We then compile a solutions proposal which needs to be advertised to get accepted for e.g. funding or management support.

Table 2. Problem classes

Problem Class	Questions
Perception/Definition Problem	What is EABV? How is EABV viewed?
Visibility/Transparency Problem	Where can we find EABV? How can we measure EABV?
Improvement/Optimization Problem	How can we improve/optimize EA adoption, collaboration, Governance, decision making, practices, maturity and BITA?

Table 3. Environmental perception and visibility problems and their solution

Environment	Problem/Business Need	Solution/IT Artifact
Stakeholders	Definition of EABV, Perception of EABV	EABVM
Strategy	Measurement of EABV	EABSC
Processes	Scope of EABV, Tracking of EABV	EABVFW, EABVM
Current EA	Measurement of EABV	EABVFW, EAMP, EABVM

Design

The main process phase of DSR is devoted to the design of artifacts because this is what DSR is all about, providing an artificially crafted solution to a problem in the

Table 4. Environmental improvement problems and their solution

Environment	Problem/Business Need	Solution/IT Artifact
Stakeholders	Improvement of EABV, EA adoption, EA collaboration, and EA Governance	EABVFW, EAMP
Strategy	Improvement of IT decision making	EABSC
Processes	Improvement of BITA	EABVFW
Current EA	Improvement of EA practices and EA maturity	EABVFW, EAMP

form of an construct, model, method, or instantiation. We already outlined our artifacts in the previous section as part of the solutions proposal. Now it's time to take a closer look at these and what they intend to accomplish. The EA Business Value Framework (EABVFW) is the main artifact since it serves as overall solution to our business needs. Besides having the other three artifacts as components, it provides a repository and guidelines how to implement the solution as well as templates on how the EABV is reported. The EABVFW takes the current EA function, i.e. EA services and processes, stakeholder information (e.g. feedback), and strategic objectives as input, measures the performance and translates it into EABV which in turn serves as input for decision making in order to improve current practices by means of better informed strategic knowledge. In order to have a clear definition and scope of what EABV is and how it is generated, we need the EA Business Value Model (EABVM). We want to achieve a common understanding and consistency in measuring performance and communicating EABV. This model also serves as means of making various entities such as metrics persistent in terms of implementation. The EA Measurement Process (EAMP) is the way we conduct continuous EA performance measurement. Therefore, we employ the process outlined in the ISO/IEC 15939:2007 standard [17] which defines a measurement process with the purpose of collecting, analyzing, and reporting data related to a product or process within an organization in order to facilitate effective management as well as providing information about the quality of those. As a tool to assist decision makers we design an EA Balanced Scorecard (EABSC) based on the well-known performance measurement approach of [18]. It relies on different perspectives where appropriate measures monitor and track the performance of chosen strategic goals.

Naturally, the objectives of our artifacts are to solve the problems and business needs that were identified earlier. These objectives are outlined in Table 5. We see that they are directly addressing the problem statements of the previous section which described our problem analysis.

Table 5. Artifact objectives

Artifact	Objectives
EABVFW	Improve EABV, EA adoption, EA collaboration, EA Governance, BITA, EA practices and EA maturity
EAMP	Improve EABV, EA adoption, EA collaboration, EA Governance, EA practices and EA maturity, find the EABV within the organizational context and represent it according to the value model
EABSC	Improve IT decision making, provide measuring of KPIs for various views
EABVM	Define integrated business value model for EA in an organization consistent way

We now know what our artifacts should accomplish, but we need to be aware of the requirements that are attached to them. We differ between business, architectural, functional and non-functional requirements. These are summarized in Table 6. For more information about requirements, see [19].

Table 6. Artifact requirements

Type	Requirement Statements	Artifacts
Business	Must be feasible.	All
	Must provide business value.	All
	Must support decision making.	All
Architectural	Must fit in with the current EA function, tools and frameworks.	All
	Must be flexible to cope with architectural changes.	EABVFW, EAMP
Functional	Capture EABV in predefined output.	EAMP
	Provide deliverables at various stages.	EAMP
	Deliverables must be usable for strategic planning process.	EAMP
	Must be executable as a process.	EAMP
	Must be executable on-demand.	EAMP
Non-functional	Deliverables must be reliable and accurate.	EAMP
	Execution must be ease-of-use.	EAMP
	Must be secure and compliant.	EABVFW, EAMP
	Must be scalable.	EAMP

Summarizing the Design phase (cf. Fig. 2) we perceive that it is split into defining objectives, defining requirements and actual design steps. The latter leaves much freedom of choice on how to actually design the artifact. The first to steps produce an artifact specification as clear basis for the design, together with the solution proposal from the analysis phase. The last document generated in the design artifact step is the comprehensive artifact description or manual respectively. The actual design phase leaves much freedom on how to build and implement the artifacts. Hereby, the researchers are able to exploit the knowledge base or even create new methodologies which themselves can be artifacts again.

Evaluation
In the Evaluation phase (cf. Fig. 2), the time has come to evaluate the artifacts. Therefore, we need to undertake a small-scale demonstration of the artifact whether it is applicable for that kind of problem and we obtain some preliminary results. The more comprehensive large-scale test and evaluation over a certain period of time to validate the artifact comes next and generates an evaluation report. The evaluation of the artifacts will take place in an organizational context. From Evaluation, it might be necessary to go back to the Analysis in case the report shows some flaws in the initial solution approach and the following design.

Diffusion
Diffusion marks the step of emitting the outcomes of the research process to different kinds of audiences through various channels by means of various media, usually in form of a publication (cf. Fig. 2). Actually, diffusion is considered the last step of this process, although diffusing results can be done at even earlier stages of a DSR project. The usual types of audiences are either management-oriented or technology-oriented which consequently calls for a different form of representation, i.e. the focus of the DSR contribution must be adapted to the intended audiences [1].

4   Research Analysis

We already described the basic layout of the research process (cf. Fig. 2) which generally is assumed to be iterative. In the initial process, there was only one way to go back in case we need to rework on our solution. This option is possible from the evaluation back to the analysis phase. In practice, we realized that this proved not flexible enough for our needs as our research process is strongly coupled with our project plan and management. Furthermore, the diffusion takes place throughout the research effort and not only in the end, be it internal distribution of milestone documents or external publications in academia.

As a result after our process analysis, we propose this process is more of an artifact build cycle where it is possible and often even necessary to step back from one phase to another in order to accommodate for requirements or changes which were not considered yet. For example, if we realize during design that we have not analyzed the problem properly, we must step back to the analysis phase to amend accordingly before we can continue. The same is true during the evaluation, where we need, depending on how grave our misjudgment of the initial solution was, step back either to the design phase or restart the cycle with an ameliorated analysis. The resulting artifact build process cycle is depicted in Fig. 3 and provides an updated perspective on our research process. It also clarifies the role of the diffusion phase which is actually done throughout a research project.

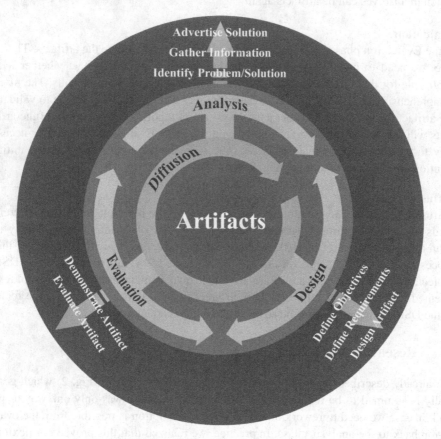

Fig. 3. DSR Artifact Build Cycle Process

As we further analyzed our research, we deem it very useful to provide the actual state of the artifacts during the whole research process. This helps to formulate milestones during project planning and execution. Being able to anticipate and capture the evolutionary state of the artifacts alleviates any collaboration efforts since a common understanding on what has to be how and when is crucial in team research. These states are outlined in Table 7.

Table 7. Artifact state during research process

Phase	Artifact State
Analysis	
Identify Problem/Business Need	First ideas and concepts how to solve encountered problems or business needs.
Gather Information	Further develop initial ideas and concepts.
Advertise Solution	Present initial solution proposal where the intention on how to solve the given issues is elaborated in order to get the support for the development.
Design	
Define Objectives	Based upon the solution proposal, the objectives of the artifact are clearly specified.
Define Requirements	An important step is to specify the requirements for the artifact, which can be business, architectural, functional and non-functional requirements.
Design Artifact	The actual design and development of the artifact is a big sub-process itself and can be achieved in numerous of ways depending on the nature of the artifact. Here, the artifact takes the desired representation in its projected end state.
Evaluation	
Demonstrate Artifact	Demonstrating the viability of the artifact in a certain form helps to justify the research effort and that the solution delivers the intended results. This is the initial test of the finished artifact in its native environment.
Evaluate Artifact	Evaluation is the rigorous assessment of the artifact and builds upon the findings from the demonstration. It shall be shown that the artifact provides the sought-after utility for the target stakeholders. Results from the evaluation can trigger another analysis or redesign of the problem or the artifact respectively.
Diffusion	
Communicate Solution	The now finally finished artifact is ready to be diffused through various inter- and intra-organizational channels although premature diffusion is possible.

5   Conclusions and Future Research

In our paper, we presented a practical DSR application in the domain of EABV assessment and therefore went through an adapted research methodology. The identified problems are solved by four artifacts: the main artifact is the EABV Framework which incorporates an EABV Model and comprises of an EA Measurement Process and an EA Balanced Scorecard. All of these artifacts are designed und evaluated with an industry partner who also provides the business environment as well as parts of the knowledge base in terms of our chosen research framework. Since the relevant business needs and the projected solutions are very complex and comprehensive in nature, we limited ourselves to a high level inspection of our artifacts to introduce the overall concept and hence, we cannot deep dive into the design of every artifact as this would be out of scope for this paper.

As we have experienced in our practical application of the DSR approach, there is a lack of flexibility in rather iterative and sequential research processes which are still predominant in DSR. We therefore adapted a research process and employed an artifact build cycle which provides the necessary flexibility and also keeps track of the evolutionary state of artifacts. In doing so, we greatly benefit in our combined research effort in terms of the surrounding project management. Our process cycle alleviates common understanding for all participants and additionally sheds light on the actual creation of the artifacts. Thereby, we contributed to the research rigor by enriching the state of artifacts in the course of various process phases. Based upon our achievements so far, we further step along the projected process path to evaluate our artifacts in an organizational environment. As a somewhat concurrent process phase, we continue to diffuse our findings in order to encourage the discussion of our solution as well as our methodology to achieve it.

Acknowledgements. This project is partly funded by the Irish Research Council for Science, Engineering and Technology (IRCSET).

References

1. Hevner, A., March, S., Park, J.: Design Science in Information Systems Research. MIS Quaterly 28(1), 75–105 (2004)
2. March, S., Smith, G.: Design and natural science research on information technology. Decision Support Systems 15(4), 251–266 (1995)
3. Curley, M.: An IT Value Based Capability Maturity Framework. MIT Sloan CISR VI(2D) (2006)
4. Österle, H., Becker, J., Frank, U., Hess, T., Karagiannis, D., Krcmar, H., Loos, P., Mertens, P., Oberweis, A., Sinz, E.: Memorandum on Design-oriented Information Systems Research. European Journal of Information Systems 20, 7–10 (2011)
5. Peffers, K., Tuunanen, T., Rothenberger, M., Chatterjee, S.: A Design Science Research Methodology for Information Systems Research. Journal of Management Information Systems 24(3), 45–77 (2008)
6. Hevner, A., Chatterjee, S.: Design Research in Information Systems - Theory and Practice. Springer (2010)
7. Schekkerman, J.: How to Survive in the Jungle of Enterprise Architecture Frameworks: Creating or Choosing an Enterprise Architecture Framework, 3rd edn. Trafford (2006)
8. Kaisler, S., Armour, F., Valivullah, M.: Enterprise Architecting: Critical Problems. In: Proceedings of the 38th International Conference on System Sciences, Hawaii (2005)

9. Ross, J., Weill, P., Robertson, D.: Enterprise Architecture as Strategy. Havard Business Press (2006)
10. Curley, M.: Managing Information Technology for Business Value. Intel Press (2007)
11. Gammelgard, M., Simonsson, M., Lindström, A.: An IT management Assessment Framework: Evaluating Enterprise Architecture Scenarios. Information Systems and E-Business Management 5(4), 415–435 (2007)
12. Schmidt, C., Buxmann, P.: Outcomes and Success Factors of Enterprise IT Architecture management: Empirical Insight from the International Financial Services Industry. European Journal of Information Systems (20), 168–185 (2011)
13. Iacob, M.-E., Jonkers, H.: Quantitative Analysis of Enterprise Architectures. In: Konstantas, D., Bourrières, J.-P., Léonard, M., Boudjlida, N. (eds.) Interoperability of Enterprise Software and Applications, pp. 239–252. Springer (2006)
14. Schelp, J., Stutz, M.: A Balanced Scorecard Approach to Measure the Value of Enterprise Architecture. Journal of Enterprise Architecture 3(4) (2007)
15. van Steenbergen, M., Mushkudiani, N., Brinkkemper, S., Foorthuis, R., Bruls, W., Bos, R.: Achieving Enterprise Architecture Benefits: What Makes the Difference? In: 15th International Enterprise Distributed Object Computing Conference Workshops, pp. 350–359 (2011)
16. Donnellan, B., Helfert, M.: The IT-CMF: A Practical Application of Design Science. In: Winter, R., Zhao, J.L., Aier, S. (eds.) DESRIST 2010. LNCS, vol. 6105, pp. 550–553. Springer, Heidelberg (2010)
17. ISO/IEC: 15939:2007 - Systems and Software Engineering - Measurement Process
18. Kaplan, R., Norton, D.: The Balanced Scorecard - Translating Strategy into Action. Harvard Business School Press (1996)
19. Robertson, S., Robertson, J.: Mastering the Requirements Process. Addison Wesley Professional (2006)

Designing-in-the-Large: Combining Local Perspectives to Generate Enterprise-Wide Integration Solutions

Sandeep Purao[1], Narasimha Bolloju[2], and Chuan Hoo Tan[2]

[1] College of IST, Penn State University, University Park, PA, USA
spurao@ist.psu.edu
[2] Department of Information Systems, City University of Hong Kong, Hong Kong
{narsi.bolloju,ch.tan}@cityu.edu.hk

Abstract. Local perspectives are important in designing effective enterprise integration solutions because they provide deep understanding of how each system may interact with others. Combining these local perspectives into a global solution is, however, equally important to develop a coherent enterprise integration blueprint. The participants in this exercise tend to be managers who have local but informal knowledge, and designers who may have a global but incomplete view that must be translated into formal models necessary for implementation. We develop a method and supporting modeling constructs aimed at such 'designing-in-the-large' that facilitates this bridging from local perspectives to global solutions, and from informal representations to formal models amenable for implementation. We present the result as design science outcomes – a Method and Modeling Constructs – that have benefited from multiple design-and-test cycles, and describe an authentic demonstration.

Keywords: Designing-in-the-Large, Systems Integration, Design Science Research.

1 Introduction

Designing of enterprise-wide systems-integration solutions is a large and complex task because it involves designing and deploying technology platforms for exchange of information and control across different organizational units separated by specialization and geography (Hobday et al., 2005; Hasselbring, 2000; Markus, 2000). Prior work shows that systems integration contributes to organizational effectiveness (Bhatt, 2000) by countering providing the natural tendency of different units to focus on local optimization at the cost of cross-unit coordination. Designing systems integration solutions is, however, expensive (Bass and Lee, 2002), and faces many challenges including technology platform differences (Lee et al., 2003; Evgeniou, 2002) and availability of local and global information. In particular, systems integration requires coordination across a large number of organizational actors including functional managers and systems integration professionals. We conceptualize the systems integration problem as Designing-in-the-Large taking our inspiration from a related

K. Peffers, M. Rothenberger, and B. Kuechler (Eds.): DESRIST 2012, LNCS 7286, pp. 122–138, 2012.
© Springer-Verlag Berlin Heidelberg 2012

term in software engineering that emphasizes this problem of scale in the context of programming (DeRemer and Kron, 1975).

In contrast, contemporary research on system integration has been limited to largely technical concerns. For example, integration platforms and approaches proposed include multi-agent coordination (Sutherland and Heuvel, 2002; Skiora and Shaw, 1998), service-oriented platforms for integration (Vernadat, 2007; Erl, 2004; Krafzig et al., 2004), and data integration (Foster and Grossman, 2003; Li et al., 2001). Although useful, these approaches focus on employing specific technologies and emphasize solution delivery instead of front-end activities such as designing integration solutions. They assume a-priori knowledge of the systems to be integrated and integration requirements from the perspective of these systems.

The conceptualization we propose, Designing-in-the-Large, highlights the need for early stage design of systems integration blueprints focusing on concerns such as understanding and capturing of integration needs and designing a cohesive solution that reflects their synthesis. Prior work that may be repurposed to resemble our conceptualization may include work and information flows (e.g., Casati and Discenza, 2001), and existing modeling techniques such as BPMN and UML to capture the requirements (e.g., Jonker et al., 2004). However, these existing approaches suffer from incomplete articulation, lack of clear conceptual foundations, and close association with vendor-specific implementation tools. We hope to overcome these shortfalls while addressing the fundamental problem of supporting Designing-in-the-Large in the context of developing systems integration solutions.

Our research is aimed at developing and demonstrating an approach - a method and associated modeling constructs - for such Designing-in-the-Large. The approach combines knowledge contained in multiple local perspectives contributed by functional managers to generate a global solution as a systems integration blueprint. Specifically, it allows (a) modeling local perspectives from multiple business managers, (b) merging these perspectives to create a global solution blueprint, and in the process, (c) bridging informal and formal representations. The systems integration domain is appropriate for developing our approach because it often presents situations that are described as 'hairball,' i.e., they include a very large number of systems with point-to-point integrations (Schmidt, 2009). The approach we develop aims at a purposeful re-orienting of this 'hairball' starting from local perspectives shared by owners of different systems followed by an approach to integrate these perspectives towards a solution blueprint.

Contextualizing in the setting of generating enterprise-wide systems integration blueprint, our proposed approach, comprising of a modeling method and associated constructs, builds on prior work such as integration patterns (Hohpe and Woolfe, 2003) and the black-box technique (Hevner and Mills, 1995). We follow the design science research method (Hevner et al., 2004) with multiple design-evaluate cycles. The key contribution of this research is a design science artifact that codifies a prescriptive theory (Gregor, 2006), including a method and modeling constructs (March and Smith, 1995) for Designing-in-the-Large in the context of systems integration.

2   Challenges for Designing-in-the-Large of Systems Integration Solutions

A canonical description of the design process is hard to pinpoint. The Simonian approach (Simon, 1996) emphasizes problem and design spaces along with search mechanisms. Studies of design processes emphasize strategies such as induction and abduction (Zeng and Cheng, 1991) as well as techniques externalization of representations (Oxman, 1997). Other perspectives include reuse-based approaches (Purao et el., 2003) and accounting for extraneous but important factors values (Friedman, 2008). Our emphasis is on an aspect that has been recognized elsewhere but for programming and implementation: the problem of scale (DeRemer and Kron, 1975). We argue that *Designing-in-the-Large* is qualitatively different from designing-in-the-small just like Programming-in-the-Large is qualitatively different from programming-in-the-small. DeRemer and Kron (1975) first argued for this distinction, suggesting the need to identify and respond to problems such as decomposition, modular approaches and coordination across members of a programming team.

Designing-in-the-Large is difficult for similar reasons. In the context of building systems integration solutions, the difficulty can be pinpointed to: (a) problems related to acquiring appropriate inputs from functional business managers who possess accurate but incomplete knowledge about the roles fulfilled by the IT platforms and human capabilities within their control, and (b) problems related to action from systems integration professionals to convert this knowledge into actionable designs such as systems integration blueprints. The first challenge is related to identification and communication of integration needs by functional business managers who possess partial knowledge of requirements from their local perspective to systems integration professionals who often seek to work with concise, often graphical representation of integration needs from a global perspective. The second challenge deals with the need to move across different sets of expectations (one from the functional business managers, the other from systems integration professionals) and in doing so, bridging the informal-formal gap between the articulations from functional business managers and the systems integration professionals (Fraser et al. 1991). A third, related, challenge deals with granularity. Interactions across systems, which may be pointed to as a key abstraction when dealing with systems integration efforts cannot scale easily because of the large number of systems and interactions (Brownsword et al. 2006).

Together, this set of challenges describes a class of problems related to supporting the process for Designing-in-the-Large. The next section describes the design science research method we used to address these challenges.

3   Application of Design Science Research Method

This research followed a design science research method (Hevner et al, 2004). Our investigation started with identifying our domain of interest as the class of problems that require: Designing-in-the-Large, and the unique context in which we would address this class of problems: building systems integration solutions. The challenges outlined in the previous section provided the set of driving concerns for our investigation. Following Vaishnavi and Kuechler (2007), our intent was to learn via building. The intended research outcomes (March and Smith, 1995) for our investigation consisted of a Method (for Designing-in-the-Large) and a set of Modeling Constructs in support of this method. To develop these outcomes, we followed an iterative, design-and-evaluate approach (Hevner et al., 2004).

Our work to develop the Method drew on several precursors such as: bottom-up methods to facilitate database view integration (Batini et al., 1986), leveraging local vs. global knowledge (Smith, 2001), bridging formal and informal specifications (Fraser et al., 1991) and approaches for eliciting functional requirements (Hull, et al., 2010). Extending these, we conceptualize the Method as one that takes into account the fragmented nature of domain knowledge by facilitating capturing the perspective of each system before merging these iteratively to arrive at an enterprise-wide systems-integration blueprint.

Our work to develop the Modeling Constructs drew on several precursors such as: considering systems interactions as first-class citizens (van der Aalst et al. 2000), box-structured modeling principles (Hevner and Mills, 1995), coordination theory (Malone and Crowston, 1994), enterprise integration patterns (Hophe and Woolf, 2003), and task dependencies in process models as surrogates for interactions among software systems (Umapathy et al., 2010). Drawing on and extending this prior work, we develop the Modeling Constructs which have the further properties of faithfully representing the domain of interest (Chan et al,. 1993), avoiding structural and implementation details (Teo et al., 2006; Topi and Ramesh, 2002), and allowing communication with non-IT professionals (Brodie, 1984).

We carried out multiple design-evaluate cycles to generate and refine the research outcomes: (a) a method to support Designing-in-the-Large by allowing modeling of local perspectives followed by mechanisms for merging the local models into a global integration blueprint, and (b) a set of modeling constructs that build on the key abstraction of systems interactions, treating them as first-class citizens. The design-evaluate cycles ensured refinement of research artifacts (see Figure 1). The initial design-evaluate cycles tested and refined adequacy of the proposed method and modeling constructs. Later design-evaluate cycle added authenticity to the constructs and method.

The evaluation cycles were started in Spring 2008 and continue still. The initial cycles consisted of application in classroom settings with groups of graduate students who employed the method and the constructs in their semester-long projects. This first round of feedback lasted three semesters and consisted of feedback related to several elements including clearer specification of the method and more concise definition of the modeling constructs, and the results were reported in Bolloju (2009). The second round consisted of feedback from three experts, senior IT professionals (a CIO, a Consultant and an Enterprise Architect not connected with this research) with extensive experiences in several large-scale systems integration projects. We relied on their experience in prior integration projects to provide feedback on our approach. Comments from these experts highlighted the strengths of our approach, and suggested enhancements such as greater documentation of local and global views to help in communication between different groups of professionals. The final round, currently ongoing, consists of controlled experiments. Improvements from the first two cycles and partially from the third are incorporated into the Method and Modeling Constructs outlined in the following section.

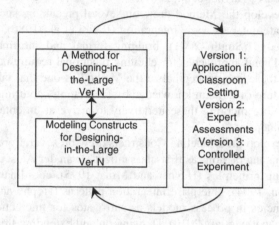

Fig. 1. Design-Evaluation Cycles

4   A Method and Modeling Constructs to Support Designing-in-the-Large

4.1   Method: Eliciting Local Perspectives and Merging

The method we have developed first helps to elicit local perspectives as interactions among systems. Each such perspective is represented by an individual model fragment captures the services consumed, events subscribed, and coordination mechanisms required from the perspective of a single system. Figure 2 outlines the method with an example.

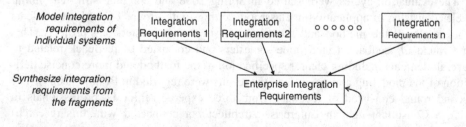

Fig. 2. Outline of the Method to Elicit Local Perspectives and Merge

An example model fragment for the Order Processing System is shown next, in Figure 3. Each such fragment may also show services provided and events published for other systems. In model fragments, the information is necessarily incomplete, for example, as may be seen in Table 1 describes information be captured from the model fragment shown in Figure 2.

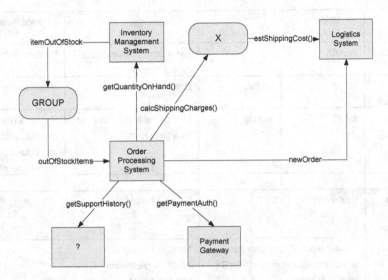

Fig. 3. Example of a Model Fragment for Order Processing System (see also Table 1)

The process of creating an individual model fragment – that is, interactions from the perspective of a given system, say, S_i, starts with eliciting and depicting interactions of the system with other systems considering the goals and objectives of processes and activities supported by S_i. An initial version of the model fragment for S_i is developed by identifying services consumed and events subscribed to by S_i. The destination nodes for such interactions may be known, unknown or not yet identified. As additional information becomes available, the model fragment may be enhanced. Model fragments may be synthesized by simply combining integration requirements captured in multiple model fragments (see Figure 4). A synthesized model fragment may contain a combination of direct links, and links through one or more coordination groups. Synthesized model fragments are created and refined by analyzing requirements such as services consumed and events subscribed, and the characteristics of services provided and events published (as shown in Table 1).

Table 1. Services, Events and Coordination Mechanisms (see also Figure 3)

Events Subscribed	Attributes		Description	Requirements
outOfStock-Items	{itemID}		List of item identifiers indicating out of stock	Medium priority
Services Consumed	Inputs	Outputs	Description	Requirements
getQuanti-tyOnHand()	itemID	quantity	Returns the quantity on hand for a given itemID	Response time should be below 0.5 sec; Volume 100 requests per min
...				
Coordination Mechanisms	Description		Mapping Details	
X	Translates calcShippingCharges() service request instances into estShippingCost() instances		fromCity <-> origin toCity <-> destination package weight <-> weight price <-> cost	
GROUP	Batches itemOutOfStock events for hourly delivery		itemID <-> {itemID}	
Events Published	Attributes		Description	Characteristics
newOrder	customerID, orderDate, orderAmount, shippingAddress, {itemID, quantity, price}		Details of a new order placed by a customer	150 events are published per min
...				
Services Provided	Inputs	Outputs	Description	Characteristics
getOrderS-tats()	fromDateTime, toDateTime	noOfCustomers, noOfOrders, totalOrderValue	Returns the order stats	Response time < 3 sec for 95% of requests
...				

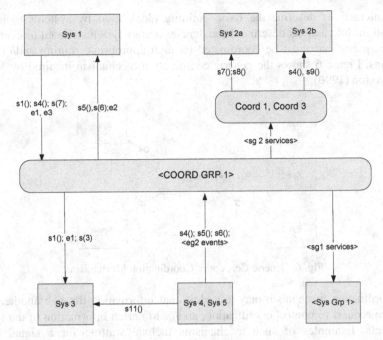

Fig. 4. A Synthesized Model Fragment

We describe the modeling constructs next.

4.2   Modeling Constructs to Represent Core Concepts and Model Fragments

We propose three basic constructs for modeling integration requirements: two types of nodes for representing systems (rectangles) and coordination mechanisms (rectangles with rounded corners), and directed links representing one of more interactions between a pair of nodes. Figure 5, for example, shows two interactions representing a service request and an event among three systems using the basic constructs.

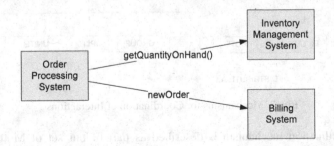

Fig. 5. Two types of interactions among systems

The interactions describe the basic building block used by systems to achieve coordination. Interactions describe dependencies across systems related to events and service requests that must be coordinated through appropriate routing and/or trans- formations. Figure 6 shows the generic coordination mechanism inspired by Malone and Crowston (1990).

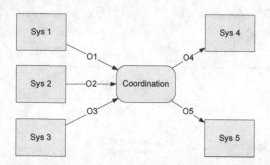

Fig. 6. Generic Concept of Coordination Mechanism

A coordination mechanism may use additional information through another event or service request to control coordination, and/or to enrich information in the incom- ing objects. Examples of such mechanisms include waiting for a signal before forwarding an object, using the results of a service request to identify one or more destination nodes, appending additional values to an incoming object, and discarding an incoming object without forwarding.   We propose nine types of coordination me- chanisms as presented in Figure 7. These go beyond the general concept from Malone and Crowston (1994) and reflect the systems integration context along with input from the formative evaluation cycles.

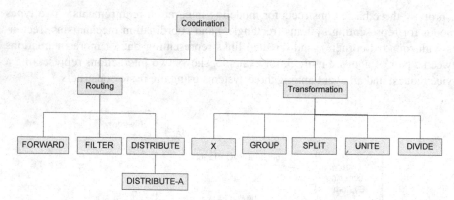

Fig. 7. Mechanisms for Coordination of Interactions

Each coordination mechanism is described as part of our set of Modeling Con- structs. The purpose of this definition is to ensure that the semantics are clear and construct overlap is avoided. For example, the coordination mechanisms FORWARD, DISTRIBUTE and SPLIT are defined as the following:

FORWARD sends each instance of each type of incoming object, from one or more source nodes, to one or more destination nodes as indicated on the link labels. Different types of objects may be forwarded to different destinations, a form of static routing.

DISTRIBUTE routes the incoming interactions dynamically based on values of an incoming object instance. DISTRIBUTE-A, a special case of DISTRIBUTE which is applicable only to synchronous service invocations, aggregates responses returned from destination nodes in preparing results to the source system. This coordination mechanism covers aggregate functions such as sum, min, max, average and count.

SPLIT separates incoming grouped objects into individual objects before forwarding to the destination nodes. The separated objects are forwarded either in the order they were presented or in the order of one or more attribute or parameter types.

Each coordination mechanism is defined in this manner and a graphical symbol is attached to this definition to allow communication with multiple stakeholders. Figure 8 shows an example of the DISRIBUTE-A coordination mechanism. It shows that an Order Processing System interacts with multiple Inventory Management Systems–aggregating the responses received to obtain the total quantity available on hand.

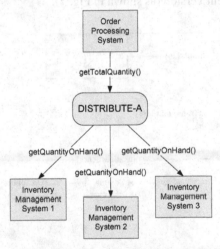

Fig. 8. Example of Coordination Mechanism DISTRIBUTE-A

Together, the Method and the set of Modeling Constructs support Designing-in-the-Large for deriving systems integration blueprints. Both were subjected to multiple rounds of design-evaluate cycles (Hevner et al., 2004). We demonstrate application of the approach next with an example drawn from an authentic setting.

5   Demonstration

The example we use for demonstration of our approach comes from the project report for a logistics company systems integration submitted by a graduate student team. To respect the space constraints for this manuscript, we limit the demonstration to a summary of the problem situation, and a brief example of the outcomes obtained.

Problem Situation: Asia Parcel Service (APS) is a global package delivery company that offers a range of supply chain solutions such as freight forwarding, customs brokerage, fulfillment, returns handling and repairs. APS provides guaranteed time-definite and day-definite deliveries based on shipment origin and destination. They have about 60 internal systems, many connected to one or more external systems. Their internal systems portfolio includes shipping, tracking, warehouse management, order processing, and dispatch systems. The external systems to which they are linked include payment gateway and labor support systems. Major drivers for their systems integration effort, apart from increasing their competitive advantage, include enhancing process efficiency by improving information flow across different systems. Some challenges they had to face include a heterogeneous mix of systems including some legacy systems, data exchange and integration problems, and difficulties in accessing information from multiple systems.

The graduate student team created several model fragments by gathering information from each functional manager. Figures 9 and 10 show examples of two model fragments (scanned from student projects) with coordination constructs updated to match those in the current version (as shown in Fig. 7).

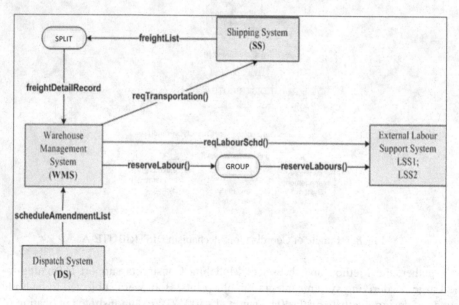

Fig. 9. WMS Model Fragment for Asia Parcel Service

The model fragments represent integration concerns from the perspective of the shipping system, the tracking system and the warehouse management system respectively. Figure 10 shows one of these, for the shipping system in greater detail.

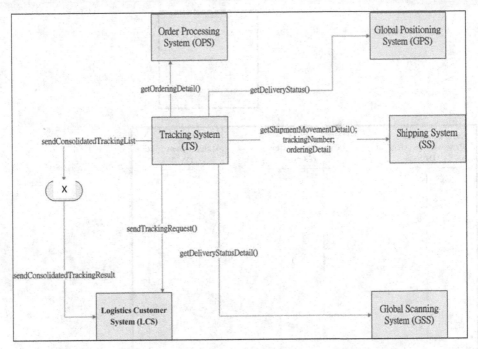

Fig. 10. TS Model Fragment for Asia Parcel Service

The synthesized model is shown in Figure 11. It contains 16 systems, multiple coordination mechanisms across the collection of systems and services. The graduate student team was able to construct the model fragments over a period of three months. The project was one among scores that used the modeling constructs and the method for moving from local perspectives to a global blueprint for integration.

6   Discussion and Concluding Remarks

We have argued the Designing-in-the-Large is an activity that is qualitatively different from smaller design efforts. Our cue comes from the classic work related to Programming-in-the-Large (DeRemer and Kron, 1975). In particular, this work has addressed problems related to eliciting local perspectives and merging them to create global blueprints – using systems integration as the context. To address this class of problems, the solution we have proposed is inspired primarily by Malone and Crowston's (1994) work on coordination but also extends my much prior work such as box-structured models, coordination theory and conceptual modeling, and related practitioner knowledge such as requirements modeling and integration patterns. Extending these prior efforts, we have identified and proposed a Method and a concise set of Modeling Constructs each of which can be customized to fit to the needs of specific integration scenarios. The research approach we have followed is canonical design science research with multiple design-evaluate cycles (Hevner et al., 2004), which have allowed us not only refinement but ongoing empirical assessments.

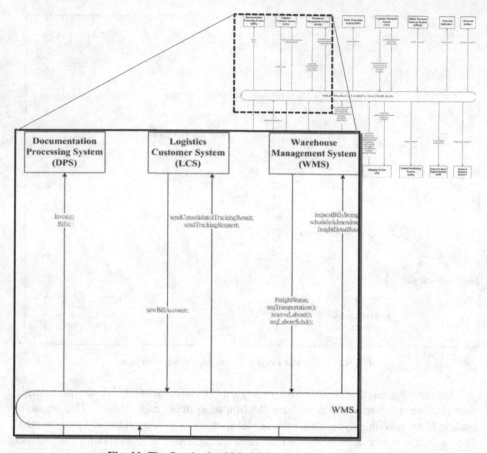

Fig. 11. The Synthesized Model for Asia Parcel Service

Based on the design-evaluation cycles so far, we have, in this paper, described the Method and the Modeling Constructs and shown a demonstration. The work completed so far and feedback from multiple evaluation cycles suggests that the model fragments one can create using the modeling constructs we propose are expressive and the models appear to be semantically close to the domain of systems integration. Each of these initial impressions is, of course, subjected to a more rigorous empirical evaluation. The set of constructs, evolved through three design-evaluate cycles, combines theoretical as well as practitioner knowledge. To further enhance the description of the constructs, semantic specification of them, which could further aid the understanding, would be feasible. Furthermore, based on the students' usage of the proposed approach in several integration scenarios, we find that the constructs offer ontological clarity as well as ontological completeness with minimal construct overload or redundancy. Here as well, these represent initial impressions and may be subjected to more rigorous evaluation.

The Method we have proposed realizes a bottom-up up approach to creating individual model fragments that are then merged. The formative evaluation cycles suggest that such an approach is likely to be more suitable for obtaining local perspectives from functional business managers who may be distributed across geographical locations and may have only limited, local knowledge. This presumed benefit of the bottom-up approach may also be tested empirically. During the formative evaluation cycles, the IT experts we interviewed commented that beginning with local integration requirements is more appropriate and practical, suggesting that the premise was found valid from a pragmatic perspective. Merging or synthesizing model fragments was, however, considered to be a demanding and potentially time-consuming task. Although relatively straightforward, it was emphasized that it would be possible to automate major parts of this process if implemented in a modeling tool. This remains on our agenda for future work, which would also facilitate empirical evaluation.

The next steps we have outlined above may be considered to be current limitations of this ongoing research effort. Further, we acknowledge that some of the formative evaluation cycles have been conducted among graduate students albeit engaged in authentic project experiences, often with external clients in real-world settings. In fact, these graduate students had an average IT experience of 6 years and held full-time IT positions. One may still, however, argue that there is still a concern about how the approach may be adopted beyond project settings in an educational environment. We acknowledge this limitation. We do argue, however, that the mix of students who used the proposals included both, students from a technology as well as business backgrounds and corresponding working experience, i.e., very similar to the target group of users. The inputs we collected during the formative evaluation cycles also included secondary sources they generated while completing their project work and therefore, were not affected by bias that may surface during conversations.

Our formative evaluations of the approach have been performed without support from existing CASE tools. With more commercial applications developed to aid system analysis, design and implementation, more significant empirical evaluations may be conducted. In addition, efforts may also be expended to develop mechanisms for resolution of differences across individual model fragments as part of merging process and building CASE tools to support our approach by providing assistance for activities such as mapping textual requirements to model fragments, tracing integration requirements, and mapping synthesized integration models to architectural solutions and suitable products for implementation.

In term of theoretical contribution, this research is one of the first to address the problem of Designing-in-the-Large in the context of generating enterprise-wide systems integration blueprints. The proposed approach with the Method and the Modeling Constructs (March and Smith, 1995) represent outcomes of multiple design-evaluate cycles (Hevner et al., 2004) and therefore, exemplify beginnings of a prescriptive theory (Gregor, 2006) in the form of a design science artifact. The work builds upon and extends several theoretical precursors, the dominant one being Malone and Crowston's (1994) coordination theory. With the outline of the Method and Modeling Constructs we have proposed, we have started to build the contours of such a prescriptive theory. Considering the systems integration context as an instance of the larger class of problems characterized by the need to work with local contexts before moving to global blueprints, our work represents a first step in developing approaches for the class of problems described as 'Designing-in-the-Large.'

The study clearly offers several suggestions to practice because it has been motivated by problems observed in practice. First, the approach provides a mechanism for assisting business and IT professionals involved in systems integration projects to collaboratively surface, represent and merge integration requirements from the perspectives of various internal and external systems. Considering the current trend of budgetary investments in systems integration related projects, the results of employing our approach, which emphasizes on graphical representation of requirements supported by textual descriptions, could provide valuable inputs to subsequent architectural design(s) and implementation of integration solutions. Further, business and IT professionals responsible for enterprise systems integration projects often have to deal with phases such as understanding integration requirements, architecting integration infrastructures, and selection and implementing suitable solutions considering enterprise wide needs and long term impacts. Our bottom-up approach can be applied to surface integration requirements simultaneously by different business and IT professionals from different divisions or departments.

With increasing recognition of understanding and supporting the design of large-scale systems, and the expressed need for fundamental research into the design of large-scale complex systems (Deshmukh and Collopy, 2010), cogent approaches to designing-in-the-large are becoming essential. Although it is acknowledged that there is no silver bullet when it comes to the design and implementation of large-scale IT systems (Rolland and Monteiro, 2002), a range of problems is being identified in the context of systems-of-systems (Boehm, 2010). The approach we have outlined – with a method that allows moving from local perspectives to a global blueprint and the associated set of modeling constructs – represent an effort to address these urgent and growing concerns. We hope that the approach along with the future research steps we have outlined will spur additional research in this direction.

Acknowledgements. The work by the second author was substantially supported by a grant from the Research Grants Council of the Hong Kong Special Administrative Region, China (Project No. CityU 110308).

References

1. Bhatt, G.D.: An empirical examination of the effects of information systems integration on business process improvement. International Journal of Operations & Production Management 20(11), 1331–1359 (2000)
2. Bass, C., Lee, J.M.: Building a Business Case for EAI. EAI Journal, 18–20 (2002)
3. Batini, C., Lenzerini, M., Navathe, S.B.: A Comparative Analysis of Methodologies for Database Schema Integration. ACM Computing Surveys 18(4) (1986)
4. Boehm, B.: Evaluating the Software Design of a Complex System of Systems. Carnegie-Mellon University, Pittsburgh (2010)
5. Bolloju, N.: Conceptual Modeling of Systems Integration Requirements. IEEE Software 26(5), 66–74 (2009)

6. Brownsword, L., Fisher, D., Morris, E., Smith, J., Kirwan, P.: System-of-Systems Navigator: An Approach for Managing System-of-Systems Interoperability. Technical Note CMU/SEI-2006-TN-019 (2006)

7. Casati, F., Discenza, A.: Modeling and Managing Interactions Among Business Processes. Journal of Systems Integration 10, 145–168 (2001)

8. DeRemer, F., Kron, H.H.: Programming-in-the-large Versus Programming-in-the-small. IEEE Transactions on Software Engineering (2), 80–86 (1976)

9. Deshmukh, A., Collopy, P.: Fundamental Research into the Design of Large-Scale Complex Systems. In: 13th AIAA/ISSMO Multidisciplinary Analysis and Optimization Conference, Fort Worth, TX, AIAA, AIAA-2010-9320 (2010)

10. Erl, T.: Service-Oriented Architecture: A Field Guide to Integrating XML and Web Services. Prentice Hall PTR, Upper Saddle River (2004)

11. Evgeniou, T.: Information Integration and Information Strategies for Adaptive Enterprise. European Management Journal 20(5), 486–494 (2002)

12. Foster, I., Grossman, R.L.: Data Integration in a Bandwidth-rich World. Communications of the ACM 46(11), 50–57 (2003)

13. Friedman, B.: Value Sensitive Design. In: Schular, D. (ed.) Liberating Voices: A Pattern Language for Communication Revolution, pp. 366–368. The MIT Press, Cambridge (2008)

14. Gregor, S.: The Nature of Theory in Information Systems. MIS Quarterly 30(3), 611–642 (2006)

15. Hasselbring, W.: Information System Integration. Communications of the ACM 43(6), 33–38 (2000)

16. Hevner, A.R., Mills, H.D.: Box-Structured Requirements Determination Methods. Decision Support Systems 13, 223–239 (1995)

17. Hevner, A., March, S., Park, J., Ram, S.: Design science research in information systems. MIS Quarterly 28(1), 75–105 (2004)

18. Hobday, M., Davies, A., Prencipe, A.: Systems Integration: A Core Capability of the Modern Corporation. Industrial and Corporate Change 14(6), 1109–1143 (2005)

19. Hohpe, G., Woolf, B.: Enterprise Integration Patterns: Designing, Building and Deploying Messaging Solutions. Addison-Wesley Longman Publishing Co. Inc., Boston (2003)

20. Hull, E., Jackson, K., Dick, J.: Requirements Engineering. Springer-Verlag New York Inc. (2010)

21. Jonkers, H., Lankhorst, M., Buuren, R.V., Hoppenbrouwers, S., Bonsangue, M., Torre, L.V.D.: Concepts for Modeling Enterprise Architectures. International Journal of Cooperative Information Systems 13(3), 257–287 (2004)

22. Krafzig, D., Banke, K., Slama, D.: Enterprise SOA: Service-Oriented Architecture Best Practices. Prentice Halll PTR, Upper Saddle River (2004)

23. Fraser, M.D., Kumar, K., Vaishnavi, V.K.: Informal and Formal Requirements Specification Languages: Bridging the Gap. IEEE Transactions on Software Engineering 17(5), 454–466 (1991)

24. Lee, J., Siau, K., Hong, S.: Enterprise Integration with ERP and EAI. Communications of the ACM 46(2), 54–60 (2003)

25. Li, H., Su, S.Y.W.: Business Object Modeling, Validation, and Mediation for Integrating Heterogeneous Application Systems. Journal of Systems Integration 10, 307–328 (2001)

26. Malone, T.W., Crowston, K.: The Interdisciplinary Study of Coordination. ACM Computing Surveys 26(1), 87–119 (1994)

27. March, S.T., Smith, G.F.: Design and natural science research on information technology. Decision Support Systems 15(4), 251–266 (1995)

28. Markus, M.L.: Paradigm Shifts – e-Business and Business/Systems Integration. Communications of the Association for Information Systems 4(10), 1–44 (2001)
29. Markus, M.L.: Toward a Theory of Knowledge Reuse: Types of Knowledge Reuse Situations and Factors in Reuse Success. Journal of Management Information Systems 18(1), 57–93 (2001)
30. Oxman, R.: Design by Re-representation: a Model of Visual Reasoning in Design. Design Studies 18(4), 329–347 (1997)
31. Purao, S., Han, T., Storey, V.: Improving Reuse-based Design: Augmenting Analysis Patterns Reuse with Learning. Information Systems Research 14(3), 269–290 (2003)
32. Rolland, K.H., Monteiro, E.: Balancing the Local and the Global in Infrastructural Information Systems. The Information Society 18(2), 87–100 (2002)
33. Scriven, M.: Types of evaluation and types of evaluator. American Journal of Evaluation 17(2), 151 (1996)
34. Sikora, R., Shaw, M.J.: A Multi-agent Framework for the Coordination and Integration of Information Systems. Management Science 44(11), S65–S78 (1998)
35. Simon, H.A.: The Sciences of the Artificial. MIT Press (1996)
36. Schmidt, J.: Lean Integration. Integration Consortium (2009),
http://www.cloudyintegration.com/uploads/
LEAN_INTEGRATION_AFE_-_John_Schmidt.pdf
37. Smith, E.A.: The Role of Tacit and Explicit Knowledge in the Workplace. Journal of Knowledge Management 5(4), 311–321 (2001)
38. Sutherland, J., Heuvel, W.J.V.D.: Enterprise Application Integration and Complex Adaptive Systems. Communications of the ACM 45(10), 59–64 (2002)
39. Vaishnavi, V.K., Kuechler, W.: Design Science Research Methods and Patterns: Innovating Information and Communication Technology. Auerbach Pub. (2007)
40. van der Aalst, W., et al.: Workflow Modeling using Proclets. In: Scheuermann, P., Etzion, O. (eds.) CoopIS 2000. LNCS, vol. 1901, pp. 198–209. Springer, Heidelberg (2000)
41. Vernadat, F.B.: Interoperable Enterprise Systems: Principles, Concepts, and Methods. Annual Reviews in Control (31), 137–145 (2007)
42. Zeng, Y., Cheng, G.D.: On the Logic of Design. Design Studies 12(3), 137–141 (1991)

Emergency Response System Design: An Examination of Emergency Communication Messages

Rohit Valecha, Raj Sharman, Raghav Rao, and Shambhu Upadhyaya

State University of New York at Buffalo, NY
{valecha,sharman,mgmtrao,shambhu}@buffalo.edu

Abstract. The current state of emergency communication is dispatch-mediated i.e. the messages from the scene are directed to responders and agencies through the dispatch. Emergency dispatch provides essential support to emergency responders during emergencies. However, there are several problems associated with the dispatch-mediated communication. Utilizing IBM's message modeling concept, we develop a messaging model to provide support for computer-mediated communication (CMC) systems.

Keywords: Computer-mediated Communication, Messaging Model, Design Science, Emergency Response.

1 Introduction

Emergency communication is the most important aspect of an emergency response [8]. The current state of emergency communication is dispatch-mediated i.e. the messages from the scene are directed to responders and agencies through the dispatch, with radio being an inseparable component. Emergency dispatch provides essential support to emergency responders during emergencies. However, there are several problems associated with the dispatch-mediated way of communication: First, since the dispatch agency employs radios for exchanging messages, there are problems relating to message reproducibility and information quality [1]. Second, since the dispatch agency handles multiple messages from a single incident on a single channel, there are problems relating to longer process time. Third, since the dispatch agency attends to messages through a single channel, there are problems relating to call prioritization.

[4], [6] provide solutions to address issues with dispatch-mediated communication in the form of computer-mediated communication (CMC) systems that utilize computer(s) for communicative transactions. [9] provides a number of objectives of CMC systems that point to improvement in communication including, but not limited to, collective intelligence, information reliability (security, privacy) and parallel communication. [9] states that the core of CMC system is the message. There have been numerous studies that focus on message characteristics (such as message cost, message size) and message transmission (such as message delay, message quality).

K. Peffers, M. Rothenberger, and B. Kuechler (Eds.): DESRIST 2012, LNCS 7286, pp. 139–146, 2012.
© Springer-Verlag Berlin Heidelberg 2012

However, there is no study that explores the current dispatch messages to develop a messaging model.

Utilizing IBM's message modeling concept, in this paper, we examine the issues associated with the current mechanisms of communication in terms of a messaging model that provides support for CMC systems as follows: First, we develop a message classification based on a detailed exploration of emergency messages. Second, we determine message frequencies and its temporal patterns for various incident types. Third, we develop a standardized messaging format. This message format improves information standardization by structuring the message.

The paper is developed based on the analysis of over 10000 messages from over 1000 incidents and inputs from first responders. The paper adheres to the design science research guidelines [3], [7]. The paper is organized as follows. In section 2, we develop the messaging model. In section 3, we provide an exploration of emergency communication messages. In section 4, we provide a case application for the messaging model. In section 5, we develop a prototype system. In section 6, we conclude with limitations and future work for this paper.

2   Development of Messaging Model

The development of messaging model is driven by Communication Theory – that studies the human process of communication. We employ Schramm's Model of Communication to identify the key entities in the process of dispatch-mediated communication including the communicator, the message objectives and the message interpretation.

2.1   Overview of Emergency Incident

The interaction among responders from various agencies is mediated through dispatch. For example, if fire agency requires police assistance for perimeter safety, they request it with dispatch, who further notifies the local area police about the request.

The initial notification of the incident is received by dispatch agency that generates an incident-related document known as the "Incident Report", which is used for various purposes like incident monitoring, resource allocation and post-incident analysis [2]. Upon receipt of this notification, dispatch alerts fire chiefs assigned to the locality of the incident. The fire chiefs respond to the notification with status of their location. Upon arrival at the scene of the incident, the fire chief may request additional vehicles or resources from the dispatch. The communication messages that are exchanged between the dispatch and the responders/agencies are logged as "Messages", which is the main focus of the paper. In this paper, we develop our messaging model based on these messages.

2.2   Development Process

We inspect raw data from 1147 major incidents responded to by North Bailey fire station from the period 2008 to 2010. The 1147 incidents provide a sample of 10411 communication messages. We then contacted first responders (two dispatchers and two fire chiefs) from dispatch and fire department with an average of more than five years of experience in dealing with emergencies. They were provided with various emergency messages. The responses included rules that facilitate the process of message classification based on message objectives.

3   An Exploration of Emergency Communication Messages

For the exploration of the emergency communication messages, we identified all the possible message types during an emergency communication. We also carried out message classification, message frequency analysis and message formatting based on our data set.

3.1   Message Classification

A classification of emergency messages helps in standardizing communication over mobile devices, other than radios, that are used during the emergencies. This classification is also helpful from the interpretation perspective after the incident for future planning and prevention. The emergency messages are classified, based on their objectives, into four message types, namely notification, request, response and update.

Table 1. Emergency Message Types

Type	Message	Scenario	Use
NOT	"MERS NOTIFYING EC HAZMAT"	The ERS issues a notification to Hazmat team	To inform an agency about the incident
REQ	"HARRIS HILL ... – MAA REQ"	The commander requests for additional ambulances	To request for additional resources
RESP	"CD142 TO CLA OPS CTR"	The deputy chief responds to Clarence Operations	To provide status of agency
UPD	"5800 LBS OF FUEL ON BOARD"	The airplane agency updates the dispatch center with fuel level	To update the bits of information

3.2   Message Frequency

The most commonly occurring incidents identified from the incident reports fall into Medical and Vehicle category. The level of response is higher depicting higher levels of resource demand, owing to number of casualties. The illustration of an emergency response communication is summarized in the Figure 1 below. The horizontal axis depicts the timeline with an interval of 15 minutes. The vertical axis depicts the frequency of message use, in percentage of total messages. The different colored graphs indicate the different message types. The incidents have been normalized to an hour for illustrative purposes. Page limitations constraint us from including a more detailed explanation of the figures below.

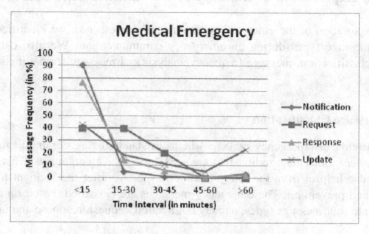

a. Illustration of a Medical Emergency

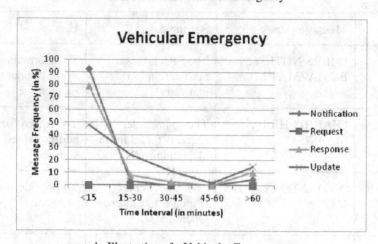

b. Illustration of a Vehicular Emergency

Fig. 1.

In general, the level of notifications is generally higher in the first 15 minutes, and gradually decreases. The level of updates follows a similar pattern except that it tends to increase a little towards the end of the incident. The level of requests is generally lower in case of vehicular and chemical incidents. The level of responses follows a similar pattern compared to updates i.e. higher in the beginning, gradually decreasing and higher towards the end of the incident. More specifically, during a medical emergency, dispatch agencies start off with additional requests, owing to fatalities.

The temporal analysis of the different types of messages by incident type allows for structuring the dispatcher interface by taking into account the need of the dispatcher with the progression of time.

3.3   Message Format

As analyzed from the incident reports, a message typically contains a communicator (the sender and the receiver), a keyword, time stamp, and an informational content such as interacting agency, resource, status of response, etc. These messaging formats are summarized in Table 2 below with the help of terminology:

DT: Date Time	AN: Agency Name	ST: Status
NOT: Notify	*: Any Agency or Responder	IN: Information
REQ: Request	IC: Incident Commander	NT: Notification Type
RESP: Response	MT: Mutual Aid Type	DR: Dispatch Responder
UPD: Update	UT: Update Type	AR: Agency Responder

Table 2. Message Format

Source	Destination	Date Time	Keyword	Attribute1	Attribute2
*	AR	DT	NOT	NT	AN
IC	DR	DT	REQ	AN	MT
AR	DR	DT	RESP	AN	ST
*	DR	DT	UPD	UT	IN

4   Case Application

For the case application, we provide a brief subset of dispatch communications with regards to the plane crash of Continental Flight 3407, from Newark Liberty International Airport in New Jersey to Buffalo Niagara International Airport in New York on

February 12, 2009. The messaging model was applied to this emergency, and some of the design and function issues were identified as a result.

5   Prototype System

The artifact exemplifies the application of our messaging model. It helps to create a better understanding of our messaging model by facilitating comparison with models from other domains. Moreover, it helps in suggesting improvement in the current dispatch system with the implementation of our messaging model.

The design of a ticker-like system for Emergency Dispatch System consists of following subsections: incident process checklist, performance logger and process feed summary. The incident process checklist provides user with a skeleton of critical messages, derived from message characteristics and frequency, for that incident. These critical messages and their status are displayed along a time line for the average length of the incident. The incident logger keeps a log of emergency messages, derived from the expert classification, during the incident. The summary of the logged messages are saved in the feed summary section of the logger, which is standardized with the help of message format. A snapshot of the ticker-like system is provided in the Figure 2 below.

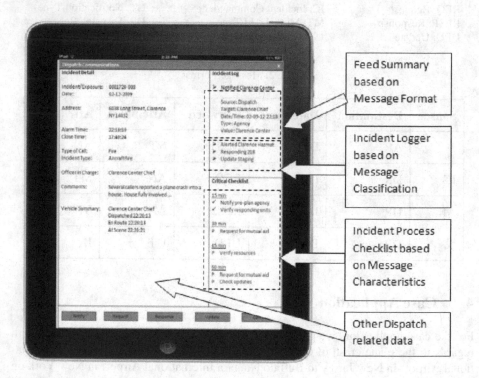

Fig. 2. Snapshot of a Ticker-like Prototype System

6   Conclusion

This paper contributes to research in the dispatch mediated emergency communication. Emergency dispatch provides essential support to emergency responders during emergencies. Radio is used as primary means of communication during dispatch mediated communication [10]. However, there are several problems associated with the dispatch-mediated communication such as message delay, channel switching, call prioritization, etc. Utilizing IBM's message modeling concept, in this paper, we develop a messaging model to provide support for computer-mediated communication (CMC) systems. With the help of four experts (two fire chiefs and two dispatchers) and raw incident communication report, emergency communication messages were classified based on their objective into four message types, namely notification, request, response and update. The messages were analyzed for identification of messaging frequency. This led to development of a message format based on messaging elements.

The paper has certain limitations. First, it considers data for only single incidents. Second, it considers data from only one dispatch agency. Third, the messaging model is not verified for applicability in case of multiple incidents. A mechanism for dealing with missed messages in the system is being addressed as one of the several future extensions to the paper. The elements of the message could be further inspected to identify a relation between them.

Acknowledgements. The research of third author (correspondent author) has been funded in part by Sogang Business School's World Class University Project (R31-20002), funded by Korea Research Foundation as well as by the Sogang University Research Grant of 2011. The usual disclaimer applies. We would like to thank Tim Olliver (Town of Amherst Disaster Coordinator, NY), James Zymanek (Town of Amherst Disaster Coordinator, NY) and Dave Humbert (Chief of North Bailey Fire Department, Amherst, NY) for their help in this research project.

References

1. Bharosa, N., Lee, J., Janssen, M.: Challenges and obstacles in information sharing and coordination during multi-agency disaster response: propositions from field exercises. Information Systems Frontiers 12(1), 49–65 (2010)
2. Chen, R., Sharman, R., Chakravarti, N., Rao, H.R., Upadhyaya, S.J.: Emergency Response Information System Interoperability: Development of Chemical Incident Response Data Model. JAIS 9(3), 7 (2008)
3. Hevner, A.R., March, S.T., Park, J., Ram, S.: Design Science in IS Research. MISQ 28(1), 75–105 (2004)
4. Jang, H.C., Lien, Y.N., Tsai, T.C.: Rescue Information System for Earthquake Disasters Based on Manet Emergency Communication Platform. In: Proceedings of the 2009 International Conference on Wireless Communications and Mobile Computing (2009)
5. IBM. Developing message models, http://publib.boulder.ibm.com/infocenter/wmbhelp/v6r1m0/index.jsp

6. Meissner, A., Wang, Z., Putz, W., Grimmer, J.: Mikobos-a Mobile Information and Communication System for Emergency Response. In: Proceedings of the 3rd International ISCRAM Conference (2006)
7. Peffers, K., Tuunanen, T., Rothenberger, M., Chatterjee, S.: A Design Science Research Methodology for Information Systems Research. Journal of Management Information Systems 24(3), 45–77 (2007)
8. Seifert, C.: Improving Disaster Management through Structured Flexibility among Frontline Responders. In: Communicable Crises: Prevention, Response, and Recovery in the Global Arena, p. 83 (2007)
9. Turoff, M.: Computer-mediated communication requirements for group support. Journal of Computing 1, 85–113 (1991)
10. Valecha, R., Sharman, R., Monteiro, J., Rao, H.R., Upadhyaya, S., Keerthana, B., Patel, M., Singh, A., Sharma, K.: A Prototype of a FIRE-RELATED EXTREME EVENTZ SYSTEM (FREEZ). In: Proceedings of WITS (2010)

Appendix

Design Science Mapping [3], [7]

Problem: Emergency dispatch provides essential support to emergency responders during emergencies. However, there are several problems associated with the dispatch-mediated communication such as delay, channel switching and call prioritization

Solution: Utilizing IBM's message modeling concept, in this paper, we develop a messaging model to provide support for CMC systems, adhering to design science principles and contributing to emergency communication literature

Design: The paper uses Schramm's Communication Model to guide this process of development as follows: First, classify different message types based on their effect (objectives). Second, we examine the message for semantic and temporal interpretation. Third, we develop a message structure.

Demonstration: Case Application, Ticker-like Prototype System

Communication: Researchers, Professionals

An Approach for Smart Artifacts
for Mobile Advertising

Upkar Varshney

Department of CIS
Georgia State University, Atlanta, GA
uvarshney@gsu.edu

Abstract. Mobile applications and services have received significant attention among researchers, developers, wireless carriers, and content providers. Many of these applications, such as Google Latitude and Find My Friends, use location-based information from GPS or wireless networks to support location-awareness. For mobile advertising, location information is certainly important, however deriving and utilizing user's dynamic context can significantly improve the effectiveness of advertisements. In this "research-in-progress" paper, we present a design-science method for building artifacts for context-aware mobile applications. The method supports sensing, processing and deriving the most current context based on both live and stored information including current activities, location, and user profile. Several important research issues are also presented.

Keywords: context-awareness, artifact, mobile advertisement, location-based services.

1 Introduction

Mobile advertisements are effective due to users' immediate and personal attention to mobile devices [3, 16]. When combined with location-based information, the effectiveness is shown to be even higher [3]. Many industry surveys estimate the potential market for mobile advertisement in billions of dollars per year in US alone. There is a need to design and evaluate artifacts to study mobile advertising and transactions.

These artifacts can derive the current context in real-time based on both live and stored information including current activities and nearness to specific services and their current offerings, people and their activities, and locations with matching contexts. To start with, the artifacts will use information available related to when (time), what (activity), who (identity), where (location) [4-6], how (process) and from whom (source). In simple cases, the user can provide some information, but in most cases the artifacts will sense, process and derive the current context based on information [8-9, 11-12] derived by a variety of wearable, portable, and environmental sensors and smart spaces. The smart artifacts should be evaluated for their effectiveness, accuracy, and real-time processing of context information.

K. Peffers, M. Rothenberger, and B. Kuechler (Eds.): DESRIST 2012, LNCS 7286, pp. 147–151, 2012.

The research questions are how to build artifacts for context-aware mobile advertising based on proximity to people and their activities, services and their offerings, and locations with interesting matching of contexts? How to evaluate such artifacts against a range of requirements? In this paper, we present a method for designing and evaluating smart artifacts for mobile advertising. In the rest of this paper, we present mobile advertising and context, a method for designing artifacts, and conclusion.

2   Mobile Advertising and Context

Location-aware mobile advertising involves sending content-rich messages to users in certain locations, where size of the location identified by advertisers or users, or to users in any location, using the history of buying preferences or specified choices [16]. The effectiveness of location-aware mobile advertising is high especially if these messages can be highly targeted and time-specific [3]. The effectiveness of location-aware advertising can be further improved by using contexts derived from multiple sets of information, both live and stored.

The basic ideas behind context awareness are to create pro-active and smart operation of artifacts by minimizing user efforts and interactions, creating a very high level of intelligence in the systems, adding adaptability and effective decision making, and increasing the level of customization and personalization for users. A system is context-aware if it uses context to provide relevant information and/or services to the user, where relevancy depends on the user's task [2]. Thus, context-aware systems have the ability to discover and react to changes in their environment. The context includes who (identity), what (activity), where (location), when (temporal) and why (reasoning for behavior and actions). Additionally, it can include how (process) and from whom (source). Personalization allows a user to specify his/her preferences, passive context-awareness includes sensing and presentation of changes in context to the user without automatic changes, and active context-awareness involves automatic changes. Context awareness can enhance the application's behavior to be more personalized for their users. Context information for an application is everything that could change the behavior of the application such as the location, user preferences, environment or properties of connectivity. For context aware applications running on mobile devices, it is vital to deal with the dynamically changing environments and to efficiently exploit the context information within limited resources of the device and mobile communication system [5].

3   The Method for Designing Smart Artifacts

Design science focuses on understanding of a phenomenon, some or all of which may be created (not naturally occurring), this leads to artifact design and evaluation. An artifact can be (a) a set of components and their organization, (b) structurally coupled to its environment, (c) working design, or (d) improved instance of a tool [14].

3.1   The General Method

We focus on how to incorporate context-awareness in the design and evaluation of smart artifacts. The artifacts can be implemented on mobile devices and will use information available from multiple sources about the user in generating highly effective advertisements. In artifact development, the "tentative" design is developed and implemented [14]. The general method used is shown in Figure 1, and is derived from [7, 14].

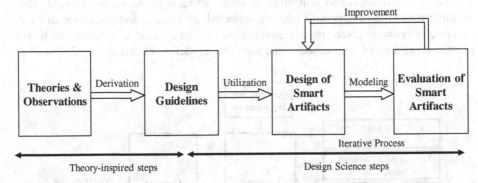

Fig. 1. The general method

3.2   Requirements and Guidelines

The introduction of context-awareness translates to the following requirements for artifacts: (a) ability to use relevant information about the user in deriving the context, (b) ability to process fast enough to allow the advertisement to reach to the user before any major changes in context, and (c) ability to gracefully degrade to at least the effectiveness of location-based application in cases of overload.

The addition of context-awareness will result in an increased amount of storage for user profiles among other things. The real-time processing requirements also increase due to added complexity of context-awareness. However, context-awareness will reduce the number and size of messages, improve the suitability and effectiveness of messages, and reduce the possibility of message transmission to an unintended receiver. The effectiveness of context-aware application can be measured in terms of (a) increased accuracy of advertisement and (b) the user's response to advertisement and starting a transaction to purchase something advertised.

The mobile advertisement can be tailored to the preference of mobile user, who may want certain information presented in a certain style. This type of personalization can be an important part of future implementations. The artifacts can be designed to address some known challenges.

There are many issues that should be addressed in implementation and testing such as (a) processing speed vs accuracy trade-off, (b) implementation complexity vs effectiveness trade-off, (c) impact of failures or malfunctions, (d) network traffic, and (e) additional distraction for mobile users.

Additional guidelines in design and evaluation of artifacts can be derived to address privacy issues in collecting user information and its potential abuse, processing complexity of context, suitability of mobile advertisements, potential distractions to mobile users, perceived similarity to "spam", and small screen and interface usability issues.

3.3   Context-Derivation and Utilization

The context-derivation and utilization in smart artifacts is shown in Figure 2. Here multiple related informational items are collected, processed, and integrated to create an effective context-aware mobile advertisement. The context generation can be implemented as a set of rules (conditional logic) or modeling of action probabilities.

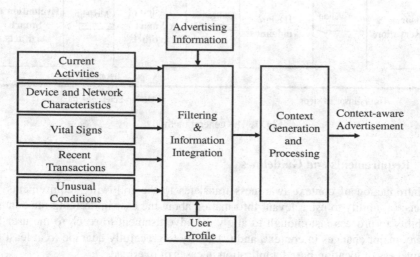

Fig. 2. Context-derivation and utilization

4   Conclusions and Research Recommendation

Our goal was to present a method for designing smart artifacts for mobile applications, specifically mobile advertising. As we build artifacts and then evaluate these, we hope to get a better understanding of how artifacts behave and how users interact with these artifacts. With improved understanding, the artifacts can be redesigned to increase their suitability and effectiveness in mobile advertising.

There are numerous questions that need be answered such as privacy in collecting user information and its potential abuse, processing complexity of context, suitability of mobile advertisements, potential distractions to mobile users, perceived similarity to "spam", and small screen and interface usability issues. We hope that this will generate some discussion on exciting research opportunities related to the application of design science in emerging areas of mobile and pervasive computing.

Acknowledgments. We are thankful to reviewers for their constructive feedback in improving this paper and for conducting future research.

References

1. Chen, G., Kotz, D.: A survey of context-aware mobile computing research. Tech Report TR2000-381. Dartmouth Computer Science Department (2000)
2. Dey, A., Abowd, G.: Towards a better understanding of context and context-awareness, Tech Report GIT-GVU-99-22. Georgia Institute of Technology (1999)
3. Dhar, S., Varshney, U.: Challenges and business models for mobile location-based services and advertising. Communications of the ACM (May 2011)
4. Favela, J., Rodriguez, M., Preciado, A., Gonzalez, V.M.: Integrating context-aware public displays into a mobile hospital information system. IEEE Transactions on Information Technology in Biomedicine 3(8), 279–286 (2004)
5. Gehlen, G., Aijaz, F., Sajjad, M., Walke, B.: A mobile context dissemination middleware. In: Proc. IEEE International Conference on Information Technology (2007)
6. Hardian, B., Indulska, J., Henricksen, K.: Balancing autonomy and user control in context-aware systems- a survey. In: Proc. Fourth Annual IEEE International Conference on Pervasive Computing and Communications Workshops (2006)
7. Hevner, A.R., Salvatore, T., March, J.P., Ram, S.: Design science in Information Systems research. MIS Quarterly 28(1), 75–105 (2004)
8. Loke, S.: Context-aware artifacts: two development approaches. IEEE Pervasive Computing 5(2), 48–53 (2006)
9. Mostifaoui, G., Pasquier-Rocha, J., Brkzillon, P.: Context-aware computing: a guide for the pervasive computing community. In: IEEE/ACS International Conference on Pervasive Services (ICPS), pp. 39–48 (2004)
10. Offermann, P., Blom, S., Schönherr, M., Bub, U.: Artifact Types in Information Systems Design Science – A Literature Review. In: Winter, R., Zhao, J.L., Aier, S. (eds.) DESRIST 2010. LNCS, vol. 6105, pp. 77–92. Springer, Heidelberg (2010)
11. Ranganathan, A., Al-Muhtadi, J., Campbell, R.: Reasoning about uncertain contexts in Pervasive Computing environments. IEEE Pervasive Computing 3(2), 62–70 (2004)
12. Schilit, B., Adams, N., Want, R.: Context-aware computing applications. In: Proc. IEEE Workshop on Mobile Computing Systems and Applications, pp. 85–90 (1994)
13. Skov, M., Hoegh, R.: Supporting information access in a hospital ward by a context-aware mobile electronic patient record. Pervasive and Ubiquitous Computing 10(4), 205–214 (2006)
14. Vaishnavi, V., Kuechler, W.: Design Science Research Methods and Patterns. Auerbach Publications, Boca Raton (2007)
15. Varshney, U.: Location management for mobile commerce applications in wireless Internet. ACM Transactions on Internet Technologies 3(3), 236–255 (2003)
16. Varshney, U., Vetter, R.: Mobile commerce: framework, applications, and networking support. ACM/Kluwer Journal on Mobile Networks and Applications (MONET) 7(3), 185–198 (2002)

Towards a Unified Design Theory for Creativity Support Systems

Matthias Voigt, Björn Niehaves, and Jörg Becker

European Research Center for Information Systems (ERCIS), University of Münster, Germany
{matthias.voigt,bjoern.niehaves,
joerg.becker}@ercis.uni-muenster.de

Abstract. A magnitude of predominantly qualitative empirical and conceptual work has indentified design principles that provide for the design of creativity support systems (CSS). Numerous kernel theories have been utilized to inform CSS design principles. However, the logical next step for design research is pending: this rich field of research may now allow for more quantitative empirical research on the actual effects of particular CSS design features on creative performance. Against the background of this research gap, we first analyze existing CSS design theories applying an analysis framework encompassing obligatory design theory components. On that basis, we extract the underlying independent (latent) variables addressed in design principles. Our contribution entails a unified design theory for CSS, laying the basis for future research in IS design science on creativity-support. Furthermore, we reflect on our approach to develop a unified design theory and discuss its implications for the philosophy of design science.

Keywords: Design Theory, Creativity Support Systems, Empirical Evaluation.

1 Motivation

Creativity is an important competitive asset for organizations (Everett 1983). New ideas for the creation or improvement of organizational procedures, services and products are fundamental to continuous adaption to rapidly changing market environments. Creativity is often defined with respect to the properties of the creative product as output of a creative process. A product is considered to be creative if it is both original, i.e. something 'new', and useful, in the sense that its fits the purpose it has been created for (Amabile 1996; Sternberg & Lubart 1995).

Creativity techniques, such as Brainstorming (Osborn 1957), have found their way in problem solution processes in many organizations. Increasingly, dedicated IT applications replace or supplement classical 'offline' approaches to creative problem solving. One prominent example is the Group Support System (GSS) ThinkTank (GroupSystems 2011), currently applied for collaborative idea generation in large governmental organizations and enterprises. The technologies that "enable people to be more creative more often" (Shneiderman 2007 p. 20). are referred to as Creativity

K. Peffers, M. Rothenberger, and B. Kuechler (Eds.): DESRIST 2012, LNCS 7286, pp. 152–173, 2012.
© Springer-Verlag Berlin Heidelberg 2012

Support Systems (CSS). Technically, the term CSS refers to a class of information systems encompassing diverse types of IS that share the purpose of enhancing creativity (Wierenga & van Bruggen 1998; Avital & Te'eni 2009). Thus research on CSS covers a broad range of systems, including Electronic Brainstorming Systems (EBS), Computer-aided Design environments (CAD) for technical and illustrative design, Decision Support Systems (DSS), Knowledge Management Systems (KMS), and GSS. Broadly, these systems can be categorized with respect to the support of creative processes of individuals or groups (Massetti 1996; Müller-Wienbergen et al. 2011). We focus on the category of individual-level CSS. Within that scope, we consider design issues that hold true for CSS in general, rather than on single types of information systems. This is in line with the statement that CSS "... can be expected to have at least some major components which are common across several domains of creative work" (Hewett 2005, p. 400).

Several experimental studies report on the effect of CSS on creative performance (Massetti 1996; MacCrimmon & Wagner 1994; Marakas & Elam 1997; Elam & Mead 1990). These insights have been partially incorporated into the design theories that are at focus of our considerations. They guide the purposeful design of IT artifacts for creativity support. However, this body of knowledge is very fragmented. We identified 23 publications stemming from diverse scientific background. In our iterative literature search process, we initiated to search for seminal psychological creativity literature and IT-related creativity literature in general. We subsequently focused on the subset addressing CSS design. Most contributions on this topic stem from conferences and journals residing to the disciplines of HCI, CSCW and IS. We then applied forward and backward search to extend our search results (vom Brocke et al. 2009).

The goal of our analysis is to identify recurring themes in the design principles that are yet scattered in the different streams of literature. We seek to provide for a unified design theory as offset for rigorous empirical CSS evaluations. Against this background, we pursue the following objectives with our study: First, we systematically analyze existent design theories on CSS design (section 3) in order to identify common design themes in design propositions (section 4). Second, we seek to lay the basis for developing a unified design theory for CSS to inform rigor design artifact evaluation and reliable evidence. The remainder of this paper is structured as follows. In the next section, we introduce the framework for design theories which we apply to systematically analyze our selected design theories. In section 3, we present the results of the design theory analysis. In the successive section we present our unified design theory for CSS.

2   Framework for Design Theories and Parameters for CSS

Before reviewing specific design theories, we seek to draw from philosophy of design science in order to base our analysis on a sound framework. IS design theories are prescriptive in nature, i.e. the "theories give explicit prescriptions [...] for constructing an artifact" (Gregor 2006, p.313). Specifically, design principles as component of design theories offer guidance in the selection or development of system features (Walls et al. 1992). Kernel theories are non-IS 'behavioral science' or 'natural science theories', provide predictions in the form of cause-effect relationships, i.e. explicitly define hypothesis (Gregor 2006; Kuechler & Vaishnavi 2008). Kernel theories inform the design of design theories. Therefore, the designer of the design theory has to conduct a transformation from cause-effect predictions to artifact design recommendations (see Figure 1). She or he hereby bridges a semantic gap 'separating' both theories (1st semantic gap). In a second transformation, the system designer has to transform the design recommendations for designing the artifact. Often, recommendations have to be interpreted to allow for implementation. This represents the bridging of a second semantic gap. Our focus is on the evaluation of the design artifact to generate rigor evidence for the validity of underlying kernel theory and design theory.

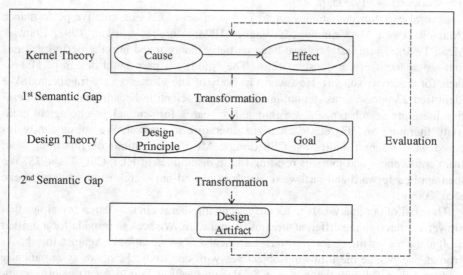

Fig. 1. Relations of kernel theory, design theory and design artifact (modified from Kuechler & Vaishnavi (2008))

We argue that for rigorous evaluation of the design artifact, the design theory has to (a) make explicit the causes (independent variable) and effects (dependent variable) incorporated in the design theory, (b) the transformation of those to design principles and goals and (c) guide the transformation from design principles to the design artifact. Some of those elements have already been addressed in the anatomy of design theories by Gregor & Jones (2007), which we take as foundation for our design theory framework. Where feasible, we define and give recommendations for each of these elements for our context of design theories for CSS:

1. Goal: The purpose of the artifact to which the theory applies, also referred to as meta-requirements, shall be explicated (Walls et al. 1992). Later analysis of CSS design theories show, that the purpose of the tool differs significantly, dependent on the chosen kernel theories and the application context it applies to.

2. Dependent variable and measurement: As to our prior claim, design theories have to indicate the causes or independent variables it incorporates in its design principles (Markus et al. 2002). Moreover, measurements for the dependent variable(s) shall be defined. In anticipation of our design theory analysis none but one design theories addressed this theory component.

3. Scope: The scope of the theory has to be defined. We refine the scope in three dimensions, each refining the origin or field of application (see Seidel et al. (2010)):

   (a) Type of information systems: design systems for product design, decision support systems, knowledge management systems and general purpose systems.

   (b) Scientific community the theory stems from: the major source of design theories we analyzed is from the field of HCI, complemented by theories from IS.

   (c) Application contexts: product designs, scientific (knowledge) work and general purpose theories.

4. Kernel Theory: Design theories shall not be developed "from out of the blue". Hence, it shall be supported by justificatory knowledge from the natural or social or design sciences. Walls et al. referred to these as product and process kernel theories (Walls, Widemeyer, & El Sawy, 1992). Later analysis of the design theories shows a broad repertoire of creativity kernel theories.

5. Method for design principle (DP) development: It has to be indicated which research methodology has been applied to derive the design principles. In the case of the analyzed design theories, literature analysis was the dominant method, partly supplemented by case study designs.

6. Design Principles: Design principles have to be explicated (Markus et al. 2002). They shall guide the CSS system designer in deciding on *what* the system should support with its features.

7. Independent variable and measurement: Design theory designer shall indicate the independent variables, measured later in artifact evaluation (Kuechler & Vaishnavi 2008). Those theoretical constructs emerge from *both* the kernel theory *and* the design principles expressing artifact properties. Additionally, measurement items shall be explicated.

8. Hypothesis: As stipulated by Gregor & Jones (2007), testable hypothesis have to be defined. For example, the theory designer has to explicate which independent variables residing from the kernel theories could be mediated or moderated by which property of the system instantiation employed in the experiment.

9. Implementation examples, prototypes: The formerly mentioned second semantic gap has to be bridged. Therefore the theory design should provide for guidance in the implementation of his or her design theory. One approach is to provide examples for concrete system features. Moreover, researchers could provide prototypes, also referred to as expository instantiation (Gregor & Jones 2007).

10. Method for DP evaluation: In cases where design artifact evaluations have already been conducted, the evaluation methodology has to be explicated (Hevner et al. 2004). We later present a single case of user observation and informal interviews.

With this analytical scheme at hand, we subsequently analyze a selected set of design theories. The results of this analysis will in turn lay the basis for developing a unified theory of CSS.

3   Analysis of Design Theories for CSS

Against the background of our formerly presented framework for design theories, we provide a concise overview of our analysis of theories. We identified 23 publications stemming from diverse scientific background. In our iterative literature search process, we initiated to search for seminal psychological creativity literature and IT-related creativity literature in general. We subsequently focused on the subset addressing CSS design. Most contributions on this topic stem from conferences and journals residing to the disciplines of HCI, CSCW and IS. We then applied forward and backward search to extend our search results (vom Brocke et al. 2009). Out of the 23 design theories, a subset of eight design theories has been selected for in-depth analysis. To gain a representative subset, we selected papers from possibly diverse disciplines (HCI and IS) addressing a possibly diverse set of CSS system types (CAD, KMS, DSS and CSS in general).

The analysis of the design theory of Hewett & DePaul (2000) according to the formerly defined design theory components is exemplarily shown in table 1. The frameworks for the other seven design theories can be found in the appendix (see table 2 to table 8). In general, the design theories expose some commonalities and differences with respect to their components. By purpose of our selection process, the design theories stem from different fields of research (which also provides for their sequential ordering in this paper): the first four design theories are on interface or interaction design respectively (see table 1 to table 4), the following two address knowledge management (see table 5 to table 6), one focuses on DSS (see table 7) and the last in sequence resides to IS (see table 8). All eight design theories are grounded in kernel theories or empirical evidence: the largest share applied the method of literature analysis for the deduction of design principles. The only two exceptions are Candy & Edmonds (1995) and (1996) following an exploratory action research and case study approach (see table 5 and table 6). With regard to the kernel theories, there is a tendency for a certain type of kernel theory: four design theories (see table 2 and table 3, table 5 and table 6) exclusively or partially apply process theories, i.e. descriptive models of phases typical for creative work. Generally, most design theories refer to psychological creativity theories, focusing on cognitive aspects promoting moments of creative insight (table 1 to table 3) or personality related issues (table 6 and table 7). The scope the design theory applies to is defined in all eight contributions. Moreover, six out of eight theories provide for implementation examples or refer to prototypes incorporating the design principles.

Table 1. Design theory framework for Hewett & DePaul (2000)

Criteria	Hewett & DePaul (2000)
Goal	Computer based working environment tailored to the system interaction flow peculiarities and cognitive aspects of scientists or engineers
Dependent variable and measurement	Not provided
Scope	Interface and interaction design (HCI), Scientific problem solving environments, Science
Kernel Theory	(1) Design principle of Norman (1988) for interaction design, emphasizing the importance of understanding the user's tasks and its proceeding in solving it. (2) Importance of analogical thinking as cognitive aspect of scientific problem solving (e.g. Clement (1988)). (3) Design for the target group of scientists and knowledge workers, drawing from the design principles of Candy & Edmonds (1995).
Method for DP development	Literature analysis
Design Principles	(1) Library of analogs, (2) multiple representations, (3) simultaneous representations, (4) flexible and tailorable usage, (5) multiple configurability, (6) multiple store and find operations, (7) multiple database access, (8) multiple communication channels, (9) logging of process and results, (10) ability to restructure the problem domain.
Independent Variable and measurement	Not provided
Hypothesis	Not provided
Implementation examples, prototypes	For some design principles, concrete implementation suggestions are provided, e.g. implementation of idea documentations in the form of "Post-it-notes" and idea sketches.
Method for DP evaluation	Not provided

However, we observe three aspects in current design research on CSS that might hamper future experimental evaluation: First, most design theories do not refer to the independent variables they manipulate (e.g. effects of task problem visualization), when the tool is implemented according to the design principles. This observation in related to in-transparencies of some design theories, not clearly explicating how the design principles were deduced from the kernel theories (see figure 1, first semantic gap). E.g. for the design theory of Elam & Mead (1990), the underlying kernel theory is Amabile's componential model of creativity, stating that domain relevant skills, creativity-relevant skills, and task motivation are crucial factors for creative performance. The first design principle, claiming that DSS (in consequence) have to allow users to stop, store work sessions in process, then resume work later, does not clearly relate to the aforementioned creative components. Second, the design theories do not refer to the dependent variable the tool is to have an impact on (e.g. creative performance). Third, for some design theories the design principles leave remarkable degrees of freedom for designing the artifact (i.e. the CSS) (see figure 1, second semantic gap) – even though some implementation examples are provided. Put simply, most design theories formulate *what* features CSS should provide, but provide only some guidance in *how* these features shall be implemented. This bares the risk that the actual intention of the design principle might not be realized. However, all design theories provide for theoretically or empirically informed guidance of CSS in form of design principles. As a result, a comprehensive orientation of the design process is provided. In the analysis of the design theories, especially of the formulated design principles, repeating themes emerged. This provided the basis for a unified design theory that allows for rigor evaluation in controlled experiments is still missing.

4   Towards a Unified Design Theory for CSS

We analyzed the design principles of all presented design theories, with the goal of identifying the underlying independent variables, i.e. the theoretical constructs that lie behind the system design properties for CSS. These independent variables can then be applied in quantitative experiments to reason about their actual effect on creative performance of users employing the system. The variables emerged in an iterative process of open coding and selective coding (Strauss & Corbin 1998): in the process of open coding, we identified themes relevant to the identification of underlying constructs in the design principles of our design theories which are manipulable by CSS tool design (see Figure 2, e.g. comparison, rich interpretation, customization). In the process of selective coding, we then used the most frequently identified themes, and systematically analyzed all design principles for occurrences of these. As a result, we had a set of eleven recurring themes. The number of occurrences of these themes found in the design principles is annotated in brackets in Figure 2 (more than one occurrence in a single design theory was counted as one occurrence). We finally reason that the themes pertain to a set of three generic CSS system properties, namely playfulness, comprehension, and specialization, which represent the underlying latent variables of our eight design theories. In the following we describe the themes we identified and provide our line of argument for "merging" them in the three latent variables.

Playfulness. In two of the presented design theories (Hewett & DePaul 2000; Elam & Mead 1990), the support of *iterative* development of (intermediate) creative products was deemed to be preferable over strict linear development process support. Accordingly, "activities may need to be performed iteratively and with the ability to halt a process, back up, modify the input or the process, and restart" (Hewett & DePaul 2000, p.15). Similar to this, the provision of *simulation* in CSS is one recurring claim. Simulation is connoted with the exploration of solutions (Shneiderman 2000) and the refinement of rules in experimental settings (Candy & Edmonds 1995). Yet another aspect of simulation is the testing of solutions in diverse contexts (Avital & Te'eni 2009). *Comparison*, as another prominent recurring theme in CSS design principles, is the simultaneous representation of diverse sets of alternative data (Hewett & DePaul 2000; Candy & Edmonds 1995; Shneiderman 2000), easing decision making. For Avital and Te'eni (2009) the fostering of human insight is supported by "juxtaposing diverse frames that are not commonly associated with one another" (Avital & Te'eni 2009, p.357). Lastly, the theme of *modification* refers to the modification of the problem of the creative task. Negotiating, changing and adding rules and constraints for the solution space shall be facilitated, so that the user can rephrase the problem to his/her current understanding of the domain (Hewett & DePaul 2000; Candy & Edmonds 1995). In later work, Candy and Edmonds (1996) state that problem formulation is an emergent process. We see all presented themes for design theories related with the latent variable (LV) of tool playfulness, which we understand as follows:

LV-1: Playfulness is the property of a tool to encourage unfettered trialability in design, helping the user to push intermediate solutions to final results iteratively.

Comprehension. Another prominent theme in our set of design principles is rich *representation* of the data used for idea development. By this, it shall be possible to "[…] model and explore an idea […]" (Hewett & DePaul 2000, p.14). For Candy and Edmonds (1995), the goal is to support user's judgment and readily incorporation of emerging knowledge in his or her activities. Rich representations shall further serve the purpose "to discover new aspects of the situation and explore them through interacting with representations" (Yamamoto & Nakakoji 2005, p.512). Shneiderman (2000) argues for inspirational functions of rich interpretations. A common example for those representations is free-hand sketches. In line with this visualization support, CSSs shall provide for "a *holistic view* of high quality visual data […]" (Candy & Edmonds 1995, p. 246). Abstraction tools shall enable the examination of objects or processes at multiple degrees of granularity (Avital & Te'eni 2009). Another claim is to design CSS in a way the users can *interact naturally* with the creative (intermediate) products. "A designer has to be able to feel as if he/she interacts with the representations rather than with the computer system […]" (Yamamoto & Nakakoji 2005, p.523). In the context of knowledge systems natural interaction shall include drawing upon terminology which is the user is acquainted to (Candy & Edmonds 1995). In order to prevent the user from loosing scope in the development of creative artifacts, *constant visual groundings* shall be provided. Dimensional structuring of representations, e.g. a two-dimensional matrix, shall serve this purpose (Shneiderman 2000; Yamamoto & Nakakoji 2005). We argue that these four presented themes of design principles characterize a tool design that fosters the comprehension of artifacts in the design process. We thus understand the latent variable of comprehension as follows:

LV-2: Comprehension is the property of a tool to foster a rapid and clear understanding of the artifacts employed for idea development.

Specialization. Different creative tasks often require support by *special purpose tools*. Users have to be able to "[...] pick and choose which pieces of functionality [they require]" (Hewett & DePaul 2000, p.15) in order to maximize their scope and control over the application (Candy & Edmonds 1996). Applying the metaphor of a workbench, special purpose tools could be re-used in a variety of tasks (Hewett 2005). Moreover, those single applications should be arrangeable in environmental tool configurations, *customized* to the needs of a task at hand (Hewett & DePaul 2000; Avital & Te'eni 2009; Hewett 2005). Finally, it is necessary to *integrate* all graphical interface components of a CSS. This includes components for simulation, comparison, modification, rich visualization and the like. "[...] the main challenge for designers is to ensure smooth integration across these novel tools and with existing tools [...]" (Shneiderman 2000, p.122). Against the backdrop of fostering creative insight, the integration of subsystems shall allow for associations across different "[...] domains, disciplines, practices and organizational units" (Avital & Te'eni 2009, p. 358). We conclude that tools have to provide the right features for the right tasks. We therefore define the third latent variable specialization as follows:

LV-3: Specialization is the property of a tool to provide the user with task specific support and to allow selecting and arranging this support for future re-use.

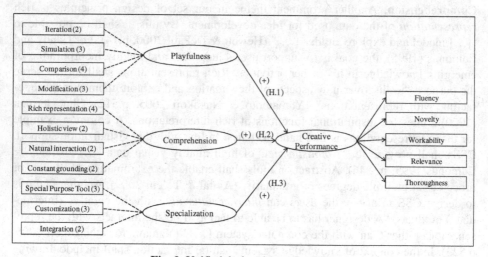

Fig. 2. Unified design theory for CSS

We subsume our analysis in a unified design theory for CSS (see Figure 2). The latent, independent variables playfulness, comprehension and specialization characterize properties of CSS, all being supposingly positively correlated to the creative performance of individuals and groups applying them in their creative work. For the design principles, the numbers in brackets indicate their occurrences in the analyzed design theories. Thus, the rich interpretation of intermediate creative products and the comparison of those is the most prominent design principle. The simulation of modifications to intermediate creative products and the customization of the CSS were each addressed in three design theories. Based on our findings, we are now able to propose the following three hypotheses (H-1 – H-3) for future design research in CSS:

H-1: CSSs that facilitate playful production of creative products will increase the creative performance of its users.
H-2: CSSs that facilitate comprehensive interpretation of intermediate creative products will increase the creative performance of its users.
H-3: CSSs that facilitate specialized support of context dependent creative tasks will increase the creative performance of its users.

Creative Performance. Three branches of creativity assessment are discussed in literature (Amabile 1996): assessment of individual creativity, of the creative process and of its outcome, the creative product. Since CSS eventually aim at fostering the production of creative outcomes, the most feasible approach for our context is the measurement of creative performance with the product-oriented approach. With the three-factor model of creativity, Guilford (1968) introduced three notions of the creative output, i.e. the quantity of ideas produced (referred to as idea fluency), the novelty of ideas (referred to as originality) and how ideas differ from each other (flexibility). Though the quantity of ideas produced can easily be assessed intersubjectively, objective assessment is still cumbersome in idea quality assessment. Amabile stated that "[…] ultimately, the assessment of creativity simply cannot be achieved by objective analysis alone. Some type of subjective assessment is required" (Amabile 1996, p. 29). An appropriate set of criteria for the assessment of the creativity of ideas has been sought in the scientific community for a long time. Dean et al. (2006) compared existent criteria and merged the most frequent occurrences in a catalogue of four criteria: novelty refers to the originality of an idea, assuming that nobody has expressed it before. Workability, also referred to as feasibility, refers to the degree to which an idea can be easily implemented and does not violate known constraints. Relevance of an idea is given if it satisfies the goals for the given creativity task. Finally thoroughness also referred to as elaboration or specificity, of an idea is the degree to which it is worked out in detail. This set of criteria, or a subset (mostly originality and relevance), has been applied in numerous experiments (e.g. Blohm et al. (2011), Gallupe et al. (1992)). For the calculation of overall creativity metrics for a set of subjects, there is evidence that good-idea-count, "which is calculated by counting the number of ideas in the session with a quality score that meets or exceeds some quality threshold" (Reinig et al. 2007, p.146), is the most reliable calculation method. We thus recommend to measure creativity by counting the ideas produced (fluency), assessing the ideas with regard to novelty, workability, relevance and thoroughness and calculate an overall value with the approach of good-idea-count.

In the next section we will discuss the relevance of our two central contributions of our paper, i.e. the systematic analysis of extent design theories for CSS and the unified design theory for CSS, for design science research in IS in general and for creativity-enhancing system design in particular.

5   Discussion

Current State of Research on CSS Design. Addressing our research goals (see Section 1), we started off with systematically analyzing extant design theories for creativity support tools. Here, we observed that there exists a plethora of research efforts in the field of HCI that addresses interface design and creative work. In contrast, in IS research and especially in IS design science, this research stream is rather underdeveloped despite the generally recognized importance of this phenomenon (Seidel et al. 2010). Our theory review revealed that the majority of work in this field provides rich information about how CSS should look like in order to be successful. Often, this research well refers to kernel theories from related disciplines, such as psychology and social sciences (Amabile 1996; Csikszentmihalyi & Sawyer 1995; Sternberg & Davidson 1995). However, extant work is beset with certain limitations. It is regularly rather difficult to extract clear construct definitions and rigorous measurement models of both the dependent as well as independent variables (e.g. generative capacity, generative fit (Avital & Te'eni 2009), multiple representations of knowledge (Candy & Edmonds 1995)). Much work on CSS provides design guidelines that inform about *what* set of features the class of IS, here CSS, should encompass in order to be 'successful'(Hewett 2005; Candy & Edmonds 1996). Less regularly, it is actually reported about *how* these desirable design features should be implemented exactly. The result is considerable ambiguities for implementation-oriented design research and rigorous design theorizing on CSS. Among other issues, it proves difficult to actually feed back into the body of knowledge that the kernel theory stems from for reasons of rigor (see Kuechler & Vaishnavi (2008) on mid-range theories). Besides some first results gained from experiments in the 1990s (Massetti 1996; Marakas & Elam 1997), literature does not yet provide a wide range of design research efforts that test the effects of particular CSS design features in controlled environments, such as lab experiments. These efforts need to be followed up, tapping on design opportunities provided by state-of-the-art technology. We consider this shortcoming a result of these ambiguities as well that the field does not yet provide an integrated or unified view on these different strands of design approaches for CSS.

CSS Design Theory Unification and Agenda Setting. Our second research objective was to identify and to consolidate prevalent CSS design themes into an integrated model. Here, our study yields three core constructs: 1) Playfulness: the property of a CSS to encourage unfettered trialability in design, helping the user to push intermediate solutions to final results iteratively, 2) Comprehension: the property of a CSS to foster a rapid and clear understanding of the artifacts employed for idea development, and 3) Specialization: the property of a CSS to provide the user with task specific support and to allow selecting and arranging this support for future re-use. We furthermore extracted differentiated sets of concrete design options that (based on prior works' findings) may be assumed to stimulated/triggered the three, as we argue, 'latent variables'. Our 'unified design theory' opens up for an array of future research. First, the effects of playfulness, comprehension, and specialization on creative performance will need to be studied in an integrated model. So far, CSS studies overlap only partially with these aspects. However, the construct playfulness is not new to IS: *Microcomputer playfulness* is a situation-specific individual characteristic and "describes an individual's tendency to interact spontaneously, inventively and imaginatively with microcomputers" (Webster & Martocchio 1992, p. 202). Being an individual trait, rather than a property of an information system, this construct has only indirect implications for CSS design. Moreover, playfulness is related to research on *hedonic information systems*, where the value of using the systems is a function of the degree to which the user experiences fun (van der Heijden 2004). As such, they are opposed to utilitarian information systems, for which the "objective is to increase the user's task performance while encouraging efficiency" (van der Heijden 2004 p.696). Our CSS design considerations focus on increasing (creative) user performance. However, fun in CSS usage may well have a positive influence on the task performance (Csikszentmihalyi 1975). Thus, both the body of knowledge on microcomputer playfulness and hedonic information systems may provide for new perspectives on the construct of playfulness in the design of CSS. Second, the relationships between concrete design choices (IT implementations) and the three abstract latent variables need to be studied. Which of the given designs is best suited for representing one of the latent variables? Can an integration of two or more suggested designs represent a latent variable better? Are there other design options, not yet discussed in the literature, that are able to represent the latent variables even more adequately? With our study and our actual propositions, we thus hope to contribute to setting an IS design research agenda that accounts for both design theorizing and IT artifact implementation issues for creativity support.

Method for Design Theory Unification. Integrating constructs from numerous potentially relevant kernel theories into a comprehensive design theory is cumbersome. For holistic design theories, a broad range of kernel theories need to be included. Moreover, the transition from kernel theory constructs to design principles may be challenging, dependent on the IT-system relatedness of these constructs. With our approach to draw on the body of different design theories in order to extract central theoretical constructs from design principles, we hope to inspire future design science research on design theory unification. We specifically propose a three step approach (see Figure 3): first, a set of design theories covering a possibly broad range of scientific disciplines and thus perspective on the design problem shall be selected. Secondly common themes in design principles shall be identified, using the data analysis method of open coding and selective coding (Strauss & Corbin 1998). Subsequently those themes shall be analyzed for underlying theoretical constructs, that cluster those theme to a 'super-topic' which may in turn represent the latent variable influenced by design properties of the design artifact.

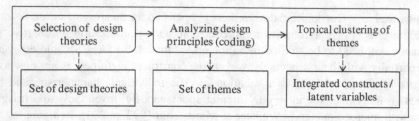

Fig. 3. Three step approach for the identification of latent variables from design theories

Limitations and Outlook. Our study yields an identification of important gaps in CSS design literature, a unified design theory for supporting creative work, and a novel design theorizing approach. However, these contributions and our findings are beset with particular limitations. First, our review of extant CSS design literature is naturally not complete. While we see that our set of articles already resulted in theoretical saturation, one may argue that a review of entirely different fields of study can give new impulse and provide new theory variables. As to our scope on individual-level CSS, we consider a review of (group) psychological literature and CSCW literature as a potentially fruitful for future construct identification. Most certainly, the suggested unified design theory needs to be empirically tested. In addition to the before-mentioned open questions, methodologically, we see great potential for conducting design science experiments in controlled environments. As for design theory unification approach, we see potential for codifying the steps in the form of a systematic procedural model in order to increase its applicability. Finally, we studied the particular area of CSS design and look forward to future research that is able to confirm or to add to our findings with regard to other fields of design science.

Acknowledgement. This paper was written in the context of the research project KollaPro (promotional reference 01FL10004) which is funded by the German Federal Ministry of Education and Research (BMBF). Moreover, we like to thank our reviewers for their very valuable feedback.

References

Amabile, T.M.: Creativity in context. Westview Press, Cumnor Hill (1996)

Amabile, T.M.: The social psychology of creativity: A componential conceptualization. Journal of Personality and Social Psychology 45(2), 357–376 (1983)

Avital, M., Te'eni, D.: From generative fit to generative capacity: exploring an emerging dimension of information systems design and task performance. Information Systems Journal 19(4), 345–367 (2009)

Blohm, I., Bretschneider, U., Leimeister, J.M., Krcmar, H.: Does collaboration among participants lead to better ideas in IT-based idea competitions? An empirical investiga-tion. Int. J. Networking and Virtual Organisations 9(2), 106–122 (2011)

vom Brocke, J., Simons, A., Niehaves, B., Riemer, K., Plattfaut, R., Cleven, A.: Reconstructing the giant: on the importance of rigour in documenting the literature search process. In: Proceedings of the 17th European conference on Information Systems (ECIS 2009), Verona, Italy (2009)

Candy, L., Edmonds, E.A.: Creative design of the Lotus bicycle: implications for knowledge support systems research. Design Studies 17, 71–90 (1996)

Candy, L., Edmonds, E.A.: Creativity in Knowledge Work: A Process Model and Requirements for Support. In: OZCHI 1995, pp. 242–248 (1995)

Clement, J.: Observed methods for generating analogies in scientific problem solving. Cognitive Science 12(4), 563–586 (1988)

Csikszentmihalyi, M.: Beyond Boredom and Anxiety. Jossey-Bass, San Francisco (1975)

Csikszentmihalyi, M., Sawyer, K.: Creative Insight. The Social Dimension of a Solitary Moment. In: Sternberg, R.J., Davidson, J.E. (eds.) The Nature of Insight, pp. 329–364. MIT Press, Cambridge (1995)

Davidson, J.E.: Insights about insightful problem solving. In: Sternberg, R.J., Davidson, J.E. (eds.) The Psychology of Problem Solving, pp. 149–175. Cambridge University Press, Cambridge (2003)

Dean, D.L., Hender, J.M., Rodgers, T.L., Santanen, E.L.: Identifying quality, novel, and creative Ideas: Constructs and scales for idea evaluation. Journal of the Association for Information Systems 7(1), 646–699 (2006)

Elam, J.J., Mead, M.: Can Software Influence Creativity? Information Systems Research 1(1), 1–22 (1990)

Everett, E.: Improving Creativity: One Organization's Approach. Public Management 65(2), 7–8 (1983)

Gallupe, R.B., Dennis, A.R., Cooper, W.H., Valacich, J.S., Bastianutti, L.M., Nunamaker, J.F.: Electronic Brainstorming and Group Size. Academy of Management Journal 35(2), 350–369 (1992)

Gregor, S.: The nature of theory in information systems. MIS Quarterly 30(3), 611–642 (2006)

Gregor, S., Jones, D.: The Anatomy of a Design Theory. Journal of the Association for Information Systems 8(5), 312–335 (2007)

GroupSystems ThinkTank (2011), http://www.groupsystems.com/ (accessed January 11, 2012)

Gruber, H.E.: The evolving systems approach to creative work. In: Wallace, D.B., Gruber, H.E. (eds.) Creative People at Work, pp. 3–24. Oxford University Press (1989)

Guilford, J.P.: Creativity, Intelligence and Their Educational Implications. EDITS/Knapp, San Diego (1968)

van der Heijden, H.: User Acceptance of Hedonic Information Systems. Management Information Systems Quarterly 28(4), 695–704 (2004)

Hevner, A.R., March, S.T., Park, J., Ram, S.: Design Science in Information Systems Research. Management Information Systems 28(1), 75–105 (2004)

Hewett, T.T.: Informing the design of computer-based environments to support creativity. International Journal of Human-Computer Studies 63(4-5), 383–409 (2005)

Hewett, T.T., DePaul, J.L.: Toward a Human Centered Scientific Problem Solving Environment. In: Houstis, A.N., Rice, J.R., Gallopoulos, E., Bramley, R. (eds.) Enabling Technologies for Computational Science - Frameworks, Middleware and Environments, pp. 1–22. Kluwer Academic Publishers (2000)

Ippolito, M.F., Tweney, R.D.: The inception of insight. In: Sternberg, R.J., Davidson, J.E. (eds.) The Nature of Insight, Cambridge, pp. 433–462 (1995)

Isaak, M.I., Just, M.A.: Constraints on thinking in insight and invention. In: Sternberg, R.J., Davidson, J.E. (eds.) The Nature of Insight, pp. 281–326. The MIT Press, Cambridge (1995)

Kuechler, B., Vaishnavi, V.: On theory development in design science research: anatomy of a research project. European Journal of Information Systems 17(5), 489–504 (2008)

MacCrimmon, K.R., Wagner, C.: Stimulating Creativity Ideas through Software. Management Science 40(11), 1514–1532 (1994)

Maccoby, M.: The innovative mind at work. IEEE Spectrum, 23–35 (1991)

Marakas, G.M., Elam, J.J.: Creativity Enhancement in Problem Solving: Through Software or Process? Management Science 43(8), 1136–1146 (1997)

Markus, M.L., Majchrzak, A., Gasser, L.: A Design Theory for Systems that Support Emergent Knowledge Processes. Management Information Systems 26(3), 179–212 (2002)

Massetti, B.: An Empirical Examination of the Value of Creativity Support Systems on Idea Generation. Management Information Systems 20(1), 83–97 (1996)

Müller-Wienbergen, F., Müller, O., Seidel, S., Becker, J.: Leaving the Beaten Tracks in Creative Work – A Design Theory for Systems that Support Convergent and Divergent Thinking. Journal of the Association for Information Systems 12(11), 714–740 (2011)

Norman, D.: The Design of Everyday Things C. Doubleday, New York (1988)

Osborn, A.F.: Applied imagination: Principles and procedures of creative thinking. Scribeners and Sons, New York (1957)

Regli, W.C., Zaychik, V., Hewett, T.T., Sevy, J.: Issues in building and evaluating networked engineering environments. In: Fourth Workshop on Knowledge Intensive CAD, p. 229. Kluwer Academic Pub., Parma (2000)

Reinig, B., Briggs, R., Nunamaker, J.F.: On the Measurement of Ideation Quality. Journal of Management Information Systems 23(4), 143–161 (2007)

Schön, D.A.: The Reflective Practicioner: How Professionals Think in Action. Basic Books, New York (1983)

Seidel, S., Müller-Wienbergen, F., Becker, J.: The Concept of Creativity in the Information Systems Discipline: Past, Present, and Prospects. Communications of the Association for Information Systems 27(1), 14 (2010)

Shneiderman, B.: Codex, Memex, Genex: The Pursuit of Transformational Technologies. International Journal of Human-Computer Interaction 10(2), 87–106 (1998)

Shneiderman, B.: Creating creativity: user interfaces for supporting innovation. ACM Transactions on Computer-Human Interaction 7(1), 114–138 (2000)

Shneiderman, B.: Creativity support tools: accelerating discovery and innovation. Communications of the ACM 50(12) (2007)

Sternberg, R.J., Davidson, J.E.: The nature of insight. MIT Press, Cambridge (1995)

Sternberg, R.J., Lubart, T.I.: Defying the crowd: Cultivating creativity in a culture of conformity. Free Press, New York (1995)

Strauss, A.L., Corbin, J.M.: Basics of qualitative research. Techniques and procedures for developing grounded theory. Sage, London (1998)

Walls, J.G., Widmeyer, G.R., El Sawy, O.A.: Building an Information System Design Theory for Vigilant EIS. Information Systems Research 3(1), 36–59 (1992)

Webster, J., Martocchio, J.J.: Microcomputer Playfulness: Development of a Measure With Workplace Implications. Management Information Systems 16(2), 201–226 (1992)

Weisberg, R.W.: Creativity: Beyond the Myth of Genius. W.H. Freeman, New York (1993)

Wierenga, B., van Bruggen, G.H.: The Dependent Variable in Research into the Effects of Creativity Support Systems: Quality and Quantity of Ideas. MIS Quarterly 22(1), 81 (1998)

Yamamoto, Y., Nakakoji, K.: Interaction design of tools for fostering creativity in the early stages of information design. International Journal of Human-Computer Studies 63(4-5), 513–535 (2005)

Appendix

Table 2. Design theory framework for Hewett (2005)

Criteria	Hewett (2005)
Goal	Human-centered computer-based support environment to facilitate innovation and creative work
Dependent variable and measurement	Not provided
Scope	HCI, Generic CSS (1)
Kernel Theory	(1) Conditions for insight (Motivation (Csikszentmihalyi & Sawyer 1995), Knowledge (Davidson 2003), Test possibilities (Ippolito & Tweney 1995), collaboration (Csikszentmihalyi & Sawyer 1995), visualization (Ippolito & Tweney 1995), constraints (Isaak & Just 1995), analogical similarity (Weisberg 1993)) (2) Iteration in the creative process (Gruber 1989) (3) Genex framework (Shneiderman 1998): non-linear four phases of the creative process, i.e. collect, relate, create, and donate have to be supported (4) Other Design theories of (Candy & Edmonds 1995) and (Hewett & DePaul 2000)
Method for DP development	Literature review
Design Principles	(1) Provide special purpose tools (2) Tools can be configured (3) Allow visualization of structures (4) Library of reusable objects (5) Auto-logging of communication
Independent Variable and measurement	Not provided
Hypothesis	Not provided
Implementation examples, prototypes	References to other publications referring to prototypes are given, e.g. Regli et al. (2001) referring to CodeLink
Method for DP evaluation	The evaluation of DP principles was out of scope of this theory

Table 3. Design theory framework for Shneiderman (2000)

Criteria	Shneiderman (2000)
Goal	If designers of CSS follow the proposed design theory, they "[…] can create powerful tools that enable users to be more creative more of the time" (Shneiderman 2000, p.115).
Dependent variable and measurement	Not provided
Scope	Interface design (HCI), evolutionary creativity
Kernel Theory	(1) Genex framework (Shneiderman 1998): non-linear four phases of the creative process, i.e. collect, relate, create, and donate have to be supported (2) Three perspectives on creativity: (a) Inspirationalists emphasize moments of insight in which a dramatic breakthrough unexpectedly appears, (b) structured approaches to creativity support apply methodical techniques to explore the solution space, and (c) situationalists emphasize the importance of social context.
Method for DP development	The design principles are deduced by means of logical reasoning.
Design Principles	Support of the four phases of the genex framework with eight activities: (1) Searching and Browsing Digital Libraries, (2) Consulting with Peers and Mentors, (3) Visualizing Data and Processes, (4) Thinking by Free Associations, (5) Exploring Solutions: What-If Tools, (6) Composing Artifacts and Performances, (7) Reviewing and Replaying Session Histories, and (8) Disseminating Results. Features to support those activities should have a high degree of integration.
Independent variable and measurement	Not provided
Hypothesis	Not provided
Implementation examples, prototypes	(1) Example implementations are provided, e.g. word processor, spreadsheets, computerized thesauri, mind maps, etc. (2) References to several commercial tools (partly still existent today) are made
Method for DP evaluation	The evaluation of DP principles was out of scope of this theory

Table 4. Design theory framework for Yamamoto & Nakakoji (2005)

Criteria	Yamamoto & Nakakoji (2005)
Goal	"[…] application systems for early stages of information design tasks" (Yamamoto & K Nakakoji 2005, p. 513). Further, the systems are to reduce the cognitive overhead in creative activities
Dependent variable and measurement	Cognitive overhead
Scope	Interaction design (HCI)
Kernel Theory	(1)"reflection-in-action" (Schön 1983), i.e. a design process in which the designer produces externalizations to interpret situations while the externalizations emerge and "reflection-on-action" (Schön 1983), i.e. the reflection of the externalization, after it has been completed (2) Issues to be addressed by computational tools supporting the early stages of information design: (a) Available means of externalizations influence designers in deciding which courses of action to take. (b) Designers generate and interact with not only a partial representation of the final artifact but also various external representations. (c) Designers produce externalizations not only to express a solution but also to interpret situations. (d) Design proceeds as a hermeneutic circle; designers proceed with projected meanings of representations and gradually revise and confirm those meanings
Method for DP development	Literature Analysis
Design Principles (DP)	(P-1) Interpretation-rich representations, (P-2) Representations with constant grounding, (P-3) Interaction methods for hands-on generation and manipulation of the representations
Independent variable and measurement	Not provided
Hypothesis	Not provided
Implementation examples, prototypes	Example of ART#001, an existing tool for the early stages of writing. Three basic system components are defined: (1) ElementEditor, for creating and modifying an element (text chunk, video chunk). (2) ElementSpace: for specifying relationships among elements (e.g. a two-dimensional space). (3) DocumentViewer: for viewing a document under construction made up of elements that have been created.
Method for DP evaluation	User observation with eye-tracking and informal interviews

Table 5. Design theory framework for Candy & Edmonds (1995)

Criteria	Candy & Edmonds (1995)
Goal	"The aim is to reduce the constraints upon the scientist's explorations and unpredictable courses of action" (Candy & Edmonds 1995, p.243).
Dependent variable and measurement	Not provided
Scope	Knowledge Support Systems, specific support for scientific knowledge work
Kernel Theory	Process model of knowledge work: exploration and evaluation, generation and invention, constraints and requirements
Method for DP development	Exploratory action research
Design Principles	(1) Exploration & Evaluation Support reflected in the activities of (a)examine data, which is supported by providing holistic views, multiple representations of data, visual data annotation, and concurrent processes, (b) evaluating rules, which is supported by multiple representations of knowledge, feedback, and domain specific evaluation, (c) refining rules, which is supported by 'natural graphical interaction', knowledge modification, and evolution. (2) Generation and invention reflected in the activities of (a) examine data, which is supported by providing holistic views, multiple representations of data, concurrent processes and evaluation of knowledge, (b) create rules, which is supported by creating objects, knowledge modification and evaluation, comparative evaluation of knowledge, (3)Constraints addressed in the activities of (a) receive and revise constraints, which is supported by 'natural' graphical Interaction, knowledge modification and evaluation and comparative evaluation of knowledge, (b)negotiate constraints, which is supported by knowledge modification and evaluation, visual data annotation, and comparative evaluation of knowledge
Independent variable and measurement	Not provided
Hypothesis	Not provided
Implementation examples, prototypes	Not provided
Method for DP evaluation	The evaluation of DP principles was out of scope of this theory

Table 6. Design theory framework for Candy & Edmonds (1996)

Criteria	Candy & Edmonds (1996)
Goal	Support of creative design
Dependent variable and measurement	Not provided
Scope	Interactive knowledge support system, support for creative design, individual support
Kernel Theory	(1) A set of criteria addressing personality traits of high profile designers (Maccoby 1991): system thinkers, insistency, learning from negative instances, confidence, intrinsic motivation, (2) Design process model of knowledge work (Candy & Edmonds 1995): exploration and evaluation, generation and invention, constraints, (3) Elements of creative design: problem formulation, idea generation, strategies, methods, expertise, (4) Case study findings: interview data in support of the aforementioned theory elements, providing the empirical basis for design principles
Method for DP development	Literature analysis, case study
Design Principles	(1) Design knowledge exploration and evaluation, (2) design space and design knowledge access, (3) design knowledge sharing, (3) tentativeness and uncertainty, (4) problem formulation and the emergence of concepts, (5) strategic knowledge and strategy development
Independent Variable and measurement	Not provided
Hypothesis	Not provided
Implementation examples, prototypes	Not provided
Method for DP evaluation	Not provided

Table 7. Design theory framework for Elam & Mead (1990)

Criteria	Elam & Mead (1990)
Goal	"[Decision support systems that] enable decision makers to develop better and more creative solutions to the problems they face."
Dependent variable and measurement	Decision making process [single step process, multi step process], creativity of response [Consensual technique for creativity assessment (Amabile 1996)]
Scope	Decision support systems
Kernel Theory	Amabile's componential model of creativity (Amabile 1983), referring to individual skills necessary and sufficient for producing creative results: domain relevant skills, creativity-relevant skills, task motivation
Method for DP development	Literature analysis
Design Principles	(1) The DSS will allow users to stop, store work sessions in process, then resume work later. (2) A DSS should provide depth and positive tenor in its feedback (3) The DSS will make available to the user a full range of qualitative as well as quantitative decision aids. (4) A DSS will be technically easy to use and conceptually challenging. (5) The DSS will provide an enjoyable or "fun" computing environment.
Independent Variable and measurement	Software treatment [no software, software version 1, software version 2]
Hypothesis	Hypothesis 1. A user of a creativity-enhancing DSS will adopt a multiple step decision process, whereas a user of no software will adopt a single step decision process. Hypothesis 2. The use of a creativity-enhancing DSS will result in higher levels of creative responses than the use of no software.
Expository Instantiation	ods/ CONSULTANT
Method for DP evaluation	Experiment

Table 8. Design theory framework for Avital & Te'eni (2009)

Criteria	Avital & Te'eni (2009)
Goal	Reach generative fit of the CSS, i.e. the highest possible "extend in which a particular information technology artifact, or part thereof, is conducive to evoking and enhancing that generative capacity in people" (Avital & Te'eni 2009, p. 346).
Dependent variable and measurement	Generative fit
Scope	Design environments and generative systems in general
Kernel Theory	Theory of generative capacity, i.e. an individual's capacity to produce creative results and theory of generative fit, i.e. "the extent to which an information technology-based system is designed to [...] enhance the inherent generative capacity of its users" (Avital & Te'eni 2009, p. 349).
Method for DP development	Literature analysis
Design Principles	Systems have to be (1) evocative by supporting Visualization, Simulation, Abstraction, integration, and communication, (2) adaptive by supporting customization and automation and (3) open-ended by supporting peer-production and rejuvenation.
Independent variable and measurement	Generative capacity
Hypothesis	Not provided
Implementation examples, prototypes	Specific examples of a 3-D CAD system
Method for DP evaluation	The evaluation of DP principles was out of scope of this theory

What Makes Corporate Wikis Work? Wiki Affordances and Their Suitability for Corporate Knowledge Work

M. Lisa Yeo and Ofer Arazy

Alberta School of Business, University of Alberta, Edmonton, AB, CA
http://www.business.ualberta.ca

Abstract. Wikis were originally intended for knowledge work in the open Internet environment, and there seems to be an inherent tension between wikis' affordances and the nature knowledge work in organizations. The objective of this paper is to investigate how tailoring wikis to corporate settings would impact users' wiki activity. We begin by synthesizing prior works on wikis' design principles; identifying several areas where we anticipate high tension between wikis' affordances and organizational work practices. We put forward five propositions regarding how changes in corporate wikis deployment procedures may impact users' wiki activity. An empirical study in one multi-national organization tested users' perceptions towards these propositions, revealing that in some cases there may be a need for modifying wiki's design, while in other cases corporations may wish to change their knowledge work practices to align with wikis' affordances.

Keywords: Wiki, Affordances, Knowledge Management.

1 Introduction

Wiki, derived from the Hawaiian-language word for fast, is a web-based collaborative authoring application [40,57]. While wikis are similar to discussion forums and blogs, these prior online collaboration tools append to the content contributed by users (e.g. discussion forums); in wikis each user edits the previous version of the page, with the most recent version reflecting the cumulative contributions of all authors. Such features have made wiki-based applications popular for knowledge management (KM) on the Internet (e.g. Wikipedia) and many organizations are now making use of wikis to meet their own knowledge management needs [23,30,42].

Wikis were originally intended for knowledge work in the open Internet environment; the most notable success of wiki technology is Wikipedia. Despite the success of wikis in the public domain, it is not clear that wikis can succeed in corporate settings as there seems to be an inherent tension between wikis' affordances and the nature knowledge work in organizations [3,24]. While the wiki system used in both Internet and corporate settings might be very similar,

K. Peffers, M. Rothenberger, and B. Kuechler (Eds.): DESRIST 2012, LNCS 7286, pp. 174–190, 2012.

wiki-based conversational KM practices may differ substantially from Internet systems such as Wikipedia. For example, over the Internet, wiki editing is open ended, while a corporation may put restriction on access privileges, provide template formats, or calculate users' relative contribution to be used in performance evaluation [6,62].

Because of this tension, wikis may be less successful in corporate environments where incentives and governance structures differ from those of the open Internet. The objective of this paper is to investigate how tailoring wikis to corporate settings would impact their successful adoption in organizations. Participation is essential to the success of communities of practice and online communities. In line with Arazy and Croitoru [2], we use participation as a proxy for the success of corporate wikis. We define 'participation' broadly, to include both active (i.e. editing the wiki by adding new content, restructuring the wiki page, or removing irrelevant content) and passive (reading the wiki) participation.

In particular, our primary research questions are: "How can we reduce the inherent tension between wiki affordances and the nature of corporate knowledge work?" and "Would such manipulations of wiki affordances affect users' wiki participation?" We put forward five propositions regarding how changes in corporate wiki deployment would impact users' wiki behavior and test users' attitudes towards these propositions using a survey of wiki users at IBM with the goal of understanding possible changes necessary for successful corporate wiki adoption.

1.1 Wiki Affordances

Gibson [22] coined the term 'affordance' and defined it as a perceivable property of an object or of the environment that allows a particular individual an opportunity for action. The idea was popularized by Norman [44,45], who brought it to the attention of the design community and, in particular, researchers in human-computer interaction [21]. The notion of affordances is increasingly being used in the information systems area [32,47,63]. The concept is useful since it emphasizes the role of the situated activity of the person who perceives the affordance, and thus allows conceptualizing the relations between the technology's features and organizational work processes.

Prior literature on wikis has described the primary design features of wikis (e.g. [40,57]). However, the notion of affordances is different than 'design feature' as it focuses on the suitability of the tool for supporting a specific task rather than on tool design per-se. Recently, studies have described some of the work practices supported by wikis [41,58,60], and have begun using the notion of affordances. Building on these prior studies [40,58,60], we can identify three broad categories of affordances: (a) affordances that simplify content creation and management, (b) affordances that reduce or remove workflow constraints and the distinction between content creation, editing and administrative tasks, and (c) affordances that support peer-based governance. A key feature of many of these affordances is to remove entry barriers that are typical of traditional knowledge management systems [9,58]. Examples include simple formatting, easy access, and incremental editing; all features that make it easy to create and update content with little technical training.

1.2   Tensions between Wikis' Affordances and Corporate Practices

Early on, organizational KM approaches focused on knowledge as objects that could be organized to support decision making, and KMS were seen as tools to manage codified knowledge, such that most KM projects were initiated top-down and driven by management. However, the rigid structure of such centrally-controlled KM initiatives exhibited poor incentives to sharing and reuse of knowledge. Peer-based production over the Internet, as exemplified by open-source software development [38] and later Wikipedia [5], has offered an alternative model of KM that emphasized principles such as open access and community governance [7,20,39,57,64]. Rather than centralized control of KM initiatives and the codification of all organizational knowledge, firms increasingly recognize that distributed collaboration is a more effective way of sharing knowledge. However, firms trying to adapt to this new open KM face some substantial challenges. Wiki is a light-weight KM system that is intended to support knowledge work in the open Internet settings, and wikis' affordances are designed for peer-production. As corporations begin deploying wiki technology it becomes apparent that there are inherent tensions between wikis' affordances and organizational knowledge work practices [3], especially in situations where the organization has not fully adapted to open KM. For example, in Internet settings, reducing recognition of individuals' contributions (non-attribution) is viewed as an essential principle for ensuring diversity and protecting users' privacy. However, in corporate settings this feature is often undesired as it impedes accountability and individual incentives; further, recognition of contributions is believed necessary for motivating user engagement. Technology affordances are malleable [47] and organizations are seeking ways to adapt wikis to their existing knowledge management practices.

Recent accounts of corporate wiki deployment [2,3,18,23,36] portray an environment that leverages on wikis' affordances in some cases and adheres to traditional organizational practices in others. In line with 'the wiki way', content is automatically published and users' contributions are not attributed; however, users are often required to register through the organizational system before allowing to access the wikis and there is less reliance on collaborative editing norms and peer-based quality control.

What, then, is the best way for deploying wikis in corporate settings? Is it possible to find a compromise between wiki affordances and corporate knowledge work practices? How could organizations drive wiki adoption? We identify a subset of five wiki affordances where we anticipate high tension with traditional organizational knowledge management procedures, and put forward propositions - one for each of the affordances under investigation - regarding how deviations from the current corporate wiki deployment practices (by either modifying the technology or by changing organizational procedures) would impact users' wiki activity. We are not aware of works in the context of wikis, or more broadly in the context of knowledge management systems, that have looked at how manipulating certain affordances will affect user behaviors (or attitudes towards behavior) within the systems.

Promoting Collaborative Editing Norms. While the role of editing norms is fairly well documented in Wikipedia [35,56,61], little is known about the extent to which corporations rely on such norms to guide users through the collaborative editing process. Wiki editing is unconstrained, which provides much flexibility, but also raises uncertainty regarding the expectations for use. Corporate users are accustomed to having training on new technology usage; however, wikis are deployed in many corporations from the ground up, with little or no training. Not providing guidance for users on such a flexible technology can have detrimental effects; the lack of norms indicating information to share across organizational boundaries was a major impediment to the adoption of a wiki in a health care setting [23]. An alternative approach for guiding users is modifying wiki technology through the use of templates, constraints placed on wiki pages, or ontologies to ensure consistent wiki page structure and terminology [14,15,25]. A recent survey of corporate wiki users suggests that the use of wiki enhancements that constrain the otherwise open-ended editing process (e.g. templates) can accelerate wiki adoption [18]. Given prior evidence on the important role of editing norms, as well as recent works that attempt to constrain wiki editing, we put forward the following proposition:

Proposition 1. *Promoting collaborative authoring norms will increase wiki participation.*

Attribution. Wikis are designed to promote group collaboration and discourage individualism [40]; pages are not associated with any single author and it is difficult to assess individual authors' contributions [6]. For example, Wikipedia often promotes high-quality articles (i.e. the output of group effort), rather than specific users. Thus, it is difficult for authors to publicize their skills and accumulate reputation [53], in stark contrast to many other popular collaboration platforms, such as Slashdot[1]. In a lab experiment studying the behavioral impact of presenting user contributions, it was found that users contribute more when they know that their work is visible and is valued [49], suggesting that attribution will motivate wiki participation. Given that corporate users are driven by career advancement [28], we expect that corporate users will increase wiki participation if their individual contributions are acknowledged and propose:

Proposition 2. *Attributing contributions will increase wiki participation.*

Allowing Unregistered Editing. Allowing users to participate without revealing their identity has the benefits of the so called "equalization phenomenon",

---

[1] http:\slashdot.org

where status and other social cues are removed from the message, allowing collaborators to focus instead on the content [13,17,19,31,48,51]. Most wikis do not include extensive access control mechanisms with the rationale that unregistered editing attracts more participation and increases the size and diversity of the author-group. Some argue that reducing the barriers to participation is the key factor to Wikipedia's success[2] [33,46], with the collective intelligence of a diverse author set resulting in higher quality content [4,7,54]. However, unregistered and anonymous contributions are usually undesirable in corporate settings, where accountability is a commonly accepted principle and free riding is a concern [34]. It is worth noting the tension between the affordance of unregistered editing and corporate users' desire to attribute wiki contributions (see above); if a user contributes without registering, it would not be possible to measure his contribution. One possible approach for resolving this tension is to allow those users who wish not to register to still edit content, while recording the contributions of those users who choose to register. We expect that allowing (but not mandating) unregistered wiki editing will drive participation, and thus we propose:

Proposition 3. *Opening the editing process to unregistered users will increase wiki participation.*

Controlled Publishing. In traditional knowledge management systems, work is structured in such a way that each role is able to perform only the tasks he is responsible for; there is a distinction between content creation, editing, and administrative tasks. Wikis remove many of these workflow restrictions [57] and eliminate the distinction between content authoring, editing, and structuring tasks, such that any writer is automatically an editor, organizer, and publisher [9,40] without requiring the authorization of any administrator [57]. In particular, automatic publishing allows for very quick evolution of page content, thus circumventing the bottleneck associated with traditional content development projects, where administrators are responsible for qualifying and publishing information [1,58]. Nonetheless, manually controlling the release of article revisions may curtail the risks of inaccurate information in a wiki and bring the process of wiki authorship more in line with existing corporate practices. The control could take the form of restricting access to pages in a manner that lets selected groups collaboratively create a page privately before publishing a final version [10] with or without the approval of an administrator. Although there is no evidence to indicate whether such controlled release of new content is effective, we expect that because controlled publishing is in line with standard organizational knowledge management practices, it would be desired by corporate wiki users. Thus, we propose:

Proposition 4. *Controlling the release of article revisions will increase wiki participation.*

---

[2] It is worth noting that since 2006, Wikipedia does not allow anonymous users to create new articles, although they can still edit existing pages.

Providing Tools for Peer-Based Quality Control. Since wikis often lack centralized governance, failing to establish peer-based quality control mechanisms could impede wiki project success. In online communities, peer oversight has been found to be as effective as expert quality control [11]; quality is attained through constant error correction and refinement by the user community, enabled by mechanisms for easy error detection and correction [40,59]. Tools such as watch lists, article quality ratings, software bots (to identify vandalism) and features to easily recover from vandalism (by reverting changes) are all used by Wikipedia to maintain high quality articles [52]. Without such tools, wiki content can quickly deteriorate, as evidenced by The Boomtown Times newspaper's editorial wiki, which was abandoned in just three days after being overwhelmed by disruptive users [60]. Prior works on wiki design have tried to enhance wikis with automatic quality control tools (e.g., tools to estimate the quality of wiki pages [27,37]) and such enhancements can motivate users to contribute to wikis [16]. An alternative mechanism for ensuring quality of pages that is specifically suitable for corporate wikis is a rating system, where users rate the quality of content on a wiki page [27]. Tools to measure the quality of wiki pages can signal the reliability of the information and could make users more comfortable relying on that information in their work. Hence, we expect that peer-based quality control tools, such as a rating system, will increase wiki use.

Proposition 5. *Incorporating an article rating mechanism will increase wiki participation.*

2   Research Method

Our research methodology is based on a web survey, where wiki users reported their perceptions on how a specific proposed manipulation (either a change to wikis' design or to the deployment procedure) would impact their wiki participation. There is an extensive body of literature in the information systems area which demonstrates that attitudes towards technology adoption are good determinants of actual adoption [8,12,43,55], thus we expect that users' self-reported attitudes are indicative of the expected effect of various proposed manipulations. The main advantage of our research method is that it enables us to explore the (perceived) effect of a relatively large number of wiki modifications in a single study.

The study was conducted at a large global organization which operates thousands of distinct wikis. The firm chosen as the subject of our study is IBM, which designs hardware, develops software, and engages in professional services. IBM has over 350,000 employees and a large user base of early adopters. An announcement regarding the survey appeared in the homepage of IBM wikis that all active wiki users could have seen, but the exact number of people who read the announcement is not known. This mass announcement would be similar to an advertisement in an industry magazine inviting survey participation. Our web survey was administered internally and was open to all users over a period of eight weeks. Of the 1,205 users who accessed the survey web site, 919 completed the survey, describing their experiences with 486 distinct wikis. Survey respondents came from various organizational units, with a significant portion from software development (capturing the experience of 5% of all wiki applications). Each subject was asked to rate statements regarding her wiki activity on a 5-point Likert scale.

Prior literature provides only little guidance on how to measure users' perceptions of proposed manipulations to wiki deployment, thus the articulation of the survey questions regarding our propositions was informed by our understanding of corporate wiki practices, and was verified through extensive discussions with IBM's wiki administration unit. This collaborative survey development process ensured that the survey questions would be interpreted appropriately by the IBM employees who chose to participate.

3   Results

IBM wiki users were asked to rate the extent to which they agree with statements suggesting that certain manipulations (changes to wiki software or adjustments in wiki deployment procedures) will enhance their activity. The results of our study show (at least partial) support to propositions 1, 2, and 5, no support for proposition 3, and evidence contradicting proposition 4. Our findings suggest that in some cases wiki users would like to see changes to align wiki deployment with "the wiki way" (e.g. automatic publishing, the use of collaborative editing norms, incorporating peer-based quality control tools such as a rating system) while in other cases corporate users would like to see modifications that are more in line with traditional organizational knowledge management practices (e.g. attributing contributions, not permitting unregistered editing). A summary of the findings is described in Table 1.

Table 1. The extent to which modifications in wiki deployment are expected to increase participation (on a 1 to 5 scale)

Modifications in wiki deployment	Proposition	Support	Mean	Median	Std. Deviation
Promote collaborative editing norms	1	Yes	3.55	4	1.00
Attribution	2	Yes (strong)	3.90	4	0.93
Allow unregistered editing	3	No	2.86	3	1.16
Control publishing	4	No (refute)	2.15	2	1.15
Add a rating system	5	Yes (weak)	3.21	3	1.11

From the five modifications we have explored, *attribution* had the largest impact on users' anticipated participation levels, with over 60% of respondents saying they agree or strongly agree that publicizing their contributions will increase their participation. On the other extreme, over 60% say they disagree or strongly disagree that *controlling the release of new content* by having an administrator first review changes would increase their activity. Figure 1 provides details regarding the distribution of responses to each of the proposed modifications.

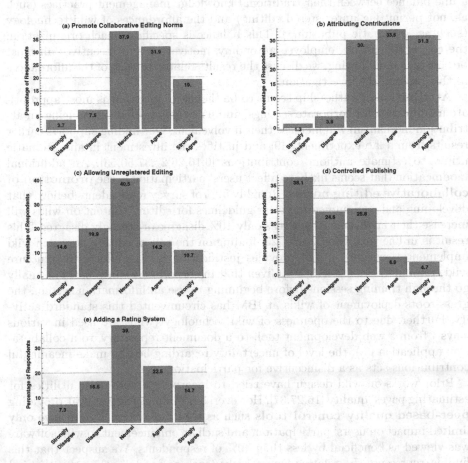

Fig. 1. Distribution of responses to statements regarding the anticipated effects of modifications in wiki deployment

4   Discussion

Wikis are designed for open and organic peer-based collaboration; however, as wikis are entering corporate walls, it is clear that some adjustments are required, since some wiki affordances run counter to traditional organizational knowledge management practices. The few empirical studies regarding wikis in corporate settings suggest that organizations are trying to find a compromise, staying true to wiki core affordances and adapting their work practices accordingly in some cases, and adjusting wiki design to fit standard knowledge management work in other cases. This work is a preliminary exploration of corporate wiki users' attitudes towards various alternative deployment schemes. To the extent that the perceptions indeed capture users' expected behavior, our findings suggest that wiki adoption would be highest when organizations are able to find a fine balance between their traditional knowledge management practices (such as, not permitting unregistered editing) and the affordances of wiki technology (such as, automatic publishing). This balance is specific to each organization; the corporate culture, employee autonomy, motivation and incentives all must be considered. Following, we discuss the results related to each of the affordances in this preliminary investigation.

Attribution of authorship seems to be the affordance that is most appropriate modification for corporate settings, and users believe that introducing an attribution mechanism will increase their involvement. Our finding supports earlier results from a lab experiment [49] and justifies the investment in an automatic utility to estimate authors' contributions [6,16,26,27,37,50,53]. An additional modification that seems likely to affect users' participation is the **promotion of collaborative editing norms**. Roughly 50% of survey respondents believe that developing and communicating clear guidelines for editing content on wikis will increase their involvement, whereas only 10% disagree or strongly disagree. This result is in line with Giordano's [23] finding on the role of editing norms in wiki implementation success, and provides justification for the efforts to structure wiki communications [14,15,25]. Given that in corporate settings users normally go through training sessions before beginning to use an information system, the grass-roots deployment of wikis at IBM has circumvented this standard activity. Further, due to the openness of wiki technology (wikis are used in various ways - from a web development tool, to a document repository, to a collaboration application [3]), the level of uncertainty regarding how to make meaningful contributions acts as a disincentive for participation.

Prior works on wiki design have tried to incorporate automatic utilities for estimating pages' quality [16,27,37]. However, our findings suggest that providing **peer-based quality control tools** such as a rating system would have only limited impact on users' participation, and such an enhancement to wiki software was viewed as beneficial by less than 40% of respondents. We suspect that this finding represents the relative lack of risks (such as vandalism) in the "behind the firewall" wiki implementation we've studied. However, we believe that when opening wiki participation to external parties (e.g. customers), quality control will be of increased importance, as demonstrated by the case of The Boomtown Times [60].

Overall, wiki users in our sample did not have a clear preference regarding **unregistered editing**: roughly 25% of survey respondents believe that allowing unregistered editors (i.e. anonymous postings) will increase their participation, while nearly 35% prefer contributions to be made by registered users. We believe that there is a link between this affordance and corporate users' interest in attribution and recognition (see discussion above), which is not feasible when editors are not identified.

Research has shown that motivational dynamics in a corporate setting have an impact on wiki participation [29]; thus we collected data to help us distinguish between self-directed use of wikis (motivational drivers such as enjoyment, self-expression, belonging to a community, learning new skills, and other direct benefits) and users who are driven to use wikis (motivational factors such as peer pressure and supervisor pressure). Please refer to the Appendix for details on survey items. Users who feel compelled to use wikis are more interested in unregistered editing (correlations are $0.17 - 0.19$; $p < 0.0001$) and in controlling publishing (correlations are $0.22 - 0.37$; $p < 0.0001$) as illustrated in Figure 2. This demonstrates that these externally-motivated users may shy away from taking responsibility and are less comfortable with features that would hold them accountable.

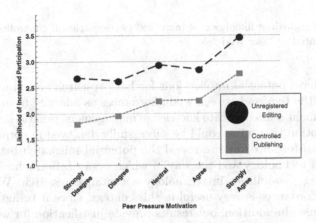

Fig. 2. Likelihood of increased participation for the affordances of (a) unregistered editing and (b) controlled publishing based on the degree to which respondents feel peer pressure to participate in wikis

Finally, **automatic publishing** of new content is expected to have contradicting consequences: on one hand it increases the risks to content quality, while on the other hand it can reduce bottlenecks in the creation of new knowledge. This dual effect was evident in our analysis of wiki roles, which found that content producers have less interest in controlled publishing since it restricts their ability to create knowledge, while content consumers have fewer objections to controlled publishing since it increases wiki content quality, as illustrated in Figure 3. Overall, users in our survey objected to the proposal to have administrators control the release of new content on wikis. We see two possible reasons for this finding. It is possible controlled publishing contradicts the notion of democracy that is associated with wikis [40] and thus is seen by users as a form of censorship and as a threat to author autonomy. Alternatively, it is possible that corporate users are less concerned with quality risks (e.g. vandalism; please refer to our discussion above) and thus do not see a need for a centralized content qualification mechanism.

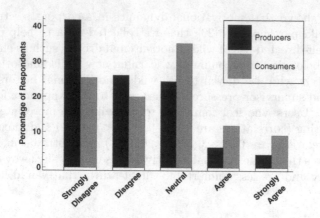

Fig. 3. Responses regarding likelihood of increased participation if controlled publishing were implemented by user wiki role

Our findings have potential implications for both research and practice. Our study highlights the tension between wiki affordances as adopted from the open Internet environment and corporate knowledge management practices, and challenges the perception that wikis could be successfully deployed in corporate settings as is [3,42]. More broadly, we reveal the potential mismatch between the intended use of a technology and the way in which organizations choose to employ it, indicating possibilities in technology acceptance research. We believe that notion of affordances is very useful in this context, since it brings together the tool and its use. In addition, our results provide justification for works that aim to enhance and modify wikis in various ways - e.g. estimating users' contributions [6], structuring the editing process [14], and automatically estimating pages' quality [16] - suggesting that this is a productive research direction.

For practitioners, we identify a need for organizations to be aware of the disparity between the type of work wikis were intended to support and existing knowledge management practices. For each of these possible incompatibilities, the organization should consider whether it prefers to change wiki's design or alternatively to adapt the organization to "the wiki way". Specifically, the results from our empirical study indicate that corporate wiki users desire recognition for their efforts, highlighting the need for both a mechanism that can estimate and publicize users' contributions as well as to provide clear guidance on the collaborative authoring process while not attempting to impose controls on wiki's automatic publishing affordances.

5   Conclusion

Following the success of internet wiki-based application, such as Wikipedia, business organizations have begun adopting wikis. However, the affordances of wikis seem to run in contrast to traditional tightly controlled corporate knowledge management practices. The findings from our preliminary study show that successful wiki adoption in organizations will require a hybrid approach to affordances, with some leaning towards settings in line with 'the wiki way' (e.g. unregistered editing, peer-based quality control) and others leaning towards more traditional corporate settings (e.g. attributing contributions). How much corporate wikis pull towards each side is a delicate balancing act, and may depend greatly on organizations' existing knowledge management practices and their ability to change.

This preliminary study has two goals. Our primary goal is in providing evidence regarding the anticipated effects of five proposed wiki modifications. While several studies have recently proposed extensions and modifications intended to adjust wiki affordances, there is no evidence to suggest which of these adjustments is more effective. In this study we investigated five wiki affordances - *collaborative authoring norms, unregistered editing, automatic publishing, non-attribution*, and *peer-based quality control* - and have reported on users' perceptions regarding the extent to which altering these wiki affordances - by either modifying the wiki system or by changing work practices - is likely to increase users' participation. Second, our conceptualization of wiki affordances goes beyond extant literature on the area with the goal of informing studies on wikis' design. While prior literature has described the primary design features of wikis, the notion of affordances is quite different than 'design features' as it focuses on the suitability of the tool for supporting a specific task (rather than on tool design per-se).

Our study provides only a preliminary probing into the suitability of wikis for corporate knowledge work. As such, an important value of this work is in pointing the direction to further research. Below, we briefly review various ways in which this study could be extended. First, we have only explored few possible modifications, and many other possibilities exist. For example, we proposed to change the affordance of 'automatic publishing' by adding an administrative control; however, an alternative modification would allow peers (rather than administrators) to qualify the content before publishing it (c.f. [10]). Second, our study of wiki affordances was based on user attitudes and, although prior research suggests that attitudes towards technology adoption are a good indicator of actual adoption [8,12,43,55], we recommend that future research would validate that actual wiki behavior corresponds to the attitudes reported in our study, either through a lab or field study. A third limitation lies in the ambiguity of the concept of participation. As we were interested in general adoption of wikis, we were less concerned about whether users would be more likely to contribute content (become 'active' participants) or to read content (become 'passive' participants). We believe that there are links between increased readers and increased active participation, and indeed it is possible that we captured cases where current readers believed they could become content creators under different affordance configurations. Follow-up work should include a more formal operationalization of wiki participation in order to provide better insights for user types as well as different user roles within both the wiki and the corporation. A fourth limitation of this study is the measurement of the likely impact of the proposed wiki modifications. We have used single-item measures, working closely with IBM's wiki administration unit to ensure that the survey questions captured our intentions and were well understood by wiki users. Thus, some terminology adopted in the survey was based on how internal IBM employees referred to the feature (i.e. 'anonymous postings' was used to refer to 'unregistered editing' and a 'rating' of wiki articles implied a peer-based control). Such terminology may have other interpretations and thus caution should be used when adapting the questionnaire items from this study to other contexts. Fifth, future research could also extend the investigation of wiki affordances beyond the impact on participation to alternative indicators of project success, such as user satisfaction or job performance. Finally, we call for further research on wikis across various industries (e.g. business, education, government) and geographical regions. We conclude with a call for future research in this exciting area and hope that others would be able to fill-in the gaps in this study.

References

1. Alavi, M., Leidner, D.E.: Review: Knowledge management and knowledge management systems: Conceptual foundations and research issues (November 2007)
2. Arazy, O., Croitoru, A.: The sustainability of corporate wikis: A time-series analysis of activity patterns. ACM Transactions on Management Information Systems (TMIS) 1(1), 6 (2010)
3. Arazy, O., Gellatly, I., Jang, S., Patterson, R.: Wiki deployment in corporate settings. IEEE Technology and Society Magazine 28(2), 57–64 (2009)
4. Arazy, O., Morgan, W., Patterson, R.: Wisdom of the crowds: Decentralized knowledge construction in Wikipedia. In: Proceedings of the 16th WITS. SSRN, Milwaukee (2006)
5. Arazy, O., Nov, O., Patterson, R., Yeo, L.: Information quality in Wikipedia. Journal of Management Information Systems 27(4), 73–100 (2011)
6. Arazy, O., Stroulia, E., Ruecker, S., Arias, C., Fiorentino, C., Ganev, V., Yau, T.: Recognizing contributions in wikis: Authorship categories, algorithms, and visualizations. Journal of the American Society for Information Science and Technology 61, 1166–1179 (2010)
7. Benkler, Y.: The Wealth of Networks: How Social Production Transforms Markets and Freedom. Yale University Press (2006)
8. Bhattacherjee, A., Premkumar, G.: Understanding changes in belief and attitude toward information technology usage: A theoretical model and longitudinal test. MIS Quarterly 28(2), 229–254 (2004)
9. Bryant, S.L., Forte, A., Bruckman, A.: Becoming Wikipedian: transformation of participation in a collaborative online encyclopedia, pp. 1–10. ACM, Sanibel Island (2005)
10. Burrow, A.L.: Negotiating access within wiki: a system to construct and maintain a taxonomy of access rules. Work, pp. 77–86 (2004)
11. Cosley, D., Frankowski, D., Kiesler, S., Terveen, L., Riedl, J.: How oversight improves member-maintained communities. In: Proceedings of the SIGCHI Conference on Human Factors in Computing Systems, CHI 2005, p. 11 (2005)

12. Davis, F.D.: Perceived usefulness, perceived ease of use, and user acceptance of information technology. Management Information Systems Quarterly 13, 319–339 (1989)
13. DeSanctis, G., Gallupe, R.B.: A foundation for the study of group decision support systems. Management Science 33(5), 589–609 (1987)
14. Di Iorio, A., Presutti, V., Vitali, F.: WikiFactory: An Ontology-Based Application for Creating Domain-Oriented Wikis. In: Sure, Y., Domingue, J. (eds.) ESWC 2006. LNCS, vol. 4011, pp. 664–678. Springer, Heidelberg (2006)
15. Di Iorio, A., Zacchiroli, S.: Constrained wiki: an oxymoron? In: WikiSym 2006 Proceedings of the 2006 Intern. Symposium on Wikis, vol. 6, pp. 89–98. ACM (2006)
16. Ding, X., Danis, C., Erickson, T., Kellogg, W.A.: Visualizing an enterprise wiki. In: CHI 2007 Extended Abstracts on Human Factors in Computing Systems CHI 2007, p. 2189 (2007)
17. Dubrovsky, V.J., Kiesler, S., Sethna, B.N.: The equalization phenomenon: Status effects in computer-mediated and face-to-face decision-making groups. Human-Computer Interaction 6(2), 119–146 (1991)
18. Edwards, P.: Managing Wikis in Business. University Business (September 2007)
19. Friedman, B., Kahn Jr., P.H., Howe, D.C.: Trust online. Communications of the ACM 43(12), 34–40 (2000)
20. Füller, J., Mühlbacher, H., Matzler, K., Jawecki, G.: Consumer empowerment through internet-based co-creation. Journal of Management Information Systems 26(3), 71–102 (2009)
21. Gaver, W.W.: Affordances for interaction: the social is material for design. Ecological Psychology 8(2), 111–129 (1996)
22. Gibson, J.J.: The ecological approach to visual perception, vol. 39. Houghton Mifflin (1979)
23. Giordano, R.: An investigation of the use of a wiki to support knowledge exchange in public health (2007)
24. Grudin, J., Poole, E.S.: Wikis at work: Success factors and challenges for sustainability of enterprise wikis. In: Proceedings of the 6th International Symposium on Wikis and Open Collaboration, WikiSym 2010, pp. 1–8. ACM (2010)
25. Haake, A., Lukosch, S., Schümmer, T.: Wiki-templates: adding structure support to wikis on demand. Structure 65, 41–51 (2005)
26. Hess, M., Kerr, B., Rickards, L.: Wiki user statistics for regulating behaviour (2006)
27. Hoisl, B., Aigner, W., Miksch, S.: Social Rewarding in Wiki Systems – Motivating the Community. In: Schuler, D. (ed.) HCII 2007 and OCSC 2007. LNCS, vol. 4564, pp. 362–371. Springer, Heidelberg (2007)
28. Igbaria, M., Baroudi, J.J.: The impact of job performance evaluations on career advancement prospects: An examination of gender differences in the IS workplace. MIS Quarterly 19(1), 107 (1995)
29. Jang, S., Arazy, O., Nov, O., Brainin, E.: "Crowding Out" in corporate wikis: the effects of job responsibility and motivation on participation. In: Proceedings of the 6th Mediterranean Confince on Information Systems (MCIS 2011), Cyprus (2011)
30. Jang, S., Green, T.: Best practices on delivering a wiki collaborative solution for enterprise applications. In: 2006 International Conference on Collaborative Computing: Networkin, Applications and Worksharing, pp. 1–9. IEEE, Atlanta (2006)
31. Jessup, L.M., Connolly, T., Galegher, J.: The effects of anonymity on GDSS group process with an idea-generating task. MIS Quarterly 14(3), 313–321 (1990)

32. Jung, J.H., Schneider, C., Valacich, J.: Enhancing the motivational affordance of information systems: The effects of real-time performance feedback and goal setting in group collaboration environments. Management Science 56(4), 724–742 (2010)
33. Kapoor, M.: Content creation by massively distributed collaboration. Tech. rep., UC Berkley School of Information, Berkeley (2005)
34. Kidwell, R.E., Bennett, N.: Employee propensity to withhold effort: A conceptual model to intersect three avenues of research. Academy of Management Review 18(3), 429–456 (1993)
35. Kittur, A., Chi, E., Pendleton, B.A., Suh, B., Mytkowicz, T.: Power of the few vs. wisdom of the crowd: Wikipedia and the rise of the bourgeoisie. In: 25th Annual ACM Conference on Human Factors in Computing Systems, University of California, Palo Alto Research Center, University of Colorado at Boulder, pp. 1–9. ACM (2007)
36. Kittur, A., Kraut, R.E.: Beyond Wikipedia: Coordination and conflict in online production groups. Communication, 215–224 (2010)
37. Korfiatis, N.T., Poulos, M., Bokos, G.: Evaluating authoritative sources using social networks: an insight from Wikipedia. Online Information Review 30(3), 252–262 (2006)
38. Lakhani, K.R., Wolf, R.G.: Why hackers do what they do: Understanding motivation and effort in free/open source software projects. In: Feller, J., Fitzgerald, B., Hissam, S.A., Lakhani, K.R. (eds.) Perspectives on Free and Open Source Software, pp. 3–21. MIT Press (2005); No. September in Perspectives on Free and Open Source Software
39. Landy, F.J., Becker, W.S.: Motivation theory reconsidered. Research In Organizational Behavior 9, 1–38 (1987)
40. Leuf, B., Cunningham, W.: The Wiki Way: Quick Collaboration on the Web. Addison-Wesley Professional (2001)
41. Majchrzak, A.: Comment: Where is the theory in wikis? MIS Quarterly 33(1), 18–20 (2009)
42. Majchrzak, A., Wagner, C., Yates, D.: Corporate wiki users: results of a survey. In: Riehle, D., Noble, J. (eds.) Proceedings of the 2006 International Symposium on Wikis, WikiSym 2006, pp. 99–104. ACM Press (2006)
43. Morris, M.G., Dillon, A.: How user perceptions influence software use. IEEE Software 14(4), 58–65 (1997)
44. Norman, D.: The Design of Everyday Things. Doubleday, New York (1990)
45. Norman, D.A.: Things that make us smart: defending human attributes in the age of the machine. Addison-Wesley, Reading (1993)
46. O'Reilly, T.: What is web 2.0? design patterns and business models for the next generation of software (2005), http://www.oreillynet.com/pub/a/oreilly/tim/news/2005/09/30/what-is-web-20.html
47. Orlikowski, W.J., Barley, S.R.: Technology and institutions: What can research on information technology and research on organizations learn from each other? MIS Quarterly 25(2), 145–165 (2001)
48. Rains, S.A.: The impact of anonymity on perceptions of source credibility and influence in computer-mediated group communication: A test of two competing hypotheses. Communication Research 34(1), 100–125 (2007)
49. Rashid, A.M., Ling, K., Tassone, R.D., Resnick, P., Kraut, R., Riedl, J.: Motivating participation by displaying the value of contribution. In: Proceedings of the SIGCHI Conference on Human Factors in Computing Systems, CHI 2006, p. 955 (2006)
50. Sabel, M.: Structuring wiki revision history. In: Proceedings of the 2007 International Symposium on Wikis, WikiSym 2007, pp. 125–130. ACM (2007)

51. Siegel, J., Dubrovsky, V., Kiesler, S., McGuire, T.W.: Group processes in computer-mediated communication. Organizational Behavior and Human Decision Processes 37(2), 157–187 (1986)
52. Stvilia, B., Twidale, M.B., Smith, L.C., Gasser, L.: Information quality work organization in Wikipedia. Journal of the American Society for Information Science and Technology 59(6), 983–1001 (2008)
53. Suh, B., Chi, E., Kittur, A., Pendleton, B.: Lifting the veil: Improving accountability and social transparency in Wikipedia with WikiDashboard. In: Proceedings of the Conference on Human Factors in Computing Systems CHI. ACM Press (2008)
54. Surowiecki, J.: The Wisdom of Crowds. Random House (2005)
55. Venkatesh, V., Morris, M.G., Davis, G.B., Davis, F.D.: User acceptance of information technology: Toward a unified view. MIS Quarterly 27(3), 425–478 (2003)
56. Viégas, F.B., Wattenberg, M., Dave, K.: Studying cooperation and conflict between authors with history flow visualizations. In: Proceedings of the 2004 Conference on Human Factors in Computing Systems, CHI 2004, vol. 6, pp. 575–582. ACM Press (2004)
57. Wagner, C.: Wiki: A technology for conversational knowledge management and group collaboration. Communications of the Association for Information Systems 13(13), 265–289 (2004)
58. Wagner, C.: Breaking the knowledge acquisition bottleneck through conversational knowledge management. Information Resources Management Journal 19, 70–83 (2006)
59. Wagner, C., Cheung, K.S.K., Ip, R.K.F., Bottcher, S.: Building semantic webs for e-government with wiki technology. Electronic Government An International Journal 3(1), 35–55 (2006)
60. Wagner, C., Majchrzak, A.: Enabling customer-centricity using wikis and the Wiki Way. Journal of Management Information Systems 23(3), 17–43 (2007)
61. Willinsky, J.: What open access research can do for Wikipedia. First Monday 12(3), 7 (2007), http://firstmonday.org/htbin/cgiwrap/bin/ojs/index.php/fm/article/view/1624
62. Yates, D., Wagner, C., Majchrzak, A.: Factors affecting shapers of organizational wikis. Journal of the American Society for Information Science 61(3), 543–554 (2010)
63. Zammuto, R.F., Griffith, T.L., Majchrzak, A., Dougherty, D.J., Faraj, S.: Information technology and the changing fabric of organization. Organization Science 18(5), 749–762 (2007)
64. Zwass, V.: Co-creation: Toward a taxonomy and an integrated research perspective. International Journal of Electronic Commerce 15(1), 11–48 (2010)

Appendix: Survey Items

Instructions. For all questions below, please indicate the degree to which you agree of disagree with the following statements. Possible answers:

- Strongly Disagree
- Somewhat Disagree
- Neither Agree Nor Disagree
- Somewhat Agree
- Strongly Agree

Table 2. Survey Items

Title	Question
Modifications in wiki deployment	
Unregistered Editing	Allowing anonymous postings will have a positive effect on my wiki participation.
Attributing Contributions	Publicizing (within and outside the wikis) the contribution of wiki users will have a positive effect on my wiki participation.
Peer-Based Quality-Control	Adding Rating to wiki articles would increase my participation.
Promoting Collaborative Authoring Norms	Clearly communicating wiki behavior norms (e.g., no personal attacks, formatting rules) will have a positive effect on my wiki participation.
Controlled Publishing	My wiki participation would increase if all wiki contributions were reviewed by an administrator who decided what to publish
Motivations	
Enjoyment	I enjoy using the wiki.
Learning new skills	Through my wiki activity, I'm learning new skills.
Belonging to a community	Participation in the wiki provides me with a sense of belonging to a community.
Self-expression	Wiki participation allows me to express my views and opinions.
Direct benefits	Using the wiki helps me to get the rewards I'm seeking.
Peer Pressure	I feel pressure from my peers and colleagues to participate in the wiki.
Supervisor Pressure	I feel pressure from my IBM supervisors to participate in the wiki.

Design Science as Design of Social Systems – Implications for Information Systems Research

Andreas Drechsler

University of Duisburg-Essen, Department for Information Systems for Production and
Operations Management, Universitätsstraße 9, 45141 Essen, Germany
andreas.drechsler@icb.uni-due.de

Abstract. There are indications that contemporary IS research is increasingly
concerned with the organizational environment in which information systems
are part of or used in. This means that IS design science approaches could benefit from concerning themselves with the organizational environment its design
artefacts are going to be implemented in, or even extend their perspectives to
organizational design, in which aspects of IS usage then play a central role. This
paper presents a design science approach for social systems from organizational
science and discusses its implications for contemporary IS research.

Keywords: design science, IS design, organizational design, social systems design, socio-technical systems design.

1   Motivation

While there is an ongoing discussion about the role and methodologies of design science in the Information Systems discipline, most of the discussions revolve around
the IT artefact and place it in the centre of deliberations [18] [27] [28]. Hevner et al.
suggest, for example, "to include not only instantiations in our definition of the IT
artefact, but also the constructs, models, and methods applied in the development and
use of information systems", while at the same time, they "do not include people or
elements of organizations" [18]. In a contrarian position, as put forth by Hess, for
example, it is suggested to make this organizational perspective the cornerstone of a
design science paradigm for IS (or rather, its German equivalent, "Wirtschaftsinformatik") [17]. This is also supported by Bygstad who classifies the IT infrastructure as an element of the organizational structure [6]. Furthermore, as shown in
greater detail in section 3.1, this also conforms to the general topical direction where
IS research seems to be heading. Therefore it could be worthwhile to explore how IS
design research could be influenced and improved by taking a deliberate organizational design perspective.

At the same time, there were discussions around rigor, relevance, and research
methods in the field of management and organizational research [34], which can be
regarded as in some ways comparable to similar discussions in Information Systems

K. Peffers, M. Rothenberger, and B. Kuechler (Eds.): DESRIST 2012, LNCS 7286, pp. 191–205, 2012.

[4]. Like in IS, there was also a development of design science approaches [30] [37] and their subsequent discussion and evaluation [26]. These approaches are not aimed at designing information systems, but social systems, like organizations. While the basic idea has been taken up in several publications in the field of IS (for example, by Alter [2], Iivari [21], McKay & Marshall [24], Hrastinski et al. [20], or Carlsson et al. [7] [8]), neither a "full-scale" transfer of a comprehensive approach from management research to the field of IS, nor a discussion of actual implications of such a transfer for key fields of IS research has yet taken place. As Kuechler & Vaishnavi note, such a transfer can serve to mitigate the "view of IS design science research as a 'hard' engineering practice" by drawing a greater amount of attention to the business environment [23]. One related field is the application of action research in the IS design science context [32]; however there are also critical voices who characterize action research as "seemingly similar, but decisively dissimilar" to design science [22].

The goal of this paper is to show potential ways and benefits of applications of design science approaches from management research to relevant fields of IS research, exemplified by the most comprehensive one by van Aken et al. In order to do this, it will first present this approach and afterwards discuss its implications as well as its limitations for the two most suitable areas of current IS research, which are identified based on a brief analysis of the tracks of recent IS conferences.

2   A Design Approach for Designing Social Systems

This section presents a generic design science approach for organizations based on the work of van Aken [37] [38] [39], Denyer et al. [9], and Huff et al. [19]. It serves as the foundation for the subsequent discussions of its implications for IS research. Of the various contributions to the aforementioned design science discussion in management research, van Aken's approach can be regarded as the most comprehensive one, which is the reason why it is chosen here. His approach is grounded on Simon's "Sciences of the Artificial" [33] and Bunge's work about technological design rules [5]. It is summarized in figure 1 and expanded by suitable research, where applicable, as mentioned.

According to van Aken, any organizational design effort should start with types of organizational problems or actors' goals rooted in the real world [38: 225]. The design artefact should aim to improve the organizational reality by solving the problems or reaching the goals [39: 68]. Ideally, the design artefact should be applicable beyond a singular case and also contain a solid, scientific foundation.

The input for the scientific design process is provided by theories of the "explanatory sciences" [9: 394]. Van Aken distinguishes here between two types of theories. Descriptive theories contain "truths" about the "real world", while prescriptive theories contain "truths" about theory-based and empirically validated, heuristic design rules [37: 235]. However, these design rules should not be causal input-output-(IO) rules ("If X, then Y").

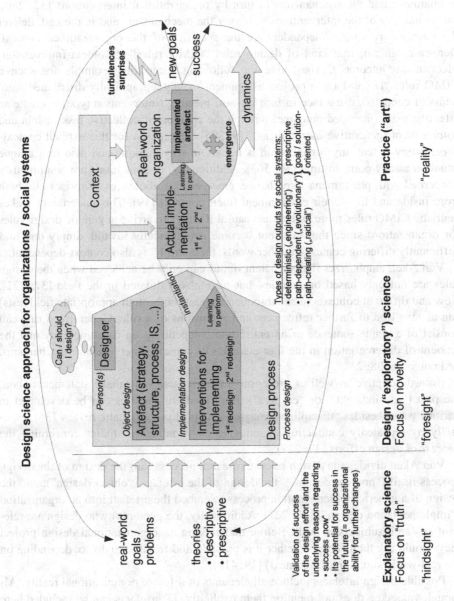

Fig. 1. Process for the design of social systems according to van Aken et al.

Instead, he suggests design rules where the final result is triggered by certain mechanisms and the mechanisms in turn by organizational interventions [37: 230]. The suitability of the interventions to trigger the mechanisms, and in the end, deliver the intended results, is dependent on the specifics of the organizational context. Denyer et al. call this kind of design rules "CIMO rules" ("Context-Intervention-Mechanism-Outcome"). They give the following, simplified example for such a CIMO rule: "If you have a project assignment for a geographically distributed team (class of contexts), use a face-to-face kick-off meeting (intervention type) to create an effective team (intended outcome) through the creation of collective task insight and commitment (generative mechanisms)" [9: 396]. The reason for this explicit context-dependency is that any organization is in certain ways unique and also in a unique situation at any point in time [30: 563]. Additionally, organizations are continuously concerned with phenomena like change, emergence, turbulences, surprises etc. both from inside and from their environment (their context) [19]. This uncertainty makes heuristic CIMO rules more suited than causal IO rules to arrive at generic design rules for organizations since they will not become automatically invalid simply due to a sufficiently differing context. In other words, their "truth" is also context-dependent.

Van Aken emphasizes that sufficient rigour can only be achieved when the design rules are not only based on theories, but were also validated in the field [37: 221]. New and different contexts (and subsequent validation through appropriate field tests) can always lead to further refinement and extensions of a rule. Generally, a rule can consist of a single sentence or an entire book, depending on its complexity and the amount of differentiation in the four elements of context, interventions, mechanisms, and outcome [38: 23].

Both descriptive as well as prescriptive theories can only make statements about the past ("in hindsight", or "ex post"). Both kinds of theories can be developed in various ways, besides "disciplined imagination" [41] or systematic review [36], especially by repeatedly conducting quantitative and qualitative studies concerning the success of design efforts [37: 229]

Van Aken divides the design science research process into the design of the design process itself ("process design"), the design of the artefact ("object design"), and the design of a generic implementation process to embed the artefact into an organization ("implementation design") [37: 227]. Additionally, the person(s) who design are relevant research subjects as well. Before undertaking an organizational design project they should ask themselves whether it is possible and feasible to do so, depending on the real-world situation (the context) [19: 419].

Possible design artefacts include all elements of a future organizational reality. Although van Aken does not mention them explicitly, IT artefacts can be included here as well since they form a core element of today's organizational realities and are often tightly interwoven with organizational structures and business processes [6]. Every implementation process is divided into three phases "by design": two redesigns followed by a final phase of "learning to perform" [39: 75]. In the first redesign phase the generic artefact needs to be formally adapted to the specific organization and its context. The second phase allows relevant organizational actors (managers and users, for example) to further adjust (deliberately and emergent) the artefact during the introduction process. These adjustments continue while every one "learns to perform" until the artefact is fully embedded inside the organizational routines.

Unlike the previously outlined approaches for explanatory science, this design science approach does not focus on "ex-post" explanations but on creating novelty "ex-ante" (or "in foresight") instead, aiming to deliver valid design propositions – manifesting themselves in design artefacts – beyond singular cases or applications [19: 418].

The implementation of a designed artefact finally is regarded as "art" of practitioners [19: 416]. They need to take their specific organization and their specific context into account, and instantiate and adapt the "design blueprints", in order to be able to successfully integrate the design artefact into their organization. In a singular case, context factors, organizational dynamics, and phenomena of emergence influence whether such an implementation effort eventually leads to success or failure. The same factors may also lead to new goals and problems which in turn may lead to a continuous cycle of evaluation, design, and implementation [12].

The success of such a design effort can manifest itself on the one hand in reaching goals or solving problems "now", but on the other hand also in sustaining and increasing the ability of an organization to solve problems or to transform itself in the future [12]. Van Aken further differentiates between "alpha tests" and "beta tests" [37: 232]. Alpha tests for him mean the repeated instantiation of a management artefact in similar contexts, while beta tests are about the subsequent application in differing contexts. The goal of these tests is to reach a broad and at the same time differentiated validation of the design artefact and the underlying design rules while deliberately taking the instantiation contexts into account. Eventually, these tests will lead not only to a validation, but also to an expansion of the underlying theoretical foundations, which in turn will benefit further design efforts.

3   Fields of Application in Information Systems Research

3.1   Relevant Fields of Contemporary IS Research

Before the implications of the presented approach for IS research can be discussed, there needs to be further differentiation of what constitutes contemporary IS research, since IS is not a unified research discipline. IS conferences are a major outlet for publication of IS research, and, unlike journals, provide a set of categories (= tracks) every conference publication is classified under. Table 1 shows the tracks of the most recent and the upcoming ECIS and ICIS conferences (2011 and 2012), further classified according to the focus of their research. Two identified categories can be characterized as having a generic focus or a focus on IS research itself. Then there is one category of IS research with a technological focus. Several other categories can be identified as having different kinds of organizational foci. The "hybrid" category finally contains tracks where both submissions with a technological and with an organizational focus could be considered appropriate.

Table 1. Classification of IS conference tracks

Category	Tracks
Generic	Alternative Genres, Breakthrough Ideas, General Track, General Topics, East meets West
Research and Teaching	IS in Education, IS Curriculum, Education and Teaching Cases (SIGED), Research Methods, Serious Games and Simulations, Engaged Scholarship through Design and Action, IS Curriculum and Education, Research Methods and Philosophy
Technological focus	Enterprise Architecture & Governance, Mobile and Pervasive Computing, Technology Substitution, Smart Mobile Media Services
Hybrid	Adoption and diffusion, IS Security and Privacy, Digital Innovation in the Service Economy, Digital and Social Networks, IS Security and Privacy, IT Global Services and Cloud Computing, Visual Media, Data and Information Quality, Global Service Infrastructures, WEB2.0 – Business Value of Social Networks, Service Science
Individual focus	Human Computer Interaction, Human Behavior in IT Adoption and Use, Human Capital
Organizational focus: IS in functions / industries	Accounting Information Systems and ERP, Business Intelligence and Knowledge Management, Enterprise Transformation, E-health, IT-Enabled Supply Chain Management, Public Sector ICT – Citizen Empowerment and Agency Transparency, IT for Health Care Management, Business Process Management, Evolution from E-Government to Transformational Government, Knowledge Management for Sustainability
Organizational focus: IS management / governance, IS project management	Information Technology (IT) Project Management, Global Sourcing Management, IT/IS Management and Development Methodologies, Economics and Value of IS, Governance and Management of IS, IT and Service Management, Project Management, Outsourcing and IS Development
Organizational focus: Aspects of IS in social systems	Co-Creating Innovations, Social Computing and Collaboration, Social and Organizational Impacts of IS, Global, International and Cultural Issues in IS, Behavioral, Social and Organizational Aspects of IS, Culture in the IS/T Service Lifecycle, Online Communities and Digital Collaborations, Organization Theory, Strategy, and Information Systems
Organizational focus: Other	IT for Global Welfare & Sustainability, E-Business and Competitive Strategy, Green IS and Sustainability, Economics and Information Systems, Green Information Systems, Innovation Theory, Research and Practice in IS

The classification shown in Table 1 supports the notion put forth in the introduction, that design science in IS should deliberately take into account the organizational perspective, because it would otherwise be limited to just a few areas of research (research methods itself, the areas with a technological focus, and arguably the topics in the "hybrid" category). Moreover, the analysis shows that there are several different kinds of "organizational contexts" IS research is concerned with. One rather large branch – at least, based on the number of conference tracks – of IS research is concerned with function- or industry-specific IS. While the particulars of each specific implementation (instance) of these IS will vary, it can be surmised that their organizational contexts will also share some similarities, which in turn means that they can be taken into account during the design phase. Another branch of IS research focuses less on IT and IS, but more on organizational management systems for the governance of the IT and IS in enterprises, or for IT project management. Here, design science would be originally concerned with organizational design. A third branch is concerned with specific fields and aspects of organizational and sociological research focusing on the topic of IS. From a design science perspective, the respective topics here are well suited to provide explanatory insight and design propositions for both IS design and organizational design. A deeper look at the topics of this category shows a great variety of research angles; therefore it is difficult at this point – and outside the scope of this paper – to discuss possible design science directions on a general, category-wide level. From the topics in the "organizational focus: other" category especially "E-Business and Competitive Strategy" stands out, on the one hand because it can also be classified as a topic of management research, and on the other hand because there are already design science perspectives on e-business and entrepreneurship discussed in the management research literature [31].

The following sections will now discuss the implications of the previously presented approach for organizational design science for design research in the IS discipline. From the categories outlined above, the discussion will focus on the two "main" categories of relevance identified in the context of design science: function-/industry-specific IS on the one hand and organizational management systems for IS management, governance and project management on the other hand. Since the latter is closer to the "original purpose" of the previously presented approach, it will be discussed first. Afterwards, the implications for IS design are discussed.

3.2 Design of Management Systems for IS Management, Governance, and Project Management

This section now will show the potential of the previously outlined design science approach to the fields of IS/IT management, governance and IT project management (henceforth, IS management). The structure of this chapter follows the elements in figure 1.

A design science approach for IS management would mean designing IS management artefacts that aim to solve real-world problems or goals of IT departments and project teams. Here, the outcomes of typical topics of IS management research (business IT alignment, IT governance, IT service management etc.) or project management research can be viewed as providing abstract, potential solutions for classes of these problems. In addition, the necessity to formulate explicit problems or goals at the start of a design effort might uncover IS management issues faced by practitioners which have not been tackled yet by IS management research.

As outlined above, according to van Aken, the explanatory sciences form the major source of input for the design process. For IS management research this generally means conceptual papers and empirical studies about IS management and project management topics. However, a "translation" of the research outcomes into CIMO design rules (or design propositions, as Carlsson et al. suggest as a potentially more appropriate term [8]) might be necessary to achieve direct applicability during the design process. Other theoretical outcomes can still be used to provide argumentative support for a certain design rule. Regarding the frequent use of causal models in IS research, Gregor and Horvorka provide a framework regarding different types of causality in different types of research settings (and hence, theories) [16]. While this issue cannot be covered in more detail at this point, it is worth noting that explanatory sciences tend to rely on different types of causality than design sciences. Therefore, a simple "interchange" of causal input-output(IO-)rules and the aforementioned heuristic CIMO design rules is not possible when grounding design decisions on empirical findings from IS management research.

Since the design process is problem- or goal-driven, it is explicitly necessary to include the designer(s) in the approach since their perceived problems and their personal goals drive the whole design effort. Potential designers here include researchers, managers, and consultants in the area of IT management. Venkatesh regards the actors or actions in the IS design science debate as "under-socialized" and sees the designer of a social system as an agent [40]. As a result of this agency issue, designers might further their own interests through the design, instead of pursuing organization-related goals, for example. A further challenge arises due to the possibility that the persons who design a generic IS management artefact are not necessarily the same who implement an instantiated artefact in a specific IS management organization in practice. Here, methods regarding stakeholder management (for example, from software requirements engineering) might be a worthwhile addition to the design process in this case. The previously outlined question "Can/should I design?" is also a relevant one to keep in mind for IS management design efforts. Pries-Heje et al. call this "artificial ex-ante evaluation" of a design artefact [28].

Any object design resulting of a design science approach to IS management consists of a model of future organizational reality (or parts thereof) of an IS management organization. It might contain elements of, e. g., an IS strategy, the organizational structure of the IT department or the project management organization, IS management or project management processes, or IT infrastructure for IS management purposes. The literature from management research generally seems to assume that a specification in natural language is the most suitable; the issue is not explicitly discussed. But in order to be able to model this future organizational reality in a rigorous way, more formal ways of specification should supplant the potentially ambiguous natural language. Here, approaches from enterprise modelling can be employed, for example the MEMO language by Frank [10], in order to model relevant aspects of the future organizational reality of the IT organization as well as relevant context factors. There is also a first outline of a modelling language specifically aimed at the area of IS management [11].

The implementation design can be interpreted as being about designing actions for "change management" which, for an IS management artefact, can include both organizational elements (establishing a project management organization, changes in IS management processes, training of IT staff, etc.) and technical elements (customizing of IS management software, its integration into the infrastructure, etc.). Since this area is arguably the least specific for the application of the generic design science approach to the area of IS management, there are several examples from the management research literature which can be drawn upon to illustrate the role of design efforts for organizational change and development (see [3] for an overview).

The instantiation in practice can be viewed as the bridge between science and the "art" of IT managers and consultants to instantiate and adapt the object and implementation design to the specific context in practice. The major challenge here for them is to account for the "uniqueness" of every IS management organization, regarding both the social and the technical elements of the respective socio-technical system. From a researcher's perspective this also means a lack of control over the application of the object design and therefore the potential end of the "chain of rigour" throughout the entire design process. Since researchers rarely get involved into organizational changes in practice, Carlsson et al. discuss the collaboration with consultancy firms in order to support a controlled transfer of design research outcomes into practice and the subsequent evaluation [8].

This evaluation of the success of an IS management design effort needs to be context specific due to the general problem- or goal-orientation of the whole approach. Any success or failure can be attributed to the (in)adequacy of the object design, the implementation design, their instantiation in practice, and/or the underlying goals for the whole effort. A thorough evaluation of each design instantiation is necessary to achieve scientific progress regarding the designed IT management artefact, the underlying theories, and the methods employed during the design process. In the end, the results of the evaluation can lead to a confirmation or revision of the object design, the implementation design, the design process, and/or the underlying theoretical foundations in form of design rules or descriptive theories.

3.3   Design of Information Systems as Future Part of Social Systems

This section now will show the potential of the previously outlined design science approach to the field of IS design. While the name of the respective category in section 3.1 highlighted the function- or industry-specific nature of IS typically discussed at IS conferences, this section will take a more generic perspective on the issue of IS design. The contents should be therefore applicable to any function- or industry-specific kind of IS design. After a brief discussion of the general relationship between IT, IS and organizations / social systems in order to draw an explicit connection between IS in organizations and the previously outlined design science approach, the remainder of this section will follow the elements in figure 1.

While there are no universally accepted definitions, the term IT commonly means either actual instances of hardware and software or, on a more abstract level, certain concepts, classes, or types of hardware and software. The term IS, on the other hand, normally includes the organizational context and purpose of IT in-use. In other words, the term IS describes socio-technical systems, consisting of people and machines (IT among them), which serve certain business purposes for information processing or communication according to economic criteria [29: 6]. Such systems are also called Human-Task-Technology systems [17] (M-A-T in the original German: Mensch-Aufgabe-Technik). This implies that, while the IT perspective highlights the technological side of IS, the IS perspective takes a more holistic stance and acknowledges that it is the human factor in the end, which can make the application of IT a useful one, creating value out of their usage within an organization. This means that a design science approach concerning organizational design is less relevant when the IT part of an IS lies in the focus in the design effort, but becomes more relevant, the more the human or organizational part of an IS design artefact stands at the forefront. The upcoming discussions will assume such a case.

As with design efforts for organizational IS management systems outlined in the previous section, designs of information systems can be interpreted as potential solutions for classes of real-world problems or goals of organizations. From a research point of view, this can be interpreted as a call for relevance through design research (solving issues at hand) [38], while from a practical perspective, it mostly are business or organizational issues which are to be solved through IS designs, and not technological issues. This further reinforces the potential of the design approach presented before for relevant IS design research.

Since the eventual solution needs to contain both technological and organizational elements (otherwise it would probably not be an issue for the IS discipline), the object and implementation design will likewise have to contain both, and additionally show (abstract, non-instantiated) ways how these two "worlds" can and should interact. For the explanatory sciences, this means likewise that conceptual and empirical research outcomes about technological aspects, organizational aspects, and their interactions are potential sources for formulating IS design propositions. The aforementioned CIMO rules are specifically aimed at formulating design propositions suitable for organizations; their suitability for IS design (or certain parts thereof) needs to be discussed in more detail than the space available here allows. Depending on the outcomes of these discussions, the remarks regarding the different forms of causality from the previous section might apply here as well.

Regarding the person(s) of the designer, an IS design encompassing a technological and an organizational perspective requires designers well-versed in both fields, or experts in each, who share a common language and are able to integrate their different viewpoints into the construction of coherent design artefacts.

At the end of the design process, the IS object design should consist of an abstract design of an IS (or rather, of a class of specific instances of IS) which is potentially suitable to solve real-world organizational goals. Since off-the-shelf software becomes more and more commonplace [35], the object design can be a software design and implementation for a new kind of IS, or a reference process model giving guidance on how to collect requirements, choose, and customize appropriate off-the-shelf software [1]. The object design should also include a link to an (abstract) implementation process, or in other words, the implementation design.

Like the object design, the IS implementation design will probably consist of technological and organizational aspects of the introduction (or instantiation) of the abstract IS in a specific organization. On the technical side, an implementation design could specify the necessary and possible ways to customize the object design and to install it into a given IT infrastructure. The organizational side can give a process framework to manage these customization and installation efforts, in addition to specifying processes of generic organizational change management, specifically tailored to the situational elements of future implementations which can be assumed as invariant due to the nature of the IS (for example, function or industry-dependent). Again, these issues can be covered by reference models [1].

Each implementation effort of the abstract IS design means a context-specific instantiation effort of both the object and the implementation design. The instantiated implementation design will concern the actual effort to instantiate and customize the object design for a specific situation, integrate it into a specific IT infrastructure, and introduce it into the organizational processes and routines through possibly several phases of redesign and a final phase where the end users "learn to perform".

After this, an evaluation phase can and should evaluate the validity of the IS designs and the underlying design rules. The split between an abstract IS object and implementation design, together with their explicit context-specific instantiation, allows an analytical distinction between phases of adoption and usage of the IS design in question. This split further allows the possibility to attribute a successful design to the IS artefacts themselves (on the design level) or to the specific customizations during a context-specific instantiation (on the instance level). At the same time, the "success" of an IS design becomes context-specific itself. Different organizations (and the actors responsible for the introduction of the artefact) may have different goals for introducing an IS. This means taking into account context- and stakeholder-specific dimensions of success for measuring success and validity of an IS design. Through the extended organizational perspective, any success or failure of an IS design can also be influenced by surprises from its environment or internal phenomena of emergence. At the same time, a skilled manager of organizational change can account for such phenomena or deficiencies of an artefact during an actual (instantiated) implementation process. In the end, an extended organizational perspective like this means the possibility of a differentiated analysis of factors contributing to success or failure of an IS artefact, but at the same time such a differentiated analysis can lead to a "dilution" of the term "IS success". Again, further discussions of this issue are limited by the space available here.

In a wider perspective, utilizing an approach as presented before can also be seen as a step towards evidence-based design of IS [25] [13]. The publication of evaluations of IS design efforts can create suitable sources of data on which the necessary studies and reviews can be based.

4   Limitations

Both the presented design science approach for social systems as well as the transfer onto the IS discipline are not without limitations. First, its underlying problem- or goal-oriented attitude excludes identification of "breakthrough", novel problems, goals, or issues through research. This indicates that a design science approach should be deliberately supplemented by suitable research approaches capable of arriving at novel research questions, for example by "theorizing as disciplined imagination", as proposed by Weick for management research [41]. The object and implementation design for the organizational part might need to be specified in potentially ambiguous natural language and simple diagrams since there are no suitable, sufficiently comprehensive modelling languages yet for modelling social systems. Due to the unique and volatile nature of social systems in practice, the instantiation, adaption, and implementation of design artefacts in practice can be more like an "art" than a science, being out of rigorous control by the researcher. This also leads to a challenge to attribute success and failure of each instantiation effort clearly to the object design, the implementation design, the underlying theories or the instantiation itself, and on top of it, to attribute it to the technological or the organizational part of the designs. Additionally, methodical support for evaluation, which is thin for design science aimed at IT artefacts as stated by Pries-Heje et al. [28], is even scarcer for the evaluation of designs of social systems.

While it is conceivable that management research might provide more in that regard, there is little to find in the literature, except for a somewhat "eclectic application" of methods from empirical research in respective papers. One reason for this might be that the design science paradigm is not a part of the management research „mainstream". Most of the relevant literature stems from a few special issues in certain journals. Additionally, most research remains on a theoretical and conceptual level. The discussions around design science in management research also are often superseded by more general discussions around rigor vs. relevance where design science serves as an example of a way of conducting more relevant management research. Additionally, Pandza and Thorpe warn against an overly deterministic, "engineering-like" interpretation of the design metaphor in the light of the design object "organization" / "social system" which is complex, dynamic and impossible to fully grasp for both (potential) designers and researchers [26].

Regarding the transfer for IS research, the classification of major streams of current IS research was based just on an analysis of conference tracks and could be expanded into journals, other conferences, more years, and an in-depth analysis of papers instead of relying on general track descriptions. This was skipped here due to space restrictions, but should nevertheless should provide a suitable foundation for the distinction of general streams of IS research. Additionally, the application and implications could only be discussed in a very broad way and with a lack of empirical grounding, so this clearly leaves a lot of room for further research regarding the possibilities and limitations of an organizational design science approach for IS research.

5   Conclusion

Drawing on an approach from management science, this paper presented a comprehensive design science approach for organizations, which was shown to be utilizable both for the design of information systems and organizational structures for IS management. The approach aims to solve real-world problems by producing designs of a future organizational reality, of which IS can form a crucial part. The theoretical inputs can consist of explanatory results from empirical research and prescriptive technological design rules. To account for the nature of organizations, each of these design rules should contain four elements: context, interventions, mechanisms, and outcome. The design artefact is divided further into an object design specifying a "blueprint" for the future organizational reality itself, and an implementation design specifying a "blueprint" for the change management effort to implement the object design in an organization. For application in an actual organization, both the object design and the implementation design need to be instantiated in a practical setting in a context-specific way. After the conclusion of the implementation effort, a thorough evaluation needs to take place, allowing the validation or refinement of the design effort and its theoretical foundations. Applied to the field of IS, this can lead to a steadily growing field-tested "body of knowledge" of IS design research. From a research perspective, rigour can be achieved by adhering to the overall research process and by following the state-of-the-art of empirical or design research in each step. At the same time, relevance is fostered due to the focus on practical application of a design artefact.

In order to evaluate the potential and limitations of such a design approach in practice, there need to be adaptations to specific research settings, subsequent practical applications and thorough validations of the approach for various forms of IS research and in several different contexts of information systems and organizations. In addition, the presented approach can potentially benefit from an in-depth discussion and a possible integration with (or distinction from) other approaches from similar directions from IS research, for example those which were mentioned briefly in the introduction.

References

1. Ahlemann, F., Gastl, H.: Process Model for an Empirically Grounded Reference Model Construction. In: Fettke, P., Loos, P. (eds.) Reference Modelling for Business Systems Analysis, pp. 77–97. Idea Group, Hershey (2007)
2. Alter, S.: Sidestepping the IT Artifact, Scrapping the IS Silo, and Laying Claim to "Systems in Organizations". Communications of the AIS 12(1), 494–526 (2003)
3. Bate, P.: Bringing the Design Sciences to Organization Development and Change Management. The Journal of Applied Behavioral Science 43(1), 8–11 (2007)
4. Benbasat, I., Zmud, R.W.: Empirical research in Information Systems: The practice of relevance. MIS Quarterly 23(1), 3–16 (1999)
5. Bunge, M.: Scientific Research II: The Search for Truth. Springer, Berlin (1967)

6. Bygstad, B.: Information infrastructure as organization, a critical realist view. In: Proceedings of the 29th International Conference on Information Systems, Paris (2008)
7. Carlsson, S.A.: Design Science Research in Information Systems: A Critical Realist Approach. In: Hevner, A.R., Chatterjee, S. (eds.) Design Research in Information Systems: Theory & Practice, pp. 209–233. Springer, New York (2010)
8. Carlsson, S.A., Henningsson, S., Hrastinski, S., Keller, C.: Socio-technical IS design science research: developing design theory for IS integration management. Journal for Information Systems & E-Business Management 9(1), 109–131 (2011)
9. Denyer, D., Tranfield, D., van Aken, J.E.: Developing design propositions through research synthesis. Organization Studies 29(3), 393–413 (2008)
10. Frank, U.: Multi-Perspective Enterprise Modeling (MEMO): Conceptual Framework and Modeling Languages. In: Proceedings of the 35th Hawaii International Conference on System Sciences (HICSS-35), Honolulu (2002)
11. Frank, U., Heise, D., Kattenstroth, H., Ferguson, D., Hadar, E., Waschke, M.: ITML: A Domain-Specific Modeling Language for Supporting Business Driven IT Management. In: Tolvanen, J.-P., Rossi, M., Gray, J., Sprinkle, J. (eds.) Proceedings of the 9th OOPSLA Workshop on Domain-Specific Modeling, Helsinki (2009)
12. Garud, R., Jain, S., Tuertscher, P.: Incomplete by design and designing for incompleteness. Organization Science 16(4), 599–617 (2008)
13. Goeken, M.: Towards an evidence-based research approach in information systems. In: Proceedings of the 32nd International Conference on Information Systems, Shanghai (2011)
14. Gregor, S.: The nature of theory in information systems. MIS Quarterly 30(3), 611–642 (2006)
15. Gregor, S., Jones, D.: The anatomy of a design theory. Journal of the AIS 8(5), 312–335 (2007)
16. Gregor, S., Hovorka, D.: Causality: The elephant in the room in information systems epistemology. In: Proceedings of the 18th European Conference on Information Systems, Pretoria (2010)
17. Hess, T.: Erkenntnisgegenstand der konstruktionsorientierten Wirtschaftsinformatik. In: Österle, H., Winter, R., Brenner, W. (eds.) Gestaltungsorientierte Wirtschaftsinformatik: Ein Plädoyer für Rigor und Relevanz, Nuremberg, Infowerk, pp. 7–11 (2010)
18. Hevner, A.R., March, S.T., Park, J., Ram, S.: Design science in information systems research. MIS Quarterly 28(1), 75–105 (2004)
19. Huff, A.S., Tranfield, D., van Aken, J.E.: Management as a design science mindful of art and surprise. Journal of Management Inquiry 15(4), 413–424 (2006)
20. Hrastinski, S., Carlsson, S., Henningsson, S., Keller, C.: On how to develop design theories for IS use and management. In: Proceedings of the 16th European Conference on Information Systems, Galway (2008)
21. Iivari, J.: The IS Core - VII: Towards Information Systems as a Science of Meta-Artifacts. Communications of the AIS 12(1), 568–581 (2003)
22. Iivari, J., Venable, J.: Action research and design science research - seemingly similar but decisively dissimilar. In: Proceedings of the 17th European Conference on Information Systems, Verona (2009)
23. Kuechler, B., Vaishnavi, V.: The Emergence of Design Research in Information Systems in North America. Journal of Design Research 7(1), 1–16 (2008)
24. McKay, J., Marshall, P.: Science, Design, and Design Science: Seeking Clarity to Move Design Science Research Forward in Information Systems. In: Proceedings of the 18th Australasian Conference on Information Systems, Towoomba (2007)

25. Oates, B.: Evidence-based Information Systems: A decade later. In: Proceedings of the 19th European Conference on Information Systems, Helsinki (2011)
26. Pandza, K., Thorpe, R.: Management as Design but What Kind of Design? An Appraisal of the Design Science Analogy for Management. British Journal of Management 21(1), 171–186 (2010)
27. Peffers, K., Tuunanen, T., Rothenberger, M.A., Chatterjee, S.: A design science research methodology for information systems research. Journal of Management Information Systems 24(3), 45–77 (2007)
28. Pries-Heje, J., Baskerville, R., Venable, J.R.: Strategies for design science research evaluation. In: Proceedings of the 29th International Conference on Information Systems, Paris (2008)
29. Rainer, R.K., Turban, E., Potter, R.E.: Introduction to Information Systems. Wiley, Hoboken (2007)
30. Romme, A.G.L.: Making a difference: organization as design. Organization Science 14(5), 558–573 (2003)
31. Sarasvathy, S., Dew, N., Read, S., Wiltbank, R.: Designing Organizations that Design Environments: Lessons from Entrepreneurial Expertise. Organization Studies 29(3), 331–350 (2008)
32. Sein, M.K., Henfridsson, O., Purao, S., Rossi, M., Lindgren, R.: Action Design Research. MIS Quarterly 35(1), 37–56 (2011)
33. Simon, H.A.: Sciences of the Artificial, 3rd edn. MIT Press, Cambridge (1996)
34. Starkey, K., Madan, P.: Bridging the relevance gap: aligning stakeholders in the future of management research. British Journal of Management 12(S1), S3–S26 (2001)
35. Strong, D., Volkoff, O.: Understanding Organization-Enterprise System Fit: A Path to Theorizing the Information Technology Artefact. MIS Quarterly 34(4), 731–756 (2010)
36. Tranfield, D.R., Denyer, D., Smart, P.K.: Towards a Methodology for Developing Evidence-Informed Management Knowledge by Means of Systematic Review. British Journal of Management 14(3), 207–222 (2003)
37. Van Aken, J.E.: Management research based on the paradigm of the design sciences: the quest for field-tested and grounded technological rules. Journal of Management Studies 41(2), 219–246 (2004)
38. Van Aken, J.E.: Management research as a design science: articulating the research products of mode 2 knowledge production in management. British Journal of Management 16(1), 19–36 (2005)
39. Van Aken, J.E.: Design science and organization development interventions: aligning business and humanistic values. Journal of Applied Behavioural Science 43(1), 67–88 (2007)
40. Venkatesh, M.: On Social Design. In: Proceedings of the 29th International Conference on Information Systems, Paris (2008)
41. Weick, K.E.: Theory construction as disciplined imagination. Academy of Management Review 14(4), 516–531 (1989)

Towards Design Engineering of Ubiquitous Information Systems

Wolfgang Maass and Sabine Janzen

Saarland University, 66123 Saarbrücken, Germany
{firstname.lastname}@iss.uni-saarland.de

Abstract. Designing complex information systems is a task performed by design teams with team members coming from different domains with different expertise. Shared understanding between members of a design team throughout a project is still a challenge. A design framework is presented that integrates individual design knowledge, explicit design knowledge used by design teams, and computational design knowledge. For each type of design knowledge, several modeling languages for expressing conceptual models are known. Translation processes between these characteristic design knowledge explications are introduced. Core elements of this design framework, i.e., modeling languages and translations, are discussed by a Ubiquitous Information System (UIS) development project that was conducted over the period of several years.

Keywords: Conceptual modeling, shared understanding, design methodology, Ubiquitous Information Systems, semantic technologies, patterns.

1 Introduction

Despite the importance of information systems for any kind of business and governmental activity, practical projects typically show poor quality of requirements, misunderstandings between members of an IS design team, insufficient communication between team members, and fuzzy business objectives. In a recent study it was described that less than 50% of requirements are captured in business-relevant IS projects and less than 20% of business needs are followed by scenarios [1]. Out of five possibilities, 43% of IT and business persons think that there is often confusion around what business stakeholders are asking for [1]. Perceived as being most frustrating about the requirements definition process are getting business to clearly state and commit to project objectives (46%) [1]. Studies like this indicate that shared understanding in design teams is one of the most pressing issues for predictable and successful information systems (IS) projects.

Research on risks in information system development projects indicate that scope and requirements are perceived as being one of the main reasons for failing projects [2]. Out of the top ten of project risks, five are related to expressing and managing knowledge between members of a design team [2]. Improved forms and methods for conceptual modeling have been investigated to find means for improving software

K. Peffers, M. Rothenberger, and B. Kuechler (Eds.): DESRIST 2012, LNCS 7286, pp. 206–219, 2012.

development productivity [3]. Several proposals exist for different kinds of conceptual modeling languages supporting different kinds of information systems and information technologies, such as UML for object-oriented system design and development [4]. These conceptual modeling languages are generally used for helping technical designers and programmers "to more efficiently translate requirements into artifacts" and, thus, support perceived common understanding between members of a design team [4]. Most of this research is descriptive and analytical, i.e. ex-post analysis of established types of information systems. For the innovative class of Ubiquitous Information Systems (UIS), traditional software engineering and IS development methods are considered insufficient because, for instance, it also requires consideration of product development and the design of physical environments [5]. Therefore, we use the innovative class of UIS for investigating knowledge transformation processes during innovative IS development projects. The key research issues are (1) a better understanding how knowledge is translated throughout a design process with the help of various conceptual models as means for expressing knowledge structures and (2) how accuracy relationships between these models can be maintained.

By taking a knowledge-based view [6], we propose an IS development framework for UIS based on a knowledge translation process [7] that supports the translation of individual representations into explicated conceptual models on a particular UIS. This framework was developed alongside the development of a UIS by a multinational and interdisciplinary IS design team. By empirical studies, we measured (1) backward compatibility as a tentative means for accuracy relationships between conceptual models and (2) fit between models and targeted usage situations with a focus on a service-situation fit.

2   Design Knowledge in Information System Development

It is informative for IS design science to note that traditional product development knows various challenges [8] that also govern IS development: trade-offs, dynamics, details, time pressure, and economical goals. Also intrinsic attributes for successful product development can be directly adopted: creation, satisfaction of societal and individual needs, team diversity, and team spirit [8]. All challenges and attributes can be summed up by asserting that product developments and also IS developments are taking place in highly volatile environments with experts from different domains working together towards mutually agreed goals. Furthermore Ulrich and Eppinger state that structured methods are valuable for three reasons: (1) Make the decision process explicit, (2) by acting as "checklists" of the key steps in a development activity they ensure that important issues are not forgotten, and (3) structured methods are largely self-documenting [8].

Following this structured approach, we perceive the whole development process as a knowledge transforming system [7] that does not distinguish between information and product. Instead we perceive a product and service as a pure realization of knowledge objects. The design process concludes when design knowledge is transformed into a knowledge object representation that can be directly realized by an appropriate matter (e.g., metal, software, humans etc.) based on existing methods, procedures, and tools.

2.1 Translation of Design Knowledge

Completeness and accuracy of representations communicated between members of a design team are central influence factors for IS project success [9]. Representations are outcomes of purposeful mental, linguistic, and social interactions in design teams that support common understandings throughout the whole IS development process [9].

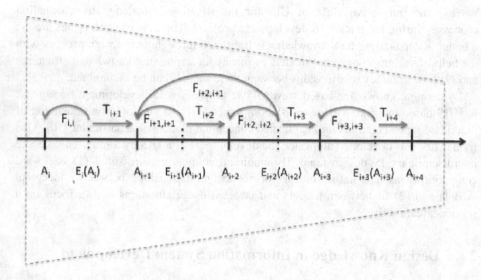

Fig. 1. Translation Process

From a knowledge perspective, design initiatives constantly translate various types of knowledge into different formats based on different languages resulting in various artifacts. Artifacts A_i are conceptually conceived by an actor through the semantics of a language and expressed by the syntactical structure of a language (cf. Fig. 1). An actor mentally conceives *implicit artifacts* while *explicit artifacts* are based on semantics that are shared in a community and expressed by syntactical structures that are used by a community. Explicit design-oriented artifacts are either *pure documentation* for humans (explicated design knowledge) or expressed in structures that can be executed by machinery, and in particular computational machinery (computational design knowledge). Design teams might use evaluations E_i of an artifact A_i for testing, for instance, consistency, compatibility with other artifacts, business fit, functional fit, and technology fit. Thus evaluations are used to improve the quality of a design process and to ensure common understanding. Translations T_i allow derivation of an artifact A_j from an individual or set of artifacts. Most product development processes but also software development process prescribe translations between various artifacts [8, 10]. Evaluations that indicate problems with a particular artifact might result in feedbacks F_i to previous artifacts [11]. Feedbacks might lead to restart of a building phase B_j with $j < i$. With this vocabulary, we will know discuss different types of design knowledge before a generic design framework is introduced.

2.2   Implicit Design Knowledge

Individual knowledge is conceived and maintained by individuals in form of mental memories in various memory systems expressed in imaginary or propositional formats [12, 13]. Individual knowledge is processed by cognitive capabilities and influenced by sensations and perceptions received via various channels, such as vision, hearing, and feeling. Individual knowledge cannot be directly shared. Nonetheless parts of individual knowledge that can be explicated and thus shared in principle (explicit knowledge [14]) while the non-expressible part can be used but not shared by explications (tacit knowledge [14]). It can be considered as an open issue whether implicit tacit design knowledge can be partially shared by non-textual and non-diagrammatic formats, such as performances or sculptures. Individual design knowledge is constantly target of change processes that are initiated when individuals are exposed to external design knowledge, for instance, in discussions with other designers. Individual design knowledge might be generally fragmented and target of fusion and fission processes.

2.3   Informal Design Knowledge

Informal design knowledge is expressed by means of conceptual modeling languages (CML) in explicit representations that do not generally comply with formal structures [11]. Terms are not fully specified but help designers to share a tentative understanding of a design issue. Informal design knowledge can be expressed by natural language descriptions, sketches, performances, or other non-formal symbol systems and can be shared between designers [11]. Informal design knowledge describes a rough understanding of a particular design issue with weak boundaries on detail level but can provide strong boundaries on strategic level. CMLs for informal design knowledge encompass metaphors, prototypical information, analogies, and other forms for expressing complex knowledge by structured items. Hence, ambiguities and misunderstandings between members of a design team are inherent.

2.4   Semi-formal Design Knowledge

The semantic fuzziness of informal design knowledge resulted in the development of various CML for semi formal design knowledge (e.g., UML [15]). Diagrammatic CMLs have been found to be appropriate in many software development projects. Diagrammatic representations of semi-formal design knowledge are often based on graph models with binary relationships between simple-typed nodes. Examples for diagrammatic CML are state-transition diagrams, UML use cases but also flow charts, Jackson diagrams, horizontal plans, circuit diagrams, urban plans, and maps in general. Instances of nodes in these diagrammatic CMLs are simple members of sets but rarely higher-order structures, such as sets of sets. Even though that some diagrammatic CML have a formal underpinning, design projects use semi-formal design knowledge in a non-formal manner for more structured communication between designers. It reduces the flexibility of informal design knowledge without formalizing it in a mathematical sense.

Semi-formal design knowledge supports narrowing down informal design knowledge by operations, such as filtering, merging, organizing, synthesizing, and summarizing [7]. Practical work shows that semi-formal design knowledge can be shared more easily if it is directly related to informal design knowledge. The relationship between informal and semi-formal design knowledge resembles the relationship between survey maps and route maps of cognitive maps where survey maps provide an overview while route maps contain more detailed, decomposed, and modularized representations [16].

Problems of UML give a good account for what happens if semi-formal design knowledge is used in isolation [17]. For instance, it is argued that use cases promote "a highly localized perspective which often obscures the true business logic of a system." In recent studies it was shown that understanding of conceptual models expressed by semi-formal CML can be supported by informal conceptual models [18].

2.5   Formal Design Knowledge

Formal design knowledge captures the meaning of a conceptual model as much as possible by mathematically formal representations [11, 19]. All statements captured by the semantics of a formal CML can be assigned a clear and undisputable meaning. For instance, logical symbols in sentences in first-order logic (FOL) have a clear meaning while non-logical symbols, e.g., the meaning of a constant "John", are used in a domain-specific way that requires agreement between designers independent of the formal CML [20]. Therefore a clear specification of the meaning of logical sentences is a "function of the interpretation of the predicate and function symbols" [20]. This means that even design knowledge expressed in formal logic still needs shared understanding on the interpretation of non-logical entities. With this agreement, logically formalized design knowledge provides precise semantics of a conceptual model. In theory, formalized design knowledge can be processed automatically but in practice only subsets of formal logic are useful with respect to effective solutions, e.g. based on SLD resolution and Horn clauses [20]. Other CMLs for formalized design knowledge could be the simpler propositional logic or more complex CMLs, such as differential equations or Hilbert spaces.

The advantages of formalized design knowledge are rigorous semantics that at least theoretically can be executed on computational machinery. A clear disadvantage is that formalized design knowledge is difficult to share between designers because it requires expertise in formal CMLs, such as FOL. For instance, the ontological part of conceptual models in FOL requires an understanding of FOL theory, of the particular logical statement, a shared understanding of the interpretation and its underlying domain.[1]

3   Generic Design Framework

Designing an information system can be understood as a translation process from one model of a particular knowledge type to another (cf. Fig. 2). The starting point are individual implicit conceptual models that are step-by-step translated into more structured models till they comply with requirements given by computational machinery (computational design knowledge), i.e. can be executed by information technologies. Thus, a distinction between conceptual models gained by system analysis and system design are encompassed by a homogeneous approach of model translation.

Translation processes incorporate additional external knowledge, such as domain knowledge that provides more details or technical knowledge that enriches models with architectural knowledge and constraints. Thus translation processes are generally complex and are based on collaborations between various members of a design team. In the following, all four translation processes are discussed (cf. Fig. 2).

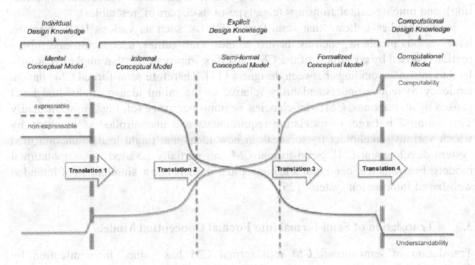

Fig. 2. Generic Design Framework

3.1   Translation of Individual into Informal Design Knowledge

Following Michael Polanyi's work, explicit knowledge can be rationalized and expressed by human communication while tacit knowledge is non-expressible and mainly resides with a person. The expressible part is translated via natural language,

---

[1] For instance, $\forall x[\exists z(Dz \& Oxz) \rightarrow \exists y(\exists z(Dz \& Oyz) \& Fxy)]$ for the representation of the informal conceptual description "Every dog owner is the friend of a dog owner".

gestures, mimics, painting or other performances into informal conceptual models. For the preceptor an informal conceptual model is less understandable than her own individual conceptual model because informal CMLs are not expressive enough and non-expressible parts of a mental conceptual model are omitted (cf. Fig. 2). With respect to computational execution, informal conceptual models provide a first handle. Text and image processing tools can analyze information CMs, search for inconsistencies, redundancies and relationships to external models. By Translation 1 informal CMs are derived that reduce understandability and increases computability relative to mental CMs. Translation 1 generally requires intensive individual mental operations, discussions in design teams before informal CMs can be explicated. In general all translation processes consist of several iterations.

3.2   Translation of Informal into Semi-formal CMs

In IS design projects translation of informal CM into semi-formal CM is considered a crucial translational step for collaborative design teams [21-23]. By "soft"-ontological approaches, key concepts and relationships are extracted from informal CMs and transformed into diagrammatic representations. Typical types of relationships are functional, time (process representations), space, organization (structural organization), and ontological relationships (e.g., type-of, is-a, part-of, resembles).

Recent studies indicate that semi-formal CMLs, such as various UML formats, have various problems, such as inconsistencies, ambiguities, adequacies, and misdirections caused by constructs of the CML itself or improper use that might eventually lead to misunderstandings between designers [17]. Therefore semi-formal CMs have a tendency to reduce understandability relative to the initial idea on individual level caused by abstractions, CML deficiencies, or improper usage (cf. Fig. 2). Additionally Translation 2 is target of escalating requirements and uncontrolled scope creep by which various stakeholder try to sneak in new ideas that might lead to uncontrolled system development [24]. Semi-formal CM can partially be used as computational models. For instance, diagrammatic conceptual models allow simulations of intended web-based information systems [25].

3.3   Translation of Semi-formal into Formal Conceptual Models

Translation of semi-formal CM into formal CM has gained large attention by frameworks for specification and verification of (early) requirements (e.g., [26]). Translation procedures are still in their infancies and require strong expertise in formal modeling and model checking (e.g., [26]). While strongly improving computability, formalization reduces understandability of formal CM by members of a design team. It is an open issue whether formal CM are part of explicit design knowledge that is useful for design work in teams or whether it only resides to computational design knowledge that is used by experts outside of design teams. The discussion on formal ontological models currently takes place within the realm of explicit design knowledge used by design experts [27].

3.4   Translation of Explicit into Computational CMs

Translation of semi-formal into computational CM is perceived as a large step called system design (Translation 4a) while translation of formal CM into system design might become a fluid process in the future (Translation 4b). Currently only a tiny fraction of all practical design projects use Translation 4b processes because of missing tools and expertise with formal models. Guizzardi [10] demonstrates the insufficiency of lightweight ontologies, such as UML and ER, for conceptual modeling issues, e.g., semantic interoperability and indicates how formal ontologies can be used. However, formal ontologies are rarely used for conceptual modeling in a practical sense but more often for specification of human knowledge that might support clarification of underlying conceptual structures of a domain.

In almost all large IS design projects semi-formal CMs are handed over from design team A (requirements and business engineering team) to design team B (system development team). If both teams have a long history of collaboration, semi-formal and informal CM are embedded into developed mutual understandings. Without this underlying mutual understanding, Translation 4a is one of the major reasons for misunderstanding, further escalating requirements, and scope creep, potentially resulting in failing projects. Final system designs are executable on computational information technologies.

4   Applying the Framework to Ubiquitous Information Systems

The proposed framework for Design Knowledge has been tested within a design project over three years by an Ubiquitous Information System (UIS). The target was to design and realize a fully instrumented and user-adaptive physical environment. All conceptual model types were carefully selected and designed so that they fit the needs of the design team. Similarly special care was given to translation processes so that no problems, such as escalating requirements and scope creep occurred. We will describe how backward compatibility of conceptual models was evaluated. The conceptual modeling framework instantiated all types of explicit design knowledge: *narrative CM* (informal CM), *pattern-based diagrammatic CMs, called Pre-Artifacts* (semiformal CM), and *formalized propositional CM* (formal CM). All CMs are framed by the *Abstract Information System Model (AISM)* that consists of *Information Sphere, Social System, Service System* and *Physical Object System* [28].

Based on translation procedures narrative CMs, i.e. the aforementioned descriptions of usage situations in natural language, are transformed into diagrammatic CMs, called Pre-Artifacts. Pre-Artifacts emphasize requirements on social structure, information objects, physical objects, and services in usage situations in a diagrammatic form. The core entities identified in narratives are assigned to these conceptual categories. Similarly, relations that connect these entities are specified. Finally, Pre-Artifacts are translated into the propositional CMs formalized in OWL. So, machine-processable CMs are gained that can be used as part of the knowledge representation representing usage situations of the UIS.

4.1   Types of Conceptual Models

Informal Design Knowledge

For capturing informal design knowledge, we deployed a situation-based approach. Situations are described by textual descriptions, called narratives. Narratives are small stories that explicitly describe on instance-level what happens if one or more actors act in an imagined UIS environment. More formally, a situation describes which social actors interact with one another or with services. Interactions can transfer information objects from one actor to another. In UIS information objects and services can be bound to physical objects. Informal design knowledge makes explicit what members of a design team think a particular IS will look like. Narratives are supposed to have a short distance to individual languages of thought [29].

Semi-formal Design Knowledge

When we began to derive diagrammatic CMs from narratives, it was detected that a more principled approach was necessary. Uncertainties occurred when defining the diagrammatic structures of narratives because of the large range of relational types as well as the comprehensive latitude in defining and modeling diagrammatic conceptual models (Pre-Artifacts, cf. [28]). Five steps were identified for deducing Pre-Artifacts from narratives [28]: (1) Extraction of terms according to AISM, (2) Assignment of terms to categories, e.g., services, (3) Representation of categorized terms and their relations according to AISM, (4) Description of Pre-Artifact, and (5) Validation of Pre-Artifact based on competency questions. Extracting and assigning terms as well as the definition of relations based on AISM, offered a wide range of opportunities that had a negative effect on the resulting Pre-Artifacts. Depending on the modeling person, each Pre-Artifact possessed other structures and relations between concepts. Analysis of Pre-Artifacts in several research projects showed re-occurring structures similar to the notion of design patterns as used in architecture [30] and Software Engineering [31]. We identified seven Pre-Artifact patterns [28].

Formal Design Knowledge

The FOL-based CML OWL [32] was used for formalization of Pre-Artifacts. The three best-performing narratives were translated into Pre-Artifacts and subsequently into formal CMs. So, the situational part of the knowledge representation consists of seven propositional CMs formalized in OWL.

4.2   Translations of Conceptual Models

Each translation consisted of two steps: (1) translation of a conceptual model CM_x represented by CML L_x into a conceptual model CM_y represented by CML L_y and (2) empirical evaluation of each CM. This allowed backward compatibility checks between CMs.

Experience with Translation 1

In Translation 1 narratives were extracted by discussions with design experts. Various brainstorming sessions resulted in narratives represented by written natural language. Several iterations were conducted till designers agreed upon a set of 12 narratives of different situations. These narratives became the baseline against which subsequent conceptual models were tested. Any design decision that went beyond the scope spanned by these narratives were intensively evaluated because major changes would have rendered earlier design steps inconsistent and potentially useless. Thus backward compatibility of conceptual models seems to be a key issue for IS design projects in general. Even though that writing narratives is generally perceived as an easy task, it came out that writing concise and useful narratives is hard.

By an initial evaluation of situations we found that test persons found three situations most interesting. In a subsequent empirical evaluation of narratives with focus on services (n=111) results of the initial study were confirmed (cf. Table 1), i.e. situations 1, 6, and 11 were rated highest with respect to intention to use a service in a situation (IU) and perceived fit of a service with a situation (PF).

Table 1. Evaluation of Informal Design Knowledge

Ra-nk	Situ-ation	Service		IU		PF	
		No	Name	Mean	SD	Mean	SD
1.	6	4	Personalized Music Service	6.28***	0.87	6.07***	1.13
2.	1	1	Weather Information Service	5.64***	1.54	4.87***	1.69
3.	6	5	Personalized News Collage Service	5.11***	1.94	4.84***	1.83
4.	1	2	Event Recommendation Service	4.65***	1.69	4.12	1.65
5.	11	6	Adaptive News Service	4.17	1.85	3.88	1.82
6.	1	3	Ticket Order Service	3.82	1.73	3.47**	1.77

We found that natural language in spoken and written form made it easy to discuss even innovative situations for complex information systems. Decomposition into narratives allowed design experts to focus without getting lost in details. Narratives supported understandability between members of the design team. In three years it did not happen that somebody claimed misunderstanding. Therefore we tentatively conclude that narratives represented by written and spoken natural language are a valid CML type for informal design knowledge.

Experience with Translation 2
Based on narratives Translation 2 was conducted for derivation of semi-formal CMs (Pre-Artifacts). In previous studies, a Pre-Artifact language has proven to be too

Table 2. Evaluation of Semi-Formal Conceptual Models

Item	Weather Inform.	Event Recom.	Ticket Order	Person. Music	Pers. News Collage	Adaptive News
	Group A, n=27			Group B, n=28		
Intention to use						
IU	6.33*** (0.73)	4.67* (1.52)	3.78 (1.74)	6.75*** (0.52)	4.86* (1.78)	5.14** (1.56)
Fit of service and situation						
Situation-Fit	6.19*** (0.96)	5.52*** (1.01)	5.19*** (1.06)	6.29*** (0.94)	5.64*** (1.31)	5.79*** (1.07)

complex for representing non-trivial narratives. Designers simply got lost. With pattern language, members of various design teams quickly assembled diagrammatic representations even for complex narratives. This positive effect of the pattern language was supported by several other design projects that were conducted in parallel. Design members evaluated whether all resulting Pre-Artifact-based CM complied with input narratives. In contrast to narratives, Translation 2 was considered a difficult task at the beginning but became straightforward by application of a five-step procedure [28]. Understandability between team members was rated high even though that the Pre-Artifact language was new to all.

Empirical evaluation of Pre-Artifacts was conducted by a fully realized prototype of the Intelligent Bathroom. The empirical study shows that all services comply with results of the empirical study conducted during Translation 1. Similarly service-situation fit was rated very high and provided evidence that the resulting prototype and realized services not only fit to the realized prototype but also to anticipations raised by initial narratives. This provides confidence to conclude backward compatibility in Translation 2 of semi-formal conceptual model with informal conceptual models.

Experience with Translation 3
Human translation of semi-formal CM into formal CM is currently a cumbersome task. Therefore we opted for an automatic solution by formalization of Pre-Artifact Patterns into FOL-based representations based on OWL. In this approach, the notion of the AISM Ontology as well as the integration of this "vocabulary" into pattern ontologies was adopted. But, for the specification of pattern-specific object properties based on the generic properties of the model, inheritance structures of object properties were used. That means each pattern defines sub properties of the relevant object properties imported from the model. Therefore, super-properties and concepts of the AISM Ontology remain unchanged. In this context, the OWL feature is used, that OWL constructs are independent, i.e. properties can exist independent of classes [19]. Based on this approach, clear assignments of specified object properties to specific patterns are realized.

Formalization of Pre-Artifacts was necessary because services and contents were processed by a semantic middleware integrated in the prototype (Translation 4b). Understandability of formal CM derived from Pre-Artifact-based CM was strongly diminished. Beside the modeler, nobody of the design team took interest in these formal CMs. This might support the conclusion that formal CMs are rather part of computational design knowledge than human-oriented explicit design knowledge (cf. Fig. 2). Computability was very high because formal CMs can be directly processed on computational machinery. Consistency checks proofed all models logically correct.

Experience with Translation 4
Both types of translation were used. All IS elements that were realized by semantic technologies used Translation 4b while all other parts used the traditional Translation 4a. Issues related to Translation 4b were already mentioned before. In general this translation took a lot of effort but allowed careful designs that could be tested for

backward compatibility. In contrast, Translation 4a appeared to be problematic when design teams for informal and semi-structured CMs differ from teams dealing with system design and realization. Forward compatibility between Pre-Artifact CMs and system designs required many meetings and changes. Scope extensions and requirement creeps occurred and had to be fixed. Backward compatibility was indirectly proven by abovementioned study (cf. Table 2).

5   Conclusion and Open Issues

The Design Framework was applied to a three-year research project and several smaller research and commercial projects. Based on these experiences all four translations and related CML for different types of design knowledge have been tested. Special focus was laid on the format and use of explicit design knowledge. Even though that many CMLs and methods for IS design and Software Engineering exist, little is known about how explicit design knowledge is created and how it is shared in teams. As far as we know, this is the first approach that tentatively investigates various types of design knowledge during translation phases supported by empirical studies that allow assessment of backward compatibilities. This explorative but nonetheless complex study left many issues open. In particular we will have to investigate knowledge sharing processes between members of a design team in more detail. Furthermore different CML for the same type of design knowledge need to be evaluated against each other for different IS types. This would give us insights on which design knowledge is supported best for which kind of IS. Eventually this could also indicate why some many IS projects fail. Even though that we tried very hard, it become obvious that formal CM are rarely useful for design teams. At least for the moment, knowledge barriers are too high, supporting tools are missing, and benefits for using formal CM are too small for members of a design team. Taking this together, formal CM tend to become part of the computational design knowledge rather than becoming a key tool for IS designers. In summary, this Design Framework provides as means for incremental design even of innovative information systems, such as an UIS. All CMs are evaluated so that design decisions can be tested and result into localized design changes if necessary.

References

1. Doomed from the Start? Why a Majority of Business and IT Teams Anticipate Their Software Development Projects Will Fail, in Geneca Research Report, Geneca LLC (2011)
2. Schmidt, R., et al.: Identifying software project risks: An international Delphi study. Journal of Management Information Systems 17(4), 5–36 (2001)
3. Wand, Y., Weber, R.: Information systems and conceptual modeling - a research agenda. Information Systems Research 13(4), 363–376 (2002)
4. Larsen, T.J., et al.: The role of modelling in achieving information systems success: UML to the rescue? Information Systems Journal 19(1), 83–117 (2009)

5. Yoo, Y.: Computing in Everyday Life: A Call for Research on Experiential Computing. Mis Quarterly 34(2), 213–231 (2010)
6. Kogut, B., Zander, U.: What Firms Do? Co-ordination, Identity, and Learning. Organization Science 7, 502–518 (1996)
7. Patnayakuni, R., Ruppel, C.P., Rai, A.: Managing the complementarity of knowledge integration and process formalization for systems development performance. Journal of the Association for Information Systems 7(8), 545–567 (2006)
8. Ulrich, K.T., Eppinger, S.D.: Product Design and Development, 5th edn. McGraw-Hill (2008)
9. Larsen, T.J., Naumann, J.D.: An Experimental Comparison of Abstract and Concrete Representations in Systems-Analysis. Information & Management 22(1), 29–40 (1992)
10. Booch, G., Rambaugh, J., et al.: The Unified Modeling Language User Guide. Addision-Wesley, Redwood City (1999)
11. Wand, Y., et al.: Theoretical foundations for conceptual modelling in information systems development. Decision Support Systems 15, 285–304 (1995)
12. Kosslyn, S.M.: Image and Mind. Harvard University Press, Cambridge (1980)
13. Pylyshyn, Z.W.: Computation and Cognition. MIT Press, Cambridge (1984)
14. Polanyi, M.: The Tacit Dimension. Doubleday, Garden (1966)
15. Fowler, M., Scott, K.: UML Distilled: Applying the Standard Object Modelling Language / UML konzentriert: Strkuturierte Einführung in die Standard-Objektmodellierungssprache, 2nd edn. Addison-Wesley, Reading (1997)
16. Chown, E., Kaplan, S., Kortenkamp, D.: Prototypes, Location, and Associative Networks (PLAN): Towards a Unified Theory of Cognitive Mapping. Cognitive Science 19(1), 1–51 (1995)
17. Simons, A., Graham, I.: 30 Things that Go Wrong in Object Modeliling with UML 1.3. In: Kilov, H., Rumpe, B., Simmonds, I. (eds.) Behavioral Specifications of Businesses and Systems, pp. 237–257. Kluwer Academic Publishers (1999)
18. Maass, W., Storey, V.C., Kowatsch, T.: Effects of External Conceptual Models and Verbal Explanations on Shared Understanding in Small Groups. In: Jeusfeld, M., Delcambre, L., Ling, T.-W. (eds.) ER 2011. LNCS, vol. 6998, pp. 92–103. Springer, Heidelberg (2011)
19. Bera, P., Krasnoperova, A., Wand, Y.: Using Ontology Languages for Conceptual Modeling. Journal of Database Management 21(1), 1–28 (2010)
20. Brachman, R., Levesque, H.: Knowledge Representation and Reasoning. Morgan Kaufmann (2004)
21. Jackson, M.A.: Principles of Program Design. Academic Press (1975)
22. Scheer, A.W.: ARIS Business Process Modeling. Springer, Berlin (2000)
23. Jacobson, I., Booch, G., Rumbaugh, J.: The Unified Software Development Process. Addison Wesley Longman (1998)
24. Verner, J., Evanco, W.M.: In-house software development: what software project management practices lead to success? IEEE Software 22(1), 86–93
25. Robles Luna, E., Rossi, G., Garrigós, I.: WebSpec: a visual language for specifying interaction and navigation requirements in web applications. Requirements Engineering 16(4), 297–321 (2011)
26. Fuxman, A., et al.: Specifying and analyzing early requirements in Tropos. Requirements Engineering 9(2), 132–150 (2004)
27. Siegemund, K., et al.: Towards Ontology-driven Requirements Engineering. In: Workshop Semantic Web Enabled Software Engineering at 10th International Semantic Web Conference (ISWC), Bonn (2011)

28. Maass, W., Janzen, S.: Pattern-Based Approach for Designing with Diagrammatic and Propositional Conceptual Models. In: Jain, H., Sinha, A.P., Vitharana, P. (eds.) DESRIST 2011. LNCS, vol. 6629, pp. 192–206. Springer, Heidelberg (2011)
29. Jackendoff, R.: Foundations of Language: Brain, Meaning, Grammar, Evolution. Oxford University Press (2003)
30. Alexander, C.: A Pattern Language: Towns, Buildings, Construction. Oxford University Press (1977)
31. Dey, A., Abowd, G.: Towards a better understanding of context and context-awareness, in GVU Technical Report, College of Computing, Georgia Institute of Technology (1999)
32. Bechhofer, S., et al.: OWL Web Ontology Language Reference. In: Dean, M., Schreiber, G. (eds.) (2004)

Technical Action Research as a Validation Method in Information Systems Design Science

Roel Wieringa[1] and Ayşe Moralı[2]

[1] Department of Electrical Engineering, Mathematics, and Computer Science,
University of Twente, The Netherlands
r.j.wieringa@utwente.nl,
http://www.ewi.utwente.nl~roelw
[2] PwC, Gent, Belgium
ayse.morali@pwc.be

Abstract. Current proposals for combining action research and design science start with a concrete problem in an organization, then apply an artifact to improve the problem, and finally reflect on lessons learned. The aim of these combinations is to reduce the tension between relevance and rigor. This paper proposes another way of using action research in design science, which starts with an artifact, and then tests it under conditions of practice by solving concrete problems with them. The aim of this way of using action research in design science is to bridge the gap between the idealizations made when designing the artifact and the concrete conditions of practice that occur in real-world problems.

The paper analyzes the role of idealization in design science and compares it with the requirements of rigor and relevance. It then proposes a way of bridging the gap between idealization and practice by means of action research, called technical action research (TAR) in this paper. The core of TAR is that the researcher plays three roles, which must be kept logically separate, namely of artifact developer, artifact investigator, and client helper. Finally, TAR is compared to other approaches of using action research in design science, and with canonical action research.

1 Introduction

Design science is the study of artifacts in context [1]. Interest for it in the information systems community arose out of a desire to make research results more relevant, by adding a problem-solving cycle to a theory-building cycle. *Action research,* taken very generally, is the intervention in a social situation in order to both improve this situation and to learn from it [2]. It arose shortly after World War II out of dissatisfaction with social science as mere diagnosis [3]. In addition to diagnosis, action research includes an intervention by scientists to improve the situation, and to learn from what happened in this "social experiment".

Both research approaches, design science and action research, are motivated by the desire to increase the relevance of research by incorporating a social problem-solving activity in research without sacrificing rigor [4,5]. This has motivated several authors to propose mergers of action research and design science

K. Peffers, M. Rothenberger, and B. Kuechler (Eds.): DESRIST 2012, LNCS 7286, pp. 220–238, 2012.

research. Lee [6] proposes an elegant extension of the framework of March & Smith [7] in which actions are treated as artifacts to be built, evaluated, theorized about, and justified. Baskerville et al. [8] integrate both action research and design science in Checkland's soft systems approach. Sein et al. [9] propose an integrated cycle that combines building, intervention and evaluation from design science research with reflection and learning from action research, emphasizing the interleaving of building and IT artifact with intervening in an organization. All of these approaches start from an organizational problem to be solved by action research, and then design an artifact to solve this concrete problem. They then reflect on this experience to draw generalizable lessons learned from this.

In this paper, we will start at the opposite end, namely artifact design, and then look for organizational problems that could be solved by this artifact. The goal of the researcher is to develop this artifact for use in a class of situations imagined by the researcher. Typically, then, the artifact is first tested, not on a real-world problem, but on toy problems under idealized circumstances in a laboratory. Next, it is scaled up to conditions of practice by solving more realistic problems with it, until it can be tested by using it in one or more concrete client organizations to solve concrete problems.

We propose to use action research in the last stages of this process of scaling up to practice. The only way to leave the idealized circumstances of the laboratory is to enter the real world. This is very similar to the way new medicines are transferred to practice, after first testing them under idealized conditions in a lab, then testing them with healthy volunteers and, eventually, with patients. To mark this artifact-driven action research off from the problem-driven action research mentioned above, we call it *technical action research* (TAR).

The primary motivation for this way of using action research is to bridge the gap between the idealizations of initial design and the concrete conditions of practice. We discuss this gap in the next section, and describe our way of using action research in more detail afterwards.

2   Relevance, Rigor and Idealization

TAR is intended to increase the relevance of artifacts just as other forms of action research aim to increase the relevance of knowledge. But the relevance gap that is bridged by TAR is the one between idealized conditions and practical conditions. To explain this, we return for a moment to the problem of rigor and relevance as originally introduced by Schön [10]. Schön is interested in problem-solving in the professions, such as in architecture, health care or law and he contrasts this with problem-solving in the technical sciences. To draw this contrast, he introduces what he calls "technical rationality", defined by him as a problem-solving approach in which possible alternative solutions are compared with respect to goals, before one solution is selected to be implemented. He identifies four assumptions about the problem made by technical rationality [10, pages 40–42]:

- The problem is framed,
- it is an example of a problem class,

- it is stable, and
- it has unambiguous goals.

Problems in the technical engineering sciences, Schön says, satisfy these assumptions, but in some professional practices, such as in the practice of architecture or law, problems do not satisfy these idealizing assumptions [10, page 42]. Technical rationality, rigorous as it is, is then not relevant for these problems and a more "artistic" way of coping with the problem is required, using Schön's words.

Schön himself frames this as the dilemma of rigor "versus" relevance, but stated like this, this is a false dilemma. First, as also acknowledged by Schön, there are many practical problems in the professions that *do* satisfy the assumptions of technical rationality, and for these problems, technical rationality can produce relevant solutions in a rigorous way. So in these cases, rigor is not opposed to relevance.

Second, Schön assumes that in the technical sciences, knowledge is developed in isolation from practice [10, pages 23–26]. All that a technical problem-solver has to do, according to Schön, is to select whatever he or she can use from this knowledge to solve the technical problem at hand. However, in the technical sciences too, knowledge developed in isolation from practice is not relevant. Cartwright [11] argues at length that the laws of physics are literally false, because they make idealizing assumptions, such as the existence of point masses and frictionless surfaces, which are false in the real world. Rather than being about the real world, these laws can better be viewed as being about abstract, "nomological machines" [12]. McMullin [13] calls this "Galilean idealization". The purposes of idealization are to enhance insight into an idealized phenomenon in isolation, and to enhance our capacity to reason and compute about this isolated idealized phenomenon. In the laboratory, great effort is exerted to approximate the idealizations assumed by these nomological machines.

This poses a relevance problem for the technical sciences, analogous to the relevance problem indicated by Schön for the social sciences. Technical professionals must design and investigate machines in the real world, where there is no budget or inclination to enforce the idealizations of nomological machines [14,15]. How then can they use scientific knowledge to develop artifacts for the real world outside a laboratory? By designing and investigating artifacts first under idealized conditions, and then scaling up in small steps to conditions of practice [16,15]. Prototypes of artifacts are first tested in the idealized conditions of the laboratory, and then these conditions are gradually relaxed until a realistic version of the artifact is tested in a realistic environment. This allows the technical scientist to develop knowledge about the behavior of artifacts in practice. The technical approach to scaling up increases relevance without sacrificing rigor.

In medical research too, medicine are first tested in safe, artificial conditions, after which the context is scaled up to more realistic conditions of practice, by first testing it on healthy volunteers, and then ill volunteers.[1] And this too is done according to rigorous standards of scientific methodology.

---

[1] http://www.fda.gov/Drugs/DevelopmentApprovalProcess/
SmallBusinessAssistance/ucm053131.htm

The problem of application-oriented research in the technical and medical sciences is, then, not one of rigor against relevance, but one of idealization versus practice. And this problem is dealt with in these sciences by starting artifact development in idealized circumstances and slowly scaling up to conditions of practice.

If this approach can be used successfully in the technical and medical sciences, then it is worth trying to do also use it in information systems design science. In this paper we will approach problem solving with Schön's technical rationality, in the form of an *engineering cycle* in which artifacts are compared and evaluated against stable goals. We will discuss the engineering cycle in more detail later, but for now it suffices to say that it is a rational decision process in which the designer generates and evaluates alternative designs by comparing them against design goals. In the first iterations through the engineering cycle, the designer makes idealizing assumptions to make it easier to find a design at all. After a proof of concept has been given, the designer improves the design by iterating through the cycle, gradually relaxing the idealizing assumptions, until all remaining assumptions can easily be satisfied in practice. Our use of TAR will be in the last stages of this iterative process, namely when the researcher tests an artifact by using it to solve a client's problem.

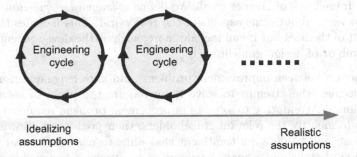

Fig. 1. Scaling up by iterating through the engineering cycle, making more realistic assumptions in later iterations

This requires a clear distinction between problem-solving for the client, artifact development by the researcher, and knowledge acquisition by the researcher. For this, we use the refinement of the framework for design science of Hevner et al. [1], discussed next.

3 A Framework for Design Science

Figure 2 shows an adaptation of the top-level framework of Hevner et al. [1], showing design science and its interfaces with the environment and the scientific knowledge base. This framework has been presented and motivated in more detail earlier, and we here briefly summarize the aspect necessary for the purpose of this paper [17].

In the new framework, the environment is the source of design goals and of a budget to achieve them. This budget can consist of money and instruments, but will at least consist of the time of the researcher, which has to be paid for in one way or the other. In return, the design researcher delivers artifacts that can be used to solve problems in the environment, i.e. to achieve goals in the environment.

The important change with respect to the framework of Hevner et al. is that the design science activity has been split into two, solving improvement problems and answering knowledge questions.

- Solving improvement problems corresponds, roughly, to building artifacts in the framework of Hevner et al. Here, we define an *improvement problem* as a difference between the actual state of the world and the world as desired by some stakeholder, where this stakeholder has made available a budget to reduce this gap. If a stakeholder has a desire but is not willing to make a budget available to achieve it, in the form of time, money or other resources, then we do not consider this desire to be a stakeholder goal. The improvement problems we are concerned with consist of designing and evaluating artifacts.
- Answering knowledge questions corresponds, roughly, to developing theories in the framework of Hevner et al. We define a *knowledge question* is a lack of knowledge about some aspects of the real world. This includes the development of theories but it can include more, such as the development of rules of thumb or of design guidelines [18].

The distinction between improvement problems and knowledge questions is important, because the attempt to solve them require the problem solver to do different things. Attempting to solve an improvement problem requires the problem solver to identify the relevant stakeholders, their goals, and criteria for the improvement, and to design a treatment that aims to change the real world in the direction of stakeholder goals. Attempting to answer a knowledge question, by contrast, requires us to identify the questions and unit of study, and define measurements that will provide the quantitative or qualitative data by which we can answer these questions.

Not only should we do different things to solve improvement problems or answer knowledge questions, the results of these efforts are also evaluated

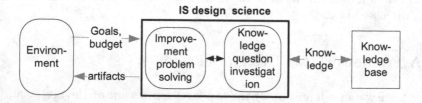

Fig. 2. Framework for design science

differently. Evaluating the result of solving an improvement problem involves the application of criteria to see if the improvement has been achieved. These criteria indicate effectiveness (has a change been achieved) and utility (has the change led to an improvement). Evaluating the result of answering a knowledge question, by contrast, involves assessing the truth of these answers and our degree of certainty about this, as well as assessing the scope of these answers.

These differences appear in the formulation of improvement problems and knowledge questions. Improvement problems can always be formulated in how-to-do form, such as

– "How to assess confidentiality risks in outsourcing IT management?"

Going one step further, they can also always be reformulated as design assignments, such as

– "Improve the assessment of confidentiality risks in outsourcing IT management."

Knowledge questions, by contrast, leave the state of the world as it is. They always can be rephrased into descriptive, explanatory, or predictive questions about the world, where descriptive questions may concern the current state of the world or its history:

– "What are the confidentiality risks in this outsourcing arrangement?" (descriptive question about current state of the world)
– "What events have led to this outsourcing arrangement?" (descriptive question about history of the world)
– "Why have these decisions been made?" (explanatory question)
– "What would be the effect of applying this new confidentiality assessment technique?" (predictive question)

Having distinguished improvement problems from knowledge questions within design science, we now turn to the engineering cycle, which is a rational way to solve improvement problems.

4   The Engineering Cycle

In the engineering cycle, an improvement problem is investigated, alternative treatment designs generated and validated, a design is selected and implemented, and experience with the implementation is evaluated (figure 3). The structure of this cycle has been extensively motivated elsewhere [19].[2] Here we give a brief summary.

---

[2] There, engineering cycle has been called the *regulative cycle*, following Van Strien [20].

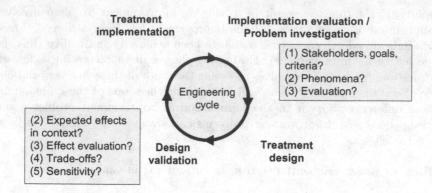

Fig. 3. The engineering cycle

4.1   Problem Investigation

In the *problem investigation* task,

(1) stakeholders and their goals are identified, and these are operationalized into criteria.
(2) Phenomena relevant for the improvement problem must be investigated, and
(3) it must be assessed how well these phenomena agree with the goals of the stakeholders.

This provides the researcher with a map of the needs for improvement.

4.2   Treatment Design

The design scientist then designs one or more *treatments*, which we here assume consist of an *artifact* interacting with a *problem context* (figure 4). This is a useful way of conceptualizing artifacts. Any IT artifact, whether it is an information system or a method or technique for developing, implementing, maintaining or using information systems, is used by inserting it in a problem context, with which it then starts interacting. Artifacts may consist of software or hardware, or they may be conceptual entities such as methods and techniques or business processes.

The interaction between an artifact and the problem context is the treatment that is expect to improve the context, just as a medicine (artifact) is inserted in a context (human body) which starts a treatment that is expected to improve the context. In our case we assume that the problem context is a social system, such as an organization, containing information systems. The problem to be solved by inserting an IT artifact in this problem context, is that some stakeholder goals need to be achieved.

Stakeholders are legal or biological persons who are affected by the artifact, and are part of the problem context. *Practitioners* are people designing particular

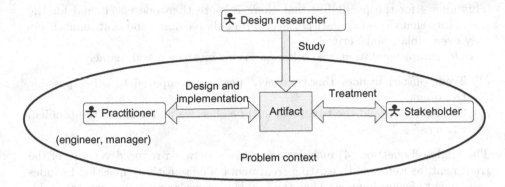

Fig. 4. Treatments and artifacts

treatments for particular problems, or managing the attempt to solve a particular problem. They are part of the problem context too. Their interaction with the artifact consists of designing and implementing it in that particular situation.

It is important here to distinguish *particular problems* that exist at a particular place and time from *problem classes*. The problem that company A has, today, of assessing confidentiality risks of company A when outsourcing the management of ERP systems to company B, is a particular problem. The problem concerns individual, named companies, and it exists at a certain time and place. But this particular problem is an instance of a problem class, namely the generic problem how confidentiality risks in outsourcing are to be assessed. In fact, a particular problem can be viewed as an instance of many related but different problem classes. We can consider the class of problems of confidentiality in outsourcing in general, or the problem class of outsourcing IT management, or the problem class of of outsourcing ERP management.

This distinction is important in design science because we are aiming at *general* knowledge about classes of problems, and so we have to be clear about the class we want to generalize to. The design scientist can study particular problems, containing particular practitioners, artifacts and stakeholders, in order to learn something about a class of problems of similar structure.

4.3 Design Validation

In the engineering cycle, when a treatment is designed, it is validated before it is implemented. In validation, stakeholders and their goals are assumed to have been identified in the problem investigation, so we skip that question. The two core knowledge questions of validation can be stated as follows:

(2) Expected effects: What will be the effects of the artifact in a problem context?

(3) Expected value: How well will these effects satisfy the criteria?

This allows for the possibility that there is more than one effect, and for the possibility that these may satisfy the criteria only partially, and that some effects may even violate some criteria.

Before implementation, two other questions must be asked, namely

(4) Trade-offs: How does this treatment perform compared to other possible treatments?
(5) Sensitivity: Would the treatment still be effective and useful if the problem changes?

The trade-off question (4) includes comparison between reduced versions of the treatment, as well as with existing treatments. The sensitivity question includes assessment of what happens when the problem grows larger (e.g. more stakeholders, more data, etc.) or when the problem is compounded with other problems.

4.4   Treatment Implementation and Evaluation

Implementation in this paper is transfer to the environment (figure 2). When a treatment is actually used in the real-world, then it can be *evaluated* by asking the same questions as before, about

(1) stakeholders,
(2) effects,
(3) value and
(4) sensitivity to problem context.

Note that in problem investigation, we ask for phenomena, which may be effects of existing technology in a context, whereas in implementation evaluation, we specifically ask for the effects of the treatments and artifacts under evaluation. The questions in both cases are the same, but the focus in different: In one case it is on problematic phenomena, whereas in the other on the effects of implemented technology.

This finishes our review of the engineering cycle. We next present TAR as one way to perform the validation task in the engineering cycle.

5   Artifact Validation by Technical Action Research

5.1   Designing an Artifact and Helping a Client with It

As explained earlier, what we call *technical action research* in this paper is the attempt to scale up a treatment to conditions of practice by actually using it in a particular problem. Figure 5 shows that TAR consists of two engineering cycles. In one engineering cycle, the researcher aims at improving a *class* of problems; in the other, the researcher improves a *particular* problem. We explain this by means of an example.

The problem in the left-hand engineering cycle is to improve an artifact, for example to improve a technique for assessing confidentiality risks in outsourcing

Problem investigation
1. Stakeholders, goals, criteria?
2. Phenomena?
3. Evaluation?

Artifact design

Design validation
2. Expected effects in context?
3. Expected evaluation?
4. Trade-offs?
5. Sensitivity?

Implementation
- Transfer to the economy

Implementation evaluation
1. Stakeholders, goals, criteria?
2. Achieved effects in context?
3. Achieved evaluation?

Improvement problem:
To develop some useful artifact

Problem investigation
1. Stakeholders, goals, criteria?
2. Phenomena?
3. Evaluation?

Treatment design
- Specify treatment using artifact
- Agree on implementation plan

Design validation
2. Expected effects in client company?
3. Expected evaluation?
4. Trade-offs?
5. Sensitivity?

Implementation
- In the client company

Implementation evaluation
1. Stakeholders, goals, criteria?
2. Achieved effects in client company?
3. Achieved evaluation?

Improvement problem:
To help a client

Fig. 5. Engineering cycles for artifact development and client helping

[21]. Confidentiality risks exist because outsourcing places sensitive information assets at the premises of a third party. In addition to the risk posed by placing information assets outside the premises of the outsourcing client, another risk is introduced because some employees of the outsourcing provider have legitimate access to confidential data of the outsourcing client, independent of where this information is placed. This creates further risks because these employees are outside the reach of internal control of the outsourcing client. Current service level agreements (SLAs) are often not sufficient to satisfy auditors of the outsourcing client that the client is in control of its information assets. However, the outsourcing provider will not allow these auditors on their premises because of the provider's confidentiality requirements; an outsourcing provider may provide outsourcing services to different clients that are each other's competitors.

The technique introduced by Morali and Wieringa [21] consists of some notations to represent the structure of the outsourcing architecture, and techniques to reason about vulnerabilities of this architecture, and about the value of information flowing through this network.

Consider the situation where these techniques have been designed, and tested on some artificial examples by the researcher. These tests have been successful and the researcher thinks these techniques can be used to solve a real world problem. How to validate this claim? One way to validate it is that the researcher uses the technique to actually do a real-world confidentiality risk assessment for a particular, real-world client. This is the right-hand engineering cycle in figure 5.

In this cycle, an intake is done (stakeholders in the client company, client goals, relevant phenomena and their evaluation) and a treatment plan is agreed on. Part of this agreement is a justification that this plan is expected to indeed deliver the results expected by the client, and this justification consists of an application of what the researcher knows about this treatment. In the very first application of the treatment in a client company, the researcher's knowledge will be abstract and uncertain, and so the risk that the expected results will not be achieved is high; but this is a risk to be taken if a real-world test of the techniques is ever to take place. The researcher then uses the technique to help the client, and evaluates the results with the client.

The goal of the client cycle in figure 5 is to answer one or more validation questions in the researcher's cycle. This is a research goal, and to make this explicit we add an empirical cycle, as described in the next section.

5.2   Inserting the Research Cycle in TAR

The four validation questions in the researcher's cycle (expected effects, expected value, trade-offs, sensitivity) are knowledge questions. Specifically, they are prediction questions: They ask for what *would* happen if the artifact *would* be transferred to the real world. In figure 6 we have inserted a research cycle to make this logic explicit.

The research cycle shown in figure 6 has the same rational problem solving structure as the engineering cycle, but this time, the goal is not to design and implement a useful artifact, but the goal is to design and implement a way of answering knowledge questions.

Research Problem Investigation. In research problem investigation, we determine what the unit of study is, what concepts we use to state the research questions about the unit of study, and what we already know about these questions. In design science, the unit of study is an artifact in context (figure 4) and the research questions are elaborations of one or more knowledge questions that appear in the engineering cycle. In this paper, we are concerned with validation research, and so the research questions will be one or more of the four design validation questions, or elaborations of these questions.

The set of all units of study make up a population. It is often difficult in design science to state in advance exactly what the population is. The precise delimitation of the population may require continued research. For example, we may be interested in the effectiveness and utility of our techniques to assess confidentiality risks, but part of our ignorance at the start of this research is that we do not know precisely for which class of companies and outsourcing relationships the technique will be effective and useful. So at the start of our research, the population is not known precisely. In the TAR approach proposed in this paper, we start from clear problem instances, i.e. we apply the technique in a client company of which we think it clearly falls inside the imperfectly known population.

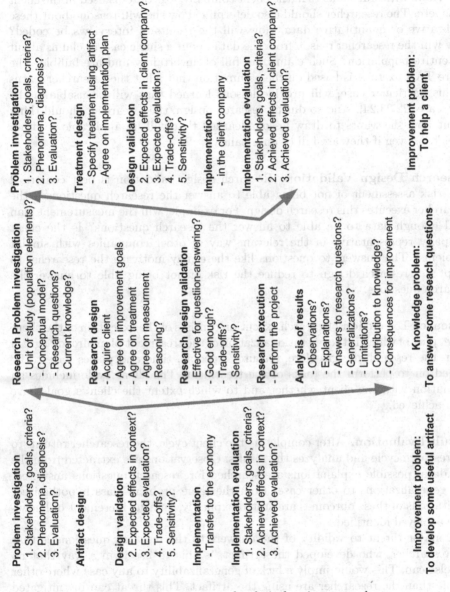

Fig. 6. The structure of technical action research

Research Design. Research design in TAR consists of acquiring access to a client company, agreeing on an improvement goal for the client cycle, agreeing on what the researcher will do for the company and on how the researcher will collect data. In TAR, data may be collected by means of a researcher's diary, interviews with stakeholders in the client company, logs of tools used in the client cycle, etc. The researcher should also determine how she will reason about these qualitative or quantitative data. How will the results of interviews be coded? How will the researcher reason from the data about a single case to claims about the entire population? Such claims are full of uncertainty and are fallible. The entire TAR exercise is based on the assumption that what the researcher learns in this particular case, will provide lessons learned that will be usable in the next case [22,23,24]. And so during research design, the researcher should think about how she wants to draw lessons learned that will be applicable to other cases too, even if they are full of uncertainty.

Research Design Validation. Research design validation is best construed as a risk assessment of not being able to answer the research questions if the researcher executes this research design. For example, will the measurement plan yield enough data to be able to answer the research questions? Is the client company representative in the relevant way of other companies with similar problems? The answers to questions like these may motivate the researcher to adapt her research design to reduce the risk of not being able to answer the research questions.

Research Execution. Research execution consists of the execution of the client cycle, part of which is the operationalization of the treatment plan already agreed on in the research design. Here, resources, people, time and places have to be agreed on to perform the tasks of the treatment. The client cycle includes an evaluation with the client whether and to which extent the client's goals have been achieved.

Result Evaluation. After completing the client cycle, the researcher returns to the research cycle and analyzes the results. Observations are extracted from the raw data, possible explanations are searched for, research questions answered, and generalizations to other cases from the same problem class hypothesized. Limitations of these outcomes are stated explicitly, and the increment of knowledge achieved identified.

A major threat to validity of the answers to the research questions is that the researcher, who developed the artifact, is able to use it in a way that no one else can. This would imply a lack of generalizability to any case where other people than the researcher are using the artifact. This threat can be mitigated by teaching others to use the artifact so that they can use it to perform the client cycle. A second major threat is that stakeholders may answer interview questions in a socially desirable way or, in a variant of this threat, that the researcher herself interprets answers in a desirable way. This introduces a risk that positive evaluations are of limited value, but it does not diminish the value of improvement suggestions and of observations of failures of the artifact. The threat can be mitigated by having others than the researcher do the data collection and coding.

Finally, the researcher identifies consequences for the top-level engineering cycle in which the treatment was designed for a problem class. For example, some elements of the technique may have turned out to be unusable or useless, and in any case the researcher may have acquired ideas for changes that would improve the artifact even further.

6 Discussion

6.1 Validations of TAR

TAR is an approach to validate new artifacts under conditions of practice. Validation research aims to answer effectiveness and utility questions about an artifact in context, and to investigate the robustness of the answers under changes of artifact (trade-off analysis) and changes in context (sensitivity analysis). What about the validation of the TAR approach itself? This too has been done by action research, where now the artifact to be validated is TAR, and it has to be validated in the context of scaling up some technique to conditions of practice.

TAR has been used in several research projects, three of which have been published. Morali and Wieringa [21] describe a project in which the researcher herself used a newly developed confidentiality risk assessment technique for outsourced IT management to do a risk assessment in two different client companies. Zambon et al. [25] describe a similar project, this time about techniques to assess availability risks in outsourcing, tested by the researcher at one client company. Engelsman and Wieringa [26] describe a project in which a technique to relate business objectives to enterprise architecture was used by enterprise architects in a large government organization to redesign their enterprise architecture in a traceable way.

Any claims that we make about the effectiveness and utility of TAR as a validation research method (design validation questions (2) and (3) of the engineering cycle) are subject to the same limitations as have been noted above for TAR: Maybe we are the only ones able to use TAR; maybe we have interpreted the data about its utility too favorably. The first threat has been mitigated by teaching TAR to Master's and PhD students, who then use it in their own research. Experience so far indicates that others can use TAR too.

We have found the use of TAR useful because it provides a structured checklist of things to do when validating artifacts in practice, and it does indeed allow us to find out how an artifact performs in practice, which, as stated in the introduction, is our goal. For researchers not interested in learning about how a technique, not yet transferred to the real world, would perform in practice, TAR would not be useful.

6.2 Rationality, Rigor and Relevance

TAR can teach us whether an artifact is applicable in practice, and by being used in one client company, it shows that the artifact is at least relevant to that company. However, relevance comes in degrees. The two companies where we used our confidentiality risk assessment technique found the confidentiality risk assessment results relevant for their goals, and they have used them. But they did not see enough of a business case to set aside resources to acquire tools and expertise to regularly use the technique. On the other hand, the government organization that used our enterprise architecture (re)design technique, invested resources to regularly use the technique.

Let us now return to Schön's idealizing assumptions of technical rationality, listed in section 2. To what extent does TAR depend on these? TAR assumes that the problem for which an artifact is designed, is not unique. It also assumes that there is a conceptual model of these problems, i.e. that the problems have been framed, and that all problems in the relevant class can be framed the same way. (It does allow that each of these problems can be framed in different ways too.) Both engineering cycles in TAR assume that agreement on goals can be achieved. And the basic assumption of validation research is that the world is stable enough to allow prediction of what would happen if the artifact were used. We conclude that TAR makes the assumptions of technical rationality identified by Schön [10].

To the extent that these assumptions are violated in a problematic situation, TAR helps us to find out whether or not this particular artifact can still be used in a particular client organization. But if all of these assumptions are violated, TAR is not applicable and other approaches should be searched, such as the combination of action research and design research in soft systems methodology proposed by Baskerville et al. [8].

6.3 Comparison with Related Work

Most approaches to action research follow the action research cycle proposed by Susman & Evered [2], which consists of diagnosing – action planning – action taking – evaluating – specifying learning. Figure 7 overlays this cycle with the multilevel structure of TAR.

This immediately makes clear that Susman & Evered's cycle is problem-driven: The cycle is triggered by a concrete need experienced by a particular client, and works bottom-up by iterating through the client cycle, to lessons learned that go beyond that particular client. Indeed, the cycle revolves around a client-system infrastructure in which the researcher and the client have built a mutual relationship of helping and learning. This contrasts with TAR, in which the researcher has identified a *class* of problems, and aims to develop an artifact to mitigate those problems. Validation of one artifact will require more than one TAR project, each for different clients. A client-researcher relationship needs to be built up for every separate client cycle. Action Design Research (ADR) introduced by Sein et al. [9] also is problem-driven and aims to build design principles based on iterative client cycles for the same client.

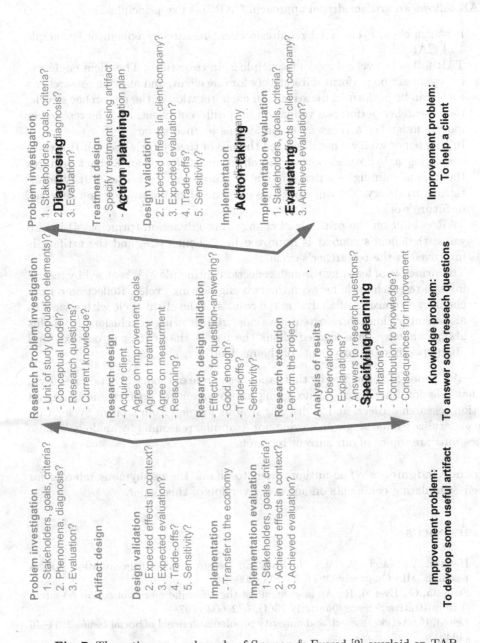

Fig. 7. The action research cycle of Susman & Evered [2] overlaid on TAR

TAR satisfies the principles of canonical action research (CAR) defined by Davison et al. [27], except that CAR assumes a problem-driven approach, whereas TAR follows an artifact-driven approach. CAR has five principles.

- For each client cycle, TAR requires a client-researcher agreement (principle 1 of CAR).
- TAR follows a cyclical model (principle 2) in two senses: The client engineering cycle can be performed iteratively for one client, and also the researcher's cycle can be performed iteratively. In each iteration of the researcher's cycle, the researcher performs a validation at a different client, and the researcher may redesign the artifact based on lessons learned so far.
- In this paper we have not discussed the use of theory (principle 3). However, specifying a hypothesis about the effect or utility of an artifact requires theory, and gaining experience in one or more client cycles can justify adaptations to theory. We will elaborate on generalization from action research in future work.
- TAR is built on the principle of change through action (principle 4) in two ways: the client's context is improved in a client cycle, and the artifact is improved in the researcher's cycle.
- The principle of learning through reflection (principle 5) is realized by inserting the research cycle between the two engineering cycles. Reflection on the client cycle consists of analyzing the results of the client cycle with a view to answering validation research questions, and drawing conclusions from this about what we have learned about the use of the artifact in context, and about possible improvements of the artifact.

A major problem untouched by this paper is the role of theory in action research. What role does theory have in designing improvements of artifacts, designing an action research project, and in drawing lessons learned from a client cycle? Can we generalize from a single case using, for example, reasoning by analogy? These questions are topics of our current research.

Acknowledgments. The authors wish to thank the anonymous referees for their stimulating comments on an earlier version of this paper.

References

1. Hevner, A., March, S., Park, J., Ram, S.: Design science in information system research. MIS Quarterly 28(1), 75–105 (2004)
2. Susman, G., Evered, R.: An assessment of the scientific merits of action research. Administrative Science Quarterly 23(4), 582–603 (1978)
3. Lewin, K.: Action research and minority problems. Journal of Social Issues 2, 34–46 (1946)
4. Baskerville, R.: What design science is not. European Journal of Information Systems 17, 441–443 (2008)

5. Järvinen, P.: Action research is similar to design science. Quality and Quantity 41(1), 37–54 (2007)
6. Lee, A.: Action is an artifact: What action research and design science offer to each other. In: Kock, N. (ed.) Information Systems Action Research: An Applied View of Emerging Concepts and Methods, pp. 43–60. Springer (2007)
7. March, A., Smith, G.: Design and natural science research on information technology. Decision Support Systems 15(4), 251–266 (1995)
8. Baskerville, R., Pries-Heje, J., Venable, J.: Soft design science methodology. In: Proceedings of the 4th International Conference on Design Science Research in Information Systems and Technology, DESRIST 2009, pp. 9:1–9:11. ACM Press (2009)
9. Sein, M., Henfridsson, O., Purao, S., Rossi, M., Lindgren, R.: Action design research. MIS Quarterly 35(2), 37–56 (2011)
10. Schön, D.: The Reflective Practitioner: How Professionals Think in Action. Arena (1983)
11. Cartwright, N.: How the Laws of Physics Lie. Oxford University Press (1983)
12. Cartwright, N.: The Dappled World. A Study of the Boundaries of Science. Cambridge University Press (1999)
13. McMullin, E.: Galilean idealization. Studies in the History and Philosophy of Science 16(3), 247–273 (1985)
14. Boon, M.: How science is applied in technology. International Studies in the Philosophy of Science 20(1), 27–47 (2006)
15. Laymon, R.: Applying idealized scientific theories to engineering. Synthese 81, 353–371 (1989)
16. Küppers, G.: On the relation between technology and science—goals of knowledge and dynamics of theories. The example of combustion technology, thermodynamics and fluid dynamics. In: Krohn, W., Layton, E., Weingart, P. (eds.) The Dynamics of Science and Technology. Sociology of the Sciences, II, pp. 113–133. Reidel (1978)
17. Wieringa, R.: Relevance and Problem Choice in Design Science. In: Winter, R., Zhao, J.L., Aier, S. (eds.) DESRIST 2010. LNCS, vol. 6105, pp. 61–76. Springer, Heidelberg (2010)
18. Vincenti, W.: What Engineers Know and How They Know It. Analytical Studies from Aeronautical History. Johns Hopkins (1990)
19. Wieringa, R.J.: Design science as nested problem solving. In: Proceedings of the 4th International Conference on Design Science Research in Information Systems and Technology, pp. 1–12. ACM, New York (2009)
20. Van Strien, P.: Towards a methodology of psychological practice: The regulative cycle. Theory & Psychology 7(5), 683–700 (1997)
21. Morali, A., Wieringa, R.J.: Risk-based confidentiality requirements specification for outsourced it systems. In: Proceedings of the 18th IEEE International Requirements Engineering Conference (RE 2010), Sydney, Australia, Los Alamitos, California, pp. 199–208. IEEE Computer Society (September 2010)
22. Lee, A., Baskerville, R.: Generalizing generalizability in information systems research. Information Systems Research 14(3), 221–243 (2003)
23. Seddon, P., Scheepers, R.: Other-settings generalizability in IS research. In: International Conference on Information Systems (ICIS), pp. 1141–1158 (2006)

24. Seddon, P., Scheepers, R.: Towards the improved treatment of generalization from knowledge claims in IS research: drawing general conclusions from samples. European Journal of Information Systems, 1–16 (2011), doi:10.1057/ejis.2011.9
25. Zambon, E., Etalle, S., Wieringa, R.J., Hartel, P.H.: Model-based qualitative risk assessment for availability of IT infrastructures. Software and Systems Modeling 10(4), 553–580 (2011)
26. Engelsman, W., Wieringa, R.: Goal-Oriented Requirements Engineering and Enterprise Architecture: Two Case Studies and Some Lessons Learned. In: Regnell, B., Damian, D. (eds.) REFSQ 2011. LNCS, vol. 7195, pp. 306–320. Springer, Heidelberg (2012)
27. Davison, R., Martinsons, M., Kock, N.: Principles of canonical action research. Information Systems Journal 14, 65–86 (2004)

Decision Enhancement for Sourcing with Shared Service Centres in the Dutch Government

Arjan Knol[1], Henk Sol[1], and Johan van Wamelen[2]

[1] University of Groningen, Groningen, The Netherlands
{arjan.knol,h.g.sol}@rug.nl
[2] Center for Public Innovation, Erasmus University Rotterdam, Rotterdam, The Netherlands
wamelen@publicinnovation.nl

Abstract. Primarily in order to save costs, many shared service centres (SSCs) are being established in organisations. However, establishing SSCs is a challenging task for many organisations, including the Dutch government. This design science research aims to enhance SSC establishment with a decision enhancement studio for sourcing & sharing in the Dutch government. The proposed studio consists of a set of services for studio participants to analyse decision alternatives and improve collaboration. In this paper a studio design is presented with four decision enhancement services for sourcing & sharing that are delivered with an online tool and predefined scripts (called sourceLets). Future research will be dedicated to the scientific evaluation of the studio design by applying it to multiple case studies in the Dutch government.

Keywords: Decision, Enhancement, Sourcing, SSC.

1 Introduction

Primarily in order to save costs, many shared service centres (SSCs) are being established in organisations [1]. A SSC is a specific type of in-house sourcing arrangement potentially capable of reducing costs and improving quality through the delivery of specialised, value-added services across an entire organisation [2,3]. In other words, a SSC is an independent centre to share supporting services within an organisation (insourcing instead of outsourcing). Although the concept of SSCs is not new, SSCs have gained considerable momentum in the past decade, mainly because of technological developments [4]. This accounts for the Dutch government also in which several (new) SSCs as part of a cost-saving incentive program called "compact government" are developed.

Even though SSCs have the potential to achieve great contributions, major difficulties with this specific type of sourcing arrangement are also recognised [5]. Achieving cost-efficient and / or quality-improving operations with SSCs proves to be a complex task [6,7]. Because of this complexity, deciding to source with SSCs is also challenging for many organisations. "The introduction of a SSC is a critical decision on a strategic level. It implies a long-term decision with significant complexity and risks." [8].

K. Peffers, M. Rothenberger, and B. Kuechler (Eds.): DESRIST 2012, LNCS 7286, pp. 239–255, 2012.

The availability of literature about decision-making and SSCs is limited. The dominant work in this field seems to be that of Janssen & Joha [8], who present a list of motives of organisations who decide to source with SSCs. And only one example of research about how to design solutions to support SSC decision-making is found with Janssen, Joha & Zuurmond [9], who have designed and validated simulation models for adopting SSCs.

The main question of this research is: how can complex SSC decisions be enhanced to achieve successful establishments of SSCs in organisations? A demarcation of which SSC decisions will be specifically enhanced with this research is necessary. In terms of Joha & Janssen [10] who have categorised SSC decision processes, this research specifically aims to enhance SSC arrangement decisions. After the decision to establish a SSC is made it needs to be decided how to arrange the SSC. Which services to source and share with the SSC? Which SSC arrangement alternative is preferred in terms of cost-saving potential, qualitative advantages and feasibility?

A decision enhancement studio is postulated as a suitable mean to enhance the complex SSC decision-making. Keen & Sol [11] define a decision enhancement studio as an environment which consists of a set of services to analyse decision alternatives and improve collaboration in complex decision processes, providing a mean for studio participants to discuss and decide on beforehand. Hence, in this research a decision enhancement studio for sourcing & sharing in the Dutch government is created consisting of decision enhancement services that provide functionalities which help users to make complex decisions.

This paper presents a design of the decision enhancement studio for sourcing & sharing. The studio design consists of four decision enhancement services that are delivered with an online tool and predefined scripts (called sourceLets as explained in further detail later).

2   Background: Shared Service Centres

In literature many definitions of SSCs are given. Based on identified SSC characteristics of Schulz & Brenner [1] and a combination of definitions of SSCs presented by Grant et al. [2], Ulbrich [3] and Ulrich [12], a SSC is defined as a specific type of independent in-house sourcing arrangement potentially capable of reducing costs and improving quality through the consolidation of specialised, common and value-added services that are delivered across an entire organization. In other words, a SSC is an independent centre to share supporting services within an organisation (insourcing instead of outsourcing).

An example SSC in the Dutch government is P-Direkt which, as a separate organisation unit, offers payroll services to multiple Ministries. Before establishment of P-Direkt multiple Ministries had their own internal payroll departments. With P-Direkt the payroll departments are concentrated into one SSC with the goal to attain cost-savings and qualitative advantages.

3   Research Approach

This research uses design science of Hevner & Chatterjee [13] as a research philosophy complemented with the inductive-hypothetic research strategy of Sol [14] in order to create the decision enhancement studio for sourcing & sharing and to achieve scientific as well as practical contributions. Following the inductive-hypothetic research strategy of Sol [14], a researcher moves from exploration and understanding of a domain (descriptive) to design and evaluation of artefacts (prescriptive). Accordingly, this research is conducted in four phases: exploration, understanding, design and evaluation (see figure 1).

This paper presents a design of a decision enhancement studio for sourcing & sharing. As shown in figure 1, the studio design is based on results from the exploration and understanding research phases. Information is retrieved from literature, case studies, expert interviews and presentations & progress meetings. Regarding the expert interviews, information and advice is retrieved from two rounds of in total 25 interviews with 20 experts working with SSCs both in and outside the Dutch government. The expert group consisted of four SSC directors in the Dutch government, six external sourcing consultants and / or researchers and ten policy makers / managers working with SSCs in the Dutch Ministry of the Interior and Kingdom relations. The experts have been interviewed in the fall and winter of 2010-2011 and in the spring and summer of 2011. The majority of the expert group has been interviewed face-to-face and some have given advice via telephone or e-mail.

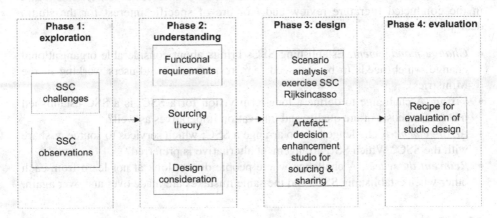

Fig. 1. Four research phases

Furthermore, during the design phase a scenario analysis exercise has been conducted based on the studio design in a case study in the Dutch government: a collecting SSC called Rijksincasso. The lessons learned from this exercise are used for the design of an online tool for SSC scenario analysis that will be used to deliver the decision enhancement services for sourcing & sharing.

Future research will be dedicated to the scientific evaluation of the studio design by applying it to multiple case studies in the Dutch government (following guidelines of e.g. Hevner & Chatterjee [13] and Venable [15]). For this a recipe [11] will be created providing a standardised description how to deploy the decision enhancement studio for sourcing & sharing for effective SSC arrangement in the Dutch government.

4   From Exploration and Understanding to Design

As shown in figure 1, the studio design is based on results from exploration and understanding research phases being SSC challenges, SSC observations, functional requirements, a sourcing theory and a design consideration. This section briefly elaborates on these results. In the next section the studio design is presented.

4.1   SSC Development Challenges

SSCs can have great contributions, but achieving cost-efficient and / or quality improving operations with SSCs is a complex task [6,7]. Knol & Sol [5] provide a taxonomy of various technological, managerial and organisational challenges that organisations can encounter when developing SSCs based on literature and three case studies of SSCs in the Dutch government. Four SSC development challenges are notable, because they were mostly mentioned by interviewees, were not found in the conducted literature review and / or are of specific interest for the studio design:

- *Change management.* Establishing SSCs brings about considerable organisational change which needs to be managed (e.g. resistance of end-users working in the Ministries).
- *Vision.* A challenge to define a long-term vision for a SSC; is a SSC established just to save costs or are quality and innovation imperatives as well?
- *Arrangement.* A challenge how to arrange a SSC; which services to source & share with the SSC? Which SSC arrangement alternative is preferred?
- *Reinvent the wheel.* A challenge where people do not look at nor learn from each other when establishing SSCs and the same mistakes are made over and over again.

4.2   SSC Observations

Based on expert interviews two SSC observations are identified:

- *Mix between rational and non-rational SSC decision-making.* SSC decision-making in the Dutch government is not necessarily based on facts and analyses, but also on interests and preferences taking place in a managerial and political context.

- *A non-linear, unpredictable SSC development process.* SSC development in practice always takes place differently and only on an abstract level generic steps can be identified. This relates to an observation that the Dutch government can be characterised as a highly dynamic organisational environment that changes frequently.

4.3   Requirements

Based on the aforementioned SSC development challenges three functional requirements regarding the studio design are formulated:

- Create a studio environment to achieve collaboration and a shared mindset when establishing SSCs (based on the change management challenges).
- Create a studio environment to share knowledge & past experiences when establishing SSCs (based on the "reinvent the wheel" challenge).
- Create a studio environment to analyse SSC arrangement alternatives to make grounded decisions that last (based on the "vision" and "arrangement" challenges).

The above shows that overall a need for a solution that enables collaboration and sharing as well as analysis of decision alternatives clearly exists in the Dutch government, confirming that the deployment of a decision enhancement studio for sourcing & sharing seems suitable to this end.

4.4   Sourcing Theory

Based on the aforementioned observation that there is a mix between rational and non-rational SSC decision-making a sourcing theory is formulated. The sourcing theory postulates that complex SSC decisions are made based on three perspectives: content (facts and analyses), considerations of stakeholders and knowledge & past experiences. For example, in SSC decision-making factual business cases are used (content), resistance to change of end-users needs to be accounted for (considerations of stakeholders) and best & worst practices from experts are taken into consideration (knowledge & past experiences). The assumption is that providing SSC decision-makers insight into these three perspectives on beforehand enables them to assess alternatives and make though-out decisions. Hence, the sourcing theory postulates that a thought-out SSC decision is a decision in which alternatives are assessed based on content, considerations of stakeholders and knowledge & past experiences.

The three aspects of the sourcing theory relate to several scientific theories / fields. First, SSC decision-making based on knowledge & past experiences relates to knowledge management (e.g. [16]). Second, SSC decision-making based on content relates to bounded rationality, implying that we are to some extent rational human beings making "boundedly rational, or "reasonable," decisions" [17] within limits such as knowledge and time [18]. Third, SSC decision-making based on considerations of stakeholders relates to stakeholder theory which "specifies how and under what circumstances managers can and should respond to various stakeholder types" [19]. In addition, the assessment of alternatives aspect of the sourcing theory relates to simulation (e.g. [14,20]), scenario analysis (e.g. [21]) and, obviously, decision enhancement services [11] in which simulation and scenario analysis are incorporated. This aspect also relates to literature about organisational decision-making stating that assessment of alternatives is "what it is all about" (e.g. [22]).

4.5   Design Consideration

Based on the second aforementioned observation of a non-linear, unpredictable SSC development process a design consideration is formulated to design a studio with loosely-coupled decision enhancement services which can be deployed situation-dependently. This means that it is not predefined when to deploy the decision enhancement services in SSC development processes.

The design consideration relates to several scientific theories / concepts, being the garbage can theory, loosely-coupled concept and agility concept. The garbage can theory of Cohen, March & Olsen [23] views organisations as garbage cans in which over time "ideas, problems and possible solutions are (metaphorically) dumped" [24], acknowledging a certain coincidental aspect or non-rational decision-making. The loosely-coupled concept can be related to Weick [25], who looks at organisations as loosely-coupled systems, and for example Chin [26] who has created a loosely-coupled portal in which services can be situation-dependently deployed. And agility is ultimately about "creating and responding to change" [27] for organisations operating in increasingly dynamic environments.

5   Studio Design

5.1   Four Decision Enhancement Services for Sourcing and Sharing

The aforementioned results show that there is a need for a studio environment with loosely-coupled decision enhancement services for sourcing & sharing which provides insight into content, considerations of stakeholders and knowledge & past experiences to anticipate on when assessing alternatives in SSC decision-making processes. Accordingly, a studio with four decision enhancement services for sourcing & sharing is created (see figure 2):

1. *Decision enhancement service for sharing knowledge & past experiences:* which knowledge & past experiences can be used?
2. *Decision enhancement service for content analysis:* the rational view: business cases, cost-saving potentials, etc.
3. *Decision enhancement service for stakeholder analysis:* who are the stakeholders involved and what are their considerations?
4. *Decision enhancement service for scenario analysis:* based on knowledge & past experiences, content and stakeholder considerations for effective SSC decision-making.

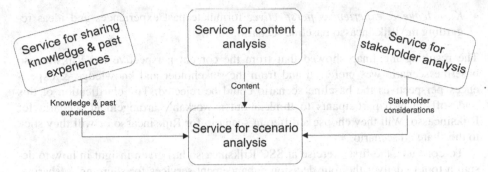

Fig. 2. Studio design with four decision enhancement services for sourcing & sharing

In essence, the studio design with the four decision enhancement services for sourcing & sharing aims to achieve workable SSC solutions by analysing scenarios based on three perspectives. The rest of this paper explains how the four services can be deployed in practice.

5.2   First Exercise: Scenario Analysis for SSC Rijksincasso in a Group Decision Session

The four decision enhancement services for sourcing & sharing are delivered with an online tool and predefined scripts. In order to achieve further insight in how to design the tool, an informal scenario analysis has been conducted in a case study in the Dutch government: a collecting SSC in development called Rijksincasso. SSC Rijksincasso aims to start next year and is currently in preparation of a potential transition of >120 collecting services of >50 governmental organisations.

The scenario analysis at SSC Rijksincasso has been conducted in a single group decision session which lasted two hours and consisted of five participants who are heavily involved in SSC Rijksincasso. The analysis is based on three standard SSC arrangement scenarios [9]:

• *Share all:* source and share all services in a domain with the SSC.
• *Share partially:* source and share a part of all services in a domain with the SSC.
• *Share nothing:* source and share no services in a domain with the SSC (null option).

During the group decision session the Rijksincasso baseline scenario: share all has been analysed by collaboratively filling in a mindmap using an online tool called MindMeister. On the mindmap the baseline scenario has been analysed based on the three perspectives of the studio design:

• *Content perspective:* clarify the cost-saving potential and formulate the qualitative advantages of the Rijksincasso baseline scenario;
• *Stakeholder perspective:* identify stakeholder concerns and potential resistance regarding the Rijksincasso baseline scenario;

- *Knowledge & experiences perspective:* formulate past experiences and ideas regarding the Rijksincasso baseline scenario.

The resulting mindmap showed that from the content perspective the Rijksincasso baseline scenario was preferred and from the stakeholder and knowledge & experiences perspectives the baseline scenario could be rejected. The clarification of this trade-off enabled participants to think about a workable arrangement scenario for Rijksincasso. Will they choose a different scenario for Rijksincasso or will they stick to the share all scenario?

To conclude, the first exercise at SSC Rijksincasso has given insight in how to design a tool to deliver the four decision enhancement services for sourcing & sharing. The lessons learned are:

- Do not only analyse baseline scenarios during group decision sessions, but analyse all three SSC arrangement scenarios based on the perspectives content, stakeholders and knowledge & experiences to enable participants to choose workable arrangement scenarios.
- Mindmapping is useful for brainstorming activities such as identifying stakeholder concerns of a SSC arrangement scenario. However, a tool for scenario analysis is necessary which aggregates the input from mindmaps to provide an overview.
- Stakeholder concerns and interests can be identified virtually using questionnaires and e-mail. Results of stakeholder analyses can be discussed during group decision sessions. This means that (parts of) the decision enhancement services for sourcing & sharing could be deployed virtually instead of in group decision sessions (also following the time-place framework of Johansen [28]).
- Using an online tool such as MindMeister is interesting because it can be accessed via any modern web browser during group decision sessions without the need of special software.

5.3   Online Tool for SSC Scenario Analysis

The aforementioned design consideration and lessons learned from the Rijksincasso case study are translated to the following requirements for a tool for SSC scenario analysis:

- A tool in which the four loosely-coupled decision enhancement services for sourcing & sharing can be deployed separately at any time in a SSC development process;
- A tool to analyse the SSC arrangement scenarios share all, share partially and share nothing based on the perspectives content, stakeholders and knowledge & experiences;
- A tool which can use input from mindmaps created in brainstorming activities;
- A tool to deploy in group decision sessions;
- A tool in which information obtained via questionnaires and e-mail can be stored;
- An online tool which can be accessed from any modern web browser.

The online tool for SSC scenario analysis is currently in development. Several wireframe sketches are provided to present an overview of the functionalities of the tool. Figure 3 provides a wireframe of the project start page in which the four loosely-coupled decision enhancement services for sourcing & sharing can be opened separately. It is to be noted that for the service for scenario analysis at least one of the other three decision enhancement services for sourcing & sharing should be completed.

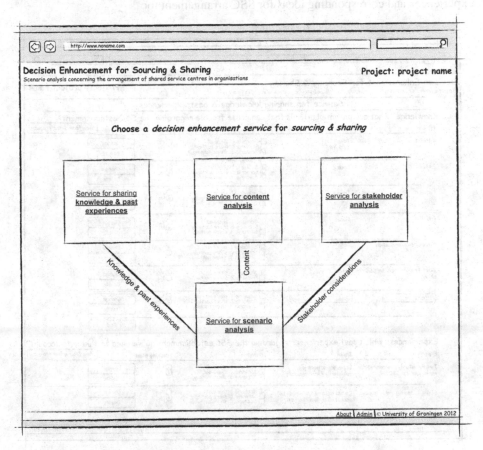

Fig. 3. Wireframe of the project start page

Figure 4 provides a wireframe of the service for sharing knowledge & past experiences page. Regarding the sharing of knowledge, the page enables participants to identify pitfalls which can cause trouble for the establishment of a SSC. For each pitfall one or multiple applicable SSC arrangement scenario(s) can be chosen. Furthermore, for each pitfall ideas can be generated to tackle them in advance. If no suitable ideas are generated a pitfall can be flagged as a breaking point which means it is likely the pitfall will become a severe source of trouble for one or multiple SSC arrangement scenarios. Pitfalls can be added, changed and deleted on the page. Also, pitfalls generated from other SSC development projects can be viewed. In this way a knowledge base with pitfalls and corresponding ideas for SSC arrangement is created. Regarding the sharing of experiences, the page enables participants to share negative and positive past experiences for the establishment of a SSC. This basically works the same as the sharing of pitfalls; for each experience ideas are generated and applicable scenario(s) are chosen. Furthermore, breaking points are flagged and experiences from other projects can be viewed, with the latter creating a knowledge base with experiences and corresponding ideas for SSC arrangement too.

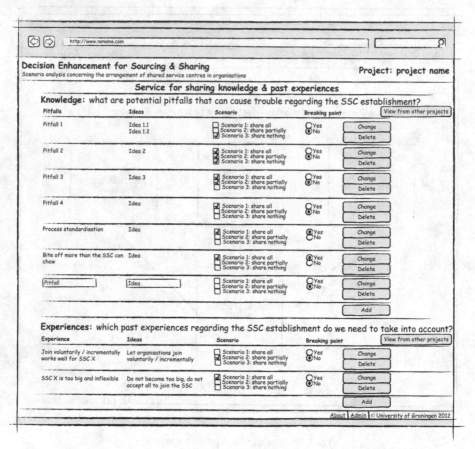

Fig. 4. Wireframe of the service for sharing knowledge & past experiences page

Figure 5 provides a wireframe of the service for content analysis page. The content analysis is divided into two aspects: cost-saving potential and qualitative advantages. Cost-saving potentials can be identified and stored by participants for share all and share partially SSC arrangement scenarios (the share nothing scenario is obsolete, because this scenario has no cost-saving potential). Qualitative advantages for the share all and share partially scenarios can be identified and stored too. In addition, qualitative advantages identified in other projects can be viewed. In this way a knowledge base with qualitative advantages for SSC arrangement is created (on top of the knowledge bases with pitfalls, experiences and ideas for SSC arrangement).

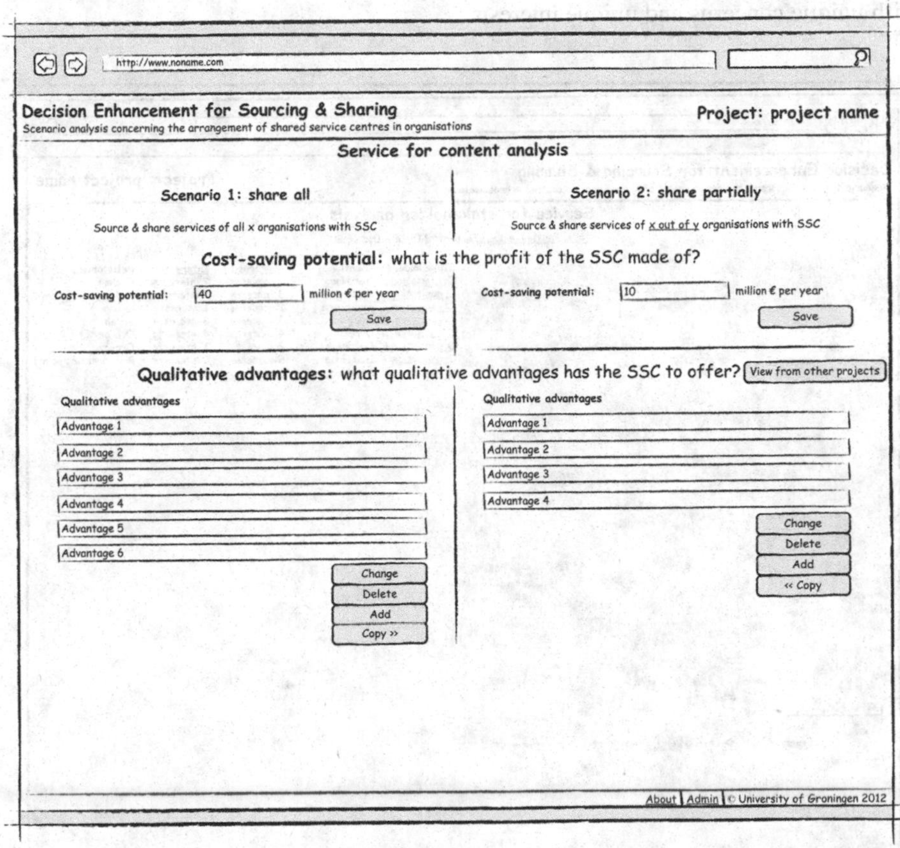

Fig. 5. Wireframe of the service for content analysis page

Figure 6 provides a wireframe of the service for stakeholder analysis page. The page provides an overview with results from stakeholder analyses in which concerns, interests and resistance of stakeholders related to a SSC in development are identified. The identification of stakeholder concerns, interests and resistance itself is done using MindMeister mindmaps (or mindmaps exported in a Freemind .mm XML format). The mindmaps can be filled collaboratively during group decision sessions or by a process facilitator having used questionnaires and e-mail to virtually retrieve information to fill the mindmap. The mindmaps follow a specified structure with three nodes per stakeholder: concerns, interests and resistance. Resistance can be assessed with the colours red, orange and green, with red meaning high resistance, orange meaning medium resistance and green meaning no / little resistance. An example is shown in figure 7. The stakeholder analysis page automatically imports mindmaps, e.g. via the MindMeister application programming interface (API). In order to visualise results from stakeholder analyses, the page provides a map (e.g. using the Google Maps API) showing all stakeholders and their resistance colour. The page also provides an overview table. Clicking on the concerns and interests table headings provides a pop-up with unique concerns and unique interests.

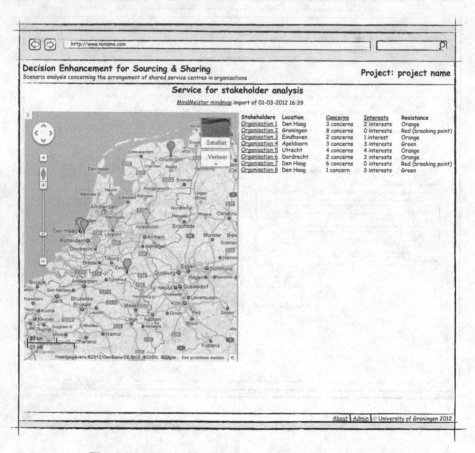

Fig. 6. Wireframe of the service for stakeholder analysis page

Fig. 7. Example MindMeister mindmap that can be automatically imported to the stakeholder analysis page in the online tool for SSC scenario analysis

Figure 8 provides a wireframe of the service for scenario analysis page, presenting an overview of the three SSC arrangement scenarios based on the three perspectives content, stakeholder considerations and knowledge & past experiences. Each block in the overview table is automatically assigned the colour red, orange or green based on results from previously conducted decision enhancement services for sourcing & sharing. The colour red presents a negative perspective, green a positive perspective and orange in between. The figure shows for example that the share all scenario is particularly beneficial from a content perspective (green), but less beneficial from a stakeholders perspective (red). Colours can also be assigned manually during group discussion if the automatically assigned colours are incorrect. The scenario analysis page forms the basis for choosing workable SSC arrangement alternatives in group decision sessions by combining and visualising the results of the other three decision enhancement services for sourcing & sharing (which need to have been deployed before).

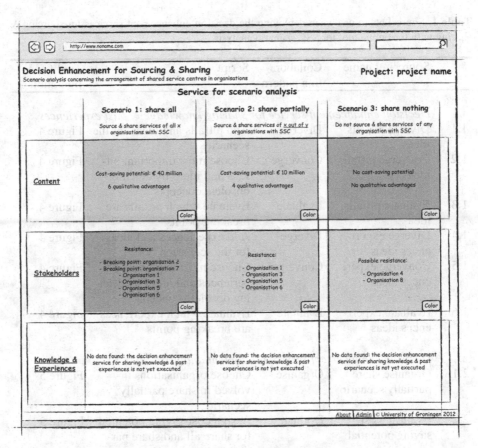

Fig. 8. Wireframe of the service for scenario analysis page

5.4   SourceLets

The four decision enhancement services for sourcing & sharing are delivered with the online tool for SSC scenario analysis as presented before and predefined scripts. Combining the predefined scripts with the online tool creates so-called sourceLets for this research (derived from the thinkLet concept as introduced by e.g. Briggs & de Vreede [29] and Kolfschoten et al. [30]). SourceLets are composed of tools, configurations and scripts and aim to achieve predictable collaboration patterns such as diverge, converge and evaluate in group activities [29].

Table 1 provides an overview of sourceLets to use when deploying the decision enhancement services for sourcing & sharing with the online tool for SSC scenario analysis. They explain how the decision enhancement services for sourcing & sharing can be deployed as well as provide a standardisation which is useful for evaluation purposes.

Table 1. SourceLets to use when deploying the decision enhancement services for sourcing & sharing with the online tool for SSC scenario analysis

#	SourceLet name	Collabora-tion pattern	Script	Tool / con-figuration
1	*Decision enhancement service for sharing knowledge & past experiences*			
1.1	Diverge pitfalls ideas	Diverge	Add pitfalls and ideas for the scenarios	Figure 4
1.2	Converge pitfalls ideas	Converge	Choose most important pitfalls and ideas by deleting obsolete concepts	Figure 4
1.3	Evaluate pitfalls ideas	Evaluate	Evaluate which pitfalls are breaking points	Figure 4
1.4	Diverge experiences ideas	Diverge	Add experiences and ideas for the scenarios	Figure 4
1.5	Converge experiences ideas	Converge	Choose most important experiences and ideas by deleting obsolete concepts	Figure 4
1.6	Evaluate experiences ideas	Evaluate	Evaluate which experiences are breaking points	Figure 4
2	*Decision enhancement service for content analysis*			
2.1	Organise share partially scenario	Organise	Choose organisations involved in share partially scenario	Figure 5
2.2	Evaluate cost-saving potential	Evaluate	Assign cost-saving potential for share all and share partially scenarios	Figure 5
2.3	Diverge qualitative advantages	Diverge	Add qualitative advantages for the scenarios	Figure 5

Table 1. (*continued*)

#	SourceLet name	Collaboration pattern	Script	Tool / configuration
2.4	Converge qualitative advantages	Converge	Choose most important qualitative advantages by deleting obsolete concepts	Figure 5
3	*Decision enhancement service for stakeholder analysis*			
3.1	Diverge stakeholders	Diverge	Add stakeholders involved	Figure 6
3.2	Diverge concerns interests	Diverge	Add concerns and interests of stakeholders	Figure 6
3.3	Converge concerns interests	Converge	Choose most important concerns and interests by deleting obsolete concepts	Figure 6
3.4	Organise concerns interests	Organise	Give redundant concerns and interests the same name	Figure 6
3.5	Evaluate resistance	Evaluate	Assign resistance color (red, orange or green)	Figure 6
3.6	Organise stakeholder analysis	Organise	Provide an overview of stakeholder analysis results with map and table view	Figure 7
4	*Decision enhancement service for scenario analysis*			
4.1	Organise share partially scenario	Organise	Choose organisations involved in share partially scenario	Figure 8
4.2	Organise scenario analysis	Organise	Provide an overview of three scenarios in which input from three services / perspectives is shown	Figure 8
4.3	Evaluate scenario analysis	Evaluate	SSC decision-making: choose preferred scenario based on overview	Figure 8

6   Conclusion and Future Research

To conclude, the studio design presented in this paper consists of four decision enhancement services for sourcing & sharing that are delivered with an online tool and predefined scripts (called sourceLets). The studio design aims to enable participants to achieve workable solutions regarding the arrangement of SSCs by assessing tradeoffs between share all, share partially and share nothing scenarios based on three perspectives. Future research will be dedicated to the scientific evaluation of the studio design by applying it to multiple case studies in the Dutch government (following guidelines of e.g. Hevner & Chatterjee [13] and Venable [15]).

References

1. Schulz, V., Brenner, W.: Characteristics of Shared Service Centers. In: Transforming Government: People, Process and Policy, 4(3), pp. 210-219 (2010)
2. Grant, G., McKnight, S., Uruthirapathy, A., Brown, A.: Designing Governance for Shared Services Organizations in the Public Service. In: Government Information Quarterly, 24(3), pp. 522-538 (2007)
3. Ulbrich, F.: Improving Shared Service Implementation: Adopting Lessons from the BPR Movement. In: Business Process Management Journal, 12(2), pp. 195-205 (2006)
4. Adler, P.S.: Making the HR Outsourcing Decision. In: MIT Sloan Management Review, 45(1), pp. 53-60 (2003)
5. Knol, A.J., Sol, H.G.: Sourcing with Shared Service Centres: Challenges in the Dutch Government. In: In Proceedings of the European Conference on Information Systems (ECIS), (2011)
6. Cooke, F.L.: Modeling an HR Shared Services Center Experience of an MNC in the United Kingdom. In: Human Resource Management, 45(2), pp. 211-227 (2006)
7. Wagenaar, R.: Governance of Shared Service Centers in Public Administration: Dilemma's and Tradeoffs. In: In Proceedings of the International Conference on Electronic Commerce (ICEC), , pp. 354-363 (2006)
8. Janssen, M., Joha, A.: Motives for Establishing Shared Service Centers in Public Administrations. In: International Journal of Information Management, 26(2), pp. 102-115 (2006)
9. Janssen, M., Joha, A., Zuurmond, A.: Simulation and Animation for Adopting Shared Services: Evaluating and Comparing Alternative Arrangements. In: Government Information Quarterly, 26(1), pp. 15-24 (2009)
10. Joha, A., Janssen, M.: Content Management Implemented as Shared Service: a Public Sector Case Study. In: IFIP International Federation for Information Processing 2010, , pp. 138-151 (2010)
11. Keen, P.G.W., Sol, H.G.: Decision Enhancement Services: Rehearsing the Future for Decisions that Matter. IOS Press, Delft (2008)
12. Ulrich, D.: Shared Services: from Vogue to Value. In: Human Resource Planning, 18(3), pp. 12-23 (1995)
13. Hevner, A.R., Chatterjee, S.: Design Research in Information Systems: Theory and Practice. Springer, New York Dordrecht Heidelberg London (2010)
14. Sol, H.G.: Simulation in Information Systems Development. Doctoral Dissertation, University of Groningen, Groningen (1982)
15. Venable, J.R.: Design Science Research Post Hevner et al. Criteria, Standards, Guidelines, and Expectations. In: In proceedings of the 5th International Conference on Global Perspectives on Design Science Research (DESRIST), , pp. 109-123 (2010)
16. Alavi, M., Leidner, D.E.: Review: Knowledge Management and Knowledge Management Systems: Conceptual Foundations and Research Issues. In: MIS Quarterly: Management Information Systems, 25(1), pp. 107-136 (2001)
17. Simon, H.A.: Rationality in Psychology & Economics. In: The Journal of Business, 59(4), pp. 209-224 (1986)
18. Gigerenzer, G., Goldstein, D.G.: Reasoning the Fast and Frugal Way: Models of Bounded Rationality. In: Psychological Review, 103(4), pp. 650-669 (1996)
19. Mitchell, R.K., Agle, B.R.: Toward a Theory of Stakeholder Identification and Salience: Defining the Principle of Who and What Really Counts. In: Academy of Management Review, 22(4), pp. 853-886 (1997)

20. Law, A.M., Kelton, W.D.: Simulation Modeling and Analysis. McGraw-Hill, Boston, MA (1999)
21. Hsia, P., Samuel, J., Gao, J., Kung, D., Toyoshima, Y., Chen, C.: Formal Approach to Scenario Analysis. In: IEEE Software, 11(2), pp. 33-41 (1994)
22. Nutt, P.C.: Public-Private Differences and the Assessment of Alternatives for Decision Making. In: Journal of Public Administration Research and Theory, 9(2), pp. 305-349 (1999)
23. Cohen, M.D., March, J.G., Olsen, J.P.: A Garbage Can Model of Organizational Choice. In: Administrative Science Quarterly, 17(1), pp. 1-25 (1972)
24. Tiernan, A., Burke, T.: A Load of Old Garbage: Applying Garbage-can Theory to Contemporary Housing Policy. In: Australian Journal of Public Administration, 61(3), pp. 86-97 (2002)
25. Weick, K.E.: Educational Organizations as Loosely Coupled Systems. In: Administrative Science Quarterly, 21(1), pp. 1-19 (1976)
26. Chin, R.: Mainport Planning Suite: Software Services to Support Mainport Planning. Doctoral Dissertation, Delft University of Technology, Delft (2007)
27. Highsmith, J., Cockburn, A.: Agile Software Development: the Business of Innovation. In: Computer, 34(9), pp. 120-122 (2001)
28. Johansen, R.: Groupware: Computer Support for Business Teams. The Free Press, New York (1988)
29. Briggs, R.O., de Vreede, G.: ThinkLets: Building Blocks for Concerted Collaboration. Lulu.com, Raleigh, NC (2009)
30. Kolfschoten, G.L., Briggs, R.O., de Vreede, G.J., Jacobs, P.H.M., Appelman, J.H.: A Conceptual Foundation of the ThinkLet Concept for Collaboration Engineering. In: International Journal of Human Computer Studies, 64(7), pp. 611-621 (2006)

Designing a Framework for Virtual Management and Team Building

Jan Pries-Heje and Lene Pries-Heje

Roskilde University & The IT University of Copenhagen, Denmark
janph@ruc.dk, lpries@itu.dk

Abstract. To cope with seven identified problems in virtual and distributed management in Danske Bank we used a design science research approach to design a conceptual framework for team building in virtual and distributed project teams. The conceptual framework combines a six-phase teambuilding model with the notion and elements of social capital. Thus in each phase of teambuilding you build up all six elements of social capital. The complete six-by-six framework was diffused in Danske Bank in January 2011, and evaluated very positively in the summer of 2011. The framework is being implemented throughout Danske Bank in 2012. This paper gives an account of the framework content and the results from the evaluation. Finally the paper discusses how the contribution can be generalized and used in other companies.

Keywords: Virtual and distributed teams, teambuilding, social capital, design science research.

1   Introduction

Globalization has arrived and influences the organization of work everywhere [cf. 1]. When a unique piece of work or a unique problem is at hand an organization typically institutes a project to solve the problem or carry out the unique task.

In the past a project team was gathered, given their own organization with a steering committee and a project manager, and often they were co-located in the same room. However, the wave of globalization means that a company will have many projects characterized by rapidly assembled project teams, geographically dispersed, but with highly specialized professionals who perform specific tasks. Individual project teams will not gather physically any more. Instead they are distributed physically and gather virtually using phone, internet, video conferences and other meeting tools to communicate.

Hence virtual teams and virtual projects will be very common in the future, where a *virtual team* in our understanding is a team separated by geography, time zones and/or culture, but never the less has to work together as a team.

In this paper we look at a concrete design science research undertaking in Danske Bank, a major Danish bank. Project work in Danske Bank is characterized by having many virtual teams with people working in both Bangalore, India and at several sites

K. Peffers, M. Rothenberger, and B. Kuechler (Eds.): DESRIST 2012, LNCS 7286, pp. 256–270, 2012.

in Denmark. These teams need to improve their collaboration. This was realized by Danske Bank at the beginning of 2010.

At the time Danske Bank was partner in a large cooperative research project called SourceIT by three companies, Roskilde University and a Technology Transfer organization named Delta. The purpose of SourceIT was to help the participating companies become better at making sourcing decisions. The results reported here on improving virtual management and project teambuilding was initiated as part of the SourceIT undertaking but continued after SourceIT ended in June 2011.

The remainder of the paper is organized as follows. First, in section 2, we carefully explain our research method; design science research, and give a short account of the outcome of an interview study conducted in Danske Bank. Then in section 3 we give an overview of existing knowledge in relation to virtual teams and management as well as the problem at hand. Then follows a section 4 where we give the details of our design of a conceptual framework solving the problem faced in Danske Bank. And a section 5 where we give an account of the diffusion and successful evaluation of our six-by-six conceptual framework (= the design). Finally the paper ends with a conclusion.

2   Research Method

In this section we carefully explain our design science research approach, the business needs we are addressing and applicable knowledge for the problem at hand.

Benbasat & Zmud [2] argue that much IS research today is irrelevant and recommend research that are more relevant, but without fundamentally challenging the existing academic value system. We believe that design science research offers the practical relevance and utility requested because it emphasizes that a design should address a need or a problem and at the same time should 'stand on the shoulders' of existing research within the problem area..

In 1992 one of the first journal papers on design science research in information systems was published by Walls et al. [3]. In the paper they argue that design is both a product and a process. Thus a design theory must on one side handle the design product and on the other side it should handle the design process. In 1995 another influential paper on design science research by March and Smith [4] was published. One of their key points is that in design science one can build and evaluate Constructs, Models, Methods and Instantiations. The conceptual framework we arrived at developing is both a Model and a Method and we have been using it in at least seven areas; making it seven Instantiations.

Continuing from the work of March and Smith [4] Hevner et al. [5] presented a design science research framework that enhances the Walls et al. [3]. At the core are the build and justify activity. And that is exactly what we are reporting in this paper.

2.1   Research Initiation and Results from an Interview Study

The research reported in this paper was initiated in the summer of 2010 when Linda Olsen, the First Vice President for Danske Bank's Outsourcing setup in Bangalore,

India (DCI), stated that they needed an improvement; they needed better virtual management. In August 2010 we interviewed Linda Olsen to obtain a better understanding of the business need for better virtual management. She told us that Danske Bank have two types of projects. One type is development projects where something new is developed often as an add-on to existing applications or from scratch. The other type of projects is system management projects where development consists of smaller changes, additions and defect corrections. The virtual projects (across Denmark-India) were mainly of the latter system management type. In Linda Olsen's opinion there was enough technology available to the virtual project teams. Thus Danske Bank had implemented tele-presence rooms at all main sites including Bangalore. They had eMeeting software and Chat at all workstations in Denmark and India. And they had several Video meeting facilities in Bangalore and at the Danish sites. Hence Linda Olsen emphasized that the need for better virtual management was in her view a *management* issue.

To address this management issue an interview study was planned and conducted to obtain a deeper and more thorough understanding of the problem. This interview study ended up concluding that the virtual management in projects had seven problems:

1. Social ties take time to build – Just putting people from different places into the same team does not create social ties within the team.
2. Not enough trust in relationships especially across Denmark and India – To work well together trust is needed
3. Lack of shared vision and common vocabulary – This is necessary to build parts of the same artifact or product at different places
4. Cultural distance – meaning that the ways and means, traditions and expectations are highly different in different parts of the organization
5. Communication Issues – Different backgrounds and different cultures often result in mis-communicate
6. Lack of reciprocity between Denmark and India – The Danish project participants often reported that they were giving more to the projects than they received back
7. Not sufficient team identification across sites – People in the same team distributed across different sites did not feel as if they were the same team

All these problems have been reported in the literature before. Cultural distance for example is a well-known problem. However, very few have undertaken a design science approach to try to cope with the problems.

2.2   Applicable Knowledge from the Knowledge Base

Quite many researchers have looked at virtual (project) management. "Much depends on experiential learning and sheer hard work" says Lacity et al [6], and they continue to say that "... outsourcing is not about giving up management but managing in a different way".

What should this different way then be? Well, our literature review of the Knowledge Base revealed a very interesting paper [7] exactly building on case studies from an Indian IT-services firm where they identified five key strategic factors essential for success using a root-cause analysis, namely (1) Shared goal; (2) Shared culture; (3) Shared process; (4) Shared responsibility, and (5) Trust.

These five key factors is a major part of what in the literature is coined social capital. That is a concept referring to connections within and between people. The concept has been used to study societies, differences between developing and developed countries, and recently to study project teams as we were interested in. Another thing that lead us in the direction of social capital was one of the conclusions from Lacity et al. [6]: "Our research found that one of the best ways to transfer knowledge is to invest in social capital. Social capital is simply the idea that knowledge and resources are exchanged, work gets done, and value is created through social relationships."

In the concrete we found a very interesting study by Evans and Carson [8] linking the performance of distributed and heterogeneous teams (equal to virtual teams as we call it in this chapter) to three core processes (communication, social integration and coordination), and social capital as a moderating structural dimension meaning that when social capital is low then distributed teams will be negatively related to group processes and positively related when social capital is high. We have showed the model in Figure 1.

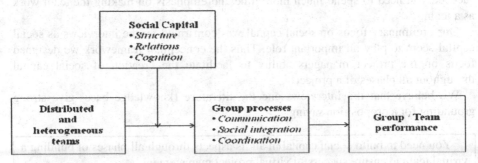

Fig. 1. Relationship between group processes, social capital and performance [8]

The concept of Social capital is relatively new and is an attempt to bring together a number of concepts such as informal organization, trust, culture, social support, social exchange, social resources, rational contracts, social networks, and inter-firm networks [9]. As a construct social capital can be defined as *"the goodwill available to individuals or groups. Its source lies in the structure and content of the actor's social relations. Its effects flow from the information, influence, and solidarity it makes available to the actor"* [9]. Social capital has three dimensions, namely a structural dimension, a relational dimension and a cognitive dimension [8, 9].

Adler and Kwon (2002) suggest that if opportunity, motivation or ability is missing it will undermine generating social capital. Thus when analysing social capital potential it is necessary to establish to what degree these three factors are present. First "opportunity", here the question is, whether a network that allow for social capital transactions is present; simply applying the idea that ties create an opportunity to act together. Both the quality of the ties (frequency, intensity, multiplicity) and the number and redundancy of internal as well as external ties matter. Especially two aspects of structural configuration has been researched; closure of the network structure; *strong ties* [10] and sparse network with few redundant ties; *weak ties* [11]. Second, "motivation" is necessary. Different motivations have been suggested such as trust and associability, socialization and shared destiny [12], enforced trust [13], career advancement [14], or to reduce transaction costs [15]. Finally the cognitive dimension focuses on ability – the competencies and resources at the nodes of the network. Thus if social capital includes the resources that any actor could potentially mobilize via their social relations then the ability of each tie is important [9].

3   Designing a Conceptual Framework for Developing Social Capital in Virtual Projects

Performance of teams is significantly varying. Barry Boehm [16] in the book "Software Engineering Economics" found a factor 1-to-4 between the best and the worst team – which on paper were equal. And DeMarco og Lister [17] in the book "Peopleware" found a factor 1-to-5; Hence to gain 400-500% difference is worth an effort.

Our overall impression from the interview study was that to make virtual teams succeed you need to spend much more time and emphasis on making the team work as a team.

Our preliminary focus on social capital was confirmed by the interviews as social capital seem to play an important role. Thus the conceptual framework we designed focus on the project managers ability to facilitate the creation of social capital throughout all phases of a project.

We believe that the interviews and the literature (knowledge base) give strong grounding for a proposition saying.

> You need to build social capital in all its aspects through all phases of building a virtual team to ensure successful virtual project management

Below we will explain the conceptual framework we designed in details. First the theoretical basis for the two dimensions in the framework is explained in section 3.1 on phases and in section 3.2 on the elements in social capital. These two dimensions result in a six-by-six matrix which is described in details in section 3.3.

3.1   Phases in the Virtual Team Process

Pries-Heje & Commisso [18] carried out a literature study on teams. They found four primary things of interest: (1) The Task; (2) Team Roles; (3) Team Working, and (4) The Process. The *task* to be undertaken by the team has an influence. For example, the more complex the task the more there is a need for a balanced team where all the *team roles* are enacted. Number three - *team-working* – is mainly about two things that we also found. It is about the importance of trust (problem #2 above). Trust is really a prerequisite for an effective team. If you do not have trust in each other you cannot work well together. You will show your 'facade' instead of your real self. The second thing of importance in relation to team working is to have a common vision within the team (problem #3 above).

Finally, the process that the team goes through is very important. We have the 'old' forming-norming-storming-performing model as a main proponent of the team process. In TSP [19] we also have the emphasis on a good team start-up in the form of a distinct launch activity. Commisso and Pries-Heje [20] have developed a model for building team with six phases as described in Figure 2.

Constitute	Team and project constituted. Do we have the knowledge and competence needed; Team gathers; We ARE a team; Who am I
Clarify	Who are the others, Clarify group dynamics; how to communicate; how to decide; rules of conduct; social contract
Commit	Aim and goals, priorities, roles, context, and vision
Carry Out	Working – preferably effectively; continued group dynamics; on-going communication and coordination
Check	How are we; Do we need to go back and repeat – build more social capital; mid way crisis
Conclude	We have come to the end; what did we learn

Fig. 2. The Six-C model for team-building [20]

3.2   Elements of Social Capital

According to Evans and Carson [8] social capital has three key elements that is of interest when studying virtual and distributed teams; a structural element, a relational element and a cognitive element, The *structural* element involves the network of ties and relationships possessed by individuals. When a new project is established all team members enter the project with a social network developed prior to the project, and they continue to develop their network as the project is progressing. The *relational* element concerns the nature and quality of the relationship ties, and refers to the trust that exists among a group. Research findings suggest that network ties that are not strengthened by mutual obligations, trusting relationships, and common language or narratives easily break down [25]. The relational element can be decomposed into: identification, trust and reciprocity. The *cognitive* element can be described as the shared concepts, vocabulary and narratives that together form a shared system of meaning. The cognitive dimension of social capital highlights the importance of shared representations, interpretations and systems of meaning among parties, and it can be split into to sub-elements: shared vision and language and concepts. Hence social capital can be understood to have 6 elements of importance in relation to virtual teams:

1. Structure
2. Relation
   (a) Identification
   (b) Trust
   (c) Reciprocity
3. Cognition
   (a) Shared vision
   (b) Language and concepts

3.3   Designing a Conceptual Framework for Developing Social Capital in Virtual Projects

We are now at the point in our design science research where we have a very good an thorough understanding of both the need and the problems as well as the existing knowledge base. After some iterations we ended up with a design combing the Six-C model – as presented above – with six aspects of social capital allowing the necessary building of enough social capital in all phases of a team.

In the concrete the design looked like shown in figure 3.

	Consti-tute	Clarify	Commit	Carry Out	Check	Con-clude
Structure / Social ties	Shield	Human behind What techn.?	Events	Celebrate Create social time	"Light" Retro-spective *	Retro-Spective *
Relation / Iden-tification	Group portrait	Imagine success Confi-dence	Short feedback loop	Create team pride Talk about success	Process observa-tion * "Light"	Retro-Spective *
Relation / Trust	*Historic trust*	Team game rules	Explore barriers Define roles	Perfor-mance and knowl. based trust	Same as above	Retro-Spective *

Fig. 3. The conceptual framework we designed consists of a six-by-six matrix combining six parts of team building with six dimension of social capital. The '*' after the name of some techniques means that the techniques is repeated in other fields.

Relation / Reciprocity	Mindset for virtual work	Mindset for virtual work	Mindset for virtual work	Identification trust	Same as above	Retro-Spective *
Cognition / **Shared vision**	Knowledge map *	Hofstede *	Front page SPOT Big Steps Game Plan	Use common vision	"Light" Retro-spective *	Retro-Spective *
Cognition / **Language & concepts**	Knowledge map *	Team-building activities Hofstede *	First meeting Devl. Model Artic. protocol Common process &archit.		"Light" Retro-spective *	Retro-Spective *
Other …			Comm. need Stake-holder matrix		Fishbone	

Fig. 3. (*continued*)

In relation to our interview study it is clear that our conceptual framework covers the problems that we identified:

1. Problem #1 – Social ties take time. This is addressed by having a conceptual framework where you go through all the phases of team build-up thereby allowing the time it takes to build social ties
2. Problem #2 – Not enough trust. This is addressed by the strong emphasis on trust building; the third row in Figure 3.
3. Problem #3 – Lack of shared vision and language. This is addressed by row 5 and 6 in our conceptual framework.

4. Problem #4 – Cultural distance. Addressed partly in the fields saying "Hofstede".
5. Problem #5 – Communication Issues. As can be seen from Figure 2 better communication is a result of the heightened level of social capital that is all six rows in all phases in the conceptual framework. Furthermore we have a row 7 "Other" that specifically addresses Communication.
6. Problem #6 – Lack of reciprocity. This is addressed by row 4 on reciprocity in our conceptual framework.
7. Problem #7 – Not sufficient team identification across sites. This is addressed by row 2 identification in our conceptual framework.

The overall idea in our design follows from the proposition: To be successful you need to build all elements of social capital in all phases of a team. To populate the six-by-six matrix we have chosen techniques that can be used in a team to build a specific part of social capital. The techniques included are coming from a number of different sources. The main source however were the book "Best Practices for Facilitation" [21]. The second most important source were Duarte and Snyder [22]. Norm Kerth's book on "Project Retrospectives" [23] were the main source for the Check and Conclude phases. Furthermore we were inspired by agile techniques especially Scrum [24]. The remainder of the techniques was taken from Commisso & Pries-Heje [20]. The choice of techniques was not incidental. We carefully discussed each of the 36 fields in the 6-by-6 model. We considered several techniques and we selected techniques that were especially well suited for both being done virtually (for example in a video or e-meeting) and best creating social capital. Research method wise this was our Build and Justify iteration (middle part of Figure 1).

Space does not permit going through all 36 felts in the matrix, but below a few examples are provided.

Under Constitute and Social Ties one can find the techniques called "Shield" (see also figure 4). What you do here is to:

- Hand out a piece of A3-paper and a thick lettering pen to each participant. This may require preparation at each site.
- Ask everyone to draw their shield where they can either draw or write something on their background (in the upper left corner), something work-related (in the upper right corner), something private for example on their family situation, sports or the like (in the lower left corner) and a tool that they feel the analogy with (in the lower right corner). Finally in the middle participants can write or draw their dream if they have one and they feel it appropriate to present it openly.
- One by one the participants then present their shield to the rest of the team. For this presentation a video camera that can zoom in on the shield and show it to all participants at all sites is necessary.

The main advantage of the shield is that is becomes "legal" to talk about other things than work. And all team participants are "whole" human beings having a work-oriented and a more private-oriented side. But the shield will allow for presentation of the "whole" thereby building stronger social ties.

Draw your Shield

Fig. 4. The Shield is a good techniques for building social ties in the Constitute phase

Under Clarify and Relation/Identification there is a techniques called "Imagine Success". What you do here is that:

- Everyone in the team thinks for themselves over the last project they participated in, which was implemented successfully
- You capture the feeling of success and transfer it to an idea of how a successful completion of this project is experienced
- Tell the team what it was that succeeded in your project success and how your success is experienced
- In the middle of a common screen or large piece of paper (seen on video) write: "The look of success" and around the write / draw in everybody's individual perception of success

Under Commit and Cognition/Shared language and concepts we urge the teams to use the Danske Bank development model with the following arguments about the advantages:

- Everyone has the same terminology in projects
- It becomes easier to register and understand data and experiences from earlier projects. The method can become a common framework for communication i.e. of successes
- With well defined phases and documentation for each phase management is much easier
- New employees without experience gets a well defined platform to start out from

4   Diffusion and Evaluation in Danske Bank

We presented the conceptual framework to management in Danske Bank the last week of November 2010. We clearly linked it to the problems we identified in our interview study as presented in section 2.1. The response was very positive. Danske Bank was confident that focusing on building social capital had potential to help them improve their virtual (project) management.

It was then decided that we, the researchers, should teach it to task managers, process-improvers and general managers within DCI. That took place in the first week of 2011. The aim of the five-day course we gave was that after the course the participants should be able to:

- Independently facilitate the start up of and the ongoing work in a virtual project team; that is a team distributed across Denmark and India that have never been together in one physical location
- Choose appropriate techniques for six phases of teamwork to use in and facilitate the building of enough social capital within the team; enough to ensure that the team can work virtually

The evaluation by the participants emphasised the following more general comments:

- The framework introduced topics that some consider very vague in a clear and perceivable manner
- Though the techniques that were discussed were familiar, put together as a package it was new and it encouraged thinking about what could be done
- It is a sensitive subject but handles it very well with good examples / tools
- The practical tools given to us will really help in day to day management
- Building social capital is the real value addition (by our conceptual framework)

We realised at the end of the first course that it was necessary to give a similar course in Denmark. The resulting course took place in early February 2011. Here – again – the evaluation was quite positive and the participants committed themselves to using the conceptual framework.

The conceptual framework was then being used in seven project areas – mainly so-called system management areas. All areas made concrete plans for how to build social capital for their team. And they have each made a cost-benefit analysis specifically for their own project showing that the benefits of building and ensuring enough social capital are much higher than the costs.

In the last week of May 2011 and the first week of June we evaluated the use of the Conceptual Framework for Virtual Management. A representative set of interviewees were selcted from both India (DCI, Bangalore) and Denmark. Interviews were recorded. For each interview a set of detailed field notes were made with the help of the recordings. Furthermore most interviews were conducted by 2 people making it possible for one person to concentrate on talking with the interviewee while the other was taking notes. In the first week of August 2011 we coded and analyzed the interview and observation data in more depth. This resulted in the following findings.

1. The framework had been used extensively in all seven project management areas
2. All the people interviewed were in agreement that the use of the framework was clearly worthwhile and that the outcome was higher in value than the "investment" in time
3. The framework had been used more in India than in Denmark. The overall satisfaction with the framework was high in India. Many examples of better / improved teambuilding and building of social capital were found among the India Interviewees
4. The satisfaction with the framework in Denmark was mixed.
5. Techniques from the first of the C's (Constitute Team, Clarify and Commit) were used considerably more than techniques from the last three C's (Carry Out, Check & Conclude)
6. Especially two techniques, the Shield Exercise and the Group Portrait, were reported to have been used with very positive results

Thus we concluded that Danske Bank could make real use of implementing the framework throughout the organization. And in fact that recommendation is being followed currently; Danske Bank is making the framework available to all projects.

In the concrete the two authors of this paper are training a number of trainers in Danske Bank in February and March 2012. These Danske Bank trainers are then expected to give courses in and facilitate the use of the framework in 100 projects by the end of 2012 (60 has already been signed up at time of writing; March 2012).

5   Conclusion

We have now reported the identification of seven problems in virtual projects with participants from several sites in Denmark and India. We have also presented a proposition stating that you need to build social capital in all its aspects through all phases of building a virtual team to ensure successful virtual project management.

Using a single case study we have confirmed the proposition and now need to consider what can be abstracted or generalized to other companies facing similar problems?

A natural question is whether it also will be beneficial in non-virtual projects to systematically build social capital? We believe the answer to this question is yes. Increasing social capital improves team performance [cf. 8]. However, the framework we have designed and discussed in this paper is aimed at virtual projects. There will be many techniques that can be useful in a "classic" co-located project team which is not part of our framework.

Hence the contribution of this paper is the design of a framework build to the contingencies of the situation at hand in Danske Bank. All the techniques included in the framework have been selected and adapted to the virtual projects in Danske Bank. That is to fit the culture of Denmark and India, and to fit the technology available to cooperate across Denmark and India.

If another company or organization wish to cope with similar problems by systematically building social capital through teambuilding then the specific organization needs to undertake an evaluation of the techniques in the six-by-six framework and for each one ask, Will this technique be possible to use here with the contingencies given here? And do we need to adapt the techniques for example to the information technology available, adapt to differences in time zone? I.e. one of the advantages between Denmark and India is that there is a 3-5 hour overlap of working hours in a normal working day. That is for example not the case between US and India.

Thus for another organization to use the results of our research they should go through the following phases:

1. Establish the challenges you are facing in your organization. This can be done through an interview study or through a survey using the seven problem areas that we identified.
2. If the challenges are similar you can benefit from adopting the six-by-six framework for systematically building social capital in projects
3. Before you can adopt the framework you need to take each of the techniques mentioned in figure 3 and make sure that they are useful in your context? You should also consider whether other techniques should be added? In considering this you should probably look at experiences from virtual projects in your organization and "harvest" positive results using different techniques.
4. When the framework has been locally consolidated we recommend that you pilot it in 5-7 projects like we did in Danske Bank.
5. When the pilot project has been evaluated and results taken into account then you can roll-out the six-by-six framework adapted to your organization

5.1   Is Our Contribution Design Science Research?

Hevner et al. [5] expressed their view on what constitutes good design science research in the form of seven guidelines that are useful in understanding, executing and evaluating design science and design research. In the following we argue that we have lived up to all seven

1. Must produce a viable artefact: We have done that in the form of the six-by-six conceptual framework.
2. Produces technology-based solutions to relevant business problems: We started out with a relevant business problem, namely to improve virtual management in Danske Bank. We identified seven specific problems. To address these problems we build a technology-based – or rather techniques-based – solution.
3. Evaluation that demonstrates of utility, quality, and efficacy: The first successful evaluation took place in November 2010 when management in Danske Bank decided to apply the six-by-six conceptual framework. The second successful evaluation took place when the task managers in the course decided to apply the six-by-six concept in their own projects. The third evaluation was carried out in the summer of 2011 and led to an organization-wide adoption in 2012. Utility was demonstrated in the pilot use in Danske Bank. So was quality. As for efficacy it was the perception that it was achieved although no measures were collected.

4. Research contribution of the design artefact, foundations, or methodologies: The research contribution is the six-by-six conceptual framework. In the March and Smith [4] notation it is a Model (with techniques in 36 fields) and a Method (of using the techniques through phases of teambuilding).
5. Rigor in construction and evaluation method: As can be seen from this paper we have been very careful and rigorous in every step of our research. We have followed and included all the steps from Hevner et al. [5]; thus making it rigorous designs science research.
6. A problem-situated means-ends search for an effective artefact: We started out with a problem given by Danske Bank and our whole undertaking was a means-ends search for an effective artefact to deal with specific aspects of the virtual management problem.
7. Communication to both technical and managerial audiences: We have communicated to both audiences in Danske Bank. We are now in this paper communicating our results outside the bank.

Thus we believe the design created in the form of the six-by-six model artefact is a valuable contribution and a good example of design science research.

Acknowledgements. The authors wish to acknowledge the valuable help of Danske Bank Group IT, DCI, ITC Infotech, Linda Olsen, Dan Schütz and the many project team members in both Denmark and India who allowed us access to their projects and helped us develop the framework.

References

1. Friedman, T.L.: The World is Flat: The Globalized World in the Twenty-First century, Updated and expanded ed. Penguin Books, London (2006)
2. Benbasat, I., Zmud, R.: Empirical Research in Information Systems: The Practice of Relevance. MIS Quarterly 23(1), 3–16 (1999)
3. Walls, J.G., Widmeyer, G.R., El Sawy, O.A.: Building an information system design theory for vigilant EIS. Information Systems Research 3(1), 36–59 (1992)
4. March, S.T., Smith, G.F.: Design and natural science research on information technology. Decision Support Systems 15(4), 251–266 (1995)
5. Hevner, A.R., et al.: Design Science In Information Systems Research. MIS Quarterly 28(1), 75–105 (2004)
6. Lacity, M.C., Willcocks, L.P., Rottman, J.W.: Global Outsourcing of Back Office Services: Lessons, Trends and Enduring Challenges. Strategic Outsourcing: An International Journal 1(1), 13–34 (2008)
7. Bhat, J.M., Gupta, M., Murthy, S.N.: Overcoming Requirements Engineering Challenges: Lessons from Offshore Outsourcing. IEEE Software 23(5), 38–44 (2006)
8. Evans, W.R., Carson, C.M.: A social capital explanation of the relationship between functional diversity and group performance. Team Performance Management 11(7/8), 302–315 (2005)
9. Adler, P.S., Kwon, S.-W.: Social Capital: prospects for a new concept. Academy of Management Review 27(1), 17–40 (2002)

10. Coleman, J.S.: Social capital in the creation of human capital. American Journal of Sociology, 95–120 (1988)
11. Burt, R.S.: Social contagion and innovation: Cohesion versus structural equivalence. American Journal of Sociology (92), 1287–1335 (1987)
12. Leana, C.R., Buren, H.J.V.: Organizational social capital and employment practices. Academy of Management Review (24), 538–555 (1999)
13. Portes, A.: Social capital: Its origins and applications in modern sociology. Annual Review of Sociology (24), 1–24 (1998)
14. Graaf, N.D.D., Flap, H.D.: With a little help from my friends: Social resources as an explanation of occupational status and income in West Germany, the Netherlands, and the United States. Social Forces (67), 453–472 (1988)
15. Baker, W.: Market networks and corporate behavior. American Journal of Sociology (96), 589–625 (1990)
16. Boehm, B.: Software engineering economics. Advances in computing science and technology. Prentice-Hall (1981)
17. DeMarco, T., Lister, T.: Peopleware: Productive projects and teams, 2nd edn. Dorset House Publishing Company (1999)
18. Pries-Heje, J., Commisso, T.: Improving Team Performance. In: Proceedings of the 33rd IRIS, Information Systems Research Seminar in Scandinavia, Rebild Bakker, Denmark (August 2010)
19. Humphrey, W.: TSP: Coaching Development Teams. The SEI Series in Software Engineering. Addison-Wesley Professional (2006)
20. Commisso, T.H., Pries-Heje, J.: The Six-C model for IS project teambuilding. In: Proceedings from the 34th IRIS, Information Systems Research Seminar in Scandinavia, Turku, Finland (August 2011)
21. Sibbet, D.: Best Practices for Facilitation. Facilitation Guide Series. The grove Consultants International, San Francisco (2002)
22. Duarte, D.L., Snyder, N.T.: Mastering virtual teams: Strategies, tools and techniques that succeed, 3rd edn. Jossey-Bass, San Francisco (2006)
23. Kerth, N.L.: Project Retrospectives: A Handbook for Team Reviews. Dorset House Publishing Company, Incorporated (2001)
24. Sutherland, J., Schwaber, K.: The Scrum Papers: Nut, Bolts, and Origins of an Agile Framework. SCRUM Training Institute (2010)
25. Burt, R.S.: Bridge Decay. Social Networks 24(4), 333–363 (2002)

Integrating Organisational Design with IT Design

The Queensland Health Payroll Case

António Rito Silva[1,2] and Michael Rosemann[1]

[1] BPM Group/QUT, Level 5 - 126 Margaret Street, 4000 Brisbane, Australia
[2] INESC-ID/IST/Technical University of Lisbon, Av. Prof. Dr. Cavaco Silva, 2744-016 Porto Salvo, Portugal

Abstract. Most existing requirements engineering approaches focus on the modelling and specification of the IT artefacts ignoring the environment where the application is deployed. Although some requirements engineering approaches consider the stakeholder's goals, they still focus on the IT artefacts' specification. However, IT artefacts are embedded in a dynamic organisational environment and their design and specification cannot be separated from the environment's constant evolution. Therefore, during the initial stages of a requirements engineering process it is advantageous to consider the integration of IT design with organisational design. We proposed the ADMITO (Analysis, Design and Management of IT and Organisations) approach to represent the dynamic relations between social and material entities, where the latter are divided into technological and organisational entities. In this paper we show how by using ADMITO in a concrete case, the Queensland Health Payroll (QHP) case, it is possible to have an integrated representation of IT and organisational design supporting organisational change and IT requirements specification.

Keywords: IT design, Organisational design, Enterprise modelling, Adaptive structuration theory, Case study.

1   Introduction

The requirements engineering discipline [15] covers the analysis and specification of IT artefacts to provide to software architects and software developers a characterisation of the functional and non-functional properties the artefacts should have once deployed. Since a software artefact is a formal entity, which is executed by the hardware, requirements engineering has focused on the complete and consistent specification of its properties in order to enforce an early identification of potential errors and reduce development costs. Therefore, a line was drawn to separate the analysis, which includes the study of the informal context where the artefact executes, from its specification, which aims to provide an implementation-ready formal description of the artefact. Although useful,

K. Peffers, M. Rothenberger, and B. Kuechler (Eds.): DESRIST 2012, LNCS 7286, pp. 271–286, 2012.

this separation has created a gap between the representation of the IT artefact environment and the specification of the IT artefact.

In a dynamic world it is necessary to continuously adapt and evolve the IT artefacts to keep pace with the environment changes. The goal-oriented requirements engineering (GORE) approaches [9] were proposed to capture the artefact's environment, and in particular the environment's active components and their intentions, and relate it with artefacts' specification through a stepwise decomposition. Therefore, GORE approaches support the definition of traceability relations between the artefact's environment and its specification.

On the other hand, social sciences and information systems research has proposed different theoretical frameworks to explain the effects of IT on organisations. Markus and Silver [11] propose a framework to represent the relations between social groups and technology. The framework considers two types of socio-technical relations, functional affordances and symbolic expressions. They consider the following concepts:

- *Technical Objects* - Technical objects are IT artefacts and their component parts. They are understood as material and immaterial "real" things of which the properties are potentially causal, that is, necessary conditions for people to perceive them and use them in particular ways with particular consequences.
- *Functional Affordances* - Functional affordances are the possibilities for goal-oriented action that are afforded by technical objects to a specified user group. Therefore functional affordances are relations between technical objects and users that identify what the user may be able to do with the object, given the user's capabilities and goals.
- *Symbolic Expressions* - Symbolic expressions are the communicative possibilities of technical objects for a specified user group. Symbolic expressions represent the qualities a user group senses in technical objects. Therefore, symbolic expressions are also relations between technical objects and users. The concept focuses on issues related to the interpretation of technical objects by users.

When comparing the social sciences frameworks and the requirements engineering approaches we realise that even though approaches like GORE consider the IT artefact's environment they are still focused on the identification and specification of the IT implementation requirements. However, after having analysed a real case of deploying a new system in an organisation, the Queensland Health Payroll (QHP) case [7], we concluded that IT design is strongly connected to organisational design and they have dynamic interdependences whose representation is not the focus of traditional requirements engineering approaches. Therefore, IT artefact design should not be represented in isolation or as a mere decomposition of organisational design.

In this paper we propose the ADMITO (Analysis, Design and Management of IT and Organisations) framework to model and capture the dependencies between IT and organisational design and provide the means to identify IT requirements in the context of a dynamic environment.

In this section we introduced the need to integrate organisational design with IT design. Next section describes the ADMITO framework. Then, the Queensland Health Payroll case is described and ADMITO is applied to it to show its advantages. Finally related work and conclusions are presented.

2   ADMITO - A Framework for the Analysis, Design and Management of IT and Organisations

The ADMITO framework for the design, management and analysis of IT and Organisations results from the extension of the Markus and Silver [11] framework by explicitly representing organisational design and differentiating between designed and emergent socio-material relations.

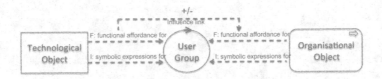

Fig. 1. ADMITO Model

Figure 1 presents the ADMITO model. This model follows Markus and Silver in the distinction between social entities, pictured as circles with an arrow to represent their proactivity, and material entities, pictured as rectangles, but extends it with the identification of two distinct sorts of materials: technical objects and organisational objects, pictured, respectively, with sharp and rounded corners. While Markus and Silver only consider *Technical Objects*, IT artefacts and their component parts, we also propose the inclusion of *Organisational Objects*, such as, organisational structure, policies and procedures [4], which explicitly define the organisational design. The incorporation of organisational objects in the model allows the representation of broad socio-material relations, depicted as arrows from the material entity to the social entity, not only technical ones, and the representation of both IT and organisational design. Moreover, the model is enriched with influence links to represent how socio-material relations have a positive or negative impact on other socio-material relations, pictured as arrows labelled with, respectively, plus and minus signs.

Another ADMITO extension to Markus and Silver model is the distinction between the model of potentialities, the *blueprint*, and the *practices* that occur in the organisation. The former characterises, from a design time point of view, the potentialities that an organisation may have and it is similar to Markus and Silver proposal. The latter integrates Orlikowski's perspective on emergence and enacted practices [14] to describe the actual practices. According to Markus and Silver model, functional affordances and symbolic expression relations between social and material entities allow the identification of the organisational potentialities of the model. To stress that the relations are potential they are pictured using dashed arrows. In other words, it describes what are the possible socio-material relations of the organisation given the social and material entities. However, due to the inherent autonomy of the organisational social entities not all the potential designed socio-material relations are actually enabled and so, a set of unforeseen socio-material relations can emerge. The model of practices describes the socio-material relations that occur in practice. To distinguish designed socio-material relations from practice socio-material relations we have called the latter functional practices and actual interpretations and they are pictured using solid arrows to emphasise their occurrence in practice.

ADMITO framework provides a particular type of organisational object to represent business processes. Besides, the socio-material relations between business processes and social entities are represented as goals.

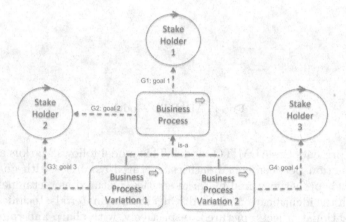

Fig. 2. Business Process Organisational Object

Figure 2 describes the generic representation of an organisational object of type Business Process and the socio-material relations with social entities of type stakeholder. A business process is an organisational object that represents a collaboration of different stakeholders towards a business goal. Each one of the stakeholders participates in the collaboration to achieve his/her goals, a socio-material relation, and all goals together contribute to the accomplishment of the final business process goal. On the other hand, it is possible to have business process variations that contribute to the achievement of specific goals, which is represented by an is-a relationship.

Since the goals of a business process for the different stakeholders are strongly connected and are interdependent it is not relevant to make it explicit in the diagram except when some of the goals are not accomplished, strikethrough is used to show that a particular goal is not accomplished. Similarly to the differentiation between functional affordances and functional practices we also distinguish goal affordances from actual goals and use solid lines to represent the latter.

ADMITO framework can also express the creation of material entities. The representation of the creation of material entities as result of socio-material relations is crucial do represent dynamic environments where redesign is constantly occurring, either explicitly (by design) or tacitly (by emergence).

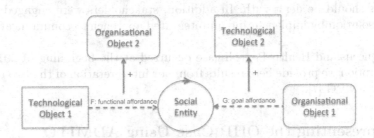

Fig. 3. Creation of Material Entities

Figure 3 shows the creation of two material entities, an organisational object and a technological object, as result of the socio-material relations. The creation is represented using a solid arrow with positive sign.

Finally, the framework can represent technical objects requirements, the use of strikethrough to show that a socio-material relation does not achieve its intent in practice, and the representation of several material entities of the same kind. Note that requirements are properties of technical objects, which represents factual qualities of the objects, whereas socio-material relations represent an appropriation of technical objects by users.

3   The Queensland Health Payroll Case

The Queensland Health Payroll (QHP) system is responsible to support the fortnight salaries payment of Queensland Health Staff. It is constituted by two subsystems, a Lattice Payroll system and an ESP Rostering system. Although Queensland Health[1] considered these two systems to adequately support the payroll business process, their maintenance costs were high and so it was decided to replace them by a new implementation to reduce costs. Since the payroll business process was adequately supported, and cost reduction was the main reason for the new system development, it is not envisioned any need to do major changes to the organisational structure at the time the deployment of the new system would occur. However, due to performance and useability problems in the new

---

[1] Queensland Health is responsible for the public health system of the Australian State of Queensland. It has approximately 78,000 employees.
http://www.health.qld.gov.au/

rostering application the health payroll staff could not fortnightly introduce the rosters for all the health staff, which resulted in employees receiving no payment, being overpaid or underpaid. The problems escalate for every new payment cycle because the inaccurate payments had to be corrected and integrated with the new fortnightly payments. To overcome this situation it was necessary, besides improving the useability and performance of the rostering system, to create a new organisational structure that centralises all the information for decision taking and to define organisational procedures that standardise how the exceptional situations should be dealt with. In addition, stakeholders were engaged in the problem solution by implementing an integrated approach to communicate with them.

The Queensland Health Payroll case occurred at the beginning of 2010 and the description we provide here results from our interpretation of the two reports issued by KMPG [7].

4   Representing the QHP Case Using ADMITO

So far the QHP case has had several stages. Our description using ADMITO follows a stepwise approach where for each stage we show the proposed design for the organisation and technology, and what resulted in practice. In the timeframe considered in this article, which is based on the two KPMG's status reports [7], three stages are considered: prior, transformation, and stabilisation. The prior stage corresponds to the period where the Lattice and ESP systems were in production and before the deployment of the new payroll systems. We use a practice diagram to describe the prior stage and show the technological and organisational context prior to the deployment of the new system. Two diagrams represent the transformation stage, a blueprint diagram describes the redesign that took place to reduce maintenance costs, and a practices diagram describes how the performance and useability problems disrupted the organisational functioning. Finally, a blueprint diagram describes the stabilisation phase, which is characterised by the changes proposed by KPMG to cope with the disrupted organisation.

4.1   The Prior Stage

In the prior stage the health payroll process was providing the expected quality of service for the different stakeholders involved in the process. However, the maintenance costs associated with the QHP system were high and the system considered obsolete.

Figure 4 represents the practices diagram for the health payroll organisation prior to the deployment of the new systems. Three social entities are considered and their socio-material relations with material entities, represented as both technological and organisational objects. The situation prior to the transformation was rather stable, the health payroll business process accomplished the goals expected by the Health Staff social group, the salaries are paid in time

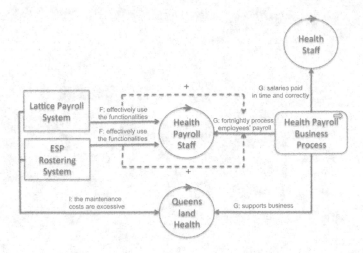

Fig. 4. Prior Stage: Practices Diagram

and correctly, and by the Health Payroll Staff social group, they can fortnightly process employees' payroll. Therefore, these goals are described as socio-material relations between the organisational object and each one of the social groups. They are represented as special cases of functional affordances, denoted by prefix *G:*. Moreover, given that the direct stakeholders had no complaints about the process, the Queensland Health considered it appropriate from the Queensland Health business viewpoint, which is represented in the diagram as an actual goal. The Lattice Payroll and ESP Rostering systems were used by the Health Payroll Staff, represented in Figure 4 as functional practices, to support their goals towards the health payroll process, represented in the diagram as influence links from the functional practices to the actual goal. However, for Queensland Health the maintenance costs associated with the two systems supporting the business process were excessive, which is represented as two symbolic expressions from the Lattice Payroll and ESP Rostering systems to Queensland Health social group.

4.2   The Transformation Stage

To reduce Lattice Payroll and ESP Rostering maintenance costs two new systems were implemented and deployed in the organisation while maintaining the organisational structure and in particular the health payroll business process.

The blueprint diagram in Figure 5 illustrates the proposed design of the organisation. Since the change's goal was to reduce the maintenance costs and Queensland Health considered the Health Payroll business process appropriate, no changes in the organisational design were devised. Therefore, the socio-material relations associated with the business process in Figure 5 are represented as actual goals and the new functional affordances between Health Payroll Staff and the new

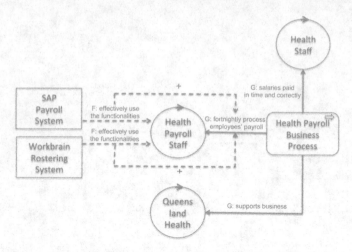

Fig. 5. Transformation Stage: Blueprint Diagram

systems are expected to continue supporting the business process operation, represented by influence links with positive impact on the actual goal. However, when the new systems where deployed, several problems associated with the Workbrain Rostering system arose which compromised the Health Payroll Staff work as illustrated in Figure 6. Note that the diagram in Figure 5 contains both practice and blueprint socio-material relations to illustrate that the socio-material relations between social entities and the organisational object, Health Payroll business process, are not expected to change.

The practice diagram in Figure 6 shows the impact resulting from performance and useability problems associated with Workbrain Rostering system. Due to these problems the Health Payroll Staff could not perform its work and the Health Staff received no payments or was either underpaid or overpaid. As an undesirable side effect, a backlog of payments requiring to be adjusted popped up and the number of problems lodged in different issues register systems increased significantly. This situation is represented in Figure 6 by two technological objects, Backlog and Issues Register, where the latter represents the five different Issues Registers existing in the organisation. Note the use of influence links, with a minus sign, to express the negative impact of the performance and useability problems on the business process goals and how the influence links, with a positive sign, represent the emergence of Backlog and Issues Register objects. Note that the SAP payroll system is omitted in Figure 6 because by applying ADMITO we do not intend to represent all the organisation but to focus on the entities and socio-material relations which are relevant to the problem at hand. This strategy is central for an ADMITO method, which should not aim to describe the whole organisation, but be a tool for designers to represent those aspects that they consider relevant.

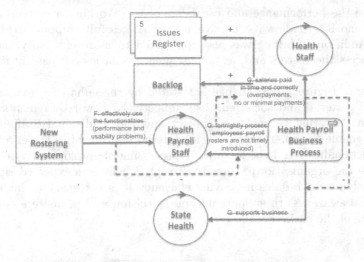

Fig. 6. Transformation Stage: Practices Diagram

4.3   The Stabilisation Stage

As a result of the organisational disruption caused by the deployment of new systems KPMG proposed a plan [7] to stabilise the health payroll business process and have the organisation back to a non-disruptive functioning, characterised by having fortnightly payments in time and correct. We use ADMITO to describe the plan from three different, but complementary, perspectives: improve efficiency, knowledge creation and sharing, and exception handling.

To cope with the organisational malfunctioning it is necessary to identify causes and repair them. The blueprint diagram in Figure 7 shows the changes proposed by KPMG to improve the Workbrain Rostering system. It is necessary

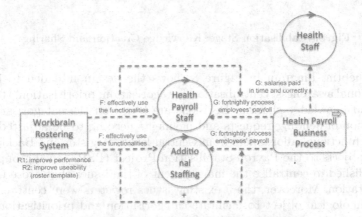

Fig. 7. Stabilisation Stage: Improve Efficiency

to improve the performance and useability of the Workbrain system, requirements R1 and R2, to allow its effective use and successfully support the business
process. Additional staffing was also contracted to more efficiently and accurately process the rosters and, as a consequence, salaries are paid in time and
correctly.

Observe in Figure 7 how change is fostered by the enhancement and introduction of material and social entities, respectively, new requirements for the
Workbrain Rostering technological object and the Additional Staffing social
group, to enable the emergence of socio-material relationships, the effective use
of the functionalities and the fortnightly processing of employees payroll. However, since the organisation is already disrupted, where unexpected situations
continuously occur, besides improving efficiency it is necessary to increase organisational awareness to support informed decision and promote a consistent
functioning of the entire organisation.

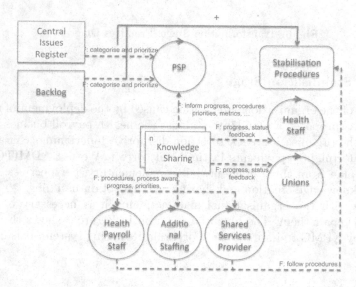

Fig. 8. Stabilisation Stage: Knowledge Creation and Sharing

The blueprint diagram in Figure 8 shows the design intended to increase
organisational awareness: centralisation, categorisation, prioritisation, standardisation and knowledge sharing. Decisions are based on the categorisation and
prioritisation of pending requests and payments needing to be adjusted, represented by functional affordances from Central Issues Register and Backlog technological objects to the Payroll Stabilisation Project (PSP) social group, which
was established to centralise the management of the issues that arose from the
implementation. Moreover, the 5 existing issues registers were centralised in a
single technological object to facilitate categorisation and prioritisation activities. Once decisions are taken and stabilisation procedures created, represented
by the Stabilisation Procedures organisational object, they are communicated

to the entire organisation using several different artefacts, which are represented as Knowledge Sharing technical objects in Figure 5.

It should be noticed how the Knowledge Sharing technical objects involve all the Queensland Health Payroll stakeholders. Their goal is to maximise the knowledge sharing to reduce organisational noise, since a significant part of the issues lodged in the Issues Registers is due to misunderstanding and lack of information, and to enforce a consistent organisational functioning according to the most recent decisions, made explicit by the stabilisation procedures. For instance, the standardisation of the ad hoc payment process to facilitate more efficient processing of payments, which is part of the Stabilisation Procedures organisational object, needs to be communicated to ensure that is consistently and effectively applied.

Finally, to deal with the set of exceptional situations it is necessary to follow the Stabilisation Procedures. In particular, it is necessary to follow an adapted and extended health payroll business process to handle the identified exceptional situations.

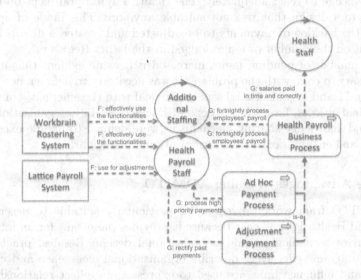

Fig. 9. Stabilisation Stage: Exception Handling

The blueprint diagram in Figure 9 shows two specialisations of the health payroll business process, which have specific goals, namely, an ad hoc payment process for high priority payments and an adjustment payment process to correct past payments. The additional sub-goals are compliant with the health process business process goals for Health Staff. Note that the Lattice Payroll System has to be used for adjustments and that the new specialised business processes are assigned to the Health Payroll Staff, which is more experienced.

5   Analysis of the QHP Case and the Advantages of Applying ADMITO

5.1   Analysis of the QHP Case

The Queensland Health Payroll case shows how IT and organisational design are strongly connected. Moreover, it shows that when the organisation is functioning in a stable environment, IT and organisational design become oblivious for the social entities in such a way that by strictly following and constantly repeating predefined procedures and group behaviour, the organisational awareness declines. Therefore, any small change in the environment may have an impact that surpasses its causes.

Actually, the substitution of the payroll system by a new system with the same set of functionalities triggered a disruption that was not foreseen during design time neither was the dimension of the impact perceived in a timely fashion after deployment. The organisation was not aware of the disruption neither had it the knowledge to react adequately. The Health Payroll Staff kept on working according to a design that was not suitable anymore. This mode of operation increased the backlog of payments to be adjusted and created a disruption that was patent on the number of issues lodged in the Issues Registers.

As the number of pending issues increased it became evident that a change was necessary to cope with the problem. It was necessary to define a new design, integrating IT and organisational aspects, to deal with the emergence of the new technological objects, Issues Registers and Backlog. Mainly, organisational procedures and knowledge sharing mechanisms were defined to handle exceptional situations and ensure a consistent organisational behaviour.

5.2   The Advantages of Using ADMITO

The ADMITO framework proved to be particularly suitable to describe the Queensland Health Payroll case because it provides the means for an integrated description of technological and organisational design. Besides, practice and blueprint diagrams effectively describe organisational emergence and constant redesign, and influence links are used to express cause effect relationships between organisational and IT design and vice-versa. In particular, in the QHP case it is shown how:

- socio-material relations between technical objects and social entities support socio-material relations between organisational objects and social entities – the functional affordances associated with the payroll and rostering systems support the business process goals for Health Payroll Staff.
- socio-material relations between organisational objects and social entities trigger the emergence of technical objects or their increase in number – the Backlog technical object results from the failure to achieve the goal "salaries paid in time and correctly". The same applies to the increase on the number of issues lodged in the Issues Register.

- socio-material relations between technical objects and social entities trigger the emergence of organisational objects – as result of the prioritisation and categorisation made by PSP a set of stabilisation organisational procedures, an organisational object, was defined.

Therefore ADMITO proved to be appropriate to be used in agile approaches for dynamic contexts where design and redesign constantly take place. Furthermore, the design of tangible entities is determined by the analysis and study of cause-effect relationships between socio-material relations.

6   Related Work

Requirements engineering is the branch of software engineering concerned with the real-world goals for, functions of, and constraints on software systems. It is also concerned with the relationship of these factors to precise specifications of software behaviour, and to their evolution over time and across software families [18]. Nuseibeh and Easterbrook [13] identify new challenges for requirements engineering as the need to model and analyse in the organisational and social context, and to focus on the environment properties instead of on the computer-based artefacts properties. In this article we show how ADMITO can describe the organisational, technological and social environment where the technological artefacts are deployed. Moreover, contrary to requirements engineering perspectives that consider that technology implements the business, ADMITO uses socio-material relations between technological objects and social entities to represent the potential implementation of business, which may or not occur in practice [19].

The goal oriented requirements engineering (GORE) approaches, reviewed in [9], are the first proposals that include the description of the systems environment. The environment is described as a collection of interacting agents that act to accomplish goals. Different GORE approaches, such as NFR [12], i*/Tropos [17, 5], KAOS [8] and GBRAM [1] have been proposed. Although differing on the concepts used to describe goals, goal decomposition and goals dependence, they have in common a focus on a static goal-centred description of the environment for the specification of computer-based artefacts. However, the goals description lacks an organisational context, the organisational styles and patterns described by Bastos et al [2] are another layer in the overall decomposition hierarchy, and agents represent active components, which do not distinguish social from material entities. Conversely, ADMITO explicitly integrates technological and organisational objects and separates social entities from technology. The former allows the representation of goals as socio-material relations while the latter distinguish tangible entities that are intentional, the social entities, from technological entities that are not. Overall, in ADMITO the organisational design and the intentionality of the social entities are explicitly addressed, which allows representing the environment as a net of dynamic socio-material relations. Lapouchnian et al [10] use a GORE approach to specify business processes. In

ADMITO we also consider the stakeholder's goals associated with a business process, yet we explicitly represent the business process as an organisational object that can have other design relations, besides an implementation relation, with technological objects.

The problem frames approach [6] proposes the description of requirements as relationships in the real world, not about the software system or even the interface with the software system. In ADMITO we follow the same approach but we include organisational design, explicitly representing it, instead of focusing on functionality only.

Agile processes [3] raise the issue of having consistent and complete requirement models in a world of constantly changing requirements [16]. ADMITO is useful to identify the parts of the environment that changed, or require change, by following influence links. This strategy conforms to agile approaches since it focus on the part of the system where the next intervention should occur, instead of enforcing a complete specification of the system requirements.

7   Conclusions

The ADMITO framework provides a set of concepts and a notation to represent the analysis, design and management of IT and organisations. In this article we focused on ADMITO's expressive power to represent the dynamic and evolving entangling of IT and organisational design.

ADMITO is based on Markus and Silver [11] framework for IT effects, enriched with the concept of organisational object, and integrates Orlikowski's perspective on emergence and enacted practices [14] by distinguishing blueprint from practices diagrams. In addition, we represent business processes as a new kind of organisational object and the stakeholders' goals in the business process as socio-material relations.

From a requirements engineering perspective ADMITO stresses the dynamic relations between IT design and organisational design, towards an agile feedback cycle where organisational and IT design are interdependent and influence each other in an endless cycle. Therefore, we propose a more pragmatic approach to the design and specification of IT artefacts than the approaches that aim at producing complete and consistent specifications of the IT artefacts. In ADMITO the requirements specification focus on the aspects that need to be changed and which are inferred from an interdependent environment. Hence, the IT requirements specification is driven by the system purpose in the environment instead of by its complete and consistent description which can be postponed to a stage closer to the implementation phase, in line with the agile software development approaches.

In this paper we use ADMITO to do a post analysis of a published report. This strategy allowed us to assess the expressiveness and conciseness of ADMITO notation and concepts to describe this kind of problems. However, we are aware that further research needs to be done to evaluate the method capability to guide on how to integrate organisational design with IT design during the development and deployment of IT. Therefore, as future work we intend to define a complete ADMITO method for organisational change that integrates the processes of organisational and technology design with strategic planning. We envision a light and agile method, integrated with strategic planning, agile software development and organisational change, that supports organisational steering by focusing, at each moment, on selected subsets of the organisation and technology that may have impact on the intended change.

Acknowledgement. The research was partially supported by the Portuguese Foundation for Science and Technology, FCT-MCTES, under grants SFRH/BSAB/923/2009 and PTDC/EGE-GES/108139/2008, and FCT (INESC-ID multiannual funding) through the PIDDAC Program funds.

References

[1] Antón, A.I.: Goal-based requirements analysis. In: Second IEEE International Conference on Requirements Engineering (ICRE 1996), Colorado Springs, USA, pp. 136–144 (April 1996)

[2] Bastos, L.R.D., de Castro, J.B., Mylopoulos, J.: Integrating organizational requirements and socio-intentional architectural styles. In: ICSE 2003 - Proceedings of 2nd International Software Requirements to Architectures Workshop, STRAW 2003, Portland, Oregon, USA, May 9, pp. 114–121 (2003)

[3] Beck, K., Beedle, M., van Bennekum, A., Cockburn, A., Cunningham, W., Fowler, M., Grenning, J., Highsmith, J., Hunt, A., Jeffries, R., Kern, J., Marick, B., Martin, R.C., Mellor, S., Schwaber, K., Sutherland, J., Thomas, D.: Agilemanifesto (2001), http://www.agilemanifesto.org (accessed June 1, 2009)

[4] Burton, R., DeSanctis, G., Obel, B.: Organizational Design - A Step-by-Step Approach. Cambridge University Press (2006)

[5] Castro, J., Kolp, M., Mylopoulos, J.: Towards requirements-driven information systems engineering: the tropos project. Information Systems 27(6), 365–389 (2002)

[6] Jackson, M.: Problem Frames: Analysing and Structuring Software Development Problems. Addison-Wesley Professional (2000)

[7] KPMG: Review of queensland health payroll implementation (2010), http://www.premiers.qld.gov.au/publications/ categories/reviews/health-payroll-review.aspx

[8] van Lamsweerde, A., Letier, E.: From Object Orientation to Goal Orientation: A Paradigm Shift for Requirements Engineering. In: Wirsing, M., Knapp, A., Balsamo, S. (eds.) RISSEF 2002. LNCS, vol. 2941, pp. 325–340. Springer, Heidelberg (2004)

[9] Lapouchnian, A.: Goal-oriented requirements engineering: An overview of the current research. Tech. rep., Department of Computer Science, University of Toronto (2005)

[10] Lapouchnian, A., Yu, Y., Mylopoulos, J.: Requirements-Driven Design and Configuration Management of Business Processes. In: Alonso, G., Dadam, P., Rosemann, M. (eds.) BPM 2007. LNCS, vol. 4714, pp. 246–261. Springer, Heidelberg (2007)

[11] Markus, M.L., Silver, M.S.: A foundation for the study of it effects: A new look at desanctis and poole's concepts of structural features and spirit. Journal of the Association for Information Systems 9(10), 609–632 (2008)

[12] Mylopoulos, J., Chung, L., Nixon, B.: Representing and using nonfunctional requirements: a process-oriented approach. IEEE Transactions on Software Engineering 18(6), 483–497 (1992)

[13] Nuseibeh, B., Easterbrook, S.M.: Requirements engineering: a roadmap. In: Proceedings of the Conference on The Future of Software Engineering, pp. 35–46 (2000)

[14] Orlikowski, W.J.: The sociomateriality of organisational life: considering technology in management research. Cambridge Journal of Economics 34, 125–141 (2010)

[15] Ross, D., Schoman, K.: Structured analysis for requirements definition. IEEE Transactions Software Engineering 3(1), 6–15 (1977)

[16] Schwaber, K.: The impact of agile processes on requirements engineering. Eberlein and Leite (2002)

[17] Yu, E.S.K.: Towards modeling and reasoning support for early-phase requirements engineering. In: 3rd IEEE International Symposium on Requirements Engineering (RE 1997), Annapolis, MD, USA, January 5-8, pp. 226–235 (1997)

[18] Zave, P.: Classification of research efforts in requirements engineering. ACM Computing Surveys 29(4), 315–321 (1997)

[19] Zave, P., Jackson, M.: Four dark corners of requirements engineering. ACM Transactions on Software Engineering and Methodologies 6(1), 1–30 (1997)

Common Citation Analysis and Technology Overlap Factor: An Empirical Investigation of Litigated Patents Using Network Analysis

Srikar Velichety and Sudha Ram

Department of MIS, Eller College of Management, University of Arizona, Tucson, USA
{srikarv,sram}@email.arizona.edu

Abstract. Companies incur huge costs in filing and defending patent lawsuits. A part of the problem arises from the fact that companies do not have a comprehensive understanding of the patents that they have cited and the patents that have cited their patents. By empirically analyzing the forward and backward citations of a set of litigated patents in the smart phone industry, we provide a method for profiling patents and identifying citation patterns. Our results show that while some patents share common forward and backward citations, others do not share any backward citations but share a lot of forward citations. We hypothesize that this maybe an indication of the convergence of different types of technologies. We also propose a new metric - Technology Overlap Factor - that can help in identifying convergence. In doing so, we provide a preliminary framework for further investigation and for building a patent analysis software system.

Keywords: Patent Infringement, Backward Citations, Forward Citations, Common Citations, Technology Overlap Factor.

1 Introduction

Patent lawsuits are disruptive, unpredictable and costly (Chien, 2011). The cost of validity and infringement opinion for a single patent averages $28,000 (Black, 2009). A recent bi-annual study of American Intellectual Property Law Association reports the typical cost of defending an infringement lawsuit at 11-77 % of the amounts at risk for a particular patent (IPISC, 2011). This underscores the need for having a comprehensive litigation prediction model that can provide clues on litigation in advance. The first step in doing so would be a thorough understanding of the patents themselves through analysis of their characteristics.

Patents almost always cite some patents - referred to as "backward citations" - and get cited by some other patents - referred to as "forward citations". This provides a starting point for analyzing patents. Forward citations were widely used in analyzing patents for a long time. While Fleming (2003) asserts that a greater number of forward citations indicate greater value, Breitzman and Thomas (2002) assert that the

K. Peffers, M. Rothenberger, and B. Kuechler (Eds.): DESRIST 2012, LNCS 7286, pp. 287–293, 2012.
© Springer-Verlag Berlin Heidelberg 2012

fact that a particular patent has been cited by many later patents indicates that the patent has ideas that many later inventors tend to build upon. Backward citations on the other hand have received much less attention in the literature. They have been used for analyzing the technological convergence of different industries (Karvonen and Kassi, 2011). While Shaffer (2011) used a network of forward and backward citations to assess a patents life time value, Daim et al., (2006) and Kim et al., (2008) used the citation network for forecasting emerging technologies.

No reported research in the literature has made a comparative analysis of the forward and backward citation networks. We argue that analyzing and extracting patterns among these citations is an important step towards a comprehensive understanding of patent litigation which is the main objective of the work reported in this paper. We focus on the Smart phone industry and report on an empirical analysis of a patent dataset from this industry.

2   Review of Patent Litigation Research

Research on patent litigation began with the assertion that the number of forward citations is a valid indicator of infringement risk of a patent (Breitzman and Mogee, 2002). However this work did not provide any empirical evidence or analytical method for calculating the infringement risk. Subsequently it moved towards analyzing the effects of policies on the patenting activities of firms in a particular industry segment (Hall and Ziedonis, 2001) - the semiconductor industry. The authors here found that patent portfolio races are driven not only by the observable scale of investments but also by the likelihood of post licensing negotiations with outside patent owners. Ziedonis (2004) found that companies patent aggressively in technology markets that are highly fragmented to avoid potential hold up problems. The first reported model on calculating the patent litigation risk (Hall and Ziedonis, 2007) used the firm level characteristics viz., R&D intensity, Size of the firm, Capital Intensity, specialization in design, patent yield, Texas instruments and year effects to calculate infringement risk. While this model helps firms assess the risk of litigation at a strategic level, it doesn't explicitly identify the litigation risk of individual patents in a portfolio. While it is important for firms to keep track of the litigation risk of their patent portfolios, given the fact that less than 5% of the patents in the portfolio of each of the companies are litigated. It would be more appropriate to know the litigation risk of the individual patents to better anticipate an imminent lawsuit. Also, since patent litigation suits are common when there is a convergence of industries (Hynes and Sinnot, 2011), it would be desirable to have a method that is independent of firm or sector level characteristics in order to be more generalizable. To our knowledge there is no reported research on patent litigation for producing such a method. We tackle this challenge by developing a method that helps comparatively analyze the forward and backward citations of litigated patents and identify interesting patterns that provide cues for predicting potential infringement.

3   Data Collection

We collected a dataset starting with 29 litigated patents as of December 2011 and gathered their forward and backward citations. The total number of patents in the final dataset is 3585. The litigated patents were obtained through a survey of literature on patent litigation (Lloyd et al., 2011), inspection of the legal proceedings section of the 10-K forms of major smart phone companies, and patent litigation news articles in major magazines.

4   Network Construction

The nodes in our network are the litigated patents and their forward and backward citations. If a litigated patent X   has cited another patent Y, then there is a directed edge from node X to node Y. Similarly, if a litigated patent X has been cited by a patent Y, then there is a directed edge from node Y to node X.

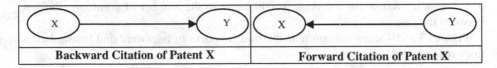

| Backward Citation of Patent X | Forward Citation of Patent X |

5   Analysis of the Network

Figures 1 and 2 show the forward and backward citation networks of the litigated patents. While we see that some patents do not share any common citations with others we also see a number of pairs of patents sharing a large number of common citations.

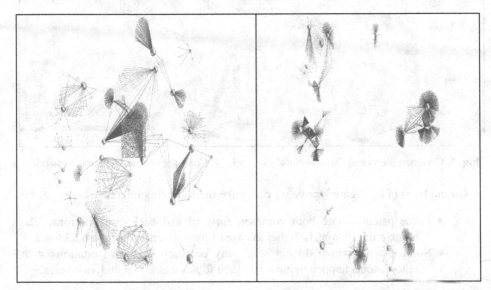

Fig. 1. Backward Citations   **Fig. 2.** Forward Citations

While the forward citation network appears to be denser, the trend of common citations between patents is clearly palpable in both the networks. This brings us to the following questions

- Do the same pairs of patents that share common backward citations also share common forward citations?
- Do the structural properties of the backward and forward citation networks show any similarity or interesting trends?

This leads us to a discussion of common citations between the litigated patents.

5.1   Common Citations

In order to analyze all common citations, we constructed an undirected, weighted common citation network with an edge between any two pairs of patents with at least one common citation and the edge weight equal to the number of common citations between the patents.

Figures 3 and 4 show the common citation networks of backward and forward citations respectively.

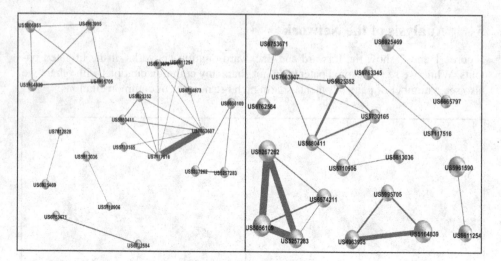

Fig. 3. Common Backward Citation Network   **Fig. 4.** Common Forward Citation Network

On the basis of the figures above we can make the following inferences.

- Some patents share both common forward and backward citations. The number of citations is higher in case of forward citations than backward.
- Some patents which do not share any common backward citations with other patents happen to have common forward citations and vice versa.

The fact that some pairs of patents do not share any common backward citations but do share a significant number of forward citations is an indication of the development of new technologies that draw upon two distinct technologies. Hynes and Sinnott (2011) argued that convergence of distinct technologies could be one of the reasons for litigation. However, no reported research on patent litigation has so far proposed a metric for quantifying the extent of convergence. Here we propose a metric called the Technology Overlap Factor to measure the extent of technological similarity between two patents.

5.2   Technology Overlap Factor

Each of the patents filed in the U.S. is assigned to one or more of the Technology classifications by the United States Patent and Trademark Office (U.S.P.T.O). The classifications can get updated subsequently and the classification structure gets updated once every 2 years. Since we are interested in measuring the extent to which the technologies of two patents overlap, we define Technology overlap factor of any two patents as the ratio of the number of common technology classes to which the patents belong to the total number of distinct technology classes to which both the patents belong. Hence for any two patents X and Y we define the technology overlap factors as follows

$$\text{Technology Overlap Factor} = n\ (X_i \cap Y_i)\ /\ n\ (X_i \cup Y_i)$$

where X_i and Y_i represent the technology class assignments of patents X and Y respectively.

For example a patent X has a technology class assignment 540/R1;560/R2 and a patent Y has a technology class assignment 540/R1;580/R2 then the technology overlap factor for these two patents is 1/3. Ideally, for those patents that share only common forward citations but no backward citations, this metric must be zero.

Our results show that for pairs of patents that do not share any common backward citations but share a lot of forward citations, the Technology overlap value is zero. Given the fact that convergence of technologies is an important factor behind litigation (Hynes and Sinnott, 2011), we argue that this type of common citation analysis provides an important clue for convergence and hence patent litigation. Also for those patents that have only backward citations but no forward citations, the values of the Technology Overlap Factor lie between 0 and 0.2. For those that share both common forward and backward citations, the value in general lies between 0.3 and 1 with the exception of pairs (US5164839, US5995705), (US4963995, US5995705) and (US5730165, US7663607). However these three pairs of patents have fewer forward and backward citations in common when compared to other pairs that have the same property. In short we find that for the three different types of common citation patterns, we see certain ranges of values that this metric takes.

6   Limitations and Future Work

Our results provide a preliminary framework for several areas of further investigation. Our dataset is a small one consisting of litigated patents drawn from a particular sector of the industry. It would be interesting to take a larger dataset of litigated patents and construct a common citation network to see if there are any other interesting patterns of citation. Also going by the fact that technological convergence is an important factor behind convergence of industries, studying the common citation patterns among patents drawn from different industries would be a rich area of study. Further, calibrating the Technology Overlap Factor to distinguish between different levels of convergence may prove to be a fruitful cue for litigation. For those patents that share common backward and forward citations, it would be interesting to construct a network of relevant patents in the technology area and see if we are able to identify the existence of a thicket. All these enhancements would require us to study a larger dataset of patents drawn from various industries.

References

1. Breitzman, A.F., Mogee, M.E.: The many applications of patent analysis. Journal of Information Science 28(3), 187–205 (2002)
2. Fleming, J.: Valuing Patents: Assessing the Merit of Patent Citation Analysis. Undergraduate thesis. University of Virginia (2003)
3. Shaffer, M.J.: Entrepreneurial Innovation: Patent Rank and Marketing Science. Washington State University (2011)
4. Breitzman, A., Thomas, P.: Using Patent Citation Analysis to Target/Value Mergers and Acquisitions Candidates. Research-Technology Management 45, 28–29 (2002)
5. Brinn, M.W., Fleming, J.M., Hannaka, F.M., Thomas, C.B., Beling, P.A.: Investigation of forward citation count as a patent analysis method. In: 2003 IEEE Systems and Information Engineering Design Symposium, pp. 1–6 (2003)
6. Choi, C., Shin, J., Yoon, B., Lee, W., Park, Y.: On the linkage between industries and technologies: patent citation analysis. In: Proceedings of 2004 IEEE International Engineering Management Conference, vol. 2, pp. 576–578 (2004)
7. Wu, H.C., Chen, H.Y., Lee, K.Y., Liu, Y.C.: A method for assessing patent similarity using direct and indirect citation links. In: 2010 IEEE International Conference on Industrial Engineering and Engineering Management (IEEM), pp. 149–152 (2010)
8. Kim, Y.G., Suh, J.H., Park, S.C.: Visualization of patent analysis for emerging technology. Expert Systems with Applications 34, 1804–1812 (2008)
9. Daim, T.U., Rueda, G., Martin, H., Gerdsri, P.: Forecasting emerging technologies: Use of bibliometrics and patent analysis. Technological Forecasting and Social Change 73, 981–1012 (2006)
10. Karvonen, M., Kässi, T.: Patent analysis for analysing technological convergence. Foresight 13(5), 34–50 (2011)
11. Chien, C.V.: Predicting Patent Litigation. Texas Law Review 90, 283 (2011); Santa Clara Univ. Legal Studies Research Paper No. 17-11. SSRN, http://ssrn.com/abstract=1911579
12. Delaney, T.Q., Pioli, J.: Navigating Recent Mobile Patent Lawsuits. Aspatore, Boston (2011)
13. Fighting the Smart Phone Wars. World Intellectual Property Review, pp. 12–19 (March 2011)

14. Hall, B.H., Ziedonis, R.H.: The Patent Paradox Revisited: An Empirical Study of Patenting in the U.S. Semiconductor Industry, 1979-1995. RAND Journal of Economics 32(1), 101–128 (2001)
15. Hall, B.H., Ziedonis, R.: An empirical analysis of patent litigation in the semiconductor industry. University of California at Berkeley working paper (2007)
16. Hynes, J., Sinnott, T.: The US International Trade Commission: smartphone patent battles. Intellectural Property Magazine 39 (February 2011)
17. Lloyd, M., Spielthenner, D., Mokdsi, G.: The SmartPhone Patent Wars. IAM Journal, March 1-30 (2011)
18. Ziedonis, R.H.: Don't Fence Me In: Fragmented Markets for Technology and Patent Acquisition Strategies of Firms. Management Science 50(6), 804–820 (2004)
19. IPISC, from AIPLA Survey (2011), http://www.patentinsurance.com/iprisk/aipla-survey/ (retrieved December 2, 2011)
20. Black, E.: from CCIA (July 16, 2009), http://www.ccianet.org/CCIA/files/ccLibraryFiles/Filename/000000000226/Ltr%20on%20Rpt%20SCP-13-51.pdf (retrieved December 2, 2011)

Environmental Sustainability in Design Science Research: Direct and Indirect Effects of Design Artifacts

Jan vom Brocke and Stefan Seidel

University of Liechtenstein, Vaduz, Liechtenstein
{jan.vom.brocke,stefan.seidel}@uni.li

Abstract. There is an increasing consensus that information systems (IS) design needs to consider effects related to environmental sustainability. While information technology (IT) can help solving environmental problems, it also causes environmental problems through emissions, wastage, and the consumption of renewable and nonrenewable resources throughout its lifecycle. Against this background, the notions of Green IT and Green IS have evolved. While the former primarily relates to the energy efficiency and equipment utilization of IT, the latter pertains to the design and implementation of information systems that contribute to sustainable business processes. In this paper, we explore how environmental sustainability can be considered in design science research. While traditionally design science research has focused on the utility of artifacts, we propose to also consider a design artifact's environmental impact. We discuss how the design goal of sustainability relates to artifact utility and suggest a framework that describes two dimensions of design artifact environmental impact, namely direct and indirect environmental impacts. While the first pertains to effects of the physical existence of an IT artifact through its production, use, and disposal, the latter relates to the potential of the artifact to contribute to sustainable business processes.

Keywords: Design Science Research, Green IS, Green IT, Sustainability.

1 Introduction

It has been argued that information systems (IS) can play a meaningful role in creating sustainable work practices and products. It has also been highlighted that the IS discipline can contribute to this development through providing information systems that enable sustainable business processes. Prominent examples include the fields of energy informatics to increase energy efficiency [24], remote work to reduce carbon emissions through travel [3], or monitoring emissions and waste to decrease the environmental impact of specific processes. While it has been asserted that information technology (IT) can help solving environmental problems, it also contributes to the deterioration of the natural environment through emissions, wastage, and the consumption of renewable and nonrenewable resources throughout the lifecycle [7, 25]. Efforts related to a more environmentally sustainable use of IT have been discussed under the labels of Green IT and Green IS. While the former primarily relates to the

K. Peffers, M. Rothenberger, and B. Kuechler (Eds.): DESRIST 2012, LNCS 7286, pp. 294–308, 2012.

energy efficiency and equipment utilization of IT, the latter pertains to the design and implementation of information systems that contribute to the implementation of sustainable business processes [25].

Sustainability has been defined as "development that meets the needs of the present without compromising the ability of future generations to meet their own needs" [27]. More specifically, Goodland [9] describes environmental sustainability as the "maintenance of natural capital," and identifies two primary environmental services: the source and the sink functions. Environmental sustainability "is a set of constraints on the four major activities regulating the scale of the human economic subsystem: the use of renewable and nonrenewable resources on the source side, and pollution and waste assimilation on the sink side" [p. 10].

Against this background, Information Systems as a solution-oriented discipline can contribute to both the worsening and the enhancement of the natural environment. The effects of information systems can be related to the above definition of environmental sustainability:

(1) On the sink side, IS produce outputs in the form of waste and emissions throughout their lifecycle.
(2) On the source side, IS require inputs in the form of both renewables and non-renewables throughout their lifecycle.
(3) IS have the potential to allow for more sustainable business processes, that is, processes that use less renewable and non-renewable resources on the source side, and that assimilate less pollution and waste on the sink side.

As the effects of information systems are intimately connected to their design, we suggest considering the environmental impact of design artifacts in design science research (DSR). This is because, in current thinking, utility is seen as the primary goal of DSR, without linking the discussion to environmental aspects [8, 13]. Design science research aims at creating innovative and purposeful IT artifacts [12, 13]. With this, it can be distinguished from the behavioral science paradigm, which typically aims at studying IT artifacts that are implemented in organizational settings [13].While the main goal of behavioral science research is to provide explanations [20], the primary goal of design science research is the utility of the resultant artifacts [12].

In this paper, we explore the role of environmental sustainability in design science research. In doing so, we aim to make three primary contributions: First, we conceptualize environmental sustainability as an explicit goal of design science research by means of a design artifact's environmental impact. Second, we discuss how the goal of environmental sustainability can be considered in design science research methodology. Specifically, we discuss the goal of environmental sustainability with regard to the general principles of design research [13, 16, 20], practice rules [13], and procedures [20], as these have been identified as mandatory components of a design science research methodology [20]. Besides, we relate the goal of environmental sustainability to the concept of design theories as a means to capture knowledge about IT artifact design. Third, our discussion of the environmental sustainability of IT artifacts allows us to propose a unified perspective on Green IT and Green IS.

We proceed as follows. In the next section, we provide a brief overview of IS research on environmental sustainability. In the subsequent section, we explore the goals of design science research as they have been discussed in recent publications. We then examine how environmental sustainability can be considered as an additional goal in design science research and propose a framework for environmentally sustainable design artifacts in IS research. Finally, we discuss our findings, and provide a conclusion where we also identify some important limitations of this research.

2   Environmental Sustainability in IS Research

Organizations are a main contributor to the deterioration of the natural environment [17], and information systems have been the most prominent contributor to economic growth over the last decades [25]. Consequently, the impact of information systems on the natural environment warrants further investigation. Recently, the concepts of Green IT and Green IS have gained increasing popularity and have been subject to research from diverse areas, most notably computer science [e.g., 14] and information systems [5]. While Green IT primarily relates to the energy efficiency and utilization of IT equipment, Green IS pertains to the design and implementation of information systems that support environmental sustainability [25]. Green IS thus targets a much bigger problem and, therefore, is said to have a much bigger potential than Green IT [25]. Watson et al. [24], for example, discuss the potentials of energy informatics to increase energy efficiency and reduce energy consumption, and propose a framework for energy informatics. Melville [17] argues that information systems research can contribute to "the creation and evaluation of systems that break new ground in environmental responsibility" [p. 1] and identifies a number of research questions that are relevant in the domain of IS innovation for environmental sustainability. Among others, he identifies different questions that are related to IS design issues: "What design approaches are effective for developing information systems that influence human beliefs about the natural environment" [p. 11]? or "What design approaches are effective for developing information systems that influence human actions about the natural environment" [p. 12]? Elliot [7] provides a "holistic, trans-disciplinary, integrative framework for IT-enabled business transformation" [p. 197]. He proposes a set of hypotheses, among others: "Technology (including IT) has a negative impact on the environment at various stages in the technology life cycle" [p. 228], thus lending an argument to the above Green IT discussion, and "Technology (including IT) has a moderating effect on the negative impact of the environment on human beings" [p. 228], thus relating to the above Green IS discussion.

This duality of IT as being both a contributor and a potential solution has also been discussed in the field of environmental informatics in terms of first, second, and third order effects of information and communication technology [14]: First order effects relate to the direct environmental impact that is due to the physical existence of the technology, second order effects are those indirect impacts due to the IT-enabled change in business processes, and third order effects result from the medium- or long-term adaption of behaviors and structure resulting from the availability of IT and IT services [14].

In summation, Green IT and Green IS offer two complementary perspectives on the role of IT in environmental sustainability. Consequently, in this study, we will explore the role of environmental sustainability in design research by considering this duality.

3   Design Science Research

In this section, we first discuss the goals of design research in order to provide a conceptual basis for integrating the concept of environmental sustainability. Second, we provide a brief overview of the DSR methodology in order to prepare the ground for a more detailed discussion on how environmental sustainability can be considered in DSR in the subsequent sections.

3.1   The Goals of Design Science Research

Design science research has emerged as a popular field in IS research, due to a widely acknowledged view that information systems is much characterized by applied research, often drawing from other disciplines, and having the purpose of providing solutions to organizations [20]. The development of design knowledge is hence of high relevance to both IS research and practice [22, 26]. Design science research is concerned with the systematic creation of knowledge about organizational problems and potential solutions through building and evaluating novel artifacts [12]. Design-science research "creates and evaluates IT artifacts intended to solve identified organizational problems" [13, p. 77]. In this context, design is both a process (i.e., a set of activities) and a product (i.e., an artifact) [13]. In current design thinking, the preeminent goal is that of utility [8, 13]. Consequently, the evaluation of the design artifact is crucial. Hevner et al. [13], for example, building upon the work of March and Smith [16], write with regard to the results of design science research: "Purposeful artifacts are built to address heretofore unsolved problems. They are evaluated with respect to the utility provided in solving those problems" [p. 78]. Similarly, Peffers et al. [20] say that in "DS research, design and the proof of its usefulness is the central component" [p. 72]. In the context of the development of design theories, Gregor and Jones [11] further state that the requirements of a system are to be understood in relation to the environment in which the system will operate. What these authors agree upon is the consideration of goals that are preeminently related to solving organizational problems. However, it is not clear how these organizational problems are related to the concept of environmental sustainability. While some solutions are intended to contribute to solving specific organizational problems, they may produce negative environmental effects at the same time. Other solutions may be developed with the explicit intention to contribute to the design and implementation of sustainable business processes.

3.2   Design Science Research Methodology

Peffers et al. [20] state that a comprehensive design science research methodology comprises of three elements: (1) conceptual principles that define design science research, (2) practice rules for design science research, and (3) procedures that describe how to carry out design science research. Table 1 provides an overview.

Table 1. Components of a design science methodology [drawing from 20]

Component of design science research methodology	Description	References
Principles	Defining what is meant by DS research	[11, 13, 16, 20]
Practice Rules	Rules that have to be considered when carrying out design research	[13]
Procedures	How to conduct and present design science research	[20]

General principles. Different authors [e.g. 11, 13, 16, 20] have coined the meaning of design science research. There is now some agreement upon its goals, typically related to utility in the context of solving organizational problems.

Practice rules. Hevner et al. [13] have notably contributed to our understanding of what principles researchers should adhere to when conducting design science research, and their work has been widely cited in IS design science studies.

Procedures. Peffers et al. [20] propose a process model for the conduct of design science research.

While a design science research methodology comprising of these three components focuses on "design research as a knowledge building activity rather than the structural nature of the knowledge or theory that results" [10, p. 317], other researchers have coined the notion of *design theory* [11], or theory for design and action [10, 11, 23].

For our study, we chose Hevner et al. [13] as the most prominent example for practice rules, Peffers et al. [20] for the procedures in design science research, and Gregor and Jones' [11] components of an information systems design theory as a recent proposal of how design knowledge can be captured in the form of theory.

4   A Framework for Environmentally Sustainable Design Artifacts

There are at least two perspectives that need to be considered when conceptualizing the sustainability of design artifacts as an additional goal in design science research: First, the environmental impact of the artifact throughout its lifecycle due to its physical existence (independent from its specific purpose) through wastage and resource consumption [e.g. 14] and, second, the impact of the use of the artifact on business processes and human behavior in more general terms [5]. Consequently, grounded in the distinction between Green IT and Green IS, the distinction between first, second, and third order effects of IT, as well as the source and sink functions as fundamental environmental services, we propose two dimensions of design artifact environmental impact: direct environmental impact and indirect environmental impact of the design artifact. The first represents the first order effects that an artifact has, viz., the environmental consequences of the use of the artifact independent from the organizational problem it tackles, due to its physical existence. The second represents second and third order effects, viz., intended and unintended environmental consequences of the use of the artifact through its impact on business processes. As the latter is closely related to organizational problems—and as an organizational problem can indeed be related to becoming more sustainable—it can be viewed as a sub-concept of utility. Table 2 provides an overview of the two sustainability dimensions of design artifacts.

Table 2. Direct and indirect environmental impact of design artifacts

Concept	Description	Example	References / prior literature
Direct environmental impact of the design artifact	The effects of the production, use, and disposal of an IT artifact, that is, the use of renewable and nonrenewable resources on the source side, and the assimilation of pollution and waste on the sink side, due to the physical existence of the artifact.	The use of a software system that runs on a computer causes waste and emissions (sink side) and consumes energy and natural resources throughout its lifecycle (source side).	First order effects [14], Green IT [18], source and sink functions [9]
Indirect environmental impact of the design artifact	The effects of an IT artifact on the sustainability of business processes and human behavior in more general terms, that is, the use of renewable and nonrenewable resources on the source side, and the assimilation of pollution and waste on the sink side, in business process that are designed and implemented using the artifact. Can be viewed as a sub-dimension of utility.	The use of software for virtual collaboration allows for reduced travel, thus limiting emissions (sink side) and consumption of non-renewable energy (source side), thus contributing to the sustainability of, for example, a sales process.	Second order effects, third order effects [14], Green IS [5, 24], source and sink functions [9]

We will explore how the environmental impact of design artifacts can be considered in (a) practice rules of design research, (b) procedures for design research, and (c) design theory, in turn.

4.1 Environmental Sustainability and Practice Rules for Design Research

Practice rules describe "good" design science research and build a foundation for evaluating such research [20]. Hevner et al. [13], in their seminal MISQ article, propose seven guidelines for conducting design science research. These are design as an artifact, problem relevance, design evaluation, research contributions, research rigor, design as a search process, and communication of research. We argue that the environmental sustainability of the design artifact (its environmental costs and benefits) can be considered in each of these guidelines. Table 3 provides an overview.

Table 3. Environmental sustainability and practice rules for design research

Guideline [13]	Description [13, p. 83]	Consideration of sustainability
Guideline 1: Design as an artifact	"Design-science research must produce a viable artifact in the form of a construct, a model, a method, or an instantiation."	In order to contribute to environmental sustainability, design-science research must produce viable artifacts that have low direct environmental impact throughout their lifecycle and/or that contribute to the design and implementation of sustainable business processes, thus being associated with positive indirect effects on the natural environment.
Guideline 2: Problem relevance	"The objective of design-science research is to develop technology-based solutions to important and relevant business problems."	In order to contribute to environmental sustainability, the objective of design science research is to develop technology-based solutions that contribute to the design and implementation of sustainable business processes while, at the same time, having low direct impact on the natural environment
Guideline 3: Design evaluation	"The utility, quality, and efficacy of a design artifact must be rigorously demonstrated via well-executed evaluation methods."	In order to ensure that a design artifact contributes to environmental sustainability, any evaluation must consider the direct and indirect environmental effects of the design artifact.
Guideline 4: Research contributions	"Effective design-science research must provide clear and verifiable contributions in the areas of the design artifact, design foundations, and/or design methodologies."	In order to contribute to environmental sustainability, design-science research must provide clear and verifiable contributions that are associated with low direct environmental effects and/or that bear the potential of contributing to the design and implementation of sustainable business processes, thus realizing positive indirect effects on the environment.
Guideline 5: Research rigor	"Design-science research relies upon the application of rigorous methods in both the construction and evaluation of the design artifact."	In order to contribute to environmental sustainability, this principle applies likewise.

Table 3. (*continued*)

Guideline 6: Design as a search process	The search for an effective artifact requires utilizing available means to reach desired ends while satisfying laws in the problem environment."	In order to contribute to environmental sustainability, design-science research must employ a search process utilizing available means that allow designs with low direct environmental impact and/or the potential to contribute to the design and implementation of sustainable business processes.
Guideline 7: Communication of research	"Design-science research must be presented effectively both to technology-oriented as well as management-oriented audiences."	The effective communication of the environmental sustainability of design artifacts can contribute to decision-making at the individual, organizational, and societal level related to the use of technology.

It thus becomes noticeable that, in order to contribute to environmental sustainability, researchers must relate the proposed practice rules to the environmental sustainability of the design artifact. Alternatively, one could propose an additional guideline labeled design artifact sustainability to capture the explicit goal of considering environmental sustainability in design science research. Table 4 provides an overview.

Table 4. Guideline of design artifact sustainability

Design artifact sustainability	In order to contribute to environmental sustainability, design science research must provide artifacts that have low direct environmental impact due to their physical existence and/or that bear the potential to contribute to the design and implementation of sustainable business processes. That is, design science research must consider the use of renewable and non-renewable resources as well as the assimilation of waste and emissions, both with regard to the physical existence of design artifacts and their indirect impact on business processes.

4.2   Environmental Sustainability and Procedures for Design Research

As indicated by Peffers et al. [20], a complete design science research methodology requires not only principles and practice rules, but also a process model. Pfeffers et al. [20] analyze prior literature on design science from various disciplines, including that of IS, and propose a method that is intended to "serve as a commonly accepted framework for carrying out research based on DS research principles" [p. 52]. The method was built upon a consensus-building approach and thus incorporates the views of different researchers [1, 4, 6, 13, 19, 21, 23]. Specifically, six activities are suggested: identify problem and motivate, define objectives and solution, design and development, demonstration, evaluation, and communication. We argue that the environmental sustainability of the design artifact can be considered in each of these activities. Table 5 provides an overview.

Table 5. Environmental sustainability and procedures for design research

Activity [20]	Description [20]	Consideration of sustainability
Identify problem & motivate	"Define the specific research problem and justify the value of a solution. Because the problem definition will be used to develop an artifact that can effectively provide a solution, it may be useful to atomize the problem conceptually so that the solution can capture its complexity. Justifying the value of a solution accomplishes two things: it motivates the researcher and the audience of the research to pursue the solution and to accept the results and it helps to understand the reasoning associated with the researcher's understanding of the problem. Resources required for this activity include knowledge of the state of the problem and the importance of its solution" [p. 52-55].	In order to contribute to environmental sustainability, define a specific research problem that is related to/considers environmental sustainability. The problem definition builds the foundation to develop an artifact that effectively provides a solution by (a) suggesting designs with low direct environmental impact, and/or (b) with the potential to contribute to the design and implementation of sustainable business processes.
Define objectives of a solution	"Infer the objectives of a solution from the problem definition and knowledge of what is possible and feasible. The objectives can be quantitative, such as terms in which a desirable solution would be better than current ones, or qualitative, such as a description of how a new artifact is expected to support solutions to problems not hitherto addressed. The objectives should be inferred rationally from the problem specification. Resources required for this include knowledge of the state of problems and current solutions, if any, and their efficacy" [p. 55].	In order to contribute to environmental sustainability, researchers must define objectives related to the direct and indirect environmental impact of the design artifact. The objectives should be rationally inferred from the specific environmental problem to be targeted (e.g., wastage, carbon emissions, energy consumption).
Design & development	"Create the artifact. [...] Conceptually, a design research artifact can be any designed object in which a research contribution is embedded in the design. This activity includes determining the artifact's desired functionality and its architecture and then creating the actual artifact. Resources required for moving from objectives to design and development include knowledge of theory that can be brought to bear in a solution" [p. 55].	In order to contribute to environmental sustainability, the research contribution in form of low direct environmental impact and/or positive indirect environmental impact of the design artifact must be embedded in the design. It needs to be argued in how far the functionality and the architecture of the artifact are actually intended to positively influence direct or indirect effects.

Table 5. (*continued*)

Demonstration	"Demonstrate the use of the artifact to solve one or more instances of the problem. This could involve its use in experimentation, simulation, case study, proof, or other appropriate activity. Resources required for the demonstration include effective knowledge of how to use the artifact to solve the problem" [p. 55].	Demonstrate the use of the artifact in a way its direct and indirect environmental impacts can be observed.
Evaluation	"Observe and measure how well the artifact supports a solution to the problem. This activity involves comparing the objectives of a solution to actual observed results from use of the artifact in the demonstration. It requires knowledge of relevant metrics and analysis techniques" [p. 56].	Observe and measure how well the artifact supports the direct or indirect environmental effects it is aimed at.
Communication	"Communicate the problem and its importance, the artifact, its utility and novelty, the rigor of its design and its effectiveness to researchers and other relevant audiences such as practicing professionals, when appropriate" [p. 56].	In addition to utility, novelty, design rigor, and effectiveness, also communicate the design artifact sustainability.

4.3   Environmental Sustainability and Design Theory

Design theories have been discussed as an important means to communicate, justify, and develop design knowledge in IS [11, 23]. At this, it must be noted that design research as an activity as described above and design theory are closely interrelated. There is some agreement that design research should rely on existent theory [2, 15, 23] and, also, that the result of design research can be a contribution to theory [15]. Peffers et al. [20] also establish a link between design research as an activity and design theory by noting that meta requirements as specified in design theories describe the objectives of a (class of) design solutions. Design theories (or theories for design and action) say how something should be done [10] by providing explicit prescriptions for constructing an artifact [10]. Gregor and Jones [11], building upon the works of others [e.g. 23], propose eight components of an information systems design theory. We argue that the environmental sustainability of the design artifact (its environmental costs and benefits) can be considered in each of these components. Table 6 provides an overview.

Table 6. Environmental sustainability and design theory

Component [11]	Description [10, p. 322]	Consideration of sustainability
Purpose and scope	"'What the system is for,' the set of meta-requirements or goals that specifies the type of artifact to which the theory applies and in conjunction also defines the scope, or boundaries, of the theory."	In order to contribute to environmental sustainability, purpose and scope should pertain to direct and/or indirect environmental impacts of a design artifact. That is, an artifact can be designed to meet a given purpose with less resource utilization or emission. In addition, artifacts can be specifically designed to contribute to sustainable business processes.
Constructs	"Representations of the entities of interest in the theory."	In order to contribute to environmental sustainability, the design theory should comprise constructs that allow to minimize the direct environmental impact and/or contribute to the artifact's potential to contribute to the design and implementation of sustainable business processes.
Principles of form and function	"The abstract 'blueprint' or architecture that describes an IS artifact, either product or method/intervention."	In order to contribute to environmental sustainability, principles of form and function can relate to both direct and indirect environmental impacts of the design artifact, that is, they describe how an artifact is designed that has low direct environmental impact and/or the potential to contribute to the design and implementation of sustainable business processes.
Artifact mutability	"The changes in state of the artifact anticipated in the theory, that is, what degree of artifact change is encompassed by the theory."	In order to contribute to environmental sustainability, the design theory describes how the artifact needs to change in order to allow for control of direct and indirect environmental impacts over time.
Testable propositions	"Truth statements about the design theory."	Truth statements about the environmental sustainability (direct and indirect environmental impacts) of a design artifact.

Table 6. (*continued*)

Justificatory knowledge	"The underlying knowledge or theory from the natural or social or design sciences that gives a basis and explanation for the design (kernel theories)."	In order to contribute to environmental sustainability, researchers can draw from a broad variety of theories both from natural and social sciences that can inform the design of artifacts with low direct environmental impact and/or the potential to contribute to the design and implementation of sustainable processes.
Principles of implementation	"A description of processes for implementing the theory (either product or method) in specific contexts."	In order to contribute to environmental sustainability, principles of implementation need to consider both direct and indirect impacts of specific systems to be implemented in a specific context.
Expository instantiation	"A physical implementation of the artifact that can assist in representing the theory both as an expository device and for purposes of testing."	The physical instantiation can be used to test the theory with regard to the environmental impacts of artifacts belonging to the class of artifacts described by that theory.

5   Discussion

We set out to examine how environmental sustainability can be considered in design science research. Drawing on prior literature, we were able to relate environmental sustainability to the general principles (and goals) of design science research, to practice rules for design science research, to procedures of design science research, as well as to design theory. We thus argue that, in order to contribute to environmental sustainability, researchers must consider the environmental impact of their artifacts in all stages of the design process. That environmental sustainability should indeed be considered in the design of IT artifacts, both in terms of direct and indirect effects on the natural environment, is consistent with prior literature from the areas of Green IT and, more recently, Green IS. For instance, Elliot [7] states that while technology per se has a negative impact on the natural environment throughout its lifecycle, it can also have a moderating impact on the negative effects of human behavior on the natural environment.

While environmental informatics has focused on hardware and software, IT artifacts can be of various natures. Specifically, there is some agreement that methods, constructs, models, and instantiations are the output of design science research [13, 20]. While for IT hard- and software (i.e., concrete instantiations) the environmental impact is rather obvious, for models, constructs, and methods this is not the case. We thus need to discuss how environmental sustainability can be related to the different types of IT artifacts. Table 7 provides some concrete examples. We contend that the direct environmental impact of constructs, models, and methods (e.g., through the construction of the artifact and its storage) is rather limited and can be neglected. However, as constructs, models and methods contribute to the design of information systems, those systems will be associated with direct and indirect environmental impacts, in turn. It thus becomes apparent that the indirect environmental consequences of a design artifact can impact on both the direct and indirect environmental sustainability of a concrete instantiation.

Table 7. Environmental impact of different types of IT artifacts

	Constructs example: building blocks of a systems design	Models example: System design	Methods example: process modeling grammar	Instantiations example: software
Direct environmental impact	The direct environmental impacts of constructs can be neglected.	The direct environmental impact of a system design can be neglected.	The direct environmental impact of a modeling grammar due to its sheer existence can be neglected.	Emissions, resource, and energy consumption of the system on which the software runs. A software tool can, for example, require more or less computational power and disk space.
Indirect environmental impact	As constructs are the building blocks of models, methods, and instantiations, they can influence both the direct and indirect environmental impact of design artifacts. In particular, they help building a sustainability-related terminology.	A systems design describes a system, or class of systems. Therefore, the system design impacts on both the direct and indirect environmental impact of the systems that are described. Principles of form and function contributing to sustainability can be incorporated in instantiations based on a specific model.	A modeling grammar may, for instance, contribute specific constructs that allow for the design of processes in the light of environmental considerations.	The environmental impact of the processes that are supported by the software. A software tool that allows virtual collaboration, for example, may reduce travel and, therefore, energy consumption and carbon emissions.

Consequently, environmental sustainability needs to be considered with regard to the different types of IT artifacts. As the different types are interrelated, the consideration of environmental impacts at one level may impact on the environmental sustainability at other levels.

In summation, from a broad level, we suggest the following primary conjecture: In order to contribute to environmental sustainability, design-science research must consider the sustainability of a design artifact, that is its direct and indirect effects on the natural environment, (a) in the general principles of design science, (b) in the rigorous application of practice rules, and (c) all stages of the design research process.

6 Conclusion

In this paper we set out to discuss the role of environmental sustainability in design science research. We contend that IS research, through its contributions to the development of novel and purposeful IT artifacts, bears a responsibility when it comes to both the worsening and the enhancement of the natural environment. Our intent was to make three primary contributions: First, to conceptualize environmental sustainability as an explicit goal of design science research by means of a design artifact's environmental impact; second, to discuss how the goal of environmental sustainability can be considered in design science research methodology; third, to propose a unified perspective on Green IT and Green IS based on our conceptualization of the environmental impact centered around a discussion of the IT artifact.

This work has some limitations. First, in this conceptual article, we focused on environmental sustainability. We acknowledge that environmental sustainability cannot be separated from economic and social sustainability, and that other foci may lead to different conceptualizations. Second, one crucial aspect that we did not explore in much depth is that of the evaluation of IT artifacts with regard to the indirect and direct impact on the natural environment. Future research must thus consider how artifacts can be evaluated with regard to their environmental sustainability, both in terms of source and sink functions.

It will be interesting to see in how far we as a discipline take responsibility for environmental deterioration by contributing to the design of purposeful and novel IT artifacts that not only have low environmental impact throughout their lifecycle, but also contribute to the design and implementation of sustainable business processes.

References

1. Archer, L.B.: Systematic method for designers. In: Cross, N. (ed.) Developments in Design Methodology, pp. 57–82. John Wiley, London (1984)
2. Baskerville, R.: What design science is not. European Journal of Information Systems 17, 441–443 (2008)
3. Bose, R., Luo, X.: Integrative Framework for Assessing Firms' Potential to Undertake Green IT Initiatives via Virtualization - A Theoretical Perspective. Journal of Strategic Information Systems 20, 38–54 (2011)
4. Cole, R., Purao, S., Rossi, M., Sein, M.K.: Being proactive: Where action research meets design research. In: Twenty-Sixth International Conference on Information Systems, pp. 325–336. Association for Information Systems, Atlanta (2005)
5. Dedrick, J.: Green IS: Concepts and Issues for Information Systems Research. Communications of the Association for Information Systems 27, 173–184 (2010)
6. Eekels, J., Roozenburg, N.F.M.: A methodological comparison of the structures of scientific research and engineering design: Their similarities and differences. Design Studies 12, 197–203 (1991)
7. Elliot, S.: Transdisciplinary Perspectives on Environmental Sustainability: A Resource Base and Framework for IT-Enabled Business Transformation. MIS Quarterly 35, 197–236 (2011)

8. Gill, T.G., Hevner, A.R.: A Fitness-Utility Model for Design Science Research. In: Jain, H., Sinha, A.P., Vitharana, P. (eds.) DESRIST 2011. LNCS, vol. 6629, pp. 237–252. Springer, Heidelberg (2011)

9. Goodland, R.: The Concept of Environmental Sustainability. Annual Review of Ecology and Systematics 26, 1–24 (1995)

10. Gregor, S.: The Nature of Theory in Information Systems. MIS Quarterly 30, 611–642 (2006)

11. Gregor, S., Jones, D.: The Anatomy of a Design Theory. Journal of the Association for Information Systems 8, 313–335 (2007)

12. Hevner, A.R., Chatterjee, S.: Design research in information systems. Springer, Boston (2010)

13. Hevner, A.R., March, S.T., Jinsoo, P., Ram, S.: Design Science in Information Systems Research. MIS Quarterly 28, 75–105 (2004)

14. Hilty, L.M., Arnfalk, P., Erdmann, L., Goodman, J., Lehmann, M., Wäger, P.A.: The relevance of information and communication technologies for environmental sustainability e A prospective simulation study. Environmental Modelling & Software 21, 1618–1629 (2006)

15. Kuechler, B., Vaishnavi, V., Kuechler, W.L.: Design (Science) Research in IS: A Work in Progress (2008)

16. March, T.S., Smith, G.: Design and Natural Science Research on Information Technology. Decision Support Systems 15, 251–266 (1995)

17. Melville, N.P.: Information Systems Innovation for Environmental Sustainability. MIS Quarterly 34, 1–21 (2010)

18. Murugesan, S.: Harnessing Green IT: Principles and Practices. IT Professional 10, 24–33 (2008)

19. Nunamaker, J.F., Chen, M., Purdin, T.D.M.: Systems development in information systems research. Journal of Management Information Systems 7, 89–106 (1990)

20. Peffers, K., Tuunanen, T., Rothenberger, M.A., Chatterjee, S.: A Design Science Research Methodology for Information Systems Research. Journal of Management Information Systems 24, 45–77 (2007)

21. Takeda, H., Veerkamp, P., Tomiyama, T., Yoshikawam, H.: Modeling design processes. AI Magazine 11, 37–48 (1990)

22. Vaishnavi, V.K., Kuechler, W.J.: Design Science Research Methods and Patterns - Innovating Information and Communication Technology. Auerbach Publications, Boca Raton (2008)

23. Walls, J., Widmeyer, G., El Sawy, O.: Building an information system design theory for vigilant EIS. Information Systems Research 3, 36–59 (1992)

24. Watson, R.T., Boudreau, M.-C., Chen, A.J.: Information Systems and Environmentally Sustainable Development: Energy Informatics and New Directions for the IS Community. MIS Quarterly 34, 23–38 (2010)

25. Watson, R.T., Boudreau, M.-C., Chen, A.J., Huber, M.: Green IS: Building Sustainable Business Practices. In: Watson, R.T. (ed.) Information Systems, Global Text Project, Athens, Georgia, pp. 247–261 (2008)

26. Winter, R.: Guest Editorial: Design Science Research in Europe. European Journal of Information Systems 17, 470–475 (2008)

27. World Commission on Environment and Development: Our Common Future. Oxford University Press, Oxford (1987)

Design Science Research and the Core
of Information Systems

Ahmad Alturki, Wasana Bandara, and Guy G. Gable

Queensland University of Technology, Information Systems Discipline, 126 Margaret St.,
Brisbane, Queensland, Australia

Abstract. Design Science Research (DSR) has emerged as an important approach in Information Systems (IS) research, evidenced by the plethora of recent related articles in recognized IS outlets. Nonetheless, discussion continues on the value of DSR for IS and how to conduct strong DSR, with further discussion necessary to better position DSR as a mature and stable research paradigm appropriate for IS. This paper contributes to address this need, by providing a comprehensive conceptual and argumentative positioning of DSR relative to the core of IS. This paper seeks to argue the relevance of DSR as a paradigm that addresses the core of IS discipline well. Here we use the framework defined by Wand and Weber, to position what the core of IS is.

Keywords: Design Science Research, Design Research, Core of Information System, Routine Design.

1   Introduction

Literature on Design Science Research (DSR) has revealed the importance of DSR and its need in the IS discipline. DSR has become an interesting approach for research in the IS discipline [1, 2], with dramatic growth in recent, related literature [5]. Since the 'design'[1] aspect is one of the main purposes for IS; many scholars believe that IS is design in nature. Therefore, some scholars show and delineate the borders of DSR and the relationships with other types of sciences [8, 9, 10]. Other scholars devote their efforts to establish how to conduct DSR and define the outputs of DSR [11, 12]. Although these efforts exist, DSR still necessitates more effort to reach maturity as a research paradigm[2] and to be well accepted by IS researchers.

IS is a complex discipline and combines many phenomena. For this reason, researchers use different methods for different purposes. It has been noted that some IS researchers mostly focus only on some aspects of IS. This observation has motivated scholars to pay much attention to design aspects of IS phenomena as design is a primary goal in IS research.

---

[1] 'Design' is "from the Latin désignàre, which means to point the way" [6 p4]; it is creating options of design that are filtered and excluded until the design's requirements are fulfilled [7].

[2] Paradigm is "the combination of research questions asked, the research methodologies allowed to answer them and the nature of the pursued research products" [5].

K. Peffers, M. Rothenberger, and B. Kuechler (Eds.): DESRIST 2012, LNCS 7286, pp. 309–327, 2012.
© Springer-Verlag Berlin Heidelberg 2012

One of the issues that needs clarification is what (core) phenomena of IS can DSR address? This paper seeks to argue the relevance of DSR as a paradigm that will address the core of the IS discipline, as defined by Wand and Weber [2, 3, 13, 14]. It mainly contributes to further encouraging the use of DSR in IS, by drawing the link between DSR related concepts and the core of IS as per Wand and Weber's view of the IS core. Wand and Weber's seminal work is adopted in this paper because it is rigorous, strongly grounded on theory, and widely accepted. We do not wish to claim that the results of linking of DSR with IS (as per the Wand and Weber's framework) is the only area IS researches should focus on; rather it is one of the key areas for of IS research.

Contributions of this paper are twofolded: 1) this paper shows what and where should we use DSR in the IS discipline; 2) it partially contributes to the delineation of many related DSR areas that are important to our argument, such as; Design Research, Design Science, and Routine Design. This helps researchers especially, novice researchers, to understand DSR paradigm of research better.

The paper is organized in the way that allows readers to understand how its contribution is achieved. The second section is the starting point of the paper which begins by showing the importance of DSR in IS and why scholars encourage to consider this type of research in our discipline. Then, most DSR related areas are covered in the third section to build the base that we use in the following section. Subsequently and importantly, a link between DSR and the IS core is established to determine the position and the role of DSR in the IS discipline. In particular, we investigate the alignment and linking between DSR and the core of IS based on Wand and Weber's [2, 3, 13, 14] IS view.

2   The Importance for Design Science Research in the IS Discipline

Here, we firstly show the importance of DSR for the IS community to justify that DSR, deserves more investigation by IS scholars. While the first subsection here shows calls for considering DSR as an important paradigm in IS, the second one brings some indicators that show the importance of DSR in the IS discipline.

2.1   Call for Design Science Research

Simon [11] could be considered as an establisher of an important agenda for IS research. Walls et al. [4] and Venable [15 p1-2] note Simon's [16] call for DSR and quoted the same citation. Simon note "Schools of architecture, business, education, law, and medicine, are all centrally concerned with the process of design." Clearly this includes the 'school' or entire field of Information Systems. ... Simon goes on to note that such schools can achieve their purpose and establish their credibility "to the degree that they can discover a science of design, a body of intellectually tough, analytic, partly formalizable, partly empirical, teachable doctrine about the design process" [15 p1-2].

Though design is implicitly an essential component of IS, neither IS practitioners nor IS researchers consider design itself to be a significant topic of study [17]. "[O]ur focus should be on how to best design IT artifacts and IS systems to increase their usefulness, and ease of use or on how to best manage and support IT or IT-enabled business initiatives" [18 p191-192]. IS as a field is concerned with design artifacts because IS practice is about the design, development, and usage of such artifact [19]. Furthermore, many believe that IS research should focus on emphasizing the discovery of the technology underneath the IS, rather than emphasizing managerial and organisational topics [20].

2.2   The Emergence of Design Science Research in Information System

Indulska and Recker [21], present how DSR is increasing in the IS discipline. The central role of Design to IS discipline [11, 22] and its importance as theory [1, 4, 23, 24, 25] are well recognized. Other indicators of the emergence of DSR are: special issues in prominent journals [26]; conferences with Design-Science tracks; a Design-Science-specific conference that began in 2006 – International Conference on Design Science in Information Systems and Technology (DESRIST); and an ISWorld Design-Science-specific website [27].

DSR is important for IS research because IS is an applied research domain which seeks to construct useful artifacts in order to solve problems and guide professionals who do the work in the real world [12]. As Gregor [23] states, DSR also complements the Behavioral Science research, which is essential and foundational in IS; while Design Science work will focus on the design of artifacts, the behavioral science work studies the intersections between people, organizations, and technology [4, 9, 11, 25, 28].

Based on Simon's [16] observations, the design aims to change the current status into the desired status. IS aims to build systems that help people to achieve the desired status. Thus, DSR and IS have the same intention, making DSR suitable for IS research. However, the leading research paradigms in the IS community are social and behavioral science [12, 29 p193] and DSR is often neglected in IS discipline [15].

Peffers et al. [12] argue that these leading paradigms are unsuitable for some IS research where construction is intended. Hence, DSR plays a crucial role in the IS discipline, because DSR gives the IS community the ability to produce applicable research solutions. Purao [6] believes that the IS discipline needs its own method because borrowed methods have failed (misled) to guide IS researchers appropriately, especially in relation to design. Winter [30] highlights this importance where the knowledge should be converted to actions (outputs) to resolve real problems. DSR is indeed suited when   a discipline aims to develop systems [31] like IS.

There is a broad consensus that IS research must respond to a dual mission: (1) make theoretical contributions and (2) assist in solving current and anticipated problems in practice [32, 33]. Employing DSR in the IS discipline increases the relevance of IS research to the real environment [9, 28, 29, 34] by helping solve industry' problems [15]. IT artifacts support organizations in achieving their goals [11]. Relevance refers primarily to the applicability of Design Research in practice [33]. Current IS research have satisfied the research community but needs to consider the application of IS research. Therefore, researchers should have a method that balances between the research's requirements (rigor) and professionals' needs (relevance); one that contributes to both academia and practice [35].

Hevner et al. [11] notice that there is a delay between academic research outcomes and its application (practice in the real world). An intensive debate has continued to occur in the IS discipline on the "crisis in the IS field"3 [29]. Using DSR will help accelerate these implementations. This delay may in part be due to the lack of a broad consensus in the IS research community on DSR issues such as methodology and common concepts and language [31, 36]. Likewise, Aken [37], in the field of management, argues strongly that there is a need for prescription-driven research; DSR, to solve the delay between practice and research. Walls et al. [4] recognized this need early and proposed Information System Design Theory (ISDT). Gregor in her seminal work proposes a design and action theory, referred to as 'Type V' in her IS taxonomy of theories [24]. Gregor and Jones [1] consider this type to be highly influential in the IS discipline because it helps professionals who work with IS.

3   Important Concepts Related to Design Science Research

This section covers mainly three of the many important concepts in DSR. These three aspects are chosen because they are important in linking and positioning DSR with the imported Wand and Weber's view of what IS core is (the goal of the paper). These concepts are DSR vs Behavioural Science, DSR vs Action Research (AR), and DSR vs Routines Design. The reader should note we recognize that other concepts such as design theory, DSR methodology, and DSR outputs are also important, but not as central (as the others listed above) to the arguments presented in this paper. Due to space limitation, we only focus on three.

3.1   Design Science Research vs Behavioural Science

Design Science research has a valid and equal place to Behavioral (Natural) Science (BS/NS) research in IS research [7, 9, 38]. Theory based (causality-related questions) and design-based (problem-solving questions) are equally important in IS research [39]. Many authors recognize the relationship between DSR and Behavioral Science and their boundaries to get a better understanding [9, 11, 25] of the phenomena of interest. A goal of this paper drives the authors to delineate two main areas: the complementary nature of DSR and BS/NS and differences between them.

The Complementary Nature of DSR and Behavioral Science/Natural Science
DSR and Behavioral Science (BS) complement each other in IS research. While the artificial phenomena is created and can be also studied, and instead of being in conflict, IT research includes both Behavioral Science (explain how and why things are) and DSR (create an artifact that helps to achieve goals) [9]. In this regard, March and Smith [9] believe that in Natural Science (NS) research, an understanding of natural

---

3 For instance see MIS Quarterly and CAIS journals.

laws governing IT systems with natural laws governing the environments in which they operate should be accomplished. The rationale behind this complementary nature is because IS consists of human-machine systems and while the artifacts (DSR outputs) represents the machine part, it is also very important to understand the performance of the artifact, with its uses in context (which is what Behavioral Science does), in order to construct new artifacts that are more effective [11].

Both DSR and Behavioral Science support IS research achieve its objectives to increase the relevance and rigor. DSR approaches this objective by developing novel artifacts. Behavioral Science, on other hand, helps by developing and justifying theories that explain and predict the phenomena. Therefore, "Each must inform and challenge the other" [11 p84]. As Aboulafia, (1991) cited in [11], Aboulafiaargues that a truth and utility are two sides of the coins, Hevner et al [11] believe this combination makes considerable contributions. Aken[40] believes and suggests that a dramatic progression in research comes from a cooperation between description-driven (Behavioral Science) and prescription-driven (DSR) research.

A kernel theory is one of the complementary forms between DSR and Behavioral/Natural Science . A design theory in DSR may use Behavioral/Natural Science theories, because DSR outputs and artifacts comprises of the same elements of interest as in Behavioral/Natural Science [4]. Gregor and Jones agree and state "who now recalls that Codd's relational database theory had a behavioral science justification? One of the reasons for advancing relational database theory was that human programmers had difficulty with the complex reasoning needed to handle repeating groups of data items" [1 p328]. Yet, it is not necessary that every part of DSR is grounded on Behavioral/Natural Science theory [1, 7, 37, 38].

Most importantly, DSR and Behavioral Science interact with each other. After an artifact is created by DSR, the artifact may become an objective of investigation in Behavioral Science Research. Also Behavioral Science helps DSR in the process of constructing the artifact by providing an explicit understanding of an environment;"truth essentially is what works in practice" [9 p255]. Furthermore, DSR gives a significant test for Behavioral Science theories and may show areas of incompleteness, opportunities, and improvement in these theories [1, 4, 5, 19].

These types of interactions are consistent with the 'Concept-Development-Impact' model proposed in [41, 42]. Fig. 1 shows how DSR and Behavioral Science complement and interact with each other. Many other papers share this view, see for example [5, 8, 10, 25, 43, 44], which present the relationship between natural science and DSR.

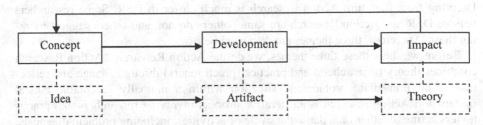

Fig. 1. DSR and Behavioural Science complement and interact with each other

Differences between Design Science Research and Behavioral/Natural Science

While complementary, there are differences between DSR and Behavioral/Natural Science from view points of definitions and activities (interest). The latter is a "body of knowledge about some class of things in the world (nature or society) that describes and explains how they behave and interact with each other" [16 p1]. For instance, scientists in Behavioral/Natural Science, attempt to understand the functioning of artificial phenomena, for example in an organization.Their activities are Behavioral/Natural Science even though scientists are interested in artificial phenomena [9]. DSR is a the knowledge about artificial objects constructed by human beings in order to satisfy certain preferred goals [16]. Aken agrees with this distinction and believes DSR is "what can be" (to develop design knowledge that is used in constructing solutions); and Behavioral Science is "what is" (explaining the causality) [37]. In other words, DSR is interested in a utility where Behavioral Science is interested in a truth [11, 27, 30, 45, 46].

The role, aim and interest of research are other points to observe differences. Scientific interest in IT is twofold: descriptive or prescriptive. The descriptive seeks to understand the nature of IT, which is Behavioral Science. The prescriptive work searches for an improvement in IT performance, which is DSR [9]. While the former concentrates mainly on an analysis to discover the components of an existing system, design focuses on a synthesis to shape these components [4]. DSR looks ahead to create possibilities by producing artifacts, but Behavioral Science looks back to explain the past through constructs theories, and laws [6]. DSR is characterized by knowing through making and Behavioral Science by knowing through observing [6]. Behavioral Science aims "at the exploration and validation of generic cause–effect relations"; and DSR aims "at the construction and evaluation of generic means–ends relations" [30 p470].

From a theoretical lens, an objective of a theory in Behavioral Science is a prediction and/or an explanation of a system. which is different to a purposeful theory like in DSR [4]. This objective is consistent with Gregor's taxonomy of IS theories [23, 24]. Gregor believes the "primary focus [Type IV (BS)] is an integrated body of knowledge – the design implications are secondary, however in design theory [Type V (DS)] the primary focus is the general design principles that inform practice" [23 p19].

3.2   Design Science vs. Action Research

Deriving from literature Action Research is much closer to DSR. Some researchers believe DSR and Action Research are same, others do not, and others suggest merging these. Therefore, three themes are discussed below.

Before we show these three themes, we define Action Research. "Action Research combines theory (researchers) and practice (practitioners) through change and reflection in an immediate problematic situation within a mutually acceptable ethical framework. Action research is an iterative process involving researchers and practitioners acting together on a particular cycle of activities, including problem diagnosis, action intervention, and reflective learning" [47 p94] . Action research is an approach that simultaneously intervenes in the real world to solve problems and gain scientific knowledge [48].

Similarities between Design Science Research and Action Research
Scholars have discussed the similarities and differences between the DSR and Action Research (AR) [35, 45, 46, 49, 50, 51], these similarities being a source of much confusion [31].

From a research process perspective, they have similar research process cycles; similar content [45], starting points, and goals [6, 35, 52]. As research methods, both DSR and AR are proactive approaches. Iteration exists in both DSR and AR cycles [52]. In terms of the intervention, they share the same objectives of interfering with and changing the real world, and solving a problem [31, 35, 38, 52]. Given this commonality of intervention, Purao [6] believes that the closest research method to DSR is AR. Both AR and DSR contribute to knowledge and to practice. They both value the need for rigor and in evaluation of results [31, 35, 52]. From a philosophical stance, Cole et al. analyze DSR and AR and state "Our analysis reveals that the two research approaches indeed share important assumptions regarding ontology, epistemology and more importantly, axiology" [35 p14]. Thus, AR and DSR complement each other and are compatible [35]. DSR and AR fit closely with one another, for more details about this comparison, see Table 1 in [45, 46].

Design Science Research and Action Research Are Different
Although DSR and AR appear similar in many ways, they have differences. DSR is a research orientation while AR is a method [49]. Iivari and Venable study DSR and AR from different points of view containing paradigmatic assumptions, interests and activities. They refute and disagree with the notion that DSR is similar to AR, like the views proposed by [45, 46].

From a paradigmatic assumptions view, a conclusion can be made that since DSR has more paradigmatic assumptions (for more details see Table 1 in [49]), AR may be a special case of DSR [49, 52]. So, "Action research is a methodology. DS [DSR] is a paradigm" [31 p442].

From a research interests' point of view, DSR has different research purposes, e.g. a new artifact invention; AR in the most cases, however, is to understand and change a complex reality. Another difference is that DSR is interested in technical problems and innovations; while AR is interested in socio-technical problems and innovations which subsequently reflect their activities [49].

DSR and AR have differences in their processes (activities). Though both of them start with a problem definition, they articulate the problem abstraction differently. Yet, both intervene into a real environment to improve the situation or solve the problem. But, AR is very clear in this goal by having dedicated steps to plan and act, while this is an implicit step in DSR [52]. Both stress on evaluation, an artifact testing in the real world, but DSR has a prior test which is an internal evaluation [7, 50, 52]. One of the activities for both AR and DSR is finding a priori theory in the domain. In AR there is a debate on whether it is compulsory or not, but in DSR it is not [7, 38, 52]. Furthermore, there is a difference of users' participation; users always participate in AR, but in DSR users may be assumed or "virtualized/imagined" by the researcher [52].

Outputs of research is another difference, AR develops an action to make change in an organization to build new knowledge. DSR, on the another hand, creates an artifact in order to learn new knowledge, and solve problems or invent new things [51]. DSR produces a general solution for a class of problems and clients; there is no "joint collaboration between researchers and the client" as in AR [49 p4]. DSR focuses on construction of artifacts and AR focuses on organizational changes [35].

DSR and AR have different roots which affect them somehow. Iivari's [38] analysis shows that AR comes from the socio-technical movement and DSR is from engineering. So, the main difference here is how they solve the problem. While AR is concerned with problem solving through social and organizational change, DSR is concerned with problem solving by creating and positioning an artifact in a natural setting. AR is based on discovery-through-action; DSR, on the other hand, is clearly centered on discovery-through-design. Likewise, Purao sees the difference coming from the arena of intervention. For AR, "it is the organizational setting, leading to theorizing using organizational metaphors ... for design research, it is in the world of signs with a view to bring to realization an artifact, leading to creation of knowledge and normative theories that employ metaphors from the plane of representation" [6 p26]. Therefore, DSR is not AR [31].

Calls to Use Design Science Research and Action Research Together
Indulska and Recker [21] observed that most methods used with DSR are AR and experiments. There are possibilities to merge DSR and AR because of their similarities [51]. Pries-Heje et al. promote that AR and DSR could be mixed to overcome the shortcoming in both approaches [53]. Venable suggests in his DSR framework that AR could be used to evaluate DSR outputs in the naturalistic evaluation phase [38, 49, 50]. Sein et al. [54] propose a new method called 'Action Design Research' which is a mix between DSR and AR. This new method is a strong evidence of using DSR with AR. In some cases DSR may be framed as AR if the research addresses an organizational problem where an artifact building needs to be added [35].

Iivari and Venable find three cases of overlap between DSR and AR: (1) completely non-overlapping (in three different ways), (2) slightly overlapping, and (3) significantly overlapping such as with Action Design Research [54]. For elaborated discussion see [49]. Iivari and Venable believe using AR within DS should be done with care. Limitations and risks should be written in an ethical framework and reported later if they still they remain [49].

3.3   Design Science Research vs. Routine Design

An aspiration of IS researchers is to produce relevant results to be used by practice [11, 15, 28]. This ambition can at times lead researchers astray, to become involved in Routine Design. The question here becomes how to distinguish between DSR and Routine Design; this helps researchers to understand, and then conduct DSR properly with their aspiration. As any types of research, the result of DSR is codified in a knowledge base and becomes a known knowledge for use in practice [11]. While IT people in the real world develop, implement, operate, and maintain IT systems [9], It seems that they are more concerned with the application of the known knowledge. This part addresses the issue of distinguishing between DSR and Routine Design.

Many authors believe that producing knowledge is a main, explicit distinction between DSR and Routine Design. Routine Design usually solves problems using current knowledge, state of practice, techniques and available components to produce a product without the creation of any additional knowledge. DSR, on other hand, produces new knowledge that yields value from a number of unknowns in the proposed design which were successfully overcome [27]. Purao [6] believes that DSR produces invention which is not known before or not just a replication. Venable [15] has a similar view and believes that the DSR is a "Technology Invention" and design practice (Routine Design) as a "Technology Application". Hevner et al. [11] states that DSR is concerned to solve an unaddressed important problem in a new or more successful, and useful way. Thus, DSR contributes to the knowledge base while Routine Design does not.

DSR addresses an abstract or a class of problems for a class of organizations and stakeholders. Routine Design, however is concerned with a particular problem for specific organizations and stakeholders [15]. Out of IS discipline edges, from a management respective, Aken [37] makes the equivalent distinction. He differentiates between an application of scientific knowledge (Routine Design) in order to solve a particular problem; and a development of scientific knowledge (DSR) which solves a class of problems. The former one is in the professional domain and the latter is in the academic domain.

The authors of this paper believe that Routine Design could be moderated and utilized if we as a research community consider Routine Design as an instantiation or a beta testing of resulting DSR, artifacts. In this view, Routine Design plays an important role like some research in behavioral or social science which tests and justifies theories by replication in a new context. Table 1 shows a summary of DSR and Routine Design comparison.

Table 1. Comparison between DSR and Routine Design

Design Science (DS)	Routine Design (RD)
General solution	Specific solution
Produces new knowledge (novelty)	Uses the current/existing knowledge
Unknowns (not known) things in the planed design	Design is known (replication)
Contributes to the knowledge base (a development of scientific knowledge)	Does not contributes to the knowledge base (An application of scientific knowledge)
Solve unaddressed important problems in a new and effective way	Solve problems using existing knowledge
Technology Invention	Technology Application
Addresses abstract or a class of problems for a class of organizations and stakeholders	Addresses a particular problem for a specific organization and stakeholders
How to resolve a type of problems	Solve one case only

4   Design Science Research and the Core of IS Discipline

Before we present how DSR fits into IS core, we stress that IS has different views and do acknowledge that there is a debate between scholars in the IS discipline on what comprises the IS core and artifacts. Investigation of IS literature reveals that there are three main views of what constitute IS core and artifact. These views are 1) IS is concerned only on Software development, 2) it also includes methods and models, and 3) a broader view that includes how people use IS, organizations implement IS, and the impact of IS on people and organization [27, 30, 35, 55].

However, having said that, in one of the seminal works[4] in IS, Wand and Weber define the core of the IS based on a strongly grounded theoretical foundation. They believe that IS is "being used to represent or to mirror, or to simulate phenomena in the real world … provides a representation of some real-world systems as perceived by someone or some group of people" [3 p66-67]. Representation is the key aspect of IS. We bring in and work upon their view and theory about IS to integrate it with the DSR paradigm. Although this integration helps in the positioning of DSR on the 'IS map', we do not wish to claim that the result of this integration is the only area IS researches should focus; rather it is one of key areas of IS research.

Aligning with our intent mentioned above, we present this section in an alternating fashion. In other words, we discuss every point linkinf both IS and DSR, before we move to another point. Thus, in the next four subsections, the main goal is to find justifications of DSR injection to the IS core, based on Wand and Weber's view, by looking at four points: 1) how DSR addressing the core of IS, 2) the representational aspects in IS and DSR, 3) the Relationships bwteeen IS and Design Science/Design Research/Routine Design, and 4) Transformation in IS and DSR development.

4.1   Design Science Research Addresses the Core of Information System

Wand and Weber studied IS to determine the core of IS and developed an IS ontology. They believe that IS has two views; external and internal views. The external view focuses on the individuals and organizations that use, implement, and deploy IS. For example, the impact of IS on the users' effectiveness in undertaking their tasks. Wand and Weber believe this view is important but is not the core of IS [2, 3, 13]. This view is consistent with Behavioural Science as explained above.

The internal view of IS consists of: (1) surface structure phenomena, (2) deep structure phenomena and (3) physical structure phenomena. Surface structure describes the facilities what is available in the IS to allow users to interact with the IS; for example: the format of a display screen, buttons that users can click to run functions, or reports. This phenomenon is mainly the concern of psychology and sociology – not IS. Deep structure describes the characteristics of the real-world phenomena that the IS is intended to represent such as Entity Relationship Diagrams or various actions that customers can take; for example when they place an order for items. The

---

[4] Benbasat considers this work is one of the few ground braking efforts that challenge our thinking and lead to new exciting directions in research and teaching.

last one is the physical structure which describes the choices that designers have made in terms of how surface and deep structure will be mapped onto the underlying technology that will be used to operate the IS. For instance, the used encryption procedures when data is to be transferred. Wand and Weber believe the deep structure phenomena is the core of the IS discipline because they manifest the representation of the real-world system and the meaning embodied in the IS. The representation is the essence and reason of the Information system's being. Fig. 2 below depicts the external view and internal view with its phenomena.

Let us now move to DSR in the IS discipline. As presented above, there is a debate between IS scholars on methodologies used in IS discipline. The complaint is that IS researchers borrow research methodologies from other disciplines to conduct IS research which take IS research away from the core of IS. Wand and Weber's IS conceptions, about the internal and external views, explain the reason behind this complaint and debate. Since most IS researchers focus on the external view, they find borrowed methodologies that suit their aim. IS, however is 'Design' in nature. Though, some researchers call for using DSR in IS, they have not yet agreed or focused on what the IS core is and what area of IS that DSR addresses.

Based on the definition mentioned above of deep structure as the core of IS and our understanding of DSR, both the deep structure and DSR share the intention of constructing things for users' need or problems. Therefore, DSR must focus on the core of IS (see Fig. 2), not on other things. This supports what IS scholars have encouraged IS researchers to do: to go back to the applied roots of IS, and see IS is 'Design' in nature.

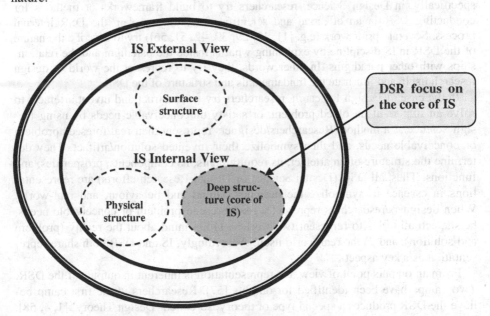

Fig. 2. External and internal views of Information System [2, 3]

4.2   Representation Aspect in IS and Design Science Research

Wand and Weber believe that representation is the key aspect of IS, it represents things in the real-world. Accordingly, IS constitutes historical representations of things in the real-world in the ways IS designers chose to envisage these things. The rationale of using representation in IS, is to know the histories of things, their behaviours, and their states in the real-world in an effective way. This is important, and there are two possible ways \ to capture these histories: 1) observe them directly; or 2) observe representations of things which are cheaper and effective (for more explanation see Chapter 2 in [3]). IS implements the effective option and its goodness is based on how well the reality is presented.

Before we cover presentation in DSR, we want to highlight that there are two types of research; Design Research and Design Science in DSR. Winter [30 p471-472] makes the distinction between '(IS) Design Science' and '(IS) Design Research; stating "while design research is aimed at creating solutions to specific classes of relevant problems by using a rigorous construction and evaluation process...(i.e., construction and evaluation of specific artefacts)... design science reflects the design research process and aims at creating standards for its rigour...(i.e., reflection and guidance of artefact construction and evaluation processes)". Similar definitions and distinctions from DSR experts are found in [17], [12] and[36].

Representation in DSR could be seen in DSR and its outputs. For the former, IS researchers may have interest in Design Science or Design Research. However, their work at its basic level is a construction of many related things which interact with each other to produce artefacts in order to solve real/foreseen problems, or build innovations. More specifically, in Design Science, researchers try to build frameworks or methods for conducting DSR in an effective and scientific way; they explain the DSR internal process. Several prior work (e.g. [11, 12, 29, 39, 42, 51, 56]) try to describe the nature of the DSR in IS discipline by explaining what is inside the paradigm and the relationships with other paradigms. In other words, they try to represent the world of design research itself, and illustrate the fundamentals and structure of the DSR.

In the case of Design Research, researchers try to construct and invent artefacts to solve an important unsolved problem, or satisfy un/conceivable needs by using Design Science as a method. Researchers/designers represent their real/foreseen problem or conceivable needs, and then symbolize their invented solution/artifact. They determine the structure of an artefact, its requirements, its components, prosperities, and functions. Thus, all DSR (Design Science or Design Research efforts) are representations in essence to symbolize the designer's mind and behaviour, and real-world. When designers/researchers represent a real/foreseen problem or conceivable needs, he/she actually tries to represent two worlds: 1) his mind about the reality (problem and solution), and 2) the real-world itself. Accordingly, IS and DSR both share representation as a key aspect.

From an outputs point of view, the representation is inherent in outputs of the DSR. Two camps have been identified for outputs [57]. Researchers in the first camp believe the DSR produces a special type of theory, so-called 'Design Theory' [1, 4, 58]. In the second camp, researchers consider only constructs, models, methods, and instantiations as outputs [9, 11]. Representation or reality is existent in both camps. Examining components of 'Design Theory' (First camp) exposes that representation is the main aspect of its components; such as constructs and principles that represent the form and function [1], and meta-requirements and meta-design [4]. For the other camp, constructs, models, and method are clearly means for representation. Instantiation is also a representation which is machine readable.

4.3   IS, Design Science Research and Routine Design Relationship

The relationship between IS and DSR is another point we should think about and make a clear view about. The IS discipline, as explained above, has different outlooks and surely DSR does not address all of them.

Based on the DSR definitions by [7, 38, 39, 40, 49] and what we see as the IS core (deep structure as per Wand and Weber's view), DSR addresses parts of the IS core (mentioned in Section 4.1). Furthermore, as we see the differentiations between DSR and Routine Design, we argue that the core of IS (deep structure) is divided into two parts: 1) IS deals with unknown problems and solutions, and 2) IS deals with known problems and solutions. DSR addresses only the first part which contains problems that are not solved or those which require the building novel solutions (new information systems), enhance current solutions, or invent something new for a conceivable need/problem. The second part of the IS core relates to known problems and solutions which are the focus of Routine Design. Consequently, we argue that DSR and Routine Design constitute the IS discipline; see the Fig. 3 below. The reader should note that Wand and Weber did not mention Routine Design and DSR (Design Science and Design Research). As per authors' understanding, Wand and Weber's view only focuses on Routine Design.

Fig. 3 can be viewed from left to right; it demonstrates the relationship between IS discipline (deep structure) and, DSR (Design Science and Design Research) and Routine Design. The light grey oval represents the Wand and Weber's view of the IS core. This view is equivalent to Routine Design as we see above; Routine Design is IS practice. The white oval is the Design Research which presents a specific part of the IS core and functions as a bridge between practice and academia. The Design Research represents the abstract knowledge developed by researchers that is converted by practitioners to a specific problem solution. Thus, Design Research and Routine Design represent the core of IS and correspond to academia and practice communities, respectively. While the left edge of the Design Research represents the relevance of research, the right edge represents the rigor of research. The last part of the first half of Fig. 3, dark grey, is Design Science which presents the work of academics. This part is related to how to conduct DSR properly.

The second half of Fig. 3 illustrates how DSR (Design Science and Design Research), and Routine Design interact with each other in IS (deep structure). This half is viewed left-right where Design Science is used in conducting Design Research and Design Research might feed back to contribute to the Design Science process. Design Research and Routine Design constitute IS deep structure. Design Research feeds Routine Design by developing abstract knowledge. Routine Design implements this abstract knowledge and converts it to actual working systems.

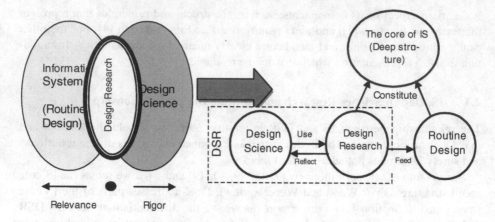

Fig. 3. The overlap between Design Science, Design Research, and Routine Design in IS discipline

In order to further support our argument in separating the IS core into Design Research and Routine Design, we use Gregor and Jones's [1 p321] explanation of the phenomena of interest for DSR. In their seminal work, they propose the relationships among IS artifacts; see Fig. 1 in [1 p321]. The phenomena includes; (1) instantiation: "artifacts have a physical existence in the real world"; (2) design theories (abstract artifacts): they are not exist in the real world except their representation means such as diagrams; and (3) human understanding of artifacts: human beings develop design theory and use them to build instantiations and then study these instantiations and their use. Using these notions within Fig. 3 above, we argue that in the IS core, human beings (designers) use and utilize Design Science to conduct Design Research in order to produce an abstract knowledge (validated Design Theory) for unsolved problem solutions or innovations. This abstract knowledge is afterward converted by human beings to build physical artefacts in different contexts; it represents Routine Design.

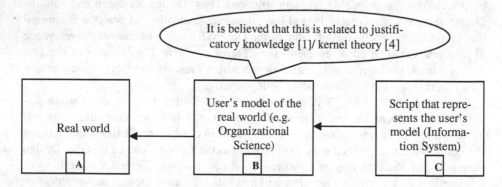

Fig. 4. Notions that represent the goodness of the representation of the real-world [2, 3]

4.4   The Transformational Nature in IS and Design Science Research

This section highlights conversions in the construction of IS, and DSR process. Both IS and DSR produce artifacts which eventually are transformed through different iterations. Generally in IS, when we build any IS, basically we generate scripts (a meaningful, ordered collection of symbols) that are intended to provide descriptions of the real-world phenomena that are our concern. Because the process of building representation is complex, we generate different kinds of scripts to meet different needs that we encounter along the way. These scripts are transformed into different forms until ultimately we produce a script that can be read by the machine; for example, we might make interview notes, pseudocodes or Entity Relationship Diagrams. All these forms of scripts ultimately represent the real-world, conform to some rules and each script can be read and interpreted by different groups of people.

Fig. 4 below shows two notions that depict representation goodness of the reality. The first one is the users' model of the real-world (box B) which represents the real-word from the viewpoints of its users and is the focus of theories from other disciplines such as organizational science. The second form (box C) is the script that represents the first model; this is the focus of IS practice. Both represent the real-world and each one goes through iterations and different forms of scripts.

Similarly, DSR is representational in nature as explained above. This representation also goes through different forms of transformation. Researchers/Designers perform many representations in the DSR until the final design is developed. Designers represent a real/foreseen problem they are going to solve or conceivably a need that they want to satisfy. They use representation quality to simplify their problem/need and to emphasize its importance. Designers then try to represent their solution and internal design of the solution. In other words, they transform important seen or feasible needs/problems to simple and understandable forms. After that, designers use their creativity and known knowledge/experience to transform these forms to a good solution/invention. This solution/invention will be also transformed to an instantiation/prototype which is also transformed to a form that can be read by machines.

Thus, going back to Fig. 4 above, we can argue that the designers in DSR execute box B and C. Based in the relationship between IS and Design Research, Design Science, and Routine Design mentioned in previous section, we see the box C represents Routine Design if the knowledge in the box B is already developed and well known. However, together boxes B and C represent Design Research because both boxes B and C are not developed or known; it means we face a problem that is not solved yet or see a need to invent something new.

DSR is the methodology to build these two forms of representations. Therefore, the role of the designer is two folds: 1) he/she needs to transform the represented real/foreseen problem (real-world) to show all aspect of the problem; 2) he/she needs to transform his solution and creativity, his mind, onto forms that solves the problem and needs to transform any justificatory knowledge imported from the knowledgebase either in the IS discipline or other disciplines. Designers ultimately generate the instantiations/scripts of representation of the real-world (box B and C).

5   Conclusion

This paper has argued that DSR is at the core of the IS discipline, in both research and practice. Specifically, the paper maps between DSR related concepts and Wand and Weber's view of the IS core. It contributes to DSR by identifying the area that DSR addresses in the IS discipline. We divide the core of IS (deep structure) into two types: 1) unknown problems and solutions; the interest of DSR (Design Research and Design Science), and 2) known problems and solutions (Routine Design). Moreover, the paper contributes to Wand and Weber's work by extending their view of the IS core. It shows how DSR is injected to IS research in order to achieve research requirements; rigor and relevance. Additionally, this paper gives a good overview of important DSR concepts which are important for novice researchers who may get confused at the beginning of conducting DSR in the IS discipline.

Nonetheless, the authors do not subscribe to the view that IS shouldn't prescribe anything outside DSR. Rather we agree with Agarwal and Lucus [59 p391-393] who state, "We believe that a major part, but not all, of the research on IS should focus on the impact of the IT artifact rather than the artifact itself (…) It is possible that Benbasat and Zmud agree with our call for more macro research given the inclusion of the impact variable in their nomological net". Gable et al. [60 p404] comment on this view, observing "the distinction made by Agarwal and Lucas between micro- and macro-level research issues is unclear as regards organizational-level research, which would seem to bridge their micro- and macro-realms …Though Agarwal and Lucas and others consider the IS-Net overly constrained, they too appear to believe it valid within its scope."

References

1. Gregor, S., Jones, D.: The anatomy of a design theory. Journal of the Association for Information Systems 8(5), 312–335 (2007)
2. Wand, Y., Weber, R.: On the deep structure of information systems. Information Systems Journal 5(3), 203–223 (1995)
3. Weber, R.: Ontological foundations of information systems. Coopers & Lybrand (1997)
4. Walls, J.G., Widmeyer, G.R., El Sawy, O.A.: Building an information system design theory for vigilant EIS. Information Systems Research 3(1), 36–59 (1992)
5. Goldkuhl, G., Lind, M.: A Multi-Grounded Design Research Process. In: Winter, R., Zhao, J.L., Aier, S. (eds.) DESRIST 2010. LNCS, vol. 6105, pp. 45–60. Springer, Heidelberg (2010)
6. Purao, S.: Design research in the technology of information systems: Truth or dare, in Unpublished Working Paper, Atlanta (2002)
7. Hevner, A.R.: A Three Cycle View of Design Science Research. Scandinavian Journal of Information Systems 19(2), 87–92 (2007)
8. Gregor, S.: Building theory in the sciences of the artificial. In: DESRIST, pp. 1–10. ACM, Malvern (2009)
9. March, S.T., Smith, G.F.: Design and natural science research on information technology. Decision Support Systems 15(4), 251–266 (1995)

10. Patas, J., Milicevic, D., Goeken, M.: Enhancing Design Science through Empirical Knowledge: Framework and Application. In: Jain, H., Sinha, A.P., Vitharana, P. (eds.) DESRIST 2011. LNCS, vol. 6629, pp. 32–46. Springer, Heidelberg (2011)
11. Hevner, A.R., et al.: Design science in information systems research. MIS Quarterly 28(1), 75–106 (2004)
12. Peffers, K., et al.: A design science research methodology for information systems research. Journal of Management Information Systems 24(3), 45–77 (2007)
13. Wand, Y., Weber, R.: Toward a theory of the deep structure of information systems (1990)
14. Wand, Y., Weber, R.: On the ontological expressiveness of information systems analysis and design grammars. Information Systems Journal 3(4), 217–237 (1993)
15. Venable, J.: The role of theory and theorising in Design Science research. In: Proceedings of DESRIST, Claremont, CA (2006)
16. Simon, H.A.: The sciences of the artificial, 3rd edn. MIT Press, Cambridge (1996)
17. Kuechler, W.L., Vaishnavi, V.K.: The emergence of design research in information systems in North America. Journal of Design Research 7(1), 1–16 (2008)
18. Benbasat, I., Zmud, R.W.: The identity crisis within the IS discipline: Defining and communicating the discipline's core properties. Mis Quarterly 27(2), 183–194 (2003)
19. Goldkuhl, G.: Design theories in information systems-a need for multi-grounding. Journal of Information Technology Theory and Application 6(2), 59–72 (2004)
20. Orlikowski, W.J., Iacono, C.S.: Desperately seeking the'IT'in IT research-a call to theorizing the IT artifact. Information Systems Research 12(2), 121–134 (2001)
21. Indulska, M., Recker, J.C.: Design science in IS research: a literature analysis. In: Proceedings 4th Biennial ANU Workshop on Information Systems Foundations, Canberra, Australia (2008)
22. Markus, M.L., Majchrzak, A.: A design theory for systems that support emergent knowledge processes. MIS Quarterly 26(3), 179–212 (2002)
23. Gregor, S.: Design theory in information systems. Australian Journal of Information Systems 10, 14–22 (2002)
24. Gregor, S.: The nature of theory in information systems. MIS Quarterly 30(3), 611 (2006)
25. Walls, J.G., Widmeyer, G.R., El Sawy, O.A.: Assessing information system design theory in perspective: How useful was our 1992 initial rendition. Journal of Information Technology Theory and Application 6(2), 43–58 (2004)
26. Baskerville, R., et al.: A response to the design-oriented information systems research memorandum. European Journal of Information Systems 20(1), 11–15 (2010)
27. Vaishnavi, V., Kuechler, W.: Design research in information systems (February 20, 2004), http://www.isworld.org/Researchdesign/drisISworld.htm (cited January 10, 2010)
28. Nunamaker Jr., J.F., Minder, C., Titus, D.M.P.: Systems development in information systems research. J. Manage. Inf. Syst. 7(3), 89–106 (1991)
29. Carlsson, S.A.: Towards an information systems design research framework: A critical realist perspective. In: DESRIST, Claremont, CA (2006)
30. Winter, R.: Design science research in Europe. European Journal of Information Systems 17(5), 470–475 (2008)
31. Baskerville, R.: What design science is not. European Journal of Information Systems 17(5), 441–443 (2008)
32. Rosemann, M., Vessey, I.: Toward improving the relevance of information systems research to practice: The role of applicability checks. MIS Quarterly 32(1), 1–22 (2008)
33. Benbasat, I., Zmud, R.W.: Empirical research in information systems: the practice of relevance. MIS Quarterly 23(1), 3–16 (1999)

34. Hevner, A., Chatterjee, S.: Design Research in Information Systems: Theory and Practice, vol. 22. Springer (2010)
35. Cole, R., et al.: Being proactive: where action research meets design research. In: Twenty-Sixth International Conference on Information Systems. Citeseer, Atlanta (2005)
36. Purao, S., et al.: The sciences of design: observations on an emerging field. In: DESRIST. Harvard Business School (2008)
37. Van Aken, J.E.: Management research based on the paradigm of the design sciences: The quest for field-tested and grounded technological rules. Journal of Management Studies 41(2), 219–246 (2004)
38. Iivari, J.: A paradigmatic analysis of information systems as a design science. Scandinavian Journal of Information Systems 19(2), 39–64 (2007)
39. March, S.T., Storey, V.C.: Design science in the information systems discipline: an introduction to the special issue on design science research. MIS Quarterly 32(4), 725–730 (2008)
40. Aken, J.E.: Management research based on the paradigm of the design sciences: The quest for field-tested and grounded technological rules. Journal of Management Studies 41(2), 219–246 (2004)
41. Nunamaker Jr., J.F., Chen, M., Purdin, T.D.M.: Systems development in information systems research. In: International Conference of System Science, Hawaii (1990)
42. Nunamaker Jr., J.F., Chen, M., Purdin, T.D.M.: Systems development in information systems research. Journal of Management Information Systems 7(3), 89–106 (1991)
43. Kuechler, B., Vaishnavi, V.: On theory development in design science research: anatomy of a research project. European Journal of Information Systems 17(5), 489–504 (2008)
44. Kuechler, B., Vaishnavi, V.: Extending Prior Research with Design Science Research: Two Patterns for DSRIS Project Generation. In: Jain, H., Sinha, A.P., Vitharana, P. (eds.) DESRIST 2011. LNCS, vol. 6629, pp. 166–175. Springer, Heidelberg (2011)
45. Järvinen, P.: Action research is similar to design science. Quality and Quantity 41(1), 37–54 (2007)
46. Järvinen, P.: Action research as an approach in design science. In: European Academy of Management. Citeseer, Munich (2005)
47. Avison, D.E., et al.: Action research. Communications of the ACM 42(1), 97 (1999)
48. Baskerville, R.L., Wood-Harper, A.T.: A critical perspective on action research as a method for information systems research. Journal of Information Technology 11(3), 235–246 (1996)
49. Iivari, J., Venable, J.: Action research and design science research–seemingly similar but decisively dissimilar. In: 17th European Conference on Information Systems (2009)
50. Venable, J.: A Framework for Design Science Research Activities. In: Information Resource Management Association Conference (CD), Washington, DC, USA. Idea Group Publishing, Hershey (2006)
51. Baskerville, R., Pries-Heje, J., Venable, J.: Soft design science methodology. In: DESRIST. ACM, Malvern (2009)
52. Rossi, M., Sein, M.K.: Design research workshop: a proactive research approach. Presentation delivered at IRIS 26, 9–12 (2003)
53. Pries-Heje, J., Baskerville, R., Venable, J.: Evaluation Risks in Design Science Research: A Framework. In: Third International Conference on Design Science Research in Information Systems and Technology. Georgia State University, Atlanta (2008)
54. Sein, M.K., et al.: Action Design Research. MIS Quarterly (2011)

55. Offermann, P., Blom, S., Schönherr, M., Bub, U.: Artifact Types in Information Systems Design Science – A Literature Review. In: Winter, R., Zhao, J.L., Aier, S. (eds.) DESRIST 2010. LNCS, vol. 6105, pp. 77–92. Springer, Heidelberg (2010)
56. Alturki, A., Gable, G.G., Bandara, W.: A Design Science Research Roadmap. In: Jain, H., Sinha, A.P., Vitharana, P. (eds.) DESRIST 2011. LNCS, vol. 6629, pp. 107–123. Springer, Heidelberg (2011)
57. Gregor, S., Hevner, A.: Introduction to the special issue on design science. Information Systems and E-Business Management 9(1), 1–9 (2010)
58. Baskerville, R., Pries-Heje, J.: Explanatory Design Theory. Business & Information Systems Engineering, 1–12 (2010)
59. Agarwal, R., Lucas Jr., H.C.: The information systems identity crisis: Focusing on high-visibility and high-impact research. MIS Quarterly, 381–398 (2005)
60. Gable, G.G., Sedera, D., Chan, T.: Re-conceptualizing information system success: the IS-impact measurement model. Journal of the Association for Information Systems 9(7) (2008)

Anatomy of Knowledge Bases Used in Design Science Research

A Literature Review

Oliver Gaß[1], Norbert Koppenhagen[1], Harald Biegel[2],
Alexander Maedche[1,3], and Benjamin Müller[1]

[1] University of Mannheim, Chair of Information Systems IV, Mannheim, Germany
{gass,koppenhagen,maedche,mueller}@eris.uni-mannheim.de
[2] University of Mannheim, Mannheim, Germany
harald.biegel@googlemail.com
[3] University of Mannheim, Institute for Enterprise Systems, Mannheim, Germany

Abstract. Several papers have addressed the theory foundation of DSR. While researchers usually emphasize that the existence of such a knowledge base (KB) is essential for high quality design science research (DSR), opinions depart what kind of knowledge comprises such a knowledge base and which qualitative requirements apply regarding the knowledge leveraged. Some researchers demand that DSR is based on descriptive formal theories, while other scholars extend the width of the knowledge base also to unverified empirical evidence, conceptual knowledge and prescriptive knowledge. In order to provide some guidance for practical DSR, we apply literature review methodology on recent DSR articles to determine the common practice regarding the use and development of knowledge bases in previous projects. Based on this investigation, we discuss current issues, derive implications for future research and suggest measures to strengthen the role of the knowledge base in DSR.

Keywords: Design Science Research, Literature Review, Theory Base.

1 Introduction

The design science approach originally goes back to engineering and has since gained significant attention in the domain of information systems (IS) research. Starting in the 60s and 70s, scholars mainly focused on distinguishing the design science research (DSR) paradigm from positivist research approaches in natural science and social sciences [1]. By that time Simon laid the foundation of the science of design in mathematics and defined designing as a search process within a closed solution space resulting in an optimized design or respective optimum [2]. Later on, researchers seemed to lose sight on design science until the beginning of the 1990s, when a variety of scholars revived design science research (DSR) in information systems (IS): Walls et al. [3] for example, broke new ground when they investigated design in light of descriptive knowledge in information systems and formulated the information

K. Peffers, M. Rothenberger, and B. Kuechler (Eds.): DESRIST 2012, LNCS 7286, pp. 328–344, 2012.

system design theory (ISDT). They concluded that rigor design science research in information systems must be informed by formal theories. Since then, much work has been published trying to define the paradigmatic nature of information system research as a design science. Such research included the ontology of design science, especially addressing the place of an artifact in its context [4-7] and the epistemology of design science, investigating the nature of the underlying knowledge base and the outcome of design science in the form of a design theory [8],[9]. Others focused on the methodology of design science by proposing particular methods to create and evaluate designs [10],[11]. By now, several papers have been published on the theory foundation of DSR. Van Aken, for example, states that, "one can design an aero plane wing on the basis of tested, technological rules, but such wings can be designed much more efficiently on the basis of tested and grounded technological rules, grounded on the laws and insights of aerodynamic and mechanics" [12, p.228]. The knowledge base of DSR comprises the theories leveraged and serves as input to DSR by providing evidence that links a design, its instantiation as an artifact and its formal representation (i.e., a design theory), to the context the design is intended to operate in. It serves to explain and predict the functionality of a design and can be used to formulate testable propositions to evaluate its impact (compare the five theory types in IS as defined by Gregor [13]). Whereas there seems to be almost an agreement on the importance of the presence of such a knowledge base in literature, the questions of what kind of knowledge exactly constitutes it and which qualitative requirements apply, remain unanswered: Though, several scholars have already tackled the topic and suggested numerous definitions and requirements for the knowledge base, the variety and divergence of their suggestions still leaves it up to the individual researchers to decide upon which theoretical framing to adopt for their own work. Our paper wants to contribute to the on-going discussion by investigating the common practice in DSR: we seek to shed light on the type and origin of knowledge that constitutes the knowledge base of DSR projects. Our analysis is guided by the following research question: What is the anatomy of knowledge bases used as input for design science research in the IS field?

Following our research questions, we focus our investigation on knowledge that serves as an input to DSR and do not intend to explicitly investigate the nature of knowledge that results from DSR projects (however we consider it as a valid input). In order to address the research question, we use the literature review methodology to determine the types of knowledge base used in published information systems and computer science design science projects. Based on this investigation, we discuss current issues, derive implications for future research and suggest measures to strengthen the role of the knowledge base in DSR.

The paper is structured as follows: chapter 2 provides an overview of several definitions of the knowledge base used in DSR, chapter 3 outlines our research methodology, chapter 4 presents the results, chapter 5 discusses the findings and chapter 6 summarizes the paper, discusses identified limitations and gives an outlook on future work.

2   Related Work

In order to determine the role of theory in DSR, it is important to examine previous work on the nature of theories in IS: Iivari [4] proposes a three-level-structure to describe the epistemology of DSR: he includes three categories of knowledge applicable for DSR: 1) Conceptual knowledge includes concepts, classifications and conceptual frameworks. 2) Descriptive knowledge comprises observational facts, empirical regularities, theories and hypotheses. 3) Prescriptive knowledge builds on design product knowledge including characteristics of an artifact, e.g., idea, concept, style or behavior and design process knowledge including technological norms and rules, determining how to achieve an intended outcome in a particular situation.

Another way to classify theories in the context of DSR is the simplified taxonomy of Kuechler and Vaishnavi [14]. They distinguish between two types of theories: 1) Descriptive theories originating from natural science and social science which serve as an input to design science by "suggest(ing) novel techniques or approaches to IS design problems". 2) Prescriptive theories which "give explicit prescriptions of 'how to do something'" [14, p.2f].

Analyzing previous work on the qualitative requirements regarding the knowledge base which is used to inform DSR, there are three major opinions in literature: First, a major contribution to the definition of this "body of knowledge" of design science has been provided by Nunamaker et al. [15] and Walls et al. [3]. Both works emphasize that design science research must be founded on and respectively informed by a comprehensive body of knowledge. Walls et al. depict four essential parts of a IS design theory: kernel theory, meta-requirements, meta-design and testable design product hypothesis. The term kernel theory, in this context, refers to the encompassed descriptive knowledge (resulting from the knowledge base) in the meta design and the meta design process. In the understanding of Walls et al. [3] this descriptive knowledge is comprised of formal theories resulting from a variety of research fields, most notable natural science and social science. Kernel theories, following their argument, serve the purpose to add truth value to a design, allowing to formulate testable propositions about the design product or the design process. However, formal theories usually build on well-defined assumptions and include rather theoretical concepts, which limit their explanatory power for more specific practical problems. Respectively, they can only provide limited truth value in particular matters. Therefore, second, Markus et al. [9] stress that the applicability of the descriptive knowledge for a particular issue is an essential factor for selecting the underlying knowledge base. Hence, they extend Walls et al.'s [3] definition of the knowledge base to practitioners' theories-in-use (PTiU) as a more applicable descriptive knowledge. In contrast to academic theories which constitute formal theoretical concepts, a PTiU includes everyday concepts from the world of practice. Although PTiUs do not make claims about some objective truth, they make claims about how to do something effectively in a particular situation. Even though, PTiUs lack the wide scope of formal theories, they can add truth value to a design too [16]. Kuechler and Vaishnavi [14] emphasize the same issue and propose a new type of theory to solve the limited explanatory power of formal theories. They introduce the term mid-range theory (MRT) to DSR. According to their definition, Mid-range theories in IS refer to formal theories that have been enriched with more explanatory knowledge to make them more applicable for particular problems. Finally, third, Gregor and Jones [8] extend the scope of the knowledge base even further; they use the term justificatory knowledge (JK) when referring to the knowledge base. Similar to Walls et al. [3], justificatory knowledge is an important part of a design theory which comprises eight components: 1) Purpose and scope, 2) Constructs, 3) Principles of form and function, 4) artifact mutability, 5) testable propositions, 6) justificatory knowledge, 7) implementation and 8) expository instantiation. Justificatory knowledge in their understanding is defined as the "justificatory, explanatory knowledge that links goals, shape, processes and materials" [8, p.326]. This includes knowledge from natural science or social science, PTiUs, (predictive) design theories as the result of previous DSR and also evidence-based justification as seen in medical research and action research [12]. Though, they stress the importance of an existing knowledge base, they accept lower qualitative requirements regarding the leveraged knowledge: their understanding includes also incomplete descriptive knowledge and practical evidence [8]. In this matter they concur with other researchers, for example Simon [2] who argues that the underlying descriptive knowledge doesn't have to be completely understood. Also, Hevner et al. [10] support this opinion: they state that design science is issue driven, rather than theory-driven, and hence the range of possible theoretical background should not be limited too much. Groaning et al. [17] argue that the knowledge used as JK does not necessarily need a scientific research background, but also allows additional knowledge.

3   Methodology

In order to determine the current role of theory in DSR we used literature review methodology. Our research design followed Webster and Watson who propose a concept-centric approach for literature reviews [18]. In detail, they suggest a framework containing five major steps: 1) Identification of relevant disciplines, 2) Selection of adequate journals and conferences, 3) Search process, 4) Structuring the content and 5) Content analysis.

Regarding the selection of relevant research disciplines, we focused on research disciplines which revolve around the nature of an IT artifact and its relation to a social context. This lead us to the obvious decision to pick information systems as the first relevant research discipline. Second, computer science, as a discipline which targets the theoretical foundations of computing and information, displayed another relevant discipline. However, computer science appears to be a wide discipline including many sub-fields which do not all directly address the design, implementation and evaluation of information system related artifacts. Therefore, we limited our research to three relevant sub-fields: The first one was software engineering which focuses on the systematic development of software, i.e., the design and development of a software artifact. The second was human-computer-interaction (HCI) which focuses on the study, planning, and design of the interaction between users and computers, i.e., the investigation of the interaction of particular IT artifacts with their environment.

The third one was information technology (IT) which revolves around the development of artifacts to process or model information. The next step included the selection of appropriate journals and conferences (see Table 1). In order to bridge the gap between objectiveness and relevance, we considered two categories of outlets and conferences: First, those which publish a wide variety of research topics (e.g., IS journals) and second those which address topics comprising a major design component (e.g., software engineering journals).

Table 1. Investigated Literature Sources

	Conference	Journal
IS	American Conference on Information Systems	European Journal on Information Systems
	European Conference on Information Systems	Information Systems Journal
	International Conference on Information Systems	Information Systems Research
		Journal of the Association for Information Systems
		Journal on Management Information Systems
		Management Information Systems Quarterly
		Transactions on Information Systems
CS[1]	Hawaii International Conference on System Science[2]	IEEE Computer
		IEEE Personal Communication
	Conference on Human Factors in Computing Systems	IEEE Internet Computing
		IEEE Software
	HCI International Conference	Computer Supported Cooperative Work
	Conference on Research and Development in Information Retrieval	International journal of HCI
		Journal of Organizational and End-User Computing
	International Conference on Management of Data	Personal and Ubiquitous Computing
		Communications of the ACM
		ACM Transactions on Computer Human Interactions
		ACM interactions
Total	9	18

The next step was to decide upon a feasible time span for our investigation. As first search run with the key word "design science" did not lead to any search results previous to 1980. Additionally, all the cited related work dates after 1990. Accordingly, we narrowed down the search period to the last three decades.

---

[1] SE, HCI and IT.

[2] Mixed IS/IT conference, here categorized as IT.

The wide selection of journals and conferences made defining a search strategy difficult. The first promising attempts on a few databases do not necessarily indicate a successful search result in total. Hence, we refined our search strategy first before conducting the actual study. The development of our search strategy followed an iterative approach: each cycle included a test run with the current search strategy, followed by an assessment of the search results and a subsequent refinement of the strategy. As a starting point, we analyzed several of the most cited articles on design science to identify an initial set of key words for the search strategy. Hevner et al.'s [10] observe that DSR exhibits a problem solving character [10]. Other literature sources define goal orientation as the key element of DSR [4]. In addition, nearly all articles name IT artifacts as a basic module for a design theory [2], [4], [10], [19]. The first test runs with different combinations of these key words and logical operators yielded a satisfying number of relevant articles. A short analysis of the findings displayed that almost every article identified, included an introduction to the methodology of DSR, mentioning the key word "design science" at least once. Exceptions to this rule were some articles focusing on design theories which do not mention "design science" explicitly. Hence, the search strategy identified as sufficient comprised an OR-combination of "design science" and "design theory". The final search run yielded 337 articles. After skimming and scanning the results and discarding all articles which d not display methodological or applied DSR, the final results comprised 67 articles about design science.

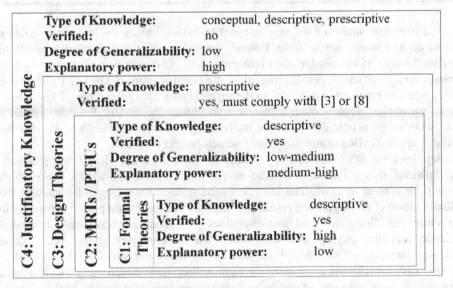

Fig. 1. Categories of knowledge bases applied for clustering

The next step included the clustering of the search results along the following dimensions. First, we defined four main categories of knowledge base used in the articles – reflecting different epistemological characteristics introduced in the related work section (compare Fig. 1): the first category comprises formal theories. This kind of theory complies with the rather strict interpretation of the knowledge base as suggested by Walls et al. [3]. The second category also contains mid-range theories as proposed by Kuechler and Vashnavi [14] and practitioner theories-in-use as suggested by Markus et al. [9]. The third category includes also results from previous DSR in the form of prescriptive theories. The theories have to comply with the definitions of Walls et al. [3] or Gregor and Jones [8]. The fourth category represents the least strict definition of the knowledge base (e.g. [2],[8]). It includes conceptual knowledge, (descriptive) practical evidence and also preliminary prescriptive results of DSR. Regarding the distinction between the different types of theory, we followed mainly the criteria type of knowledge (descriptive, prescriptive, conceptual [4]), degree of generalizability, explanatory power for a particular problem class and whether the knowledge was scientifically verified. If several types of knowledge were used, the segmentation was conducted based on the least formal knowledge leveraged in the article.

Table 2. Segmentation of methodological DSR articles

Category	Information Systems	Computer Science
Formal Theory	[3] [21] [22] [23]	
MRT / PTiU	[19] [24] [25]	[26]
Design Theory		
JK	[8] [10] [27] [28] [17] [29]	[30]

The manifold nature of the implemented knowledge bases made a categorization based on key words not feasible. Instead, we had to skim and scan each article to derive the type of knowledge used (compare [20]). This step was conducted by two researchers. Conflicts, especially regarding the classification of MRTs / PTiUs, were discussed and resolved. Additional to the segmentation along the types of knowledge base, we applied several other dimensions to cluster the results: One differentiator was whether the article described the methodology of DSR (Table 2) or whether the authors applied DSR methodology in a research project (Table 3).

Articles about DSR methodology usually do not apply a knowledge base practically; however they promote a specific interpretation of the knowledge base which should be applied in DSR. The analysis of the utilized knowledge also enabled the identification of its originating research discipline. We used a simplified taxonomy to structure the disciplines and sub-disciplines. We distinguished between natural science, including physics and mathematics but not computer science (CS), social sciences including all sub-disciplines such as psychology or sociology but not information systems (IS) and a category for various disciplines which includes all articles that utilize more than one of the latter (sub-) disciplines as a source of their knowledge base.

Furthermore, we analyzed the types of artifact which are investigated in the DSR project. We distinguished between four types of artifacts: constructs (vocabulary and symbols), methods (algorithms and practices), models (abstractions and representations) and instantiation (software components and information systems) [15],[30].

The publication target is determined by whether an article was published in a journal or a conference. We did not apply any further rankings to define an order within these two categories. All articles were assigned to the different categories disjointedly.

Table 3. Segmentation of applied DSR articles

Category	Origin	Information Systems	Computer Science
Formal	Natural Science	[31] [32]	
Theory	Social Science	[33] [34] [35] [36] [37] [38] [39]	[40] [41] [42]
MRT / PTiU	CS	[43] [44]	
	Social Science	[45]	
	IS	[46] [47] [48] [49]	
	Various	[50]	
Design Theory	IS	[9] [51] [52]	
JK	CS	[53] [54] [55] [56]	
	Social Sciences	[57] [58] [59]	
	IS	[60] [61] [62] [63] [64] [65] [66] [67] [68] [69]	[70] [71]
	Various	[72] [73] [74] [75] [76] [77]	[78] [79] [80] [81] [82]

4 Results

Table 4 presents an overview of the number of methodological and applied DSR articles and the category of knowledge base they promote (methodological) or the category of knowledge base they implement (applied DSR). We identified 14 papers on DSR methodology and 53 papers which apply DSR methodology to address a research topic. All methodological articles share that they suggest at least some kind of knowledge base. We did not encounter any articles which deny the importance of an underlying knowledge base for DSR altogether. Knowledge bases built on formal theories are promoted by four articles, the application of MRT / PTiU for the knowledge base also by four. Six methodological articles advertise a less formal interpretation of the knowledge base.

Table 4. Categorization results in absolute numbers

Category	Method	Practical
Formal Theory	4	12
MRT / PTiU	4	8
Design theory	0	3
JK	6	30
Total	**14**	**53**

We could not identify any articles which solely solicit design theories as underlying knowledge. However, most authors of methodological papers who suggest a wide interpretation of the knowledge base also consider design theories as a valid part of it (Table 4). Our analysis uncovered an apparent preference (30 articles) for a wide interpretation of the knowledge base.

Table 5. Origin of KB in absolute numbers

Category	Natural Science	Social Science	IS	CS	Various	Total
Formal Theory	2	10				12
MRT / PTiU		1	4	2	1	8
Design Theory		3				3
JK		3	12	4	11	30
Total	1	14	18	6	12	53

Formal theories and MRT / PTiU also find widespread application (20 articles). Examples for formal theories originating from the social sciences are the "theory of symbolic representation" [36] or the "social constructive learning theory" [41]. Examples for theories originating from the natural sciences are the "theory of form" [40] or the "recursion theory" [32]. Examples of mid-range theories are the two major IS theories, such as the "technology acceptance model" and its derivations [47], [48], [49] or the "task-technology-fit model" [50].

Only three papers leverage a design theory [9], [51], [52]. In all three cases, the papers use the "design theory for emergent knowledge processes" [9], [51], [52]. Even though, we identified many articles which also implement results from previous DSR in their knowledge base, for example enterprise integration patterns or meta models, these previous results do not comply with the definition of a design theory as provided by Walls et al. [3] or as provided by Gregor and Jones [8] and were therefore classified as justificatory knowledge only.

The origins of justificatory knowledge are manifold. Researchers apply conceptual, prescriptive and descriptive knowledge of a variety of disciplines and sub-disciplines. Often researchers leverage knowledge of more than one discipline (e.g., IS and CS knowledge) to inform their designs (11 articles). Examples for applied justificatory knowledge are agile development methods [81], system development lifecycles [56], the interaction model of SOA [54], grid-based architecture principles [82] or the wide-audience-requirement engineering method [81]. In contrast to formal theories or MRT / PTiU which often originate from other sub-disciplines of the super ordinate research field (e.g., psychological theories), justificatory knowledge is often very context specific and results from the same sub-discipline (see Table 5).

Regarding the types of artifacts (see Table 6), the most common types found are models, mostly abstractions and representations of business processes (20 articles). Almost with the same frequency appear instantiation in the form of software components, light-weight applications and full-fledged information systems.

Table 6. Type of artifact in absolute numbers

Category	Con-struct	Model	Method	Instan-tiation	Vari-ous	Total
Formal Theory		1	4	7		12
MRT / PTiU	1	2	2	3		8
Design Theory			1	1	1	3
JK	2	16	2	7	3	30
Total	**3**	**20**	**9**	**18**	**4**	**53**

DSR that works with model artifacts often build on related justificatory knowledge, mostly represented by conceptual knowledge in the form of meta models. Instantiations, on the contrary, rely more on formal theories (7 articles) and MRT/PiTU (3 articles). Regarding the correlation between the publication target and the type of knowledge base used (see Table 7), our analysis shows that DSR published in journals leverage a higher percentage (58,9%) of scientific theories (Formal theories, MRTs/ PTiUs and Design Theories). DSR which is published in conferences instead, mostly relies on context specific, but scientifically less verified justificatory knowledge (64.9%). Furthermore, DSR which targets the development of models and does not implement a comprehensive knowledge base based on formal theories are usually published only in conferences.

Table 7. Publication target in absolute and relative numbers

Category	Conference	Journal
Formal Theory	6 (16.2%)	6 (35.3%)
MRT / PTiU	6 (16.2%)	2 (11.8%)
Design Theory	1 (2.7%)	2 (11.8%)
JK	23 (64.86%)	7 (41.1%)
Total	**36 (100%)**	**17 (100%)**

5   Discussion of Results

In general, all DSR works utilize one or various knowledge sources and none of the ones in our sample negate the necessity of a solid knowledge base. The first core finding is the more or less equal distributions of theory grounded articles and justificatory knowledge based articles (23 vs. 30 articles). In particular, the research papers originating from the IS field reflect an equal distribution (20 vs. 23 articles) whereas we observe a tendency towards JK based grounding in the CS discipline (3 vs. 7 articles). However, the significantly lower number of identified DSR papers in CS does does not seem to allow for drawing reliable conclusions. The slightly higher number of articles that build their research on justificatory knowledge (30 articles) as compared to theory grounding (23 articles) can be explained by the fact that DSR is often problem driven [10]. When solving a concrete problem, a researcher's first choice seems to be mostly knowledge that is closely related to the problem and can provide a high degree of explanatory power for the particular context. Such knowledge results usually form related research or is collected empirically by the researchers themselves as our analysis shows. Formal theories seem to be only the second choice: especially when researchers attempt to generalize their results, theories are used to frame the results into a wider context. Very rarely is a DSR project initiated in response to the need to further prove descriptive theories or to extend results from previous DSR research. More surprising is the finding that the distribution of methodological articles does not show a significant tension towards theory grounding (8 vs. 6). With regard to articles that promote formal theories in contrast to justificatory knowledge, we detected that a majority of articles address theory grounding from a paradigmatic perspective. Another way to promote theory integration in DSR could be to provide researchers with more concrete guidelines how to utilize formal theories in their work. For example, how can theory X from social science be used in DSR to address problem class Y.

The second finding is that the origin of knowledge shows a clear focus on IS and social science rooting. This phenomenon could be explained by the abstraction level of how technology is analyzed in the course of DSR: DSR in IS usually focuses on the application of technology in a social context. Technology is often examined from a rather abstract point of view and not elaborated in detail. Social science theories seem to be more applicable than natural science theories in this case since they include constructs for various social factors and sometimes also provide constructs to cover technological aspects. However, we need to point out that according to our data this statement applies only on the level of formal theories and when the artifact is an instantiation (e.g., a full-fledged IS). DSR research which focuses on very specific design problems (e.g., models), does not solely rely on formal theories from social science but utilizes knowledge from various disciplines. The explanatory power of the leveraged knowledge seems to be the most important factor in this case; no matter what the origin of the knowledge is. Also, more technology focused DSR projects, especially in the CS domain (e.g., algorithm design), draw greater benefits from CS or natural science theories and justificatory knowledge. These disciplines seem to be perceived as offering better theories for the design and advance of solutions to technical problems.

The third finding is that design theories are rarely utilized as knowledge base in DSR projects. The explanation for this deficit could be twofold: i) lack of design theories and ii) existing DSR theories are not applicable. Both statements are supported by the fact that we found only one DT, which is actually utilized three times in DSR projects, the "Design theory for emergent knowledge processes" suggested by Markus et al. [9]. Specifically analyzing this design theory, one could condense the following key features: 1) the design theory is based on an established framework for information system design theory, 2) it is highly generalized regarding its context (emergent knowledge creation) and characteristics (impossibility to predict process participation and tool usage, knowledge distribution, and emergent processes) and c) it is highly tangible in terms of the artifact, applicable requirements, recommendations, system design and development principles. One could argue that these features are relevant prerequisites for a design theory to be utilized in later DSR. However, these high qualitative requirements which seem to be hardly ever met are also a probable explanation for why only few design theories exist which are applicable for further DSR research. We think additional methodological work should aim on clarifying the nature of design theories and also provide practical guidelines how to create applicable design theories.

A fourth finding is that DSR work published in journals leverages a higher percentage of (formal) theories in contrast to DSR which is published on conferences. As the evaluation of the scientific quality of particular outlets or the rigor and relevance of DSR projects is out of scope, we can only speculate about the reasons: One possible explanations could be that DSR work addressing real world problems is more often found on conferences, and such targeting the development, verification or extension of theories more often in journals.

6   Conclusion, Limitations and Future Work

Our literature review on the anatomy of the knowledge base in DSR lead to the following results: 1) There is no extreme – both formal and less formal knowledge are used for the knowledge base of DSR in IS and CS. 2) Researchers harness knowledge from a variety of disciplines, however there is a tendency towards the use of social science and IS knowledge. 3) Design theories play almost no role for the knowledge base. 4) DSR research published in journals leverages more formal knowledge, while those published on conferences more informal. Our work is subject to several limitations: first, we cannot obviate that we have missed important work on DSR in IS. Second, we are aware of the fact that we couldn't cover all IS and especially CS literature sources which are potential targets of DSR. Third, our results are very dependent on our segmentation of the knowledge bases applied. While methodological articles on the nature of the knowledge base provide a good basis for segmentation of social science theories, natural science theories, especially leveraged CS theories and theorems, often do not fit in these patterns. In addition, it was not always clear to which research discipline an article belonged, especially when an outlet addressed both CS and IS topics (e.g. HICSS). Despite the shortcomings of our study, we believe that our research succeeds in shedding some light on the anatomy of the knowledge bases used in DSR. Especially our third finding reveals a critical issue since a significant number of DSR scholars stress the importance of DTs as the outcome (e.g., [3]), and more importantly, contribution to the scientific knowledge base. Therefore, the lack of applied design theories raises the question if previous DSR has already made these contributions and if not why. As concluded, further methodological work could help to achieve some clarity here. In addition, our results offer the possibility to investigate further correlation between the category of the knowledge base and the quality of DSR works. A more comprehensive study, using official rankings, could show the type of KB used in high quality publications. Citation backtracking could reveal a connection between the KB used and the amount of citations of an article.

References

1. Orlikowski, W., Baroudi, J.: Studying information technology in organizations: Research approaches and assumptions. Information Systems Research 2(1), 1–28 (1991)
2. Simon, H.: The sciences of the artificial, 3rd edn. MIT Press, Cambridge (1996)
3. Walls, J., Widmeyer, G., El Sawy, O.: Building an information system design theory for vigilant eis. Information Systems Research 3(1), 36–59 (1992)
4. Iivari, J.: A paradigmatic analysis of information systems as a design science. Scandinavian Journal of Information Systems 19(2), 39–64 (2007)
5. Orlikowski, W., Iacono, C.: Research commentary: desperately seeking the 'IT' in IT research-A call to theorizing the IT artifact. Information Systems Research 12(2), 121–134 (2001)
6. Benbasat, I., Zmud, R.: The identity crisis within the IS discipline: Defining and communicating the discipline's core properties. Mis Quarterly, 183–194 (2003)
7. Baskerville, R.: What design science is not. European Journal of Information Systems 17(5), 441–443 (2008)
8. Gregor, S., Jones, D.: The anatomy of a design theory. Journal of the Association for Information Systems 8(5), 313–335 (2007)
9. Markus, M., Majchrzak, A., Gasser, L.: A design theory for systems that support emergent knowledge processes. MIS Quarterly 26(3), 179–212 (2002)
10. Hevner, A., March, S., Park, J., Ram, S.: Design science in information systems research. MIS Quarterly 28(1), 75–105 (2004)
11. Sein, M., Henfridsson, O., Purao, S., Rossi, M., Lindgren, R.: Action design research. MIS Quarterly 35(1), 37–56 (2011)
12. Van Aken, J.: Management research as a design science: Articulating the research products of mode 2 knowledge production in management. British Journal of Management 16(1), 19–36 (2005)
13. Gregor, S.: The nature of theory in information systems. Management Information Systems Quarterly 30(3), 611 (2006)
14. Kuechler, B., Vaishnavi, V.: Theory development in design science re search: anatomy of a research project. European Journal of Information Systems 17(5), 489–504 (2008)
15. Nunamaker, J., Chen, M.: Systems development in information systems research. In: Proceedings of the Twenty-Third Annual Hawaii International Conference on System Sciences, pp. 631–640 (1990)
16. Sarker, S., Lee, A.: Using a positivist case research methodology to test three competing theories-in-use of business process redesign. Journal of the Association for Information Systems 2(1) (2002)
17. Groaning, A., Wendler, R., Leyh, C., Strahringer, S.: Rigorous selection of input artifacts in design science research – tavias. In: Processings of the 16th Americas Conference on Information Systems (2010)
18. Webster, J., Watson, R.: Analyzing the past to prepare for the future: Writing a literature review. MIS Quarterly 26(2), xiii–xxiii (2002)
19. Kuechler, B., Park, E., Vaishnavi, V.: Formalizing theory development in is design science research: Learning from qualitative research. In: Proceedings of the 15th Americas Conference on Information Systems (2009)
20. Machi, L., McEvoy, B.: The literature review: Six steps to success, 1st edn. Corwin Press, Thousand Oaks (2009)
21. Buckl, S., Matthes, F., Schweda, C.: Utilizing patterns in developing design theories. In: Proceedings of the 31st International Conference on Information Systems (2010)

22. Gregory, R.: Design science research and the grounded theory method: Characteristics, differences, and complementary uses. In: Proceedings of the 18th European Conference on Information Systems (2010)
23. Weber, S.: Design science research: Paradigm or approach. In: Processings of the 16th Americas Conference on Information Systems (2010)
24. Ofer, A., Kumar, N., Shapira, B.: A theory-driven design framework for social recommender systems. Journal of the Association for Information Systems 11(9), 455–490 (2010)
25. Hovorka, D., Germonprez, M.: Tinkering, tailoring and bricolage: Implications for theories of design. In: Proceedings of the 15th Americas Conference on Information Systems (2009)
26. Zimmerman, J., Forlizzi, J., Evenson, S.: Research through design as a method for interaction design research in hci. In: Proceedings of the 2007 Conference on Human Factors in Computing Systems CHI 2007, New York, p. 493 (2007)
27. Gonzalez, R.: Validation of crisis response simulation within the design science framework. In: Proceedings of the 30th International Conference on Information Systems (2009)
28. Roland, M., Thoring, K.: Understanding artifact knowledge in design science: Prototypes and products as knowledge repositories. In: Proceedings of the 17th Americas Conference on Information Systems (2011)
29. Weedman, J.: Client as designer in collaborative design science research projects: what does social science design theory tell us? European Journal of Information Systems 17(5), 476–488 (2008)
30. Hevner, A., March, S.: It systems perspectives - the information systems research cycle. Computer 36(11), 111–113 (2003)
31. Woolridge, R., Hale, J., Hale, D.: Towards a reference architecture of intent for information systems strategic alignment. In: Proceedings of the 14th Americas Conference on Information Systems (2008)
32. Heinrich, B., Bolsinger, M., Bewernik, M.: Automated planning of process models: The constructions of exclusive choices. In: Proceedings of the 30th International Conference on Information Systems (2009)
33. Chatterjee, S., Sarker, S., Fuller, M.: A deontological approach to designing ethical collaboration. Journal of the Association for Information Systems 10(3), 138–169 (2009)
34. Siponen, M., Baskerville, R., Heikka, J.: A design theory for secure information systems design methods. Journal of the Association for Information Systems 7(11), 725–770 (2006)
35. Zhang, X., Brown, S.: Designing collaborative systems to enhance team performance. Journal of the Association for Information Systems 12(8), 556–585 (2011)
36. Kasper, G.: A theory of decision support system design for user calibration. Information Systems Research 7(2), 215–232 (1996)
37. Xu, J., Wang, G., Li, J., Chau, M.: Complex problem solving: Identity matching based on social contextual information. Journal of the Association for Information Systems 8(10), 525–545 (2007)
38. Mittleman, D.: Planning and design considerations for computer supported collaboration spaces. Journal of the Association for Information Systems 10(3), 278–305 (2009)
39. Vranesic, H., Rosenkranz, C.: The role of boundary objects and boundary spanning in data warehousing -a research-in-progress report. In: Proceedings of the 17th European Conference on Information Systems (2009)

40. Steiger, D., Steiger, N.: Decision support as knowledge creation: An information system design theory. In: Proceedings of the 40th Annual Hawaii International Conference on System Sciences, p. 204a (2007)
41. Zhang, X., Olfman, L., Firpo, D.: An information systems design theory for collaborative eportfolio systems. In: Proceedings of the 44th Annual Hawaii International Conference on System Sciences, pp.1–10 (2011)
42. Benjamin, S., Schooley, L., Alnosayan, N.: Development of a disability employment information system: An information systems design theory approach. In: Proceedings of the 39th Annual Hawaii International Conference on System Sciences (2006)
43. Lau, R., Liao, R., Xu, K.: An empirical study of online consumer review spam: A design science approach. In: Proceedings of the 31st International Conference on Information Systems (2010)
44. Lau, R., Lai, C., Ma, J., Li, Y.: Automatic domain ontology extraction for context-sensitive opinion mining. In: Proceedings of the 30th International Conference on Information Systems (2009)
45. Nickerson, R., Varshney, U., Muntermann, J., Isaac, H.: Taxonomy development in information systems: Developing a taxonomy of mobile applications. In: Proceedings of the 17th European Conference on Information Systems (2009)
46. Becker, J., Karow, M., Mueller-Wienbergen, F., Seidel, S.: Toward process modeling in creative domains. In: Proceedings of the 15th Americas Conference on Information Systems (2009)
47. Gass, O., Mädche, A.: Enabling end-user-driven data interoperability – a design science research project. In: Proceedings of the 17th Americas Conference on Information Systems (2011)
48. Golding, P., Donaldson, O.: A design science approach for creating mobile applications. In: Proceedings of the 30th International Conference on Information Systems (2009)
49. Nan, N., Johnston, E.: Using multi-agent simulation to explore the contribution of facilitation to gss transition. Journal of the Association for Information Systems 10(3), 252–277 (2009)
50. Baloh, P.: The role of fit in knowledge management systems: Tentative propositions of the kms design. Journal of Organizational & End User Computing 19(4), 22–41 (2007)
51. Markus, M.: Toward a theory of knowledge reuse: Types of knowledge reuse situations and factors in reuse success. Journal of Management Information Systems 18(1), 57–93 (2001)
52. Vizecky, K.: A design theory for knowledge transfer in business intelligence. In: Proceedings of the 17th Americas Conference on Information Systems (2011)
53. Collins, J., Ketter, W., Gini, M.: Flexible decision support in dynamic inter-organisational networks. European Journal of Information Systems 19(4), 436–448 (2010)
54. Hoyer, V., Stanoevska-Slabeva, K.: Generic Business Model Types for Enterprise Mashup Intermediaries. In: Nelson, M.L., Shaw, M.J., Strader, T.J. (eds.) AMCIS 2009. LNBIP, vol. 36, pp. 1–17. Springer, Heidelberg (2009)
55. DevelAkesson, M., Kautz, K., Eriksson, C.: Engaged design science: oping design decisions for the future e-newspaper. In: Proceedings of the 31st International Conference on Information Systems (2010)
56. Böhringer, M.: Towards a design theory for applying web 2.0 patterns to organisations. In: Proceedings of the 19th European Conference on Information Systems (2011)
57. Williams, K., Chatterjee, S., Rossi, M.: Design of emerging digital services: a taxonomy. European Journal of Information Systems 17(5), 505–517 (2008)

58. Urbach, N., Würz, T.: Designing a reference framework of it/is outsourcing steering processes. In: Proceedings of the 19th European Conference on Information Systems (2011)
59. Boehm, M., Stolze, C., Breitschwerdt, R., Zarvic, N., Thomas, O.: An integrated approach for teaching professionals it management and it consulting. In: Proceedings of the 17th Americas Conference on Information Systems (2011)
60. Sarnikar, S., Deokar, A.: Towards a design theory for process-based knowledge management systems. In: Proceedings of the 29th International Conference on Information Systems (2008)
61. Chung, W., Tseng, T.-L.: Extracting business intelligence from online product reviews: An experiment of automatic rule-induction. In: Proceedings of the 31st International Conference on Information Systems (2010)
62. Umapathy, K., Purao, S., Barton, R.: Designing enterprise integration solutions: effectively. European Journal of Information Systems 17(5), 518–527 (2008)
63. Mueller, B., Ahlemann, F., Riempp, G.: Towards a strategic positioning method for it management. In: Proceedings of the 30th International Conference on Information Systems (2009)
64. Martin, J., Conte, T., Knapper, R.: Towards objectives-based process redesign. In: Proceedings of the 17th Americas Conference on Information Systems (2011)
65. Hertlein, M., Smolnik, S., Riempp, G.: Knowledge centers in professional services firms: Design and empirical evidence. In: Processings of the 16th Americas Conference on Information Systems (2010)
66. Becker, J., Weiss, B., Winkelman, A.: Developing a business process modeling language for the banking sector – a design science approach. In: Proceedings of the 15th Americas Conference on Information Systems (2009)
67. Albert, T., Goes, P., Gupta, A.: Gist: A model for design and management of content and interactivity of customer-centric web sites. MIS Quarterly 28(2), 161–182 (2004)
68. Xie, J.: Sustaining quality assessment processes in user-centred health in formation portals. In: Proceedings of the 15th Americas Conference on Information Systems (2009)
69. Blinn, N., Lindermann, N., Fäcks, K., Nüttgens, M.: Web 2.0 in SME Networks - A Design Science Approach Considering Multi-perspective Requirements. In: Nelson, M.L., Shaw, M.J., Strader, T.J. (eds.) AMCIS 2009. LNBIP, vol. 36, pp. 271–283. Springer, Heidelberg (2009)
70. Cleven, A., Wortmann, F.: Uncovering four strategies to approach master data management. In: Proceedings of the 43rd Annual Hawaii International Conference on System Sciences, pp.1–10 (2010)
71. Hain, S., Back, A.: Towards a maturity model for e-collaboration -a design science research approach. In: Proceedings of the 44th Annual Hawaii International Conference on System Sciences, pp.1–10 (2011)
72. Aaen, I.: Essence: facilitating software innovation. European Journal of Information Systems 17(5), 543–553 (2008)
73. D'Aubeterre, F., Singh, R., Iyer, L.: Secure activity resource coordination: empirical evidence of enhanced security awareness in designing secure business processes. European Journal of Information Systems 17(5), 528–542 (2008)
74. D'Aubeterre, F., Singh, R., Iyer, L.: A semantic approach to secure collaborative interorganizational ebusiness processes (ssciobp). Journal of the Association for Information Systems 9(3), 231–266 (2008)

75. Samuel-Ojo, O., Schooley, B., Hilton, B., Horan, T.: Sharing behavior in emergencies: An instantiation of a utility-focused prototype of a secure mobile near-real-time content device in pre-hospital and hospital settings. In: Processings of the 16th Americas Conference on Information Systems (2010)

76. Andrade, E., Reynoso, J.: Enhanced learning using mutimedia-interactive systems: An experimental study. In: Proceedings of the 15th Americas Conference on Information Systems (2009)

77. Hochstein, A., Brenner, W., Schindlholzer, B.: Service consumer model: Understanding and describing consumers for new service development. In: Proceedings of the 14th Americas Conference on Information Systems (2008)

78. Gaspoz, C., Pigneur, Y.: Preparing a negotiated r&d portfolio with a prediction market. In: Proceedings of the 41st Annual Hawaii International Conference on System Sciences, p. 53 (2008)

79. Druckenmiller, D., Acar, W.: Engineering dialectical inquiry: Lessons learned from lab explorations. In: Proceedings of the 42nd Annual Hawaii International Conference on System Sciences, pp.1–10 (2009)

80. Rittgen, P.: Collaborative modeling -a design science approach. In: Proceedings of the 42nd Annual Hawaii International Conference on System Sciences, vol. 42, pp.1–10 (2009)

81. Schooley, B., Hilton, B., Abed, Y., Lee, Y., Horan, T.: Process improvement and consumer-oriented design of an inter-organizational information system for emergency medical response. In: Proceedings of the 44th Annual Hawaii International Conference on System Sciences, pp.1–10 (2011)

82. Weber, S., Beck, R., Wolf, M., Vykoukal, J.: Portfolio performance measurement based on service-oriented grid computing: Developing a prototype from a design science perspective. In: Proceedings of the 43rd Annual Hawaii International Conference on System Sciences, pp.1–10 (2010)

Characterizing Design Science Theories
by Level of Constraint on Design Decisions

Bill Kuechler[1] and Vijay Vaishnavi[2]

[1] Information Systems
University of Nevada, Reno, 1664 N. Virginia Street, Reno, NV 89557
kuechler@unr.edu
[2] Computer Information Systems
Georgia State University P.O. Box 3965 Atlanta, GA 30302-4015
vvaishna@gsu.edu

Abstract. A current issue in Design Science Research in Information Systems (DSRIS) is the manner in which to capture and present the knowledge gained in the course of a DSRIS project. Different conceptions of design science theory have been suggested. The most firmly established of these is Information Systems Design Theory (ISDT). Recently a number of authors have suggested that additional theory formulations are needed to capture higher-level knowledge: *higher level design science theories* (HLDST). As more types of theory to capture different types of information are proposed the question arises: how do these different theory types relate, to each other and also to the artifact that is constructed in the course of most DSRIS projects?

In this paper we develop a design-decision-constraint framework for characterizing design science theories. Additionally we relate design decisions to the dependent and independent variables of the theories; these traditional elements of theory have been lacking in most discussions of design science theories. By (re)introducing dependent and independent variables to the design science theory conversation we hope to bridge the gap between traditional explanatory theory and ISDT, and thereby help to clarify the discussions of theory in DSRIS.

Keywords: design science research, theory categorization, mid-range theory, theory taxonomy.

1   Introduction

Many recent publications on design science research in Information Systems (DSRIS) have expressed the desirability of a prescriptive design theory as one of the outputs from a DSRIS project. Walls, et al. (1992, 2004) set out the first and most commonly understood form for this prescriptive information termed an ISDT – Information Systems Design Theory. Each ISDT captures design information on the *class* of artifacts of which the specific artifact in the DSRIS project is an instantiation. Walls et al. suggested a specific format for an ISDT (see Table 1), and many DSRIS exemplars (Markus et al. 2002; Hall, et al. 2003; Jones and Gregor 2006) have followed this definition to varying degrees.

K. Peffers, M. Rothenberger, and B. Kuechler (Eds.): DESRIST 2012, LNCS 7286, pp. 345–353, 2012.
© Springer-Verlag Berlin Heidelberg 2012

Table 1. Content Categories of Information System Design Theory (from Walls et al. 2004)

		Theory Component of ISDT
Design Product	1.	Meta-requirements
	2.	Meta-design
	3.	Kernel theories
	4.	Testable design product hypotheses
Design Process	1.	Design method
	2.	Kernel theories
	3.	Testable design process hypotheses

One suggested component of the Walls, et al. (1992, 2004) ISDT framework is kernel theories – high level theories from natural and social sciences that can inform both the Design Product and the Design Process portions of the ISDT. However, the framework gives no guidance on how the kernel theory relates to or suggests the prescribed meta-design and/or design method. In order to fully capture that knowledge a more abstract type of design science theory is required.

In the next section of the paper we present the suggestions of various authors for alternative forms of design science theory. All of the alternative forms operate at a higher conceptual level than ISDT (cf. Gregor's (2006) type II, III, IV theories; ISDT is classified by Gregor as type V). All of these alternative forms of theory have significant value and focus on different aspects of design science research. For convenience we refer to these theories by the group designation, *higher level design science theories* (HLDSTs). Without a framework to classify and relate these different theory formalisms, confusion is inevitable as to what knowledge each formalism captures and how each relates to the other and the DSRIS artifact itself. A framework for classifying design science theories according to the degree to which they constrain design decisions is then proposed and exercised with an example. A concluding section summarizes the contribution of the theory classification framework to DSRIS.

2   Higher Level Design Theory Representations for DSRIS

Vaishnavi and Kuechler (2004; Kuechler and Vaishnavi, 2008) were early proponents of a design science theory formalism that was less prescriptive and more general and explanatory than the Walls et al. (1992, 2004) ISDT. They described their theory conceptualization as mid-range in scope just as ISDT, but lying between kernel theories and ISDT in conceptual level. They termed such theory *design relevant explanatory / predictive theory* (DREPT) and describe it as explicit *translation into the design domain* of specific aspects of a technology and design neutral kernel theory (Kuechler and Vaishnavi (in press)).

Gregor and Jones (2007) also issued a call to DSRIS researchers to capture more of the knowledge generated in a DSRIS effort than is possible in the Walls, et al. (1992, 2004) definition of an ISDT; they suggested extensions to the Walls, et al. template including an explanatory component they termed *justificatory knowledge*. We interpret justificatory knowledge to be very similar to HLDST: explanatory knowledge that details how the physical and/or psychological principles embodied in the artifact give rise to the useful behaviors it exhibits.

Baskerville and Pries-Heje (2010) propose a design theory formulated as requirements-components pairs [of a designed class of artifact], and demonstrate that this formulation satisfies both the prescriptive how-to aspect of the traditional Walls, ISDT while offering additional explanatory information on how the artifact functions. In the formalism they term *explanatory design theory* (EDT) requirements are explicitly related to artifact components. This is a parsimonious and elegant construction; however, the level of explanation offered by *EDT* seems to be lower than either *justificatory knowledge* or HLDST. EDT operates at the level of component, HLDST and *justificatory knowledge* at the level of basic-cause-of-functionality, and so neither can substitute for the other. This suggests that design science may eventually fully accept an array of different theory conceptions, each working most effectively at a specific level of abstraction as may be most appropriate for a specific discussion.

Arazy, et al. (2010) propose another variant on design science theory which they call *applied theory*. Applied theories are derived a-priori from kernel theories and effect a linkage between those theories and the DSRIS artifact design. Along with the Gregor and Jones (2007) and Kuechler and Vaishnavi (2008), Arazy, et al. believe that "Although we cannot expect to find a direct one-to-one mapping [between kernel theory constructs and design goals] the correspondence should be clear." *Applied theory* as they present it establishes that correspondence. We understand *applied theory* to be outside the range of HLDST in that it remains a technology neutral specialization of kernel theory and so does not make the transition to the design domain. We have included it because it is obviously motivated by the same need to link kernel theories with design theories that has resulted in multiple proposals for HLDST and helps to underscore this need as a continuing trend in DSRIS.

The design theory formulations discussed above are all significantly different from the traditional Walls, et al. (1992) ISDT. Understanding how these new types of design science theory relate to each other, to ISDT and to the process of design science requires a robust categorization framework. The framework developed below typifies theories in a manner that aids in understanding the conceptual level of the theory by focusing on the constraints on design imposed by each theory formulation.

3   A Design Constraint Theory Categorization Framework

Figure 1 distinguishes three levels of knowledge capture in DSRIS: high level theories including both kernel theories and experience based insights and intuitions into design, mid-range design science theories[1] and at the most concrete level, the designed artifact itself. Figure 1 also illustrates a common understanding of how theory is 'ordered' in IS design science research (e.g. Walls, 1992; Venable, 2006). It implies, for example, that kernel theories are at a higher level than ISDT and

---

[1] From a conceptual standpoint they could be called 'mid-level design science theories'. They are called 'mid-range' theories to convey the scope of their use.

'precede' it; however the common understanding leaves ranking criteria tacit. Figure 1 actually represents a tree since each of the arrows in the figure can lead to multiple forms of knowledge capture at the next level. For example, a kernel theory can lead to multiple HLDSTs.

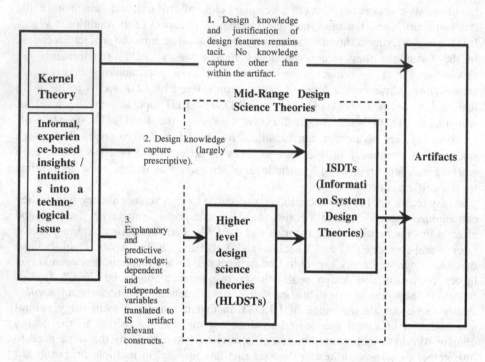

Fig. 1. ISDTs and higher level design science theories (HLDST) as mid-range knowledge representations in design science research (adapted from Kuechler and Vaishnavi, in press)

Figure 2 expands on Figure 1 in three significant ways. First, it adds *Models* as the final level of design specification, that are more concrete than ISDTs in that they specify specific implementations (specific rather than *meta* level). Second, the level of *Artifacts*[2] is broken into implemented template systems and operational systems levels. Third and most important, the figure indicates the design decisions that are specified and constrained by each level of theory. The framework of Figure 2 provides a classification-by-level scheme for design science theories that is orthogonal to Gregor's (2006) theory typology. The arrows in the figure indicate transitions from higher to lower conceptual levels. The classification provided by the framework is unique in that it orders theories by the number and kind of design decisions it constrains or leaves open; there is an exact inverse correspondence between conceptual level and degree of design constraint. That is, the higher the conceptual level, the fewer design constraints it entails.

---

[2] Including designed artifacts in the model and thus treating them as (concrete) theories is arguable. It may, however, be noted that they have been proposed in HCI as the best way to expose and explore theory in complex realms (Carroll and Kellogg 1989).

Kernel theories leave almost all design decisions open - even leaving open the application(s) for which the phenomena described by the theory may be useful. In fact, kernel theories are typically technology neutral. Occasionally, kernel theory can be serendipitously related to technology through the use of IT apparatus in the testing of the theory. An example might be a psychological theory of the subjective perception of time intervals that was tested in a published paper using PC displays and speakers. The experimental apparatus used to test the theory may inadvertently suggest an IT application for the otherwise technology-neutral theory.

HLDST is positioned one step to the right of comprehensive (kernel) theory in Figure 2. This movement takes theoretical statements from the natural/social science domain into the design domain. HLDSTs in our definition specify an IS application domain and an effect to which the theory is applicable. The translation of comprehensive theory DVs (dependent variables) to *effects* potentially useful in the business environment and the translation of the comprehensive theory IVs (independent variables) to one or more artifact-achievable *behaviors* (that cause the effect), is visible in all HLDSTs. However, while the translation is explicit in some HLDST formulations (*DREPT*; Kuechler and Vaishnavi, in press) it is implicit in others (*justificatory knowledge* (Gregor and Jones, 2007); *explanatory design theory* (Baskerville and Pries Heje, 2010))

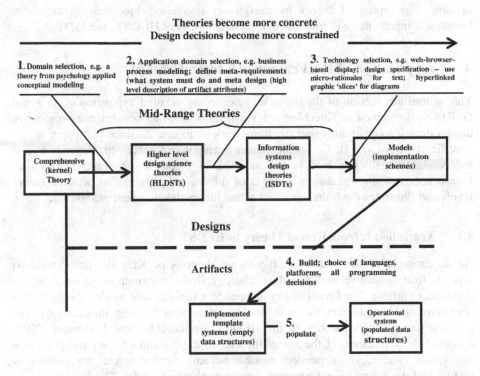

Fig. 2. Design decision constraint across design theory levels

ISDTs specify lower level design decisions: the specific technology and the specific artifact functionality (attributes or requirements) by which the desired effect might be obtained. At a still more concrete level, *models* in the computer science and engineering sense specify all of the above plus the implementation details of the functionality. Models are the most concrete level in the design domain.

In the artifact domain the implementation is fixed – there are no more design decisions to be made. It is consistent with the rest of the framework however, to distinguish between an artifact with unpopulated data structures – where the specific application environment has yet to be determined – and an operational system, fully embedded in a specific work domain. Once in use with populated data structures and procedures, only operational decisions concerning the use of the artifact remain.

We feel this categorization mechanism is natural to design science research and specifically to DSRIS. We believe it will allow the design science researchers to finally, firmly define the level at which various design science theories and models operate; as DSRIS researchers ourselves and readers and reviewers of substantial numbers of DSRIS research papers we have seen considerable confusion over the design science theory level issue (is it a theory in the same sense as kernel theory?; is it closer to a computer science model which is more constrained?) Venable (2006) has also explicitly raised the question of the level at which design science theory should operate. The typing of theory by design decision also objectively distinguishes between comprehensive (kernel) theory, different types of HLDST, and ISDT.

4   Application of the Framework to an Example

Throughout this section of the paper we refer to the detailed exposition of an actual DSRIS project given in Kuechler and Vaishnavi (2008) to demonstrate progressive design decision constraint using the framework of Figure 2. Since that paper uses a specific type of HLDST, which makes explicit reference to dependent and independent variables in both kernel and HLDST theories, our example does also. Please note that the discussion below is of the *logical progression* between theory levels and illustrates the framework, not actual theory development techniques.

4.1   Transition 1, from Kernel Theory to HLDST

As an example of this transition, the kernel theories of Kuechler and Vaishnavi (2008), from cognitive and social psychology, have *information salience* as the dependent variable. The kernel theory independent variables are *modes of information presentation* (textual, numeric, with or without various framing information). The mapping from kernel theories to the HLDST for Kuechler and Vaishnavi (2008) involved the application of the kernel theories to the domain of *computer presented conceptual models*. The dependent variable became more concrete: the salience of textual and diagrammatic information about a conceptual model. The DV translation maps a general theory into one of specific interest to IS. The independent variable becomes technology dependent: computer mediated display of a conceptual model.

The IV translation maps the general theory into the design realm. Note however that the HLDST is still quite general and *potentially* applicable to any of the multiplicity of conceptual models used in IS. Kuechler and Vaishnavi (2008) termed their HLDST: A theory of grammatical element salience in [computer mediated] conceptual modeling (GESCM).

4.2 Transition 2, from HLDST to ISDT

In moving from HLDST to ISDT, a single area of interest was specified. In the running example, the specific conceptual modeling area of *business process modeling* was chosen. Also, necessarily, the HLDST DV of conceptual model information salience was specialized to: salience of business process modeling notations and their related design rationale. The IV was specialized to on-screen presentation of data: textual presentation of non-functional requirements displayed in some manner or sequence with a diagrammatic notation. Detail on the DV constitutes the Walls et al. ISDT *meta-requirements*. Detail on the IV constitutes the Walls et al. *meta-design*. ISDT *testable hypotheses* (another component of the Walls, et al. ISDT) were easily derived from the nature of the effects specified in the meta-requirements (and explained by the HLDST).

It is easy to see that the transition from HLDST to ISDT is truly one of conceptual level on demonstration that a single HLDST can yield multiple ISDTs. For the Kuechler and Vaishnavi (2008) HLDST, for example, an alternate specific domain could be conceptual modeling of data. An alternate IV could be on-screen presentation of multiple notational representations of the same data, each intended to make salient a different aspect of the data set, and so on.

4.3 Transition 3, from ISDT to Model

In moving from ISDT to the artifact design *model* the final high level design details – conceptual, as opposed to construction – were made. BPMN was chosen as the *specific* process notation from several widely used alternatives. The *specific* mode of presentation was conceptualized as a hyper-link between BPMN symbols or logical groupings of such symbols, termed 'slices' and the textual description of a portion of the process design rational for that portion of the process, termed the 'micro-rationale' for that 'slice'. Note that, just as when transitioning from HLDST to ISDT, many alternative choices of notation and presentation could have been made yielding many different models from a single ISDT.

4.4 Transition 4, from Model to Template System

This transition is the implementation step during which the artifact is actually constructed, guided by the Model/ISDT. As part of this transition, concrete decisions must first be made as to development languages, IDEs, programming frameworks, etc. Following these decisions, the multitude of actual implementation decisions – how to partition the program into functions and subroutines, specific algorithms and data structures, etc. - are made routinely in the course of programming the artifact – in the example case, the Business Process Design Display System.

4.5   Transition 5, from Template System to Operational System

The system (in the running example), which had been tested with partial and stub data, was, on completion, fully loaded with data. In this project as in most DSRIS projects, the data consisted of carefully selected test cases intended to determine the satisfaction of design requirements – evaluating the effectiveness of the artifact. In a production environment – since DSRIS results are intended to be used in practice – the data would be some subset of the actual and proposed business processes in effect at the organization implementing the system.

5   Summary and Discussion

In this paper we have briefly described a design-decision-constraint framework for design science theory categorization in DSRIS. The framework specifies the design decisions that are constrained at each theory-level-to-theory-level transition and the manner in which dependent and independent variables become more concrete as the theory levels progress from comprehensive (kernel) theory to actual artifact. We showed briefly how the framework could be used with an example taken from an actual DSRIS project, and sketched the manner in which the framework is compatible with all recently proposed formulations for design science theory.

Note that the framework as illustrated by Figure 2, especially from ISDT through Operational System, bears a striking resemblance to an IS system development methodology. We do not see how it could be otherwise and still accurately reflect design practice; indeed we see this resemblance as adding substantial face credibility to the framework. The primary difference between the framework and a development methodology is that the framework is focused primarily on the knowledge that can be captured and expressed at each "development phase" while a development methodology is exclusively focused on the activities performed at each phase. Additionally, the design science DSRIS theory categorization framework extends to higher levels of abstraction than a development methodology: HLDST and kernel theory. These levels are rarely of concern to IS development in practice.

References

1. Arazy, O., Kumar, N., Shapira, B.: A Theory-Driven Design Framework for Social Recommender Systems. Journal of the Association for Information Systems (JAIS) 11(9), 455–490 (2010)
2. Baskerville, R., Pries-Heje, J.: Explanatory Design Theory. Business and Information Systems Engineering 5, 271–282 (2010)
3. Carroll, J., Kellogg, W.: Artifact as Theory Nexus: Hermeneutics Meets Theory-Based Design. In: CHI 1989. ACM Press (1989)

4. Gregor, S.: The Nature of Theory in Information Systems. MIS Quarterly 30(3), 611–642 (2006)
5. Gregor, S., Jones, D.: The Anatomy of a Design Theory. Journal of the Association for Information Systems 8(5), 312–335 (2007)
6. Hall, D., Paradice, D., Courtney, J.: Building a Theoretical Foundation for a Learning-Oriented Management System. Journal of Information Technology Theory and Application 5(2), 63–85 (2003)
7. Jones, D., Gregor, S.: The Formulation of an Information Systems Design Theory for E-learning. In: DESRIST 2006, Claremont, CA (2006)
8. Kuechler, B., Vaishnavi, V.: On Theory Development in Design Science Research: Anatomy of a Research Project. European Journal of Information Systems 17(5), 489–504 (2008)
9. Kuechler, W., Vaishnavi, V.: A Framework for Theory Development in Design Science Research: Multiple Perspectives. Journal of the Association for Information Systems (JAIS) (in press)
10. Markus, M.L., Majchrzak, A., Gasser, L.: A Design Theory for Systems that Support Emergent Knowledge Processes. MIS Quarterly 26(3), 179–212 (2002)
11. Vaishnavi, V., Kuechler, W.: Design Science Research in Information Systems (January 20, 2004), retrieved from http://desrist.org/design-research-in-information-systems/ (last updated September 30, 2011)
12. Venable, J.: The Role of Theory and Theorizing in Design Science Research. In: DESRIST 2006, Claremont, CA (2006)
13. Walls, J.G., Widmeyer, G.R., El Sawy, O.A.: Building an Information System Design Theory for Vigilant EIS. Information Systems Research 3(1), 36–59 (1992)
14. Walls, J.G., Widmeyer, G.R., El Sawy, O.A.: Assessing Information System Design Theory in Perspective: How Useful was our 1992 Initial Rendition. Journal of Information Technology Theory and Application 6(2), 43–58 (2004)

On the Relationship between the IT Artifact and Design Theory: The Case of Virtual Social Facilitation

Björn Niehaves, Kevin Ortbach, and Asin Tavakoli

University of Muenster, European Research Center for Information Systems (ERCIS)
{bjoern.niehaves,kevin.ortbach,asin.tavakoli}@uni-muenster.de

Abstract. Both the IT artifact and design theory are fundamental elements of a design science project. While literature provides an extensive discussion on why IT artifacts and design theory can be regarded as two sides of the same coin, an operational detailed model on how to actually decode and translate the one into the other is not yet to be found. In this paper, we address this important issue taking the example of social facilitation, a theory perspective that informs us about how the integration of social media features in IT-based routine work can increase task performance. With the help of this example we are able to demonstrate how a lack of discussion regarding the relationship between the actual implementation (IT artifact perspective) and corresponding variables (design theory perspective) can create significant issues of scientific rigor. In order to overcome this gap, we develop a design theorizing framework that differentiates between the structural model (inner model), the measurement model, and the design model (both outer model components). Based on our findings, the paper concludes with discussing potentially fruitful avenues for future research and theory development in design science.

Keywords: Design theory, Framework, Artifact-Theory Relationship, Instantiation, Virtual Social Facilitation.

1 Introduction

The design science research paradigm is highly relevant to information systems research. In recent years, there have been several efforts to bring design research into the IS discipline because it addresses the perceived lack of practical relevance (Hirschheim & Klein 2003) as well as the need to focus on the IT artifact (Hevner et al. 2004). While the importance of the latter within the design science research paradigm has been discussed controversially, it today appears to be generally accepted that a pure focus on the IT artifact is too narrow for a socio-technical discipline (McKay & Marshall 2005; Carlsson 2010). It has been proposed that the phenomena of interest for design research in IS should also include, on a more abstract level, theories (Gregor & Jones 2007). Thus, in addition to the need to increase practical relevance by developing useful IT artifacts, theorizing can be considered an important aspect of design research as well. Design theories, as a specific theory type, define how to do something, i.e. are prescriptive in nature and concern the principles of form

K. Peffers, M. Rothenberger, and B. Kuechler (Eds.): DESRIST 2012, LNCS 7286, pp. 354–370, 2012.

and function as well as methods and justificatory theoretical knowledge that are used in the development of IS artifacts (Gregor 2006).

However, while the interdependencies between kernel theory and design theory are widely discussed, not much attention has yet been given to the relationship between design theory and the IT artifact. Generally, artifact instantiation from theory is important to demonstrate feasibility of both the design process and the design product (Hevner et al. 2004). However, literature on specific design problems in IS shows that the principles developed by a certain design theory may be instantiated in different ways (e.g. Hardless, Lindgren, & Schultze, 2007). With this paper, we seek to show how the absence of this discussion leads to issues of scientific rigor and support our argument with the help of an example: virtual social facilitation. Based on our findings, we then develop a design theorizing framework that integrates the discussed aspects.

The remainder of this paper is structured as follows. Section two outlines related work on design science and identifies achievements as well as gaps with regard to the relationship of design theory and IT artifact. In Section three, the case of virtual social facilitation is presented and evaluated with respect to specific design choices and their motivation. Section four then builds upon this analysis and derives implications for design theorizing.

2   Related Work in Design Science

There are different views on what constitutes design theory and how it relates to the implementation of an IT artifact.

Design theory is non-existent. In an early work on design science in IS, March and Smith (1995) stated that the term theory should be preserved for natural sciences and could not be applied in a design context. They point out that "an appropriate framework for IT research lies in the interaction of design and natural sciences. IT research should be concerned both with utility, as a design science, and with theory, as a natural science" (March & Smith 1995, p. 255). Nevertheless, they briefly refer to the relationship between general IS theories and the IT artifact by stating that "theorizing in IT research must explicate those characteristics of the IT artifact operating in its environment that make it unique to IT and require unique explanations" (March & Smith 1995, p. 259). For design science in general, they identified four major outputs: constructs, models, methods and implementations. Here, they argued that design science – similar to natural science – would need a basic language of concepts (constructs) which could then be used to describe tasks or situations in terms of models. In addition, design researchers would also develop certain practices of performing design activities (methods) which may be instantiated in a particular implementation. This argument is developed further by Hevner et al. (2004). However, while recognizing the importance of the other products, they see the "purposeful IT artifact created to address an important organizational problem" (Hevner et al. 2004, p. 82) as major output of design science. Again, the relation between theory and implementation is only addressed on a very abstract level and only refers to IS theories in general and not IS design theories. It is stated that behavioral science addresses the development and justification of theories that explain or predict phenomena related to the identified business need whereas design science is concerned only with building and evaluating the artifacts.

Design theory is informed by kernel theories. In contrast to this view, there has been the notion of a design theory in IS research as initially developed by Walls et al. (Walls et al. 1992) based on the idea of a "science of the artificial" proposed by Simon (1981). Here, not only the IT artifact is considered the core research objective of the IS discipline in general and IS design research in particular (as in e.g. Benbasat & Zmud 2003; Hevner et al. 2004) but also a theory on how to design these artifacts. This information systems design theory (ISDT) is defined as a "prescriptive theory based on theoretical underpinnings, which says how a design process can be carried out in a way which is both effective and feasible" (Walls et al. 1992, p. 37). In this context, Gregor and Jones adopted the concepts of March and Smith stating that "'constructs, models and methods' are all one type of thing and can be equated to theory or components of theory, while instantiations are a different type of thing altogether" (Gregor & Jones 2007, p. 320). Thus, they emphasize the need to differentiate design theorizing from implementing a particular instance of the developed theory in terms of an IT artifact. For the theorizing function, kernel theories, i.e. theories from natural and social sciences that govern design requirements, have been identified as core components. Walls et al. (1992) state that their utilization can be considered essential for both design product, i.e. the actual artifact, and design process. Iivari (2007) even sees the "danger that the idea of a 'design theory' will be (mis)used just to make our field sound more scientific without any serious attempt to strengthen the scientific foundation of the meta-artifacts proposed" if no kernel theories are used within the design theorizing process. Thus, in this view of design science, it is recognized that there has to be a relationship between the underlying kernel theory and the instantiated artifact. The exact structure of this relationship, however, is not elaborated in further detail. It is described on a rather high level and not analyzed with respect to the constructs of the kernel theories in-depth. Furthermore, in this understanding, it is assumed that kernel theory only informs the design, but is itself not systematically refined or further developed by the findings of the design research.

Reciprocal relationship between kernel theories and design theories. Gregor (2006) sees design theories as being strongly related to all other theory types (theories for analyzing, theories for explaining, theories for predicting, and theories for explaining and predicting). More specifically, she sees a strong interrelationship between theories of explanation and prediction (EP) and design theories stating that "knowledge of people and information technology capabilities informs the design and development of new information system artifacts" and that "these artifacts can then be studies in terms of EP theory" (Gregor 2006, p. 629). Kuechler and Vaishnavi (2008) add the concept of a mid-range theory and argue that that kernel theories can both inform design science and in turn be refined and developed by it.

It can be noted from this review that there has been a comprehensive discussion in literature about the outputs of design science, the general distinction between design theory and the IT artifact and the relationship between kernel theories and design theory. However, not much has been published yet on the exact relationship between design theory and particular instantiations of this theory in terms of IT artifacts. Design theories are normative theories, i.e. they are prescriptive and evaluative rather than only descriptive, explanatory, or predictive (Markus et al. 2002). Kuechler and Vaishnavi (2008) state that design theories consist of prescriptive statements where a prescribed action is intended to lead to a certain goal. The relationship between prescribed action and goal correspond to the cause-effect-relation within the underlying kernel theory. However, one could argue that a design theory may include alternative prescribed actions i.e. alternative design choices that are aimed towards the same goal. One concept that points into a similar direction is that of a design theory nexus by Pries-Heje & Baskerville (2008). Referring to Carrol and Kellog (1989) they state that a "design theory nexus extends the deductive view of the relationship between theory and artifact to a reciprocal relation between the articulation and rearticulation of theoretical claims and iterations of design" (Pries-Heje & Baskerville 2008, p. 3). Here, however, alternative solutions do not concern particular design choices but competing design theories and, thus, are aimed towards different goals. Therefore, to our knowledge, there is no theoretical view that includes a discussion of the relationship between alternative prescriptive statements, i.e. prescriptive designs and the implemented artifact.

3 The Case of Virtual Social Facilitation

3.1 Background and Motivation

Looking at the developments within the 20th century, it is observable that information technology has been primarily used to capture and structure data within organizations and to streamline business processes by means of automation. There has been a plethora of studies focusing on how IT can contribute to more efficient processes (Broadbent et al. 1999; Bala & Venkatesh 2007). Innovations in IT were introduced by the global players and have then been adopted by smaller businesses before arriving at a consumer level. Recently, however, there has been a turnaround regarding this trend (Moore 2011). Now, IT innovations are oftentimes induced on a consumer level and then diffuse into organizational context. The systems of record, i.e. core IT systems of the companies that support their daily routines, are "no longer a source of competitive differentiation for organizations" (Moore 2011, p. 3). They are increasingly complemented by systems of engagement, i.e. systems that allow for communication and collaboration across enterprise boundaries. In a world of complex supply chains and a plethora of stakeholders involved in each business process, this concept of boundary spanning has been outlined as one key aspect for competitiveness (Levina & Vaast 2005). In this context, Web 2.0 in general and social media in particular are often seen as enabling technologies (Kaplan & Haenlein 2010). Research and practice calls for the Enterprise 2.0 that extends and complements existing systems of record with Web 2.0 technologies thereby integrating social media into the organization.

In this context, social psychology in general and social facilitation theory in particular may assist in determining and explaining possible effects these implementations have with regard to work performance. Moreover, researchers have argued that the latter may be a suitable foundation for research on emerging technologies (see Aiello

& Douthitt 2001; Feinberg & Aiello 2006) and, thus, may also be utilized in a social media context. Therefore, within this case, we will use (virtual) social facilitation (VSF) theory to analyze the effects social IT-features may have on simple task performance.

3.2   Social Facilitation Theory

In its core, social facilitation theory is concerned with the impact of social presence on the performance of a particular task (Aiello & Douthitt 2001). It can be traced back to early studies by Triplett (1898) who observed that bicycle racers performed better when racing against others than when being alone on the track. The term itself was coined by Allport (1924) who defined it as "an increase in response merely from the sight or sound of others making the same move". Later studies moved away from the coaction principle and showed that social facilitation could also be achieved by means of a passive observer (e.g. Dashiell 1935). In his milestone article on drive theory, Zajonc (1965) suggested, that the mere presence of others increases arousal which in turn leads to a higher level of individual drive towards the investigated task. However, it was found that this only applies to simple and well-learned tasks. Performance on complex or novel tasks, on the other hand, is impaired by the presence of other individuals (Bond & Titus 1983; Zajonc 1965; Feinberg & Aiello 2006). In addition, Cotrell et al. (1986) suggested, that only an audience who has the ability to evaluate the task will stimulate arousal. In their study, the presence of blindfolded individuals did not yield a significant effect on task performance. Taking up this view, Carver & Scheier (1981) postulated that the feeling of being observed will lead to an increased awareness of differences between actual and anticipated behavior. They used this feedback-loop as explanation for the observable increase in task performance.

Table 1. Overview of related studies on VSF and their variables

Authors	Description	Treatment		Implementation	
		Name	Origin	Description	Origin
(Aiello & Kolb 1995)	Experiment study on the impact of electronic performance monitoring on productivity and stress by using a data-entry task and group brainstorming.	Monitoring	Prior work (e.g. U.S. Congress 1987)	Data-entry transmitted to controlling client	The author(s) do not provide specific information
(Kolb & Aiello 1997)	Experiment study on the effects of computer-based performance monitoring on work productivity by using a data-entry task and a moderate vowel/consonant identification task.	Monitoring	Prior work (e.g. U.S. Congress 1987)	Screensharing	The author(s) do not provide specific information
(Davidson & Henderson 2000)	Laboratory experiment on the effects of electronic performance measurement on performance, mood state and stress levels by using an anagram-solving task.	Measurement	Prior work (e.g. George 1996)	Rotating icon indicating performance measurement	The author(s) do not provide specific information

Table 1. (*continued*)

(Rafaeli & Noy 2002)	Experiment study on the effects of virtual presence (none, text chat, pictures from other participants) and feedback (winner of auction) on behavior and performance in Dutch auctions.	Monitoring	Prior work (e.g. Aiello & Svec 1993)	Displaying number of other bidders, Displaying name and picture of bidders, Text chat with bidders	The author(s) do not provide specific information
		Feedback	The author(s) do not provide specific information	Displaying winner of auction (picture and name)	The author(s) do not provide specific information
(Zanbaka & Ulinski 2004)	Experiment study on the effects of virtual human presence on task performance by using a pattern recognition and categorization task.	Monitoring	Prior work (e.g. Hoyt et al. 2003)	Interactive 3D character projected to wall (virtual human)	Haptek Corporation
(S. Park & Catrambone 2007)	Experiment study on the effects of presence by virtual humans on task performance by using different tasks: anagrams, mazes, and modular arithmetic.	Monitoring	Prior work (e.g. Zanbaka & Ulinski 2004)	Interactive 3D character on computer monitor (virtual human)	Haptek Corporation
Our Study (cp. Authors 2012)	Experiment study of the effect of monitoring, measurement, and feedback dialogs - in a virtual presence setting - on IT-based anagram solving.	Monitoring	Prior work (e.g. Aiello & Kolb 1995)	Screensharing	Prior work (Kolb & Aiello 1997)
		Measurement	Prior work (Davidson & Henderson 2000)	Icon indicating the measurement	Prior work (Davidson & Henderson 2000)
		Feedback	Prior work (Rafaeli & Noy 2002)	Text chat tool and indicating icon	Prior work (Rafaeli & Noy 2002)

However, with regard to the increasing digitalization of workplaces, researchers started to investigate the effects of virtual social facilitation by replacing the former human facilitator with a virtual equivalent. Here, studies found that e.g. presence of computer monitoring has similar effects on the work performance than that of a physical person (e.g. Aiello & Svec 1993; Aiello & Kolb 1995). However, the actual implementations of the monitoring efforts differed significantly among studies and included screensharing (Kolb & Aiello 1997), virtual humans (S. Park & Catrambone 2007; Zanbaka & Ulinski 2004), or simple icons indicating the observation (Davidson & Henderson 2000). Table 1 shows an overview of relevant variables within the different studies on virtual social facilitation. All of these studies were concerned with low complexity tasks.

3.3 Research Model

From literature, we can identify three treatments as being potentially relevant for social applications: monitoring, measurement, and feedback dialogs. These were used

Table 2. Experiment variables used in our study

Category	Variable	Definition	Implementation
Dependent variable	Performance (PERFORM)	Performance is defined as the performance gain/loss in comparison to the control situation, using a combined performance measure, taking into account correct and wrong answers as well as completion times for an anagram puzzle task.	Median over the individual response times of each participant
Independent variable	Monitoring (MONITOR)	Monitoring describes the presence of the supervisor. In the virtual presence setting, the participants are told that IT is used to monitor their doings, e.g. via screensharing.	Screensharing and indicating icon on user interface
	Measurement (MEASURE)	Measurement describes the fact, that work performance is explicitly measured and evaluated. Within the virtual test setting, performance recording was achieved by means of automated time saving.	Verbal notice and indicating icon on user interface
	Feedback (FEEDBCK)	Feedback is used to inform the participants about their performance, while the test is in progress. We define feedback twofold: (1) Continuous feedback of measured performance throughout the experiment at given times and (2) a comparison of the participants performance to a peer group.	Text chat tool (every 25% completion) and indicating icon on user interface.

as constructs for analysis. The research presented here is part of a bigger study on social facilitation (Niehaves & Tavakoli 2012). While monitoring, i.e. presence of another (virtual) person, can be found in all identified related studies, measurement is specifically addressed within the research of Davidson and Henderson (2000). Feedback, on the other hand, relates to the feedback-loop model as proposed by Carver and Scheier (1981) and has been one aspect in the work of Rafaeli and Noy (2002). The dependent variable (performance) has been measured by calculating the median over the individual response times of each participant. Here, wrong answers have been replaced by a time of 99 seconds. Table 2 gives an overview of the variable definitions within this study.

Based on the described model, we derived three main hypotheses stating that all monitoring (H_1), measurement (H_2) and feedback dialogs (H_3) would have a significant positive impact on simple task performance. In our understanding all three treatments can be seen as instances of virtual presence. Fig. 1 shows a graphical representation of our research model.

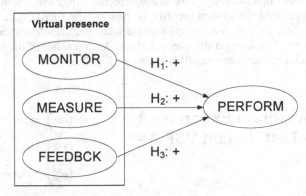

Fig. 1. Research Model

3.4   Methods and Results

Our study was conducted in 2011 with 40 individuals (average age: 22.75 years, 16 females, 24 males) who received a small monetary compensation for their effort. We measured the simple task performance using an IT-based anagram test thereby tying in with related studies on the subject (Aiello & Svec 1993; Davidson & Henderson 2000; S. Park & Catrambone 2007). Suitable anagrams (160 in total) were determined with help of a pre-study with 14 participants.

Table 3. Experiment design

Setting	Treatments			N	Task performance	
	MONITOR	MEASURE	FEEDBCK		Mean (in Seconds)	Standard Deviation
Control Situation	No	No: Participants unaware of measurement	No	40	6.535	2.810
Setting 1	Yes	No: Participants unaware of measurement	No	40	5.561	1.934
Setting 2	Yes	Yes	No	40	5.098	1.603
Setting 3	Yes	Yes	Yes	40	4.186	1.198

The experiment itself started with introducing the participant to the test tool and an initial solving of 20 anagrams for practicing purposes. Afterwards, four test variants were conducted, divided into two distinct settings: the control situation (CTRL) and the virtual presence setting. An overview of the four variants and their basic performance results is given in Table 3. Within virtual presence setting, monitoring (MONITOR) was implemented by means of screensharing, MEASURE through telling the participant that the system records the results, and FEEDBCK by using a text chat tool after each 25% of task completion. In addition, each treatment was communicated by means of an icon on the user interface. A screenshot of the implemented IT artifact (with all treatments activated) is shown in Fig. 2.

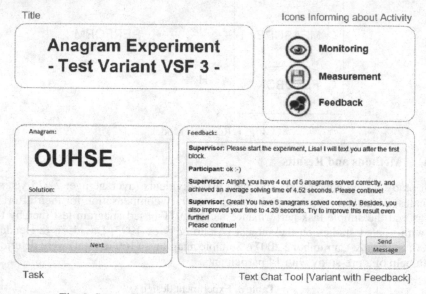

Fig. 2. Screenshot of the implemented IT artifact (translated)

In the virtual presence setting, the adjusted coefficient of determination, adjusted R^2, shows that around 12% of the variance can be explained with the three independent variables. MONITOR has the highest positive impact on task performance, followed by FEEDBCK. MEASURE shows the lowest impact on task performance and is not significant (see Table 4 for details).

Table 4. Results of the regression analysis (n=160)

F / Sig.	8.001 / .000			
R2 / adjusted R2	.133 / .117			
Var	*B*	*β*	*t*	p-value (sig.)
MONITOR	.975	.182	1.995	.048
MEASURE	.463	.100	.946	.345
FEEDBCK	.912	.170	1.865	.064

p-values below .1 can be considered as significant.

The regression formula thus looks as follows:

PERFORM = -3.858E-15 + 0.975 * MONITOR + 0.463 * MEASURE + 0.912 * FEEDBCK

As a result, hypothesis H2 cannot be confirmed as MEASURE has not proven to exert significant influence on performance. However, both MONITOR and FEEDBCK impact significantly on simple task performance in the virtual setting, thus, leading us to confirm hypotheses H1 and H3.

3.5   Discussion of Findings

We found that certain virtual social facilitation treatments are able to increase performance on simple IT-based tasks. On the one hand, our study revealed that monitoring by means of digital features may yield a positive effect on completion time. Screensharing, i.e. the way we implemented the construct, can be one possible way to stimulate the monitoring effect through IS design. However, we have to acknowledge that the implementation of such monitoring efforts outside an experimental setting may come along with certain barriers and negative connotations. Feedback dialogs, however, are usually not associated with these downsides, but also exerted a positive influence on task performance in our study. Thus, our design choice of a text chat tool may be a suitable addition to existing IT-based task systems. Against this background, the presented study can be understood as a step towards a design theory of virtual social facilitation trying not only to explain the relationship between the variables but also to provide guidance for the design of a specific IT artifact (Gregor 2006: theory type V; see also Kuechler & Vaishnavi 2008). By selecting screensharing as instantiation for monitoring and a text chat tool for feedback, we undertook two distinct design choices that turned out to positively impact performance of the investigated tasks. However, alternative design choices (for instance, audio-visual approaches to implement monitoring (by web cam) and feedback dialogs (by video chat)) may equally or even better stimulate relevant social facilitation effects and thus need to be subject to further investigation.

4   Conclusion

Implications for Design Theorizing. The current debate in design science has put great effort into discussing the relationship between kernel theories and design theory. It appears to be widely acknowledged today that theories not only input into design activities (for instance Hevner et al. 2004; Gregor & Jones 2007; Peffers et al. 2007; Iivari 2007), but that (design) theories are a highly desirable output of a design science project themselves (for instance, Gregor 2006, Gregor & Jones 2007, Pries-Heje & Baskerville 2008). In addition, literature provides arguments that design science projects should even feed back into the original body of social science theory (for instance, Kuechler & Vaishnavi 2008 on mid-range theories). Here, the IT artifact is commonly regarded as an instantiation of a design theory (Gregor & Jones 2007). With the help of an IT artifact, design scientists demonstrate the feasibility of their arguments and put their theories to a test. So far, however, the discussion in this area stays on a rather abstract and general level in the sense that, habitually, the relationship of the one entity "design theory" and the other entity "IT artifact" is discussed. With the further conceptualization of design theories as a system of prescriptive statements and the exploration of design theory variables on a more detailed level (for instance, Gregor & Jones 2007, Kuechler & Vaishnavi 2008), the question arises of what this more detailed and differentiated view of design theory implies for the theory-artifact relationship. Taking the example of Virtual Social Facilitation (VSF), we draw from social psychology and adapted social facilitation as our kernel theory. Our review of this body of knowledge shows a gap between the very rigorous approach to conceptualize theory variables (such as MONITOR, MEASURE, or FEEDBCK) on the one hand, and the rather "careless" approach to select or to develop actual implementations of these theory variables in terms of the IT artifact on the other hand. One might say that the literature in that field does not appear to show primary interest in the actual IT implementation of the basic theories. With the prominent calls, however, for building our design science efforts on kernel theories (for instance, Iivari 2007, Gregor & Jones 2007), we will possibly run into significant issues here. As design scientist, we may have a genuine interest in the way things are implemented in terms of the IT artifact. With the help of virtual social facilitation, we were able to demonstrate that the design theory variables and corresponding IT artifact characteristics are not equating with each other. For instance, we discussed alternative audio-visual approaches to implement monitoring (web cam instead of screensharing) and feedback dialogs (video chat instead of text chat). Why is it crucial then to differentiate between the abstract design theory variable and a concrete IT artifact characteristic?

1. The discrepancy between the theory construct (e.g., MONITOR) and the actual implementation (e.g., screensharing) is a potential source of error. Outer model discussions are an integral element of assessing the quality of, for example, a structural equation model (see, for instance, Wetzels et al. 2009; Venkatesh et al. 2003). The measurement items (manifest variables) do not necessary indicate the theory construct (latent variable) sufficiently. Also, actual IT implementation choices may not represent the best possible solution to relate to an abstract design theory variable. Comparing a) screensharing or b) audio-visual surveillance or c) both measures to implement MONITOR, we may argue that the three solutions could represent the theory construct to different degrees. That being said, we call for an explicit discussion of both the abstract design theory construct (normally strong in related disciplines & habitually weak in IS design research) and the concrete IT implementation (habitually weak in related disciplines and their potential "kernel theories" (see the example case of social facilitation) & often strong in IS design research). With an explicit discussion of the theory construct and the implementation, one can better assess the quality of a design theorizing effort. If

these two sides do not match perfectly in one study, this at least opens up for a more mature discussion of design alternatives.

2. An explicit distinction between the abstract theory constructs and the concrete IT implementation characteristics supports artifact and theory mutability (see Gregor & Jones 2007, Pries-Heje & Baskerville 2008). IT artifacts in practice might be subject to constant change (Gregor & Jones 2007) and the design theory should be robust against certain degrees of change. The suggested differentiation between theory constructs and IT implementations is supposed to offer a potentially feasible path. For instance, if an IT system in practice is moving from text chat to a video chat, one could still argue that the two alternative designs do relate to the design theory variable FEEDBCK. However, we can now explicitly discuss the potentially different effects and workings of the two implementation alternatives. This might lead to different variables of a design theory turning out to exert a stronger/weaker influence with different levels of significance. As for the given example of virtual social facilitation, video chats could prove to contribute stronger to creating a virtual presence of a person than text chats. Against this background, artifact mutability is desirable, but it requires an explicit and differentiated discussion in order to avoid potential design theorizing errors (see again point 1).

Addressing this gap, we argue for a novel design theory framework that explicates the discrepancy between abstract, latent design theory constructs on the one hand and concrete, manifest variables and IT implementations on the other hand. We suggest understanding a design theory as entity composed of two major elements, an inner model and an outer model. Fig. 3 provides a graphical model of the proposed design theorizing framework while Table 5 offers definitions and examples of the key terminology used.

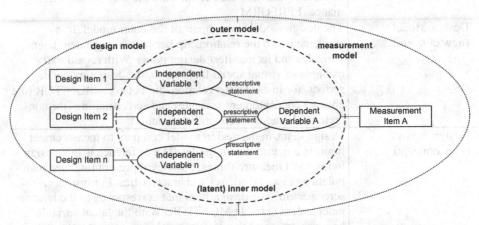

Fig. 3. Design Theory Framework (Example with One De-pendent and Three Independent Variables)

Table 5. Key Terminology of the Proposed Design Theory Framework (with Definitions and Examples)

Inner Model (see, for instance, Wetzels et al. 2009)	The inner model, often synonymously referred to as structural model, is concerned with the relationships between the latent variables (dependent and independent) in a theoretical model. Path coefficients are used to describe the inner model relationships between the latent variables. As for the example of virtual social facilitation, the inner model represents the relationship between the independent latent variables MONITOR (significant), MEASURE, and FEEDBCK (significant) and the dependent latent variable PERFORM.
Outer Model (see, for instance, Wetzels et al. 2009)	The outer model is concerned with the relationship between the latent variables and their indicators/items (one or more manifest variables). In our proposed design theory framework, the outer model consists of the two subparts measurement model and design model.
Measurement Model (see, for instance, Thompson et al. 2012)	The measurement model is a classic concept of structural equation modeling. In our design theory framework, a measurement model is a subpart of an outer model. Here, measurement items constitute manifest variables and they are utilized to measure a latent variable. As for the example of virtual social facilitation, the measurement model describes the relationship of the only "measured" variable, PERFORM, and its single measurement item.
Measurement Items (see, for instance, Thompson et al. 2012)	Measurement items are manifest variables that are utilized to get an understanding of a related latent variable. As for the example of virtual social facilitation, the (only) measurement item is the mean time to solve a series of 20 anagram puzzles in seconds which is used to indicate the participants' performance (PERFORM).
Design Model (new concept)	The design model is a subpart of the outer model. It is concerned with the relationship between independent latent variables and its manifest design items. With regard to the example of virtual social facilitation, the design model describes, for instance, the relationship between MONITOR (the abstract concept/latent variable) and screensharing (the concrete implementation/manifest variable).
Design Items (new concept)	Design items in the design model compare to measurement items in a measurement model. The difference is that design items don't measure things, but they represent intended manipulations of an IT artifact's characteristics. For instance, screensharing is a design item that corresponds to the latent independent variable MONITOR. With the latent variable being abstract and the design item being concrete, the two things are not equating with each other. As for the given example, MONITOR could be implemented by audio-visual surveillance or keyboard activity monitoring alternatively.

On the one hand, the inner model is concerned with the relationship between independent and dependent variables which we regard as latent ones. They are latent because they are not directly observed. As for the example of virtual social facilitation, the inner model describes the relationship between MONITOR, MEASURE, and FEEDBCK (independent) with PERFORM (dependent). On the other hand, the outer model is concerned with the relationship between the latent variables and other directly observable variables including IT implementation characteristics. In our proposed design theory framework, the outer model consists of two subparts: the measurement model and the design model. As in traditional research on structural equation modeling (SEM), the measurement model consists of a latent variable that is measured by manifest variables. Taking the example of virtual social facilitation, we find the dependent variable PERFORM the only one to be "measured", in this specific case by the mean time [in seconds] of the individual participants to solve a series of 20 anagram puzzles. In contrast, the design model is not concerned with latent variables that are "measured", but with latent variables that are "designed", meaning that they are related to an intended manipulation of an IT artifact's characteristics.

For instance, screensharing is a deliberate design choice embedded in an IT artifact and it corresponds to the latent independent variable MONITOR. While certain variables of a design theory are not passively measured but actively designed, we argue that a design theorizing framework has to provide a distinction in order to account for the different nature of the two areas.

Strengths and Limitations. With this paper, we can make several contributions to the body of knowledge, especially in IS design science. First, we develop an (experimentally tested) design theory for virtual social facilitation that is based on social psychology and social facilitation theory specifically. We deliver a concrete answer to the question of how an integration of social media and IT-based routine work can be designed in order to increase work performance. With the help of this exemplary case, we reveal challenges and potential pitfalls in IT artifact design and design theorizing that is built around kernel theories. We demonstrate that a missing distinction between the abstract design theory construct and the concrete IT artifact characteristic can be a source of error and that it can diminish the scientific rigor of a design science effort. We argue further that such a missing distinction leaves out potential for accounting for artifact mutability in design theorizing. In order to overcome this challenge, we propose a novel design theorizing framework takes into account latency of variables. In order to improve the applicability of our framework, we provide comprehensive definitions as well as examples of key terminology. However, our research is beset with particular limitations. We conducted only 160 experiments to test our VSF design theory and acknowledge that further evaluative research is recommendable. Future research should in fact test the effects of alternative design choices to implement the given theory constructs (e.g., video chat instead of text chat for FEEDBK). Moreover, we have analyzed studies from the field of social psychology to develop our theory. It might be that the design theorizing challenges, especially the underprioritized discussion of the actual IT implementation characteristics, is only found in this body of knowledge. Future research should investigate whether design theorizing challenges are alike in other areas. Finally, we acknowledge that our proposed design theory framework needs to be tested and evaluated further for feasibility. We have developed it on the basis of the given VSF example. Future research will need to show in how far the design theorizing framework is able to provide constructive guidance if applied in a design science project from the beginning on.

Acknowledgement. This paper was written in the context of the research project WeChange (promotional reference 01HH11059) which is funded by the German Federal Ministry of Education and Research (BMBF).

References

1. Aiello, J.R., Douthitt, E.A.: Social facilitation from Triplett to electronic performance monitoring. Group Dynamics: Theory, Research, and Practice 5(3), 163 (2001)
2. Aiello, J.R., Kolb, K.J.: Electronic performance monitoring and social context: impact on productivity and stress. The Journal of applied psychology 80(3), 339–353 (1995)
3. Aiello, J.R., Svec, C.M.: Computer Monitoring of Work Performance: Extending the Social Facilitation Framework to Electronic Presence. Journal of Applied Social Psychology 23(7), 537–548 (1993)
4. Allport, F.H.: Response to social stimulation in the group. In: Allport, F.H. (ed.) Social Psychology, pp. 260–291. Erlbaum, Hillsdale (1924)
5. Bala, H., Venkatesh, V.: Assimilation of Interorganizational Business Process Standards. Information Systems Research 18(3), 340–362 (2007)
6. Benbasat, I., Zmud, R.W.: The identity crisis within the IS discipline: Defining and communicating the discipline's core properties. MIS Quarterly 27(2), 183–194 (2003)
7. Bond, C.F., Titus, L.J.: Social facilitation: A meta-analysis of 241 studies. Psychological Bulletin 94(2), 265 (1983)
8. Broadbent, M., Weill, P., Clair, D.: The implications of information technology infrastructure for business process redesign. MIS Quarterly 23(2), 159–182 (1999)
9. Carlsson, S.A.: Design science research in information systems: A critical realist approach. Design Research in Information Systems (2010)
10. Carroll, J.M., Kellogg, W.A.: Artifact as Theory-Nexus: Hermeneutics Meets Theory-Based Design. In: Proceedings of the SIGCHI Conference on Human Factors in Computing Systems, pp. 7–14 (1989)
11. Carver, C.S., Scheier, M.F.: The self-attention-induced feedback loop and social facilitation. Journal of Experimental Social Psychology 17, 545–568 (1981)
12. Cottrell, N.B.: Performance in the presence of other human beings: Mere presence, audience, and affiliation effects. In: Simmel, E.C., Hoppe, R.A., Milton, G.A. (eds.) Social Facilitation and Imitative Behavior, pp. 91–110. Allyn and Bacon, Boston (1986)
13. Dashiell, J.F.: Experimental studies of the influence of social situations on the behavior of individual human adult. In: Murchison, C. (ed.) A Handbook of Social Psychology, pp. 1097–1158. Clark University Press, Worcester (1935)
14. Davidson, R., Henderson, R.: Electronic Performance Monitoring: A Laboratory Investigation of the Influence of Monitoring and Difficulty on Task Performance, Mood State, and Self-Reported Stress Levels. Journal of Applied Social Psychology 30(5), 906–920 (2000)
15. Feinberg, J.M., Aiello, J.R.: Social Facilitation: A Test of Competing Theories. Journal of Applied Social Psychology 36(5), 1087–1109 (2006)
16. George, J.: Computer-based monitoring: Common perceptions and empirical results. MIS Quarterly 20(4), 459–480 (1996)

17. Gregor, S.: The Nature of Theory in Information Systems. MIS Quarterly 30(3), 611–642 (2006)
18. Gregor, S., Jones, D.: The Anatomy of a Design Theory. Journals of the Association for Information Systems 8(5), 312–335 (2007)
19. Hardless, C., Lindgren, R., Schultze, U.: Technology-Mediated Learning Systems For Project Work A Design Theory. Scandinavian Journal of Information Systems 19(2), 3–36 (2007)
20. Hevner, A.R., et al.: Design science in information systems research. MIS Quarterly 28(1), 75–105 (2004)
21. Hirschheim, R.A., Klein, H.K.: Crisis in the IS Field? A Critical Reflection on the State of the Discipline. Journal of the Association for Information Systems 4(5), 71–146 (2003)
22. Hoyt, C.L., Blascovich, J., Swinth, K.R.: Social inhibition in immersive virtual environments. Presence: Teleoperators & Virtual Environments 12(2), 183–195 (2003)
23. Iivari, J.: A paradigmatic analysis of information systems as a design science. Scandinavian Journal of Information Systems 19(2), 39 (2007)
24. Kaplan, A.M., Haenlein, M.: Users of the world, unite! The challenges and opportunities of Social Media. Business Horizons 53(1), 59–68 (2010)
25. Kolb, K.J., Aiello, J.R.: Computer-based performance monitoring and productivity in a multiple task environment. Journal of Business and Psychology 12(2), 189–204 (1997)
26. Kuechler, B., Vaishnavi, V.: On theory development in design science research: anatomy of a research project. European Journal of Information Systems 17(5), 489–504 (2008)
27. Levina, N., Vaast, E.: The emergence of boundary spanning competence in practice: implications for implementation and use of information systems. MIS Quarterly 29(2), 335–363 (2005)
28. March, S.T., Smith, G.F.: Design and natural science research on information technology. Decision Support Systems 15(4), 251–266 (1995)
29. Markus, M.L., Majchrzak, A., Gasser, L.: A design theory for systems that support emergent knowledge processes. MIS Quarterly 26(3), 179–212 (2002)
30. McKay, J., Marshall, P.: A review of design science in information systems. In: Proceedings of the 16th Austalasian Conference on Information Systems Science, Sydney (2005)
31. Moore, G.: Systems of Engagement and The Future of Enterprise IT - A sea change in enterprise IT (2011)
32. Niehaves, B., Tavakoli, A.: When Routine Work Becomes Social: How Virtual Social Facilitation Increases Performance on Simple IT-Based Tasks (unpublished manuscript, 2012)
33. Park, S., Catrambone, R.: Social Facilitation Effects of Virtual Humans. Human Factors: The Journal of the Human Factors and Ergonomics Society 49(6), 1054–1060 (2007)
34. Peffers, K., et al.: A design science research methodology for information systems research. Journal of Management Information Systems 24(3), 45–77 (2008)
35. Pries-Heje, J., Baskerville, R.: The design theory nexus. MIS Quarterly 32(4), 731–755 (2008)
36. Rafaeli, S., Noy, A.: Online auctions, messaging, communication and social facilitation: a simulation and experimental evidence. European Journal of Information Systems 11(3), 196–207 (2002)
37. Simon, H.: The Sciences of the Artificial. MIT Press, Cambridge (1969,1981)
38. Thompson, R.L., Higgins, C.A., Howell, J.M.: Personal Computing: Toward a Conceptual Model of Utilization. Management Information Systems 15(1), 125–143 (2012)
39. Triplett, N.: The dynamogenic factors in pacemaking and competition. The American Journal of Psychology 9(4), 507–533 (1898)

40. U.S. Congress, The electronic supervisor: New technology, new tensions Office of Technology Assessment, ed. U.S. Government Printing Office, Washington, D.C. (1987)
41. Venkatesh, V., et al.: User Acceptance of Information Technology: Toward a Unified View. MIS Quarterly 27(3), 425–478 (2003)
42. Walls, J.G., Widmeyer, G.R., El Sawy, O.A.: Building an information system design theory for vigilant EIS. Information Systems Research 3(1), 36–59 (1992)
43. Wetzels, M., Odekerken-Schröder, G., Van Oppen, C.: Using PLS path modeling for assessing hierarchical construct models: Guidelines and empirical illustration. MIS Quarterly 33(1), 177–195 (2009)
44. Zajonc, R.B.: Social facilitation. Science 149(3681), 269–274 (1965)
45. Zanbaka, C., Ulinski, A.: Effects of virtual human presence on task performance. In: Proceedings of tthe 14th International Conference on Artificial Reality and Telexistence, Seoul (2004)

Towards a Formal Approach to Information Systems Design Theory Using Category Theory

George R. Widmeyer

Durango, Colorado, USA
george.widmeyer@gmail.com

Abstract. This paper reports research in progress for the formalization of the notion of information systems design theory within the framework of formal logic and category theory. The formalization starts with the concept of four relational systems (empirical, subjective, conceptual and formal) that are linked by the four activities for design science research proposed by Venable (2006). Category theory is used as the basis of representing the concept of an information systems design theory as a formal framework by representing each of the four relational systems as either types (theories) or tokens (models). The arrows (morphisms) between the four concepts are explained using Barwise and Seligman's (1997) definition of "infomorphisms". The contributions of this research are that it explicates the role of kernel theory (background theory) in information systems design theory and it links this design theory to information fusion and information flow research efforts. It thus provides structures that represent a formalization of the design of information systems.

Keywords: Design Theory, Representations for Design, Category Theory.

1 Introduction

An early activity in structured information systems design is some form of problem diagnosis or requirements specification; generally, this information is developed from discussions with affected users, customers or clients of various types. Information systems design theory efforts include the identification of a domain kernel theory as part of the problem diagnosis (Walls, Widmeyer and El Sawy 1992). A key purpose of the research in progress reported in this paper is to explicate the role of this background information in the construction of formal conceptual models used in the development of information systems. We do this in terms of (1) goal theories, (2) information theories and (3) kernel theories.

A second goal of this research in progress is to formalize the structures that represent the meaning of information in information systems design as either types (theories) or tokens (models). This effort draws upon category theory, which is a relatively young branch of pure mathematics (Pierce 1991). It might seem esoteric but category theory has been used in computer science in the design of programming languages and in the formal verification of program correctness (examples are given in Chapter 3 of Pierce 1991).

K. Peffers, M. Rothenberger, and B. Kuechler (Eds.): DESRIST 2012, LNCS 7286, pp. 371–380, 2012.
© Springer-Verlag Berlin Heidelberg 2012

The contribution of this research is the attempt to show how formal methods like category theory ought to be applied at the system level to such elements as mental models, which are not inherently mathematical in nature. Category theory has been used at the program level to generate software (Williamson, Healy and Barker 2001), but this research proposes using similar methods in the design specification phase of systems development. The intent is to provide a formal method for describing design theories and to provide some analytical tools for working with that formalism. The concepts of classification and infomorphism are key to this effort.

The next section of this paper presents four information structures linked by the four activities for design science research proposed by Venable (2006). Section three provides a description of category theory and information flow theory that is a sufficient introduction for the general reader. Section four presents an example formalization of information systems design theory using Barwise and Seligman's (1997) definition of "infomorphisms". The final section reflects on the role of background theory in information systems design, the contribution of a formal theory of design, and future research.

2   Four Relational Systems

This section presents four relational systems (empirical, subjective, conceptual and formal) that are linked by the four activities for design science research proposed by Venable (2006). We claim that information systems designers must understand the structures of each of these four and, in fact, work within each one as they develop the specification for an information system.

Figure 1 shows the four relational systems, which are motivated by a paper from Turoff (1997) where he identifies four components and human processes between pairs of the components. His purpose is to compare how the processes changed from a pre-computer understanding of the world to post-computer virtuality processes. Our research uses the concept of his components but replaces the processes with the four activities for design science research proposed by Venable (2006), which are shown on the arrows in Figure 1. We also think of these components in terms of four "worlds" as opposed to the three worlds of Popper or Habermas. Gregor and Jones (2007, page 321) identified the three worlds as the objective world of material things (empirical), the subjective world of mental states (subjective), and an objectively existing but abstract world of man-made entities (conceptual). To these three we add a fourth world of the artificial that runs in a computer or virtual environment (formal).

We think of the two worlds on the left side of Figure 1 as representing the requirements for an information system. It is important that the system designer understands the entities that exist in the objective world and the processes between these entities that need to be represented in the information system. The two worlds on the right side of Figure 1 represent the design of the information system. The concept of requirements and design are important in an information systems design theory and this distinction is captured in our proposed formalization based on category theory, which is presented in Section 4 of the paper in the discussion of Figure 3.

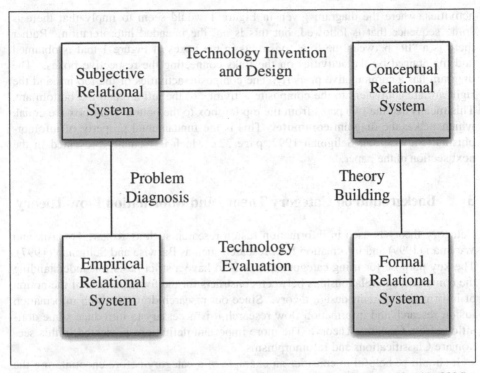

Fig. 1. Four Relational Systems and Four Activities Between Them (based on Venable 2006)

The meaning of our four constructs is given in Table 1.

Table 1. Description of the Four Relational Systems (based on Turoff 1997, page 39)

Empirical Relational System [Objective Reality]	A representation of the entities and relations that exist in the objective world.
Subjective Relational Systems [Mental Models]	An individual's internal representation of an understanding of the external world.
Conceptual Relational System [Metaphors and Theories]	The abstractions and analogies guiding our formation of understandings and design of models and representations.
Formal Relational Systems [Models and Representations]	Explicit and formal descriptions or simulations that can be mutually understood and shared by knowledgeable individuals.

The mappings between the four constructs are taken from Venable (2006) and their meaning should be clear to the reader since they are intended to be exactly what the words say. Venable (2006) states that one moves back and forth between the four activities, where the diagram given in Figure 1 would seem to imply that there is some sequence that is followed, but this is not the intended interpretation. Rather there is a "fit" between the four constructs in the boxes of Figure 1 that is obtained and maintained by the activities on the links connecting the respective boxes. The diagram has a commutative property. The composite activities of the top arc and the right arc are equivalent to the composite activities of the left arc and the bottom arc. This means that the two paths from the top left box to the bottom right box are equal, which makes the diagram **commute**. This is the fundamental property of infomorphisms (Barwise and Seligman 1997, page 32), which is formally presented in the next section of the paper.

3   Background on Category Theory and Information Flow Theory

Category theory is used in information fusion research such as Kokar, Tomasik and Weyman (1999) and information flow research such as Barwise and Seligman (1997). The key purpose for using category theory is to have a strict basis for understanding the constructs and relationships between constructs for the formalization of the notion of information systems design theory. Since our research draws on both information fusion research and information flow research it is necessary to introduce some definitions from Category Theory. The more important definitions presented in this section are Classifications and Infomorphisms.

It should be helpful to consider an example of a category before encountering the definition. The category of finite sets (SET) has as an Object a finite set or collection, for example, the set of all participants in a conference. A map f in this category consists of three things: (1) a set A, called the domain of the map, (2) a set B, called the codomain of the map, and (3) a rule assigning to each element a in the domain exactly one element b in the codomain. This b is denoted by $f(a)$; another way of denoting this is $f: A \to B$. Other words for map are function, transformation, operator, arrow or morphism (Lawvere and Schanuel 1997). Category theory is a generalization of similar concepts from mathematical structures such as sets, groups, algebras, vector spaces and topological spaces (Pierce 1991). The following definition is based on Pierce (1991, page 1) and Lawvere and Schanuel (1997, page 21).

Definition 1. A **category** is a mathematical structure consisting of:

1. A collection of **objects** (e.g., A, B)
2. A collection of **arrows** often called **morphisms** (e.g., f, g)
3. Operations assigning to each arrow f an object called the **domain** (e.g., A) and a second called the **codomain** (e.g., B), [which can be written $f: A \to B$]
4. For each pair of arrows $f: A \to B$ and $g: B \to C$ there is a **composite** arrow with domain A and codomain C denote as $g \circ f: A \to C$ satisfying associativity
5. For each object A there is an **identity** arrow that has domain A and codomain A denoted as I_A satisfying the identity law such that for any arrow $f: A \to B$, $I_B \circ f = f$ and $f \circ I_A = f$

A diagram in a category is a collection of objects and a collection of arrows between these objects (Pierce 1991, page 11). An important diagram from information flow research is that of an infomorphism that is built from classifications. The following definition is based on Barwise and Seligman (1997, page 69).

Definition 2. A **classification** A = <tok(A), type (A), $\models_A$> consists of:

1. A set, tok(A), of objects to be classified, called the **tokens** of A
2. A set, typ(A), of objects used to classify the tokens, called the **types** of A
3. A binary relation, $\models_A$, between tok(A) and typ(A)

If $a \models_A \alpha$, then a is said to be *of type α in A*. Figure 2 shows two classifications, these are A and B.

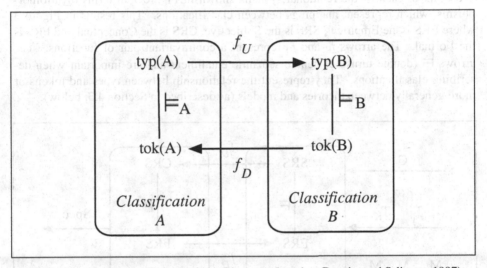

Fig. 2. Classification and Infomorphism Diagrams (based on Barwise and Seligman 1997)

Now that the definition of classification has been introduced then we can define an infomorphism. "Infomorphisms are important relationships between classifications A and B and provide a way of moving information back and forth between them. The classifications can be of the same objects or they can be of different objects" (Barwise and Seligman 1997, page 72). The fundamental property of infomorphisms is that the diagram commutes. The following definition is from Barwise and Seligman (1997, page 72). [Note: read f_U as "f-up" and f_D as "f-down"]

Definition 3: An **infomorphism** $f: A \leftrightarrows B$ from A to B is a contravariant pair of functions f = <f_U, f_D> satisfying the following Fundamental Property of Infomorphisms:

$$f_D(b) \models_A \alpha \text{ iff } b \models_B f_U(\alpha)$$

for each token $b \in$ tok(B) and each type $\alpha \in$ typ(A).

An infomorphism consists of two things: a pair of classifications (A, B) and a contravariant pair of functions between A and B satisfying the above condition. Note that the arrows f_U and f_D go in opposite direction; this is the contravariant property. Classification *diagrams* are used to depict infomorphisms as shown in Figure 2.

4   Formalization of Information Systems Design Theory

The section describes the construction of an information systems design theory, sketches an example application area, and amplifies on the goals of this research.

4.1   Construction

We think of each of the relational systems shown in Figure 1 in terms of infomorphisms, which represent mappings between classifications. This results in Figure 3 where ERS is the Empirical, SRS is the Subjective, CRS is the Conceptual and FRS is the Formal. The arrows f_U and f_D represent a contravariant pair of functions. The arrows $\models$ (double turnstile) denote semantic entailment and are important when describing classifications. They represent the relationship between types and tokens or more generally between theories and models (as described in Section 4.3, below).

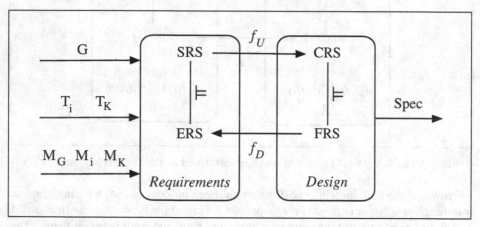

Fig. 3. Information Fusion (informed by Kokar, Tomasik and Weyman 1999)

The additional arrows at the left in Figure 3 represent inputs to the information fusion process of an information systems design theory. The research of Kokar, et al. (1999) describes the problem domain of that research as information fusion or more particularly sensor fusion, what we in the information systems field would call a data fusion problem. They use category theory to formalize the fusion of data from physical sensors to identify the type of sensed object. The result is an algorithm and computer program for identifying the properties of physical objects. Our research builds on the distinction of knowledge of sensors used, knowledge of the goal for a fusion system, and background knowledge. Their data fusion problem becomes our information fusion problem.

The G, T's and M's in Figure 1 are parts of an information systems design theory. The G stands for Goals. These are queries about the world that are to be answered by the information system. The symbols T_i and T_K stand for information theories and kernel theories, respectively. They represent the knowledge used in interpreting events observed in the empirical world and background knowledge about the world such as constraints on what can and cannot happen in the empirical world. An example of a constraint could be that if event X has happened then event Y cannot have happened since they are mutually exclusive. T_K is the kernel theory (Walls, et al. 1992) of an information systems design theory. The three M's with subscripts are models associated with the three corresponding theories. The Spec arrow at the right of Figure 3 represents a formal, executable specification of an information system. It is an instance of the design theory; it is an Expository Instantiation – a component of an information systems design theory (see Gregor and Jones 2007).

The theories and models on the Requirements side of the Information Fusion diagram (Figure 3) must be fused into a single set of types and tokens on the Design side of the diagram. This is where category theory provides the rigor for a formalization of design theory. The construction required is that of Colimit and Limit. The Colimit operation (the f_U arrow in Figure 3) is syntactic theory construction and the Limit operation (the f_D arrow in Figure 3) is semantic model construction (Kokar, et al. 1999). A special case of the (co)limit construction is used to combine or "add" classifications by taking the Cartesian product of tokens and the disjoint union of types (Barwise and Seligman 1997, pages 33 and 81). The (co)limit operation combines the goal, information and kernel theories along the common parts. It is the shared union of theories that we need for an information systems design theory.

4.2   Example

Consider the illustrative example of the event management process in ITIL (IT Infrastructure Library). Events in a computer system are detected and classified as Informative, Alert (a process has reached a threshold and action must be taken to prevent an exception) or Exception (van Bon 2007). These are the subjective *types* of events. A signal is the *token* transmitted by the system and must be classified. The theory for processing these signals is part of the T_i information theory. The kernel theory T_K has to include logical axioms that express specific background knowledge such that if a signal is classified as type Alert then it cannot be classified as Informative or Exception. The models in this case can be based in Boolean Logic. This means that the kernel theory T_K needs to have general knowledge of Boolean Logic such as operators AND and OR. These theories and models are the Meta-Requirements for an information systems design theory.

4.3   Research Goals

Our formalization of information systems design theory has the proposed structure and properties since we base this formalization in category theory in general and information flow research in particular.

There is more structure in each relational system shown in Figure 3 than just types and tokens. There are also logical relationships between types, which is called a "regular theory" (Barwise and Seligman 1997, Chapter 9). For example, the SRS in Figure 3 represents a Subjective Relational System or Mental Model. The SRS includes types (i.e., typ(A) in Definition 2) and constraints. A regular theory generated by a classification includes the types and logical relationships between them built using standard propositional logic. The combination of a classification with a regular theory and tokens that satisfy domain constraints is a "local logic" (Barwise and Seligman 1997, Definition 12.1). A local logic satisfies the Fundamental Property of Infomorphisms stated in Definition 3; in which case, the arrow f_U in Figure 3 is then a theory interpretation (Barwise and Seligman 1997, Definition 12.6). These concepts provide a start on achieving the second goal of this research, which is to formalize information systems design theory based on category theory. The key challenge of the current research in progress is to apply the concepts of classifications and infomorphism to treat the SRS, ERS, CRS and FRS in Figure 3 as theories and models. This has yet to be completed.

The first goal of this research is to explicate the role of background information in information systems design theory (ISDT). Walls, et al. (1992) introduced the term "kernel theory" as a starting point for ISDT. Kernel theories come from the behavioral and natural sciences and give necessary and sufficient conditions for the cause and effect relationships of technology with consequences (Gregor and Jones 2007). This research proposes to separately identify goal theories and information theories from kernel theories. Goal theories are the formal representation of the inquiries that are addressed by an information system. Information theories are formal representations of the properties of the information sources and how to process information from these sources. They can address the situation where an information source is noisy or unreliable. This final type of knowledge is what can be called the kernel theory (Walls, et al. 1992); this knowledge provides the way to reason with the information – what Barwise and Seligman (1999, page 22) refer to as providing "inferential information content." Think of this as being able to respond to queries about the world that cannot be answered in general by using any one information source. These kernel theories are domain dependent.

Walls, et al. (1992) also meant kernel theories to be the basis (the kernel) of an information systems design process in addition to the product design. This research does not address this other usage of kernel theory. We propose the distinction between (1) goal theories, (2) information theories and (3) kernel theories as an important addition in ISDT.

5   Conclusion

This paper reports research in progress for the formalization of the notion of information systems design theory within the framework of formal logic and category theory. This final section summarizes our position on the characteristics of background theory in information systems design, describes the contribution of a formalization of information systems design theory, and suggests future research areas.

The first goal of this research is to explicate the role of background information in the construction of formal conceptual models used in the development of information systems. The requirements for an information system come from various sources. There is specific domain information that must be represented in the system. There are specific goals that represent queries that can be answered by the system. Finally, there is background information about generally accepted practices and processes that must be faithfully represented by the information processing functions of the system. We adopt the distinction between (1) goal theories, (2) information theories and (3) kernel theories as a new basis for information systems design theory.

A second goal of this research is to create a framework in which the requirement of consistency of representation (in terms of types and tokens, theories and models) is formally and explicitly specified. This research proposes to show how this can be achieved by building on category theory for information systems design theory. The framework builds upon the prior research of Walls, et al. (1992), Venable (2006) and Gregor and Jones (2007) in the IS design research area. It specifically proposes the concept of four relational systems (empirical, subjective, conceptual and formal) that are linked by the four activities for design science research proposed by Venable (2006) as depicted in Figure 1 and Table 1. The concepts of classification and info-morphism from information flow research are key to this effort. Whereas, both information fusion research (Kokar, et al. 1999) and information flow research (Barwise and Seligman 1997) are at the sensor and signal level, our research is aimed at the systems level shown in Figure 1. This should be a significant contribution of this research.

The next step of this research is to explicitly show how the Colimit and Limit constructions described in Section 4 actually function in moving from requirements to design. Another next step is to expand the ITIL Event Process example (based on van Bon 2007, pages 273 – 277) and go even further by considering the ITIL Incident Management and Problem Management processes since these are well documented in ITIL publications. This can provide an evaluation as suggested by Venable (2006) of the designed artifact shown in Figure 3. A second extension is to apply the formalization to other design science research efforts such as Explanatory Design Theory (Baskerville and Pries-Heje 2010), which also focuses on the requirements and design parts of information systems design theory.

References

1. Barwise, J., Seligman, J.: Information Flow – The Logic of Distributed Systems. Cambridge University Press, Cambridge (1997)
2. Baskerville, R., Pries-Heje, J.: Explanatory Design Theory. Business & Information Systems Engineering 2(5), 271–282 (2010)
3. Gregor, S., Jones, D.: The Anatomy of a Design Theory. Journal of the Association for Information Systems 8(5), Article 19 (2007)
4. Kokar, M.M., Tomasik, J.A., Weyman, J.: A Formal Approach to Information Fusion. In: Proceedings of the 2nd International Conference on Information Fusion, pp. 133 140 (1999)

5. Lawvere, F.W., Schanuel, S.H.: Conceptual Mathematics: A First Introduction to Categories. Cambridge University Press, Cambridge (1997)
6. Pierce, B.C.: Basic Category Theory for Computer Scientists. The MIT Press, Cambridge (1991)
7. Turoff, M.: Virtuality. Communications of the ACM 40(9), 38–43 (1997)
8. van Bon, J.: Foundations of ITIL V3. Van Haren Publishing, Zaltbommel (2007); ITIL stands for IT Infrastructure Library. ITIL is a major resource for IT Service Management concepts and approaches
9. Venable, J.R.: A Framework for Design Science Research Activities. In: Khosrow-Pour, M. (ed.) Proceedings of the 2006 Information Resource Management Association Conference, Washington, DC, USA, May 24-26 (2006)
10. Walls, J.G., Widmeyer, G.R., El Sawy, O.A.: Building An Information System Design Theory For Vigilant EIS. Information Systems Research 3(1), 36–59 (1992)
11. Williams, K., Healy, M., Barker, R.: Industrial Applications of Software Synthesis via Category Theory—Case Studies Using Specware. Automated Software Engineering 8(1), 7–30 (2001)

Evaluations in the Science of the Artificial

–

Reconsidering the Build-Evaluate Pattern in Design Science Research

Christian Sonnenberg and Jan vom Brocke

University of Liechtenstein, Fuerst-Franz-Josef-Strasse 21,
9490 Vaduz, Principality of Liechtenstein
{christian.sonnenberg,jan.vom.brocke}@uni.li

Abstract. The central outcome of design science research (DSR) is prescriptive knowledge in the form of IT artifacts and recommendations. However, prescriptive knowledge is considered to have no truth value in itself. Given this assumption, the validity of DSR outcomes can only be assessed by means of descriptive knowledge to be obtained at the conclusion of a DSR process. This is reflected in the build-evaluate pattern of current DSR methodologies. Recognizing the emergent nature of IT artifacts this build-evaluate pattern, however, poses unfavorable implications regarding the achievement of rigor within a DSR project. While it is vital in DSR to prove the usefulness of an artifact a rigorous DSR process also requires justifying and validating the artifact design itself even before it has been put into use. This paper proposes three principles for evaluating DSR artifacts which not only address the evaluation of an artifact's usefulness but also the evaluation of design decisions made to build an artifact. In particular, it is argued that by following these principles the prescriptive knowledge produced in DSR can be considered to have a truth-like value.

Keywords: Design science research, evaluation, design theory, epistemology.

1 Introduction

Design science research (DSR) in information systems comprises of two primary activities: build and evaluate [1]. Although the evaluation of DSR artifacts as well as of design processes is regarded as being "crucial" [2, p. 82] much of the contemporary information system DSR work focuses on the build activity and the creation of prescriptive knowledge in the form of IT artifacts [3]. This is consistent with the view that prescriptive knowledge is the basic outcome of DSR (cf. [4], [5]). However, the prescriptive knowledge created during the build activity is assumed to have no truth-like value [5] which basically questions if such knowledge is worth to be accumulated. Moreover, if prescriptive knowledge cannot be validated until it is applied in practice a design science researcher runs the risk of devoting a significant amount of time to building insignificant solutions to practical problems.

K. Peffers, M. Rothenberger, and B. Kuechler (Eds.): DESRIST 2012, LNCS 7286, pp. 381–397, 2012.
© Springer-Verlag Berlin Heidelberg 2012

This paper suggests, however, that prescriptive knowledge can have a truth-like value if DSR is conducted according to three principles. These principles relate to the problem of evaluation of DSR artifacts and spur reconsideration of the build-evaluate pattern incorporated in many current DSR methodologies. These principles are derived from the work on modes of DSR inquiries [4], on design theories [6], and on evaluation patterns for DSR artifacts [7]. The paper aims at contributing to the body of knowledge on DSR methodologies in that it tries to clarify some epistemological implications of current DSR practices. Moreover, it links existing but still not integrated and isolated contributions regarding evaluation and theorizing in DSR with the purpose of providing guidance for design science researchers to rigorously produce valid DSR artifacts.

The paper proceeds as follows. After discussing knowledge types involved in DSR as well as current DSR practices the paper points to important epistemological implications of these practices. The paper then proposes and discusses three principles to circumvent the implications of current DSR practices. The paper concludes with a summary and an outlook on future research.

2   Knowledge Types in DSR and Their Truth Values

IIVARI [5] made the point that design science research in IS, just like research in economics, is basically conducted at three levels of research: (1) a conceptual level, (2) a descriptive level, and (3) a prescriptive level. Research on each level creates different types of knowledge having different truth values. Conceptual knowledge captures "what things are out there" [5] in terms of concepts, constructs, conceptual frameworks, classifications, taxonomies, or typologies. Conceptual knowledge forms the foundations upon which both descriptive as well as prescriptive research build. Descriptive research is concerned with describing, understanding, and explaining 'how things are out there' [5] and produces descriptive knowledge in the form of observations, empirical regularities, theories, and hypotheses [5]. Prescriptive research yields prescriptive knowledge in the form of IT artifacts (design product knowledge) and recommendations for practice (design process knowledge) [5]. Prescriptive research is interested in answering 'how one can effectively achieve specified ends' [5].

Among the three knowledge types DSR activities predominantly focus on the creation of prescriptive knowledge (cf. [2], [4], [5]). More particular, DSR essentially aims at building artifacts that have utility for practice [2]. Statements of truth in DSR therefore relate to the fact that an artifact is actually useful or not for solving a given class of practical problems. IIVARI [5] emphasizes that prescriptive knowledge has no truth or truth-like value. Ultimately, an artifact or recommendation as prescriptive knowledge has to prove its utility in practice. This evidence, however, materializes in descriptive knowledge about an artifact. According to IIVARI [5], only descriptive knowledge, i.e. observations, empirical regularities, and theories have a truth value.

As a consequence evaluations in DSR are located at the descriptive research level and are considered to not differ much from evaluations conducted in other sciences like the natural or human sciences (cf. [2], [5], [8]). However, the science of the artificial is different to other sciences in that it deals with analyzing phenomena (artifacts) that usually have not been existent at the beginning of scientific inquiry [4]. Thus, it can be challenged if evaluations in DSR should be conducted in a similar way as in the natural or human sciences. The following sections briefly outline how evaluation is considered in current DSR practices and subsequently discusses the implication of these practices with regard to achieving 'true' knowledge in DSR.

3   The Build-Evaluate Pattern in DSR

Although suggesting that prescriptive knowledge as the central result of DSR has no truth value, IIVARI [5] also emphasizes that prescriptive knowledge "forms an area of its own and cannot be reduced to the descriptive knowledge of theories and empirical regularities" [5, p. 56]. According to his understanding, DSR is concerned with creating prescriptive knowledge that is assumed to have no truth-like value and with gathering evidence through descriptive research that an artifact proves to be useful. Current DSR methodologies reflect this sequencing of prescriptive and descriptive research. In DSR terms, design science researchers conduct two high level activities: build and evaluate [1], [3]. A prominent example of such a DSR process is provided by PEFFERS ET AL. [9]. Their DSR methodology has been synthesized from prior DSR process proposed in the literature and is depicted in Fig. 1.

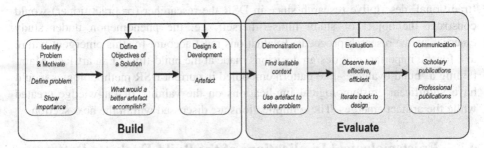

Fig. 1. Build-Evaluate in a representative DSR methodology (cf. [9])

What can be seen from Fig. 1 and what is also a typical assumption of other DSR processes is that evaluation activities and thus the articulation of truth statements about an artifact occur ex post, i.e. after an artifact has been constructed [3]. Truth about an artifact according to the build-evaluate pattern is known not until the evaluate phase which creates descriptive knowledge about an artifact. This applies also for DSR methodologies envisioning a concurrent or interweaved building and evaluation, like for example in Action Design Research (ADR) as proposed in [10].

Although ADR evaluation cycles appear to be much shorter when compared to a DSR process according to Fig. 1 evaluations still occur ex post, i.e. after an artifact has been constructed or revised. Thus, a validation of design decisions and the design principles incorporated by an artifact already in the design and construction phase is not a central theme in DSR evaluations. Evaluations rather focus on proving the usefulness of an artifact and less on the artifact design itself, i.e. on an artifact's rationale and specifications that are a constituent part of the prescriptive knowledge created in DSR.

In this regard it is interesting to note, however, that existing DSR methodologies emphasize the build activities, i.e. the actual artifact design, over evaluation activities [10]. This is consistent with what can also be observed in actual DSR projects. Much time is spent on designing and building an artifact, like for example when building new software systems or (re-) designing business process models. Given the significant amount of time on building an artifact and provided that the magnitude of a design decision's impact on the applicability and usefulness of an artifact is significantly higher at design-time than at run-time, i.e. when the artifact is actually constructed and instantiated (cf. [11]) it is less satisfying for a design science researcher to assume that the prescriptive knowledge holds no truth value.

It is the claim of this paper, however, that the evaluation of DSR artifacts should be approached differently compared to the study and evaluation of phenomena in the natural or human sciences. This difference emerges directly from the scope and interest of DSR which is not to explain or predict how the world is (through observations, theories, etc.) but to shape the world by means of artifacts [5]. Moreover, as GREGOR [4] points out, the truth value of DSR knowledge cannot be evaluated in terms of 'traditional' descriptive research since in DSR the researcher (or practitioner) would construct the object of study himself/herself, i.e. the phenomenon under study emerges as the research proceeds. Evaluations must account for this emergent nature and for the importance of design decisions made at the build-time of an artifact. Maintaining a 'build-evaluate'-like pattern embodied in current DSR methodologies would have significant epistemological implications on the validity of knowledge created while the artifact emerges. These implications are discussed within the next section.

4   Epistemological Implications of the Build-Evaluate Pattern

From a descriptive research point of view an artifact is considered to be true if some theory, observation, or empirical regularity exists that tells 'how an IT artifact actually behaves', 'why an IT artifact exists in the world', 'how an IT artifact actually relates to other things in the world' or 'if an artifact proved to be useful' (cf. [2], [5]). However, statements of truth in DSR do not primarily relate to 'what is' and 'how things are' but to 'what could and what should be' [5] and 'how useful things are expected to be'. This is consistent with the view of SIMON [8] who suggests that the sciences of the artificial "*are concerned not with the necessary but with the contingent*

– not with how things are but with how they might be – in short, with design" [8, p. xii]. In this regard, GREGOR [4] argues that the study of IT artifacts by means of traditional descriptive research has to be reconsidered both in the building and the observation of IT artifacts in order to accommodate the particularities of the science of the artificial [5]. Notably, the sequencing of build and evaluate activities hardly accounts for the emergent nature of IT artifacts [10].

If DSR evaluations would be limited to descriptive knowledge it would only be possible to infer ex post if an artifact proved to be useful and why it did so. However, DSR requires IT artifacts to be built in a disciplined and "informed" way [2], [5] which necessitates making inferences on the truth contained in the prescriptive knowledge created throughout a DSR process. Therefore, it is important to infer on an artifact's expected impact on the world ex ante, i.e. before an artifact has been applied to some real world problem. A designer could refer to descriptive knowledge to justify and inform the design of a new artifact and thus ingrain descriptive truth into it. This would require the existence of kernel theories, a so called design theory, or meta-artifacts [5], [6], [12]. Nevertheless, an IT artifact emerges throughout a DSR process. The construction of an artifact precedes the knowledge of why it works [6] and thus design decisions also relate to conceptual and mainly prescriptive knowledge of an emergent design theory. These decisions have to be justified and validated by means of evaluations long before an IT artifact has been put into use.

Eventually, the assumption that the truth of an artifact cannot be inferred from prescriptive knowledge embodying an artifact's ideas, purpose, and structure ultimately affects the validity of early phases of a DSR process. If prescriptive research would result in knowledge that cannot be assumed to have truth value then no reasoning could be made about it. As a result, it can be questioned if prescriptive research could be characterized as research at all since no valid knowledge is created. Prescriptive knowledge as the major outcome of DSR would not be worth to be accumulated. Reusing parts of an artifact by other researchers of within other contexts might not be justifiable since these parts are also assumed to have no truth value. In this regard, a design science researcher would hardly be able to build an artifact in a rigorous and informed way as required by DSR guidelines [2] since design decisions could be validated not until an artifact has been constructed and applied to some reality. Some might argue that the science of the artificial would no longer be a science but rather a practice. In fact, PURAO [12] remarks that the scientific foundations underlying design research have remained largely undeveloped.

Is there a way to circumvent these epistemological implications? The key to a solution must be to acknowledge that the science of the artificial is different to the natural and human sciences and requires different modes of inquiry to reason about the truth of the knowledge created [4]. The most significant difference is that the phenomena under study cannot be assumed to be existent at the outset of a DSR endeavor but it emerges in the course of scientific inquiry. The next sections outline how an inquiry in DSR might be conducted in order to make truth-like statements about prescriptive knowledge while it emerges through design science research.

5   Progressing Towards a Truth – Principles for Evaluating DSR Artifacts

5.1   Three Principles for Evaluating DSR Artifacts

To demonstrate the validity of an artifact already in the design phase and to provide a rationale for the design decisions a design science researcher has to resort to a truth residing in conceptual and prescriptive knowledge, i.e. the ideas, metaphors, analogies, or other artifacts from which the artifact under study has been deduced. In order to make truth statements about an artifact corresponding prescriptive knowledge should be documented and accumulated in a way that allows for step-wise evaluations of an artifact as it emerges in the DSR process. In particular, such a documentation should not only allow for making inferences on the usefulness of an artifact but also on an artifact's expected suitability and importance as well as the validity and correctness of its design and construction. That means evaluations should also address the validation of incremental design decisions right from the start of a DSR process.

Prior work already pointed out that evaluation in DSR may address either the artifact design (i.e. the artifact characteristics) or the actual artifact as it is used by some relevant stakeholders. The former refers to *ex ante* evaluations occurring prior to the artifact "construction" whereas the latter refers to *ex post* evaluations after an artifact has been constructed [3]. However, ex ante evaluations in DSR are usually interpreted as a means to anticipate the effort required as well as the (economic) consequences implied by the envisioned artifact characteristics. Ex ante evaluations thus often employ complexity or profitability measures at the outset of a DSR project (cf. [3]). What has been neglected so far in ex ante evaluations is the emergent nature of IT artifacts. As has been outlined above, current DSR methodologies treat the inherent structure of an artifact, its principles of form and function, as a black box in both the build and evaluation phase. In particular, the evaluation of design decisions made by a researcher during the build phase is well out of scope of existing DSR methodologies.

It is the claim of this paper that the prescriptive knowledge that emerges throughout a DSR process has a truth-like value. This implies that incremental additions made to the prescriptive knowledge base throughout a DSR process, if evaluated and documented in a rigorous way, can be communicated early by design science researchers to interested peers or research communities. For example, a researcher could present intermediate products of a DSR process to the research community in order to build consensus on the relevance, novelty, and importance of a chosen problem domain, to discuss design objectives and features, to disseminate an initial blueprint of an IT artifact spurring joint or distinct developments of artifacts for a particular problem domain, or to demonstrate that an artifact can be put into practice by means of a prototype.

Building on prior work on DSR evaluations this paper extends the notion of ex ante evaluations by emphasizing that in order to achieve rigor in DSR it is not sufficient to just letting the IT artifact emerge in the build phase and evaluate its use but to ensure that a design science researcher makes design decisions in a disciplined way order to consistently and rigorously converge to a feasible and useful artifact. To do so it is suggested that evaluations in DSR should be conducted according to three principles. These principles have been synthesized and combined from prior literature ([4], [6], [7]) and are summarized in Table 1. It is hold that by following these principles the unfavorable epistemological implications of the build-evaluate distinction of current DSR methodologies can be alleviated.

Table 1. DSR evaluation principles

Principle	Description
Distinction between **interior and exterior modes** of DSR inquiry	This principle directs the foci of evaluations on two aspects: (1) the constituents of the artifact and the design decisions taken as well as on (2) the evaluation of the usefulness of the artifact.
Documentation of prescriptive knowledge as **design theories**	This principle necessitates the prescriptive knowledge to be documented in a structured way. This would facilitate the communication and dissemination of the prescriptive knowledge produced within a DSR process. Moreover, such documentation would already have a truth-like value that is worth to be accumulated in a DSR knowledge base.
Continuous assessment of the DSR progress achieved through ex ante and ex post evaluations	This principle prompts the design researcher to have multiple evaluation episodes throughout a *single iteration* of a DSR process.

These principles are interrelated in that one principle supports the other principles. Their implications on DSR evaluations are explained in detail in the following sections.

5.2   Distinguishing Modes of DSR Inquiry

This principle directly points to the implications of the build-evaluate pattern. DSR should not only describe and predict "'what is'" and "'why it is'" (descriptive knowledge produced in the evaluation phase). DSR predominantly builds IT artifacts producing prescriptive knowledge. The question is how a design science researcher might infer on the truth residing in that prescriptive knowledge. GREGOR [4] proposed a framework which clarifies on a high level how knowledge creation, theory building and thus truth assessment can be achieved in DSR (cf. Fig. 2).

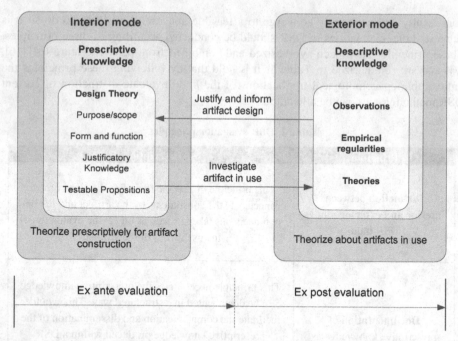

Fig. 2. Modes of DSR inquiry (based on [4, p. 8])

In their work [4] distinguishes two separate but linked modes of research activities that particularly affect the way artifacts should be evaluated: (1) an *interior mode* of DSR, and (2) *exterior mode* of DSR. The interior mode is concerned with producing "*prescriptive statements* about how artifacts can be designed, developed and brought into being" [4, p. 7, emphasis added]. The exterior mode aims "primarily at analyzing, *describing* and predicting what happens as artifacts exist and are used in their external environment" [4, p. 7, emphasis added]. Research in the interior mode would make use of inductive reasoning on prior descriptive or prescriptive knowledge when building an artifact. It is in this mode that prescriptive knowledge is produced. In the external mode descriptive knowledge about the artifact is produced treating the artifact more as a *black box* and only assessing significant design features with regard to achieving some utilitarian ends [4]. The relationships between interior and exterior research mode and the involved knowledge types are depicted in Fig. 2. The figure also illustrates how the application of each of the three evaluation principles stated above supports the creation of valid DSR knowledge.

In order to theorize in the interior mode, i.e. to add truth to prescriptive knowledge, a design science researcher has to document the emerging IT artifact in a way that allows for reasoning about its purpose, its rationale, its inner structure, the conditions under which the artifact is expected to work, the steps required to actually use the artifact in practice, or testable propositions that can be evaluated in the exterior mode.

Such prescriptive design knowledge can be documented by means of a *design theory* [6]. The next section briefly outlines the anatomy of a design theory according to GREGOR & JONES [6] and discusses how such an anatomy supports DSR evaluations.

The distinction between interior and exterior mode not only requires design knowledge to be documented as design theories. It also widens the perspective of how evaluations in DSR should be approached. Instead of only resorting to ex post evaluations in the exterior mode (i.e. analyzing and creating descriptive knowledge), evaluations should also be conducted ex ante during the build phase as part of the interior mode. Ex ante evaluations would then refer to design theories and the progress achieved in designing an IT artifact would be assessed by means of evaluation criteria pertinent to different aspects of a design theory. This will also be discussed further below.

5.3   Documentation of Cumulative Prescriptive Knowledge as Design Theories

Reasoning about IT artifacts in the interior mode, i.e. its build phase, requires the design researcher to document prescriptive knowledge in a particular way. GREGOR & JONES [6] refers to such a documentation as (information systems) *design theory* (ISDT) showing *"the principles inherent in the design of an IS artifact that accomplishes some end, based on knowledge of both IT and human behavior. The ISDT allows the prescription of guidelines for further artifacts of the same type. Design theories can be about artifacts that are either products (for example, a database) or methods (for example, a prototyping methodology or an IS management strategy)"* [6, p. 322].

According to [6] a design theory consists of eight components:

1. Purpose and scope (causa finalis)
2. Constructs (causa materialis)
3. Principle of form and function (causa formalis)
4. Artifact mutability
5. Testable propositions
6. Justificatory knowledge
7. Principles of implementation (causa efficiens)
8. Expository instantiation.

Some components could be specified and reasoned about right at the outset of a DSR project, while other components are specified and reasoned about as the IT artifact emerges throughout the build phase. What can be seen, however, is that documenting artifacts according to the eight components readily serves to evaluate an artifact in terms of 'what should be' and 'how it would be able to shape the world'. Reference to descriptive knowledge and thus to exterior modes of DSR is made through components (5), (6), and (8). Testable propositions can be investigated in ex post evaluations to create descriptive knowledge about the utility of the artifact. Justificatory knowledge serves to explain or anticipate why an artifact might work in a given context and ingrains truth of prior knowledge. Justificatory knowledge can be of a descriptive (theories, observations) or of a predictive type (other design theories that proved to be useful or principles of form and functions that are reused). Expository instantiations may help to reason about an artifact's feasibility and applicability at build-time (artificial evaluation in interior mode) or to reason about its usefulness when applied to some reality (naturalistic evaluation in exterior mode). The descriptive knowledge gained by evaluating instantiations in the interior mode can serve as additional justificatory knowledge for further developing the artifact in a subsequent build cycle (e.g. benchmark results).

Documenting IT artifacts as design theories is a prerequisite for enabling the interior mode of DSR and thus to create prescriptive knowledge that ingrains truth value. Moreover, it immediately affects the way evaluations can be conducted in DSR. The distinction of interior and exterior modes of DSR together with a dedicated means for documenting the IT artifact enables the reasoning about the validity of the artifact ex ante, i.e. before it has been put into use. The predominant build-evaluate pattern of DSR methodologies along with its unfavorable epistemological implications can be reconsidered in favor of a more fine-grained consideration of research rigor in the design process. Evaluations should not only be conducted at the conclusion of a DSR project but they should be conducted on a continuing basis to assess the progress achieved as the artifact emerges [3]. In this regard, principles (1) and (2) discussed above support principle (3) leading to an expansion of the common build-evaluate pattern into a *design-evaluate-construct-evaluate* pattern (e.g. as has also been put forward in [3].

5.4   Continuous Assessment of the Progress Achieved in a DSR Process

By following principles (1) and (2) prescriptive knowledge in the form of design theories can be regarded as having truth-like value. Thus, it is possible and also reasonable to consider the evaluation of design decisions ingrained in the artifact and not just its usefulness by means of continuous assessments of the progress achieved in the DSR process. Two aspects are central to enable such a continuous assessment. First, *evaluation criteria* have to be defined to be able to systematically demonstrate the progress achieved in DSR and to guide evaluation activities [14]. Second, it should be clarified how ex ante and ex post evaluations can be positioned in a DSR methodology leading to the definition of *evaluation patterns* in DSR (cf. [7]).

Evaluation Criteria

Table 2 below lists DSR evaluation criteria proposed by [1]. These criteria could be applied in both ex ante and/or ex post evaluations. While this criteria set is considered being comprehensive [14], however, the proposed evaluation criteria are not independent of the artifact type under consideration. AIER & FISCHER [14] suggest criteria that are independent of an artifact type and particularly apply for evaluating design theories. These criteria are: utility, internal consistency, external consistency, broad purpose and scope, simplicity, fruitfulness of further research. Another set of evaluation criteria is proposed by ROSEMANN & VESSEY [15]. Their criteria set aims at particularly ensuring the relevance of a DSR artifact, i.e. if an artifact is expected to be applicable in practice. The suggested criteria are: importance, suitability, and accessibility of an artifact [15]. Applicability checks in that sense are considered particularly suitable for ex ante evaluations.

Table 2. Evaluation criteria for DSR artifacts (cf. [1])

	Construct	Model	Method	Instantiation
Completeness	X	X		
Ease of use	X		X	
Effectiveness				X
Efficiency			X	X
Elegance	X			
Fidelity with real world phenomena		X		
Generality			X	
Impact on the environment and on the artifact's users				X
Internal consistency		X		
Level of detail		X		
Operationality			X	
Robustness		X		
Simplicity	X			
Understandability	X			

Depending on the type of object to be evaluated and on the point in time an evaluation should be conducted some criteria might better reflect the progress achieved in designing an artifact then others. To structure evaluation activities and corresponding evaluation criteria the concept of evaluation patterns for DSR artifacts has been proposed in [7]. The core ideas behind these patterns as well as their specifications are presented in the next section.

Evaluation Patterns

Patterns are useful to describe a good solution to a recurring problem (cf. [16], cited in [17]). Patterns can be useful for both researchers and practitioners in that they incorporate "high-level solutions to classes of problems that can be converted into specific best practices" [17, p. 9]. For researchers patterns may serve to "synthesize and capture knowledge in a given domain as well as highlight areas for future research"

[17, p. 9]. SONNENBERG & VOM BROCKE [7] introduced the concept of evaluation patterns for DSR artifacts. Such patterns should provide design science researchers with an orientation when configuring particular evaluation strategies. Essentially, these patterns can be positioned within a global design-evaluate-construct-evaluate pattern.

Fig. 3 below sketches a cyclic high level DSR process incorporating a design-evaluate-construct-evaluate pattern. The DSR process includes the DSR activities *problem identification*, *design*, *construction*, and *use* followed by corresponding evaluation activities. As can be seen, the process suggests that evaluations in DSR should be conducted throughout the whole process. In such a process, ex ante evaluations validate the *design of an artifact* and ex post evaluations validate *artifact instances* and *artifacts in use*. In particular, ex ante evaluations are conducted before the construction, ex post evaluations are conducted after the construction of any artifact [3].

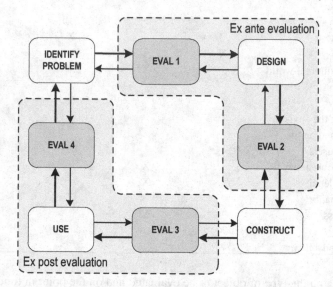

Fig. 3. Evaluation activities within a DSR process

The evaluation activities in Fig. 3 have been given generic names. Depending on the context and the purpose of an evaluation within the DSR process different evaluation methods and evaluation criteria could be applied for an evaluation activity [18]. Such a combination resembles 'best practices' in the form of evaluation patterns.

Design science researchers could benefit from such evaluation patterns as they would be able to disseminate their (validated) research findings also in early stages of their research. Ultimately, a design science researcher has to proof the utility of an artifact. However, even design objectives or principles of form and function, if related to a generic problem and evaluated rigorously might already inform other researchers and thus present a useful contribution to a DSR knowledge base.

In order to formulate such evaluation patterns it is required to broadly understand the purpose and scope of individual evaluation activities of the DSR sketched in Fig. 3. The nature of these activities as well as possible evaluation criteria and methods are summarized in Table 3 and are further discussed below. Moreover, their purpose and scope as well as their significance for supporting the accumulation of (incremental) prescriptive knowledge by means of design theories is discussed below.

Table 3. DSR evaluation activities and evaluation criteria

Activity	Input	Output (mandatory)	Eval. Criteria (exemplary)	Eval. Methods (exemplary)
Eval 1	Problem statement/ Observation of a problem Research need Design objectives Design theory Existing solution to a practical problem	Justified problem statement Justified research gap Justified design objectives	Applicability, suitability, importance, novelty, (economic) feasibility	Literature review, review of practitioner initiatives, expert interview, focus groups, survey
Eval 2	Design specification Design objectives Stakeholders of the design specification Design tool/ design methodology	Validated design specification Justified design tool/ methodology	Feasibility, accessibility, understandability, clarity, simplicity, elegance, completeness, level of detail, internal consistency, applicability, operationality,	Mathematical proof, logical reasoning, demonstration, simulation, benchmarking, survey, expert interview, focus group
Eval 3	Instance of an artifact (prototype)	Validated artifact instance in an *artificial setting* (proof of applicability)	Feasibility, ease of use, effectiveness, efficiency, fidelity with real world phenomenon, operationality, robustness, suitability	Demonstration with prototype, experiment with prototype, experiment with system, benchmarking, survey, expert interview, focus group

Table 3. (*continued*)

			Applicability, effectiveness, efficiency, fidelity with real world phenomenon, generality, impact on artifact environment and user, internal consistency, external consistency	
Eval 4	Instance of an artifact	Validated artifact instance in a naturalistic setting (proof of usefulness)		Case study, field experiment, survey, expert interview, focus group

Eval1 Activity

The evaluation of the problem identification activity serves the purpose of ensuring that a meaningful DSR problem is selected and formulated. It should be demonstrated whether the envisioned design science research project is important for practice, is novel and thus adds to the existing knowledge base. The Eval1 activity might have different inputs depending on what actually triggers the interest in the DSR project (cf. [9]). A DSR process might start with a problem observed in practice, with a research need observed in the literature, with an existing artifact (design theory) which needs refinement in a given context, or with an existing practical solution that has not been rigorously documented or developed. Mandatory outputs of this activity are a justified problem statement, a justified research gap, and justified design objectives which serve as input for subsequent activities. Thus, the evaluation criteria and methods all serve to justify the engagement in a DSR project. Therefore, an evaluation pattern pertinent to the Eval1 activity could be termed "Justification" describing how a design researcher can justify the value of a solution and the prospective artifact. Criteria to be used here may predominantly refer to applicability checks regarding the suitability of a design idea and the perceived importance of the problem. With regard to developing an artifact, i.e. to specify a design theory, the Eval1 activity is concerned with validating the purpose and scope as well as the constructs to be used. The appropriateness of constructs might be justified by referring to constructs that have been used for solving similar problems (justificatory prescriptive knowledge). An artifact's idea could be further validated by means of descriptive justificatory knowledge in the form of results from surveys or interviews. Moreover, a design science researcher may already derive testable propositions at this point.

Eval2 Activity

The evaluation of the design activity result serves the purpose of showing that an artifact design progresses to a solution of the stated problem. Since the artifact has not yet been constructed (instantiated) and thus not been applied to some reality this evaluation is artificial [19]. Possible inputs to this activity are a design specification ('blueprint', initial principles of form and function), the design objectives, information on the stakeholders of a design specification, as well as the tools and methodologies used for creating a design specification. The design specification is evaluated against its correctness and completeness to assess whether the design flawed. In particular, it should be evaluated whether the constructs used in the design specification as well as their relationships correspond to the stated design objectives. Moreover, it should be assessed whether the design specification is understandable and meaningful to all of its stakeholders (e.g. managers, IT staff) Thus, the use of particular design tools and methodologies has to be justified. Possible evaluation patterns pertinent to the validation of the design specification could be termed "demonstration" (show analytically that an artifact behaves as intended for a single test case), "simulation", or "formal proof". With regard to the justification of the design tool or methodology a pattern could be termed "tool evaluation". With regard to a design theory, the Eval2 activity validates the principles of form and function which have been specified during the design activity. Moreover, a design science researcher might want to formulate principles of implementation. Demonstrations and simulations may result in descriptive justificatory knowledge in the form of observations and empirical regularities. A formal proof may yield prescriptive justificatory knowledge in the sense that a formal proof confirms the consistency of assumptions about "what should be".

Eval3 Activity

This evaluation activity serves to initially demonstrate if and how well the artifact performs while interacting with organizational elements. In this activity, some inferences on the utility of an artifact could already be made. Since this activity links ex ante as well as ex post evaluations it is central for reflecting an artifact's design and stimulate subsequent iterations of the design activity if necessary (see feedback loop). The "realities" considered here may comprise of subsets of "real tasks", "real system", and "real users" (these "realities" have been suggested in [20]). Inputs to this activity are instantiations of artifacts ("constructed" artifacts) which should be evaluated regarding their applicability. At this point, the application context of the artifact instance tends to be artificial (in the sense of [19]) and might only prove that an instance is applicable to a task, within a system, or by a real user. The interplay of all three realities together with the artifact instance would be the focus of the Eval4 activity. Prototypes are frequently used at this stage. Besides demonstrating the applicability of an artifact instance, this evaluation activity should also proof that the artifact instance is consistent with its specification, i.e. that it ingrains the principles of form and function validated in the preceding evaluation activity Eval2. Possible evaluation patterns pertinent to the Eval3 activity could be termed "prototyping" and "experimentation". With regard to developing a design theory this activity is concerned with validating the component "expository instantiation" as well as artifact mutability. Moreover, evidence is gathered with regard to the ability of the artifact to behave according to its purpose and scope.

Eval4 Activity

This evaluation activity serves to ultimately show that an artifact is both applicable and useful in practice. Evaluations reflect the organizational context by means of all "three realities" (real tasks, real systems, and real users). Inputs to this activity are artifact instances that are fully embedded within the organizational context. Possible patterns pertinent to the Eval4 activity could be termed "case study", "field experiment", "survey", or "applicability check". With regard to design theories the main focus of the Eval4 activity would be to finally validate the artifact based on the testable propositions specified in the design theory.

6   Conclusions

This paper suggests reconsidering the build-evaluating pattern of current DSR methodologies in favor of a more fine grained evaluation pattern that accommodates the emerging nature of IT artifacts. Therefore, three principles for DSR evaluations have been proposed that particularly support a design science researcher to make inferences on the truth contained in the prescriptive knowledge produced by individual DSR activities.

These principles have not been invented from scratch but have been synthesized from prior literature in the field and combined to fit the purpose of this paper. However, some aspects need to be explored in more detail. In particular, the definition of a comprehensive set of evaluations patterns related to the outlined evaluation activities is expected to be particularly beneficial to better guide design science researchers and to foster the rigor and discipline of the artifact development throughout the whole DSR process. Future DSR methodologies could build on the principles put forward in this paper and verify, whether they prove to be effective.

References

1. March, S.T., Smith, G.: Design and Natural Science Research on Information Technology. Decision Support Systems 15(4), 251–266 (1995)
2. Hevner, A.R., March, S.T., Park, J., Ram, S.: Design Science in Information Systems. MIS Quarterly 28(1), 75–105 (2004)
3. Pries-Heje, J., Baskerville, R., Venable, J.: Strategies for Design Research Evaluation. In: 16th European Conference on Information Systems (ECIS 2008), Galway, Ireland (2008)
4. Gregor, S.: Building Theory in the Sciences of the Artificial. In: Proceedings of the International Conference on Design Science Research in Information Systems and Technologies, DESRIST 2009, Malvern, PA (2009)
5. Iivari, J.: A Paradigmatic Analysis of Information Systems As a Design Science. Scandinavian J. Inf. Systems 19(2) (2007)
6. Gregor, S., Jones, D.: The anatomy of a design theory. Journal of the Association of Information Systems 8(5), Article 2, 312–335 (2007)
7. Sonnenberg, C., vom Brocke, J.: Evaluation Patterns for Design Science Research Artefacts. In: Proceedings of the European Design Science Symposium 2011, Dublin, Ireland. CCIS, vol. 286. Springer (2012)
8. Simon, H.: The sciences of the artificial, 3rd edn. MIT Press (1996)

9. Peffers, K., Tuunanen, T., Rothenberger, M.A., Chatterjee, S.: A Design Science Research Methodology for Information Systems Research. Journal of Management Information Systems 24(3), 45–77 (2007)
10. Sein, M.K., Henfridsson, O., Purao, S., Rossi, M., Lindgren, R.: Action Design Research. MIS Quarterly 35(1), 37–56 (2011)
11. vom Brocke, J., Recker, J., Mendling, J.: Value-oriented process modeling: integrating financial perspectives into business process re-design. Business Process Management Journal 6(2), 333–356 (2010)
12. Walls, J., Widmeyer, G.R., El Sawy, O.A.: Building an information system design theory for vigilant EIS. Information Systems Research 3(1), 36–59 (1992)
13. Purao, S.: Design research in technology and information systems: truth or dare, unpublished paper, School of Information Sciences and Technology, The Pennsylvania State University, University Park, State College, PA (2002)
14. Aier, S., Fischer, C.: Criteria for Progress for Information Systems Design Theories. Information Systems and E-Business Management 9(1), 133–172 (2011)
15. Rosemann, M., Vessey, I.: Toward Improving the Relevance of Information Systems Research to Practice: The Role of Applicability Checks. MIS Quarterly 32(1), 1–22 (2008)
16. Alexander, C., Ishikawa, S., Silverstein, M.: A Pattern Language. Oxford University Press, New York (1977)
17. Petter, S., Khazanchi, D., Murphy, J.D.: A Design Science Based Evaluation Framework for Patterns. The DATA BASE for Advances in Information Systems 41(3), 9–26 (2010)
18. Vaishnavi, V.K., Kuechler, W.: Improving and Innovating Information & Communication Technology: Design Science Research Methods and Patterns. Taylor Francis (2008)
19. Venable, J.: A Framework for Design Science Research Activities. In: Proceedings of the 2006 Information Resource Management Association Conference, Washington, DC, USA (2006)
20. Sun, Y., Kantor, P.B.: Cross-Evaluation: A new model for information system evaluation. Journal of the American Society for Information Science and Technology 57(5), 614–628 (2006)

Design Science Research Evaluation

Ken Peffers[1], Marcus Rothenberger[1], Tuure Tuunanen[2], and Reza Vaezi[3]

[1] Lee Business School, University of Nevada Las Vegas, Las Vegas NV USA
{ken.peffers,marcus.rothenberger}@unlv.edu
[2] University of Oulu, Oulu Finland
tuure@tuunanen.fi
[3] University of Houston, Houston TX USA
srvaezi@uh.edu

Abstract. The consensus view is that the rigorous evaluation of design science (DS) artifacts is essential. There are many types of DS artifacts and many forms of evaluation; what is missing is guidance for how to perform the evaluation, more specifically, what evaluation methods to use with specific DS research outputs. Here we find and review 148 DS research articles published in a selected set of information systems (IS), computer science (CS) and engineering journals. We analyze the articles to develop taxonomies of DS artifact types and artifact evaluation methods; we apply these taxonomies to determine which evaluation methods are associated in the literature with particular artifacts. We show that there are several popular "artifact - evaluation method" combinations in the literature. The results inform DS researchers of usual and customary combinations of research artifacts and evaluation methods, potentially providing them with rationale and justification for an evaluation method selection.

Keywords: Design Science, evaluation, artifacts.

1 Introduction

The importance of evaluating DS research artifacts is well supported in the literature [1, 2]. These articles provide justification for the publication of DS research efforts and outcomes in quality information systems (IS) research outlets, provided that the artifacts are, in addition to other attributes, rigorously evaluated. That such evaluation is an essential component of a DS research contribution is emphasized as "crucial" in Hevner et al. [2] and in Peffers et al. [1], as well as in discussions about how to conduct DS research, e.g., [3-5]. Other researchers have also emphasized the importance of evaluation, e.g., [6-11].

Notwithstanding the consensus that evaluation is essential, there is little guidance about what is desirable, acceptable or customary in evaluation. Artifacts should be evaluated with criteria based on the requirements of the context in which the artifact is implemented, according to Hevner et al. [2]; for example, in terms such as "functionality, completeness, consistency, accuracy, performance, reliability, usability, fit with the organization and other relevant quality attributes." Evaluation methods might

K. Peffers, M. Rothenberger, and B. Kuechler (Eds.): DESRIST 2012, LNCS 7286, pp. 398–410, 2012.

include case studies, field studies, static analysis, architectural analysis, optimization, dynamic analysis, controlled experiments, simulation, functional testing, structural testing, informed argument, or scenarios [2, p. 86, Table 2.]. Peffers et al. [1] advocated "observ[ing] how well the artifact supports a solution to the problem." Case studies reported in Peffers et al [1] were evaluated using field studies, observation of reuse rates, performance testing, and client feedback about usefulness.

How are DS research artifacts evaluated? There is considerable variety in the artifacts that result from DS research efforts. Are there, consequently, characteristics of these artifacts that tend to lead to certain kinds of evaluation? These are important questions because the evaluation and presentation of DS research outcomes is essential to the efficacy of DSR research, as well as to the professional success of researchers. DS research papers are unlikely to be published in influential outlets, unless authors can make persuasive arguments that artifacts were appropriately evaluated.

In this paper, we locate and examine DS research papers from IS and from engineering research journals. We classify the papers to create taxonomies of the DS research artifact types and of the evaluation method types in use. Using these classifications, we observe associations between types of artifacts and the methods used to evaluate them, showing which evaluation methods have been used to evaluate which types of artifacts. We then develop case studies of exemplary studies to show how the artifacts have been evaluated.

2   Data

The data consists of published DS research papers in major IS and engineering journals. We selected ten well-regarded journals that we judged were likely to publish some design science articles (Table 1). Since DS researchers in the IS discipline have traditionally published at least some of their research in engineering journals, we included those engineering journals that are most important to the IS discipline as well. Five selected journals are in the core MIS discipline and five are in computer science and engineering. All of them are listed in prominent positions on the AIS Journal ranking lists [12].

From each of these journals we identified up to 25 articles, searching up to five volumes and stopping when we had identified 25 articles or completed five volumes, whichever occurred first. One researcher included all articles that he classified as design science into the candidate set of articles, taking an inclusive approach; including an article when in doubt, rather than omitting one. This resulted in a total of 159 articles.

Two additional researchers independently audited each candidate article to determine whether it was correctly classified as DS research. Each researcher identified articles for which the classification as design science was not clear. The two auditing researchers discussed the doubtfully classified articles and made a decision about whether to include the article by consensus. This process resulted in the removal of eleven articles from the study because the auditors agreed that they were not DS research. The auditing step ensured that all papers entered into the study were actually DS research papers. This resulted in a sample of 148 articles. As we expected more DS articles appeared in computer science and engineering journals than in IS journals, as DS is a more prevailing research approach in those disciplines. The final total included 117 articles in computer science and engineering journals and 31 in IS journals.

Table 1. Information systems and engineering journals included in search

Journal Name	Acronym
ACM Transactions on Database Systems	ACM TDB
European Journal of Information Systems	EJIS
IEEE Transactions on Engineering Management	IEEE TEM
IEEE Transactions on Knowledge and Data Engineering	IEEE TKDE
IEEE Transactions on Software Engineering	IEEE TSE
IEEE Transactions on Systems, Man & Cybernetic	IEEE TSMC
Information and Management	I&M
Information Systems Research	ISR
Journal of Management Information Systems	JMIS
MIS Quarterly	MISQ

3   Analysis

We classified the papers by artifact type and evaluation method. The two researchers independently evaluated the content of each paper for these two characteristics and established item categories in the two dimensions, in order to develop sets of artifact types and evaluation methods. We used an open coding approach; two researchers independently categorized the papers, defining and naming their own categories without an established list. After the independent assessments, the two researchers compared their results; 91 percent of the artifact classifications and 81 percent of the method classifications were consistent between the two researchers. Different category names with the same meaning were consolidated into one category name without counting that as a difference. To resolve the remaining classification differences, the two researchers reread the respective articles and obtained consensus in a discussion in which they explained their reasoning to each other. Differences were resolved in an iteration of this process and the codes were consolidated into six artifact types and eight evaluation method types. At the same time they established the artifact and evaluation method labels and definitions, checking paper content to ensure that the resulting categorizations were consistent and that the definitions were consistently exclusive.

The artifact classification includes conceptual artifacts like constructs, models, and frameworks, as well as methods, which are conceptual actionable instructions. Formal logical instructions are classified as algorithms and actual hardware or software implementations are classified as instantiations (Table 2).

Table 2. Artifact Types

Algorithm	An approach, method, or process described largely by a set of formal logical instructions.
Construct	Concept, assertion, or syntax that has been constructed from a set of statements, assertions, or other concepts.
Framework	Meta-model
Instantiation	The structure and organization of a system's hardware or system software or part thereof.
Method	Actionable instructions that are conceptual (not algorithmic)
Model	Simplified representation of reality documented using a formal notation or language.

The evaluation method classification includes technical experiments as a means to evaluate the performance of an artifact without the involvement of research subjects, and subject-based experiments that use research subjects to assess the validity of the assertions that motivated the development of the artifact are true. The classification further differentiates between prototypes, illustrative scenarios, case studies, and action research. Prototypes are the implementation of artifacts to demonstrate their utility; illustrative scenarios apply the artifact in a synthetic or real world situation to demonstrate its utility; and case studies implement the artifact in a real-world situation to evaluate not only its utility, but also its effect on its environment; action research also implements the artifact in a real-world situation to evaluate its effect on the environment, but does that in the context of a research intervention. Logical arguments and expert evaluations are also part of the evaluation method classifications (Table 3).

3.1   Clusters of Artifacts and Evaluation Methods

Table 4 shows the results of our analysis, in terms of the count of the number of papers at the intersection of each artifact and evaluation method. It shows that, in this sample of papers, algorithms, methods, and models are the most popular artifact types across all journals; however, the other artifact types were also well represented. Technical experiments and illustrative scenarios are the most commonly used evaluation methods.

To differentiate between IS vs. CS and engineering DS research, we split the results from Table 4 into Table 5 for IS journals and Table 6 for CS and engineering journals. Since the majority of DS research papers in our sample appeared in the CS and engineering journals, the results for those journals fairly closely mirrored those for the whole sample. The results for the IS journals reflected the much smaller representation of DS research in those journals. Nonetheless, despite the small numbers, discernible patterns of association appeared. In particular, case studies and illustrative scenarios figured more predominantly in the counts of evaluation methods. The choices of artifact type appeared to be much more evenly distributed in the IS journals than they were in the CS and engineering journals.

Table 3. Evaluation Method Types

Logical Argument	An argument with face validity.
Expert Evaluation	Assessment of an artifact by one or more experts (e.g., Delphi study).
Technical Experiment	A performance evaluation of an algorithm implementation using real-world data, synthetic data, or no data, designed to evaluate the technical performance, rather than its performance in relation to the real world.
Subject-based Experiment	A test involving subjects to evaluate whether an assertion is true.
Action Research	Use of an artifact in a real-world situation as part of a research intervention, evaluating its effect on the real-world situation.
Prototype	Implementation of an artifact aimed at demonstrating the utility or suitability of the artifact.
Case Study	Application of an artifact to a real-world situation, evaluating its effect on the real-world situation.
Illustrative Scenario	Application of an artifact to a synthetic or real-world situation aimed at illustrating suitability or utility of the artifact.

As one might expect, the choice of evaluation methods is driven by choice of artifacts; particular artifacts lend themselves to evaluation with particular methods. To analyze these clusters, we created groups of articles employing unique artifact type / evaluation method combinations. Tables 4 through 6 show the number of articles that belong to each artifact/evaluation method pair. The tables demonstrate that certain artifact / evaluation method combinations occur far more frequently than others. For example, in IS journals, methods are most frequently evaluated using case studies, while in computer science and engineering journals, methods are most commonly evaluated using technical experiments. In both disciplines algorithms are most frequently evaluated using technical experiments.

Table 4. Distribution of Evaluation Methods by Artifact Type (all journals)

	Logical Argument	Expert Evaluation	Technical Experiment	Subject-Based Experiment	Prototype	Action Research	Case Study	Illustrative Scenario	none	Total
Algorithm	1		60	1				3		65
Construct	3		3	2	2			2		12
Framework	1	1			1		1	4	1	9
Instantiation			5	1	1			1		8
Method	2		14	4			7	6		33
Model	3		10		2	2		4		21
Total	10	1	92	8	6	2	8	20	1	

3.2 Exemplar Papers

For each research artifact / evaluation method cluster, we identified an exemplar paper for further analysis. The objective in this selection was to obtain a typical representative for each included specific artifact / evaluation method pair. This is consistent with a theoretical sampling approach in qualitative research, treating the papers as cases to be entered into further analysis. This final analysis step examines the reasoning provided in the exemplar papers for the choice of evaluation method.

4 Two Exemplar Studies

Here we examine the reasoning provided in the exemplar papers for the choice of evaluation method. We believe that artifact type, context, and data availability are issues that contribute to the selection of an evaluation method, but we expect that a more refined set of criteria will emerge from the analysis. Because space in this publication is limited, we present here just two of the selected exemplar papers.

Table 5. Distribution of Evaluation Methods by Artifact Type (IS journals) [EJIS, I&M, ISR, JMIS, MISQ]

	Logical Argument	Expert Evaluation	Technical Experiment	Subject-Based Experiment	Prototype	Action Research	Case Study	Illustrative Scenario	none	Total
Algorithm			4							4
Construct	1				1					2
Framework	1	1					1	1	1	5
Instantiation			3					1		4
Method	1		2	2			6	1		12
Model			1		1	1		1		4
Total	3	1	10	2	2	1	7	4	1	

Table 6. Distribution of Evaluation Methods by Artifact Type (CS/Eng journals) [ACM TDB, IEEE TEM, IEEE TKDE, IEEE TSWE, IEEE TSMC]

	Logical Argument	Expert Evaluation	Technical Experiment	Subject-Based Experiment	Prototype	Action Research	Case Study	Illustrative Scenario	none	Total
Algorithm	1		56	1				3		61
Construct	2		3	2	1			2		10
Framework					1			3		4
Instantiation			2	1	1					4
Method	1		12	2			1	5		21
Model	3		9		1	1		3		17
Total	7	0	80	6	4	1	1	16	0	

4.1   Exemplar Paper 1: Instantiation Evaluated by Prototype

Chen et al (2003) designed a flexible database system (FDS) to provide superior query performance in production systems, e.g., that of an airline or large retailer, where the database is very large and the number of read queries is much larger (perhaps 1000 times larger) than that of write queries and where read queries are very diverse, often requiring joins among diverse tables.

To achieve improved performance the FDS employs a number of read-only, de-normalized database systems that are each intended to field queries of different characteristics. The FDS consists of a query analyzer, DBS_0 (a normalized database system), DBS_1 – DBS_n (de-normalized read-only systems), a scheduler, and a performance monitor.

Designed Artifact: System Instantiation

We classified the designed artifact as an instantiation because it represents in idea or concept that is or is intendedly expressed by an example system, rather than, for example, in a modeling language. The query analyzer receives a queries from system users and assigns each to one of the DBS, such that if the query is an update it is assigned to DBS0or if the query is a read-only it is assigned to one of DBS1 – DBSn, depending on which DBS is predicted to produce the best performance for the query.

The design of the FDS follows the steps:

1. Design of the update data structure, DBS_0, using a conventional database design approach.
2. Design of the read-only candidate structures, scaling down from an exhaustive set of de-normalized designs through use of expert database knowledge to a feasible set.
3. Build a knowledge base of queries to determine which DBS provide the fastest time for queries with given characteristics.
4. Decide which read-only DBS to keep active.
5. Assign queries to the most appropriate structure.
6. Determine conditions to refresh the read-only DBS from DBS_0.
7. Restructure the FDS when the distribution of query types warrant it.

Evaluation: Prototype

Chen et al [13] develop two prototype FDS, one of which is based on a very simple data structure and the other a more complex, production level system, with seven tables, each with 10 to 40 attributes, and from 625 to 6250 tuples, and they use them to demonstrate six of the seven steps above. Experiments using the two prototypes show an average of 40% less processing times can be achieved using the FDS, compared with a 3NF DBS. They estimate that this savings is easily sufficient to offset the cost of additional storage, refresh and restructuring required to implement and maintain the FDS.

The use of a prototype instantiation to demonstrate the efficacy of a design can provide strong evidence when used to show that a design works as intended, is useful for its intended purpose, or has the potential to achieve an expected performance level. The use of a specific instantiation suggests that the artifact should be evaluated on its directly observable performance, e.g., processing time.

4.2   Exemplar Paper 2: Method Evaluated by Case Study

Peffers, Gengler, and Tuunanen [14] designed a method intended to facilitate wide participation in data collection for IS planning activities, while maintaining a focus on ideas that are important for the firm. Wide spread participation should allow the firm to take advantage of knowledge about the value of potential systems that is widely dispersed among people in and around the firm, rather than only the knowledge that is held among a small circle of executives. The method needed, however, to overcome the limitation of traditional bottom-up planning processes, where the participants overwhelm managers with many self-serving ideas that are difficult to evaluate, but are mostly valueless.

The method is based on personal construct theory [15]. PCT holds that every observer has models for how the universe works, such that states of the universe have consequences and these consequences impact the values of the observer. PCT is extended in this research to a designed method for data collection, analysis, and ideation that can produce ideas for potentially valuable new systems for the organization.

Designed Artifact: Method

The designed artifact, critical success chains (CSC), consists of a set of procedures that informs the beginning of the IS systems planning process, from initial data collection, to analysis, and to ideation, to produce a set of feasible ideas for new systems. We classify this as a method because the instructions are actionable and conceptual.

CSC proceeds in a series of four phased activities:

- pre-study (scope the study, determine sample participant, gather stimuli),
- discovery (data collection through intensive one-on-one interviews),
- analysis (aggregating and modeling the data),
- integration (transforming the modeled ideas into feasible system ideas)

Evaluation: Case Study

Peffers, Gengler, and Tuunanen [14] demonstrated the CSC method in two case studies, an initial exploratory case study at Rutgers University and a more extensive and thorough study at Digia, a Helsinki software development firm. At Digia the scope of the study was ideas for 'killer applications' for mobile financial services. Data collection with a sample of 32 lead users and experts resulted in 147 chains, or arguments for specific system functionality. Analysis reduced this data to five graphical network models, each describing functionality, reasoning, and value, for a product bundle. An ideation workshop used these results to develop feasible ideas for three new products that the firm intended to explore further.

We classified this evaluation as a case study because the method was demonstrated in the context of use to affect real phenomena in the organization. The case study lends itself for use in evaluating the efficacy of a designed object that is intended to be used in a complex organizational setting where a simple experiment or other simple test could not be used to adequately show the efficacy or performance of the object. Case studies can provide much stronger evidence of efficacy or performance than simple arguments or illustrative scenarios. They vary greatly in the strength of evidence of efficacy or performance, often depending on how far the case carries the results of use of the method towards an impact on the firm. In this case the firm intended to explore the ideas further, however, the case study does not follow the story through to full execution, because, as is often the circumstance, full execution would occur well outside the desired time frame of the case story.

A potential weakness of case studies comes from the specificity of the context; the more idiosyncratic the case story, the less generalizable the evidence. While an illustrative scenario can be tailored to an ideal context, a case study, based as it must be on a real context, is likely to come with less than ideal observed facts.

5   Discussion

This research has led to the developed of a taxonomy of design science research artifacts and a taxonomy of artifact evaluation method types, based on use in publications in the IS and CS and engineering disciplines.   Six artifact types and eight evaluation method types have emerged. The analysis of the publication count in each of these categories has shown that some artifact types and evaluation methods are more commonly used than others, that there are some differences between IS vs. CS and engineering publications with respect to artifact types and evaluation methods, and that there seem to be clusters of artifacts and evaluation among the papers.

Overall, technical experiments are dominant, representing a clear majority of the evaluations (92 of 148). Illustrative scenarios, with 20, follow this. Algorithms make up a near majority of the artifacts, followed by methods and models. When we look at the disciplines separately, the results do not differ much, except that for the papers published in IS journals there is a cluster of methods evaluated by case studies that represent a significant part of the instances.

An analysis of the artifact / evaluation method clusters was less conclusive: clear clusters are missing in the overall data set, except for the "algorithm - technical experiment" combination. The same holds for the IS article sample, however, to little surprise it was confirmed that IS researchers are more keen to use qualitative evaluation methods such as case studies and action research. Similarly CS and engineering researchers use often more technical evaluation methods for their research. Therefore, we can see more differences between the research disciplines. Nevertheless, the analysis has supported the notion that the artifact, as well as the culture of the discipline drive evaluation choices.

While certain artifacts are almost exclusively evaluated using a specific evaluation method (for example, algorithms are almost exclusively evaluated using technical experiments), other artifacts lend themselves to a choice with regards to the evaluation method selection.   Methods are frequently evaluated using technical experiments, but also using case studies; CS and engineering outlets seem to favor the former, while IS outlets most frequently publish the latter. The analysis of the exemplar cases is shedding light on the motivation and the tradeoffs with regards to the evaluation method choice.

The Peffers et al. [14] evaluated a method using case studies; the discussion of this exemplar paper emphasized that the evaluation method chosen demonstrated the efficacy (performance) of the design artifact in an organizational context, however, the discussion also highlighted that a potential weakness of case study evaluation is their lack of generalizability. Technical experiments, which is the prevailing alternative evaluation method for methods, was evaluated in the context of another exemplar paper (not included in this version of the article for space considerations); this evaluation method would potentially address this weakness, as technical experiments can be designed for generalizability. However, this evaluation method demonstrates efficacy in a synthetic environment (its technical performance), and thus falls short of the case study in demonstrating performance in real world context. This discussion on the tradeoffs of evaluation choices for the method artifact is exemplary for several other artifacts that offer evaluation choices to the researcher. The extended version of the paper will include a larger set of exemplar papers that will help us to explore these choices in detail.

6   Conclusions, Limitations and Future Research

In this paper, we have reviewed a selection of journal articles, 148 in total, in order to assess what is the current practice of evaluating outcomes of DS research. More specifically, we were interested in understanding the connections between different artifacts and evaluation methods. The results of our study show some patterns of evaluation for DS artifacts and evaluation types in each of information systems and engineering. The patterns of evaluation potentially provide authors with examples and templates to support their own use of evaluation methods in future DS research.

As limitations to the study, we see that a more detailed analysis is needed. First of all, due to space limitations we were not able to do detailed analysis of all combinations of artifacts and evaluation methods. In this paper, we do provide two exemplars that would represent the range of artifacts and evaluation. What remains to be done in this research is to examine the papers in this sample to understand the reasoning and tradeoffs behind the use of specific methods to evaluate specific artifacts. We plan to address this limitation in an extended version of this paper. A deep analysis of the reasoning and tradeoffs behind evaluation choices will, we hope, illuminate good practices. In addition, a more complete set of exemplar papers will help future DS researchers with a valuable set of examples to support good evaluation method choices and to help justify those choices.

It can be also argued that more comprehensive review of literature should be done in order to provide better overview of the matter in the literature. Although, we see that the current sample of articles is well justified as means for doing the analysis we do see that this argument can be made. For example, the bias in the current sample is towards more technical papers in software engineering. For this reason, the set of IS journals could be extended and journals that entertain publishing DS research outputs, such as Information & Management, Journal of Information Technology Theory and Application and Scandinavian Journal of Information Systems, could be included in the review. There are also a number of DS research specific tracks in well respected IS conferences, which could be considered including the conference this paper has been written for. However, the current sample of articles has allowed us to develop the artifact and evaluation method taxonomies and helped us to identify the prevailing artifact / evaluation method combinations; this, in turn, has led to the identification of the exemplar articles that drove the analysis of the reasoning and tradeoffs of evaluation method choses. Thus, we consider that the sample is justified for the given purpose.

In the future, we should be able to develop heuristics for researchers to follow in order to choose the appropriate artifact / evaluation method combination for their research. Contingency theory based research in IS literature offers interesting examples of how to do this, see, e.g. [16]. However, we also recognize that the practitioner, in our case the researcher, should be involved in this research process as well. Therefore, this stream of research may call for more action research [see, e.g., 17], or perhaps action design style research [11].

References

1. Peffers, K., Tuunanen, T., Rothenberger, M., Chatterjee, S.: A Design Science Research Methodology for Information Systems Research. Journal of Management Information Systems 24, 45–78 (2008)
2. Hevner, A.R., March, S.T., Park, J.: Design Research in Information Systems Research. MIS Quarterly 28, 75–105 (2004)
3. McNaughton, B., Ray, P., Lewis, L.: Designing an Evaluation Framework for IT Service Management. Information & Management 47, 219–225 (2010)
4. Cleven, A., Gubler, P., Huner, K.: Design alternatives for the evaluation of design science research artifacts. In: Proceedings of the 4th International Conference on Design Science Research in Information Systems and Technology. ACM, Philadelphia (2009)
5. Son, S., Weitzel, T., Laurent, F.: Designing a process-oriented framework for IT performance management systems. The Electronic Journal of Information Systems Evaluation 8, 219–228 (2005)
6. Eekels, J., Roozenburg, N.F.M.: A methodological comparison of the structures of scientific research and engineering design: their similarities and differences. Design Studies 12, 197–203 (1991)
7. Nunamaker, J.F., Chen, M.: Systems Development in Information Systems Research. Journal of Management Information Systems 7, 89–106 (1991)
8. Walls, J., Widmeyer, G., El Sawy, O.: Assessing Information System Design Theory in Perspective: How Useful was our 1992 Initial Rendition. Journal of Information Technology Theory & Application (JITTA) 6, 43–58 (2004)
9. Walls, J., Widmeyer, G., El Sawy, O.: Building an Information System Design Theory for Vigilant EIS. Information Systems Research 3, 36–59 (1992)
10. Takeda, H., Veerkamp, P., Tomiyama, T., Yoshikawam, H.: Modeling design processes. AI Magazine 11, 37–48 (1990)
11. Sein, M.K., Henfridsson, O., Purao, S., Rossi, M., Lindgren, R.: Action design research. MIS Quarterly 35, 37–56 (2011)

12. AIS, http://ais.affiniscape.com/
    displaycommon.cfm?an=1&subarticlenbr=432
13. Chen, A.N.K., Goes, P.B., Marsden, J.R.: A query-driven approach to the design and managment of flexible database systems. Journal of Management Information Systems 19, 121–154 (2003)
14. Peffers, K., Gengler, C., Tuunanen, T.: Extending Critical Success Factors Methodology to Facilitate Broadly Participative Information Systems Planning. Journal of Management Information Systems 20, 51–85 (2003)
15. Kelly, G.A.: The Psychology of Personal Constructs. W W Norton & Company, New York (1955)
16. Mathiassen, L., Saarinen, T., Tuunanen, T., Rossi, M.: A Contingency Model for Requirements Development. Journal of Association of Information Systems 8, 569–597 (2007)
17. Baskerville, R., Wood-Harper, A.T.: Diversity in information systems action research methods. European Journal of Information Systems 7, 90–107 (1998)

Design of Software Agent-Populated
Electronic Negotiation System and Evaluation
of Human – to - Agent Negotiations

Rustam Vahidov and Gregory E. Kersten

InterNeg Research Centre, Concordia University, Montreal, Canada
{rvahidov,gregory}@jmsb.concordia.ca

Abstract. Negotiation is a flexible mechanism for facilitating effective economic exchanges. Electronic negotiations allow participants to negotiate online and use analytical support tools in making their decisions. Software agents offer the possibility of automating negotiation process using these tools. The purpose of this work is to make progress towards outlining design-theoretical principles for agent-enhanced negotiation systems (AENS). This paper describes an electronic marketplace named DIANA (Deal-making system Incorporating Agents in Negotiations and Auctions) that allows involving software agents in negotiations. It also presents the results of experiments in agent-to-human negotiations. Various types of agents have been configured and paired up with human counterparts for negotiating product sale. The paper discusses the results and presents a set of rules for the design of AENS.

Keywords: electronic negotiations, software agents, design theory, experimental studies.

1   Introduction

In a dynamically changing global business environment negotiations represent an important mechanism for facilitating economic transactions. It offers flexibility and active involvement of the participating parties, which other major mechanism categories, such as fixed price, and even auction models, lack. In the course of negotiations parties exchange offers in order to jointly explore the possibilities of finding acceptable solutions. Negotiations involving more than a single (typically price-based) issue allow for more degrees of freedom in search for agreements, which would be beneficial to the negotiators due to the asymmetry of their preference structures. Properly managed and conducted negotiations promise to maximize the mutual benefits of the participants and avoidance of situations characterized as "leaving money on the table".

Online negotiations supported by electronic negotiation systems (ENSs) allow the parties to exchange offers over the internet [1]. In addition to enabling any-time/anywhere mode of interactions, they may also incorporate analytical facilities for supporting negotiators in their preparation and conduct of negotiations in order to achieve the benefits mentioned above. This support can range from such tools as those

K. Peffers, M. Rothenberger, and B. Kuechler (Eds.): DESRIST 2012, LNCS 7286, pp. 411–422, 2012.
© Springer-Verlag Berlin Heidelberg 2012

used for capturing and modeling negotiator's preferences, to providing active advice and critique, and all the way to complete automation of the negotiation conduct.

Despite the promises and potentials, the existing ENSs have mainly been used in research and educational contexts. Catalogs and auctions have been predominantly employed as means of transacting between businesses and their customers. Could it be that ENSs do not option for the real-world economic parties, and represent, as it were, the "phantom meta-artifacts" [2]? We do not consider this being the case, and further research is needed into the factors related to ENS adoption and usage. One possible explanation to the scarcity of real-life ENSs and negotiating websites is that negotiations imply a relatively high cognitive load, especially if multiple issues are involved (e.g. price, warranty, product attributes, shipment, etc.). This load may translate into a prohibitive cost when day-to-day transactions involving people who are not negotiation experts are concerned. Investigating the modes of human-ENS interactions, as well as automation of some structured aspects of negotiations may serve as the key to promoting ENS adoption and usage. Software agents may alleviate the problem of cognitive effort by automating negotiation process while working with customers towards an acceptable deal. Moreover, they can also ensure consistency in reaching negotiation outcomes according to the set policies.

The purpose of this work is to investigate the prospects of negotiations involving humans and software agents in order to make progress towards outlining design-theoretical framework for agent-enabled ENSs. The work represents an early stage towards developing components of design theory for an agent-empowered ENS (AENS). To this end an electronic marketplace system called DIANA (Deal-making system Incorporating Agents in Negotiations and Auctions) has been built. The system was used in experiments with human subjects in order to investigate the effects of various agent strategies on negotiation outcomes, with the purpose of deriving guidelines for AENS design.

2   Related Work

Ever since the publication of the seminal paper by Hevner et al. [3], design-oriented research in IS has attracted a considerable community of followers. Works by numerous researchers have helped to establish the legitimacy of design-type studies and lay the groundwork for theoretical approaches to design science [e.g. 4, 5, 6]. A recent book on the subject explores the similarities between the traditional notion of science and advocates application (with interpretation) of scientific principles to design science research [2].

We posit that theoretical approach is required to accumulate and apply design knowledge. In this regard, an ideal formulation of a meta-artifact should be in form of a design theory for that class of artifacts. The concept of a design theory introduced by Walls et al. [6] includes both type of requirements and type of system solution as key components. The development of these components is guided by the kernel theories. In Gregor & Jones [4] [4] formulation one of the key components includes "the principles of form and action", which could be related to the "type of system solution" mentioned above. These important contributions do not stipulate the exact forms in which different components of a design theory should be formulated structurally and dynamically. Vahidov [7] has proposed a representational framework for design researcher's meta-artifacts that includes analytical, synthetic, technological, and implementation layers. Carlsson (2005, p.) has introduced the notion of technological rules to represent design knowledge. The form of such a rule could be expressed as: "If you want to achieve A (outcome) in Situation B (problem) and C (context) then something like action/intervention D can help because E (reason)". In this work we present a number of such rules for the design of AENS, which are derived from the results of our experiments. To this end we first need to investigate the related work in electronic negotiations involving software agents.

Research on automated negotiations involving software agents has been extensive [8, 9]. While thorough coverage of the past work in the area is well beyond the scope of this paper, we will review the representative publications in the context of business exchanges. One could categorize these in accordance with the context of interactions (i.e. C2C, B2B, B2C), and the extent of automation.

One well-known early work in this direction was the construction of the Kasbah electronic marketplace [10, 11]. Targeting primarily the C2C domain the marketplace allowed human users to configure agents, which would then be sent to the marketplace to negotiate with each other. Three types of agents ranging from competitive to the conceding ones were provided. Negotiations included a single issue, i.e. price. In B2B applications software agents have been proposed for automating various aspects of supply chain management. For example, in [12] an agent-based architecture has been proposed for dynamic supply chain formation. The agents acting as brokers representing various entities within supply chain negotiated agreements with each other in building up the chain.

There has also been work targeting the B2C transactions. In [13] the authors proposed an agent-based architecture for automated negotiations between businesses and consumers. The buyer agents incorporated such components as searcher and negotiator, while seller agents featured negotiator module whose strategy was set by the sales department. It has been argued by many that complete automation of real-life negotiations, in particular in business contexts does not seem to be a viable solution (e.g. [14]. Automation in general is applicable only when tasks concerned are well-structured, which is rarely the case in many business situations. However, since efficient policies can be set for multiple daily interactions with the customers regarding the sales of products and services, it seems that a relatively high level of automation may be feasible.

While the work reviewed above concerns fully automated negotiations, there has been some research into sharing responsibilities between human negotiators and negotiation agents. In [15] a system has been proposed where agents actively supported human decision making in the negotiation process. An agent advised the human user on the acceptability of the received offer, helped with the preparation of the counter-offer, and critiqued offers composed by the users when it deemed necessary to intervene. [16] proposes an agent-based architecture with the purpose of multiple negotiation management. In this architecture a fleet of agents negotiated deals with customers. These negotiations were monitored by a coordinating agent, which--based

on the analysis of situation--instructed the negotiating agents to modify their strategies and adjust reservation levels within the limits of its authority. The overall process
was monitored by a human user who could intervene to make changes if necessary.

The current work aims at informing design of electronic agent-populated marketplace and investigation of software agents' performance as compared to human-
human dyads while in multi-issue negotiations. Various types of agents following
different strategies have been configured for the comparison of their performance.

3   Architecture of DIANA and Configurations of Agents

Kersten et al. [17] proposed a general framework for electronic marketplaces involving humans and software agents called Shaman. The design of DIANA system has
been inspired by this framework. Figure 1 shows the simplified architecture of
DIANA, focusing on its negotiation support facilities. Negotiation case library stores
information on different negotiation cases, including such specifics as the subject of
negotiations, issues involved, options for the discrete issues, and other details. The
cases can be created by the system administrator. Negotiation engine uses the information from the case library to manage the exchange of offers and counter-offers
between the parties. The negotiating parties could be both humans, or mixed human-
software agent dyads. The analytical toolbox allows modeling of preferences and
evaluating received and prepared offers in terms of their overall utilities. These could
be used both by humans, as well as agents in the process of exchange. A human user
maybe the principal of the agent who delegates the task of negotiation to the agent. In
this case the principal has to configure the agent to specify its behavior.

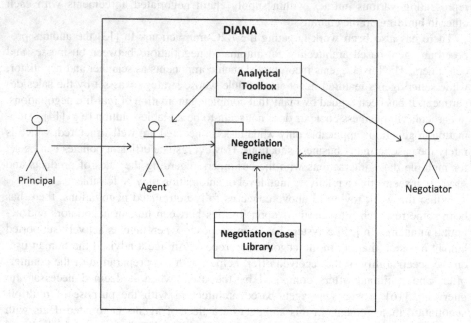

Fig. 1. Overall architecture of DIANA

Agents can be configured, in part, by specifying the concession schedule they must follow. In our experiments, we have chosen to use five different concession schedules, three of which were similar to those used in Kasbah experiments (Chavez et al. 1997). These included: competitive, neutral, collaborative, competitive-then-collaborative, and tit-for-tat strategies. The competitive agents (CM) tend to make smaller concessions in terms of utility of generated offers in the beginning of the negotiation period. However, as they approach the end of the period, they would start making larger concessions in search of an agreement (figure 2).

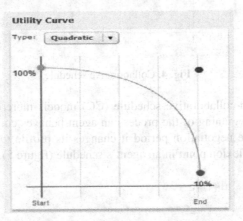

Fig. 2. Competitive schedule

Neutral strategy (NT) dictates that an agent concedes the constant amount of utility regardless of the time period, i.e. the concession schedule is linear (figure 3). Collaborative schedule (CL) implies making large concessions in the very beginning of the negotiation period in search of a quick agreement. This represents the case where an agent is anxious to sell the product. However, as the agent quickly drops the utility close to the reservation levels, it cannot make large concessions later in the process (figure 4).

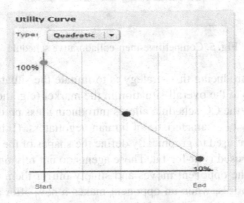

Fig. 3. Neutral schedule

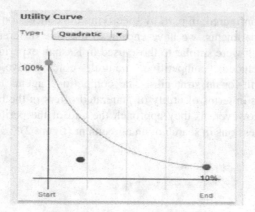

Fig. 4. Collaborative schedule

Competitive-then-collaborative schedule (CC) models more complex behavior of the agents. In the beginning of the process an agent behaves competitively, however, in the middle of the negotiation period it changes its profile to a collaborative one. Thus, there is an inflexion point in an agent's schedule (figure 5).

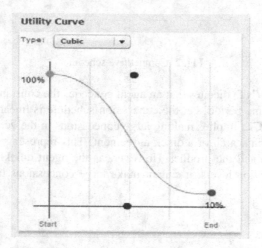

Fig. 5. Competitive-then-collaborative schedule

The reason for introducing this strategy is to imitate the situation when an agent's behavior adjusts due to the overall situation in the market (e.g. the product is not selling well). Moreover, the CC schedule allows introducing less predictable non-obvious behavior, which may be characteristic of human negotiators. (Little circles appearing on the screenshots are used to graphically define the shapes of the curves.)

The final strategy used is tit-for-tat. These agents do not rely on utility calculations. Rather, they watch the opponent moves and simply mirror them in composing counter-offers. In other words, when an opponent makes a new offer an agent determines the difference between this offer and the previous one made by the opponent, and applies the same difference to its own offer. If, say an opponent made a large change to a price, the agent would do the same.

The agent follows the following algorithm. In the beginning of the process it makes an offer that has highest utility to an agent. It then waits for the opponent to respond. If an opponent agrees, the process terminates. If an opponent makes a counter-offer the agent calculates its acceptable utility level according to the concession schedule employed. If the opponent's offer is equal or higher than the acceptable utility, the agent accepts the offer. Otherwise, the agent generates a new offer according to the acceptable utility level. It takes the opponent's offer as a starting point, and employing hill-climbing algorithm changes it to get close to the set utility level. This heuristic method is used instead of analytical one, since most of the issues are not continuous variables. It then sends this offer to the opponent.

4   Experiments

The negotiation case developed for the experimental study concerned the sale of a desktop computer. There were five issues including the price, type of monitor, hard drive, service plan, and software loaded. Each option for each issue had a corresponding level of utility (attractiveness), these levels being different for the buyers vs. sellers. In order to calculate the total utility of the offer the issues were assigned different weights. These were then used in an additive utility function to estimate the level of attractiveness of an offer. Agents used this information in order to decide on the acceptability of the received offers and generate offers.

All agents acted on the seller side, and they were not aware of the buyers' preference structures. The weights were slightly different for sellers than buyers to facilitate tradeoffs, which have been considered one of the key integrative negotiation characteristics [18]. Thus, agents would decide on the utility of the next offer first, according to their concession schedules, and then generate the corresponding offer.

In the current work we were interested in the objective outcomes of agent – human negotiations, as well as subjective variables capturing human perceptions of the process, outcomes and system. The measured variables included the utility of the agreements, and the proportion of agreements achieved. These relate to the economic benefits of agent-human negotiations.

The subjects in the study were university students enrolled in the introductory course on information technology. Thus, the negotiation case was well in line with the learning objectives of the course. The treatments included pairing up the subjects with various types of agents described in an earlier section. We also paired up humans with humans in a control group.

The experiment was conducted via the web, whereby subjects could perform their tasks from any location in an asynchronous mode during a two-day period. The subjects were invited to join the negotiations via email containing the link to the system. Negotiations began by sellers making the first offer. The agent sellers then checked for the status of negotiations at fixed intervals of time (every 3 hours). At those points of time, if they have not received new offers, they would wait until the next period of time elapsed. If an offer was received they would evaluate it and would either accept it, or would make a counter-offer.

Human subjects were free to terminate the negotiation at any time without reaching an agreement with their counter-parts. Upon the completion of the experiment the subjects were asked to answer: "I was negotiating with: 1) a human; 2) a computer: 3) not sure."

5   Results

For the analysis of the results we have selected only those negotiation instances, which featured at least four offers in total. The rationale for this decision was to include only those cases where the subjects took the task seriously. Thus, we ended up having 436 usable negotiation instances. Of these, 65% ended up in an agreement, while in 35% of cases the agreement was not reached.

Figure 6 shows the results of the question related to whether the participants guessed correctly if they were negotiating with humans or computers. The left side shows the results from human-agent dyads, and the right side shows human-human ones. The leftmost bar in each group indicates the number of responses that read "human", the middle one relates to "computer" responses, and the last one shows "not sure" responses.

As one can see, the majority of subjects in the agent-human dyads were not sure if they were interacting with the humans or agents (183 responses). This was followed by the group of subjects who had thought they were negotiating with other humans (114). The smallest group consisted of those who guessed correctly that they were interacting with agents (65). It is interesting to note that some subjects in the human-to-human dyads thought they were interacting with a computer (2 out of 30).

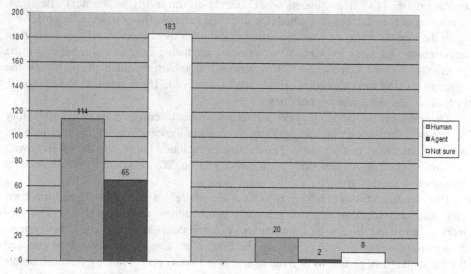

Fig. 6. "I was negotiating with…" agent - human dyads vs. human – human dyads

The distribution of answers depended on the type of the agent strategy employed. For example, in competitive-then-collaborative category much larger proportion of subjects thought they were negotiating with a human counter-part as compared to those who had an impression they were dealing with a machine (25 vs. 8). This can be explained by the fact that CC concession schedule results in more complex behavior, less obvious behavior that could be more readily ascribed to humans, rather than machines. Similar, though less prominent results were obtained in competitive agent category (33 vs. 15). On the other hand, the collaborative category was the only one where the number of "human" vs. "machine" responses was equal (21 each). Perhaps, the subjects expected their human counterparts to be more competitive, rather than conceding.

Table 1 shows the proportions of agreements for different compositions of dyads. The largest proportion of agreements was reached in the collaborative agent category. This an intuitive result, since collaborative agents make large concessions early in the negotiations process, and thus they have a higher chance of making a deal with the human counterparts. It is interesting to see that human-to-human dyads have a second-lowest record in terms of proportion of agreements made. Thus, the majority of agent-involved dyads have reached more agreements than purely human dyads.

Competitive agents were able to reach an agreement in 53% of cases. Competitive-then-collaborative agents have made agreements in 75% of cases, falling between the CL and CM categories, but higher than neutral category. The lowest number of agreements was achieved in tit-for-tat category. This is the only agent strategy that does not employ utility function, and, thus it does not necessarily drop its utility level to the minimum towards the end of the period. Overall, agent-human pairs achieved agreements in 66% of cases vs. 50% exhibited by HH dyads.

Table 2 compares the utilities of reached agreements for sellers and buyers across different categories. In human-human dyads the sellers achieved much lower utility levels than buyers. This could be explained by the adopted reference frames. Since both sellers and buyers in this category were undergraduate student subjects, they tended to shift the price levels downwards to what they consider to be acceptable regions. Nonetheless, as it can be seen from the table, the human sellers had reached the lowest levels of utility.

Table 1. Proportions of agreements

Category	Agreements, %
All agent categories	66
Competitive	53
Neutral	70
Collaborative	82
Competitive-collaborative	75
Tit-for-tat	43
Human-human	50

The highest average utility was achieved by tit-for-tat agents (72.4). However, as already mentioned, they performed worst in terms of proportion of agreements reached. In terms of proportion of agreements the competitive agents have performed slightly better than human sellers. However, utility-wise these agents have considerably outperformed their human "colleagues" (63.2 vs. 35.9). Collaborative agents did only slightly better than humans, reaching 36.5 utility. However, they had much higher proportion of agreements. Competitive-then-collaborative agents have reached the average utility level of 40.4, and the neutral ones had a slightly higher value of 43.8. Overall, agents did better than human negotiators (46.8 vs. 35.9).

Table 2. Utilities of agreements

Category	Seller utility	Buyer utility
All agent categories	46.8	65.6
Competitive	63.2	44.9
Neutral	43.8	69.7
Collaborative	36.5	79.0
Competitive-collaborative	40.4	71.9
Tit-for-tat	72.4	36
Human-human	35.9	73.0

In addition to dividing agents into various above configurations we have also had two versions of their algorithms for generating offers. Passive agents generated their offers without taking into account the opponent's counter-offer, while reactive agents took the opponent's offer as a starting point and tried to modify it to fit the desired level of utility. As the results indicate, reactive agents were able to achieve 72% agreement rate, while the passive agents only managed to secure 64% rate. This difference was significant, while there was no significant difference in the utilities of agreements.

6   Design Implications

The results show that employing agents in the majority of cases lead to superior results as compared to using human negotiators. The findings also allow us to draw blueprint for the set of design guidelines for the AENS in form of technological rules [19]. The rules, to remind, have the form "If you want to achieve A (outcome) in Situation B (problem) and C (context) then something like action/intervention D can help because E (reason)". In our case, the problem on hand is agent – to human negotiation. The reasons for these rules derive from the results of the experiments. Thus, we end up with context/outcome/intervention components. The following text summarizes the empirically supported rules.

1.   Overall, taking into account counter-part's offers while generating counter-offers lead to increased likelihood of agreements. In other words, being adaptive to the opponent pays off.

2.   If you want to achieve higher agreement utility, when number of agreements is not of primary concern, use competitive strategies for your agents. For example, in the absence of considerable competition, competitive strategies pay off.

3.   If you want to achieve high proportion of agreements, while the utility can be somewhat sacrificed, use collaborative strategies. This could be the case when the competition is high, or the negotiator wants to maintain relationships with the counter-parts, or has excess resources, and under other circumstances when the transaction is very much desirable.

4.   If the desired outcome/context may change during the course of negotiations, dynamically adjust the strategies.

If it is important that human counter-parts should not guess that they are interacting with a counter-part use complex or dynamic strategies. This rule is supported by the finding that in a relatively complex compete – then collaborate scenario the human counter-parts were least convinced that they are negotiating with a machine.

7   Conclusions

The purpose of this study was to make a progress towards the design an agent-populated marketplace, experimentally investigate the promises of agent-human negotiations in B2C context, and outline rules that could guide the design of AENS. To this end various types of agents were configured to conduct negotiations with human subjects. The question of whether humans were able to tell if they were negotiating with machine has important implications, since if they did they would be, in principle, able to predict the opponents moves. Findings indicate that, in most cases, the subjects were not able to make a correct guess. This is especially true when agents employed a complex concession pattern, i.e. compete-then-collaborate.

In regards with the outcomes the results show that human negotiators performed worst as compared to agents in terms of utility of agreements. They were also second worst in terms of number of agreements. One possibility for future work could be conducting experimental studies where agent and human negotiators could add issues in the course of negotiations.

Acknowledgments. This work has been supported by grants from the Social Sciences and Humanities Research Council of Canada (SSHRC), the Natural Sciences and Engineering Research Council of Canada (NSERC).

References

1. Kersten, G., Noronha, S.J.: WWW-based Negotiation Support: Design, Implementation, and Use. Decision Support Systems 25, 135–154 (1999)
2. Vahidov, R.: Design-type research in information systems: findings and practices. IGI Global, Hershey (2012)

3. Hevner, A., March, S.T., Park, J., Ram, S.: Design Science in Information Systems Research. MIS Quarterly 28, 75–105 (2004)
4. Gregor, S., Jones, D.: The Anatomy of a Design Theory. Journal of the Association for Information Systems 8, 312–335 (2007)
5. March, S.T., Smith, G.F.: Design and Natural Science Research on Information Technology. Decision Support Systems 15, 251–266 (1995)
6. Walls, J.G., Widmeyer, G.R., El Sawy, O.A.: Building an Information System Design Theory for Vigilant EIS. Information Systems Research 3, 36–59 (1992)
7. Vahidov, R.: Design Researcher's IS Artifact: a Representational Framework. In: 1st International Conference on Design Science Research in Information Systems and Technology, DESRIST 2006, Claremont, CA (2006)
8. Beam, C., Segev, A.: Automated Negotiations: A Survey of the State of the Art. Wirtschaftsinformatik 39, 263–268 (1997)
9. Jennings, N.R., Faratin, P., Lomuscio, A.R., Parsons, S., Wooldridge, M.J., Sierra, C.: Automated Negotiation: Prospects, Methods and Challenges. Group Decision and Negotiation 10, 199–215 (2001)
10. Chavez, A., Dreilinger, D., Guttman, R., Maes, P.: A Real-life Experiment in Creating an Agent Marketplace. In: Nwana, H.S., Azarmi, N. (eds.) Software Agents and Soft Computing: Towards Enhancing Machine Intelligence. LNCS, vol. 1198, pp. 160–179. Springer, Heidelberg (1997)
11. Maes, P., Guttman, R.H., Moukas, A.G.: Agents that Buy and Sell. Communications of the ACM 42, 81–87 (1999)
12. Wang, M., Wang, H., Vogel, D., Kumar, K., Chiu, D.K.W.: Agent-based negotiation and decision making for dynamic supply chain formation. Engineering Applications of Artificial Intelligence 22, 1046–1055 (2009)
13. Huang, C.-C., Liang, W.-Y., Lai, Y.-H., Lin, Y.-C.: The agent-based negotiation process for B2C e-commerce. Expert Systems with Applications 37, 348–359 (2010)
14. Lin, R., Kraus, S.: Can automated agents proficiently negotiate with humans? Communications of the ACM 53, 78–88 (2010)
15. Chen, E., Vahidov, R., Kersten, G.E.: Agent-supported negotiations in the e-marketplace. International Journal of Electronic Business 3, 28–49 (2005)
16. Vahidov, R.: Situated Decision Support Approach for Managing Multiple Negotiations. In: Gimpel, H., Jennings, N.R., Kersten, G.E., Ockenfels, A., Weinhardt, C. (eds.) Negotiation, Auctions, and Market Engineering. LNBIP, vol. 2, pp. 179–189. Springer, Heidelberg (2008)
17. Kersten, G.E., Kowalczyk, R., Lai, H., Neumann, D., Chhetri, M.B.: Shaman: Software and Human Agents in Multiattribute Auctions and Negotiations. In: Gimpel, H., Jennings, N.R., Ockenfels, A., Weinhardt, C. (eds.) Negotiation, Auctions, and Market Engineering. LNBIP, vol. 2, pp. 116–149. Springer, Heidelberg (2008)
18. Raiffa, H., Richardson, J., Metcalfe, D.: Negotiation Analysis. The Science and Art of Collaborative Decision Making. Harvard University Press, Cambridge (2003)
19. Carlsson, S.: Developing Information Systems Design Knowledge: A Critical Realist Perspective. The Electronic Journal of Business Research Methodology 3, 93–102 (2005)

A Comprehensive Framework for Evaluation in Design Science Research

John Venable[1], Jan Pries-Heje[2], and Richard Baskerville[3]

[1] Curtin University, Perth, Western Australia, Australia
j.venable@curtin.edu.au
[2] Roskilde University, Roskilde, Denmark
janph@ruc.dk
[3] Georgia State University, Atlanta, Georgia, USA
baskerville@acm.org

Abstract. Evaluation is a central and essential activity in conducting rigorous Design Science Research (DSR), yet there is surprisingly little guidance about designing the DSR evaluation activity beyond suggesting possible methods that could be used for evaluation. This paper extends the notable exception of the existing framework of Pries-Heje et al [11] to address this problem. The paper proposes an extended DSR evaluation framework together with a DSR evaluation design method that can guide DSR researchers in choosing an appropriate strategy for evaluation of the design artifacts and design theories that form the output from DSR. The extended DSR evaluation framework asks the DSR researcher to consider (as input to the choice of the DSR evaluation strategy) contextual factors of goals, conditions, and constraints on the DSR evaluation, e.g. the type and level of desired rigor, the type of artifact, the need to support formative development of the designed artifacts, the properties of the artifact to be evaluated, and the constraints on resources available, such as time, labor, facilities, expertise, and access to research subjects. The framework and method support matching these in the first instance to one or more DSR evaluation strategies, including the choice of ex ante (prior to artifact construction) versus ex post evaluation (after artifact construction) and naturalistic (e.g., field setting) versus artificial evaluation (e.g., laboratory setting). Based on the recommended evaluation strategy(ies), guidance is provided concerning what methodologies might be appropriate within the chosen strategy(ies).

Keywords: Design Science Research, Research Methodology, Information Systems Evaluation, Evaluation Method, Evaluation Strategy.

1 Introduction

There is widespread agreement that evaluation is a central and essential activity in conducting rigorous Design Science Research (DSR). In DSR, evaluation is concerned with examining DSR outputs, including design artifacts [6] and Information Systems

K. Peffers, M. Rothenberger, and B. Kuechler (Eds.): DESRIST 2012, LNCS 7286, pp. 423–438, 2012.

(IS) Design Theories [3], [20]. March and Smith [6] identify "build" and "evaluate" as two DSR activities. Hevner et al [5] identify evaluation as "crucial" (p. 82). In their third guideline for Design Science in IS Research, they state that "The utility, quality, and efficacy of a design artifact must be rigorously demonstrated via well-executed evaluation methods" (p. 85).

Evaluation provides evidence that a new technology developed in DSR "works" or achieves the purpose for which it was designed. Without evaluation, outcomes of DSR are unsubstantiated assertions that the designed artifacts, if implemented and deployed in practice, will achieve their purpose. Rigorous, scientific research requires evidence. If Design Science Research is to live up to its label as "science", the evaluation must be sufficiently rigorous.

But how should rigorous evaluation be designed and conducted? What strategies and methods should be used for evaluation in a particular DSR project? How can the evaluation be designed to be both effective (rigorous) and efficient (prudently using resources, including time)? What would constitute good guidance for answering these questions?

Unfortunately, there is little guidance in the DSR literature about the choice of strategies and methods for evaluation in DSR. A notable exception is Pries-Heje et al [11], who develop a 2-by-2 framework to guide selection of evaluation strategy(ies) for a DSR project. They identify that evaluation design needs to decide what will be evaluated, when it will be evaluated, and how it will be evaluated. However, beyond providing the framework and an idea of what needs to be designed in the DSR component of research, they provide very little guidance in how a research should or could actually design the DSR evaluation component. This state of affairs in DSR constitutes what we can call an "evaluation gap".

The purpose of this paper is to address this evaluation gap by developing a DSR evaluation framework with clear guidance for how one could design and conduct evaluation within DSR. Making a strong, published evaluation framework available to design science researchers, particularly novice ones, can simplify the research design and reporting. Such guidance would help DSR researchers make decisions about how they can (and perhaps should) conduct the evaluation activities of DSR.

It is important to clarify that the framework developed here is to aid DSR researchers in the design of the evaluation component of their DSR. The framework proposed here is not a framework for evaluating DSR projects as a whole or after the fact. Conducting DSR involves much more than the evaluation of the resulting DSR artifacts and IS Design Theories and such broader evaluation of a whole DSR project is outside the scope of this paper.

This next section of this paper discusses relevant literature on evaluation in DSR to elucidate the "evaluation gap" addressed in this paper. Section 3 describes an extended framework and method developed to address this gap. Section 4 describes the evaluation of the method in use by novice design science researchers. Finally section 5 discusses the findings and presents conclusions.

2   Literature on Evaluation in DSR

This section considers the DSR literature concerning the purposes for evaluation in DSR, characteristics or aspects to be evaluated in DSR evaluation, kinds of artifacts (evaluands) in DSR, design goals to be addressed in the design of a DSR evaluation method, methods proposed for evaluation in DSR, and guidance for designing the evaluation component of DSR.

2.1   Purposes of Evaluation in DSR

As noted above, evaluation is what puts the "Science" in "Design Science". Without evaluation, we only have an unsubstantiated design theory or hypothesis that some developed artifact will be useful for solving some problem or making some improvement. This section identifies and discusses five different purposes for evaluation in the DSR literature.

1. Evaluate an instantiation of a designed artifact to establish its utility and efficacy (or lack thereof) for achieving its stated purpose

March and Smith [6] define evaluation as "the process of determining how well the artifact performs." (p. 254). The central purpose of DSR evaluation then is to rigorously demonstrate the utility of the artifact being evaluated (known as the "evaluand" [13]). DSR design artifacts   "are assessed against criteria of value or utility – does it work?" [6]. A key purpose of DSR evaluation then is to determine whether or how well the developed evaluand achieves its purpose.

2. Evaluate the formalized knowledge about a designed artifact's utility for achieving its purpose

Evaluating the design artifact's utility for purpose is closely related to the concepts of IS Design Theories (ISDTs) [3], [18], [20], design principles [7], [10], [12], or technological rules [16], which are formalizations of knowledge about designed artifacts and their utility. When an artifact is evaluated for its utility in achieving its purpose, one is also evaluating a design theory that the design artifact has utility to achieve that purpose. From the point of view of design theory, a second purpose of evaluation in DSR is to confirm or disprove (or enhance) the design theory.

3. Evaluate a designed artifact or formalized knowledge about it in comparison to other designed artifacts' ability to achieve a similar purpose

In addition to the first purpose above, Venable [17] identifies a third purpose – evaluating the artifact "in comparison to other solution technologies" (p. 4). A new artifact should provide greater relative utility than existing artifacts that can be used to achieve the same purpose.

4. Evaluate a designed artifact or formalized knowledge about it for side effects or undesirable consequences of its use

Another purpose that Venable [17] identifies is evaluating an artifact for other (undesirable) impacts in the long run, i.e. for side effects (particularly dangerous ones).

5. Evaluate a designed artifact formatively to identify weaknesses and areas of improvement for an artifact under development

A fifth purpose of evaluation is formative evaluation, in which an artifact still under development is evaluated to determine areas for improvement and refinement. Sein et al [12] use evaluation formatively in early (alpha) Building, Intervention, and Evaluation (BIE) cycles (*cf.* ex ante evaluation in [11]) of their Action Design Research Methodology (ADR). The last BIE cycle in ADR is summative evaluation of a beta version, which is in line with the first purpose for evaluations given above.

Next we turn our attention to what is evaluated.

2.2   Aspects and Characteristics to Be Evaluated in DSR

Utility is a complex concept and not the only thing that is evaluated in DSR. Utility may depend on a number of characteristics of the artifact or desired outcomes of the use of the artifact. Care must be taken to consider how utility for achieving the artifact's purpose(s) can be assessed, what characteristics to evaluate or measure. Each evaluation is quite specific to the artifact, its purpose(s), and the purpose(s) of the evaluation.

Nonetheless, it is useful to consider what kinds of qualities for evaluation are discussed in the literature. As noted earlier, Hevner et al [5] identify utility, quality, and efficacy as attributes to be evaluated. Hevner et al [5] further state that "artifacts can be evaluated in terms of functionality, completeness, consistency, accuracy, performance, reliability, usability, fit with the organization, and other relevant quality attributes" (p. 85). They later identify "style" as an aspect of an artifact that should be evaluated.

Checkland and Scholes [1] proposed five properties ("the 5 E's") by which to judge the quality of an evaluand: Efficiency, effectiveness, efficacy, ethicality, and elegance. Effectiveness and efficacy are sometimes confused. Effectiveness is the degree to which the artifact meets its higher level purpose or goal and achieve its desired benefit in practice. Efficacy is the degree to which the artifact produces its desired effect considered narrowly, without addressing situational concerns.

All of these properties of the artifact in some way contribute to the utility of the developed artifact and act as criteria that are candidates for evaluation in determining the overall utility.

2.3   Kinds of Evaluands in DSR

Next we consider the different kinds of evaluands. Based on the literature, we can identify two different classifications of artifacts.

First, we can distinguish product artifacts from process artifacts [3], [18]. Product artifacts are technologies such as tools, diagrams, software, etc. that people use to accomplish some task. Process artifacts are methods, procedures, etc. that guide someone or tell them what to do to accomplish some task.

Second, we can distinguish between technical artifacts and socio-technical artifacts. Some artifacts are in some sense "purely" (or nearly purely) technical, in that they do not require human use once instantiated. Socio-technical artifacts are ones with which humans must interact to provide their utility.

Relating the technical vs socio-technical distinction to the product vs process distinction, product artifacts may be either (purely) technical or socio-technical, while process artifacts are always socio-technical, which will have implications for their evaluation.

2.4 Goals of Evaluation Design in DSR

Next we consider what goals there are for the design of the evaluation itself. There are (at least) three possibly competing goals in designing the evaluation component of DSR.

- Rigor: Research, including DSR, should be rigorous. Rigor in DSR has two senses. The first is in establishing that it is the artifact (instantiation) that causes an observed improvement (and only the artifact, not some confounding independent variable or circumstance), i.e. its efficacy. The second sense of rigor in DSR is in establishing that the artifact (instantiation) works in a real situation (despite organisational complications, unanticipated human behavioral responses, etc.), i.e. its effectiveness.
- Efficiency: A DSR evaluation should work within resource constraints (e.g. money, equipment, and people's time) or even minimize their consumption.
- Ethics: Research, including DSR, should not unnecessarily put animals, people, organizations, or the public at risk during or after evaluation, e.g. for safety critical systems and technologies. Venable [19] discusses some ethical issues in DSR.

The 5 E's [1] are also relevant to the design of the evaluation part of a DSR project. Each of the above goals corresponds to one of the 5 E's. Only Elegance is missing, although presumably an elegant evaluation would be preferable to an inelegant one. Importantly these goals conflict and DSR evaluation must balance these goals.

2.5 Evaluation Methods in DSR

Next we consider what methods there are for evaluation (from which a Design Science researcher might choose).

Different DSR authors have identified a number of methods that can be used for evaluation in DSR. Hevner et al [5] summarize five classes of evaluation methods with 12 specific methods in those classes. (1) Observational methods include case study and field study. (2) Analytical methods include static analysis, architecture analysis, optimization, and dynamic analysis. (3) Experimental methods include controlled experiment and simulation. (4) Testing methods include functional (black box) testing and structural (white box) testing. (5) Descriptive methods include informed argument and scenarios. They provide no guidance on method selection or evaluation design.

Vaishnavi and Kuechler [15] allow for both quantitative and qualitative methods and describe the use of a non-empirical analysis. They do not provide guidance for selecting between methods or designing the evaluation part of DSR.

Peffers et al [9] divide what others call evaluation into two activities, demonstration and evaluation. Demonstration is like a light-weight evaluation to demonstrate that the artifact feasibly works to "solve one or more instances of the problem", i.e. to achieve its purpose in at least one context (*cf.* ex ante evaluation in [11]). Evaluation proper is more formal and extensive, and takes a fairly positivistic stance that the activity should evaluate "how well the artifact supports a solution to the problem" (p. 56). Methods for evaluation identified include the collection of "objective quantitative performance measures such as budgets or items produced, the results of satisfaction surveys, client feedback" (p. 56), or the use of simulations or logical proofs, but they provide no guidance for choosing between methods.

Nunamaker et al [8] identified a number of methods for evaluation or what they termed experimentation. These included computer and lab simulations, field experiments, and lab experiments. Additionally, they identified several methods of observation, including case studies, survey studies, and field studies, although they did not see these as evaluation methods. Moreover, they did not provide much guidance in choosing among these evaluation methods, except to say that the evaluation method must be matched to the designed artifact and the evaluation metrics to be used.

The activities that Nunamaker et al [8] called experimentation and observation, Venable [17] instead respectively called artificial evaluation and naturalistic evaluation, explicitly recognizing the evaluative nature of the observation activity. Artificial evaluation includes laboratory experiments, field experiments, simulations, criteria-based analysis, theoretical arguments, and mathematical proofs. The dominance of the scientific/rational paradigm brings to artificial DSR evaluation the benefits of stronger scientific reliability in the form of better repeatability and falsifiability [4].

Naturalistic evaluation explores the performance of a solution technology in its real environment i.e., within the organization. By performing evaluation in a real environment (real people, real systems, and real settings [14]), naturalistic evaluation embraces all of the complexities of human practice in real organizations. Naturalistic evaluation is always empirical and may be interpretive, positivist, and/or critical. Naturalistic evaluation methods include case studies, field studies, surveys, ethnography, phenomenology, hermeneutic methods, and action research. The dominance of the naturalistic paradigm brings to naturalistic DSR evaluation the benefits of stronger internal validity [4].

Artificial and naturalistic evaluation each have their strengths and weaknesses. To the extent that naturalistic evaluation is affected by confounding variables or misinterpretation, evaluation results may not be precise or even truthful about an artifact's utility or efficacy in real use. On the other hand, artificial evaluation involves abstraction from the natural setting and is necessarily "unreal" according to one or more of Sun and Kantor's [14] three realities (unreal users, unreal systems, or unreal problems). To the extent that an artificial evaluation setting is unreal, evaluation results may not be applicable to real use. In contrast, naturalistic evaluation offers more critical face validity. Evaluation in a naturalistic setting is "the real 'proof of the pudding'" [17, p. 5].

Further, Venable noted that more than one method could be used, mixing artificial and naturalistic evaluation as well as positivist and interpretive evaluation methods, leading to a pluralist view of science, where each has its strengths in contributing to a robust evaluation depending on the circumstance. Nonetheless, Venable [17] provided little or no guidance about selecting among methods and designing an evaluation strategy.

In summary, the DSR literature identifies a fairly large number and variety of evaluation methods, but gives little advice as to choice among methods, i.e. how to design an evaluation strategy for a particular DSR project.

2.6 Guidance for Designing Evaluations in DSR

While the DSR literature provides almost no guidance on how to design the evaluation component of DSR research, there is one notable exception: the paper by Pries-Heje et al [11], which proposes a 2-by-2 framework of strategies for evaluation in DSR (see figure 1 below) and provides some guidance for considerations about how to choose among them. Their framework combines one dimension contrasting artificial vs naturalistic evaluation [17], as discussed in section 2.5, with a second dimension contrasting ex ante and ex post evaluation. Ex post evaluation is evaluation of an

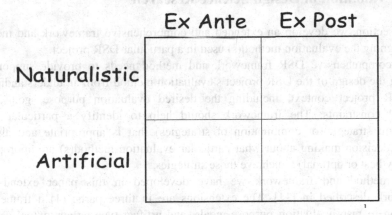

Fig. 1. A Strategic DSR Evaluation Framework (adapted from [11])

instantiated artifact (i.e. an instantiation) and ex ante evaluation is evaluation of an uninstantiated artifact, such as a design or model. This distinction is similar to the later distinction in ADR concerning evaluation of alpha versions of an artifact for formative purposes vs evaluation of beta versions of an artifact for summative purposes [12]. The paper also takes into account that what is being evaluated – the design artifact - can either be a process, a product or both (as discussed in section 2.3).

Some key points that Pries-Heje et al [11] make concerning the design of evaluation in DSR are that:

1. The distinctions of ex ante vs ex post and artificial vs naturalistic evaluation surface a variety of ways in which evaluation might be conducted.
2. Ex ante evaluation is possible and building an instantiation of an artifact may not be needed (at least initially).
3. Artifact evaluation in artificial settings could include imaginary or simulated settings.
4. Naturalistic evaluation can be designed by choosing from among multiple realities and multiple levels of granularity for measurements or metrics.
5. Multiple evaluations, combining multiple evaluation strategies, may be useful.
6. The specific evaluation criteria, measurements, or metrics depend on the type of artifact (product or process) and intended goals or improvements.

While the above suggestions to guide the research design of evaluation in DSR are useful, we believe they are incomplete and less useful than they might be. There is no guidance for considering how the different purposes, evaluation design goals, available resources, etc. can or should be considered when choosing a DSR evaluation strategy or strategies. Moreover, they provide no guidance about how to select evaluation methods. These difficulties are addressed in the next section.

3   A Comprehensive Framework and Method for Designing Evaluation in Design Science Research

In this section, we develop an extended and comprehensive framework and method for designing the evaluation method(s) used in a particular DSR project.

The comprehensive DSR framework and method needs to provide support for deriving the design of the DSR project's evaluation method from an understanding of the DSR project context, including the desired evaluation purpose, goals, and practical constraints. The framework should help to identify a particular DSR evaluation strategy (or combination of strategies) that is appropriate and also to support decision making about what particular evaluation method(s) are appropriate (possibly best or optimal) to achieve those strategies.

The method and framework we have developed in this paper extends the framework described in [11]. The extensions are in three parts: (1) a framework extension to map evaluation purpose, goals, and artifact type as contextual aspects that set the criteria for the evaluation design to a potential evaluation strategy or strategies (see figure 2 and section 3.1), (2) an extended framework to map a chosen evaluation strategy or strategies to candidate evaluation methods (see figure 3 and section 3.2), and (3) a process or method to use the two extended frameworks (see section 3.3).

3.1   First Extension: A DSR Evaluation Strategy Selection Framework

The first extension relates or maps various aspects of the context of the evaluation in the DSR project to the framework by Pries-Heje et al [11], as shown in figure 2 (A DSR Evaluation Strategy Selection Framework). Relevant aspects of the context of the DSR evaluation serve as the starting point and input to the design of the DSR evaluation. Relevant contextual aspects include (1) the different purposes of evaluation in DSR, (2) the characteristics of the evaluand to be evaluated, (3) the type of evaluand to be evaluated, and (4) the specific goals that must be balanced in the design of the evaluation part(s) of a DSR project. These four contextual aspects were discussed in sections 2.1 through 2.4 respectively.

In figure 2, the above four contextual aspects are combined into criteria that should be considered as input to the DSR evaluation design. These criteria include the following and are mapped to ex ante vs ex post and artificial vs naturalistic evaluation as shown in the white areas of figure 2,

- The extent to which cost and time resource limitations constrain the evaluation or the whole research project
- Whether (or not) early, formative evaluation is desirable and feasible
- The extent to which the artifact being designed has to please heterogeneous groups of stakeholders or if there is likely to be conflict, which will complicate evaluation
- Whether the system is purely technical in nature or socio-technical in nature, with the consequent difficulties of the latter (cf. artifact focus as either technical, organizational, or strategic [2]
- How important strong rigor concerning effectiveness in real working situations is
- How important strong rigor concerning whether benefits are specifically due to the designed artifact, rather than some other potential cause (or confounding variable), is
- Whether or not access to a site for naturalistic evaluation is available or can be obtained
- Whether the level of risk for evaluation participants is acceptable or needs to be reduced

To use the framework, a design science researcher begins with an understanding of the context of the DSR evaluation, maps that understanding to the criteria in figure 2, and selects an evaluation strategy or combination of strategies based on which rows, columns and cells in figure 2 are most relevant.

		Ex Ante	Ex Post
DSR Evaluation Strategy Selection Framework		•Formative •Lower build cost •Faster •Evaluate design, partial prototype, or full prototype •Less risk to participants (during evaluation) •Higher risk of false positive	•Summative •Higher build cost •Slower •Evaluate instantiation •Higher risk to participants (during evaluation) •Lower risk of false positive
Naturalistic	•Many diverse stakeholders •Substantial conflict •Socio-technical artifacts •Higher cost •Longer time - slower •Organizational access needed •Artifact effectiveness evaluation •Desired Rigor: "Proof of the Pudding" •Higher risk to participants •Lower risk of false positive – safety critical systems	•Real users, real problem, and somewhat unreal system •Low-medium cost •Medium speed •Low risk to participants •Higher risk of false positive	•Real users, real problem, and real system •Highest Cost •Highest risk to participants •Best evaluation of effectiveness •Identification of side effects •Lowest risk of false positive – safety critical systems
Artificial	•Few similar stakeholders •Little or no conflict •Purely technical artifacts •Lower cost •Less time - faster •Desired Rigor: Control of Variables •Artifact efficacy evaluation •Less risk during evaluation •Higher risk of false positive	•Unreal Users, Problem, and/or System •Lowest Cost •Fastest •Lowest risk to participants •Highest risk of false positive re. effectiveness	•Real system, unreal problem and possibly unreal users •Medium-high cost •Medium speed •Low-medium risk to participants

Fig. 2. A DSR Evaluation Strategy Selection Framework

In using figure 2 to formulate a DSR evaluation strategy or strategies, it is important to prioritize these different criteria, as they are likely to conflict. For example, obtaining the rigor of naturalistic evaluation may conflict with reducing risk to evaluation participants and the need to reduce costs. If cost and risk reduction override (or preclude) rigorous evaluation of effectiveness in real settings, then an artificial evaluation strategy may be chosen as more appropriate.

In formulating an evaluation strategy, figure 2 can advise the DSR researcher in the choice. Identifying relevant, higher priority criteria in the white and blue cells supports identifying an appropriate quadrant or quadrants, i.e. the relevant blue cell(s) in figure 2. Note that picking a single box may not be the best strategy; rather, a hybrid strategy (more than one quadrant) can be used to resolve conflicting goals.

3.2   Second Extension: A DSR Evaluation Method Selection Framework

The second extension is to relate the different evaluation strategies in the framework by Pries-Heje et al [11] to different extant evaluation methods, which were also discussed in section 2.5. This extension is expressed as a mapping of DSR evaluation strategies to relevant evaluation methods (see figure 3). By combining these two figures, the extended framework provides a bridge between the contextual factors relevant to the DSR evaluation and appropriate means (methods) to evaluate the DSR artifacts.

DSR Evaluation Method Selection Framework	Ex Ante	Ex Post
Naturalistic	•Action Research •Focus Group	•Action Research •Case Study •Focus Group •Participant Observation •Ethnography •Phenomenology •Survey (qualitative or quantitative)
Artificial	•Mathematical or Logical Proof •Criteria-Based Evaluation •Lab Experiment •Computer Simulation	•Mathematical or Logical Proof •Lab Experiment •Role Playing Simulation •Computer Simulation •Field Experiment

Fig. 3. A DSR Evaluation Method Selection Framework

Having decided the high level strategy to be used for evaluation (i.e. which of the quadrants in Figure 2 will be used for the evaluation), then the particular evaluation research method(s) need to be chosen and the evaluation designed in detail. Figure 3 gives a mapping of different possible DSR evaluation research methods map into each quadrant of the framework in Figures 1 and 2. This mapping may omit some potential evaluation methods and other evaluation methods may be developed or adopted for DSR.

Depending on which quadrant(s) were chosen as the DSR evaluation strategy (using figure 2), figure 3 suggests possible evaluation methods that fit the chosen evaluation strategy. The specific choice of evaluation method or methods requires substantial knowledge of the method(s). If the DSR researcher is unfamiliar with the possible methods, he or she will need to learn about them. Further characteristics of the evaluation method will need to be assessed against the specific goals and other contextual issues of the specific DSR project. Detailed advice on which method or methods to select to fit a particular DSR evaluation strategy is therefore beyond the scope and available space of this paper.

3.3   A Four-Step Method for DSR Evaluation Research Design

The third extension is a four-step DSR evaluation research design method that relies on the extended framework as shown in figures 2 and 3.

The development of the extended framework as elaborated in figures 2 and 3, together with our collective experience conducting and supervising DSR projects, enables us to deduce and design a four-step method (or process) for designing the evaluation component(s) of a DSR project. In general, these are to (1) analyze the requirements for the evaluation to be designed, (2) map the requirements to one or more of the dimensions and quadrants in the framework using figure 2, (3) select an appropriate evaluation method or methods that align with the chosen strategy quadrant(s) using figure 3, and (4) design the evaluation in more detail.

1. Analyze the context of the evaluation – the evaluation requirements
   As a first step, we need to identify, analyze, and priorities all of the requirements or goals for the evaluation portion of the DSR project.
   a. Determine what the evaluands are/will be. Will they be concepts, models, methods, instantiations, and/or design theories?
   b. Determine the nature of the artifact(s)/evaluand(s). Is (are) the artifact(s) to be produced a product, process, or both? Is (are) the artifact(s) to be produced purely technical or socio-technical? Will it (they) be safety critical or not?
   c. Determine what properties you will/need to evaluate. Which of these (and/or other aspects) will you evaluate? Do you need to evaluate utility/effectiveness, efficiency, efficacy, ethicality, or some other quality aspect (and which aspects)?
   d. Determine the goal/purpose of the evaluation. Will you evaluate single/main artifact against goals? Do you need to compare the developed artifact against with other, extant artifacts? Do you need to evaluate the developed artifact(s) for side effects or undesired consequences (especially if safety critical)?
   e. Identify and analyze the constraints in the research environment. What resources are available – time, people, budget, research site, etc.? What resources are in short supply and must be used sparingly?
   f. Consider the required rigor of the evaluation. How rigorous must the evaluation be? Can it be just a preliminary evaluation or is detailed and rigorous evaluation required? Can some parts of the evaluation be done following the conclusion of the project?

g. Prioritize the above contextual factors to determine which aspects are essential, more important, less important, nice to have, and irrelevant. This will help in addressing conflicts between different evaluation design goals.

2. Match the needed contextual factors (goals, artifact properties, etc.) of the evaluation (from step 1) to the criteria in figure 2 ("DSR Evaluation Strategy Selection Framework"), looking at the criteria in both white portions relating to a single dimension and the blue areas relating to a single quadrant. The criteria statements that match the contextual features of your DSR project will determine which quadrant(s) applies(y) most or are most needed. It may well be that more than one quadrant applies, indicating the need for a hybrid methods evaluation design.

3. Select appropriate evaluation method(s) from those listed in the selected, corresponding quadrant(s) in figure 3 ("DSR Evaluation Method Selection Framework"). If more than one box is indicated, selecting a method present in more than one box may be helpful. The resulting selection of evaluation methods, together with the strategy(ies) (quadrant(s)), constitute a high level design for the evaluation research.

4. Design the DSR evaluation in detail. Ex ante evaluation will precede ex post evaluation, but more than one evaluation may be performed and more than one method used, in which case the order of their use and how the different evaluations will fit together must be decided. Also, the specific detailed evaluations must be designed, e.g. design of surveys or experiments. This generally will follow the extant research methods literature.

4   Evaluation of the Framework

When writing about evaluation it is obvious that the framework derived needs to be evaluated. We should take our own medicine so to say. To some extent we have. For three years, the authors have taught various versions of the evaluation framework as it has evolved to a variety of students and scholars carrying out design science research at our and other universities. They have been taught the four steps presented above as well as different evaluation methods. In particular, at Roskilde University, they have been asked to apply the framework in real DSR projects with an average size between 1 and 2 man years (6 people, 3 months full time, is a typical project).

One example from Roskilde University was a group that redesigned a bike lane to make people behave better when biking, i.e. less rude to other people biking and people walking. They designed with Ockham's Razor of simplicity in mind. They used the theory of planned behaviour to inform their design. The group decided that their redesign should be evaluated with a real user (biker) focusing on real problems, i.e. naturalistically. However, access was a problem since it would not be possible to fully implement the real solution without obtaining a lot of permissions and red tape from the Ministry and the Municipality, suggesting an ex ante naturalistic evaluation instead, based on figure 2 (DSR Evaluation Strategy Selection Framework). Thus they instead chose ex ante evaluation and used a Focus Group for evaluation as suggested by figure 3 (DSR Evaluation Method Selection Framework) and deferred instantiation and ex post evaluation to another project with sufficient access and other resources.

Another example from Roskilde University was a group that designed and constructed a digital collaborative workspace. Here material from an existing but completed project was used to evaluate the project. Material included among other things the requirements specification, the project plan, and some Scrum artifacts on tasks. As a full ex post naturalistic evaluation would be too time consuming and resource intensive for the project group, the team chose an ex post artificial evaluation strategy (shown as appropriate in figure 2) and the project outcome was evaluated using a kind of Computer Simulation of the digital workspace (as suggested by figure 3).

The third example is called ChickenNet. Here the group investigated how the use of a digital learning game can give elderly people the ability to achieve the necessary skills for using the internet. The project was inspired by another project called BrainLounge, the purpose of which is to help elderly to exercise their brain through interactive games. The group used an iterative design process, collecting expert and user feedback after each iteration, i.e. it focussed on formative, ex ante evaluation as suggested by figure 2. The product at the end was a mock-up that illustrated the final game design. Here a combination of naturalistic evaluation (real users) and artificial evaluation (experts) was used. The first iteration was ex ante and then the following iterations moved towards ex post, ending with a mock-up. Again figure 3 turned out to be useful in choosing evaluation method.

Overall, the result of the evaluation of our evaluation framework is quite positive. Hundreds of students and scholars (around 500 in total) have been able to use the framework, have made decisions on how to evaluate their design artifact, and have carried out the evaluation in accordance with the comprehensive framework as presented in this paper. In most cases, they chose appropriate evaluation strategies and methods.

Thus far our own evaluation has been naturalistic, ex ante, as the methodology has not stabilized until this writing (indeed it may further evolve). Given the lack of other guidance, the risk to participant users is quite low. As a sociotechnical artifact, a naturalistic evaluation seems natural. During evaluation, we have observed our students, sought more general feedback and listened for suggestions for improvement (as well as deducing our own ideas for improvement based on user reactions and problems experienced). A more formal, rigorous evaluation seeking clear ratings as well as open comments about different aspects of the framework and method and their goals will be sought in the next round of usage. As the risk remains fairly low and the artifact is a socio-technical one, a naturalistic, ex post evaluation is suggested for such rigorous evaluation, perhaps using surveys or focus groups of the method users.

5   Conclusion

Evaluation is a very significant issue in IS Design Science Research, yet there is little guidance concerning how to choose and design an appropriate evaluation strategy.

To address the above need, we have developed and presented three enhancements to the existing DSR Evaluation Strategy Framework proposed by Pries-Heje et al [11], which are based on an analysis and synthesis of works on DSR as presented in section 2. The first part of the extended framework (figure 2) maps aspects of the context of a DSR evaluation, such as resources, purpose, goals, and priorities, to the two dimensions and four quadrants of the Pries-Heje et al [11] DSR Evaluation Strategy Framework. The second part (figure 3) maps the quadrants (or the selected relevant DSR evaluation strategy or strategies) to available and relevant research methods that could be chosen to conduct the evaluation or multiple evaluation episodes. We have further developed a detailed four-step method for the design of the evaluation components in a DSR project. This new framework and method should assist DSR researchers, particularly those new to the field, to improve the efficiency and effectiveness of their DSR evaluation activities.

The primary aim of the enhanced framework and method is to guide Design Science researchers who may need assistance in deciding how to design the evaluation component of their DSR projects. The framework could also be used by reviewers of DSR publications or research proposals in evaluating research design choices, but that is not our intent.

We have tried out and evaluated the extended framework and method in numerous design research projects, including our own and student projects. Nonetheless, further research is needed to gain more experience using the comprehensive DSR evaluation framework and the DSR evaluation design method, further evaluate their utility, and further develop and improve the method, especially as new DSR evaluation methods are developed.

References

1. Checkland, P., Scholes, J.: Soft Systems Methodology in Practice. J. Wiley, Chichester (1990)
2. Cleven, A., Gubler, P., Hüner, K.: Design Alternatives for the Evaluation of Design Science Research Artifacts. In: Proceedings of the 4th International Conference on Design Science Research in Information Systems and Technology (DESRIST 2009). ACM Press, Malvern (2009)
3. Gregor, S., Jones, D.: The Anatomy of a Design Theory. Journal of the Association for Information Systems 8, 312–335 (2007)
4. Gummesson, E.: Qualitative Methods in Management Research. Studentlitterature, Chartwell-Bratt, Lund, Sweden (1988)
5. Hevner, A.R., March, S.T., Park, J., Ram, S.: Design Science In Information Systems Research. MIS Quarterly 28, 75–105 (2004)
6. March, S.T., Smith, G.F.: Design and natural science research on information technology. Decision Support Systems 15, 251–266 (1995)
7. Markus, M.L., Majchrzak, A., Gasser, L.: A design theory for systems that support emergent knowledge processes. MIS Quarterly 26, 179–212 (2002)
8. Nunamaker, J.F., Chen, M., Purdin, T.D.M.: Systems Development in Information Systems Research. Journal of Management Information Systems 7, 89–106 (1990/1991)

9. Peffers, K., Tuunanen, T., Rothenberger, M.A., Chatterjee, S.: A Design Science Research Methodology for Information Systems Research. Journal of Management Information Systems 24 (2008)

10. Pries-Heje, J., Baskerville, R.: The Design Theory Nexus. MIS Quarterly 32, 731–755 (2008)

11. Pries-Heje, J., Baskerville, R., Venable, J.R.: Strategies for Design Science Research Evaluation. In: Proceedigns of the 16th European Conference on Information Systems (ECIS 2008), Galway, Ireland (2008)

12. Sein, M.K., Henfridsson, O., Purao, S., Rossi, M., Lindgren, R.: Action Design Research. MIS Quarterly 35, 37–56 (2011)

13. Stufflebeam, D.L.: The Methodology of Metaevaluation as Reflected in Metaevaluations by the Western Michigan University Evaluation Center, pp. 95–125 (2000)

14. Sun, Y., Kantor, P.B.: Cross-Evaluation: A new model for information system evaluation. Journal of the American Society for Information Science and Technology 57, 614–628 (2006)

15. Vaishnavi, V., Kuechler, W.: Design Research in Information Systems. AISWorld (2004), http://desrist.org/design-research-in-information-systems/ (accessed March 3, 2012)

16. van Aken, J.E.: Management Research Based on the Paradigm of the Design Sciences: The Quest for Field-Tested and Grounded Technological Rules. Journal of Management Studies 41, 219–246 (2004)

17. Venable, J.R.: A Framework for Design Science Research Activities. In: Proceedings of the 2006 Information Resource Management Association Conference, Washington, DC, USA (2006)

18. Venable, J.R.: The Role of Theory and Theorising in Design Science Research. In: Hevner, A.R., Chatterjee, S. (eds.) Proceedings of the 1st International Conference on Design Science Research in Information Systems and Technology (DESRIST 2006), Claremont, CA, USA (2006)

19. Venable, J.R.: Identifying and Addressing Stakeholder Interests in Design Science Research: An Analysis Using Critical Systems Heuristics. In: Dhillon, G., Stahl, B.C., Baskerville, R. (eds.) CreativeSME 2009. IFIP AICT, vol. 301, pp. 93–112. Springer, Heidelberg (2009)

20. Walls, J.G., Widmeyer, G.R., El Sawy, O.A.: Building an information system design theory for vigilant EIS. Information Systems Research 3, 36–59 (1992)

Author Index

Printed in the United States
By Bookmasters